Wartime Letters:
Hamp and Peggy Smith

1942 – 1945

Hamp and Peggy's daughters, Pat Adamson and Joan Noble, typed out the letters. Joan Noble wrote the introduction and compiled the book. All their children contributed photographs and articles.

Wartime Letters:
Hamp and Peggy Smith

1942 – 1945

Joan Noble

Matador
9 Priory Business Park,
Wistow Road, Kibworth Beauchamp,
Leicestershire. LE8 0RX
Tel: (+44) 116 279 2299
Fax: (+44) 116 279 2277
Email: books@troubador.co.uk
Web: www.troubador.co.uk/matador

ISBN 978 1784620 455

British Library Cataloguing in Publication Data.
A catalogue record for this book is available from the British Library.

Typeset in 11pt Aldine401 BT Roman by Troubador Publishing Ltd, Leicester, UK
Printed and bound in the UK by CPI Group (UK) Ltd, Croydon, CR0 4YY

Matador is an imprint of Troubador Publishing Ltd

I would like to thank my husband Peter Noble for his love and encouragement, for coming up with the title *Wartime Letters: Hamp and Peggy Smith* and for his very generous gift in funding the publishing of the book.

This book is in memory of our parents, Christopher Hampton Smith (Hamp) and Margaret Cowell Smalley Smith (Peggy), and for their grandchildren: Michael, Peter, Christopher, Cameron, Lauren, Rob, Jeff, Stewart, Andy, Erin and Caroline, and their great-grandchildren: Angelina, Nikhita, Ayden, Harriette, Cameron, Colton, Seth, Keane, Andrew and Nathan.

Joan Noble
Doug Smith
Pat Adamson
Ian Smith

April 2014

CONTENTS

INTRODUCTION

S ome of our earlier childhood memories involve a skeleton in the attic of our house. It had been acquired to assist our father's medical studies and it was kept in his blue Air Force trunk along with Air Force uniforms and paraphernalia, old photographs and stacks of blue airmail letters tied into neat bundles with white satin ribbon. At that time the skeleton was the most fascinating of the contents of the trunk. The letters though didn't go unnoticed. We were always aware of them and knew they were letters written by our parents to each other when our father was 'overseas' during the war. A few letters were even vandalised to make contributions to childhood stamp collections.

In this book we have reproduced the letters from the trunk. The letters were written by our parents to each other during their courtship (1942) and after their marriage when Father was overseas during the war (1944-45).

Our parents, Hamp and Peggy Smith, were married on 15th January 1943 at the First Baptist Church in Edmonton, Alberta in the middle of a prairie winter snowstorm. Peggy's father, the Reverend Doctor William Cameron Smalley, officiated. Hamp and Peggy met at the University of Alberta Hospital when he was studying medicine and she was a nursing student, a conventional doctor-nurse romance. After graduating in 1941, Hamp joined the Royal Canadian Air Force (Squadron 423) and spent some of 1942 touring rural Alberta doing medical examinations for potential recruits. He wrote to Peggy from small rural Alberta towns charting the progress of RCAF recruitment and his day-to-day travel in Northern Alberta. Peggy saved all these letters (hers have gone missing) so the early letters are a one-sided account of his work and their romance. After their marriage they were posted to the RCAF base at Claresholm, Alberta. Their daughter Joan was born in Edmonton on 17th October 1943. Hamp was posted overseas in April 1944. He was a Medical Officer stationed at Topcliffe, Yorkshire from May to December 1944. In January 1945 he was posted to Castle Archdale, Lough Erne, Northern Ireland with Coastal Command at the Royal

Air Force flying boat base. In June 1945 after V-E Day he was posted to Number 22 Canadian General Hospital in Bramshott, England as a Medical Officer in the venereal diseases unit. He was repatriated in December 1945. During this time Hamp and Peggy wrote to each other three to four times a week. They carefully saved their letters and for many years they were tied in bundles with white ribbon and stored in a trunk in the attic of our home in Camrose. All their letters, and a few from other members of the family, have been reproduced in this book.

Our mother and her parents

Our mother, Margaret (Peggy) Cowell Smalley, was born 25th November 1919 in Winnipeg Manitoba, the only child of William Cameron Smalley (born in Southport, Lancashire, 9th December 1880, died Camrose, Alberta 3rd December 1972) and Margaret Alice Smalley nee Cowell (born Blackburn, Lancashire 14th December 1891, died Camrose, Alberta 8th April 1979). WC (we called him Ba) went out to Calgary, Alberta, Canada in 1903. He was the son of a Baptist minister, and once in Canada, became interested in the ministry himself. In 1905 he moved to Brandon, Manitoba to attend Brandon College and work as a student pastor and in 1912 he was ordained as a Baptist minister. He was engaged to be married before going out to Canada and he returned to England and married Margaret Alice Cowell on the 4th September 1913 – a ten-year engagement! They set up home in Canada where he served as a pastor in rural Manitoba (1913-1924) and then the Fourth Avenue Church, Ottawa until his appointment as General Secretary of the Baptist Union of Western Canada in 1930 when they moved to Edmonton, Alberta. He was awarded an honorary degree of Doctor of Divinity from the Northern Baptist Seminary in Chicago in 1945. Searching Google for 'WC Smalley' brings up many references to his work in the Baptist church as well as this photograph of him taken when he attended Brandon College.

Margaret (Nana) was also a leader in her own right and served for a time as president of the Women's Home Mission Convention of Ontario East and Quebec. They were presented to King George VI and Queen Elizabeth and were present at a dinner in honour of Their Majesties at the Macdonald Hotel in Edmonton on 2nd June 1939. Margaret represented Canada in London in

Figure 1: W.C. Smalley, editor of the Brandon College paper, The Critic, 1912-13.

1951 at the Festival of Britain, Women's Department of the Baptist World Conference. Our mother, Margaret Cowell (Peggy) Smalley, born 25th November 1919 in Winnipeg Manitoba, was their only child. Peggy graduated from the University of Alberta School of Nursing in May 1943.

Our father and his parents

Christopher Hampton Smith (Hamp), born 28th October 1917, grew up in Camrose, the youngest and third child of Percy Frank and Ella Blanche Smith (nee Johnson). His father, known as PF, was a general practitioner. The Smith family antecedents left Clack Farm, Osmotherley, Yorkshire in 1817 and sailed from Hull to Prince Edward Island on *The Valiant*. They settled in Crepaud, PEI and the first church (Methodist) in Crepaud was built on their farm. PF was born in Bedecque, PEI on 25th March 1873, the eighth of nine children. He was a cousin of Lucy Maud Montgomery who wrote *Ann of Green Gables*. His mother, Margaret, was the eldest daughter of Speaker MacNeill, the first speaker of the House of Parliament in PEI after confederation. PF studied medicine starting in Dalhousie but then in 1902 changed to Physicians and Surgeons Medical, an annex of John Hopkins in Baltimore, Maryland so he could attend lectures by Sir William Osler. He graduated in 1906 and was awarded a gold medal in surgery.[1] He met our grandmother, Ella Blanche Johnson, in 1907. They planned to marry in August 1909 and settle in

Oklahoma City but he was stricken with diphtheria and the wedding was postponed. They were married in Arkansas on 30th March 1910 and after this, while convalescing, he made a trip home to PEI and then out to Alberta to visit friends. He was persuaded to stay in Alberta and joined in practice with Dr JG Stewart in Camrose. Blanche joined him in Camrose in December 1910.[2]

Blanche was born 6th February 1878 in Memphis, Tennessee the second of nine children. Her father was William Henry Johnston (the 't' was later dropped from the surname) who was educated at Marshal Institute, Mt Pleasant Mississippi reading law. He married Luella Florence Hughes in 1874. She was the daughter of Dr John Powell Hughes, a medical doctor and plantation owner at Collierville near Memphis where Blanche remembers spending many happy summers. Luella was a graduate of La Grange Female College in Tennessee. William Henry died suddenly when Blanche was quite young and the family was left in difficult circumstances. Luella later ran a boarding house in Arkansas Hot Springs and Blanche was working there at the time of her marriage.

Blanche and PF settled permanently in Camrose and had three children: Frank MacNeill (Mac) born 11th April 1912, graduated in medicine from the University of Alberta in 1936; Margaret born 8th March 1916, a teacher, and our father, Christopher Hampton born 28th October 1917. Mac married Irene Thibaudeau and they had three children: Alan (13th December 1936), Frank (1937) and Neill (14th May 1946). Margaret married William (Bill) Norton and they had two children: David (23rd May 1944) and Jean (30th September 1952).

What happened to everyone

Although Hamp and Peggy had other intentions, after the war they moved to Camrose so Hamp could provide some temporary relief for Mac and PF in their extremely busy medical practice. As it happened they stayed on and settled in Camrose. Hamp joined Mac and PF in the Smith Clinic and he and Peggy bought the old Burgess House at 4718-51 Street and that became our family home. Mac and Irene and Margaret and Bill also eventually built houses on 51st Street. The Smith Clinic became a large and successful group practice.

Hamp and Peggy had three more children: Douglas Hampton (11th December

1946), Patricia Louise (13ᵗʰ December 1947) and Ian William (2ⁿᵈ April 1955). The family lived at 4718-51 Street until Hamp retired from the Smith Clinic in 1978. Summers were always spent at Pigeon Lake and in the 1950s they bought a lot at Grandview Beach and built a cottage on the lakeshore. Hamp did much of the interior carpentry with some help from the family, and it became a focus of family holidays and gatherings for children, friends and later grandchildren. Hamp and Peggy settled there permanently after his retirement. In the summers they had all the grandchildren together for a week at the lake without parents. The cousins became friends and have many memories of their grandparents and 'the lake'. Michael Hollihn had written a short article about his grandfather as well as a poem about a visit to the lake cottage years after Hamp and Peggy had died and the cottage had been sold. These are in the appendices at the end of the book. Hamp died on the 25ᵗʰ October 1992 and Peggy stayed on at 'the lake' until her death on the 22ⁿᵈ April 1994. The eulogy to Hamp written by Doug and read at his funeral is also appended at the end.

Joan followed her mother's career and graduated from University of Alberta School of Nursing (Diploma Nursing 1965, Diploma Public Health Nursing 1966). She married Bernd Gert Hollihn on 14ᵗʰ June 1969 and they had two children: Michael Bernd Hollihn (14ᵗʰ May 1970) and Peter Christopher Hollihn (17ᵗʰ June 1972). Michael married Kamiljit Gill in 2001 and they had three children: Angelina Sky (2ⁿᵈ December 2001), Nikhita Sage (23ʳᵈ November 2005) and Ayden Arjuna (9ᵗʰ August 2007). Peter married Debra McRitchie in 1998 and they had two children: Harriette Tallulah (28ᵗʰ August 2002) and Cameron James (14ᵗʰ July 2004). Joan and Bernd were divorced in 1982. Joan married John Mason Sneddon in 1984 and divorced in 1988. Joan married Peter John Noble in 1992.

Doug also attended the University of Alberta graduating in 1967 with a Bachelor of Science in Biology and 1972 with a Bachelor of Science in Electrical Engineering. He married Gail Peterson (BSc Nursing 1971, U of A) in 1970 and they had three children: Christopher Douglas Hampton (18ᵗʰ October 1973), Cameron Gordon Hampton (27ᵗʰ July 1976) and Lauren Kierston Margaret (7ᵗʰ May 1979). Cameron married Olivia Godfrey in 2013. Lauren married Jon Cockerton in 2003 and they had two children: Andrew (18ᵗʰ August 2006) and Nathaniel Robert Gordon (27ᵗʰ December 2012).

Pat attended McTavish Business School in Edmonton and married Robert Garry (Bob) Adamson on 8th June 1968. They had two children: Robert Douglas (Rob) (22nd October 1969) and Jeffrey William (Jeff) (21st October 1972). Rob married Tarie Ann Frazier on 22nd July 2012. Jeff and Cheleen McBeath, together since high school, had one son, Colton Ray (1st December1994). Jeff and Cheleen separated in 1996. Jeff married Candace MacDonald on 14th September 2002 and gained a stepson, Keane Michael Lamoriss (11th May 1996). Jeff and Candace had a son Seth Arvid (2nd June 2002).

Ian attended the University of Lethbridge graduating with a BA in 1979 and then Queens University graduating with a degree in law in 1982. He married Cheryl Stewart on 30th June 1979. They had four children: Stewart Hampton (17th February 1981 – 4th April 2002), Andrew Charles (30th July 1983), Erin Jane (16th September 1985) and Caroline Anne (3rd November 1988). Erin married Cassidy Tutsch on 8th September 2013.

NOTES

1   Now in the possession of Joan Noble.

2   Blanche saved letters and cards that Percy wrote to her from 1907-1910 as well as letters from both of their mothers and other relatives over many years. Jeanie Parker (Norton) has typed them up and they have provided dates and interesting information about the family at this time.

THE LETTERS

1942

Hamp and Peggy met at the University of Alberta Hospital probably sometime in 1941. He was studying medicine and she was a nursing student. Hamp graduated in Medicine in 1941 and along with many of his contemporaries, joined the Royal Canadian Air Force (RCAF). In May of 1942 he was sent to Toronto on a training course. After this he was temporarily posted as a medical Officer at the RCAF base in McLeod, Alberta and then posted to the RCAF Recruiting Centre, Edmonton. He wrote to her regularly from Toronto, Fort McLeod and then many small rural Alberta towns giving an account of his daily life, news of mutual friends and his thoughts of her. Peggy saved all these letters (hers have gone missing) so the 1942 letters are a one-sided account of Hamp's activities and their romance. After his return from Toronto at the end of May there is much mention of their serious intentions and in his letter of 14 July Hamp mentions, "getting some jewelry". Their engagement must have become official in the late summer of 1942.

Unless indicated, all letters were addressed either to Miss Margaret Smalley 11034 – 89 Avenue, Edmonton, Alberta (her parents' home) or Miss Margaret Smalley, Undergraduate Nursing Staff, University Hospital, Edmonton, Alberta. Unless specified all Hamp's letters from 3 May to 27 May were headed Suite 401, Frontenac Arms Hotel, 306 Jarvis Street, Toronto.

Post Mark: Winnipeg May 1, 11:30 P.M., 1942

Dear Peggy (i.e. Peggy dear)

Just a line to let you know that I am alive and well and still out of the danger zone. We are getting near Winnipeg so will mail this to you from there. Have not had a very exciting journey (The train started here) thus far. Last night we sat around and talked for a couple of hours with Jonesy and then met Jim Saks who is in the navy and going back to Halifax where he has spent the past year. Listened to a monologue on the navy for over an hour but it was fairly interesting. Then I brought my bottle of rye and everybody had a nightcap and went to bed. Woke in Saskatoon at 6:00 A.M. and couldn't go back to sleep so the day has been a bit long.

We wired ahead to the Westminster last night and it will probably get reservation there (if the prices are right) but will keep you posted.

The people ahead of me have 2 children the youngest about 2 years and the mother just announced that it was no use trying to put him to sleep if he wasn't sleepy and he definitely is not sleepy. Unfortunately.

Well since I have run out of material I will stop. Could go on but you've heard all *that sort* of thing before now. Hope you got in O.K. last night. With love, Hamp

Toronto

Frontenac Arms Hotel
306 Jarvis Street
Toronto
May 3

Dear Peggy,

Well as you see we arrived this morning and are temporarily settled. We are staying at the Frontenac Arms but do not move to our permanent suite until tonight and am not yet sure of the number but this address will get us. (me in particular however).

Had very pleasant trip although not exciting – wish you were here. Second day out of Edmonton played penny ante poker all afternoon with a chap named Clark from Edmonton (lost $.50 which will have to go on my swindle sheet somewhere. Met a chap and his wife in the air force. Graduated in medicine with Johnnie Macgregor and Jimmie Calder and Max Cantor and formerly interned at the U of A Hosp. so we had a lot in common. We even shared our ryes and so spent our evenings in the club car and had a tall cool one or two and celebrated.

The country was really dull until we came towards Toronto and then it was beautiful. My first experience with farms with split rail fences, silos, etc. Trees are all in leaf and some bushes covered with white blossoms – to us farmers they looked like Saskatoon bushes from the train but were probably dogwood or something. Certainly am envious of the countryside here when I think of all the trouble we have to in order to find a place to drop a case of beer and here the whole country side is suitable. Certainly wish you were here.

The James Street Baptist Church is just across the street and very handy and certainly have gone if I was not slightly travel worn (pure propaganda for home consumption).

Have not had to salute anybody as yet but am afraid it's going to pretty tough down here.

We have a suite which has 2 bedrooms, sitting room, kitchen, bathroom for $80.00 a month so it really is a good set up – quite modern and all that so figure we did pretty well. As a matter of fact 2 could live as cheaply as one (more propaganda). I didn't copy down your ~~Dad's~~ pardon me, I mean your old man's address but will probably be able to dig it out of the phone book or somewhere. It has leaked out the sieve I call my mind.

Has rained all the way from the Saskatchewan border and is still raining. All Manitoba was about 6" under water but is just drizzling here. Very nice to look out your window and see fresh washed green leaves and grass. I certainly like their maples here – the one outside goes up past our window and we are on the 6th floor at present. Well I'll quit now and write you soon and would like to hear from you (and see you).

With love, Hamp

May 4, 1942

Dear Peggy,

Hope you don't think I am just writing my diary and sending it to you for safe keeping but have a lot to say so will proceed. Certainly miss you – nothing like you in Toronto or anywhere and can't express it.

Today we moved over to the #6 I.T.S. for our first class. Just signed in and told that was all for today. Met Harry Cooper (better known as Red Cooper) who graduated the year before I did. He I were very good friends previously although he was formerly quite a reprobate. Dave & Johnnie and I took him up to the room and we phoned down for beer. The desk clerk said their beer room wasn't open and we couldn't get it but soon there was a knock on the door and he appeared with 3 quarts of beer – said their license had been taken away from them but they kept a "little illegally to help the patrons". Charged $.50 a quart for Labatts Capital Lager which isn't bad.

We are just beginning to suspect that we are probably not in a first class hotel. Went down to have breakfast in the dining room and the desk clerk said "oh I wouldn't eat there if I were you – go up to the restaurant" and he walked out on the sidewalk and pointed to a place down the street. Apparently they run a dining room so they can sell beer and now they can't sell beer.

Went with Harry to the Manning Depot for women to see friend of Harry and his wife's (he's been married 5 days now and says he can recommend it). Quite interesting to see the joint. Then went to the Royal York to go to have a beer and met 2 other fellows from the course and drank beer until 12:30 noon and then went up to Harry's room had a bottle of rye – in other words it was damp and I am ashamed of myself dear but I must say nobody got drunk.

Ate lunch and met Peter Rule who graduated in architecture from U of A, then Harry, Johnnie, Dave and I with Peter to drive and Harry's wife to chaperone rented a Drive-UR-Self car and rode out to the Manning Depot and picked up Doug Ritchie. He's been working there and in the air force for 4 days and is already in uniform which is something. He took over the driving and we drove all over the city (or practically!) and sight saw and then around and found a suite for Harry and his wife and then a beer at a very nice B. Parlor and then a big steak and then around to the Royal York to the B P(arlor) I'm getting ashamed to write it and picked up Harry and his wife and Peter Rule and his wife and a girl named Nancy Smith who is a corporal in the women's air force and took Home Ec in Edmonton and whom Doug Ritchie is at presently pursuing (his intentions are honorable this time I really believe however) and 2 friends of the Rules (both married and so it was OK dear even though their husbands are overseas). Drank beer until 11:30 and drove them all home in a cab which was bad but and so home to bed at 1:00 A.M. but am first writing about it.

We have moved our suite again and our address will be Suite 401, Hotel Frontenac Arms, 306 Jarvis Street. This one has a hall, 2 bedrooms, a living room, kitchen, bathroom & dinette. Somebody wouldn't take it because he said smelled of cabbage (that chap Werthenback I told you about) but we had a beer and couldn't smell a thing and so took it. Apparently we aren't in a very good district and verging on a red light district but we say we are comfortable and the place looks OK to us, is 3 blocks from the school and to hell with it. Well my next letters won't be so wet – we get down to work tomorrow and so this will all go by the board. Will write you again. With love, Hamp

P.S. My last letter should have reached you late Monday but Dave forgot to post it (passing the …)

Post Mark: Toronto May 6, 3:30P.M., 1942

Dear Peggy,

Well am now commencing to get home sick but we don't finish the course until May 30 and then home. We are getting quite critical of Toronto and it has now been unanimously decided that there is nothing like the good old west with its straw stacks and stooks. Johnnie is quite bitter today and says $.50 buys the biggest haircut in Canada if you get it in Toronto – they have long ago thrown away the soup bowl pattern and are using saucers.

Went to school for 3 hours this A.M. and then had an hour's drill and then off for the rest of the day. Walked all over downtown Toronto and then ended up at a movie and then home where we read until couldn't keep our eyes open. Woke up at 11:00 when Dave came home from his Mother's and am now writing. Have been sending my letters to you to 11034 – 89 Avenue and don't know whether this is exactly correct or not so will send this one to the hospital to check (maybe I am getting a little impatient).

Well since this is just a line to let you know I still love you and that weather is OK and the beer is terrible and I still love you and the days have cloudy and cool here since we arrived but it has only rained once. Will close now and keep you posted. With love, Hamp

Post Mark: Toronto May 8, 12:30P.M., 1942

Dear Peggy,

Hope your mail isn't piling up on you but must keep my diary up to date. Had school until 4:00 P.M. again today. Included 2 hrs. of movies on principles of aircraft flight which were a little out of our line

7

but interesting. One lecture on the worries and trials of the student pilots another on air force organization. Also an hours drill in which we learned that if we didn't swing those arms we would keep the class back and furthermore would be a menace to the morale of the air force and undermine the defense effort of our country.

Tonight we went to a wrestling match at the Maple Leaf Gardens (which is 3 blocks from our apartment). Haven't had so much fun in a long time – a real show. There were 3 kids in front of us who cheered the villain and booed the hero. They were so unpopular with the rest of the crowd that we joined them and had the time of our lives but almost got involved in some arguments. Two women in front of us fainted when the villains got really tough and all in all we had a swell evening. Went with Werthenback and his wife and tomorrow he invited us over to his apartment. There is going to be a blackout sometime tomorrow night so he says he's going to lay in a supply and have a blackout party so that everybody won't know if the lights are on or off.

Have forgotten your Dad's address but will try to dig him up tomorrow if at all possible if I can do it without cutting into his schedule. Am putting up with quite a bit of heckling from Johnnie and Dave so I guess I better stop. Johnnie got his first letter away to home and loved one today. He's still laughing about a fellow sitting beside us at the wrestling matches – wearing a Christie stiff & pince nez and black evening coat and looking like our conception of the typical easterner – he was all for the heroes and we disgusted him utterly by cheering the bums. Well, hope I hear from you sometime and I miss you. Only 24 more days and we finish here. With love, Hamp

8/5/42

Dear Peg

Got your letters tonight – was certainly glad to hear from you. Was just about getting to the point that I was going to phone just to hear from you again.

Haven't contacted your Dad yet as was going up to Yonge Street today saw a sign on a church saying the Rev W C Smalley was speaking there on Sunday May 10 at 11AM. We are more or less planning to go to Niagara tomorrow but if we don't I am going out & listen to him.

Tonight we went to Dave's mother's apartment for dinner and sat around and played hearts etc. with his mother and sister and sister-in-law. Had a very enjoyable evening.

Just took time out a read your letter again – went through it so fast the first time that didn't get it all. Really now dear you will have to cut down on your smoking. I'm sorry you haven't heard from Marg & Doc etc. but hope you manage to entertain yourself. I feel a bit guilty about my holiday but my company is all male and will remain so. Glad to hear you are taking our prayers seriously. Thanks for reminding me of Freddy – to tell you the truth I kind of forgot and will get a letter off to Line Station and repeat what I've told you (except I won't tell him I love him).

Tomorrow we get our knocks – Schick, Dick, vaccination and TABT so don't know whether we'll want to go to Niagara or not after that. Well better quit and will keep writing from you. Can't tell you how tickled I was with everything when I heard from you.

With love, Hamp

June★ 7/ 42
(★Time sure is flying but would like to
believe it so won't cross it out)

Dear Peggy,

Should really write diary dearest but am a bit shy. Well we survived the blackout. Went over to Werthenbach's and sat with he and his wife and ate and also drank as you probably know. I'm not criticizing the blackouts here but I must say I certainly enjoyed the ones in Edmonton more and wish I was there for more (providing the company is yourself). Had a very dull day and nothing to report. Lectures all day and drill for an hour. Have now got a routine in which we come home everyday with anybody we can pick up and have a bottle of beer and then eat. Very nice routine as far as bull sessions go but I am not losing any weight – will cut down out of deference to you (if you still care). (The radio is just playing a rather depressing tune – "Somebody else is taking my place" – so guess I better go cry myself to sleep and quit bothering you. Hope you are OK and hope o hear from you soon. With love, Hamp

Dear Peggy

Well I didn't write you last night because I had nothing to write about except I miss you and I hope you take that for granted. Sat up at 6.60 am today and decided it was a good day to go to Niagara Falls. Went by bus and it was really a nice trip – fruit trees were in full blossom although I believe they are going off a bit now – beautiful country to say the least. As soon as we got there took a sight seeing tour of falls, rapids, etc. and then ate dinner and went up to the falls on the boat "Maid of the Mist". That properly impressed us but all the rest seemed highly commercialized and Johnnie thought they carried it so far that he wanted to stay there tonight and see if they turned the water falls off at night and put them back on again for the tourists in the morning. Also went across on the cable car but were not impressed. However a little bit burned. Slept yesterday afternoon and went to a show last night and went to bed early and OK today but everybody is still very cautious when they pull their coats on over their arms.

Didn't tell you that Nat Heath came over and took a couple of lectures with us. She isn't in uniform yet and her hats are still too big for a crowded room. Only spoke to her for a minute so don't know if she loves her work or not. Have not yet phoned Mrs Birrell and suppose I'll have to do it soon although I think I'm going to feel a bit stupid.

Well, wish you were here – if you get tired of nursing hop a train for Toronto. Much love, Hamp

Postcard

Post Mark: Niagara Falls, May 11 10 AM, 1942
P11 Front View, Horseshoe Falls of Niagara, Canada

Wish you were here because we stopped having a wonderful time after having seen the falls
    Love, Hamp

Dear Peggy,

Well have nothing to write about but hate to get out of practice. We stayed home tonight for a change. – We were going to go to a night ball game but was too cool and looked like rain. I decided to be the student of the crowd but Johnnie and Dave were thoroughly obnoxious and turned on the radio and kept talking to me. When that didn't work they went out and got two cases of beer and that finished it. At present Johnnie is standing behind Dave's chair – Dave's reading a magazine and when he gets the story well started Johnnie butts in and tells him how it ends so as you see we might just as well go out as stay in.

Got another letter today and glad to hear from you. Can't make me any more homesick than I am. We all are starting to talk about how pleasant Alberta is. Sorry to hear about Leona Carruthers – let me know how she gets along and what they found – if you think of it. Have ceased to be surprised at what Sam Epstein does and am sorry to say that Mrs. Smith's son is no longer numbered among his well wishers.

Today we had tropical medicine all day and all feel slightly infested with snakes, scorpions, mosquitoes, worms, etc. Haven't had any drill since last Friday and kind of miss it – will get 2 hours tomorrow. Everybody is complaining about the arduous schedule – by the way 90% of the school is pot bellied and feel like my figure is a bit brumby but comparatively passable but will still start on the salad-a-day regime – probably next week.

Got a bee in my bonnet I looked up hotels today – phoned the Prince George – "Mr. Smalley checked out today" so I guess I missed him. Apologies again dear.

Phoned up Mrs. Birriet tonight. She was out thank goodness.

Johnnie is getting very discouraged as he has not yet had a letter from Helen (he has written one by the way – last Tuesday). Is stubbornly resisting the temptation to break down and write another letter.

Have not yet done any shopping and if you can think of anything you would like me to look for down in the town here don't hesitate to let me know. Have just about finished my writing pad and realized that your budget is probably a bit strained after providing me with the means to correspond (which by the way is one of the handiest things I've ever had) so will enclose some stamps .. as an incentive. If it hurts your feelings – give me hell *Kid*! We had better sign off with love and kisses. Hamp

P.S. would add more but am afraid you don't burn my literary efforts. Love Hamp

The writing is worse than usual but I wrote while half lying on the chesterfield – not an excuse but ? just an explanation.

Enclosed in letter Toronto public transit ticket with notation written on it:

"Nearly forgot this but sliding it in. Have not been making a collection since I left you. – I'm one up anyone cares.

May 13, 1942

Paper wrapped around other card and letter:

INSTRUCTIONS ON HOW TO READ THIS LETTER

STEP I
Shake it all out on a large flat table. OR else remove envelope and mix contents in any handy box (beer box generally is handiest but this of course depends whether you are living at home or you aren't)

STEP II
Arrange contents in an orderly fashion starting at part A and keep going – if you lose interest keep going anyway – it'll prove you still love me. (over)

ALTERNATE INSTRUCTIONS ON HOW TO READ THIS LETTER
Burn it! It isn't worth the effort.

PART A (Letter)

Dear Peggy,

Well got your letter today and glad to hear you are getting out occasionally – I don't know who J. Levees is but consider him a very fortunate fellow. The chap who dishes out the rose's sounds sick enough to be safe for a while so won't worry about him.

Had rather a dull day – will enclose my notes on lectures today on the Dental Corps – am sure you will be interested in their organization. Had drill for 2 hours today and it was work. Wasn't hot today but sticky and your clothes seemed to glue themselves. Had a thundershower today (tonight) and boy saying it was a shower is an understatement, it was a cloudburst. Johnnie and I went to a show and just sat there and steamed after being out in the rain and left after seeing most of one of the pictures of a double feature and came home.

Certainly did well today in my mail. Got a letter from Margaret (in reply to one I wrote by the way – boasting again). Says she has been run ragged by showers etc. and has seen Bill about twice in 2 weeks. States she is going to start sending out invitations or something to the wedding. Says she doesn't want to send you one and have you feel obligated to buy a present – asked my opinion and I'm writing her and telling her not to because I know your salary and if you get a chance to go to the wedding *we* will go down together (providing my posting is right and you are willing – maybe I'm presuming a little too much – if I am, hell *Kid*!).

Johnnie got a letter from Helen today and is writing a return tonight – very pleased with himself. Dave is out at his Mother's place so we're just sitting looking at the wall.

Well had better sign off with love and a lot of other stuff that's silly – but nice. Only 18 more days. Hope you continue to get around a bit as I feel a bit guilty about my holiday realizing that in the past year I've kind of limited your activities and reduced your contacts.

Much love, Hamp

P.S. Had a letter from Dad today and he enclosed a cheque for $50.00 – force of habit I suppose. Will be one of the few of his that I have returned although is a temptation not to invest it in Kimberly

(Alpine) products. Figure I can about do this on my own hook however but Pappy's heart is sure in the right place.

More love, Hamp

PART B (Written on back of pkg. of Sweet Caporal Cigarettes)

Here are my notes on the organization of the Dental Corps. Took 3 hours to get them down but consider it time well spent as these facts are all of value and interest. (Consider them a military secret however.)

PART C

Putting a lot of trash in your letter but not very busy. Not a hint because it ain't needed but just some extras.

Photographs! (Not Autographed)

P.S. I found it only costs $2.85 to telephone (mercenary chap) – well have to talk about by mail sometime.

PART D (Postcard of Niagara Falls with locations X and Y marked on it)

Have an extra post card and lots of time so might as well take up some more of yours as well as your patience (also a good excuse to sign "with love") Can't remember any landmarks in the picture except X where we lost Dave and didn't find him for 3 hours which we spent looking for him by lying down reading at about Y. With love, Hamp

May 13/42

Dear Peg,

Nothing much to report as usual – suppose your mother has her postcard by now and that I am now on the family black books. Don't know how to get off of them but hope I'm not on yours.

Doug Ritchie came over tonight and we all had a long bull session. He sent you his very best regards and meant it. He hasn't changed a bit – asked him how he really liked the east and he leaned back and said "Well, I'm not one to boast about my conquests or mention my defeats but etç." – so you see he hasn't changed a bit but I like him just the same. Says he was over at the Western the other night and he & Joe

Chamberlain gave us a buzz. but we weren't in so will have to give Joe a buzz and see if he is as unhappy about Toronto as we are although I imagine he is quite pleased with the hospital.

Say I'd better improve my writing. Eventually it got out tonight about my daily correspondence and Ritchie said she probably can't read them and just uses them as an indication that you are still thinking of her. I'm ashamed to admit this is probably correct.

School today as usual – had a number of movies on the effect of gravity on the human body with blacking out, loss of consciousness, etc. – quite interesting. Things will begin to brighten up a bit next week when we start inspecting the various westigatan units and their equipment.

Glad to hear from you letter today that Sam is doing so well – hope he proves so invaluable down there that the gov't hears about him and drafts him. Sorry to hear you are getting broke. Say *kid*! How about going to a show on your night off – don't know if I can get there on time or not but will get the tickets (if you will allow me) – take one of your girl friends (e.g. A. Boyd) and don't mention the fact that I invited you. Will give you the necessary for tickets and meal and you get mine and wait for me and if I don't show up go on in anyway. (If this build up doesn't sound so good – consider it a loan) to be paid back as formerly and won't hold you to it if your ideas (in my regard change).

Glad you have your mother and aunt started on the idea – hope you keep it up – for my sake – doubtful if you are thoroughly convinced but I sure discourage hard. Well had better quit and I will write you soon (in about 24 hours). Give my regards to Freddie et al. Still wish you were here (one track mind I have). Much love, Hamp

May 14/ 42

Dear Peggy,

Nothing to report. Weather has been very sticky and another rainstorm tonight. Went to a double feature at 5:00 p.m. and got out just before 9:00 so you can see we are not very busy. Are not very happy with our work. No mail today so was a bad day all around. Well had better quit squawking because one can't have everything. Are getting to the stage where we can see the beginning of the end of the course so things will look progressively brighter. Had my first salad today – lobster & mayonnaise so you can see my good intentions don't amount to much. Well had better quit as haven't got anything to write about. Miss you as usual. Much love, Hamp

May 15/42

Dear Peg,

Glad to hear from you again (that's putting it mildly – maybe I'm getting spoiled by these daily letters.) Sorry to hear you're overworked again – have worked out a scheme so you can avoid it – will have to explain it to you sometime. — Time out while everybody gets excited about school being half over. Johnnie and myself are unanimous that the time has certainly dragged & Dave said it went pretty fast so far. That all goes to prove that Dave is a confirmed bachelor. Everything has been day to day except the weather. If we hadn't been bored to tears for about half of our 6 years or so in medicine, I'm sure we wouldn't have been able to tolerate some of our lectures today. Has rained steadily all day. We sat around all evening and were just about to start to study and then realized what a rut we were getting in and so went for a long walk in the rain and got thoroughly soaked. Came home, found I'll have to stand in the back now at drill tomorrow as my only other pair of pants is at the cleaners.

Phoned up Joe Chamberlain tonight at the Western. He and the rest of the boys are apparently quite pleased with the place. He was on duty tonight so is coming over tomorrow afternoon to see us (Saturday and our P.M.) suppose will end up at a show as there is so damned little else to do down here.

Nat Heath showed up at school today in her uniform. Was very disappointed that it was raining and told everybody it was the first time in her life she ever paid $10 for a hat and on top of that put it on for the first time & walked out into a rainstorm. Got so mixed up in her saluting that says she saluted a street car conductor. She's posted to Rockcliffe – a training centre for women 5 miles out of Ottawa. There is MO for about 800 women and is not particularly overjoyed.

16

Had a letter from Mother and she says Bill Waterton[1] (a chap in the RAF back from England and who I've only seen once since he went over 3 years ago – that about a month ago) – anyway he told her I was contemplating matrimony – at least I was trying to persuade somebody else it would be a good thing. So Maw writes that's very nice and hopes its true – although not too soon. You may be interesting to know that she thinks the Smalley girl very pretty and very lovely girl, etc. Well not much more to write about except I heartily concur in above statements and could say much more. Will write you and report my activities. Was certainly pleased with the reiteration of your sentiments regarding myself and will never take them for granted (by that I mean I'll always make sure I deserve them). Much love, Hamp

May 17, 1942

Dear Peg,

Well Sunday afternoon and just sitting and looking at the wall. Still cloudy and cool and trying to rain but rather welcome it as we are too lazy to do anything anyway. Yesterday afternoon Joe Chamberlain and Doug Florendine came over. We got a dozen and sat around for 3 hours discussing the east. They like the Western very well and are too busy to worry about Toronto itself. From what they say they should have a real good internship this year. Went out and had a chicken dinner and then walked up and down Yonge looking for a show but then we didn't want to see them or we had seen them so got another couple of dozen and came home and sat and listened to the radio. We all went to sleep about 11:30 and woke up at 1:30 and then the boys went home saying how they enjoyed the evening – rather doubted it but we enjoyed them anyway.

Joe got busy writing a letter to you. Put it in an envelope and wouldn't let me censor it so I will enclose it (unread by me so help me). Don't know whether its contents are OK or not as he had several of the dozen but will take a chance.

Dave is out at his mother's and Johnnie is writing a letter also so is very peaceful here. (too damned peaceful). We will probably get our postings this coming week and then will know whether it's at

Moosebank or Labrador and how long approximately. I applied for overseas or #4 training command (west of the Saskatchewan border approx) so have lots of leeway – hope it is Edmonton of course but can't be sure.

Johnnie went downtown for 2 hrs yesterday to buy a present for Helen. Got thoroughly worn out but didn't see anything to get for her – says its all junk. Expect to have the same trouble shortly.

Well am beginning to get even more dull than usual in my literary efforts so had better stop. Your mother has probably gotten her postcard by now so I suppose diplomatic relations have been broken off – hope isn't contagious and spreads to rest of the family. Well, hope to hear from you tomorrow – quite a silence – Saturday, Sunday and to Monday, at 5:00 P.M. when we get our daily mail. Hope you are well and weight continuing to improve. Much love, Hamp

May 16, 1942

Dear Peggy,

We have been over at the F.O.'s suite since about 3 P.M. It is now about 11 – drinking beer in fairly large quantities. We went out and had a chicken dinner at the usual time, then went to the Royal York for a beer and decided it would be more comfortable back at the suite so a 2 dozen job was purchased and here we are. The lads are suggesting what I should write but I am deaf to their suggestions. We are well satisfied with the Western Hospital but of course are a little critical here and there after being in U.A.H. There are an awful lot of good men here of course and quite a few that aren't – we have seen a lot of stuff we don't agree with. The nurses are nothing extra as far as I have seen.

Chris tells us Rentries got hitched. Give him our best will you? Also Bunny and tell him I'll write him soon.

Tuesday night I took a girl from T.W.H. to hear Glen Gray and Cara Lowaorch in a place here – it was the real stuff. I mean the band was! I haven't taken the girl out again – yet.

Chris felt pretty lonely at Niagara they tell me but they didn't stay there long so he didn't do anything about it. That's about all for now. I'll let Chris finish this off. Sincerely, Joe.

Dear Peg,

Two letters today – you certainly did yourself proud and made life worth living once again. Glad to hear the stamps were favorably received and sorry that you couldn't go to a show with me but admit it was a bit far fetched but seemed like a good idea at the time. Glad to hear that you were able in some measure to talk your mother out of having a hatchet hung for Hampton – or at least making it a dull one. Now all I have to worry about is your Pappy getting the ax and grinding it a bit.

Sorry Johnnie and I couldn't horn in on your beer bust but if everything you say is so the beer went farther – less people to drink it and well diluted by you and Helen weeping into glasses. Say kid! I notice you said you didn't start to get mournful until 11:10 – it wasn't the alcohol was it – (you don't have to reply on this one as I'm just making conversation).. Glad to hear you got to a show without financial backing from myself and really overjoyed to hear the competition isn't too keen.

Got a letter from Freddy Day today and told me that you were over at his place – he wrote it while giving an anesthetic. Yesterday dropped him a line asking him why in hell he didn't write so if you see him tender profuse apologies in my part and that his epistle was gratefully received and contents avidly assimilated.

Tonight we went down to a show – King's Row – quite a good picture but not too cheerful – people going crazy and others having their legs cut off and other entertaining but not too happy incidents. Had quite a good organ which played between parts and was very enjoyable. – vaguely remember similar one in Capital in Vancouver.

By the way darling (affectionate creature, isn't he") that line in the letter that you couldn't read has gotten me beaten. Am making a special effort to improve but doesn't seem to make much difference. The part in your letter stating that you will never change your views is certainly pinning yourself down and expresses my sentiments exactly and want you to know I've made up my mind about you and want no one else and will never change my views.

Tomorrow our day is taken up with instruction in how to do the M2 examination for aircrew and since did this for the first two months in the RCAF don't expect much new but will admit you learn something everyday. The class is divided in two groups – our group works tomorrow night and are off tomorrow afternoon and so in our time off have arranged to go to the shooting range and practice revolver shooting. Johnnie bought and read a western story yesterday and so is all prepared to uphold the traditions of Alberta and impress these Easterners how we were brought up shooting rustlers and running sheep herders off our ranges. (Will let you know just how bum we are)

Our social whirl has kind of hit a backwash but are invited out to dinner on Wednesday. Harry Cooper's wife is going to put on a demonstration and show us the advantages of home life.

Well had better quit. Still love you more than ever and wish you were here. Much love, Hamp

P.S. As far as pinning me down to name the day – you name and then just try to get out of it.

P.S. What do mean *supposed* to be the luckiest man in the world – I am (re you anyway).

May 19 /42

Dear Peg,

Well, nothing to report as usual. Am writing this in face of great odds – namely my roommates. But just can't pass up the opportunity to tell you I love, miss you & wish – oh well – I wish. (that line is beginning to get a bit stereotyped although have not yet figured out another combination of words to express the fact that I miss you and wish you were here.)

Had the afternoon off and went revolver shooting – did very poorly but was a lot of fun. Tonight went to school for an hour and then picked up Werthenback and sat for a while and then his wife came down and spent the evening with us. They brought rye but we steadfastly refused to drink it and consumed Ontario beer – they ended up very punchy and had a very nice evening and we all only moderately so. Tonight is my last night – tomorrow start that reducing diet for sure (says he now). Have the whole day off until tomorrow at 3:30. I then only work an hour, so they are really beginning to bread down – up to now in our schedule of 9 to 5 we have only had one lecturer who has failed to show up so we really can't grumble about the school being poorly organized – although would like to.

Tonight it isn't raining but is steamy hot so have always something to complain about. Well had better quit. Much love, Hamp

P.S. The finger – how Big? – ? ? ? ? ? (Get it?)

P.S. *The next day – Time 2:20 P.M.*

Have just gotten up and eaten and read my mail – a letter from Johnnie Hunt. He's in practice with his brother in Lethbridge and joining the RCAF in the fall. No mail from Edmonton – 2 days running – an all time low. Had better keep quiet before I put my foot in my mouth. Am now off to school.

Much love, Hamp

May 20/ 42

Dear Peg

In the last letter at 2pm today (it is now midnight) I said if I didn't quit my foot would end up in my mouth-well it did – received your letter about 2 hrs after mailing mine. Certainly apologize because anyone of those 12 pages you wrote more than compensated for the day before. Sorry to hear you aren't feeling so well & hope you are OK by the time this arrives – keep forgetting that you are still working as hard as ever & that it isn't easy to sit down & write a letter after you are too tired to hold up your head. In the future if I don't hear from you will take it for granted and you certainly don't have to apologize.

Went over to Harry Cooper's for dinner and had a home cooked meal and it certainly didn't help the diet at all – his wife sets up a pretty good dinner. After dinner we went out to a night baseball game. We didn't' have to pay anything to get in because we were in uniform and so really can't criticize the game but it was pretty poor baseball. After the game went back to Harry's for coffee and sandwiches and the home to you – next best thing anyway to talk to you via the mail.

Tomorrow have limited amount of school again and plan on going to the wrestling match and watching the "Angel", You probably remember having seen his picture – an acromegalic that makes the Neanderthal man look like a matinee idol. Should be corny but fun.

This weekend have Saturday off. Don't know what we will do-probably sleep and then after that we can really start counting the days in earnest. No word yet of the postings. In a way it would be rather a good thing for your Dad if he accepted the church in Vancouver. He isn't getting any younger and that job he's got now is a dickens of a lot of work and responsibility and worry for a man without an ulcer let alone a man with one. But I must say dear he probably would work just as hard anywhere so what difference and besides who would fill his present job-nobody as capably I can tell you and I'm not just boasting about my girlfriend's old man but heard it from many directions.

Let me know how Sheila Beauchamp comes along and when. Have not got them a wedding present and have to get something for the baby. If you have any ideas on the subject whether you think them good or bad send them along. Please I mean.

Well Peg I had better sign off for the night. Apologize for my letter of this afternoon and hope you aren't displeased. Hope your summer complaint is transient and that your next letters don't report "bismuth (sic) as usual". In future when you are tired don't stay up to write (I mean it) – providing you spend about 10 minutes dreaming. Give my very best regards to your family and your Dad – I was sorry to have missed him. That I look the same as everybody else in uniform if I keep my stomach in and the hayseeds brushed off. Had definitely better quit although it is quite a temptation to go on just because this is the nearest thing to talking to you that I can get. By writing and looking at you (your picture) am practically carrying on a conversation – one sided however. Much love, Hamp

PS Hope you understand the 1st PS in the last letter – more love – Hamp

May 22 /42

Dear Peg

Received your letter and surprised to hear I missed a day – haven't been writing Saturday night and that must be the answer – will take steps to correct the omission. Nothing to report as usual – you apparently have recovered from you indisposition & glad to hear it. As for Mrs Wallace one just has to taker her for granted with other things that mar perfection – like ants in a picnic or caterpillars on the trees on a summer night with a full moon shining over the riverbank onto the Saskatchewan.

Did not go to the wrestling matches tonight. We saw a show called Mr V or something-was quite good. Had a bad day today – in drill today it was my turn to get out and give commands – afraid yours truly ("with much love") will never make a general. Today had our Schick and Dick tests and apart from these things did very little.

You and Helen are apparently seeing quite a bit of each (I mean the little bit of each other is seeing the other quite often). I keep Johnnie informed of your activities so he doesn't worry about Helen sitting home of an evening knitting. He at present is sitting here reading a Western story and too lazy to write so really shouldn't pass along any news.

Well have nothing much to say except a lot which you very well expressed as possibly better kept for a few days and then passed along in person (assuming very hopefully that the posting is going to be OK – but even if I get to Labrador its going to be via Edmonton and that's positive and definite. Well better sign off & goodnight & —-Much love, Hamp

PS How is the stamp supply? If you don't want to go to a show alone don't hesitate to invest in stamps and send them back (cancelled stamps are legal tender to me)

PS

Sun	Mon	Tues	Wed	Thurs	Fri	Sat
					1	2
3	4	5	6	7	8	9
10	11	12	13	14	15	16
17	18	19	20	21	22	23
24	25	26	27	28 ★	29	30 X
31						

X-on the train, ★-if you should write on Thurs it would get here on Sat.-our last day here

Dear Peg,

Nothing to report but am doing it twice anyway – to explain. Wrote one letter to you tonight so far explaining in some detail how very little there was to write about. Have tomorrow off and knowing me to be as lazy as I am I figured it would be a good idea to mail it tonight. (Are you still following me?) Anyway put on the coat, the hat, the gloves and goes out into the rain (it's rained hard all day and we haven't seen the sun for a week) and got out and hear a voice 4 flights up saying "Say Chris – here's your letter." It fluttered down 2 stories and then stopped on a windowsill and there remains. Johnnie, after he quit laughing, figured he better apologize and said he'd write a note and here it is enclosed forthwith. (Are you still following? and if you are do you wonder why?).

Had another bad day at school – Medical Statistics explained to us for 3 solid hours with only a 5 minute break after 1 1/2 hours. and then a chalk-talk or drill for an hour. This afternoon learned how to don respirators in the approved fashion and then went into the gas chamber. Took them off and then 30 people tried to crown out at once – the small people got shoved to the back and so I was the 29th out and really weeping by then.

Tonight saw Bob Hope in My Favorite Blonde – quite good if you like the type. Hope at 8:30 P.M. and have been writing letter to you steadily ever since. While Johnnie is sitting drinking beer and throwing my efforts out onto the windowsills. To repeat what I said in the first letter (some soul may see it and mail it) – I hope you don't get small pox and don't know why they should pick on you to nurse the case when you haven't been vaccinated recently (Except of course understand that they wanted the best nurse ~~in the hospital, in Alberta, in Canada~~ in the world).

We had better quit now.

Much love, Hamp

P.S. Couldn't figure out what was written on the back of the envelope of your letter today or who wrote it.

More love, Hamp

Dear Peg,

I'm starting this letter to apologize for the fact that the last letter written you're not going to receive. Having started it via Air Mail by throwing it out the 4th floor window to expectant Chris on the street below, and fully expecting the same to land safely either on or shortly off the side walk and having duly considered relative humidity, wind currents, laws of gravity and several bottles of beer, the release was grand. It fluttered like a gull in the breeze, for a while. Anyway to make a long story short its now laying on the windowsill of the 2nd floor. I think something went wrong.

Signed CH Smith for J. H. Young (the heel)

May 23/ 42

Dear Peg

Here we sit Johnnie, Joe Chamberlain and myself – I'm being quite rude and disregarding the conversation and writing to yourself. Nothing to write about except yourself and could write on this subject all night but probably not interest you as great deal. So far today have read my lectures for a couple or 3 hours, gone to a show (Shores of Tripoli and not good) and then ate and came home. Joe phoned and told him to come over and we would go out somewhere but instead have sat here and drunk beer and discussed the worries of the world. So far this evening have gambled 50 cents – 25 cents to Johnnie that you couldn't buy a wedding ring for $300 – still think they are very plain and secondly that the sun will shine before Tuesday (25 cents) – Also bet 25 that we would both be posted to recruiting centre at Edmonton. Has been quite a daring evening if my expenses continue at present rate I doubt I will be able to afford an engagement ring (this is my 6th bottle of beer that's talking but is the expression of what my subconscious self has on my mind). Will now attempt to write legibly and carefully as the contents of this letter to now probably quite illegible.

No letter today and take it for granted by now you probably have the communication stating that you don't have to write if you are too tired (magnanimous bloke ain't I?) You can kick me when I'm accessible if you want to.

Have now 10 letters from you and saving them all to read them over at every opportunity-can cover missed day by re-reading so it's OK.

Had better quit as I don't imagine this is very entertaining. Will see you in about a week. Miss you more as the days go by instead of acclimatizing myself to the idea of not having you where I can see you every day. Much love, Hamp

PS The writing is terrible but statement very sound

Canadian National Telegram

Confirmation of Telegram Telephoned
To: Miss Margaret Smalley
11024 – 89 Avenue
Edmonton
May 25 7:03 P.M., 1942
Posted to Recruiting Centre Edmonton Love Hamp.

May 24, 1942

Dear Peg,

Absolutely nothing to write about so will proceed to write about nothing with a clear conscience as you have been warned. Set aside today to study and managed to do about everything but that. You may have gathered that when Joe Chamberlain was over last night we all got quite happy. Went out about 1:00 A.M. and had onion sandwiches and then home to sleep to noon today. Joe wrote you another letter but this one kind of petered out (so did Joe by the way) so it was censored by myself.

After getting up have written letters home, read a couple of magazines, listened to all the radio programs, eaten a couple of meals and since it is now about 11:00 PM am practically getting to the stage where my conscience will drive me to my books. Have now got a pile of mimeographed sheets about 5"high (I'm not exaggerating) and are expected to know them. Johnnie is sitting across the room – he reads about 3 pages and then reads for a while from a western story and then carries on after a smoke and changing the radio a couple of times and remarking that its only 5 more days to the last day – so you see we are very hard up for something to do.

By the way wrote Roy Bunap and asked him to give you my stethoscope and percussion hammer which I left at the recruiting centre – that is if he ever happened to near UAH or your residence. Hope you don't mind me piling more junk on you.

Dave has spent the day at his uncle's so we have had nobody to annoy all day and find it very dull.

Well had better sign off again. Hope to hear from you tomorrow and no doubt will (getting a bit overconfident isn't he). Much love, Hamp

May 25, 1942

Dear Peg,

Posting to #3 Recruiting Centre Edmonton. Leave here Saturday night and guess will arrive in Edmonton on Tuesday morning – not sure but believe that is correct. Posting in a way is everything I wanted but to be honest had it 5th in my preference list which in order was 1} Overseas 2} #4 Training Command a) SFTS b) EFTS c} B & G School d) Recruiting Centre. Reason is that there is the least medicine to be obtained at a Rec. Centre but in the final analysis they are all essentially the same and the recruiting centre has the advantage that may never be achieved at the others. Suspense is finally ended. Johnnie goes to Patvela Bay on Vancouver Island & Dave goes to Uculet or some such place on the west side of Vancouver Island. We all wanted to stay in the west but they really went as far west as it was possible to go.

Today went over to #1 I.T.S. Dull morning but this afternoon went for a ride in the low pressure chamber. Quite an interesting experience. Went up to 30,000 feet and then got one of us to volunteer to take off our oxygen masks – mine wasn't very comfortable and I thought would be a cheap drunk so tried it. Quite interesting experience – I got very dizzy in about 3 minutes, lost track of what was going on after 5 minutes and was just blacking out about 6 minutes when somebody thought it would be a good idea to give O2. The instructor went 13 minutes – a record – the only reason he made it was because after about 8 minutes

27

he had passed out and we didn't realize it as he could still move and let him go until somebody looking in a port hole said either we give him oxygen or he was going to let the machine down with a rush.

Tomorrow we go over to the clinical investigation unit and see their setup – giant centrifuges etc. for reproducing the effect of gravity on the boys and so will try to stand in front of the line and get knocked out again.

Well will quit and mail this. Hope you are pleased with the posting too. Will see you soon.

Much love, Hamp

P.S. Got a letter today from my gal and glad to hear that she is happy in work – hope they don't overwork her.

May 26, 1942

Dear Peg,

Wrote in kind of a hurry last night to be sure it got mailed – really glad to go back to Edmonton but still have to wear a uniform around the hometown. Oh well, my company compensates and don't feel too conspicuous in the street with you as I know nobody is looking at <u>me</u> anyway.

Last night we took the ferry out to the island and walked all over hell's half acre but saw it all and came home tired but feeling that we were conscientious sight seers again. Today spent the morning at the Clinical Investigation Unit. Quite interesting with giant refrigerators etc. After that stopped for Kaki shirts and then came home and spent the afternoon reading our précis. Went to a show tonight Abbot & Costello – not very good and on top of that we had seen the news reel 4 times (inclusive) and so weren't particularly impressed.

May 27, 1942

Dear Peg,

Well business as usual and as usual there is no business – just sitting looking into space (and reading the Sat. Evening Post). I'm getting a little hard to get along with I guess – Dave & Johnnie went to the "Water

Follies" but was damned if I wanted to go sit for a couple of hours and watch people get wet when we have been doing nothing but that for 3 weeks. Sun really shone today and weather couldn't be complained about at all which is a hardship because that's the main topic of conversation (as you probably realize by now).

Spend the morning at the Link trainer and had a lot of fun although in my present state find I am not much of a pilot. Johnnie got it into a spin and practically bailed out before the instructor told him what to do to get out of it. This afternoon had our night vision tested – sat for 45 minutes with dark goggles on and then sat 15 minutes in the dark and then got tested at various levels of illumination equivalent to night without moon, moonlight night, etc. – quite practical but a waste of time – even if I had flunked I didn't think it would have let me out of night work at the recruiting centre.

Tomorrow we are supposed to go the recruiting centre and to the Manning depot but if the sun is shining Mrs. Smith's son is going to get a sunburn (a bit complicated when reread by the writer). Had a letter from home today. Preparations for the wedding are apparently going full blast and to a neutral observer there seem to be a few cases of acute nervous exhaustion in the offing. Showers are a dime a dozen and there have been several dollars worth to date and Margaret seems to be making a better haul than the average individual who used to sail the seas and stick up galleons. If she keeps on

Letter post marked Toronto

May 28 3.30 PM 1942

1 page in envelope page marked 5 and 6 – may be continuation of above

keep harping on this but figure that one donation from this side of the Smith combine is adequate. Now don't get your feelings hurt again dear.

Arrive in Edmonton Tuesday morning and on arrival will get settled and then phone your mother as to what your hours are etc. so you aren't disturbed at your work. Have to start the routine of finding another place to stay and all that which won't be any fun. Report to work on morning of May 4th.

Saturday afternoon in Camrose there is a wedding reception[2] (to me it sounds as though the people they've swindled presents out of won't be able to afford to eat for a while and are going to serve accordingly. You of course have been invited if you can make or want to. All this may sound as if the Smith's are trying to put the pressure on you so it looks like your opportunities for springing the trap before you put your neck in it are getting fewer.

Johnnie arrives in Edmonton Tues AM and leaves Wed AM so hasn't very much time at home.

Well had better sign off now as the continuity of the epistle has just ceased to exist. Will see you some Tuesday. Much love, Hamp

PS The writing of some of this is so bad can't even attempt to proof read it. Don't let it fall into unfriendly hands or they'll probably haul you up for receiving letters in Japanese. However, as Ritchie says – it at least proves I'm still thinking of you – which proves something.

Margaret and Bill's wedding 6th June 1942. From left: Hamp, Ella Blanche (Grandma Smith), Margaret, Frank Smith (in background) and Bill

MacLeod, Alberta

Station Hospital
#7SFTS
Macleod, Alta
June 14, 1942

Dear Peg

Well have finally got a little bit settled. Would have written before but strange place, strange room, no ink, didn't know where to get ink etc. To begin at the beginning had a pleasant trip down – met a Major who commands an army unit at Trail, B.C. and he was very pleasant and gave me a lot of fatherly advice about what to do and what to expect at a new station. First night had transport waiting at the station and then taken to Officer's Mess where Sq. Ldr. Brewster, the senior medical officer waited up for me and gave me the low down on the set up – he is a very swell fellow and is going to make it very pleasant here.

The hospital is a 35 bed one enlarged to hold 42. They do all their own surgery here and have a swell set up. Their own x-ray, a nice operating room and facilities for practically anything you want. At present there are only about 15 patients in a couple of post op hernias, fracture, mumps, G.C., head colds and the like. Yesterday morning somebody got hit on the head by an air screw (propeller to me – up to yesterday) – got a gash clean across his scalp but no fracture. I consider he was fairly lucky.

To describe the station to you – its a swell place by the way. There are about 1200 men here at present and it is going to be increased to 15 – 1600. They fly nothing but Anson's here (2 engines) and have between 75 to 80 on the station so there are always some flying and haven't got used to the noise at night yet. They have about 180 – 200 student pilots and mostly RCAF except for a few Aussies. The Officers Mess is very nice and there are about 110 officers on the station, most of them young and all very friendly but as yet haven't gotten to know any and consequently am more or less a lost sheep but not grumbling about it yet (except I wish my girl were here).

This morning went down to the hangars for the first time and went for a flip (getting very colloquial very rapidly) in an Anson. Flew across the country and ended up over Lethbridge and then back here. They say the air was quite bumpy but fortunately didn't get ill on my first trip.

My work here isn't too bad. At present, Sq. Ldr. Brewster and myself are the only M.O.'s here with another one coming. In the morning get breakfast by 8:30 and then to hospital by 9:00 A.M. and make ward rounds. Just a matter of looking at everybody and writing their diet for the day. Then at 10:00 A.M. there is morning sick parade and then generally do M2's. – not much change from the recruiting centre in that respect. Have about 50 to be done on people who are remustering to aircrew and this at the recr. centre would seem a bit of a chore but don't feel to badly about it down here because of doing them in the hospital, etc. The station here is a mile and a half from MacLeod. There is a bus service from here to town and so are not too isolated – except I haven't got anybody to go in with anyway. Have a room to myself in the Officer's Quarters. Cool and light but not exactly cozy – the rooms are all double but have no roommate as yet anyway.

Really feel I'm going to like it here and am going to try hard to anyway. We are just barely in the foothills with snow-capped mountains in the distance so it's quite a nice spot. The wind started to blow today and guess it will just keep on although it was calm for my first day here (yesterday). Feel a little bit isolated but don't mind staying here (too much) now that we have discussed things with each other and have reached an understanding with something definite to look forward to and to wait for.[3] I'm afraid my posting will be temporary here only since they have their full complement of M.O's when they all get back from leaves, etc. but at least will have had a taste of what goes on.

The mailing here is a bit vague to me as yet and this is another excuse for not giving my address sooner. Another is I wanted to look around a bit so could give you an idea what it was like.

There are 2 nursing sisters here – one is a Nancy Smith who graduated from U.A. Hosp – about my brother's vintage. Have only seen them twice for about 2 minutes each time. Because I have stuck pretty close to the hospital – I don't know where they stuck. One of the former ward aides of the UAH is here – a blondish girl with glasses and sharp nose and quite pleasant and who used to work on the 3rd. She is a hospital assistant here and seems very capable.

Well have kind of run down so will close and write you soon. Hope you didn't get pneumonia. Much love, Hamp

P.S. Paper isn't very fancy but just grabbed what was handy – will improve.

14/6/42

Dear Peg

Well wrote you this afternoon and gave you the low down. Tonight am not so cheerful (summer night, warm breeze, nothing to do—-& my gal ain't here-it might just as well be snowing). The postal facilities here are a bit limited so decided to begin an epistle to be added to daily and mailed bi-weekly. If this isn't sufficient to maintain my contacts will double or even triple production but as it would largely be drivel don't think this would be very satisfactory either. It's a good thing one doesn't have to worry about accommodation in MacLeod – one officer started looking for a house for he and his wife last March and has just succeeded in finding one. As nothing has happened since last writing except night has fallen (& that is a fairly routine happening here) will sign off and continue later.

June 15

Well another day written off and quite a day. This morning 2 Ansons from the station collided about ten miles from here. Students soloing in each of them were instantly killed and pretty well mangled and both aircraft are total losses. Didn't go to the crash but was all day at the hospital – sick parades, sprained ankles, burns and various minor stuff as well as writing boards for discharging air women and doing examinations for aircrews have been busy all day. Also a couple of aircraft ran in to each other while taxiing and another ran out of gas and made a forced landing on the edge of the field – nobody hurt in these. All in all was enough activity. A new medical officer is supposed to arrive tonight but hasn't shown up yet.

The wind has blown hard all day and everybody seems to take it for granted – various arguments as to its velocity some saying its 60mph but most saying it probably isn't more than 30-40 mph which apparently is just a breeze. The letter I wrote you yesterday left today so suppose it will be a few days before I hear from you. One certainly gets to look forward to mail after even a short time. Wrote Fred and Alix today and thanked them for their many kindnesses. The morning I left Fred got very confidential with me and told me that one of the reasons Alix got a little tired a little early was that they are 3 months along towards having a family. Nobody knows this apparently except them and Dr Vant and Alix wants to keep it quiet for some reason or other. He didn't ask me to say nothing but assumed I would. Don't know whether you knew or not but anyway don't let on to Freddy or Alix that you know or that I told you. Alix apparently has had a little trouble with nausea etc. so guess I should feel quite ashamed for buying beer etc.

Keep kicking myself for not seeing you the morning I left. Figured it would be better at the time – didn't want to embarrass you at your work. Now I wish I had. Oh well will see you on my first 48 hr leave which should be coming along in 2 or 3 weeks. Putting in an early bid for a date with my best gal (& only one in case you didn't know). Have only got about 2 mos to go now before I can apply for my annual leave – whether to take it in the fall or wait until February depends on yourself and secondarily on your family but want you to worry about it for a while anyway. Hope your conscience and constitution stood up OK to our last evening & hope it didn't alter your views any. Well am beginning to wander so will say goodnight.

Much love, Hamp

June 16

Well another day is put away – nothing to report. Usual routine & quite busy all day (thank goodness). Wind is still about 40mph and no sign of let up and guess it won't subside for the rest of the summer so might as well get used to it. The other new MO still hasn't arrived yet so am still very much on my own. When some more help arrives I hope to get into Lethbridge and see Hunt. Also will be able to get a 48 possibly and get up to Edmonton via TCA or Anson if they happen to be ferrying any aircraft there. Won't be for 3 or more weeks but it's something to look forward to – unless the medical strength is increased I am likely to be stationed here permanently.

This letter when reread by myself begins to show signs of repetition so had better terminate and mail it. Started off the routine in earnest today – tea at 4.00pm every afternoon in the nurse's outing room. There are two nurses here, one whom is getting married at the end of the month and one who is here on a temporary posting like myself. They have very nice quarters at the hospital but are not exactly overworked. Too bad one isn't yourself but can wait. Much love Hamp

Dear Peggy

My correspondence slipped yesterday – no excuse except fairly busy & very lazy. Is raining hard today and almost consider it a pleasant change from the wind. Are having a bit of surgery down here— a hernia yesterday and 2 today. I at present am the staff anaesthetist and pouring drop ether. Am certainly no hell at it but just getting by O.K. so far. Miss the joys and comforts of the anaesthetic machine but not too much.

Had a letter from Dad yesterday. He's going to drive off for a short holiday and is coming through MacLeod & will probably be through this afternoon or evening. Phoned yesterday and tried to talk him out of it for a week because since I'm the only M.D. around I can't get away to drive around and also have been too busy to get to know too many people around here so really don't know an awful lot about what we actually have here. Anyway he is coming so I'll do what I can to entertain him. He asked if there is any possibility of you getting off and driving down with him but I told him no hope that is correct.

Hamp's father, Percy Frank Smith

My posting is very definitely temporary here. Two M.D.s are coming Monday and then I leave fairly soon and will no doubt go back to the recruiting centre at Edmonton. Rather disappointed in a way but guess it doesn't matter a great deal. Also will have all the advantages of being able to see yourself whenever you'll let me.

Find it a little lonely here at times as I really don't know anybody but have made a few acquaintances and hope to make more – am too tied down a present to worry much about it though. Will sign off and get this in the mail. Hope to hear from you soon. Much love, Hamp

RCAF Recruiting Centre, Edmonton

Miss Margaret C. Smalley
3445 Point Grey Rd, Vancouver

> #3 Rec Centre, RCAF
> Edmonton Alberta
> July 8/42

Dear Peg

Certainly had an agreeable surprise today – got a letter from the one and only. You certainly are prompt. Your description of the first part of your holiday sounds like the perfect set up and it's going to be hard to get acclimatized to Edmonton and the muddy Saskatchewan after the blue Pacific. Glad to hear you ate on the train and glad to hear that the Lieut was married although after all, you are on holiday.

Your old man sounds like quite a fisherman. Would like to have been along when he was rowing against the tide and the anchor – that would be enough to make even him cuss just a bit with a clear conscience.

Haven't been exerting myself very strenuously. When I left you at the station Sunday came home and found my company was Ches. Tanner and Cecil Tredger and the two Newland girls. Don't know if they were glad to see me or not. They stayed to about 1 o'clock in the AM – in a way I was glad to see them as the place was a bit depressing. The other roomers were in the hall discussing the accident in the basement and stayed until 1.30 talking outside my door – I think they were afraid to leave each other and go to bed. I finally went out and asked them if they would like a night cap. (Ches & Cec left part of a bottle of Scotch – I drank some of it by the way). Gave each a couple of ounces and they took the hint and went to bed.

Monday night after finishing work Fred and Ted Bell came in for a while. Drove around for an hour and so to bed.

Last night went out to Charlie Baker's for supper and them golfing with Fred and Charlie. Played 3 holes and the retired in disorder leaving the field to the mosquitoes. Have never seen them so many, so big and so vicious. However we each had a small transfusion and are now taking iron and hope to have our blood up to normal again in about 2 months. Just a steady cloud of them over all the time and the noise they made, made the radio's "green hornet" sound pretty feeble. Today was busy but dull until your letter came this afternoon and now must admit that things look pretty rosy again.

Apparently the mobile recruiting trip isn't going out next week but is going the week after – the reason for the postponement being the Exhibition. So it looks like you're going to be in town and I'm not. Don't know for sure yet and will know by the weekend.

Well, better mail this. Hope you continue to have the best holiday ever. If your finances show any signs of getting strained, don't let them break but just drop a line and I can put a mortgage on your next months salary (or next years) and send funds forthwith. Well, much love, Hamp

PS This letter may look a bit bent by the time you get it but have to carry it around looking for an envelope. More love

PS I certainly wish I were there and hope that some time in the not too distant future something similar can be arranged.

#3 Rec Centre, RCAF
Monday
(sent to 3445 Point Grey Rd, Vancouver 14/7/42)

Dear Peg

Well got the *3rd* letter today. Am certainly getting spoiled. You and your family are apparently getting down to brass tacks on your future and I'm certainly glad to hear it – it will save a lot of stammering on my part when you return. Speaking of salting away the King's cash – I bought a new suit and then am buying some jewellery for sure and then after that am going to be a real miser. Glad to hear you phoned Jean Gil – but don't see too much of her – she's a lot of fun and I like her but I don't like her reputation (after all it isn't the Victorian age though is it? and after all I'm not married to the girl but after all I damn near am).

Went out to Pigeon Sat afternoon and came home last night (Sun night). Had a very quiet time but enjoyable. It rained hard all day Saturday but yesterday was nice. Had the boat & motor out & was just getting away from home when the motor gave a couple of grunts & gave up the ghost – out of gas – so I rowed home (& the five other people in the boat) – have come to the conclusion that motor boating is good exercise. Dad came out for the afternoon and we are now on somewhat more friendly terms.

Have been looking for a place to stay and may stay on 89th on the south side – quite a ways from your place so you needn't think I'm camping on your doorstep (although I'd like to – I sure miss you). Not very definite however.

Drove around by your house with Marg and Bill on the way home. Grass is well cut & everything seems to be in good order. Mac & Irene are coming up Wednesday to go to the Exhibition so will probably go out with them. I phoned Fred last night as I hadn't heard from him since last Tues. – figured he was busier that I was so didn't bother him at all last week. We may go out to the fair together on Tuesday night although I more or less feel he's just looking after me since he knows my interests at present are on the west coast – feels I might be getting a bit dismal. not quite correct but can't say I enjoy Edmonton with yourself not here.

Marg and Bill got your card – said you wrote a real letter on it and were certainly glad to hear from you. My family keeps cautiously feeling around to see what our intentions are – haven't told them anything and am just letting them wonder. If you think this is not a good idea I will enlighten them.

On looking over this page quickly there are too many 'Is' so had better stop talking about myself. Well your boyfriend certainly misses you but feel compensated by the fact that you're having a swell holiday. Keep it up and see you the picture of health in a couple of weeks. Much love, Hamp.

Dear Peg

Well am leaving on mobile this morning. Leave here and go to Camrose today and down as far as Provost on Friday and back to Camrose on Saturday again. Will be here Saturday night (July 23) about 8 o'clock and would like to see you if you're home.

Fred Day has my golf clubs if you want to use them. Alix confided in me on Friday night about their family. Didn't tell her that Fred had already told me because he hadn't told her that he had. So when she tells you be properly surprised although I told her that we suspected.

Three or more people have told me that they hear I'm getting married. I have replied that it's a good idea and all I have to do now is persuade the girl that it is. So I'm afraid you've been put in a rather embarrassing position & I'm sorry. Will talk it over with you and your family if I may when I get back so rumours that may be embarrassing to you can be properly countered. Well will close now and see you at the end of the week – if you'll let me. Much love, Hamp

(PS forgot to leave the letter in the mail box)

(same envelope)

Dear Peggy

Had intended to write you and leave the letter in your mail box – as a matter of fact have got the letter I my pocket and then forgot to leave it. I am at present in Camrose – for this afternoon and evening and then move on tomorrow to Daysland and so on down the line. Come back here on Saturday (July 23) and then proceed up to Edmonton. Will be in Edmonton about 8 o'clock at night and would like to see you. Hope you are at home and will see me.

I have got us in quite a lot of talk and am afraid that you will be quite displeased. Several people have said "I hear you are getting married". I have tried to pass it off and say it's a good idea and wish I could convince my girl of the same. This sort of thing seems to have practically gone by the rumour stage and I'm sorry for your sake. It may make it very embarrassing for you with your family. Hope you aren't too displeased but don't know how it got started (or do I?). The pay off was when Ron Homer who is living at the same place as I am while looking for a house – told me that he heard I was getting married. As the only person he has talked to is Dr Vant it looks like you are in pretty deep now and that it is no secret that my intentions are honourable. I thought I had better warn you now so that you'll be prepared when you get back. It has got to the stage where I want to talk it over with you and if you are agreeable discuss it with your family.

Alix confided in me that they were going to have a family. I was agreeably surprised and didn't tell her that I knew because Fred hadn't told her that we knew. She will no doubt tell you and hope you are surprised although I told her we thought she was looking very smug for sometime. Well better sign off and will see you Saturday night – if you'll let me. Certainly will be glad to see you. With much love, Hamp

Peace River
Oct 23/42

Dear Peg

Well have gotten this far at least. This may sound a little pessimistic but it's snowing fairly heavily and is damned damp. Had better account for myself so far. Spent Monday night in Athabasca-did about half a dozen medicals and then were invited out for the evening to the local telephone operator's. Had a pleasant evening with beer, piano and lunch. Not very hilarious but spent the time.

We have a sergeant major from the army along with a driver and another station wagon. They a both a lot of fun. The driver is an old Imperial Army and was shell shocked in the last war. Now he stutters whenever he gets excited and repeats furiously "whoa-but-say, whoa-but-say!" and stamps his right foot and then manages to get in gear again. Whenever we lose him we comb the beer parlours for him and then start again. They come along and pick up what we can't use and also get a few of their own but so far I've done as many medicals for them as I have for us and haven't been overworked.

Tuesday we went through and stopped a short time at Smith. Slave Lake, Kenuso and then stayed overnight at High Prairie. That night Major Gainor, the man in charge of recruiting for MD13 for the army came through and spent the night. Had a very pleasant evening playing bridge with him – he and I made 4 small slams and sundry games so he must be a good bridge player. Very interesting man who has been around a bit and since the last war has been in China, Japan and Burma.

Stayed the next day and night in High Prairie –didn't see anything except and few breeds and some farmers who didn't want to fly. Went out with the army boys and picked one man off the section gang and did a quick medical in the middle of the road.

Yesterday went out into McLennan and spent the forenoon there – we met Wilf Barrell there – he had been in Calgary and then took the train up there. Did 5 medicals then came on to Peace River. Have shot a several things but so far all I've hit is a hawk.

Peace River town is completely overrun by the American Army. They have a big camp across the river and are putting a winter road through to McMurray. There were no rooms in the hotel and we got a double room in the back of what seems to be an old garage. There are 2 double beds and so four of us stayed there.

We had a 26 of scotch and had that before supper and the place looked a little better. After supper we went over to the theatre to see the "Zeigfield Girl". Had to wait about an hour in the lobby and the boys started to play cards on the floor and some Americans joined them so it was quite cosy for a while.

Well have arrived to Friday and the snow again so better stop. Met George Casper last night and he invited me over tonight. We may goose to Grimshaw tonight however because it isn't going to be very busy here. The restaurants are crowded and you can't get a drink of water because apparently the town's water supply has been condemned so I'm getting tired of tea and beer and will be glad to leave the place. Wish you were along until we hit this place and then I changed my mind – don't wish you any hard luck of this description. Well will write you again and miss you. With much love, Hamp

Dear Peg

Well today is the day. Woke up this morning and Bob and the army driver gave me many happy returns of the day etc. and shoved a bottle of rye in my hand. – this is the first time I've ever had a big slug of rye before breakfast. Have had a very pleasant trip so far. After Peace River we stayed a day in Fairview (a night at least) and stopped on the way to Berwyn. Were quite busy. Got there in time for a Saturday night torchlight parade for the victory loan and some of the party led the parade – I unfortunately was still doing medicals at 10 o'clock at night and couldn't go. Went down to Dunvegan on Sunday morning and spent the morning sightseeing. That afternoon after doing some medicals we drove on to Sexsmith where we spent the night. Went out and saw Mr and Mrs Umbach for a few minutes. They have a lovely home and were very pleasant. First, however, believe it or not! – we went to church. After there was a party though at some army wife's place and we met a bunch of Americans and went home early.

The next day we went to Grande Prairie – met Art Beauchamp in the morning and went out to the army camp. Met the CO of the RCAF unit at the airport – he was in bed with a beautiful black eye – he's apparently a fine fellow but inclined to tipple and says he ran into a door. That afternoon we saw about 50 people and I did 18 medicals – the majority were aircrew and I worked all afternoon and evening without a break.

Yesterday we drove to Wembley and then to Beaverlodge last night. Met Cy Young a classmate of mine and saw him for a while in the afternoon. The church was having a chicken supper and we were invited to it. The businessmen of the town clubbed together and paid for the meal of about 40 American boys who were working on the airfield at Grande Prairie and we came with the invitation. Had a very fine dinner then spent the evening at Cy's place (until 2AM) and so all in all it was very enjoyable. Well had better quit – we are now on our way to Hythe, Pouce Coupe and Dawson Creek. Well had better stop and get this on the train-much love-miss you. Much love, Hamp

Mobile Recruiting Unit in northern Alberta

Air Force Medical Given on Tracks

Railway Section Worker Is Given Speedy Service

GETS INTO UNIFORM

The armed forces give plenty of service when it comes to giving medical examinations for potential recruits.

On a mobile recruiting trip into the north country, Flt. Lt. C. H. Smith, of the Edmonton air force recruiting centre, came across a youth in a railway section gang who wanted to get into uniform. He didn't waste any time but gave the youth a medical examination right on the railway tracks while the rest of the gang went on working.

The youth was found fit and was enlisted in the army. It was a joint recruiting trip by the army and air force and Flt. Lt. Smith was in charge of medical examinations for both services.

It was the first joint recruiting drive ever undertaken by the army and the air force out of Edmonton. The parties traveled in two station wagons and visited many towns and villages between Edmonton and Ft. St. John, B.C.

Seven women and 28 men were recruited for the army, and 33 air crew and 34 ground crew, including women, for the R.C.A.F. The recruiting parties were away 16 days. They had no trouble finding accommodation along the way, except at Peace River where they slept in a garage.

Army recruiters were led by Sgt.-Maj. B. J. Barnes, of Edmonton, formerly of Castor.

Air Force recruiters included FO. W. C. M. Barrell, Sgt. Jack Grossman and Cpl. Christine McKinnon, of the women's division.

Clipping probably from The Camrose Canadian

Hamp and Peggy, 1942

1943

There were no letters in 1943 because they were together. It was an eventful year for them. They were married on a very snowy day in January. Write-ups from the Edmonton Journal and The Camrose Canadian describe the wedding. They had a honeymoon on the west coast and then settled in Claresholm at the RCAF base where Hamp was posted. Peggy must have become pregnant on their honeymoon and their daughter Joan Margaret was born on October 17 1943 just 9 months and 2 days after the wedding. Peggy often joked that her mother made her 'sit on eggs' so she wouldn't deliver before nine months had passed.[4]

EDMONTON JOURNAL, SATURDAY, JANUARY 16 1943

Margaret Smalley Becomes Bride
Flt. Lt. Christopher Hampton Smith

Rev. W. C. Smalley Officiates at His Daughter's
Wedding Friday at Baptist Church

Potted palms and giant yellow chrysanthemums interspersed with blue iris, formed the background for the wedding Friday in First Baptist church of Margaret Cowell, only daughter of Rev. W. C. Smalley and Mrs. Smalley, and Flt. Lt. Christopher Hampton Smith, younger son of Dr. and Mrs. P. F. Smith of Camrose. The bride's father officiated, assisted by Rev. Daniel Young.

The bride, who was given in marriage by Dr. W. Carpenter, wore a gown of Duchesse satin, fashioned with heart-shaped neckline edged in rose-pointe lace, long medieval sleeves tapered over the wrists, and a full-gored skirt that fell in molded lines to the floor, finishing in a slight train. Her veil of embroidered tulle, fastened to a coronet of orange blossoms that had been part of her mother's wedding ensemble, fell the entire length of her gown. Her bouquet was of red American Beauty roses, combined with white freesia.

Attendants were Miss Eleanor Greenleese and Miss Alison Boyd McBride. Miss Greenleese, as maid of honor, wore a toe length gown of daffodil yellow sheer styled with long bodice, sweetheart neckline, and elbow-length sleeves. Her hat was a quaint bonnet of yellow sheer, tied at the back with yellow ribbons and topped by a cluster of spring blossoms. She wore elbow-length white kid gloves and carried a bouquet of spring blossoms. Miss McBride's slipper-length frock was in chartreuse green sheer and with it she wore a matching bonnet of chartreuse sheer, elbow-length gloves and a bouquet of spring flowers. Both attendants wore gold charm bracelets, gifts of the bride.

Best man was Flt. Lt. Fred Day of Red Deer. Ushering guests to pews marked with tulle bows were Flt. Lt. Douglas Ritchie of Calgary, Flt. Lt. Raymond Burnap and FO Wilfred C. Barrell, the latter two of Edmonton.

Wedding marches were played by Mrs. Barber Smith and Mrs. Malcolm MacLeod sang "Because" during the signing of the register.

Wedding reception to 75 guests was held later at the Corona. Receiving guests, Mrs. Smalley wore a formal dress of American gold crepe fashioned with a deep V neckline and long sleeves. Her hat was a brown Gainsborough model, and she wore a corsage of Talisman roses. Mrs. Smith, mother of the groom, wore a toe-length ensemble of dove-blue crepe. Her flowers were cream tea roses.

The bride's table was centered with a three-tiered wedding cake, topped with orange blossoms.

Toast to the bride was proposed by Hon. John Campbell-Bowen, Lieutenant Governor. Dr. G. Fred McNally was master of ceremonies.

For their wedding trip the couple left for the Pacific coast, the bride traveling in a mulberry wool coat.

THE CAMROSE CANADIAN, JANUARY 20, 1943

Flt. Lieut. Hampton Smith and Margaret C. Smalley Married Friday Evening

Ferns, palms and large gold chrysanthemums banked the altar of First

Baptist Church on Friday evening, in setting for the wedding of Margaret Cowell Smalley, only daughter of Rev. W. C. Smalley and Mrs. Smalley, to Flt.-Lt. Christopher Hampton Smith, R.C.A.F., younger son of Dr. and Mrs. P. F. Smith of Camrose. Officiating was the Rev. W. C. Smalley, assisted by the Rev. Daniel Young

The bride was given in marriage by Dr. William Carpenter of Calgary. She wore a formal gown of white duchess satin, styled with a sweetheart neckline, lily point sleeves, long torso bodice and flared princess skirt slightly en train. Featuring the neckline and forming a square yoke at the back of the bodice was a narrow band of white lace inset. Her full-length veil of silk embroidered net was held in place by a coronet arrangement of orange blossoms and 'mums, which were part of her mother's wedding ensemble. Her only jewelry was a double strand of pearls, and she carried an arm bouquet of deep red roses and white freesias. White lace gloves completed her ensemble.

Attending the bride were Miss Eleanor Greenlees, maid-of-honor, and Miss Alison Boyd McBride as bridesmaid. Miss Greenlees wore a toe-length gown of gold silk crepe fashioned on similar lines to that of the bride's, with three-quarter length sleeves, a matching net headdress, Victorian style, accented by a tiny cluster of flowers beneath the brim, and long white kid gloves. Her flowers were a mixed spring bouquet of irises, carnations and daffodils.

Miss McBride chose a frock of lime green net over heavy silk, featuring princess lines, a sweetheart neckline and three-quarter length sleeves worn with long white kid gloves. Her headdress of matching green was styled on similar lines to that of the maid-of-honor and she carried an arm bouquet of spring flowers to match. Both attendants wore tiny gold bracelets, gifts of the bride.

Best man was Lt. Frederick Day, R.C.A.M.C., and ushering the guests to their places were Flt.-Lt Douglas Ritchie, R.C.A.F., Flt.-Lt. Raymond Burnap, R.C.A.F. and FO. Wilfred Barrell, R.C.A.F.

Mrs. F. Barber Smith supplied the wedding music, and during the signing of the register Mrs. Malcolm McLeod sang "Because".

A dinner reception to 75 guests was held at the Corona Hotel following the ceremony. Mrs. Smalley received in a floor-length gown of American gold crepe, styled with a V-neckline, draped bodice, bracelet-length sleeves, and gracefully draped skirt. Her flowers were a shoulder corsage of sweetheart roses, daffodils and pink carnations. Mrs. Smith chose a toe-length gown of dove blue, with silver brocaded bodice, and shoulder corsage of orange roses and blue irises.

A three-tiered wedding cake centered the bride's table with was set with a white linen cloth, and decorated with tall white tapers and baskets of spring flowers.

His honor, J. C. Bowen, Lieutenant Governor, proposed a toast to the bride. Dr. G. Fred McNally, Edmonton was master of ceremonies.

Following a two weeks wedding trip to the Pacific coast Flt. – Lt. and Mrs. Smith will take up residence at Claresholm.

The bride is a graduate nurse of the University hospital, receiving her degree at the Christmas convocation. The bridegroom was graduated in medicine from the University of Alberta in 1941.

Traveling, the bride wore a two-piece silk crepe suit of earth brown, with a Gainsborough model fur felt hat, and matching brown accessories.

Invited guests were Dr. and Mrs. P. F. Smith, Dr. and Mrs. F. M. Smith, Mr. and Mrs. L. A. Laird, Camrose; Dr. and Mrs. W. Carpenter, Dr. and Mrs. A. Spankie and Mr. and Mrs. James Smalley, Calgary; Mr. and Mrs. Wm. Umbach, Sexsmith, and FO. John Hunt, R.C.A.F., Macleod.

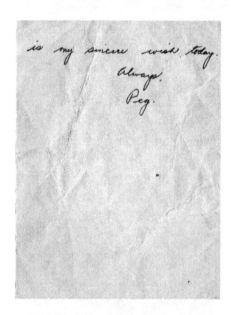

11024 - 89 Avenue
Edmonton.
January 15. 1943.

Dear Hamp,

Just a little gift, my dear, from me to you, which, I trust will be on your own office desk in the near future & will always remind you of me.

Along with it goes the sincere thought — one which cannot be

verbally expressed but is none - the - less sincere — that through the changing days & years & through a world of shattering ideas there are four things which nothing can change my believe & trust in you; my hopes & my love for you.

May our coming days together be as happy as our memories. That

is my sincere wish today.

Always,

Peg.

Peggy gave this letter to Hamp with a framed picture of herself on their wedding day.

1944

H amp was with Squadron 423 of the Royal Canadian Air Force and was posted overseas in April 1944. He was stationed at Topcliffe, Yorkshire from May to December 1944. Peggy and Joan went to live with her parents in Edmonton.

College of Arms,
March, 1943.

Chester Herald
and Inspector of Royal
Canadian Air Force Badges.

Hamp, Peggy and Joan 1944

Peggy's parents (Nana and Ba)

The Smalley House, 11024 – 89th Avenue, Edmonton

APRIL 1944

Unless stated otherwise, letters to Peggy are addressed to Mrs C H Smith, 11024-89th Avenue, Edmonton and letters to Hamp are addressed to FL/LT Smith, C 10858, Medical Officer, RCAF, Overseas

Postcard
Winnipeg
April 18, 1944

Dear Peg

No. 1 of a series. Very dull trip. Nothing to report. Practically home sick already. Will write tomorrow but nothing but prairie to write about.

Love, Hamp

April 19, 1944

Dear Hamp,

It seems like ages since you were with us and you're not even at Lachine yet. Do wish we knew when you'd be coming home, then the passing days would mean more than they do. However the time will pass as it always does and we'll be together again.

Have got more settled now. Put up our own bedroom curtains and covered the trunk with our own cover. Have taken out the big rug and put down our own mats. Will change the pictures when I get to them in the trunks and then with our own bedspread on, the room should look quite cozy and partly like "home". Have changed the room around so that it looks like this:

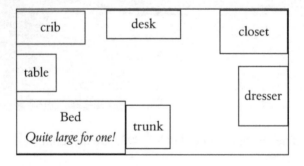

The room is out of proportion don't you think? So you see I've been quite busy.

Yesterday went over to see Doris Fleming and we had a long talk, catching up on gossip etc. They bought a car last week, 1929 Chrysler, much like our new limousine and so at night they took me for a ride so I could hear the motor purr. To put them through the old grilling I talked about all the rattles and squeaks and what our car had that theirs hadn't but ended up by admitting that it was pretty good and hoped it would run.

Met Betty and Gordon Bell and they are expecting a family next month. Gordie was saying that Bickam(?) is now at Manning Pool, Edmonton, so he certainly is seeing the country.

Had you heard about Charlie? *(See clipping below)* Imagine it will be quite a shock. It was to me.

Went over to see Alix and Sandra for a few minutes today and everyone there was quite taken with Joan, so she's still the A1 child.

She has a grand time in her bath kicking away at the water and splashing the walls. I almost have to wear a bathing suit. She can sit up when she's in the water and so really tires herself out. The rubber tub leaks but as it drains out slowly and into the bathtub it doesn't matter.

Margaret and I went back from the Station feeling quite blue and blubbery and so split a bottle of beer and smoked until twelve o'clock and talked about this and that, then went for Bill at the plant and arrived home about a quarter to one. Sat up till two talking to the folks and then went to bed and really slept until 12:30 P.M. Mother came in for Joan and tried to wake me up but didn't succeed and so let me sleep it out.

Joan went back on egg yolk yesterday and really loved it. Couldn't feed her fast enough to please her and so she yelled between each spoonful. It sure was funny. She's getting back in her routine now and slept outside this morning and this afternoon.

Am going to get my banking affairs straightened out this week and next week am going to see about Joan. So will be quite busy for awhile. How was the trip down? Did you see any interesting things? What is Lachine like?

Margaret just phoned and says "Hi" to you. She had a letter from Ma and Dad.

Got home about suppertime but didn't eat any supper. Also left my hat and a pair of pants mixed up with Ma's. Don't usually leave things like that lying around – just goes to show you what type of girl I am, when you're around.

Joan is awake roaring for food so must away and look after "l'enfant." By the way – do you "parley-vous" yet? All of our love, dearest Joan and Peg.

P.S. If you can, sign your last letter "As Ever – Hamp" so I'll know not to expect mail for some time. More love

Clipping enclosed:

Flt. Lt. Baker
Edmonton Medico Is Dead Overseas

Flt/Lt CO Baker, 27, medical officer at an operational base overseas and son of Mr. and Mrs. HG Baker, 1119 - 61 St., has died on active service, according to a telegram received by his parents from RCAF headquarters. Born in Edmonton, Flt/Lt Baker went to highlands public and Eastwood high schools and graduated in medicine from the he University of Alberta in 1941. He interned at the Royal Alexandra hospital for one year before enlisting with the RCAF in April, 1942. He served with the RCAF as a medical officer at Edmonton and the Pacific coast before going overseas. While at the university he played hockey and tennis and was a member of the Parnassus club. His family was notified several days ago that he was to undergo an operation.

Surviving are his parents; two brothers, PO HS Baker, a staff pilot at Lethbridge, and DB Baker who is taking first-year medicine at the University of Alberta and has enlisted in the RCNVR; and a sister, Alice C Baker, a former member of the CWAC, who was discharged because of ill health.

Canadian National Railways
April 19/44

Dear Peg

I now have an excuse for my poor writing since this letter is being written in the observation car. We are at present traveling through Ontario and looking out there is nothing to see but spruce, rocks and frozen water. The snow is still lying under the trees and makes the scenery even less interesting than it might otherwise be.

The trip yesterday was very dull. While in Rivers?, Manitoba managed to tear out to the hotel and have two beers. Picked up a Liberal MP for the Fraser Valley for company. In the evening we split my bottle of rye and so from here it will be quite a dry trip.

I have not met anyone I know and have had little desire to when I get this far for I keep thinking I wished you had been talked into taking the trip east with me, but realize that it would have been foolish for you to go back by your self.

According to a couple of boys I have met I won't be long in Lachine but you never know.

Had the good fortune to miss dinner yesterday – went to sleep and woke too late. I certainly felt better for it so will try it again today.

Hope Joan doesn't cause you too much concern – you certainly will have a full time job there in a few weeks – the daughter will provide few dull moments.

I didn't thank your Mother and Dad and Margaret for their kindnesses. Wish you would for me. Certainly miss you already Peg. Well, goodbye for now. All my love, Hamp

On Active Service
#1 Y Depot, Lachine, Quebec
April 20, 1944

Dear Peg

Arrived this morning and am not too impressed yet. Had a very uneventful day yesterday. Did nothing for amusement but play cribbage and Russian Bank with a kid from Winnipeg (aF/c air gunner) back from overseas. He also had a bottle of very poor rye which we tasted and decided that the train ice water was as good.

Got here at 11AM this morning and wandered around trying to get settled. I have the upper half of a double-decker bunk in a barrack block which houses 26 men. This is a little more convivial than what I am used to but I guess it is the beginning of a long time of this sort of thing. Excuse the paper – it is a little grubby but it is all I have available at the moment.

Some of the boys down here have been waiting 6 weeks for a posting, so I'm not very happy at the start. Met three other MOs but didn't know any of them previously. Haven't seen anyone else who I have ever met with the exception of a number of students from Claresholm's last graduating class. I had them all in hospital at one time or another but can't remember any of their names – which is a trifle embarrassing.

I don't know what one does to occupy their time here – time seems to drag. We are about half an hour out of Montreal by bus and streetcar but won't go in until I can get to know someone to drag along with – which may take some time.

Tomorrow morning at 9AM have to go to a lecture and there will apparently get issued with kit, blood typed, etc.

The train trip here was not so bad. The train was surprisingly light and there was never any wait for dining cars etc. – apparently traffic has fallen off markedly in the past 2-3 weeks.

Down here there is a lounge for transient officers like myself. You have to wait in line for meals and just about everything else you do. They had a good stock of camera film today-was tempted to buy some and get the camera to fit them. Haven't seen any sign of Father Monaghan so I guess he has gone on already.

If you write me here put a return address on the envelope just in case.

Am anxious to know how the daughter is getting on without me. Hope she didn't cause too much trouble when she woke up and realized I had sneaked out on her. Be sure and get Bill and Margaret's offspring a bang-up present if you can afford it.

Have already started to brush up on my French – learned the phrase "Les passagers sont pries de ne pas fumer dans la chamber de toilette avant 8.30 AM." As soon as I learn a few no spitting signs I can venture out and converse with the habitants.

Met a kid who was with Johnnie Hunt overseas – as a matter of fact Johnnie repatriated him because of sinus trouble. He says Johnnie hasn't changed a hell of a lot – went over on the boat with him and saw Johnnie get in a fight with some F/O who tried to tell him off – so I guess he's about the same as ever. Got Johnnie's address from him.

Well, That's about all the news so will close now and write tomorrow and let you know how my day fills.

Certainly miss you Peg. Hope you don't have too much difficulty filling your time but imagine that you have enough friends to keep occupied.

Goodbye for now All my love, Hamp

Dear Hamp,

Got a beautifully long letter today and only mailed yesterday! Made you feel almost next door to me figuratively speaking. Also got a letter yesterday written on the train. I always phone Margaret and keep her posted. She is talking of mailing you a camera on Monday and the size of the film is 120. Also the camera we gave her takes a 120. Hint!!

Yesterday was busy repacking the trunks and airing bedding and washing used sheets of ours etc. and in the afternoon pushed Joan to see Sandra Day. The daughter is beginning to make strange now with certain people. Mrs. Robertson looks at Joan and Joan breaks down and weeps. The nice character is certainly changing a lot. Seems to have grown an awful lot even since you left. She certainly likes to be played with and grins and gurgles merrily while I cut up capers. She sits up straight in the buggy by hanging on to the sides but still can't manage it alone. She's been a stinker again too. Gets hungry and grabs her bottle pushing the nipple into her mouth – all on her own, then sucks furiously for 2 ozs. and stops to play around so we have had a few fights over the meals of late. Right now we're not speaking – put her to bed disgusted.

Last night Mother and Dad went over town to a show. Kay Bartleman dropped in and stayed for the evening.

Today I finished repacking and have all our stuff together so it will be easy to locate. Then I did the ironing. Put the finishing touches on my room and it looks real cozy so Joan and I will be very comfortable.

Got tidied up and took Joan to the store and she spread Arrowroot biscuit all over everything and was quite a mess when we got home.

Am going down to Alix's tonight to pay bridge. Ha! Ha! Yes, dear, I'll remember not to trump my partner's ace!

It will sure be something new to sleep with 26 in a room. Don't forget you're on the top or you might roll out and get a black eye!

Do hope you won't have to wait too long for a boat although for myself I'd just as soon you were here for ages.

As you can see my days have been quite busy but now that I'm settled guess I'll have to look around a bit.

Joan seems to miss you. At times she looks as though she thought something was different but she's being a good kid without you so don't you worry about giving me too much trouble, darling. (Ha! Ha!) Two like her would be quite a job, I imagine which reminds me that Jenny hasn't paid me a visit as yet. Maybe she's just fooling around and will call when she's good and ready. At any rate we sure hope so, don't we, darling. However if she doesn't arrive we'll just move Joan over and make room for David.

Sure like your French lesson. Quite a place for a classroom I must say. But one usually likes to read something when in the rooms of rest and relaxation.

Hope you get up nerve to venture to the Big City and look around. How's the Quebec beer? Wet anyway no doubt.

Dad is going to Toronto in early May and says if you are still around he'll come up to Montreal to see you if he has the time.

If you stay in Lachine for 6 weeks I'll sure wish I'd gone East. In fact I do now. But there probably isn't much living accommodation down there and you would have to be away most of the time. But it would be wonderful. Have the feeling inside of me that it's about time for you to come home. Can't quite comprehend that you'll be gone for months. We're sure looking forward to your return. I hope it's soon, darling, so very soon.

That seems to be all the news for now. We'll write again tomorrow. All my love, dearest, Peg

i Y Depot
Lachine
#4, April 22, 1944

Dear Peg

Excuse the scruffy writing paper. It was all I could find and I forgot to get some last night. Have had quite a busy time. Spent the morning filling out documents and the went out and got my pay book, got my picture taken, blood typed, checked by the dentist again and then was issued with a tin helmet, gas mask, webbing, gas cape and so forth.

Have not yet carried my trunk up. You have to carry it 3 blocks and the handle got kind of bunged up in transit so I said to hell with it. Have met several other MOs in transit but knew none of them before.

Met Doug Tempest and Paddy O'Flynn from Claresholm last night. They have been here 3 weeks and so far done nothing of note except go into Montreal a couple of times. We are through here on Friday noon and have nothing to do until Monday morning. I think it will probably make for long dull weekends.

Met Bill Saunders today – you may remember him at the Edmonton Rec Centre. Tomorrow afternoon I may go into Montreal and look around.

I went to bed at 9pm last night and slept until 7am. I certainly was tired after the train trip and running around etc. They had a dance for the station personnel last night but somehow those things hold very little interest without yourself as partner.

The weather down here has been perfect but there is still a chilliness in the air and spring is a little further along in the west I believe.

The other MOs have been trying to wangle rooms in the staff officer's mess. That is the mess for the station officers and also repatriated officers who are returning again to the old country are quartered there. They have had no luck but we will be able to have mess privileges for eating there possibly. It doesn't particularly matter to me because food is food wherever you find it.

There are several hundred officers around now so the place is a little congested. Everybody is a little lost so we're all in the same boat.

Well there isn't much more to report on my activities. Will say goodbye for today and write tomorrow. Give my regards to Joan and tell her I'd be glad to hear from her. All my love, Hamp

Dear Peg

Didn't write yesterday because I was in town. Friday night found an empty bed in the barrack block with Paddy O'Flynn and Doug Tempest so I moved my stuff over again. I'm getting quite dextrous at slinging baggage now but imagine I'll get a lot better before I quit. Friday night the Rotary club of Montreal put on a show on the camp – it was very good indeed and helped put in the evening.

Got up about 10.00 on Saturday and went into Montreal about noon. It takes about 45 minutes by bus and streetcar and costs 11 cents. I bought myself a flashlight and some batteries. Was unable to get any spare flashlight bulbs so I wonder if you could stick some in a bundle some time if you happen to think of it.

Also got some trunk straps since my trunk is beginning to bulge at the hinges. Haven't had the courage to open my trunk because I don't think I'll be able to close it if I do. Am getting short of laundry though so I guess I'll have to begin the struggle.

Also got a cigarette case (very cheap) because cigarettes are apparently sold in bulk in England & got a bullet cigarette lighter since matches are apparently hard to get. Then we went over to the Mount Royal Hotel and had 3 bottles of beer (quarts) and by the time we got Doug's pants pressed (after he spilled a bottle of beer on them) it was 5PM so we went over to bars of some description and drank rye and ginger and had dinner. After that we went and looked at about 4 more so called cabarets. To me they are just a bunch of crummy joints that clip you at every opportunity – drinks are about 75 cents each and are very poor. Then we wound up at a place that Doug Tempest liked to see the floor show. It certainly stank. After that we ate again and arrived home about 3AM.

I wished that you were with me to see the places although I don't think that you would have found them very interesting. Well Peg, that about brings my diary up to date. I would certainly like to know how you are getting along, what you are doing, how the daughter is and all about you. Will close and write tomorrow. All my love, Hamp

PS Wrote to you before I got out of bed and then went down to the PO and got 2 letters from you and was really thrilled. That is the best thing that has happened to me since I left home. You seem to have kept yourself busy with one thing and another. The arrangement of the room sounds cosy and I hope you and Joan can be comfortable. That clipping about Charlie Baker was certainly a shock – nothing seemed more remote. I got a letter from Doug Ritchie today also – he wrote that Charlie had been found by x-ray to have a sarcoma of the stomach and was being flown back to Canada for a laparotomy. Doug didn't sound very optimistic but it was certainly a surprise. He didn't have much to say but just wanted the news from home.

Joan seems to be really coming along well and if she continues she may turn out half as well as her mother which would satisfy me completely. There is no mention of Jenny coming and I hope for your sake that Joan doesn't acquire any brothers or sisters for a while – for my own sake it would be 100% OK – but enough of that.

Be sure and write me as soon as you now what the Norton is and how everybody is. It's a lovely Sunday afternoon and we have nothing to do but sit. I'm writing this from my bunk and after that see little in the offing except to roll over and go to sleep.

Well darling, sure wish we could take a walk together about now, but it won't be long and then we won't have to worry again about being separated. Your letters are very cheerful – hope you are.

All my love again, Hamp

#6, April 25, 1944

Dear Hamp

Thank you for the lovely long letter we received today. Was very glad to know you had been around for awhile. It made me feel much better as I hate to think of you just sitting around with time on your hands – but guess most of the time is accounted for by the R.C.A.F. at that.

Haven't been out of the house today. Was going to trot Joan down to Dr. Orr's but it was such a cold windy day that I couldn't take her out. It felt almost like snow and it wouldn't surprise me to see it by morning.

Dad left this morning for Calgary but will be back on Friday to go to Toronto. So he is running around again.

One hour later

Time out while I talked to Helen Campbell – the neighbor on the left – who came in to weigh a parcel for her sailor husband. Am going to her place for tea tomorrow and to a show with Alix at night.

Phoned Marg Norton today to keep her up to date. She is fine and Bill was busy cleaning the hot air pipes and was apparently quite dirty to look at.

Had a letter from Irene Smith asking for your address as they have a going away present for you. A special watch, no less, which hadn't arrived when we were home so they didn't say anything. Marg is also sending a camera to you or have I mentioned that before. Feel very mean that I didn't give you something sometimes I wonder how I can be so stupid.

Must say – it certainly looks like Joan is going to have a brother or a sister. Please note the singular – you made them plural in your letter and if you don't mind, darling, I think I'd rather just have one at a time. The symptoms are heading up the same way 1) cystitis and 2) the great fatigue. Nausea hasn't arrived yet. Maybe I'm all wrong and Jenny may come but I've a feeling; – women's intuition I guess, – an inner knowledge, or something that you are going to have a bang up Christmas – come Christmas!

Haven't decided yet what we're going to do but if a junior is coming I'll have to look for a place of my own but there's lots of time to plan for that.

It will be a busy time for me but I'm not worried so don't you be anxious – will just take things in their stride. It really is a good time to raise a family as we can be together and do things together when you come home instead of having to start on a family. Of course it's too bad you can't see Joan grow up but we'll have one sometime just for you. What say old man? That's if we can get accustomed to sleeping together again. Which reminds me that I sure miss you to warm my feet at night – have been wearing ankle sox of late to get warm.

Joan pulled her 4 A.M. gag again last night and then was wide awake and ready to get up at 6 A.M. She's just 2 hours too early. Her eczema has subsided since I cut out the pablum. I know you said she didn't need it but you know me I have to try everything once. At any rate she's improved and a good kid in her own way.

That seems to be all the news for now. Hope you are getting along OK and having a fairly good time. Do take a look around now 'coz it will probably a long time before we can see it together.

All my love, dearest, Peg

Lachine, April 25, 1944

Dearest Peg,

Didn't write you yesterday and have no good excuse except I missed the mail and figure that I would add it in today's letter. Didn't do much yesterday and delayed writing because I thought there might be something to add to the letter. It rained heavily all day yesterday. Didn't go out on parade in the morning but just slept. In the afternoon at 3.00 there was a parade and we watched them present DFC's and DFNu's to boys back from overseas. There are a lot of repatriated officers here who have been back in Canada on a month's leave and are now returning overseas. Also the ferry command pilots stay over here – Dorval is just a few miles from here and that is the main stop in the flying command overseas. Saw one sergeant who was 57 hours out of Cairo and that appears to be commonplace around here. Last night went downtown and had 2 glasses of beer and then came home. We were tired of sitting around here and since the trip there and back takes about 2 hours it filled in the evening. I certainly don't think much of Montreal and don't want to see the place again. Had a parade this morning and it was full of interest for us. We are leaving shortly and don't write me here after you get this letter. You can start writing RCAF overseas and I shall certainly be glad to hear from you Peg. It seems ages since I saw you and Joan. Hope neither one of you change – I won't unless I lose some weight-that will be the only alteration. I have gotten a kit bag and officers knap sack and am sending my suitcases home to you. Paddy and Doug are also leaving – we don't know where from.

The weather this morning is raining with occasional flakes of snow – a glimpse of sunny Alberta would be welcome but I suppose it won't be much different there. Didn't get a letter from you yesterday but hope to get one today.

Bought a couple more shirts down here at the canteen and am going to fill up my baggage with cigarettes etc. I wonder Peg if you would send some cigarettes overseas to me as soon as possible. They will be there when I arrive then – there is some arrangement whereby 300 a week or some such figure can be sent. I wonder if you can check on it – they are quite cheap and apparently delivery is good. I will try to increase your allowance when I get over there and find how much money I need. I didn't buy a bond here this time but may do so later.

Well darling look after yourself and the infant. If you get ill see John Scott or Irving Bell. Also you had better get a check up from Dr Vant and make sure that all is OK. I'm sorry I never did check you over but kept procrastinating as usual. Spent the morning putting strong bolts into my trunk – the hinges got sprung out and also the handle so it was rather hard to handle but I've now repaired it and hope that it holds.

Have gotten myself pretty well plastered with white paint from painting my name on my luggage.

It certainly is going to be a struggle to get our baggage on. I have the trunk, a kit bag, and the officer's kit bag (haversack). Then there is a haversack for the gas mask, a tin helmet and the webbing which consists of a haversack with shoulder straps and belt around you on which there is a water bottle, revolver holster and sundry gadgets. When I get all this on over my great coat and add gas mask and cape to it Hampton is really going to be sweating.

Tomorrow we are going to try and get a pass for the day and go down to see Don Hills (NZ F/O from Claresholm). He is passing through on his way to Summerside, PEI. There are a bunch of RAF pilots in our hut. They have been around for a long time. Talking about flying mosquitoes-120 miles in 18 minutes – quite fast I thought.

Well dear, I'm just rambling because I hate to stop writing. Will probably get 3 or 4 more letters away to you. Well, will write tomorrow. All my love, Hamp

Dear Peg

Writing this from the Mount Royal Hotel in Montreal. We were allowed out the gate for 4 hours this afternoon and I hurtled downtown and got myself some fur lined slippers because I heard that you needed them overseas. This will be my last letter for a few days. It should take about 6 days to cross but we may hang around our embarkation port for a while before we leave.

It certainly was grand to hear your voice last night and know that you were there. I couldn't get a phone over in the phone building and so went into the mess where there was a dance going on and so it was a bit noisy. That is why I phoned you collect. I am enclosing 10 dollars to pay for the call. I got paid $69 today and got it converted into pounds so that it will be available on arrival. I am banking with the Royal Bank of Canada overseas.

Well Peg, I had better stop because we have to dash back to camp and hand in our blankets and finish packing. I am duty MO on the trip and have to travel on a train with the boys and be responsible for their health – also on the boat. I understand we get special quarters on the boat and the train so it is OK. Am enclosing the receipt for my suitcase which I expressed to you. Well honey – all my love. Jenny may not come and if she doesn't – well, we'll talk about it later. All my love, Hamp

#7, April 26, 1944

Dear Hamp,

It was a real thrill to hear your voice last night. Had just come home from mailing a letter to you and I don't have to tell you what a grand surprise the phone call was. Have thought of lots of things I could have told you but we both wanted to hear each other talk and I couldn't think of anything but "It's Hamp." It really was swell. Sure got my money's worth and hope you did too.

Phoned Margaret today and she has sent the camera all ready so you may get it. If you do, hope you can take it with you as we may be able to send you a film from time to time.

Joan must have known it was her dad on the phone as she got real lively and didn't settle down until after 1 AM. However she slept until 6 A.M. so it wasn't too bad.

Mother, Joan and I went next door for tea this afternoon and Joan and I had our pictures taken on the lawn. We have been doing very well at horning in on other people's films so when they are developed will send them along to you.

Had a letter from your Mother today and she wrote that the box of books had arrived. Your summer uniforms by the way were in one of the trunks so I have them here. They had heard from you in Camrose and were very pleased.

Mother had to go out tonight so instead of going to a show Alix is coming over here.

Am going to write you at least twice a week after your letters stop and imagine they will catch up to you sooner or later. 'Thought it would bridge up a long gap of waiting.

Didn't get a letter today but hardly expected one. Any way am still in the clouds from the phone call.

That seems to be everything for now. Hope you are fine and do take care of yourself darling.

All my love, Peg

Mount Royal Hotel
Montreal
April 27, 1944

Dear Peg

Here I am again. Got down yesterday and all ready to go when the draft was cancelled for 24 hours. We will leave tomorrow I believe. I believe I told you I am conducting MO. I have a trainload of ground crew to look after and it won't be much fun. They gave me a tin box of medical supplies so it is just more bloody stuff to carry. Came down today and bought a pair of shoes so I won't need any for another 2 years – also stocked up on magazines and reading materials.

Got a letter from you yesterday. You seem pretty well settled now and apparently have managed to keep busy.

I have never done so much walking for years and my dogs are really barking.

Well I had better dash back to camp and see if we are all set again.

Good bye for now. All my love, Hamp.

PS We are up in Dan Hill's room so that accounts for the stationery. He is leaving this afternoon for PEI.

April 30, 1944

Dearest Hamp,

It's a long time since I wrote to you – or so it seems and it's an even longer time since I heard from you but guess there will be news in a week or so. Got the suitcase the other day so now have everything here.

Took Joan to Dr. Orr last Thursday and he gave me coal far for the eczema. It was different than ours so used it and her legs are 100% improved – in fact almost cured. Sure hope it lasts. He looked at the birthmark and gave her 12 minutes of radium. It didn't seem to have any effect but can't tell yet. Am to take her back in 3 months for another treatment.

After seeing Dr. Orr, Joan and I took the streetcar out to Margaret's. Our daughter is certainly getting heavy and I sure was glad to get to Margaret's. One block away I almost sat on the curb for a rest but managed to make it. Had a bottle of beer upon arrival and it sure tasted good – but definitely! Joan had her milk and went to sleep until 11:30 PM when we wakened her up to take her home. She sleeps on her stomach now and can sleep for 6 or 7 hours straight.

Margaret looks very well indeed but doesn't get any fatter or thinner – but is really quite huge. Take a dim view of their adoption of "David" as a name for Buster and sure hope they have a girl – serve them right. However guess we had one chance.

Aunty Lena and her daughter-in-law came over for supper last night and were quite impressed with Joan – said she looked like a Smith. For people who seldom make remarks they seemed quite impressed.

Went for a walk with Alix at night and to Tuck for a "coke". She had heard from Freddy and he sent her a cameo and carved coral bought in the city near his station. Al Reid is still with him but Bob Zender has been moved.

Saturday was as usual. Dad came in from Calgary at 1 A.M. – spent 2 hours at Carstairs because of a railway crash – so it was really quite a boring trip – he thought.

Decided it was time to rake up the front lawn – spring is in the air – so put on slacks and as it was a warm day dressed Joan up & put her in the buggy and out in the sun. She enjoyed it very much and we cooed to each other while I worked. It was fun and really felt good when it was done.

Went to see "Government Girl" at the Garneau after and it was quite good. In fact am just in bed after feeding Joan. Dad had just made his usual last minute dash to the train. He left for Toronto and will be gone for 4 weeks.

Bought a $50 bond the other day for cash and another one on the installment plan. Also paid Mother $20 for half of April's board and room. Bought the bonds from the money I brought up from Claresholm and my next cheque should come on Monday so am OK financially. Think it's a good idea to put some money in bonds as they pay 3% interest as compared with 1½ % bank interest. As Dad says if the bonds depreciate after the war our savings in the bank wouldn't be worth much either so I figured I could save some money and also buy bonds – and too, darling, the idea is to "Speed the Victory" and then you can come home so why shouldn't I buy bonds to a certain extent but don't worry we'll have some money anyway when you come marching home.

We both miss you so much but there's no sense writing like that so will never mention it again but you will understand we can hardly wait for you to come home. Will write soon. Take care of yourself.

All my love, darling, Peggy

MAY 1944

May 1, 1944

Dear Hamp,

How are you doing, old boy? Think of you all the time and wish we could see you. However one of these days — – Be sure to let me know if there is any little or big thing you want and I'll send it to you. What about your Medical Journals? They are starting to arrive. Also got my own cheque today and so went downtown with Alix in her car and opened a bank account.

Had $30 left over from last month so deposited it and cashed *my* cheque and gave $40 to Mother for my May rent and kept the $26 out for incidentals.

Also ordered 600 British Consel cigarettes for you. If you find 600 is not enough let me know and I'll increase it to 1000. Alix thinks they take some time to get there. Also if you want another brand – let me know. And by the way am sending to you because *I want to* – not because you asked for them. Ha! Ha! Guess you weren't listening when I said I'd send them to you – eh dear?

Yesterday was quite a day – really poured down. Went over to see Alix in the P.M. and my stockings were wet to the knees before I'd gone 1/2 block. But it was grand walking in the rain.

Our pictures arrived from Camrose and they really are quite good so will be sending them around. Would you like one?

Had a letter from Hughie Lawson and she is coming to the medical convention with Bob next week so will share my bed with her. Bob is staying at I.T.S. Haven't heard from Doris yet so guess she's busy with Larry.

You'll never guess what happened to me this morning. Well at 6 A.M. when I was thinking about getting Joan some food, I stretched into wakefulness and somehow twisted my neck and so now I'm going around with my head on an angle and unable to turn left. Frequently I forgot my misery and turned suddenly and then you should have heard the bursts of – Oh! Oh! Oh! filling the house. Margaret thinks it's a good joke and sort of hopes my neck's dislocated so that I can wear a dog-collar on my neck and a pie plate on my upper lip and be a Ubangi – but I refuse. A fine sister you've got. Have been putting moist heat on most of the day and it feels much better tonight so guess I'll survive.

Joan is getting to be quite the brat. She can race anywhere now and so we find her scratching on various chairs with her finger nails – or trying to climb the trilight – or pulling out the hairs on the buffalo robe – or like today knocking or rather pulling over a stack of books and magazines from table by the radio chair and gnawing on the corner of a

Digest quite unconcerned. Maybe she can read and was following instructions – Reader's – Digest. At any rate she's still quite a little character. She can almost sit up on the floor without any help. Today she sat alone for about 1 minute and then toppled over. She gets quite a bang out of her bath in the A.M. and sure does a lot of kicking and splashing. As for food she has cut herself down to 6 oz. of milk each feeding but gets about 4 oz. of porridge, 4 oz. of vegetable, 4 oz. of fruit and 1 egg yolk daily plus 1 or 2 arrowroots so guess she doesn't starve.

Her eczema has certainly improved after using Dr. Orr's coal tar. No redness or roughness and only little white shiny scars where the eczema broke out. These should go away in time. Don't you think. Must take Joan to Dr. Leitch next week but it's really quite a trip by streetcar.

Have been having small bouts of nausea lately – in the mornings. Does that mean anything I wonder? Will wait awhile before going to Vant however.

As you may know by now Jenny has not arrived. I think we arranged all that before we left Claresholm – quite unknowingly. Can think of one or two possible incidents when we might have caused some disturbance. Do you think that is so?

Mac Young has been sent to Calgary (Col. Belcher) now. Saw Carol in town last week. Also met Elliot Cowan and they are expecting an addition to the twosome next month.

That seems to be all for now. Hope to hear from you soon. When you come home you'll have many tales to tell. All my love, dearest – Peg

Remember me to Doug, John, Dave and others when you see them.

May 3, 1944

Dearest Hamp,

Wonder what you're doing now? It is quite a game with me to stop and think of all the different things you may be doing at various hours of the day. A very good pastime and makes you seem not so very far away.

Bought some things for your parcel the other day and hope to get it off by weekend. Won't tell you what is in it so it'll be a surprise. Anyway its chiefly food. And you think you're going to lose weight. Ha! Ha!.

The other night just after I'd written to you Jo Aiken and Biel Pace phoned me. They were room-mates and up on a Refresher Course. Biel is now at Vulcan. It was swell of them to phone. Jo called at the house the next afternoon and stayed for an hour. He said Claresholm was much the same and very few postings. Irvin was the only one he could remember and then didn't know where he was going. They are getting another M.O. in your place next week. His name is McKean (?). He was on the course in tropical Med. in Washington and Jo says you have talked about him. I can't place him.

Joan as usual showed off for the company. She sat in her swing and grinned away as though she had done something very smart – and she hadn't done a thing. But the funny part was she kept this silly grin all the time Jo was here and then go sobersides again. Would really love to know what was going on in her wee mind.

The daughter is sure happy lately – more than usual. Tonight heard her gleefully enjoying herself instead of sleeping so went in to settle her down. Her feet were where her head should have been and she gave me that well known toothy grin thru the bars of the crib – so I stayed and played for awhile and we had a great time grinning and cooing at each other like two nuts. She finally settled down.

Was over visiting Alix and Sandy today with Joan. Sandy is just at the training stage and today when Alix turned on the hose, Sandy said politely "Go-Go?" at which Alix and I howled with laughter.

You should see the city now. It is just beautiful with the first bursting of spring. The leaves are all new, shiny and very green and some early flowers and fruit blossoms are out. The days are very warm and sunny. Edmonton is really at its best.

Alison's engagement was announced tonight. The write-up was very funny I thought, gave how many medals she had – well – almost! And her picture was in too. Quite the stuff. I've been invited or asked to show the presents and trousseau on May 12 from 6 to 7 at the "Big Tea". Am not invited to the wedding as it is only a family affair. McB had a letter from Dick today and he was busy washing windows and waxing floors on Gander Island so McB is thrilled. Etc & etc!!!

Fred wrote Alix that he would be moving on and further up shortly so guess he'll be quite busy.

Joan's eczema continues to improve and her appetite is really good. She does weigh over 17 lb. now. At night she usually sleeps from 6:30 to 11:30 form 12 to 6 and 6 to 8. then has 3 or 4 hours sleep most days and plays hard between times. She's going to be a concern shortly.

Am feeling fine myself although still a bit tired but will get rested shortly. My stiff neck is almost cured. Can't turn my head all the way to the left yet but I'm getting there. That'll teach me to stretch and loiter in bed.

Big surprise – especially to me as I didn't expect it – Jenny just arrived! Am glad – as I haven't been feeling well in the mornings and her arrival may help me somewhat. Am sorry too in a way because David won't be able to come and keep Joan company. However I guess it really is the best thing that could happen at this time so will welcome Jenny with open arms. Sure feel silly too! Because you always said she'd come sometime and right you are.

Will be glad to get some mail from you soon – if only a few lines and please don't laugh over Jenny's arrival until I'm near to enjoy the joke with you.

This letter seems rather patchy as I've had to scratch from some of the news items. But whether I've anything to say or not – just have to write to you. Am writing every second night now so that you'll really have a newsy letter. It's quite hard to write every night when it's the same routine every day and no mail. Will improve however. All my love, darling – Peg

May 6, 1944

Flash!

Joan just sat up in her playpen by herself. At least I sat her up and she kept on sitting. Thought it great sport. I grinned away.

Dearest Hamp,

Its way passed the time to write you again at least one day or so out but the days seem to slip away as routinely as my work – each day almost the same as the last.

Jessie Horne phoned me on Thursday and we went shopping. I bought Joan a playpen and a highchair so will be staying pretty close to home for the rest of the month.

When the chair arrived I put Joan in it and she immediately pounded on the tray and had a great time. She sure loves to sit in it and looks so tiny propped up in a great big chair. Figured it was best to get in a pen before she learned to creep. She likes that too because she can bang on the sides of it with her rattle. Really quite a noisy daughter we have! Looked in her mouth the other day and discovered two new teeth just through – lateral incisors. She's really quite the kid! And getting fatter every day – now over 17 lbs.

Went to a show last night with Kay Bartleman. Madam Currie – quite good – but I wasn't in the mood for that type of thing.

The days are very dull and quite cold and windy. There are several large bush fires in various parts of the province and so the sky is very smoky – can hardly see across the fire. Several planes are missing and 2 people have been burned so guess they're quite large. Enough of this morbid news!

Alix is alone now as her mother has gone to the Coast so she is enjoying being her own boss and is seriously thinking of trying to find a place for herself. Not a word to Fred yet please!

Had a letter from Doris yesterday giving me the low down on Claresholm and inviting (us,me) to go to Waterton with them in July. Haven't made up my plans as yet. The Bothwells are all fine. Biel is at Woodhouse and Larry weighs over 8 lbs. The Flowers have moved where McKean's lived and guess what – this will slay you – Mrs. McKean is expecting a baby in 4 months — that's something I'd like to see to believe. I must be like you – you know, "seeing is believing".

Had a letter from Mother today and Dad is in hospital again. Ma says with his cough and heart but Margaret says he and Hills were competing to see who'd be "Queen of the May".

Margaret is fine and expects to go to hospital any day now. Have finished the bonnet and one bootie so will have something for "it" at any rate.

Didn't get your parcel off as I'm still looking for stuff to put in it. Figure it will take me about a month to make up each parcel as you can't always get what you want every time you go downtown.

Did you buy yourself a pipe? If not do you want one? What kind? and What brand of tobacco? What about your brand of cigarettes – would you like a different kind? Sent you British Consols. Please let me know.

Have been feeling quite chipper since Jenny arrived. Not nearly as tired. I don't think I was worried about the babies but I feel almost a free woman since she arrived that sometimes I wonder just what type of mother I am. However looking after two small babies can be just a bit too much at times. Everything is running smoothly again so you need have no worry about us in any way.

Joan is in her high chair, banging the tray with her spoon and practically crying out "Supper" so had better away to the "wee bairn".

Will write you soon, my darling, and I do hope we hear from you soon. All my love, dear – Peg

P.S. What facilities have you for making a snack? & what do you crave in line of food?

May 7, 1944

Dear Peggy,

A lot of water has passed under the bridge since I last saw you. I was duty M.O. on a troop train to "an eastern Canadian port". Another chap and I had a drawing room to ourselves and had quite a nice trip of it. I had no casualties except a couple of head colds and a kid who got drunk and took a poke at himself in the mirror with a little trouble resulting to his hand. We had to carry our baggage over a quarter of a mile to get to our ship from the station. I was darn near dead by the time I finally staggered up the gag plank – my arms are 4 inches longer than they were when I left Edmonton. I was quartered in a cabin along with 19 other officers – double decker bunks and never more than a foot away from anybody. Also the 20 on the other side of us used the same bathroom with its 4 wash basins – you can imagine the congestion in the morning because the water was only on from 6:00 AM to 7:45 AM. I was with a good bunch fortunately. We had two meals a day – we ate in relays – I was on the first sitting and so ate at 7:00 AM and 5:00 PM. The food was only fair but whenever we complained some boys returning after

30 days leave in Canada told us that those were banquets compared to English meals so we shut up. The trip was quite uneventful. I didn't get seasick. Our first two days out were very smooth and then it got a bit rough. I certainly didn't enjoy my meals for a couple of days but ate them anyway and hoped for the best. We were on quite a large ship but it was *very* crowded. The lounge would accommodate about 400 and never had less than 800 in it. I managed to get a seat in it on 3 occasions only. Paddy O'Flynn and Doug Tempest were a few cabins away and we played a little knock rummy but mostly read and slept. Didn't see anything except a few icebergs, some porpoises and the odd Liberator overhead. Boat drill was a daily chore which helped pass the time. We lined up for everything as usual. The canteen continually ran out but I managed to get about a month's cigarette supply. I was advised to get cigarettes sent over in lots of 7000 – the larger packages aren't lost so easily and don't tend to get stolen as do smaller lots of 1000. If you could fix that up then I would have everything I want except some of these air mail forms. We are apparently rationed to four a month of these and so if you could send some over in some sort of a parcel it might help.

I am writing this at night on the train. We left for our destination in mid-afternoon and will arrive during the night. These English trains are really an experience. We are in a 3rd class coach – every place has a table up and they brought a big pot of stew down the aisle and gave us each a plateful and then followed bread and margarine. The bread is very dark but tastes OK to me. We got up at 3:30 this morning and had breakfast at 4:00 AM and then sat and waited until 2:30 PM to disembark from the troopship. When we got on the quay an RCAF band was out playing and some women were passing out tea and buns. It was quite a pleasant reception.

I can truthfully say I have never seen more beautiful country side than I have here. As we sailed in the whole country looked like a series of golf courses with trees in leaf and an occasional old castle sprinkled on the landscape.

If I ever get leave I am going to Edinburgh and see more of the Scottish country side. I have no desire however to see much of Glasgow as it seems to be quite sooty in spots. We are getting the impression more and more that there is a war on but the country side itself looks so serene that it is difficult to contemplate.

When we first got on the train one felt that you were crowding yourself into a toy railroad but when you have been on them awhile you seem to have as much room as you need and they certainly travel. We blacked out about 10:20 but the ventilation is good on the train. After we first got on and started to travel the tracks were lined with children and adults. The boys tossed out everything they had to them – cigarettes, candy, and their Canadian change. Everybody had a wonderful time.

Well Peggy I have only been gone about 3 weeks but it seems about 3 years. Hope you and Joan are both well and happy. I am anxious to hear from you two and get all the news. I sent a cablegram today but heard that it might be delayed a few days – I hope not. It was kind of a routine thing with numbered messages. Well I'll say goodbye for now. The writing is poor but the train is a little jerky at times. I will try to write often. Hope Joan's eczema is not too troublesome. It may be a few days before I write to the folks so pass the news along if you can. Would like a finished picture of you and Joan and a snap of you.

All my love, Hamp

May 8, 1944

Dearest Hamp,

Isn't it funny how quickly the days go? They go for us here for we are kept busy with one thing and another. This week it will be the Lawson's. Bob is up on a refresher course & Hughie came along too. She is staying with me so am quite busy taking her around.

There is not much news from Claresholm. McEwen is the new MO – not McLean as Jo said.

Saturday night went to see Alix – her mother being away keeps Alix at home. We had a good time – way over 3 weak drinks of Scotch – and as you know it must have been weak for me to drink Scotch – & a continuous smoke. Not very exciting but quite daring – we thought. Sure slept well that night – should try it more often.

Margaret was up at Dr. Vant's on Friday and she may be going any day now. Seems to me I have already mentioned that to you.

Joan sure likes her teeth. The other day when I picked her up, my arm got in her mouth so she bit it and drew blood. Maybe I don't feed

82

her enough. And yesterday – you should have heard the racket she kicked up. Joan was in her high chair and I was mixing up her vegetables at the stove and turned to put the spoon in the sink. Poor Joan must have thought the food was not coming because she opened her mouth and gave only long loud yell and big tears trickled down her cheeks and you know what a face she makes anyway. It really was funny. When I came up with her dish she broke into a great grin so everything was hunky again.

You'll die when you hear what I did today. Well I bought a bond for Joan and one for you. That makes $200 worth this campaign but that will be all for a time until I save some more money. Hope you think I took out enough and not too much.

Was looking at flashlight bulbs today but couldn't buy any as I didn't know how large your flashlight was. The bulbs are sold depending on the number of batteries you use and also on whether the bulbs screw in or push in. so please let me know about that some time. Also if you need batteries.

Am fine and getting pretty healthy but not fat enough to please Mother but then I'm more pleased if I'm on the thin side.

Joan too is healthy and getting quite fat and really growing. Sure wish you could see us. We'll have a picture for you soon. Hope to hear from you shortly. All my love, Peg

May 9, 1944

Dear Peg,

Didn't write yesterday because I wasn't able to obtain paper or stamps. Hope you get my first letter OK. I am starting to number my letters from overseas and this is #2. If you will do the same then we'll know if we are getting all our mail.

Have gotten a bit settled finally and am getting caught up on rest. Slept right through from 9 last night to 7 AM today. I have never been so cold as I was this morning. Got up at 7:30 and made a mad dash into my clothes – our huts have no heat and since the time is advanced 2 hours it was cold. There are outside wash houses and we have to walk a couple of hundred feet to them. There are bathtubs and showers – I really had a good soak in a tub last night. Am going into town this afternoon with Wilson, another MO and look around. We are all cleared from the station here but have no indication as to our postings yet. There is no disembarkation in leave for ground crew so I hope we don't have to sit around here too long. We have certainly been busy since we arrived – getting documented and so forth – my dogs have really been barking. I certainly have a lot of admiration for the English – they are really working. There are WAAFS in the mess and they certainly work hard. They also look after the barrack and so forth. We have to clear the barracks between 9 and 12 AM and 2 & 4 PM so they can clean them up – there is no place to go so it rather leaves you at loose ends. The food is substantial and after we get used to it will not seem too bad – but dear, if I ever see sausages on the table at home I will get up and leave.

We were issued army K rations for the trip down here – they are meat – they were a real luxury compared to present rations – but don't think I'm grumbling because the food here is quite OK.

We won't get any mail here for at least another 5 days.

It's rather hard to get used to the cars and trucks running on the wrong side of the road. Everybody seems to have a bicycle and if I even get settled I am going to try to get one. We are paid in rather a peculiar fashion – the money is deposited in your account in a London bank and you write checks on it. Apparently all the local banks will cash a check up to the sum of £5. I have nearly gotten used to the money here but you certainly get an awful weight of money in your pocket after you get a pound note changed. Apparently money doesn't go far here and they say a pound note is worth about the equivalent of a dollar while you are in London.

I am going to try to contact Hunt one of these days but so far haven't had much desire to do anything but sleep. The weather here has been wonderful – sunny days without clouds. However the sun doesn't shine like in Alberta because there seems to be a perpetual haze in the skies. When it starts to rain we will really freeze I'm thinking. Have seen a number of people I knew before but no real friends.

One certainly sees a lot of aircraft in the skies over here and I guess I will gradually be able to identify a few of them.

The country is beautiful and I certainly wish that you were here so we could see it together. I have seen a number of people with whom I can compare family pictures so you are seeing a bit of England. Certainly miss you Peggy. The daughter is getting smarter every day I imagine and soon should be getting into a smart alec stage. Don't let her forget who her old man is. Was only able to get two of these forms so will save them for you and not write home. If you could explain to them and tell them I'll write when I can get more time. All my love, Hamp

Penciled on envelope RCAF Wimbledon

May 10, 1944 8 P.M.

Dearest Hamp,

We are having quite a busy time with Hughie and Bob in town. Was asked to dinner at the Corona with them. Bob was staying there and Hughie with me. After dinner we went out to visit Nora and Bob McLean. You may remember him – Claresholm a year ago and an Admin. Officer – now at A.O.S. During dinner it started to snow. That heavy wet stuff. We phoned for a taxi at 11:30 and phoned the same company every 1/2 hour for 2 hours before it finally came. It had been on its way from the very first – so the company said. At any rate the car arrived about 1:30 A.M. It was still snowing and about 2 inches deep and of course we got stuck on one of Edmonton's good mud roads. Managed to get out after 3/4 hr. of coaxing so it was quite late when I got home. Felt wider awake then of course and so lay in bed thinking about various things for 2 more hours. It was really a lot of fun being stuck – I thought – of course I just sat. Guess it wasn't much fun for the driver sweating at the wheel. Kept wishing you were along so we could laugh at the good taxi rides one gets now adays. You just never know.

Before we went to dinner we were asked down into Bie's room for a drink – rye & water. A F/L Baker was there also. Bie asked to be remembered to you and sends you all the luck in the world. Bie is now at #3 Recruiting centre here – & quite happy.

Bob was talking to Easton and the R2-11 (?) Bob made out on you was your ticket overseas. According to Bob (from Easton) they are hand picking the MOs for overseas and only sending over the most promising ones. Ahem!

Saw Ron Horner today and he was asking about you. Also wanted to be remembered.

When we wakened up this morning most of the tree tops were broken off by the weight of the snow. One large tree was split in half – from top to bottom. Hard to believe that the snow could be so destructive. Most of the trees have some branches broken off. One in Mrs. Henderson's yard fell into ours and snapped the electric light cables and we were without electricity until almost noon. It started snowing again this afternoon but the sun is out now. It sure looks funny to see the tulips blooming through the snow. Dad says it's cold in Chicago too, so it must be right across the country. Monday we were going without coats and today we're wearing overshoes. Silly isn't it.

Joan is certainly cute these days. Just went in to see if she was covered and she was lying with her seat skywards. A newly acquired pose – quite impressive. She has acquired an increased appetite and bangs impatiently on the tray when food is in sight. You put a spoonful of food – like spinach in her mouth and in goes her left hand. Then another spoonful and the right hand. This process alternates with each spoonful. Then if you don't watch, one hand will wander into the dish and come out with a handful of stuff which is smeared over anything she touches. Towards the last of the food she starts to blow and spinach flies all over the kitchen. Today she had peas, spinach and string beans from chin to eyebrow and ear to ear. Quite a mess. Had to buy her a bib that could be wiped off with a rag to save time and energy.

Monday night after Hughie and I had stopped talking and were putting out the light, I glanced over at Joan and there was the little tyke holding up the blanket on the crib rail and peeking out from under, grinning all over the little face. Hughie and I burst out into gales of laughter she was so cute.

Had to send Joan's play pen back as there was a flaw in it and the top rail split right through. The play pens these days are just made from scrappy wood and not very substantial. Cost $9.50 too.

Am thinking of making you some cookies tonight so I can get the box off real soon so had better get cracking as it'll probably take me till midnight to get them made. Hope you like them.

Margaret is still waiting. She got Sam Gablehouse's sister to come in each A.M. when she gets home. A very good idea and Margaret is happy about the whole thing.

Am waiting patiently for some word from you, darling. It will be a great day when it arrives.

All my love, dearest – Peg

#3 – May 10, 1944

Dear Peg,

Have been quite busy sightseeing since I wrote you yesterday. Have been sightseeing in Gloucester. It was just another city but quite an experience never the less. Did nothing but window shop and walk – my feet are again killing me. Saw the Gloucester Cathedral and went through it. I was really impressed. I don't know if you have seen it or not – the windows in themselves were really impressive – one of these is the largest in England and is said to be the largest in the world. The stonework of the place was also a revelation to me. After seeing the cathedral, we (MO named Wilson) and I proceeded to window shop. The clothes are surprisingly cheap. For instance a suit that looks of fair quality can be bought for about 25 to 30 dollars. Women's clothes looked more expensive and a very cheap looking dress might cost upwards of 55 shillings. We were given 107 clothing coupons and it's 21 for a suit, 7 for shirt etc. We have more coupons than we need actually. There doesn't seem to be a shortage of anything but things you would expect to be short are very expensive, e.g. radios, electrical goods – one of the boys bought a metal soap dish for 2/6 and at that it was too small for Canadian soap. The people are all in war work and all very cheerful. We went to two or 3 small pubs and had a glass of beer but they are open after 8 at night and we had to catch a bus at 9:30 so we didn't get any beer to speak of. You have to get in a queue up for nearly everything including the bus. The double-decker buses are an education – this business of paying after you get seated is an innovation. We walked all over Gloucester downtown and ended up in a park where we cooled our feet off a bit. The English kids all holler at you "any chewing gum". One little kid very scornfully refused an English penny because he couldn't spend it but fell all over himself to get a Canadian dime for a souvenir. Still no news of possible posting but it will come sometime soon. Would rather like to get to London sometime but am in no great rush. You can see so much so cheaply that it seems a shame to go there and spend your money and then have nothing to travel with.

I don't know when I will have the opportunity to get to see all your relatives. Will do it sometime when I get a few days leave.

Have also been to Cheltenham. It is very pretty in spots and we wandered through it and saw quite a lot of it. The hub seems to be the promenade which is a wide street with large old trees which completely shade it. I haven't yet become accustomed to the kinds of trees but the birds seem familiar – sparrows. Someone is going down to the post office so I will rush through this and get it down with him. Am going out on a trip into the country this afternoon and will tell you about it when I get settled again. Certainly wish you were with me but wouldn't wish sore feet like mine on anyone, particularly yourself.

Well certainly be good to hear from you and see what is doing at home with all of you. Well goodbye for now and all my love. Hamp

#4 – May 11, 1944

Dear Peggy,

Writing this in the morning and it's foggy and cool. This English climate certainly will make a rugged type out of me unless I get to a place with a fire in it. Felt a little warmer after breakfast – sausages and beans – the beans were good and the sausages taste a little better every day.

Yesterday went into the country. Went to Strand and caught a bus from there to a place called Middlehampton and on the way got off at an old inn in the country. The trip went up a hill most of the way and when you finally got to the top you could see for miles. On the top was a common with a golf course on it. It was the most beautiful countryside I have yet seen in England – occasional thatched cottages, trees hanging over the roadside, fruit trees in blossom. I had imagined that you would see most of the countryside under cultivation. On the contrary all of it is green and greener than I imagined anything could be. It all looks like one huge park. When we got off at this inn we asked for supper. They said they didn't have any food to feed us but could give us tea. We had a *fresh* egg, buttered bread, tea, cakes and a little jam for /6. It was really nice and was probably the last fresh egg we will taste in a long time. After that we went across to another old inn and had a couple of pints of ale. It was dark stuff and tasted the most like Canadian ale that I have tasted so far.

May get a letter tomorrow and that is indeed something to look forward to. No news of posting yet. When I get it I may miss a day or two in my writing.

Haven't been asked by the station MOs for any work yet but some of the other MOs in my draft have been – would like to get back to work sometime. Am going to try to phone Johnnie Hunt today but don't know if I will make it or not.

Well honey will close and write tomorrow and let you know what I am doing. All my love, Hamp

Mrs. C. H. Smith
Canadian National Telegram
11024 – 89 Ave
Edmonton, AB

May 11, 1944 7:20 AM

ARRIVED WITHOUT INCIDENT AM WELL TRUST YOU ARE
THE SAME LOVE
HAMP SMITH.

May 12, 1944 – 8 P.M.

Dearest Hamp,

Today is a wonderful day for I got your cable this morning. Was really quite surprised to get it so soon and had been prepared to wait another week for word from you. Phoned Marg right away and then your Dad. The Lawson's stopped in at night to say goodbye and they were pleased to know you had arrived. They had spent the last two days with relatives so haven't seen too much of them since our episode with mud and snow.

The weather has cleared since then and I'm outside on the back lawn. The crabapple trees and cherry trees are in bloom and apart from several broken branches cluttering the lawns, the town looks very pretty.

Was at McBride's trousseau tea yesterday and it really was quit a "do". All the West end crowd was there exclaiming "My dear" and "Isn't it exquisite" etc. until Horne and I – we went together – thought we would burst out laughing any moment. McB really had a lot of lovely things – sterling silver in scads, tea service, Dresden china dinner set (only one in Canada) monogrammed linen etc. & etc. She is being married on the 24th of May and as far as Jessie and I are concerned she has slipped back into the snooty class. It was really quite a day. You and I gave McB a lunch (linen) set but she hadn't opened it when I left so don't know if she liked it but who cares. Or is that the right attitude? Told Margaret all about it and she wished she could have been there so we could really discuss the matter at length.

Margaret went to see Dr. Vant yesterday and he said she'd still be around by the 24th. He also told her he was going away and may not be back in time so Margaret feels kind of pushed around although she doesn't mind having Dr. Hutton. However your Dad will probably not like the idea.

Your mother sent me a box of chocolates for Mother's Day and also something for Joan. They are at Margaret's so haven't seen what it is yet. Dad sent me a Mother's Day card from Toronto signed by Joan "per her private secretary her grand-dad" and Mother sent me a card signed by you and Joan. I sent a card and a letter to your Mother signed by all of us and also one to Mother so it looks like a good weekend.

Alix was very thrilled yesterday as she got a dozen roses and a card from Fred and Sandy and so she sat down and cried. Am going over tonight to see the flowers and Alix.

Baked some cookies for you yesterday and so today put the finishing touches on your box and it is now ready to be taken to the PO when I go over town. As I've said before if there's anything you want please let me know.

Wrote to the Reader's Digest to readdress your copy to you so start looking for it in a month or so.

How are you liking England and what have you been doing? I'll bet it's very interesting over there and very busy too, especially now.

Jessie has had several letters from Sid. He is an F/O now and still in India.

Joan has developed a new trick. When she smiles now she wrinkles up her nose like a rabbit and snorts. It is really very funny and she gets quite a bang out of it. She's getting harder to feed as she likes to help you along by putting her hands in her food and stirring it up, so she usually ends up quite a mess.

The daughter just woke up and so is now beside me in her play pen – just a-lying there and a-looking around. Her hands are still quite an object of amusement. Her hair has grown in at the back so she is no longer called "Baldy", but it is not long enough to curl yet. She weighs about 17 3/4 lbs. so is getting to be quite an armful. Her newest teeth are right out in the open now so she's got quite a mouthful.

As for myself, I've lost the few pounds I gained at Camrose so will have the fun of starting all over again. Have been running around too much and staying up too late. Will have to mend my ways ere I get to be a shadow. Feel wonderful however.

That's all for now, dear All my love, Peg

Canadian Pacific Telegram
Post Mark: Edmonton May 15, 9 PM, 1944
from Great Britain
Mrs. C. H. Smith 11024 – 89 Ave. South Edmonton

ALL WELL AND SAFE. BEST WISHES TO ALL AT HOME ALL MY LOVE
DEAREST
HAMP SMITH

4:10 PM MAY 15   TELEPHONED

#5 – May 15, 1944

Dear Peggy,
Have been pretty lax about writing but have been traveling and

apparently these letters have to be mailed from an Air Force station. Left my last station after I wrote you the mail might be delayed. From there went to London. We were supposed to spend one afternoon there and then proceed but decided to take a day off and see the place. We stayed at a club called the Constitutional Club, just off Trafalgar Square. It was quite a stuffy old place but was supposed to be very classy – Winston Churchill was the president of it but actually he didn't drop in and look us up. I guess he was busy. It was just off Trafalgar Square and so we didn't have much trouble finding it when we left it to explore the town. The afternoon we got settled we had some cocktails at the club and then went over to the Canadian Officers Club just across the way. We had a meal of spaghetti which was the best food we had tasted. It was served to us by Mrs. Vincent Massey. The club is just two rooms and a kitchen. From there we went to the headquarters mess and picked up some of the big boys who run our medical services here. They took us into a place called the Exhibition Club. We went there by tube underground and that was my first experience with the London underground. It certainly is a long ways under and it really travels. This club was a bottle club where a bottle of scotch (small) cost 3 pounds. We left there about 12 midnight and found ourselves in the blackout. It was really quite dark. One of the boys walked straight into the side of a bus beside the curb. So you can imagine. The taxis don't seem to slow down much in spite of that. We finally found the entrance to the underground and got out at Trafalgar Square. Went to Lyons to eat – it was the only place in London that was open all night for food. We had to queue up as usual and finally got in and had some powdered eggs scrambled and toast. Then we tried to get a taxi home and didn't succeed and finally ended up at the club about 3:00 AM telling each other what a good time we had had and each wondering if we believed it.

The next morning went to Buckingham Palace and watched the changing of the guard. They were all in battle dress but it was nice to see and there were two bands – one the pipes and the other a large military brass band. Then back to the Club and sat and had dinner – fish, cabbage and boiled potatoes – the usual. Went out after lunch and was standing on a corner in Trafalgar Square when Dave Moffat came up – it's funny how you meet people. He and I got on the underground and went out to Kew Gardens – you know, Kew in lilac time. It was very pretty but I was a little disappointed because it was more of a park than a flower garden and since all England looks like a park to me, it didn't impress me as much as I thought it would.

That evening we went to a show called "The Love Racket". It was a musical comedy and very good in spots but I couldn't understand all the dialogue and so missed part of it. It seemed funny to have coffee and biscuits served to you during intermission. By the way I don't know how the English make coffee but I suspect that they use rain water and dandelion roots – it tastes like nothing on earth.

After the show we went to a place for our meal – the shows are all on very early because of the blackout – at a place called Poissins. I had scallops which I don't like and the meal cost me a pound so I was not very pleased. After that we went home and sat in the lounge in the Club and drank beer. The club was very stuffy and very old. Everybody was horribly proper. I may become a gentleman over here if I don't look out. I even had to argue to get Dave Moffat up to my room so I could wash. The next day in the morning we left London and I'll tell you about my trip in my next letter. Before leaving we had breakfast – sausages and scrambled eggs (powdered). I repeat that I'll never look at sausages again. I imagine I won't get any mail from you for several weeks and it will certainly be welcome. I would kind of like you to keep my letters – diary you know. I'm certainly going to save yours. I've reread yours several times already.

All my love, Hamp

Written in pencil on envelope, RCAF Wimbledon

May 15, 1944

Dear Hamp,

You're just wonderful my darling. Did I ever tell you? Well you are. Got another cable today and was surprised, thrilled, excited etc. all rolled up together so you can guess I'm not good for very much.

I suppose by now you are all settled in your new quarters. Hope you run into some of the old crowd soon and have a good get-together – which it undoubtedly will be.

My present from Mother Smith wasn't a box chocolates but a box of "three Flowers" perfume, eau de cologne and powder – real good stinky stuff. Joan got a box of arrowroot biscuits. Sure thought it grand of Mother to remember us.

Saturday night I meandered over to Alix's and with another war mother we sat and chatted until 1:00 A.M. so it was another late night for no reason except that I didn't want to go to bed until I was ready to sleep. Alix had another letter from Fred and he is now the C.O. of something and is in the Medical Inspection branch.

Met John Waddell on the street today. He has been posted back here to I.F.S. and is on the M.S.B. as a nose and throat man – so guess Jean and I will be getting together one of these days.

Alix and Sandy came over for supper last night. We went for quite a stroll on the campus first and was it ever hot! It is Convocation tomorrow and so everything is humming on this side of the river.

Have two more pictures of Joan – one with Sandra and one with me so will write you ordinary mail and send the snaps to you soon. Have to wait for a reprint on one as they are pictures taken on Alix's camera. I still am unable to get film and Alix is without now too. However the Flemings have a film and no camera so I may be able to strike up a bargain.

Mailed a parcel to you today and I do hope it arrives OK and soon and that it contains things you can use. If however there is something in it you don't like, want or need you might let me know so that you won't get it a second time.

Joan is trying her darndest to crawl but so far without success. She has the right idea however as she gets up on her hands and knees and rocks trying to shove herself forward usually collapsing on her face. But one of these days she'll break into a crawl and then – heaven help us! She'll be a terror. She certainly has a Smith appetite – sits in her high chair leaning forward as far as she can – with her eyes just about popping from her head as she watches her food coming. And as I've said before she has to help too by mixing it up again – with her hands! Mother and I laughed tonight because Bud got his supper a few seconds before Joan and she let out one yell and almost jumped out of the chair. She was that eager. She rolled off the chesterfield yesterday and fell on the floor before I could get to her. There was quite a noise for a few minutes but

Joan was more scared than hurt – in fact she wasn't hurt a bit. Must have fallen on her head I guess.

Had a letter from your Mother last week and Dad is home from the hospital – much improved. Everyone is fine and the same as ever. Dad is still in Toronto and will be away 3 more weeks. He wanted to know if you were still in Montreal as he would have looked you up.

Your little wife is just in the best of health and humor and still gets mad at people who remark on how thin she is – and really it isn't any worse than it was 3 years ago. Guess I need you home, dear, to fatten me up like you did the last time.

Alix and I are talking about going to Pigeon with Sandy and Joan this summer. What do you think about it?

Will write on Wednesday darling. All my love, as ever – Peg

#6 – May 17, 1944

Dear Peg,

Well, have done a bit of traveling around since I last saw you. While I think of it – these letters are very hard to get – if you could send me a hundred or two it would help a lot. If you send registered parcels they apparently get here quite quickly so I would be very glad to get some. You would be surprised how much satisfaction there is in writing you – it seems to bring you that much closer. I notice by the date that it's a month today that I left so the time is going.

Have had some more experience with English trains. It's quite a game to get your luggage into the baggage car and haul it out yourself. You can't leave it alone a minute because there are so many people about that you are bound to lose some of it. This business of getting on the train and wondering when you get off is also new. The conductor doesn't tell you because he doesn't seem to exist and none of your compartment mates seem to know, you just keep looking for the sign in the station and if it is the right one you dash off and haul out your baggage.

I spent a few hours in York. It was quite a nice city to look at in spots. It is entirely surrounded by a very old stone wall. Went up and walked around it for a way. The stonework was really built to last. It apparently surrounds the older part of the city and seems to go for miles. Johnnie Hunt and I met in York and then drove over and saw Doug Ritchie at his station. They are both much the same as usual. They are pretty well settled in their routine and seem happy about it all.

After that I went and reported to my unit. I am at present at a station where I will stay for about 2 weeks and learn how they do things over here. After that I will proceed to my unit which will be more or less permanent. The leave situation is out of the question for us so I suppose it will be some time before I get to see any of the relatives.

Will write tomorrow. XXX to the daughter. All my love, Hamp

#7(renumbered 6)   May 18, 1944

Dear Peg,

Well, am more or less settling into sort of a routine. I told you I would be here about 2 weeks and then go to another place. My mailing address is this next place so I won't get a letter until I arrive there (if then?). The work here is much the same as at home except you become much more conscious of the venereal diseases. It is peculiar how promiscuous some people become. Out of curiosity I have asked them how they would like it if the people they left at home acted in the same way, and they all were indignant to think that such a thing might be possible. The sick parade runs about 20 to 25 – the usual line of stuff with a few more people in it who want to go home. The present hospital I am in is quite nice – a more or less permanent setup and is quite well equipped. We of course send nearly everything to nearby base hospitals which are largely staffed by the RAF.

The first day I arrived here I met W/C Burgess who is just here temporarily while recuperating from a foot injury. He received it when he baled out of his aircraft when it was shot up by flak after returning from a raid. He landed in a ploughed field and fractured a metatarsal. The next night he and I went into a nearby small town and had a steak – yes, a genuine tender, juicy steak. It was really quite a treat. Food apparently can be gotten if you know where to go.

The food at this mess is excellent and I think compares favorably with a good many Canadian stations. The one drawback I have found to date is – my wife isn't here with our daughter. However they tell me there is a war on and I realize it when I look around the mess and see all the DFCs and DFMs etc.

There should be quite a stack of mail when it arrives and it certainly will be welcome. I am curious to know how long it takes to get mail. I have lost track of the number of letters I have written you but will call this one No. 6 and try to keep it right number. Goodbye for now and all my love, Hamp

#8 – May 20, 1944

Dear Peg,

Nothing much to write about today but I won't let that deter me. The weather is as usual – damp with fog and occasional rain. If the temperature in the mess gets up to 60 it is sweltering and it averages nearer 50. One gradually becomes accustomed to it – I hope.

Not very busy today – had a crash on the drome tonight – just a ground loop and nobody seriously hurt but it provided a little excitement for a while. Tomorrow I'm going to scrounge a bike and get out and see a little of the countryside in the evening.

The hospital had a big event today – the RCAF sent us 2 books – one on the diseases of the skin and the other on minor surgery.

I wouldn't trust myself doing minor surgery – the orderly who hangs around me is named Adderley. A little fellow with a mustache named Adderley who hails from Nassau. He apparently thinks the germ theory is obsolete so you have to keep watching him and telling him to comb his hair and wash his hands and take his fingers off the middle sterile dressings etc. Adderley described himself as a psychopathic personality (he read a psychiatry book of one of the MO's) and it happens that he is correct.

The nursing sister here is away on her honeymoon at present. She married an MO from a nearby station. Apparently the NSs don't stay single very long. I have never met the girl who is here. At present there are about the usual run of patients in sick quarters – nobody sick. Anybody who is at all ill is evacuated to RAF hospitals so actually our work doesn't vary much from the Canadian routine.

Well Peg it certainly will be nice to hear from you. (This statement may get a little monotonous to you but that's the way I feel). All my love, Hamp

Normal Letter No Envelope

May 18, 1944

Dearest Hamp,

This letter is just a change from the "blue forms" – not that I'm out of them but because I wanted to send the snaps of Joan to you. Three of them are quite good and one only fair.

They are numbered on the back and according to the numbers the comments of each are as follows:

(1) Taken in front of our place (note the fir tree) on April 30. The film was one that had been in our camera for 3 years and had 2 pictures left – one was spoiled and the other is not very good. Supposed to be a "close-up" of Joan in her buggy.

2) Joan and Sandra taken in front of Robertson's one hot Sunday. Sandra kind of hogged the lime-light but Joan was lucky to have friends take her picture.

3) Joan and I on the same day – Joan as usual scowling at the sun and Me – I'm just astanding there.

4) Taken in front of Hedley's (next door-neighbor) after we'd been in for tea. Joan was in quite a happy mood. A good picture of her I thought. I really have other things to wear but people always want to take my picture when I have my blue suit on.

As you can see from the snaps we aren't looking sick or anything like that so don't worry about us.

I believe I wrote to you rather sketchily about Victory bonds so guess I'd better elaborate. To get down to finance – they had business men call at your house to sell bonds so I bought two, one $50 bond for cash and another on time. That was from the money we had in Claresholm which was $110. Well – $5 went on the 2nd bond as first payment; opened a bank account with the Bank of Montreal and deposited $30; gave Mother my board and room money for two weeks and kept the change. Along came my cheque on the 1st of May so paid my month's room rent of $40 and kept the change. Then along came the bond salesman again so I took 2 more on time – One in Joan's name and one in yours and gave him the down payment of ten dollars. So this is how we stand. Each month I put $27 into bonds and the remainder of your allowance into the bank. From my cheque I pay my board and room and keep the rest for pin money. Then if I need any more I draw from the bank. So its really quite a simple setup and I think it will work. I'll be banking the interest from all our bonds & Joan's which now total $750. Which reminds me Bob Lawson said he would have S/L Chandler send me the bond from the 5th loan. Am going to get a box when Dad comes home so everything will be intact.

Just went in to cover up our daughter and put her down in bed. She was lying at the head of the bed with feet through the side – banging on the wall. She keeps me awake until 2 A.M. some mornings by rolling around and banging. Guess I'll have to take her in hand one of these days.

She has discovered how to kneel in the bath and look over the sides, really quite cute. She sure loves to splash the water about. It isn't just splashing – she seems to scoop it up and toss it over the sides.

I certainly wouldn't change her for all the money in the world. She's grand company and I'm glad she's ours.

I've been wearing your identification bracelet. Do you mind? It can be fastened anywhere along the chain so it fits me. Decided it was too nice to have sitting in a drawer. I'd use your beer mug too if I had the reason for doing so. Guess I'll have to celebrate when "Buster" Norton arrives.

That seems to be about everything for now as I wrote last night and will be writing tomorrow too.

Have you any ideas about our finances? If so write them down some day will you, dear?

Will try to get more snaps for you. Hope to get a film one of these days and use it.

Trust you are fine and getting along OK and not too lonely. We hope to get a letter from you soon. Have they still got the rotation system in effect for the MOs? If you find out anything about it you might let me know. All my love, darling, as ever, Peg

Dearest Hamp,

Am still living on the pleasure of your cables – although as a rule cables and wives are supposed to be pretty cold affairs but to me your cables were the most thrilling things that have happened to me for ages and ages. Am still trying to figure out the reason for two cables – most girls aren't lucky enough to get two. We have thought up many reasons for the two but whatever it may be I think it was darn swell of you to be so considerate darling and it just goes to show that you are the very, very best.

Am writing you my thoughts tonight as I haven't been doing very much and figure that you would want to know just how the old brain is percolating even if it isn't very brilliant.

Haven't mentioned Jenny for quite some time, have I? At first I was very disappointed that she had come as I was all prepped up for David – even at such an early date. Of course I realize now just how silly it all was but time at that point was going so quickly that each minute seemed to be another day nearer to your leaving. However now that Jenny has arrived and I've got settled down to a routine and as Joan grows and becomes more active each day I realize just what a time it would have been with David and believe me saying I'd be busy was putting it mildly. But it really boils down to the fact that whether Jenny or David had come I'd have been very happy and contented – as much as possible without you here.

Through all of this you may be gathering that now the rush of settling and meeting of old friends is over, that I'm missing you terribly and have more time to think of the happy days we had together. Well if you have such a glimmering you are quite right. I often wonder if its stage one gets into which reaches a climax and gradually gets more settled. Time will tell. I certainly admire the girls whose husbands have been away for years – not mentioning the husbands. But enough of this – and into a lighter frame of mind.

It certainly has been hot the past two days and Joan has been having a few regulated sun baths and is getting quite a tan. Her eczema is still good and flares up once in a while on her legs and face. However the coal tar keeps it in place and she can eat almost anything so it is not a worry anymore. Wish you could see her play with Buddy[5]. She's crazy about him and he of her. She leans out of her high chair to watch him go by and comes up beside her when she's on the floor. She pats his head and grabs his fur and than laughs out loud – of course she is grinning all the time. Bud rolls around for her and noses up beside her – but confidentially I think he's after arrowroot crumbs more than her petting. Yesterday was over at Day's and Joan and Sandra took a great shine to each other. Joan of course is at the stage where she likes to pull hair – which isn't very good as far as Sandra is concerned and Sandra is not allowed to touch "little babies" so we haven't had any rows as yet but in a few months it may be a different story.

It was convocation yesterday but I didn't go – figured one was enough for me. There were some big "do's" to celebrate and everyone I saw seemed to be having a very merry time.

Started sewing again for Joan. Her sun suit fits her just swell so am making a sunbonnet to match. It's blue as you may remember so she'll look a prize packet.

Margaret is still waiting but she claims she's going to do nothing but sit on cotton until Dr. Vant returns. Their "Buster" can't have the same desire to get out and see life as Joan did!

An old school friend of mine lost her husband at sea recently. His boat was escorting a convoy about the same time you went over. She has a little boy of 2 and I really don't know just what she's going to do. Wish there was some little or big thing I could do but she says "No thanks I'll manage." It sure must take an awful lot of "guts" at times.

Am wondering if your cigarettes have arrived yet. I hear it takes about a month to get them started so of course its too soon yet – but its almost a month. In fact its a month today since you left and that means that Joan is 7 months old today. It doesn't seem possible does it? Do you feel ancient at all, having such a grown up family? Ha! Ha!

It is again time to feed our "little character" and also time I went to bed so will say "good Night" for now.

Hope you are very, very well and getting used to being with the boys again. Have a good time while you can, darling, coz when you come home, I'm going to stay right beside you for years to come. It's a threat and also a promise. All my love, dear, As Ever, Peg

Dear Peg,

Well another day has gone by. The days go by quite quickly but the evenings tend to drag a bit since I don't know anyone here to speak of as yet. Johnnie Hunt was in today for lunch and we had a chat. He certainly hasn't changed much and is as happy go lucky as usual.

Today I learned how to drive one of the ambulances. I went in one of the little ambulances. These are very small and you feel as if you are sitting right down on the road. There are 4 speeds ahead but beyond that are very simple. It's quite a novelty keeping on the left side of the road though and I'm not going to be very ambitious for awhile until I get more used to the traffic.

Got in touch with Doug Ritchie yesterday and he is going to try to get over one of these evenings. I don't know the country well enough to do much traveling. We are on call every other night – each night I have had to get up and sew up the head of somebody who fell off a bicycle. There are apparently more injuries from that than from a lot of other things.

This climate is cold – the first 3 days I was here I was quite unable to keep warm. Have gradually started to become accustomed to it and am wearing my battle dress which is much more comfortable than a uniform.

In my letters I cannot tell you what goes on at the station so they will get duller and duller (if possible). Will be glad to hear from you regularly and so be able to keep up a conversation. Will write tomorrow. All my love, Hamp

Dearest Hamp,

I wrote to you last night and sent the letter by ordinary mail because it contains some snaps for you. Hope they get through all right but if anything should happen to them I can get the negatives printed again.

Went downtown yesterday with Helen Campbell – the girl next door – as she was going to Dr. Vant so I waited for her and saw Mrs.

MacDonald who used to be in Claresholm. She is expecting a baby in 6 weeks. He was the education officer and is now at I.T.S.

Dr. Vant is away on his holidays until June so it looks like Margaret will get Dr. Hutton. I haven't gone to see Vant yet but its a "must do" for June.

Today Alix and I went on a "Buggy Parade". We push the buggies with our children in them up and down the sidewalks. It's really quite a new idea, don't you know? Any way it was quite a lot of fun and Sandra talks to Joan all the time calling her "little baby Joan". After strolling up and down for about an hour we came home and had tea and cookies in the back garden inviting Helen Campbell to join us. Buddy of course was "Johnny-on-the-spot" for cookies and Sandra kept feeding her's to him. Our daughter was in her play pen and of course ate all her biscuits by herself (note the plural).

Joan is beginning to creep. She can manage quite well for about 2 feet and then collapses. She pushes with her left foot and pulls herself with her hands and arms and kind of wriggles the rest of herself along. In another week she'll be a-crawling all over the place.

She's getting to be the "real miss" now. When she sees her food coming both arms fly out and she bounces up and down and the episodes of blowing and stirring the food carry on from there. And if you want her to do something she doesn't want, you hear about it. She makes real sounds of disgust and wrinkles up her nose. You remember how the storm cover fits on her buggy – a two inch fold up the front to prevent a draught? Well she has that all bent down by chinning herself on it to look out when she's supposed to be asleep. And when I tease her now or play "Bore a Hole" she gets awfully excited and chuckles away loudly with frequent squeals. She's really quite a "tomboy" even now. Hope you are home to control her when she gets over a year old because when I scold her she just looks at me and grins so what will she do as she gets older. A real character yessiree!

I'm just fine and have made it a point to stay home these nights and get some sleep.

That seems to be all for now. How are you getting along and what have you been doing lately? Have you been sight seeing yet? Guess that's a silly question. Well g'bye for now.

All my love, darling As Ever – Peg

Dear Peg,

Well another day has progressed. Sunday is the same as any other day now. Was quite busy with the usual line today. Doug Ritchie came over today and had supper with me and then we went cycling with a dental officer named Reg Ball who came with him. It was my first glimpse of the country from up close. It is very pretty indeed – everything very green, the fields all divided by hedges and the villages every few miles, each consisting of a large church and a small number of brick houses. The houses temporary buildings here are brick and it seems funny to me to see such permanent looking structures called temporary. Apparently brick is much easier to get than wood, so that explains it.

Stopped at a little country inn and had a beer. They are apparently all much the same – a fireplace, a bar and a place to seat about a dozen people. Have a very good opinion of English beer now.

The nursing sister who got married came back today – all radiant and not looking very tired (they had good weather in Edinburgh so that probably accounts for it) – not like a foot of snow in Vancouver. She was a classmate of Harriette Rainsforth's.

Well there isn't much to write about. In about 2 weeks time I'm going to have to resort to sneaking English cigarettes. Some of them aren't bad but they cost about 3 cents a piece. I bought some White Owl cigars on the boat (2 boxes) and gave a box to Johnnie Hunt. He was tickled to get them and it gave me a lot more satisfaction than smoking them myself. The only reason I got them was because they were available and cheap. Demonstrated yours and the daughter's picture to Doug and he said she was a wonderful looking child so he's still my friend.

Well, goodbye for now again. All my love, Hamp

#9 – May 22, 1944

Dear Peg,

Another day. Have lost track of my letters again but believe that his is No. 9. Wrote yesterday and didn't get it mailed in time so you may get two at once. At present I have a very limited number of forms so I am writing to you only and then if I can scrounge more will write to the rest. If you could pass the news along and explain the situation it would be a help.

Have to go into town and get a new flash for your picture. I packed and repacked it about half a dozen times (got it out whenever stopped for more than 24 hours) and had no trouble but the glass got cracked coming up from London. May get into Harrogate this week and get some. It certainly is nice to be able to look at your picture if nothing more. I've traveled a long way but without any exaggeration, you are the best looking girl I have seen or will see.

I haven't discussed Jennie with you at all because there wasn't very much more *I could* say. It would be good news to me in that our first effort was so wonderful, that with that practice, the second would be even more so, if that were possible. However it's no fun for you and I can't be of much help to you here, so for that reason I would rather Jennie kept coming until my return.

Had a big day today. Worked in the hospital until noon. Then had lunch. Then there was a mess meeting that lasted an hour. And then I painted – a bunch of us painted the dining room. Got thoroughly splattered with paint and had a wonderful time. The dining room is a very large room – quite long with large windows about 12 feet high along one side of it. Painted it light blue with cream trim – it looked very good if I do say so myself (not that I did enough to be proud of). This was an old RAF mess so didn't exactly conform to Canadian standards of interior decorating. The bar officer kept big jugs of beer available so it was about as pleasant an afternoon as I have spent in this country.

Saw a show in the mess tonight – about the American nurses on Bataan – forget the name of it. It was quite good but a little dramatic.

Well, will say goodbye for now again and will write. Say hello to Joan for me. All my love, Hamp

#10 – May 23, 1944

Dear Peg,

Well there isn't much to write about. The weather has really been wonderful the past 2 days. The sun has shone and it has been warm.

Have gotten used to no longer seeing direct sunlight and feel that seeing the sun through the haze is practically as good as the real thing.

Was very busy today. Had a large sick parade and then kept going all day with boards, ulcers, sinusitis and what not. By the time I was through, the place seemed pretty grim so I came over to the mess and met Charlie Burgess and we had a couple of beers – which improved the situation slightly. Then sat around for the rest of the evening and just talked – about post-war Canada and how wonderful Alberta was – with some of the chaps from the West.

Phoned Tommy Ellison – he used to be at Claresholm and was Curly Ellison's brother, the fat, reddish, baldish chap in maintenance – he wasn't home. I was going to cycle over to see him but will do so tomorrow or the next day. Something to do.

I don't know how much longer I will be on this station but it will be 3 or 4 or 5 more days and then I will move along. It's getting to be a habit – this living out of a suitcase – but I don't think I will really become used to it.

Sent my laundry out yesterday – the first since Lachine P.Q. – 10 shirts, 18 hanks etc. etc. – hope that it comes back before I move. Davy Moffat said that laundry was a real problem with him – he was moving all over the country and it never did quite catch up with him.

Well dear, there is not much to write about and my room is too chilly to stay out of bed in, so will say goodbye and write. It'll be good to hear from you. All my love, Hamp

11 – May 23, 1944

P.S. Joan got hold of this letter and you almost didn't get it. You know what she does with paper – well!

Dearest Hamp,

Congratulations old man! You are now an uncle of a wee boy born at 6:19 this A.M. and weighing 6 lb. 9 oz. Both are going well.

Margaret went to the hospital last night after supper. She wasn't having any pains but her membranes had ruptured in the morning so Marg Hutton – who delivered the baby – told her to go in at night so guess they had to give a medical induction. Margaret phoned me at five o'clock to tell me she was going but didn't quite know why. I phoned the hospital this morning and Miss Fane and I had a long chat about this and that but she said Margaret came through nicely. Am going to see her tomorrow.

Was over at Norton's on Sunday and Marg was really huge especially for an average baby. I thought she was going to have twins. We played 3 handed crib, nines and bridge. Bill and I had a bottle of beer a piece and Marg had a glass of tomato juice. She was feeling very well indeed.

I took Joan with me and we put her to bed in Margaret's room with all the dining room chairs lined up on the outside of the bed. But she managed to get stuck between the bed and the wall and her pride was hurt because she had to be hauled out. She wasn't hurt however, but for safety's sake, she ended up in Buster's bassinet so you may guess how large it is.

I should have written you Sunday night but we didn't get home until midnight.

Saturday afternoon Alix had a small tea on her back lawn. Lois McCrea and Betty Stark were there with their boys so we had quite a lively time. Spent Saturday night at home embroidering the letter "S" on some serviettes your Mother sent me last Christmas.

Yesterday it rained all day so stayed in and made a sun bonnet to go with Joan's playsuit and finished her dress that I had cut out in Claresholm. So you see I'm gradually getting all the things I planned to do, finished.

Joan is getting to be a wild Indian. At night she moves around her bed so much I can't go to sleep and anyway I have to wait till she goes to sleep so I can cover her up. It doesn't matter how you pin the covers down now she always manages to get on top. When she wants to turn over nothing can stop her even if you hold her down. Am really worried about her because when she gets older she'll be an awful brat and I won't have that so we are going to be in for stormy days, I guess. Maybe she'll tame down a bit after a while.

The sweater, bonnet & booties I made for Margaret are going to look awfully sissy on a boy. They'll be OK if Margaret uses them while he's small.

Am thinking of going down to Camrose in 2 or 3 weeks or if Dad comes up to see Margaret I may go back with him for a few days.

I hope you're getting your mail all right. We of course are not getting any as yet and the rumor goes around that mails from Britain are held up due to invasion plans. So am not worried about you. Far be it for me to crab about no mail when such big things are brewing. But a letter would be nice though as it is awfully queer to write every other day and not know whether you get them or not. One of these days though the mail man will carry good tidings.

Had a letter from your mother yesterday and everyone is fairly well – in other words "as usual".

As for myself, I feel well, look well and am well but that seems a waste of time as there's no one here who enjoys it. All for now "Uncle" All my love, dearest, as ever, – Peg

#11 – May 25, 1944

Dear Peg,

Didn't write yesterday because I was running so low on these forms that I was afraid that there would be no letters for awhile. Have managed to scrounge a dozen now so that will help out a bit.

Yesterday was just another day except it was a little cooler than usual. Very busy all day with the routine run of things. Johnnie Hunt's brother Bill went missing yesterday. He was an observer and had completed his first tour and took an extra trip before going on leave before his second tour. Johnnie feels pretty down because somebody says they saw him spin in just inside the French coast, so it doesn't leave him much hope.

Last night they had a party in the mess. There was a dance and a few people brought their wives and girl friends and the rest sat around and got drunk. I was on duty so didn't do that. They all decided it was a good party but personally I found that I missed my wife.

Today was another quite busy day with bags of people to see. Tonight Charlie Burgess and I went over the station cinema and saw a show. It was a Red Skelton picture which I think you and I saw somewhere – in Camrose I think – with him a pants presser who married a Broadway star. Enjoyed it because it provided the passage of an evening.

Doug Ritchie phoned and wanted me to go golfing this evening but I was too busy so wasn't able to get away.

Hope to get some mail next week. My cigarettes have run down pretty well but hope to get some, sometime. I think you can arrange through one of the cigar stores (Miles') to send them over via Imperial Tobacco Company at the overseas rates of $3.00 a thousand or something.

Well Peg, nothing much to write about but will keep on anyway because I like talking to you.

All my love, Hamp

12 – May 25, 1944

Dear Hamp,

Time seems to be slipping along but where it goes to and what I do with it I can't say. I've spent the last 3 hours trying to get Joan to go to sleep but she's so full of play that she figures sleep is not for her. She's quite the wild Indian still these days and my guess is she'll have her carriage wrecked shortly if she keeps on bouncing away in it like she does. I have to strap her in now for I daren't leave her in it as she is just as likely to face out as not. Today she discovered that her high chair would rock as the front legs were up on the linoleum and the back ones on the hardwood so she had quite a time rocking it and bouncing around. She certainly gets a big bang out of life, let me tell you, and she's such a darling I don't know what I'd do without her. Am afraid she's going to be spoiled though as I take your share of my loving out on her and then she gets her own as well.

I went up to see Margaret yesterday and of course David William. Margaret is very well and very happy. She went into the hospital Monday night and didn't start with pains until 4 A.M. Tuesday and David was born at 6:19 A.M. so it wasn't too long. The baby was a breech presentation so Margaret really had quite an easy time considering everything. Wee David is a fine boy and although he is quite small at present is fine and healthy. He has dark hair, red face and blue eyes and I think looks more like a Norton than a Smith but he's real cute. Bill of course is very excited and awfully proud and all he could say was "And it's a boy!". Dad and Irene drove up on Tuesday afternoon, had a look at Margaret and the baby and as everything was all right they left the hospital in 15 minutes. Tuesday night they dropped in to see Joan and I for about 10 minutes. Dad looked about the same although he had another bout of pneumonia after you left and even admitted that he is tired. He had an enlargement of our picture made for the house and is going to send one to Mother and Dad. Very sweet of him I thought.

Alison was married yesterday and for a quiet home wedding it made quite a splash in the paper with a big write up and quite a good picture of McB. The groom was not in the picture but they did mention his name in the paper along with an *antique* silver vase on top of the cake. Meow! Maybe it's a case of sour grapes as I wasn't invited & Margaret thinks I was gypped but whether I was or wasn't doesn't bother me at all.

Alberta is certainly having some very queer weather. Last night snow fell in Mountain Park and Luscar to a depth of 55 inches – if you can imagine and it was the heavy wet snow so guess there was considerable damage done. The roof of a skating rink fell in at Mountain Park as it couldn't stand the weight. Approx. 250 tons so they figure. I'll bet the trees are a mess as ours were with only 4 1/2 inches of snow. We've had rain the last 8 days and its been very bleak and cold but today the sky released in the afternoon so I guess its fair weather ahead. The city really looks very pretty after the rain with the new green of the trees and hedges of the bright reds and yellows of the tulips with blue iris and purple lilacs. The little green shoots of the peas, radishes, lettuce and carrots are up in our garden now and we have been eating our own green onions and rhubarb for a week or more. How does the green onion sound darling, or is that being mean?

Mother is out at a show tonight with Mrs. Henderson so Joan and I are holding the fort alone. I've been getting more sleep lately as I haven't been going out at night except to mail your letters and drop in for a coke somewhere.

Dad is not home yet although we've been expecting him for the last day or so. He's probably gadding around somewhere and loath to turn his footsteps to our happy abode. However he'll probably turn up one day and off again the next. I'm getting the wanderer's itch for something for I feel its about time I went home to Claresholm and then I remember that the Smith's don't lie there anymore so I pull in the reins and settle back again.

Flash from the home front – our daughter is at last asleep but we'll probably go through it all again at 11 o'clock as usual and than a repeat at 6 A.M. But for all the racket she makes I still think she's the best baby – at the least the best one we've ever had. All for now dear! All my love, dearest, Peg

#12 May 27, 1944

Dear Peg,

Didn't write again yesterday – no excuse except I fell asleep on my bed after supper and didn't wake up until midnight so rolled in. Had my best news since arrival tonight. Johnnie Hunt phoned up that there were two letters from you. I am going to the station he is at present stationed on, so had my mail forwarded there. I believe he said they were dated May 11 and May 15 so at that rate, the service is pretty good. Can hardly wait to get them – it certainly will be good to hear from you.

Nothing happened yesterday of note. Was on duty but it was very quiet with the usual routine on sick parade.

Today was a repetition, was going to take the afternoon off but had nowhere to go so just hung around the hospital and tended the sick and afflicted. There are 2 MOs on this station at present – a fellow named Hicks and myself. The station strength is considerably greater than Claresholm so we manage to keep occupied. The other chap is a very good sort and I have liked it here. I am just getting "genned up" on the RAF forms and procedures etc. before I proceed to what will be my more or less permanent posting and Johnnie Hunt will come back to civilization here for a change.

Tonight cycled over to see Tommy Ellison. You may remember him at Claresholm. Went to the station and found the MO and he drove me around in the ambulance and located Tommy. Tommy was just out of briefing for an op and was a little preoccupied but it was good to see a familiar face. He is about 1/4 through his tour of ops. I think he was glad to see someone from Claresholm.

Tomorrow I am going to try and cycle out in the country with Charlie Burgess and scrounge more eggs from the farmers – if I can get away – we probably won't have any luck but it will be something to do. Certainly hope I get my mail tomorrow. Miss you. All my love, Hamp

#13 May 28, 1944

Dear Peg,

Had a banner day today, got two letters from you. This is the happiest I have been since I left you. They were written on May 10 (#16) and May 12. Bob and Hughie must have been up for the Medical Convention. It was nice to hear that Hughie stayed with you and you got an opportunity to more or less even up the score. McBride trousseau tea was apparently quite an event – glad to hear that Allison is getting married at last. Margaret should have her family by now and I certainly hope that all is O.K. Sorry I didn't send you anything for Mother's Day honey – makes me feel a little sheepish but was in transit at the time. Will try and make up for it sometime. Still haven't got my bank account fixed up so am a little short of funds. (That should be enough of excuses but I'm still sorry.) Am looking forward to your cookies. The food is good here but you miss certain things e.g. cookies, meat etc. – but it's nothing to worry about because we are very well fed and eat better than the civilians. Joan sounds like she is getting cuter every day (if that were possible). It certainly will be good to get a look at her again. You can't write too much about her (or about yourself). You seem to keep quite busy and am glad to hear it. Glad to hear that it was Bie's room you went to have a drink of rye in – he is one person you would never have to worry about. That snow storm must have been quite something just about as bad as the one we got married in. At the rate Joan is going she will soon be feeding herself and then still take some chasing I imagine. I hope her skin is doing well and becoming less of a problem.

Tonight was on duty. Hung around doing nothing much and then Johnnie Hunt came over (he sent the letters this afternoon). He brought the dentist with him – Ken Moore an Alberta graduate – we had a beer and then shot snooker with Charlie Burgess and managed to fill in the evening.

112

Johnnie also gave me 600 cigarettes which should last until some start to come.

He went back about 10:00 PM and then I saw a couple of "casualties" at the hospital and then reread my letters for the 4th time and am writing.

It has been a gorgeous day – actually hot and sunny – people say that it is our one day of summer. If it continues tomorrow I am going to try to get away for a couple of hours cycling.

Also had a letter from Mother today – written on April 23.

Well, will say goodbye for now. Your letters are really morale lifters. All my love, Hamp

13 – May 28, 1944

Dearest Hamp.

I've been quite busy the last few days going to see Margaret and David. They are both fine and doing remarkably well. I took Joan on Friday afternoon in her buggy and left her outside but she didn't seem to like that very well and really cried with great tears rolling down her cheeks so I had to cut my visit short. At night Mary Hall, Marie Collins and I went to the Garneau – a good show and we all wept. It was "Lost Angel" and all about a little girl. Saturday was so very hot and I couldn't stay awake so slept most of the day. Today was another hot one and haven't had much ambition except to seek shade and breeze.

Dad came home last night and of course was very tired as he's been away ever since you left. He brought Joan a cute wee dress from Winnipeg and Mother and I blouses. Mine is red and Mother's white so we really did all right by ourselves.

Fred sent Alix some sandals from Italy with a grass top (woven) and wooden soles. He sent a pair to Sandra and his sister Helen. Alix's were too small and so she had me try them on and after quite a struggle on my part to be polite and yet not take them she finally brought them to the house and left them. The whole thing nearly broke up a beautiful friendship for a few days. I thought she should at least keep them as souvenirs as Fred had sent them but she thought that was a silly idea. So I now have a pair of Italian sandals.

Alix and I have decided not to go to the lake as it wouldn't be much of a holiday for us having to haul and heat water every day to wash, and build fires to heat baby bottles etc. so we've decided to relax and take it easy at home. It sounds so much easier but if we can get someone to take our "kids" for a week-end we may go.

I met Ken Gordon and his wife today. He is now stationed at Camrose as a dentist. They said our picture is in Langbell's, a big one and a small one so guess we're a feature attraction or a feature at any rate.

The reason Joan was so fussy the other night is that she is cutting more teeth – her lower lateral incisors. She also has a mild enteritis too but is not hard to handle. Can't say I blame her for fretting with all the heat as well.

Joan sure doesn't think much of her new bath setup. I think I told you she had ripped the bath off the frame by kneeling and bouncing in it so she now gets bathed in the big tub and all that expanse of water scares her, there's nothing to hang on to and she skids around on the porcelain. A towel on the bottom just slithers around but she's getting more used to it each day.

Mother bought Joan a little sun suit yesterday and she looks like a little boy in it but a cute one.

When Joan sees anything particularly interesting she sits up, reaches out to the object and says "Ugh ugh". It's the Indian in her – I guess. And you know, dear, she's just like her dad. Ha! Ha!

Helen Magee and Philip were up seeing Margaret today. They are getting married in July sometime. Leonard Loveseth left for Brockville and was apparently quite upset at leaving Flora – tears in his eyes and such. Marg and I say "aw nuts!" because he wasn't going far enough away for that.

Just discovered today that we can collect $3 of interest on some bonds and so increase our rather flat bank account. It won't be flat when my next check comes in though which should be tomorrow, I hope. Have gone the last four days on seven cents as I've been too lazy to go to the bank and anyway there wasn't a thing we needed.

Am taking Joan to Dr. Leitch on June 6 the first time I could get an appointment – that's 3 weeks in advance to get in not bad eh? Then I'll have the same struggle again with Dr. Vant and then it'll be time to take Joan back to Dr. Orr so its quite a round of reception rooms.

Am sorry my letters are not more interesting but its rather dull right now even though we're busy all the time. I'll certainly be glad when you come home. It'll be fun starting our home again.

All my love, dearest – Peg

#14 May 29, 1944

Dearest Peg,

More good news today – Johnnie phoned that more mail had come in and he would try to get it over tomorrow.

Today was a very hot summer's day. I didn't think the country could produce two in a row. It was a pleasure to perspire. Took the afternoon off and went cycling with Charlie Burgess, his navigator and the station padre. We cycled into Thirsk and watched them. It was market day and everybody seemed to be in there selling something or just visiting. The Yorkshire accent is really something to write home about – they might just as well be talking Greek until you get a bit accustomed to it. Then we cycled in to a place – forget the name of it – and had a beer in the pub and watched the local farmers play dominoes and then came home. Cycled about 15 or 18 miles and had a very nice afternoon. The countryside is lovely with its creeks and stone bridges and lanes and hedges on all sides.

Tonight bummed around – saw about 1/3 of a show in the mess – played at pool and then one of Charlie's air gunners produced a box from home. Canned chicken, pork & beans, dill pickles – it was damned good.

This is Monday and they have steak on Monday. It was very good. Drove in, in Charlie's car (he bought it for about £50 after had his accident and was still in plaster).

So you see the afternoon got filled in. It certainly would have been nice if you were along – you would have enjoyed it. All my love & kisses, Hamp

Dear Peg,

Really hit the jackpot today – got 8 letters from you and they were all wonderful. Two were written on April 25 and 26 and sent to #1 Y Depot. In them you told me about the watch Mac and Irene were sending and said you were sorry you hadn't given me a going away present. You underestimate the value I place on your affection. You're goodbye kiss was more to take away with me than anything you could have bought me and I keep seeing you as I left you – the most beautiful girl in the world. In them you discussed Jennie and David and were being very brave. The later letters kind of put David out of the picture and I'm very glad for your sake dear – you have quite enough to do without accepting any more responsibilities for the present. I won't say that I'm relieved – but am glad for your sake that Jenny showed up – imagine that it was one visitation from her that you enjoyed.

The next two letters were April 30 and May 1. Joan's eczema seems to be doing well and you had her birth mark fixed up – it was very good news. Was hoping the little tyke wasn't too uncomfortable and am much relieved – want for her to grow up as nice as her old lady and have no blemishes even if they aren't in the public eye.

Your bond buying is a good idea but save some money to spend on yourself. It's always nice to have a couple of hundred dollars cash available – it keeps you from being dependent on anyone and give you a feeling of independence – you know you can do what you want if you want. You should get yourself a safety deposit box for your accumulating valuables.

The medical journals would be very welcome. Reading material is scarce except for newspapers and the journals are nice to browse through. The British Consuls will be really nice to get – apparently they take 4 – 6 weeks to arrive. Would be very glad to get one of the pictures of you and Joan and also would appreciate as many snapshots of you two as you can get hold of. By now your sore neck is nothing but a memory (I hope). Joan seems to be really storing away the groceries these days – she will have to be paying more board if she doesn't look out. You asked me in the letter on May 1/44 if I could recall any incident in Claresholm that might account for Jenny's absence (Heh! heh!) – to be frank I can recall about a dozen and the memory is very pleasant – but I better stop kidding or you'll get annoyed. By the way, got a letter from Johnnie Young today and expect to see him some day soon. Miss you 26 hrs a day.

All my love, Hamp

Written in pencil on envelope-RCAF Topcliffe

14 – May 30, 1944

Dearest Hamp.

It sure is a long time since I have heard from you. How goes the struggle anyway, old dear?

We are doing almost the same as usual. Got my check yesterday with my increase so am on easy street now. Went downtown today to look after my financial affairs & did quite well for one day I thought. I picked up the bond which was paid for completely and then paid $9 on each of the other 3 bonds and deposited $73 in our savings accounts plus $3 interest from our other bonds. Felt like it was a good day. Also paid my rent.

Bought myself a bathing suit – not that I'm planning to do much swimming but I intend to get a sun bath. The suit is a rose shade with white trim. Will have to get a picture for you when I get some film. Also bought a sport shirt for Bill on request from Margaret for their Anniversary on the 6th. Yes dear I'll remember to remember its their anniversary.

Last night I went to the Garneau with Alix and Betty Stark. We saw "Lady in the Dark" about a gal who couldn't make up her mind until a psychoanalyst got hold of her. Quite funny in most parts.

Alix had a letter from Fred today and he has been posted to #5 base hospital in the same country to do surgery and orthopedics' and he is very thrilled at the change from MI. A very nice opportunity for Fred, I'd say.

Jack Day has received his posting overseas but don't know when it is effective. It's too bad just when they're expecting a family in September. We were really lucky weren't we, darling?

Saw from the paper tonight where Nat Heath has been posted to the Betcher as the radiologist for Army, Air Force and Navy. There's

117

quite a write-up and her picture. She was posted from St Thomas.

The Gordon Bill's have a 9 lb. 3 oz. boy born last night. So there are more proud parents now and another boy.

Joan has been a bit troubled the last two days with a mixed diarrhea. So yesterday I stopped all food and gave her nothing but water and apple juice and today she is much better. Had to cut out her SMA as there's too much fat in it, I guess, as it says on the tin not to be used in case of diarrhea. So put Joan on pasteurized milk and water (50:50) and no sugar today. She seemed very hungry tonight so I increased the milk content and cut down on the water. It was not a bad attack but might have been if it had gone on. Don't know what caused it maybe her teeth – at any rate its one of those things that goes with the upbringing of children. I don't know whether to put her back on SMA again or not if the cow's milk agrees. We still have 12 tins of it downstairs. However I'm taking Joan to Dr. Leitch on Tuesday and will see what he has to say about it all.

Mother and I did a washing yesterday and what a wash! Dad had been away for five weeks and wasn't in one spot long enough to get a washing done so we really went to the cleaners. I don't mind washing with the machine but it's the ironing that gets me. But I don't do much.

Joan is almost better and will be so by the time you get this so worry not, my dear. I'm disgustingly healthy so don't even turn a hair with worrying over me.

All my love, my darling As ever, Peg

#16 – May 31, 1944

Dearest Peg

Well another day is chalked on the board and I'm that much nearer to you. Very busy today with sick parades and sundry ill. It's quite nice here in that you are too rushed during the day to have to worry about everything outside and haven't got time to think about how homesick you are.

Tonight had a party. Tommy Ellison came over and Chuck Burgess and I got together and talked about Claresholm for hours and how wonderful our wives were. Then I brought out a 26 of rye which I had bought and we drank that with Bert Swan and Jack Watt (a Wing Co in Aeronauts) and rehashed the situation and then went to the bar and had a few Scotch's and then to bed. A very pleasant evening. The universal topic was Claresholm and Alberta and our wives and families so we all enjoyed ourselves.

Reading over your letter of May 3 – you start by saying "I wonder what you are doing now". Well, I'm just in my pajamas and about to roll into bed, having brushed my teeth and washed my face and spent about 5 minutes looking at our picture. So now you know. I miss you and am not morbid about it, actually quite cheerful, but count the time until we are together again and will wait 50 years for you and only you – you may see my 26 of rye creeping into the letter a bit, but want to tell you occasionally how much I love you so you won't have any doubts in the matter. Bawl out about half a dozen people a day found thinking the other way and will continue to do so.

This parcel you are sending me is beginning to intrigue a bit. Am getting tired of fried spam and cauliflower so something else will be a change and a pleasant one.

You may wonder a bit about some of my letters (re interest value) but every day is much the same and I like to write to you, so will do so regardless.

XXXXX – for Joan

XXXXXXXX – to you   All my love, Hamp Excuse very poor writing please dear.

JUNE 1944

Peggy's letters to Hamp have written in pencil on envelope SHQ Topcliffe followed by varying numbers (614, 811) unless indicated otherwise.

#25-June 1, 1944

Dear Peg,

Still no mail. Things are getting a little bleak but I guess it's just a matter of being patient.

Took the rest of the roll of film today and am having them developed – hope they turn out OK. Will send them off to you as soon as I get them back.

It has been very quiet for the past 2 days and very little to report. (Last night I was on duty but it was quiet).

Tonight Bill Scott (the dentist), myself and Bill Carter – a new MO just over – went for a long bicycle ride. We must have gone between 15 and 20 miles. We went to the old estate where they quarter some of the air crew and wandered through its gardens. They have gone to ruin but they are still beautiful – there was a path about 1/3 of a mile long with rhododendron bushes bordering each side. They were in bloom with bright red, white, violet and pink blossoms and they were really lovely. The path was shaded with huge old oak trees so it made a nice cycle. After that we went scrounging eggs and fell on a place where we were about to get 2 1/2 dozen so that gives quite a supply. Eggs cost 3/2 a dozen which makes them about 75 cents so that isn't bad (I guess).

On the way back we stopped in at a pub and had a beer and it was a nice evening.

Merlin Hicks came back from his course down south last night. He saw the glider bombers in action and said they were no worse than the newspapers described them. Am certainly looking forward to mail and hearing how you are all doing.

Will write tomorrow if I hear from you. All my love and kisses. Don't let Joan forget her old man – bet she's a handful now. Hamp

14-June 1, 1944

Dearest Hamp,

This letter may be a little news sparse but I'm going to glean and see what can be turned out of my brain. So here goes!

Went up to see Margaret yesterday and she looks healthier every time I see her – like a contented cow (which she calls herself as she's nursing David). She rather hoped she wouldn't be able to but now she has to be fair as she said that if she could she would and so far so good. Little David is thriving too and is 6 oz over his birth weight all ready and has a very good appetite. It started to rain just as visiting hours were over but I stayed until the rain was over – about 5:30 PM Margaret and I got quite giggly over nothing at all and Miss Fane came down to see what was going on. It looked for a minute as though I was going to be put out but we all got very chummy. The hospital is quite strict about visitors now and only one is allowed in at a time. It rather complicates matters at times. Last night it poured again so I settled down and altered dresses, shortening some and doing a few needed repairs. Then got all set to wash my hair and decided to cut my hair. Cut off about 6 inches – it was really long, and put it up on pins. Now I only have to comb it and it's all curled and still to my shoulders. It will be swell for summer – nice and cool and all that sort of thing. Of course when I saw all my hair in the wastebasket I wondered if I'd done the right thing but it turned out better than I'd dared to hope. Margaret says she likes it very much and they have a film so maybe I can wangle a picture soon. Now that it's June perhaps I can get some film – sure hope so.

Joan is all better now and back to eating like a horse. She is still struggling with the crawling business but she manages to get around the room by rolling and pushing – pulling herself along so that I can't leave her anywhere by herself. She certainly notices and gives her Indian grunt of Ugh! Ugh! when anything catches her eye.

Irene phoned me yesterday to see when Margaret leaves the hospital – which will likely be Sunday – as she is planning on coming up for a few days. I think Joan and I will go back with her and stay about two weeks and then come home as Mother and Dad are going to a convention in Calgary. Mother and Dad went out tonight with Dr. & Mrs. McQueen so I'm spending an "at home".

Mother and I were up to see Margaret today and gave the babies in the nursery the once over. The Bell's have a whopper of a boy. He looks about 3 months old all ready. Haven't seen Betty yet as she's not allowed visitors so far.

Alix phoned me last night to say that Sandra still had her cold and it was much worse. Sunday had spent the day sleeping 1/2 hour of every hour and was very listless. She was sneezing and her eyes were puffy. So cheerful Peggy kindly told Alix to be on the look out for measles adding that she hoped it was only a cold. This morning Alix again phoned me to say I was right. Dr. Leitch had been over and Sandra is quarantined for 10 days. Fortunately for us Joan has not been over to

Days all week as I've kept her near home. So we won't be seeing much of the Days for awhile.

Jo Aiken sent me a picture of you like the one Hughie gave me. There was no letter just the snap but I thought it was darn decent of him to mail it to me. As I had two I gave one to Margaret and she was pleased to get it.

Your cigarettes are on the way as I got a card from the manufacturer today saying that they were in the post office so you may get them in a few weeks. Have already ordered a second lot for you so they should come along in July sometime.

Had a letter from Mother yesterday and Dad is much better and everyone else is fine.

I can't remember having said what a cute note I found in the suitcase you sent. I often think about it and read your other letters just to keep in close touch with you. The waiting for mail is sure hell but I at least know that when they start coming there'll be scads of letters.

I hope you are well and enjoying the English life. How do you like the beer? It's too bad I couldn't send my unused ration to you. Have you had any leave yet and what have you seen?

All my love darling, as ever Peg

P.S. Margaret's room is #8 right opposite the door to the nursery. Can you remember it?

#17-June 2, 1944

Dearest Peg,

Didn't write you yesterday since there was absolutely nothing to write about. The same today again – was on duty last night so just sat around and read and then went to bed early and wasn't disturbed so it was quite quiet. The days keep busy – the amount of paper work that goes through is really something to wonder about. Johnnie Hunt is going down to London for a five day course so I am staying here another week. Reread your letters and am answering them by degrees. Charlie Burgess and Tommy Ellison pretty nearly ruptured themselves laughing when I told them that Mrs. McKrechan was expecting – I'd hate to be the infant wouldn't you? Got myself a pipe in Montreal and have

122

smoked it a bit. Don't care what kind of tobacco I use in it but don't smoke it very much.

The daughter must certainly be getting to be a big girl – sitting in her chair and wandering around in a play pen and a mouthful of teeth – that grin of hers must really be toothy by now. Wonder when she'll start trying to say something. Find that I can scrounge flashlight batteries here – may need a bulk sometime (screw in type) but use the torch very little at present. May use it more at my next station.

You had better start putting on some weight and quit admiring that nice slim figure of yours. Certainly miss seeing you around, when I'm not busy and have time to reflect – but will never get morbid as I did in my last letter.

The weather is still cold. It's funny how you have a hot day which is really steamy and the next day is like midwinter. Can't figure out where all the heat goes.

Should get another batch of mail any day now – hope so. Wrote Bob Lawson, the Bothwells, Mother, Dad and Margaret. So if any of them answer, it will bring a bit of extra news along.

Have started PT on the station here and it certainly boomed sick parades – about 10 people every day trying to dodge it. It will frizzle shortly I expect. In the meantime I have been too busy to get out.

Well goodbye for now. *Much* love. All of Mine. Hamp

16-June 4, 1944

Dearest Hamp,

I numbered the last letter incorrectly – it should have been #15 instead of 14 so don't thing you've missed a letter.

It rained all day Friday so Joan and I stayed at home and amused ourselves. She surprised me by shouting merrily "Oh! Mum! Mum!" all day but I know she doesn't know what it means. She's quite a good rug cleaner now that she is creeping a bit better, for she crawls around picking up the fluff off the rugs and trying to put it in her mouth before I stop her and not to mention the dust she gathers up on her knees. (We do clean the rug almost daily). So you see we were quite busy but we are that way most of the time. You won't hold her now to amuse yourself because she won't allow it – she's too busy crawling all over you. Today she discovered two things. 1) that she can stick her tongue out – so Joan spent most of the day with her mouth open and tongue out 2) that she can stand on her feet and use them as support while she reaches for things – so tonight when I thought she was asleep I discovered her standing at the foot of the bed playing with the lamp. She wasn't standing up straight but she's getting the idea. Dad calls her Joan E. Brown because she tries to put all of her teething ring into her mouth – she get 1/2 of it in now so perhaps with a bit more practice she'll be able to compete with Hoe E. Brown. She's completely cured of her complaint and really loves the new formula – takes 7 ounces each feeding and not a drop left. Have strengthened the formula twice now and she has so much energy it's wearing me down. You should hear the noise she makes just talking to herself instead of going to sleep and she's awake at 7:45 every morning ready to go again. Thank goodness she's not a twin!

Friday night I went to the Capitol to see the "Desert Song" with Kay Bartleman. It was in Technicolor and very good with a modern plot – Hitler was of course the indirect cause of all the trouble. Rather a different plot than the original but very timely – I guess.

It of course rained on Saturday but I went to see Margaret anyway. She was up walking around and looking very well. She came home today and David now weighs 6 lb. 14 oz i.e. 8 oz over birth weight so that's pretty good.

Irene came up yesterday supposedly to help but Margaret figures she's giving home to visitors. I hope she is wrong and that Irene does her share.

Sandra still has the measles so haven't been going to see them. It makes the days rather dull as there's not much to do when it rains. Fred has definitely been posted to #5 base hospital and is now attached to that hospital unit which has been overseas since 1940 and has been in Africa, Sicily and now Italy. The hospital is under canvas and has 1200 beds. Fred is under some Lt Col from Halifax, a specialist in orthopedics and they are assigned to traumatic surgery and from his letters I gather he is very thrilled. As who wouldn't be?

I hope you'll be able to get a lucky break like that one of these days darling because I think you deserve it – naturally. I stayed in last night and red the "Strangled Witness" – and Saturday night too, the second in a row. Will be banging up quite a record soon.

Today it is still raining so haven't been beyond the veranda. Alison and her husband dropped in for 5 minutes – back from their honeymoon and on their way east, stopping at Winnipeg, Toronto and Montreal traveling the Great Lakes by boat and from Montreal to Gander Bay by air. Quite a trip and do I envy them even if the destination is Gander Bay. Gee I'd go to Timbuktu if you were going to be there.

Be a good boy, you lug. We still love you even more than ever. All my love, dearest Peg

P.S. Are you losing any weight yet? As if you could.

#18-Sunday June 4, 1944

Dear Peg,

Had a good day – two letters from you and a parcel. The parcel was Margaret's camera which finally caught up to me from Lachine. Have no film so if you can find any 120 film sometime I'll get some pictures. Your letters were written on May 9 and May 23. You hadn't received any mail from me and I can't understand it. Hope that it has all caught up with you by this time. Joan has just started to creep when you wrote – she'll certainly be a going concern by now. Would like to be around to help you chase after her.

That was big news about being an uncle of a 6 pound 9 oz nephew. It was good to hear that it was over and that all were fine. That was kind of a puny effort compared to your 8 lb. + but you kind of outdid yourself I guess. If our David had come along you probably would have had to have an induction at 7 mos. to get him through. Will send a belated cable of congratulations tomorrow and will also cable you just in case the mail is slow.

Glad you are feeling well now. Save all your good looks dear because I will have a lot to catch up on when we get together again. The way the daughter sounds, she'll be the boss of the family when I get home and I'll just have to keep quiet and do as she says.

Am off the evening but it is rainy and cold so I'm just sitting around as usual. Have read all the magazines in the mess now so will have to start brushing up on my snooker.

The meals here are fair but miss the meat. If you should happen to be able to get canned meat it would be good – corned beef etc

There are about 6 pictures left on the roll in the camera and as soon as the sun comes out again will try to get some pictures to send along.

My writing is a little worse than usual tonight but am shivering as I write and that doesn't help – too lazy to get up and put on my sweater.

Well goodbye for now darling. Give my love to Joan. All my love, Hamp

17-May 5, 1944 [*probably meant to be June 5 1944*]

Dearest Hamp,

At long last the silence is broken, perhaps I should say quartered for I received 4 letters today and you well know how welcome they really were. I hope darling that by now you are getting some mail too.

The letters from you were written on May 16 to 19 inclusive and your letter saying that "mail might be delayed" has not as yet arrived. Was glad you had met Doug, John & Dave and gather that you are stationed near Doug & John in the county where your father was born. I may be wrong but its fun trying to be smart.

Don't worry about my throwing out your letters because you see they're a part of you until you return and I wouldn't want to toss you in the ash can. I was very amused at one of your letters when you mentioned all the trouble it is to look after your "luggage". Luggage is a real good English word and you really must be "catching on" very quickly.

I have all ready been saving "blue forms" for you. I think I wrote something about them to you before. However your next box will have some in and I'll send more at frequent intervals. The Post Office don't like to hand out very many when you don't buy stamps as well. But I'm gradually getting quite a collection.

I can't say how really swell it is to get letters again. The postman was so cute about the whole thing. He counted out the letters (I was watching from the window as I'd been waiting for him as usual) put them in the box, knocked on the door (quite unusual) and scurried down the steps with a very pleased look on his face. Of course I've just been walking on air and had to rush to the phone after reading and tell Margaret & Alix – even though I'd been talking to them 1/2 hour before. Just think how excited we'll be when you're coming home.

Joan says "Thanks for the kisses, Daddy and I gave one to Mummy coz she wanted one too". Speaking of Joan – she's really crawling now. Today she kept making a bee line for trilight cord and putting it in her mouth. So I say "No, no Joan" – tap, tap, softly on the diapers and haul her off to the other end of the room. She promptly turns around and heads right back. She did it 5 times and ended up in her playpen.

This afternoon we both had a sun-bath as the rain has cleared – first sunny day since I got my bathing suit. We lay on a rug on the back lawn. I was going to reread your letters and look at the newspaper but Joan kept crawling off the rug to eat grass so I gave up and crawled after her.

Who said England wasn't cold dear? Oh yes, Mrs. Atkinson. Just wait until you see her again eh? Or do you hope you won't? Is there anything I can send you to keep you warmer? Let me know. Could do with something at night to keep my feet warm myself.

You seem to have spent a busy day in London. It was sure funny how you bumped into Dave. I can just see the two of you carrying on at Trafalgar Square. I'll bet even the pigeons stopped to watch or have the pigeons all gone?

At any rate it sounds as though you're going to have a pretty fair time if John and Doug are close – that is of course until you get "browned off". Here's hoping you won't get "browned off" but here's hoping you'll want to come home.

All my love, dearest. As ever, Peg

#19-Tuesday June 6, 1944

Dear Peg,

Well, today is a memorable occasion – the invasion has begun[6] – I hope that it is successful. Did nothing tonight but sit around the mess and listen to the news. I imagine that over in Canada there is a flash every 15 minutes. Well, over here the news comes on at noon and 6:00

PM etc but there are no extras – the usual English reserve – so you wait 2 to 4 hours and wonder how things are going in the mean time. Interruption of 24 hours – someone phoned and wanted heat in the control tower because the temperature was down to 55. After a couple of hours found that it was impossible so they just had to sit and shiver – well the invasion is along another day – I imagine you get as much news as we do about it. Everybody is really hoping and praying for success. It certainly means a lot to the boys here. It decides whether or not they get home this year or next year or 5 years from now. Most of them that we see have been here for 2 to 4 years so they have something to wish for.

Have been doing the usual thing for the past 3 days, sick parades, paper work all day, usual minor ailments and complaints at night. Nothing doing tonight except had a collar fracture of a kid playing softball – usual procedure – splint him and send away for an X Ray etc

Got a letter from Mother yesterday – most of the news was in your letters but it's nice to get mail anyway.

Things are in a little confusion here as far as MOs go. Two S/C's have been posted in from Canada and now I don't know whether I move or stay here. It doesn't matter except it delays me getting my mail because I am having it forwarded to the place I expected to go to.

Expect to get the cigarettes you sent before long – in the meantime, I have enough tobacco to last me. It's surprising how rapidly they go – you smoke 2 for every one you give away and they just seem to vanish.

How is the daughter doing now on her conversation – is she making any noises you can understand? How long is her hair? Am getting anxious for more mail although it is only 4 or 5 days since I heard from you. By the time you get this will probably have a stack of it from you.

Goodbye for now. All my love, Hamp

18-June 6, 1944

Dear Hamp,

Today is D day as you well know and every one over here is very excited after all these months of waiting. Every house had their radios on very loud and as you walked down the street you could hear the news without missing a word. In town Mike's had a loudspeaker playing on the street so that the people could be kept up to date. In all the churches there were services of prayer for all the boys taking part and believe me the whole country is right behind them. It's really an all-out effort this time and no fooling. For myself I can't express all I feel but I can tell you my thoughts are always there kind of pushing them on. I wish I were there to give my bit to Hitler and his gang. Maybe I should have been a fighter instead of a wife and mother but then again I've got a full job here looking after the daughter and staying as I was when you left.

Have just finished making two almost complete copies of your letters to me and sending them to Mother and Dad. I thought that was the best way for me to let them know just what you have been doing a way back in May. You will have written them by now and perhaps they have a letter too but just in case the mail is delayed I went ahead anyway. I hope you don't mind my doing that and I can assure you that I'm a very good censor – keep out the personal stuff and send all the juicy bits of gossip. I haven't used the typewriter in four years or more and find I'm still quite good at it, ahem. Please pardon any errors in spelling because it may not be all my fault. The fingers seem to get in the wrong places at times as you can no doubt see.

I took Joan down to Dr. Leitch today and he seemed quite impressed with your daughter – particularly when he found that her dad was one of the Smith boys from Camrose. Joan is fine; is 27" long and weight 17 and 1/4 pounds. She had her inoculation for whooping cough and diphtheria put into the mound of fat above the gluteal muscle. Of course she just about broke the needle by deciding to get up on her knees at the crucial moment but all went well considering that she had missed her afternoon nap. We kept her quiet by letting her chew on a tongue blade which she brought home quite proudly as a souvenir I guess. She is to be on cow's milk now in a formula for a little while longer but will soon be on straight milk which will cut out a lot of bother for me. You should see the daughter stuff down a bowl of pablum and follow that with 7 ounces of milk. Really quite a little pig – and what a howl goes up when she sees the food coming. She's really cute now as she makes noises as if she were trying to talk. When she sees something she wants she goes into all kinds of gibberish to attract your attention. And is she ever fast when it comes to moving some place she wants to go. I have to be sure she's in a very safe place now or else she gets into mischief.

The phone bill arrived today for your call from Lachine. You just about guessed it. The total was $10.25. I of course have spent the money you sent me ages ago but think I can afford to pay for it.

It has been rather lonely around here the last two days as there is a convention on in the church and Mother and Dad have been spending all their time down there from about ten in the morning until ten at night so I have been the head of the house for these days. I really like it but don't know how I ran the house in Claresholm and looked after you as well. It seems to take me all my time to do the routine work and look after Joan too. Yesterday I turned out the wash for the first time and really enjoyed it. Of course I used the machine. Then after receiving your letters I had such an abundance of energy that I cut the lawns both back and front. Very good exercise and I felt very pleased with myself chiefly because I didn't have to do it.

In two weeks Mother and Dad go to another convention in Calgary for a week so I will be on own again. There's one disadvantage to living alone and that is that you have to spend your evenings by yourself unless you can get someone to come in for awhile.

I won't be going to Camrose until July. I had thought of going back with Irene but she went back today and I couldn't arrange it. Just phoned Margaret to see how they are getting along. Margaret is a bit tired from having Irene – not that she didn't appreciate what Irene did for her but she got very weary of Irene talking all the time. Said she thought she'd go crazy before she left. Mac was supposed to come up with Gus and Grace as they were going to buy new furniture for the office but Irene went back by bus so I guess Mac couldn't get away. Dad is apparently having the office remodeled now and everything is well under way. I notice that I have just got a new spelling in the last sentence – that was not the typewriter this time but your own dumb wife.

I didn't get any mail today other than the phone bill but then I can't expect such gifts every day. Am getting your next parcel lined up as it's about time I sent another. Will be sending it by registered mail as you suggested and will make them smaller and send more of them. Right now it is hard to know what to send as I don't want to clutter you up with a bunch of junk that you can't use. But I suppose anything from home will be welcome. I hope you will enjoy the tie I sent you last time. It was sent back from Lachine in your suitcase and as it looked like a very good tie to me I sent it on again to you. You no doubt were trying to get rid of it or some such thing but it's a small world after all and you can't get away from your wife's good intentions even so far away as England. That seems to all the news and gossip etc for today. Will be writing tomorrow. Have you noticed how my will to write oftener has picked up since I got your letters. I rather felt before as if you weren't even there, – as though I were just writing letters and telling someone what I was doing – but the will to write was there to a certain degree. You probably felt the same way although you could picture me at home and I didn't know where you were. All my love, my darling – Peg

#20-June 9, 1944

Dearest Peg,

Got 4 letters today and they all were wonderful. Am sorry that you are not getting any mail but I guess it will all get there in time. Your last was written on May 19. The one with the snapshots was really swell – all the pictures were clear and made me kind of homesick to see my lovely wife and charming daughter. That close-up of Joan was typical – she had her hand in her mouth. She looks quite the young lady sitting up in her carriage beside Sandra in #2. You can tell that she's really beginning to sit up and take notice now. The other two of Joan and you are just like being home with you – certainly is nice to see you Peg – just standing there as if you were going to look up and speak to me and say "you old b–". You asked in your letter about the rotation system for MOs. Well now everything is very unsettled of course – before now – we were told that we would rotate home every 18 mos. at the maximum – by that time it will matter or else we'll be home anyway so I can't tell you anything very definite.

The next 3 letters were #8, #12, & #13. It's funny that it doesn't matter whether they don't get here in the right order or not – they are all full of news and I reread them. You apologized in one for not writing more – what you write is what I want to hear – what you and the daughter are doing. On May 15 you had mailed a parcel so it should be here shortly. Hope that you get away for a holiday somewhere – it's a lot of work traveling but the change is pleasant and when you get back you realize what a good place home really is. It's quite a change for one of the Smith products to have dark hair and am glad to hear that Bill asserted himself. You spoke of green onions – we had them for supper tonight and I made a great big sandwich out of them and am still enjoying my suffering from it.

Yesterday took half the afternoon off and went over to Doug Ritchie's station. Johnnie Young was up and we had a bull session. Johnnie is living under canvas – he is very tanned, gaining weight and looks very well. He's as full of BS as ever but you like to hear it. He is very happy in his present set up. In the evening he and I sat around and drank beer until 11:00 AM and then I came home. Doug was busy with a casualty and so we didn't see very much of him.

Merlin Hickes – the S/C on this station – MO – is going to London tomorrow to take a course on VD – it is just a week and an excuse to get away.

VD is quite a problem here. The erks (ground crew) are a major source of trouble. It certainly makes you wonder – however we have very few married personnel coming in and the ones over here that play around are the exception.

Well that's about all I have been doing on duty tonight and may be up quite late but not doing very much but waiting for aircraft etc

I am going to stay at this station now. More people posted so I'm to remain – am getting my mail readdressed and will get it a little more promptly. All my love, (+bags of kisses) – Hamp

Written in pencil on envelope '61 RCAF Base'   # 19-June 8, 1944

Dearest Hamp,

I am rather worried about the way I ended your last letter – feel that you may get the wrong idea. What was meant was that it was very hard to write every day when there wasn't very much to write about and no letters to carry on a conversation. However now that mail is coming through, it will be a lot easier. I want you to understand darling that you don't have to write every day – just as long as I get two or three letters

132

a week I'll be contented. Am going to try and write you every day and at least every second day. If I don't write every day I'm not going to feel as though I were doing wrongly because some days as we all know it is almost impossible to get one written. Take yesterday for example. I always have a busy day doing my chores of washing (Joan's), bed making, dishes, feeding and looking after Joan, taking her for a walk, and at night sterilizing and making the formula. If I don't go out which is quite often I write to you but when I go out its sometimes hard working in a letter. So there we are, or are we? Let's forget the whole thing – but I'll write often. *[often crossed out]*

Last night went out to Margaret's. She is doing fine and looks like her old self – almost. She lost 25 pounds but still weighs 118 and so is a bit on the plump side. However she'll lose that as David gets older. That's the voice of experience talking. Had 2 beers so it was a very good evening. David looks so tiny compared to Joan and doesn't weight 7 pounds yet but he's contented so that's half the battle.

Margaret phoned at noon today to say she had just received your cable of congratulations. We all thrilled to hear from you. I gather you are now getting your long awaited mail for I don't think anyone cabled you. If my assumption is correct it didn't take very long for you to get the mail and an answer back. It is really wonderful when you think of it.

I got another letter #8 written on May 20. Your first letters haven't arrived yet so its fun wondering when they will arrive. I imagine you were rather sad to leave Adderly behind when you left – he sounds like a very good type to know. Intelligent and all that.

Was out shopping today at Safeway and the Drug store – for you and Joan. Joan got some talcum, oil and pablum. You will see what you got shortly. Am going to bake some cookies tomorrow and try to get some more blue forms and then will mail your parcel – registered.

Jenny arrived this morning again for the second time since you have been away. She really knocked me for a loop with her boisterousness and volume. However she won't be here for long – I hope – and then I can settle down to normal.

Joan's inoculation has not bothered her very much or I should say not at all unless to make her more bubbling over with the good life. Honestly she is such a live wire that when she begins to walk I'll be a wreck trying to keep up with her. She tries to talk so much that I wouldn't be surprised if she came out with a sentence one of these days.

How is the cold damp weather affecting your sinuses? Can you pull anything? But then we wouldn't want you to do that or would we?

That's all for now dear – am going to bed with a Frost. All my love, Peg

Written in pencil on envelope '61 RCAF Base'   # 20-June 9, 1944

Dearest Hamp,

How are you doing after that huge rain and hail storm you had on May 29? Read about it in the papers today. You should be getting used to the climate by now I guess. Do you want some nice long plum colored woolies for winter, dear? Maybe I could scare up a suit or two or go out and kill off a couple of Americans and send you their fleece lined suits. But seriously honey let me know. How about your nice white flannelette pajamas? Guess I've carried this far enough now or you'll be getting rather annoyed.

After mailing your letter last night Helen Campbell (next door neighbor) and I went into Tuck and had a coke. It was very lively and we found it quite amusing from the sidelines. The farm boys and girls were in for a course at Varsity and they were definitely making the most of their holiday. Course 102 had just finished writing exams at ITS so the tamer ones were in Tuck but we saw a taxi go by crammed full of airmen and one of said airmen leaning out the window completely "out cold" after having been more than slightly nauseated. Not a pretty sight but we felt as though we were seeing a bit of the night life of some folks.

As you perhaps remember, Helen is 19 and married to a petty officer in the Navy now overseas on loan to the RM. They are expecting a family early next month so we feel as though we have a lot in common. We usually drift out during the day or early evening to mail letters and sip cokes – our usual form of amusement.

Yesterday I dressed Joan up in her blue playsuit and bonnet that I made in Claresholm and we went shopping. While I was in the store someone gave Joan a copy of the Family Circle – a mag on homemaking and recipes etc. You can imagine what Joan did with it. When I came out the carriage was rocking back and forth violently and legs and feet were sticking up in the air. The poor magazine was torn to shreds and Joan was covered with print but enjoying herself very much. Today I put her on the rug in the front room and inside two minutes I'd lifted her away from some flowers at one end of the piano, taken her from the plug by the trilight and picked up the blue vase and several magazines by the radio. So Joan went into her playpen. That's how fast she can move and a moderate example of the mischief she gets into. She is learning to wave her hand for goodbye but always does it beautifully when I say "Da! Da!" She's got her wires crossed somewhere but I'm convinced she's more than normal – though of course is only her mother's opinion. Excuse please Joan is awake.

[SCRIBBLINGS]

The above was not my brightest of ideas I find, as I almost ended up without the letter because Joan thought it made the loveliest sound when grasped in a fist – so Joan is in her play pen again.

Alix and Sandra are at last out of quarantine so I'm going over there tonight. It will be quite a gossip session as Alix and I have only talked on the phone a few times.

Just thought that your cable reached the Norton's on their wedding anniversary and so they were more than pleased.

Didn't get a letter today but have had five this week and feel wonderful. All my love, darling – Peg

Written in pencil on envelope '61 RCAF Base'

21-June 10, 1944

Dearest Hamp,

Well old boy how are you doing? I rather expected a letter today but as it didn't arrive I will be waiting for one on Monday.

Am out on the back lawn with Joan trying to write to you, get a sunbath and look after your daughter, but the first few minutes and even while I write am trying to keep Joan from getting the letter. She manages to crawl up and play with the corners. It looks like I'll have to quit for now. The wee one is crawling on my lap all the time. Bye for now.

She has finally found something to amuse herself – picking up grass – so have only to keep my eye on her although I feel I'm going to be invaded right now. She just crawled from one end of the blanket hell bent for this letter. Am now using her for a desk so that fools her for a few minutes.

We had a good time last night for we celebrated Alix's return to activity by drinking half a bottle of Italian rum sent by Fred. He warned Alix that it was potent stuff and half the fellows were sick on it. Guess we didn't have enough although we drank it straight. It didn't make us very merry – just warm all over. It was very sweet and tasted more like wine. (Have just avoided another invasion.) Needless to say we were rather disappointed but perhaps it's a good thing we didn't get tight on it.

Merick Drug Store had films on today so we each got one and are now set to take pictures galore and send them to you. Also ordered some more cigarettes (1000) Sweet Caps. They will arrive some time.

It is Father's Day on June 18 so for that day I send you the very best of wishes my darling and hope you'll be home to celebrate the next one with us. Joan sends her love and many kisses too.

Am going to Margaret's tonight to stay with her until Sunday night as Bill is going fishing with Mr. Heller. Mother offered to look after Joan for me and I thought it was swell of her. Dad leaves for the coast tonight so Mother will be alone again. I hope Joan won't wear her out too much for she certainly is a live wire. I can't take many late nights as she is ready to get up by 7:30 AM.

While I'm on the subject I must thank your from the bottom of my heart for letting me sleep in, in the mornings at Claresholm. I really appreciated that. It is too bad you weren't home now so I could get you your breakfast.

Joan is roaring "Da! Da!" at the top of her lungs right now and will wave to anybody who waves to her – but it doesn't matter what you say as long as you wave.

Mother bought Joan a plastic ball today. They don't bounce but they certainly roll around and she has a good time crawling after it.

Alix says Fred is very busy in Italy these days working from dawn to dusk and falling into bed at night.

Sheila Beauchamp had a queer cable from Art on June 7 which she can't understand so she thinks Art has been moved to France with a

Field Ambulance Unit. But you probably know more about that than we do.

By now you should be settled, with your unit and getting more mail. Is a unit the same as a squadron? Won't it be wonderful when we really get in contact with our mail? Another two weeks should do it I think.

It is time to feed Joan her supper and then I must away to Margaret's after I sterilize the bottles. That is all for now. Will write again tomorrow. Take good care of yourself my darling and best wishes for Father's Day. Heaps of love, Peggy XXXXXXX from Joan and me!

#21-June 11, 1944

Dear Peg,

Another two days have rolled by with very little to report. Have been quite busy with routine during the day. After I wrote my last letter I rolled into bed and about 1:30 had to get up – somebody yelled "Crash Doc" so I lit running and could see the aircraft burning off the edge of the field and figured that it didn't matter whether I hurried or not. However the crew all got out OK so by the time I had gotten the injured fixed and away, my rest was ruined.

Last night Johnnie Hunt got back from London and he had quite a "flap" as the saying goes. We sat and shot the bull and gradually got squiffed and then played pool and went to bed – very enjoyable evening because Johnnie always manages to communicate a little of his enthusiasm to you.

Tonight Doug Ritchie moved over. He is going to be posted here for awhile at least. Merlin Hicks is now away in London for a week so Doug and I are here – we will probably stay on for a time at least. We had quite a bull session again – Doug is "brassed to buggary" (as the saying goes) at present. He is being shunted aground because of the arrival of S/L's from Canada and is disgusted with things in general for a very short period. It is certainly wonderful to have a wife you think the world and more of and a super infant – when you talk to Doug you realize that he has no one to tie to and is unsettled and more or less at loose ends.

The invasion seems to be going well and I certainly am praying that it continues well. We all guess at the duration of the war over here. The optimists say 3 to 6 months and the pessimists say 2 years – nobody has a clue of course so it is nice to speculate and hope.

The last few days have practically been a class reunion – it's certainly nice to see the boys and talk over old times and show them the pictures you sent – you don't realize how much those snapshots mean.

I got a couple of snaps taken of me when we were cycling a couple of weeks ago but they didn't turn out so I will just have to wait for some more.

The sun shone for a couple of hours tonight after rain so it made the country look a little better.

Johnnie Hunt and I tentatively plotted a trip to Blackburn on a day off but find that with present uncertainty of transportation we might not be able to make it in one day and so will have to postpone it.

Have actually only been off one half day so far (the day I went cycling) but may take some time later if I feel the urge to sightsee.

Well goodbye for now darling. Loads of love to Joan. All my love, Hamp

Written in pencil on envelope '61 RCAF Base'   # 22-June 11, 1944

Dearest Hamp,

Here I am at Margaret's and if the letter reads a bit incoherently it's because your loving wife has a mild hangover from two bottles of beer. Imagine that!

I came over last night about 8 o'clock after putting Joan to bed and making her formula. Margaret was very glad to see me as Bill and Mr. Heller had left for Lobstick Lake about 11 AM and by 8:30 she was quite lonesome. But we soon got chummy and I had a bottle of beer and then another about 11:30. Margaret had one too although she knows it's not the very best thing as it makes David very burpy. After talking over every situation we could think of, as only Margaret and I can, we went to bed at midnight. Wee David woke up about two quite hungry and ready to eat – but he was an hour too early so he fussed until 3 AM and then continued to fuss after for an hour. Margaret finally told him to go to sleep as he'd had everything and – a miracle – he went to sleep and so did Margaret and I. David gets fed every 3 hours and the hours certainly roll by. Marg feels kind of stuck with the nursing and thinks it a very uncertain thing. Don't think she'll be doing it much longer as she is not still long enough – you know not the contented cow type that just sits all day.

At 9:00 AM the baby was bathed and fed and then we had oranges and shredded wheat and went back to bed until noon when hunger dragged us all from bed. David had the usual and Margaret and I bacon, eggs, toast, honey and coffee plus about five cigarettes. We sat around the kitchen table until 2:30 PM reciting incidents of being tight etc – because I felt as I'd been on a party. Then we had another sleep until 5:30 when we rallied for the evening at 6 PM I started making supper so that Marg could feed David and then eat too but she started to play with him until he started to put his fists in his mouth. Then Marg realized what time it was – she was in a fog somewhere before that. But after supper we smartened up a little and now feel very spry indeed.

Mac and Irene are planning to come up on Tuesday – if Mac can get away this time – to buy the office furniture. Dad has been busy with the Red Cross Blood Clinic in Camrose the last two days and is apparently very pleased with every thing.

Haven't heard yet whether they were pleased to get copies of your letters or not but I guess they will be even if they don't tell me so.

That seems to bring us up to date again. We are now waiting for the fishermen but the Magee's have just arrived. All my love, dear – Peg

Written in pencil on envelope 61 RCAF Base

23-June 12, 1944

Dearest Hamp,

Well the fishermen finally arrived home last night and the big catch – one greyling. We all had a big laugh over it all but guess they had a good time anyway.

Eleanor phoned this morning. She is in town for a few days from Lethbridge so we went to the Corona for lunch and then to a show –

"Lifeboat". It was quite good and dramatic of course. The scene was always in the lifeboat but even so didn't get monotonous. Eleanor is very well.

It was quite a thrill to come home to 4 letters again. Mondays must be my day. These were dated May 21 to May 25th and it seems funny to hear you write about things that are all squared by now as you must have had some mail, to cable Margaret. Am really sorry that you have had all those months of worry about Jenny needlessly but maybe you were quite sure she would come and as you now know come she did. However the whole thing was very queer because I was so sure I was right (will tell you all when I see you) and it wasn't worrying me so it couldn't have been mental – or could it? However I feel rather silly about my spouting off my mouth so early. I've really learned my lesson now.

I do hope your cigs arrived before you rant out however I don't think they could have but perhaps by now you have got them. I hope so.

By your letter I was right about your posting to Yorkshire. Was very pleased to know my picture is of use and very flattered to think that I'm the best looker on two continents. Say no more my darling, else I get vain. On the other hand it's music to my ears and I think I can control the vanity so carry on me sweet. Am glad you are learning a useful trade while away – you know painting. It will come in handy for later use – or will you have had enough? Did you mean in your letter that your posting to a unit is only a temporary arrangement? You talk about living out of a suitcase and so I wondered if you are going to be moving about quite often.

Do you ever write by ordinary mail? If you run out of blue forms you could write anyway and they would eventually catch up with me. Am having quite a time rounding up some blue forms to send, however have managed to get around 20 and hope to have more to put in. If I were in town every day it would be quite easy to collect them as they only let you have a few at a time.

Was sorry to hear about Johnnie's brother. It would be quite a shock for him.

Am glad to see you get to the "cinema" quite often "old chap". Are they quite good on the whole? Bet you'll have a few English expressions

140

when you come home and "By jove, old thing, I'll tease the living daylights out of you. That's what I'll do, sir, that's what I'll do".

Joan and I are very well and getting quite a tan. Mother is really swell about looking after Joan and really does a good job too. I certainly owe her a whole lot. It's much better than living alone and I'm doing what I please and everyone is getting along just swell.

Alix is coming over and we are going out to the "post". All my love, dearest – Peg

#22-June 13, 1944

Dear Peg,

Nothing new to report. Have been quite busy for the past two days but nothing very exciting. Last night saw a show which I had seen before – it was quite enjoyable in spite of that.

Johnnie Hunt phoned today that a registered parcel had come in for me. It is probably that watch that you spoke of. There has been no mail from you for several days but it is apparently being held up in the south somewhere and will be along in a bunch some time soon.

Had a little trouble sleeping last night – there is a big water tank outside my window, kind of a miniature swimming pool. They practice diving drill in it. Some of the boys got feeling happy and pulled one of the chaps out of bed and threw him in the tank and then got out the dinghy. When that was over they hauled the dinghy down the hall past my room and left it in the mess sitting room. Since it is about 10 feet by 6 feet (a rubber affair) it took a lot of maneuvering so the quiet was broken for some time.

We had a visit from our PMO from London today – he wanted to know if I was interested in a tour of duty in the Middle or Far East for 18 to 24 months. I told him no and so that is one list I am not on.

The invasion seems to be going quite well and I hope it continues. The original excitement here has gone and now it's settling down to the same old routine. Charlie Burgess will be going back to work some time this week I imagine – don't envy him.

Had a duck egg for breakfast this morning – Martin Hicks gave it to me and didn't taste too bad either.

141

Doug and I have got pretty well established in our routine now and are gradually getting organized to suit ourselves. We re trying to revive the germ theory and tell people to boil things occasionally but it is pretty hard to start. Well, goodbye for now. All my love, Hamp (miss you)

24-June 14, 1944

Dearest Hamp,

It's still raining after 3 days and has only let up for a few minutes now and again. Last night at the height of the rain I went out to the West end to Kay Bartleman's. She was having some of the old crowd in to see Eleanor again – and Eleanor same as usual arrived at 10:15 PM. She'd been somewhere else first so that kind of dampened the doings a bit more. Came home at 11:30 and the rain and wind were so strong that I was soaked to the skin in five minutes. By the time the street car came I felt as though I was in a stormy sea and about to capsize and I had my umbrella too. But it was quite a lot of fun and I didn't catch cold. When I got home the daughter was awake and crawling around her crib like a lion in a cage. She had been awake over an hour and wouldn't take her bottle but just wanted to play. I put up with her grunting and growling for another hour and a half but finally resorted to a well known method to let her know she was not the boss. However I didn't assert myself too much but Joan got the idea and went to sleep at 2:30 AM.

Even though the rain is falling it's still sunny to me. I got four more letters today dated May 9, 10 & 11 and May 27 so that just about makes us all caught up. Your first letter is still traveling around somewhere. I was very pleased to know you were getting your mail. You're like me getting the middle ones first. You certainly have been seeing the country so far in your short time there. I can just see the English country side again with their shady lanes and green hedges and do I wish I could be there with you! You have seen several places that I did not visit for I spent most of my time in Lancashire – which by the way is not so many miles from where you are – with visits to London & Scotland. Do go and see Scotland before you come home, darling, as it's quite different than England although if it's raining it tends to be very gloomy and quite depressing.

142

Joan at last cut another tooth today. You will be tired of my writing about Joan getting teeth sometime but at last we have another – a lower lateral incisor (right) so the mate should be along soon. Right now Joan is crawling from the front room to the back of the house with several detours of inspection en route but as I've said before you have to keep an eye on her all the time. She says "Da Da" and "Ma Ma" now and waves goodbye. When you say "Joan, where are the pretty flowers?" or "Where's Buddy, Joan?" she looks around and if she sees either one she gets very excited and almost climbs out of my arms. And talk about being a toughie. You should see her some day after she's been crawling around and has her hands, face and knees all dirty and suddenly gets hungry, she just sits down and howls. I think she tends toward temper tantrums too coz if she has to go to bed when she doesn't want to she lies on her back and bounces up and down on her feet and back of her head and yowls. But don't worry darling, one real tantrum and we'll settle up so fast that she'll be good for a few days. It's just that she's so full of life and old mick that she's a going concern. Of course what can we expect when we mix up the Smiths and the Smalleys.

Have your parcel all wrapped and ready to send but it's still raining cats and dogs. The Imperial cheese came from Margaret and the can of milk from Mother. It's one she's been saving for quite a while – ever since canned milk was rationed. The books I scrounged from Dad's supply. The cookies are not very good this time. The oatmeal crisps will probably be crumbs and the other ones I bought as they were sold for overseas parcels but I think they will dry out – anyway they aren't very good. I also must apologize about the gum. It smelled so good as I was packing and my mouth drooled so I couldn't resist taking a piece. I thought you wouldn't mind so very much so please forgive me, darling. I feel like such an old meanie robbing you of some of the luxuries of life. The shoestrings were bought from a man at the door who hopes you'll come home safely.

Mr. McDomand called around yesterday to see Joan and me. You probably remember him as you drove him from Camrose to Edmonton once. Remember?

Am going to put on my seven league boots and battle my way through the rain to the mailbox.

Hope the parcel arrives OK. Ten pounds of parcel is quite a lot of parcel let me tell you. Am going to try and send smaller ones and oftener. I imagine you would like that way better. All my love – Peg

Dear Peg,

Had a parcel today. Got the watch that Mac sent. It is an Oyster and is really a beautiful one. Not much of a note with it but it was good to hear from Mac and Dad.

Yesterday went into York for the morning. It was quite a pretty drive (by ambulance). York's kind of a quaint old city with its narrow gates through the wall which surrounds the old part of the town. I didn't stay for long because we wanted some white counting pipettes, microscope cover slides, syringes, basins, etc Also I got myself a wedge cap so that now with battle dress and wedge I am getting to look like another "erk". After doing that I dashed back and then kicked myself that I hadn't stopped and gone through York Cathedral and looked about – will do so sometime.

Johnnie Hunt came down this afternoon and we and Ritchie had some pictures taken of ourselves. Have two more to take and then will get them developed – hope they turn out OK – will send them.

Last night was off but just sat around – am doing the same tonight but am on duty. Charlie Burgess officially went back on ops today (boarded him up to flying category) – he leaves tomorrow and I hope he makes it.

We are gradually getting our sick quarters worked into shape. I don't believe I have described them in much detail to you.

This was more or less permanent station at one time so there is a central building with offices and rooms for about 8 patients. It is quite nicely fixed up but there is no heat in it to speak of, at this time of year, so you are always cold. Leading off from this is a long corridor to two Nissan huts which are the wards and these we use mainly. They each have two coal stoves in them so they can be kept fairly warm. Each ward has about 8 beds. Between the wards is a bath room with good plumbing. A "bomb proof" corridor leads from the main building in another direction to a "bomb proof" room about 8 feet high and 20 ft x

40 ft. It is for the treatment of casualties and broken up into units for treatment of gas casualties. It is very dark and rather damp so we don't use it much. Well, have run out of paper. Still miss you. All my love, Hamp

25-June 16, 1944

Dearest Hamp,

It's still raining but just intermittent showers today. You know it stops raining for five minutes or so – just long enough to catch a breath and lure people from their homes and then it starts to pour twice as hard.

Dad was held up for 12 hours at Blue River, B.C. on his way home from Vancouver because of a washout on the line but he arrived home this morning none the worse for looking at the same scenery all that time.

The river rose 17 feet in 48 hours and has flooded some of the houses on the flats but the crisis is supposed to be over and the water should be receding by midnight. I think the heavy fall of snow west of here early in June is responsible for most of the increased water. Then too a steady downpour for four days has to go somewhere.

Because of the weather, we haven't been doing much outside activity but I've got a lot of things done that have been hanging fire for a long time. Yesterday I pasted all our wedding cards and Joan's birth cards in a scrapbook plus the write-up of our wedding, Margaret's, Eleanor's and Alison's and am going to put in anything else of interest so you can catch up on the news and local gossip more fully when you return.

Joan has been wilder than a wildcat these last few days. I keep thinking that she can't possibly get any wilder than she is now but each day proves that I'm wrong. Maybe I shouldn't throw her around so much or try to bring her up tough. You certainly wouldn't recognize our once quiet child. She started in a bit at Camrose if you remember those nights we tried to put her to sleep but now she's four times as active so perhaps you can figure out what she's like. But I'm glad she's so active for apart from being a normal and quite clever child (ahem!)

she keeps me from getting fat and lazy. Right now she's on the floor on her hands and knees looking at me with a big grin and a mischief look in her eye and growling like a dog. I don't know how she can make a noise so long at a time because if I growl back at her I soon have a sore throat. We had to move all the books and magazines from the table by the radio chair because she kept pulling them down and tearing them up so now she's crawled over and is sitting on the lower shelf of the table pounding it with her hand. By now she's over by the fireplace playing with the little vents on the hearth. Pardon me while I lift her away. Back again but not for long as she's eyeing it again and is now at the buffalo robe – pardon me! Here again. I think we're going to have to have apple box furniture in our home. Would you like that dear? Pardon me again! Something tells me someone is going in a playpen real soon. Joan's now lying on the mat between the living and dining rooms so perhaps I can get the letter written without any more interruptions.

How would you like a sleeveless pullover for the winter? Would you be allowed to wear it under your tunic? If the idea appeals to you let me know soon and I'll knit one for you this summer. I've started on a winter sweater for Joan and it's almost finished so I thought if I could get the wool in an air force color I'd make you one too but not until I hear from you.

Everyone at home is wondering just what will happen now that the CCF is in Saskatchewan. It may become quite a mess. The war news sounds good what with the bombing of Japan so maybe with quite a struggle you'll be home in a year. Here's hoping. All my love, Peg

#24-June 17, 1944

Dear Peg,

Today is an anniversary. Two months today that I left and it seems like two years. No mail for nearly two weeks now and Ritchie says he's going to outlaw me from sick quarters if I don't stop complaining about it. However, it should be a nice bunch when it does arrive.

Haven't been very busy lately. Last night, Bill Scott (a dentist) and myself got on our bikes and went out scrounging eggs. We managed to

146

get 9 apiece and so we will have an egg for breakfast for the next 6 days (we each ate 3 after we got home – cooked them over at sick quarters). Merlin Hicks was posted today and is going into a Can. Gen. Hospital – a nice break. The SMO coming is a chap who has been down south for some time and is supposed to be kind of a screwball so it will be interesting. Also another MO came in tonight – used to be in Manitoba – it is possible that one of us will be posted shortly but we all stay in the same neighborhood more or less.

Johnnie Hunt phoned tonight – nothing to say but just being sociable. He and the chap who came in with him are getting along well. Johnnie was down the other afternoon – I told you – didn't describe how he looked. His battle dressed looked like he had been working on the engine of a Halifax for the past 6 months and his "Guss Edwards" hat (flat hat) appeared to have lost an argument with a truck – Johnnie really looked like an operational type from away back.

Doug is out tonight in Harrogate so I'm kind of on my own.

If I don't get mail by Monday, I'm going to cable – things are getting pretty desperate. Am getting anxious to know how you and Joan are doing these days. Must get those films developed and get them on their way. Wish I had more film so I could take some pictures of the Yorkshire countryside.

Well goodbye for tonight. Will hope to hear from you shortly. You should be thinking of a holiday shortly. All my love, Hamp

26-June 18, 1944

Dearest Hamp,

Yesterday was an anniversary – 2 months since you went away and 8 months since Joan was born, but we didn't celebrate. I bought Joan a red wooden soldier for a birthday present and she had it about half an hour when she banged the arms off it but she still enjoys playing with the casualty.

Speaking of casualties Joan took a header out of her buggy – to celebrate I guess. I put her out on the verandah in the morning as usual and she was out for 20 minutes when I heard a softened thug and then a yell. Rushed out to find Joan on the verandah by the buggy. How she

147

got out I don't know because her covers were still in place and the storm cover was on and fastened. She was also strapped in – so she couldn't fall out – but she succeeded anyway so guess I'll have to buy her a new and better harness.

It finally stopped raining yesterday but the sun didn't shine until today when it became like the good old Alberta weather that you remember and talk about.

Went to a show last night "The Gangs All Here" – Benny Goodman, Alice Faye and Carmen Miranda who sang the "Girl in the Tutti-frutti Hat". Maybe you remember that we saw the runner of it at Claresholm. It was quite good and I enjoyed it.

Walked across the High Level today with Helen to look at the river and see a parade in the grounds of the Parliament buildings. It was quite windy on the bridge as usual and my was I tired when I got home. After bucking the wind I felt rather wobbly when we reached the other side and decided that it was a good way to have a cheap drunk. Rallied around enough to walk back again, however.

We received quite a blow yesterday from our landlady. She gave us our notice to vacate by next May 1. We had been expecting something because she called at the house a few days after you had left. She seemed rather surprised to see me at home and after poking her nose into every corner she withdrew with the remark that she might want the house herself by fall. She is due to be superannuated as a teacher but has not given us any reason for wanting the house. So right now we are all wondering what to do. Houses for rent are very scarce and houses for sale are a way up. Mother & Dad don't really want to buy a house here as they hope to retire to the Coast in a few years, but Dad is still working so there's no point in buying a house at the Coast now and if we can't rent one here we may have to buy one. It's all very confusing right now but when Mother and Dad start working on it I guess it will all clear up. If they can get a house here that's any good we'll be moving as soon as we can get it. However, it's all in the air right now but I'll keep you posted as to the moves and ideas etc. It should do as news interest if nothing else. But don't worry until there's something to worry about because I think something will turn up. Maybe I'm the great optimist.

Margaret was out of the house yesterday for first time since May 21st with David too. Guess they'll be going out now regularly.

Last night Joan stood up in her crib and started to cut her teeth on the bed rail. It looks as though I'll have to put a harness on her in bed too to keep her from falling overboard!

Guess there should be mail tomorrow. Sure hope so. All my love, Peg

Dear Peg,

Got 5 letters from my darling wife today. Yorkshire looks very bright indeed for a change. It certainly is marvelous to hear from you and what you were doing. The last was written (typed) on June 6 and your typing is darn good Peg – wonder how long it took to bang off that letter – quite awhile I'd wager.

Also got a chit informing me that I have a parcel – it was probably cigarettes – will write tomorrow and let you know. The mail certainly gets all mixed up – you write every day and know that the letters won't come in sequence but it's kind of a lot of satisfaction to be able to talk to you this way.

The daughter is apparently going to be a live wire just like her mother. She must be crawling well by now. I was glad to hear that you had taken her to Dr. Leitch and had her inoculations started. It will be a big help for you not have to worry about formula or SMA – hard to realize that she is 8 months old now. Margaret seems to be doing well, can just imagine that she, being as hard headed as she is, wouldn't appreciate Irene coming up and telling how she raised her family.

Sandra should be well over her measles by the time you get this and you'll have somebody to bum around with again.

You said in one letter for me to be a good boy – that is something you never need worry about until you see me again whether it's 2 years or 5 years – you rank so high above anyone else that I'm yours and yours only.

Tonight am on duty – had a little business so far – a couple of minor fractures (metacarpals). Bill Scott and I went over to the sick quarters and played 5 games of cribbage. He beat me 4 times and skunked me one of them. I had to buy him a beer. Certainly miss you to play cribbage with – you mentioned my ego as a cribbage player for me (let me know if you consider that a slam at your ability at the game).

You said you were sending parcels by registered mail – for ordinary purposes it doesn't matter, just if there is something of particular value (not that they all aren't priceless).

Well goodbye for now honey. All my love, Hamp

27-June 20, 1944

Dearest Hamp,

Monday is always a good day for me and yesterday was Monday and I got six letters and all from my beau. It is certainly grand to hear from you and now that we are both getting letters it is far more interesting. Your first letter arrived yesterday dated May 7 along with some from the last of May and June 2nd. It is very peculiar the way they hold up the first letters and let the others through.

Your trip across sounds like quite an experience and I was very glad it was uneventful as now I don't have to worry a great deal about you. I'll send over some of the Medical Journals in the next parcel as they won't let us send a bunch of magazines over so if you don't mind I'll take the liberty of sending only the important and interesting ones and keep back the editions about conventions etc. The letter written while under the influence on a 26 was a gem because you let yourself go and wax eloquent for a while and say such lovely things about me that I glowed for a week after reading it. Our letters are usually so very sedate, darling, that I get a bang out of the ones where you throw convention to the wind and get down to some honest to goodness "mugging". Guess I'll have to go on a party and give you a thrilling letter too, coz I hate to write how much I love you and how much you mean to me because then I get to missing you so very much that I get just a trifle depressed and ache with wanting you back . If I don't write about it and everything goes OK but please read between the lines and you'll know how much your missed.

Went downtown yesterday and at last mailed your parcel. I feel ashamed as its been a week since I got the parcel ready but it was not good weather for moving about. Helen Campbell took me in their car.

150

She was visiting Dr. Vant so I usually go down with her and do my shopping. I cashed in my June permit on a case of beer and a 13 of Scotch – yes dear, Scotch.

Mother leaves tomorrow so I'm planning to pay Alix and the girls back a few drinks. Dad is already in Calgary so Joan, Bud and I are going to hold down the fort. In case you're worried – my liquor is residing next door pro temp. Really felt quite guilty going into the vendors – north side – as I felt I might meet someone I wouldn't want to and it would have been very embarrassing all around. But nothing happened except very curious glances from employees of said outfit but as I'm of age, married and a mother I felt I could cope with them all. Maybe it was a false sense of security but at any rate I'm at home safe and won't be going down there again for quite a while.

About the house situation – we will be living in Edmonton whatever happens until Dad quits his job or get fired which will not be for quite a while yet. Miss Munro, our landlady, may be out too because of all the new rental regulations as it is the people who buy the house who give the notice of vacation and then you have a year to get out. Well apparently Miss Munro hasn't sold the house yet and so she can't put us out, what ho! So it looks like a very interesting fight from the sidelines. However, time will tell and in the meantime why worry. Who knows but what you might be home before we get thrown to the wolves, I hope, – but what a hope. However, darling, this being apart is not so terribly bad – could be a lot worse in fact and it won't be forever.

Got myself a permanent today. The old gal is picking up since coming to the city – but it really all springs from the fact that I cut my hair – like I told you and it didn't turn out quite as expected after a few days – so got me a permanent. Mr. Davidson said I'd sure murdered my hair (Ha! Ha!). It's a good thing I'm getting all these ideas out of my head while you're away so you can't see what a very stupid person your wife is. I'm gradually getting sensible however but it's a long and slow road.

Joan is as usual – cute as a bug's ear. She is beginning to get the idea of standing on her feet and it won't be long before she's walking by hanging onto the furniture. She gets up on her knees and reaches for things now. Her eighth tooth is just about through so the wee character is growing up. That's all for now darling and will be writing again tomorrow. Marg got your letter too. All my love dearest, Peg

Dearest Peg,

Well, here I am eating cookies and writing my wife – yes, I got the parcel and it was really swell. Am going to hoard it for awhile and then will pool it with some of the boys and have a banquet. Everything got here in fine style – some of the cookies were a bit bent but they still taste delicious to say the least. That tie was one of the new ones I bought in Camrose and it is now my best tie. That hot chocolate will be good some cold evening because the tap water here is warm enough to dissolve it. Have stopped on the cookies now and about every 4th word take time out and crack a peanut. Thanks very much dear for it all – it's a lot of work putting these things together.

Also got 3 more letters from you and they were all more than welcome. This is the most cheerful I have been since I got here. I counted up my letters last night – I have all the first 18 you sent and today got 19, 20 & 21.

Glad to hear that the money is coming OK. Don't tie it all up in bonds. We will need at least $1,000 cash when this is over and I expect to bring about $500 of it back with me (those are minimum figures) – however think it is a damn fine idea to have the bonds and am glad you are getting them. Don't cut off too much of your hair honey – I like it the way it was but of course I'm in no position to criticize am I? Anything you do is OK. You asked me in one letter (#15) how I liked the beer – am beginning to think it is OK. Doug says that it's the only thing in England I seem to really approve of. We generally go in at lunch time and have a half pint before lunch.

I don't imagine we will have leave for some time since it is still cancelled indefinitely for ground personnel, when I get some I will spend a day or two looking up your relatives. Have been planning to write them but never seem to get around to it. If Joan can stand on her feet now (#16) (June 4) it won't be long before she is running all over the place. Glad to hear that Freddy Day is getting a break – in about 8 or 10 months I will have a chance of getting into a decent hospital but not before. The MOs are just beginning to rotate in hospitals now and it goes in order of seniority overseas.

By the way I am not losing any weight now – am about 188 but the food here is very good at present so will probably gain. Have just about recovered from a bad head cold and am feeling a little more cheerful about the English climate again.

I have managed to scrounge a few blue forms and now have a slight surplus but will be glad to get a few extras. You asked me if I wanted anything warm. I would like some kind of sweater which can be buttoned up the front. Will let you know about underwear but actually I don't need it and can get some over here if I do (I think). You asked in letter #17 if "here's hoping you'll want to come home". Don't give that a second thought – I guess the tone of my letters is indication enough – try not to be too morbid in them but don't always succeed.

It certainly makes a difference when you get mail. It's so easy to write – I like to hear what you do so don't ever worry about not having anything to write about. All my love, Hamp

28-June 22, 1944

Dearest Hamp,

Mother left yesterday noon for Calgary and as Dad had already gone, Joan and I are on our own. We are pretty busy at times though as I get stupid notions and get myself rushed off my feet. Like this morning, I did the family wash instead of Monday and it wasn't really my day at all. In the first place the hose that runs water into the machine kept falling from the top so that boiling water spurted all over the basement. I finally got control of the situation and had a machine full of water and tore upstairs to turn down the gas under the tank as I had visions of the back of the house exploding across the river. When I got back to the basement again the whole place was flooded with hot soapy water. Oh me! I'd left the hose in the machine and it had siphoned out the water. Such a stupid wife you have my darling. Where on the God's green earth did you pick her up? Finally got the wash on the line at 12 noon and felt as though I'd accomplished quite a job – 4 sheets and pillowcases, Joan's bedding & diapers, personal clothes, etc & etc But it's fun and I love managing a house. You feel as though you'd really accomplished something when it's all spic and span.

Had Kay Bartleman over for supper last night and she slept here.

Needless to say we didn't go to bed very early. Jessie Horne came in about 8 PM and Alix and Betty Stark came over after a show. Jessie and I had 2 bottles of beer and Kay 2 or 3 drinks of Scotch as she doesn't like beer so we were quite merry when Alix and Betty arrived. So we then tried to get them merry too but they never succeeded in catching up to us as we kept on with them when they arrived. It was quite a night.

Went to the store yesterday and bought some bologna – about $.10 worth which is almost a pound. At night was defrosting the refrigerator and discovered that Mother had bought some also so I'm eating bologna 3 times a day almost.

Tonight Jessie and the two nurses next door – Clark and Eckmeyer – are dropping in so it will probably be another good do – on their rations this time.

Bought a canvas harness to keep Joan in bed as she get up on her knees and chews the rail so it won't be long before she's up on her feet and out on her head. Also bought a leather one for the buggy so the poor wee tyke is really tied down to a certain extent. The canvass harness looks like this: [diagram] Part "A" fits on top of mattress and ties to the springs. Part "B" is fastened to "A" with two tapes about 6" long which enable Joan to roll around and sit up – but she can't pull her lion in the cage act. "B" fastens under the armpits and "C" are straps which go over the shoulders and fasten at the front to "B" – something like a parachute harness. She didn't like the apparatus at first as you can well imagine but she's getting used to it now. It will be real handy when we go to Camrose coz the single bed would not have suited our "Bronco". I had visions of piling up pillows on the floor at the side of the bed for softer landings.

Got a letter today dated June 7 and you had received the camera. I have three 120 films that I managed to scrounge for future use as they are hard to get. However will let you have one – our camera uses 120 also – and will write Eleanor to ask Bill to send me some from Lethbridge when each shipment comes in. Apparently Bill is sending 2 films each month to Gordon Blott so maybe can work something. It's an angle anyway.

Joan and I are going to Camrose about the 7th of July – after Joan's second inoculation. Mother is supposed to be coming up today with Eileen and Bill Duggan as she hasn't seen David yet so we may get to see her too.

154

Am trying to cut out Joan's 6 AM feeding and feed her at 8 – 3 meals a day stuff. She eats at 8 OK but wants to eat at 10 and 2 as well. We'll get organized soon though and everything will be plain sailing – I hope. She's on cow's milk still and really thriving. We will have 12 cans of SMA for our next Junior by the looks of things. All my love, darling, Peg

#28-June 22, 1944

Dear Peg,

Am not sure if this letter if #27 or #28 but am calling it #28. You spent a page of #19 telling me that it was sometimes hard to write every day. Don't worry about skipping a day or even two (generous of me, eh honey?). I know you are busy with the daughter and there is no reason to worry about a day or two – don't let it bother your conscience I mean. Every letter I get I read it about 3 times so it makes up for it. Also the mail is irregular so that if you miss a day or two it doesn't actually matter – well, enough of that, I am getting a little involved. Glad to hear that my cable got there OK – after I sent it I kicked myself for not saying that I was getting mail OK but at that time didn't have enough money to send one to you – as a matter of fact I was broke for 4 or 5 days until the bank sent my cheque book. Jenny's arrival is getting to be a regular occurrence – if she keeps coming so violently you might start to think that David would be just as welcome. The daughter saying Dada is pretty wonderful – don't teach her to say buggerlugs until I get home to counteract it. That note from Joan was welcome – she said she thinks her old lady is wonderful – that makes two in your family who dote on you.

Sorry I can't get a bottle of rum to send to you but maybe it's just as well. Thanks for the Father's day wish – am still kicking myself for slipping up on Mother's day.

Had rather a quiet day today. Nothing went particularly well so I bawled hell out of everybody on general principles – does you good occasionally. Jean MacIntyre (our recently married nursing sister) is no hell at times so I cloud up and rain on her occasionally.

Last night the WD concert party from Canada was on the station (didn't have room for this last night to tell you). The whole caste consists of 11 girls – the show lasted about 1:15 hours and was quite good – the RAF blokes didn't particularly appreciate it because they didn't get the Canadian connotation of some of it.

Ritchie and Merlin Hicks are off golfing this afternoon and I held the fort. Nothing much to do. Had to give a lecture on VD and show a film. Hate doing it but it sure is necessary here – am getting tired of urethral smears m sulfathiazole levels, white blood counts etc-some of these birds never get a clue and think that the girls they meet are just wonderful – very disgusted about it at present.

Well, will say goodbye for now honey and will write. The films are apparently OK but they are just being printed. Will send them. All my love, Hamp

#29 June 23, 1944

Dear Peg,

Another good day. Got two letters from you. In one you had (June 11) been over at Margaret's for the week end and had gotten beered up. You seem to have had a nice time in kind of a quiet way. June 12 you got 4 letters from me – hope the mail starts coming a little better – you haven't gotten the ones in which I did my only sightseeing – the Gloucester Cathedral etc – I suppose they will arrive.

Tonight Doug Ritchie and Bill Scott and Blair Purvis (one of the engineering officers) and I went over to the show – we stayed for the news reel (of the invasion) and a couple of shorts which included Donald Duck and then left when the main feature came on (a western). Dave and Blair and I then bought ourselves a pint of beer and came down to my room and had Camembert cheese and crackers with it – it was really good – we finished the cheese before we quit. Then we opened a can of pears and had that and then had another one and then we ate cookies and finished up with a big hunk of fruit cake followed by peanuts. Really quite a feed. I'll be gaining weight again. Really did appreciate the parcel honey – it was all swell and thanks again. The weather has been fairly warm lately so I am saving the chocolate to have hot one of these cold damp evenings.

156

The days are quite quiet now and Doug and I shoot an awful lot of bull back and forth. Had an inoculation parade yesterday and did about 125, so you see that things are just about the same.

I didn't tell you I had a ride in a Halifax about 3 weeks ago. They certainly are a huge aircraft and have a lot of room to move about in. I didn't tell you about it because I thought you would worry about me flying. I won't be doing any more flying around so you don't have to worry about it. England from the air looks very pretty but I wouldn't want to be a pilot here particularly – the weather is certainly rotten for flying compared to what we have on the prairie. Gusts of rain, fog etc

Merlin Hicks leaves tomorrow but his replacement hasn't arrived so we are still curious as to how we will get along with him once he comes.

I am on duty tomorrow and the usual routine in sight. We have really been giving the blast to the "erks" on VD for the past 3 days – films, lectures etc and I'm getting a little fed up with the routine – not browned off though dear. I must be careful that I don't get too many English expressions (eh dear). Well so to bed and read for a few minutes. Those magazines (Post and Readers Digest) were a stroke of genius.

All my love. Give Joan a hug and kiss for me. Hamp

June 25th 1944

Dear Peg

Well the snaps are finally on their way. They aren't particularly good but they will give you some idea what your husband looks like – you may notice that he hasn't lost any weight.

#i Johnnie and myself and F/S Maddox who is the NCO in charge of our hospital and a very good chap – his home is in Toronto, he is married and he has been overseas over 3 years

#ii & #iii Johnnie and Doug and myself (telling you just in case you don't recognise us

#iv myself actually smiling the reason being that the sun is actually shining for a change. You may notice that the battle dress looks a little baggy – actually it is comparatively well pressed in that picture so you can see how I need you to look after me. The old ambulance in the background is quite a machine.

Didn't write you last night – will write a blue form now and mail this and it together and see how soon they each arrive.

Won't say much more or I won't have anything to put in the blue form. Will try to get some more snaps from time to time – if you can scrounge any 120 film (extra to your own for pictures of you and Joan) it would be nice to have. If you go to Camrose see Bert Groves and he will fix you up with some (in the Camrose Drug Store). Well, goodbye for now, all my love, Hamp

PS There is a picture of Doug and Johnnie and myself which is very similar to another. Could you send the one you don't like to Camrose.

#30-June 25, 1944

Dear Peg,

Well tonight I got the snaps mailed. They aren't too good but you can tell who they are at least. The day's rather dull when they were taken so they are a little dark.

Have had a very peaceful weekend. Yesterday afternoon fell asleep in the sun, behind the hospital and got quite a burn. Johnnie Hunt came down from Wimbledon and he and Doug and I went to Harrogate. We had dinner and then had some beer and then we went over to a dance – I didn't dance honey because you are the only one who I seem to get along with – sat and watched with Bill Scott and Al Gardiner (another Dentist) and then we went home to the hotel and went to bed. Doug and Johnnie followed in a few minutes – came home early because they found nothing better to do. Johnnie and I got up at 7:00 AM and caught the train back and I went to work as usual. Doug stayed and played golf today.

I've had a room with a double bed (which Johnnie and I slept in) and a single in which Doug slept. Neither one of them got any rest because I snored so loudly (still have quite a cold – ahem?) I guess I never realized how long-suffering you were. You never told me I snored but they certainly rubbed it in.

It is kind of nice to get away from the camp occasionally – you get kind of fed up with the place. I am going to try to get up to Scarborough sometime – it is supposed to be a rather pretty seaside resort town. Probably won't make it for some time. Certainly wish you were here so we could see these places together – I haven't much desire to travel around and sightsee by myself.

Well dear, will say goodbye for now. Give the daughter my love and kisses and try to show her who her old man is when the pictures come. All my love, Hamp

29 June 25, 1945

Dearest Hamp,

Just in case you think I'm neglecting you I'll hasten to explain that I wrote you on Saturday, dear, by ordinary mail so that I could send you some more snaps of Joan. Since I've been alone time is going so quickly that I lose track of the days and get rather bawled up in my writing schedule, however, I think its been every second day that I've written this last week so don't know why I feel slightly guilty about my mail to you. Guess it's because I almost forgot to write today and intended to write yesterday but didn't get around to it.

Saturday afternoon Joan and I went over to Day's and had a wonderful time. Stayed for supper too. Joan and Sandra played around on the floor together. It's hard to realize that the daughter is getting big enough for such things. Just after I got Joan to bed Margaret phoned to say Mother was up with Bill and Eileen Duggan and Mother had to see us right away. So the Duggans – in your Dad's car – came over for us and we stepped out. Joan of course wakened up promptly and stayed awake until after 10 PM, Ma finally putting her to sleep by pushing her back and forth in David's buggy. We ate and came home at 1 AM I could see things were not going very well between Marg and Ma and Ma wanted to come home with me as she thought it terrible for Bill, Marg and the baby to be sleeping in one room and of course expressed herself quite clearly. I didn't bite at the bait and everything calmed down for awhile. We – the Duggans too – were invited back for Sunday dinner and at 3 PM the Duggans picked us up again and away we went. As soon as we got in the door Ma said Margaret was tired, the baby was sick and she was coming to have supper with me – even had her bag packed. What to

159

do was a $64 question. So I talked to Marg and she said she didn't give a God damn what Ma did as she was tired of all the talk about the baby being hungry and sick and how puny he looked and how exhausted Marg was etc & etc – so after an hour of misery for everyone Ma came home with me and the Duggans went to Aunt Maggie's and finally came for Ma at 8 PM to go back to Camrose. So it was quite a day. Margaret phoned this AM and David fell asleep as soon as we left and had slept all night and most of the morning. Bill and Marg got quite giggly in the evening and have chalked up another experience and know where not to go for a summer holiday even if Ma thinks Marg should go home and go to bed for a couple of weeks. A great life – don't you agree?

Ma and Pa are expecting Joan and I down there very soon now as they have the room all fixed over – new rug and new drapes – so it looks like they expect us for a year or so. However I can't say I want to stay quite that long as I don't think I could take it for very long at one stretch. Things are beginning to look bright again today so it's going to be O.K. again.

Was just in rubbing the wee one's gums as her 8th tooth is giving her some trouble. She lay there and let me rub it for quite awhile and then gave me a coy look and a big grin. She's settled down again. Today she pulled herself up on her feet in her crib so it's a good thing she's broken into her harness for night time. She loves to have you stand her up on her feet and hold her arms so that she can practice walking. Where she learned that I can't imagine but she's certainly got the idea and thinks it's great sport. Looks as though she'll be walking before long. A very clever child eh darling?

Tonight Joan and I were out for early supper at my cousin Netta's. She is the deaf one. Aunty Lena was along too. Netta has four girls between the ages of 16 and 3. Isn't that awful? Hope we have better luck than that with our brood, how ever many there may be.

Mother and Dad are coming back from Calgary tomorrow night and I must say I'll be glad to see them. Not that I'm tired of being alone but I find it rather hard looking after the house and rearing Joan. Guess I'm just not made of the strong, tough, work-in-the-field stuff. Haven't done much work around the house. Guess I can't take these bar parties. Kay and Jessie came over twice and we drank beer – also the nurses next door – & scotch. That could be the answer.

Haven't heard from you since Wednesday but am not worried as the mails do some funny things. Received a card today saying your 1000 cigs are on the way. In future we can only order 300 as they are going air mail but we can order any number of 300's. So you may get 3 or 4 separate parcels of 300 cigs at a time. Won't that be quite a day? Will write tomorrow. All my love, darling Peg

#30-June 27, 1944

Dear Peg,

Didn't write last night because there was nothing to say. Haven't done much for the past 2 days but sit around. Last night I went to a show – Deanna Durbin in "The Butler's Sister". I though it was pretty poor but provided a means of passing the evening. The show was in the mess so it is a consolation when you can sit and have a pint of beer and smoke and watch the film if you want to. After the show I went over to sick quarters and looked around and then got beaten in a couple of games of cribbage. I generally play two games each night I am on with Cpl McKinnon, one of our NCOs in our orderly room. He is a chap about 40 – used to farm in Saskatchewan – very nice chap. After that picked up Doug and Blair Purvis (Eng. officer) and adjourned to my room and ate some fruit cake and had a little cheese and crackers (finished them) and fought the war for about an hour. Every night Doug and I get here and argue about how long the war is going to last and how and when and where it will finish. Doug is one of those optimists who believe it will be over in Europe in a few months – hope he is right.

I should be about due for some more mail from you soon. It is nice when it comes in bunches but I haven't enough control to kind of ration it.

It has rained hard for the past 2 days. I rather enjoy the rain because it was quite warm – much warmer than the usual cloudy day with the wind blowing.

Have had quite a sock darning bee the past few nights and am gradually getting them up to date – the darns are a bit lumpy and don't compare with your product but they are improving.

It was PT today so we had a very large sick parade again (just like

161

GO's parade at home) – the hour of sick parade coincides with that of PT so some of them figure that they might as well spend a little time chatting to the MO.

Have a hard time getting my sleep still – it is bright daylight until 11:30 PM or later and you still don't feel that it is time to go to bed until it gets dark.

Well honey, haven't much to write about so had better sign off for now. The daughter should be practically walking by the time you get this – give her my love and loads of love and kisses to yourself.

All my love, Hamp

30-June 28, 1944

Dearest Hamp,

The days are certainly slipping away and it's almost July. Where the days ago to is a mystery but they sure go and fast.

Mother and Dad came home last night. They had a good time at the Convention – as good a time as one can have at these affairs. I got a pair of silk stockings and Joan a pair of blue overalls to help her to crawl so we did OK don't you think. Mother brought you some chocolate bars and some gum so you did OK too.

The house business if finally over and Dad just finished the negotiation today to buy our house. So now it's ours and we don't have to move. The terms were $4,000 cash and so we snapped it up because most houses in Garneau are selling for $6,000 up no matter what the house. Dad of course has had to turn his bonds over to get the place and he has borrowed $250 worth of your bonds. They will be returned to me with interest but I don't care about that as it's a safe investment anyway and helps out the family.

Had a letter from Aunt Annie – Mother's sister – in Fleetwood Lancashire and she says they'd be very proud if you could manage to visit them some time and it is not very far from where you are. I think you could go in a few hours if the train service is as it used to be. They own a butcher shop so maybe you could wangle a steak. Aunty Lena had a letter from Eddie and he has left England to the northern part of Ireland.

162

Haven't had any mail for 10 days but guess it will arrive again soon.

Joan is still a going concern. When she crawls it's almost a run and she's trying to stand on her feet now. She eats like a horse and seems to be hungry all the time. At breakfast she gets the juice of an orange – but doesn't like it very well – her porridge bowl of pablum and 7 oz of milk, for dinner – vegetables and fruit, toast and 7 oz of milk' at supper a whole egg, fruit, toast and 7 oz of milk and at 11 PM 7 oz of milk. During the day she has several pieces of toast and arrowroot biscuits. She has finally got rid of her 6 AM feeding so we have a better sleep. Tonight after Joan's bath and when I was drying her hair it went into little curls so maybe we have a blue eyed curly blond. Sure hope so at any rate.

Kay Bartleman has asked me to go with her on her holidays for two weeks in September. She is going to Banff. I think it's a good idea and although there's not much at Banff in September still I think we can have a lot of fun.

Got some more canned milk from Aunty Lena on Monday so am almost ready to send another parcel to you.

Am going out to see Alix as I haven't been out at night for some time – that is without Joan.

I hope you are very well and still enjoying life and still love me – which I know you do etc & etc and me loves 'OO! Ugh! All my love, Peg

#32 ?-June 28, 1944

Dear Peg

Well, had another good day today. Got 4 letters from you – June 15, 17, 19 & 21. When I realize that you are only 8 days away it doesn't seem so bad – but bad enough.

Have been doing little of late. Last night I kind of got led astray – went into the bar to have a beer with the boys and didn't leave for about 3 hours and a dozen beers. Certainly felt awful this morning and have resolved to drink English beer in moderation in the future.

The bar here is a separate little room – old oak beams, paneling, pheasants and foxes for decoration – actually it is quite quaint – no seats in it however.

163

Today I took off and went up and spent the morning with Johnnie Hunt. He is in a lovely part of the country. The countryside is beautiful now with green fields and fields of poppies in bloom. I guess they are a weed here but they create quite a splash of color to see a whole field red with them. All the houses have beautiful gardens and the roses were all in bloom and some bushes of them were really lovely. We stopped at several places and went and looked at them and managed to scrounge some ("we" meaning a chap named Stafford who is one of the accountant officers here – he was up on business and I went along for the ride). We stopped and got some eggs at a farm and also someone sold us some turkey eggs. It's going to be quite interesting to see what they are like – if I get enough nerve up to have one cooked. Then on the way back we stopped at Harome, Yorks. That is the place my grandfather was born (quite a coincidence). We were passing through it so we stopped at a little old inn had a pint of beer. The inn had been there for over 600 years – low beamed ceiling, thatched roof, and worn flag stones – quite a picturesque little spot. The landlady referred us to a chap named William Smith who is a descendent of Christopher Smith who I imagine was my great grandfather. We saw the old farm which is just on the edge of the village. It is not owned by a Smith now however. This chap, William Smith, wasn't at home and his wife was as deaf as a post so I gave up in disgust. I knocked on the door and when she came I asked 4 times if this was where Wm Smith lived – she finally said she didn't have any eggs for sale so I started all over again and then she thought I was trying to rent a room and proceeded to show me the house. I got her stopped and finally wrote it out who I wanted to enquire about and she couldn't figure it out, so I gave up. Old Stafford was nearly splitting by this time. I intend to go back again sometime. Well, will write tomorrow. All my love, Hamp

31-June 30, 1944

Dearest Hamp,

There isn't very much to write about as I've stayed close to home for the last few days except for a night out to see Alix.

Alix hasn't much news either except that Fred writes from Rome and Tiber River 600 yards from Vatican City and is very busy. We were feeling a little disgusted with life – partly due to the heat which made us tired and partly due to our children who had been quite a strain on us with the activities so we sat and discussed the situation and then had several drinks of Scotch. We are not getting to be drunkards and neither are we complaining but we sure like a "bitching" session once in a while so don't get us wrong.

Have just returned from locating Joan. She's in the bathroom on the floor with her wee pot in one hand and the handle of the diaper pail in the other trying to lift the pail from the floor and believe you me she is almost succeeding and with one hand too.

Must tell you about this morning as I think you would enjoy this choice bit. Had Joan in bed with me as it was only 7:30 and I thought too early to get up. She of course was wide awake. I had on my yellow pajamas – which you might remember – and the top was unfastened. Joan was sitting on the far side of the bed and spied a pink rose bud (?) on my fair chest so she made a bee-line and tried to get it off. I can tell you we were out of bed very quickly as I had been dozing prior to the little episode. Oh me! There is no privacy at all not even with you away.

If the letter seems a bit incoherent dear it's because I'm now playing peek a boo with Joan around a door. She spends most of her time while in the play pen standing up and hanging on the top rail sort of chinning herself but she's afraid to let go when her knees cave in and so she hangs by the hands and hollers until I rush out and take her down. Once she's down she wants to get up again and so we spend a very busy day as you can well imagine. I now have Joan in her pen and she's trying her little trick but has her feet crossed and can't figure out what is wrong. But we are sure busy trying to get up. We are on 3 meals a day with a bottle during the night when and if we waken for it and we eat just before the family so we're really growing up and quickly too.

It's hard to realize that tomorrow is the 1st of July. The days are speeding away although I feel as though time has stood still since you went away. It's very bad thing I know but I can't quite get the same enthusiasm for things as when you are here. However I try my hardest to get interested in things and so far am not doing too badly.

Haven't had any mail for two weeks and the last letter was June 4th so guess the invasion held up the mail or else you have been moved

165

elsewhere. However I don't worry about you dear as you are my "superman" Yippee. Alix just phoned and asked me to go to a show tonight in an hour's time so must away as Joan has to be bathed, bottles done, my get spruced up and eat my supper so –

Bye for now, all my love, darling – Peg

#33-June 30, 1944

Dear Peg,

Nothing much to report today. Tonight Doug and Bill Scott and myself went out scrounging eggs on our bikes. We got about 10 miles away and it started to rain and it really poured. We were soaked right down to our underwear when we got back. Had a hot bath and then went over to sick quarters and cooked ourselves a couple of eggs – we each ate a turkey egg – they taste like chicken eggs but are better because they are bigger. By the way, that pair of fleece lined slippers I bought in Montreal for $5.00 – Bill Scott saw a pair in Harrogate priced at 8 pounds 10 shillings – so I guess I got quite a bargain.

We just about finished the box you sent last night – had the tin of Prem and some tea and ate about 10 cookies each. All very delicious. Wonderful wife I have you know and I certainly miss her. The cigarettes arrived today – 600 British Consuls. I can not stop smoking my fine cut.

I was a little worried about that letter in which you said you would have to move. Of course you can always go to Camrose Peg. But in a way I would like to see you more or less independent until I get home. Your Mother and Dad have been so swell to you and to me that I hate the thought of you leaving them now. There are so many people in Camrose I don't approve of – I would sooner we more or less started out in the place together. However I guess it will be a few months before you have to move and we will wait awhile and see how things work out before I start putting in my oar and worrying you. Hope that you don't have to move though.

Got a letter from Margaret and one from Mother. Margaret's letter wasn't particularly cheerful – I would gather that motherhood is quite an ordeal – you never said very much honey and I certainly admire you for it – and for a thousand other things.

166

Well will write tomorrow. This is kind of a scribble because I am trying to get it in the mail.

All my love, Hamp.

JULY 1944

Dearest Hamp,

A very happy July to you my darling, and may the next one be spent together. So far it has been a very busy month. Yesterday morning Helen Campbell phoned me and wanted me right over. So I went and she had started into labour. Her mother – Mrs. Hedley – was rather excited and wanted Helen to go the hospital right away but as her pains were 10 minutes apart we talked her out of it and Helen and I had tea, toast and cigarettes and more or less just sat and waited. Of course Helen did a bit more than just sit. However four hours later when the pains were 3 minutes apart I drove Helen to the hospital in Hedley's car and had her admitted, etc and then came home. It was a miserable day for the 1st of July and poured down most of the time. I spent the day knitting, reading and sticking pictures in our album. Am almost finished all the ones you've collected through the years.

At night I went over to see Margaret and Bill. They have gotten over the wee bout with Mother and just make a joke of it now. David is gaining and sleeping like a top and Margaret is still nursing him. Some sister you've got there kid!

On the way to Margaret's I met Sigert Balfour and he was going overseas almost immediately. Also Jack Day, Jack Thompson, Pete Hudson, Frank Dorsay, Stan Warshawski and a couple of others. So maybe you'll run into them sometime.

We hear that Ted Bell and Beauchamp are in the invasion. The war news is certainly very encouraging but we have a long way to go yet.

Mother had two letters from you on Saturday but as it was the 1st of July, we of course had no delivery. I should get some tomorrow however as it's been two weeks since your last letter. I really should get a haul tomorrow. I hope! I hope! Was very good though to know everything was OK with you.

Bill, Margaret and I drank to your health and safe return last night with a beer. I almost felt as though you were in the room and how I wished it! If wishing could will things you'd be home now. But no matter.

Helen finally came through at 1 AM with a 7 lb 13 oz boy so everyone is very thrilled and excited. Poor Helen was in labour 17 hours (17) and I was sure when I took her in that she'd be a mother in a few hours. But one never knows and apparently she went into a slump after she got to the hospital.

The baby is cute with a round face, pug nose, dark hair and is fat and funny like Joan was. I'm going to bath him for two or 3 times after Helen comes home and then am going to Camrose about the middle of July. Had to postpone the visit as I'd promised Helen.

While I was at the hospital I ran into Robby the RCMP who used to be a patient at A & B. We ran into them on Jasper Ave before you left – remember? Anyway he is a proud pappy of a wee girl.

Joan is still a-doing. She's discovered how to sit down after she's been standing for a while so I don't have to dash around quite as much. She's trying to pull herself up on the furniture and succeeds most of the time so it won't be long before she's shunting back and forth around the room. I was up until 2 AM this morning with her as she's getting a molar I think. At least she always sucks her index finger and rubs her gums and also makes quite a to do about her thumb. Something she's never quite forgotten but if I watch her I can keep her from it very well. She was restless yesterday and last night and wouldn't go to sleep so I had to end up by rocking her and humming a tune. Our daughter has rhythm too as she jives to music. Think I'll go to the bed now and get some shut eye. All my love, dearest, Peg

#34-July 2, 1944

Dear Peg,

Well Dominion Day went by yesterday without much fuss. We had a sports day here yesterday which was very successful in spite of the fact that every half an hour it would start to rain and this would last 5 to 10 minutes. Johnnie Hunt came down in the evening and there was a party in the mess. Johnnie and I stuck together all night and dashed around meeting people we knew – Charlie Burgess came and several more chaps who I had run into – a couple of MOs who came over on the boat with me etc. I was more or less standing by and about midnight somebody was brought in who was hit by a car – so my evening was a bit held down. Fortunately this person was just bruised, scalp wounds etc so nothing serious.

Pardon me while I get up and close the window. About 100 yards from my window there are the buildings of the station pig farm and when the wind blows this way, you realize just how bad 300 pigs can smell.

I am certainly anxious to see what Joan looks like now – try and get a picture of her with her teeth showing. You also honey had better try to get away for a holiday – give yourself a bit of a change. If you have any further worries about your health you had better get a chest x-ray etc – which I slipped up on before I left. Certainly kick myself now at all the things I should have done for you before I left.

I suppose you have that case of beer and 13 of Scotch put away by now honey. Hope you didn't get too merry and hope you got merry enough. Hope your housing situation solves itself – certainly wish we were more or less settled somewhere – however, we are not, so I better stop making us feel sorry for ourselves.

Today it rained all day and after spending about three hours seeing the sick and afflicted, I had nothing to do, so played cribbage with Bill Scott, the dentist. Beat him 5 games in a row – ahem! Get a picture of yourself with that new permanent wave and in your new bathing suit honey.

Well, will close now and write tomorrow. Hope I get some news from you tomorrow but generally don't expect it until about Wednesday of each week. Well goodbye for now honey.

Bags of kisses. All my love, Hamp

#35-July 3, 1944

Dear Peg,

Nothing much to report today. Had another moderately busy day but wasn't rushed by any means. Merlin Hicks left today for his hospital appointment and his replacement – Jack Perverself came in. He has been with a squadron down south and is now due for his squadron leader – he has about 4 year's seniority in now.

Tonight Doug, Blair Purvis (Engineering Officer) and myself went out in an armoured car. Blair looks after some on the station so he drove us around the countryside "testing" the vehicle. While we were testing it we picked up a couple of dozen eggs. Also we got wet a bit again – Blair only had a slit about 3" x 12" to see through so we had to keep our heads out and look for traffic. Very enjoyable ride – I was surprised at how smooth it was.

There was a show on in the mess tonight but I only saw about half of it and then had to leave to see some bloke with diarrhoea.

That flood in Edmonton must have really been something. I doubt if it was wetter than Yorkshire though. That idea of a scrapbook is a darn good one – I always had an ambition to keep one but never had the initiative.

You asked me about a sleeveless pullover sweater. I would be very glad to have one but there is no use you putting all your spare time into it (not that I wouldn't appreciate it) – any kind of a sweater that you can pick up and that is warm would be swell.

There is a rumour that leaves may begin again for ground crew sometime – if they do I'm certainly going to follow your advice and go up to Scotland. Your selecting the best Medical Journals is a good idea – we get the BMJ, J of War Med, etc over here and I would appreciate the odd "who done it" mystery occasionally.

Well, have run out again and it gets monotonous to you for me to say how much I love my wife but I am beginning to believe the statement that absence makes the heart grow fonder, more every day. Well, will sign off and say hello to the daughter for me and tell to grow up as tough as she wants to – she can boss me and I'll like it. All my love, Hamp

33 July 4, 1944

Dearest Hamp,

Today was my lucky day again as I had 8 letters from my beau. It was wonderful to hear from you at last. We seem to be having the same trouble with our mail – it is rather depressing this no mail business isn't it? Guess we have to expect such things. Was glad you said "no" to the PMO about the eastern tour as I sure hope you will be home before two years are up. It would be an interesting trip though. About cribbage you old goat, I was just learning to play the game. Guess you can't be very good eh, if an amateur can maintain your ego. Just wait till you get home old man and I'll stand a couple of games against you. I know more about it now so your ego may suffer. It will be fun to play together no matter who wins though. I'm not worried about you not being a good boy but just thought that when you get home you had better not be as good as you were when we were on our honeymoon. By that I mean I want a real good time with you and Joan for about a year. Get it? Of course I won't care if you are a super good boy however and things happen.

Joan is saying Da da and Mum-m-m quite a bit and also "ba ba" which is said to her when bad so she gets back at us quite often. She of course is always blowing and gurgling. Bought Joan her first real boots yesterday – white with cushioned soles. She thinks they are the real McCoy and really struts her stuff when she tries to walk. I hope she won't be bowlegged as she is till quite young to be standing and trying to walk but I can't hold her down.

Dad and Mother settled up the little matter of the house today so it is now theirs. Dad just used $150 worth of bonds and so gave us back $100. Haven't heard anything about the bonds from Claresholm by the way but guess it isn't lost anyway.

Alix was over last night and we sat and knit for awhile and then went to Joan's. Saw Helen Gun for the first since she went to the San and she looks very well indeed and says she feels fine. Gordy Bell has been posted to Winnipeg and Betty and the baby are going too in a month's time.

Went to the hospital to see Helen today and she is getting along fine. While there I saw Elliot Cohen and he (is) (was) a proud daddy of a little girl and just what they wanted. It was born either yesterday or today.

Coming from the hospital I stopped in to see Mrs. Lawton and have a cup of tea. She had been in bed last week with guess what? Yes sir, her old trouble "with my uterus and bladder" but she seems to be better this week. Nora Horner was operated on for a toxic thyroid about a month ago and is doing very nicely now.

Had a letter from Ma yesterday and she sent me one of the letters you wrote her. She said Mac was going to try and get some 120 films for you and perhaps I can get some extra ones and send along. Can hardly wait for your pictures. Hope they turn out OK. Are you losing any weight with all your cycling? Bet you look cute as an "erk". I'm going to call you that some day just to annoy you. I'm already lining up a campaign of teasing you and loving you so you'd better be prepared too. Won't it be fun darling? I do hope it won't be very much longer now. Dad belongs to the pessimists and doesn't see how it can be over in 2 years. I'm set for at least a year but refuse to think of it being any longer. However I'll settle for less any day.

Ordered some cigarettes for you yesterday – 300 – and as they go air mail you're supposed to get them in 10 days so they may arrive before your 1000. I'm going to send 300 a week from now on.

Have another parcel almost ready to send – just have to make the cookies. There are 2 parcels – one will contain medical journals and some stuff to eat and the other contains canned food etc. There is a special part parcel – but don't celebrate unless its on your being a good girl. Pardon me, I mean, boy. Must have been thinking of myself.

That seems to all for now darling except that Joan and I miss you very much and send you barrels of love and kisses and hugs. All my love, dearest – Peg

#36-July 5, 1944

Dearest Peg,

Today I got your letter dated June 22/44 you seemed to be having quite a hectic time, what with doing the wash and getting yourself in a minor schnozzle in the process and the family away. You are apparently having a minor fling and I think it does you good occasionally to wake up with a hangover and realize that parties you miss don't do anything but make you feel like hell the next morning.

The daughter seems to be more or les corralled for the time being

172

with her harness. I have been intending to ask you for quite awhile and kept forgetting – how long is Joan's hair now and what does it look like? Has she still got some of her bald spot? Am certainly waiting for more pictures.

Doug Ritchie dug up a roll of 120 film today so the next nice evening we will go out and try to get some picture of the countryside – some of it is nice.

Last night "Staff" Stafford (accounts officer from Eastern Canada) and myself went out bike riding. We came on a place where there were very extensive green houses and so went in and looked around. There was a very obliging type there who showed us around – he had apples and apricots and cherries outside and plums, grapes, figs, tomatoes under glass. It looks like a good place to remember when they get ripe. As you can now see honey, in Yorkshire the food is good – the farmers have as much as they do in Canada and so you needn't worry about me except that I will keep my weight up too much.

Doug and Perverseff went into Harrogate tonight for dinner and the evening. The place doesn't interest me very much since I can have a beer in the mess if I want one, and bum around here and fill in time.

The war news is good. Ritchie bet me a pound today that Berlin would be under the allies by Christmas. I was the pessimist who bet against it.

I should get a couple of more letters this week – maybe that is being overly optimistic but you have spoiled me so now that I get to expect them and look for them daily. (I don't mean that I look for a daily letter.) Well will say goodbye. Give my regards to your Maw and Paw. All my love, Hamp

34-July 7, 1944

Dearest Hamp,

More mail today. This is my lucky week even with the rain et al it has been very wonderful. Five letters today which brings us up to June 27 and you were munching on cookies and peanuts. By now you should have another parcel and again let me apologize for the cookies – they were one of my worst efforts and you know how my cooking can vary.

Mailed a couple of 9 pound parcels to you today and if they don't arrive at the same time do wait for both as the feast will not be perfect without the works. One has about 6 medical journals – just to keep you up to date and also provide educational reading material. Let me know when the Reader's Digest starts coming under separate cover as I readdressed mine to you through the company. If it should go astray I can try and locate it. Perhaps!

Didn't write you on Wednesday as Joan and I were busy all day trying to cut molars. We have 8 teeth now but still aren't satisfied so we are starting on the big ones. They are pretty tough however and so we didn't sleep all Wednesday until 11 PM when aspirin finally soothed our shattered nerves. It was a pretty bad day as we didn't know what to do and nothing pleased us very much. Yesterday it rained and rained and so we stayed in and were ourselves again and trying to get our sleep at the right time which never seemed to work out. But today is a wonderful day. Rain and the sun shines and the daughter her usual very bright self – muttering away all day and laughing at any old thing which seems amusing. Joan is sitting in her swing – swaying back and forth with a big grin on the wee face. We swing ourself now.

Just finished taking a couple of pictures of Joan standing up in her playpen. She's very good at it now and is really learning things very quickly. Quite a brainy child if I do say so. It's funny to watch her rocking to music. Last night in the bath she splashed so hard with her feet and hands that I was soaked and the clothes on the door were quite damp so you can imagine the fun and also the mess we had.

How is your clothing supply doing? – socks, shirts, etc. Let me know dear. Also your razor blades, soap etc Guess it won't hurt to send along a little next time as your stock must be dwindling somewhat. But you can let me know. Won't you be a wonderful husband able to darn your own socks etc? Maybe you could take over the cooking too and I'll raise the family. How's about it old boy?

I don't mind you going up in a plane for the *odd* ride, darling, but none of this hopping over Germany stuff. Just to be morbid – Joan and I can't manage without you forever. We can be brave about your absence now but anything else would knock the props out from under that we could not take.

Can hardly wait to see the pictures of you and the boys. They will be something to show the girls – just like you show our pictures around.

I was thinking of knitting you a pullover as already mentioned but will look at patterns and see what would be quite high at the neck. I guess you'd rather have one that buttons as it won't rumple your hair so will see what I can do along those lines. Rumpling your hair is something I'd like to do right now but guess I'll have to add that to my "torment list for future use."

Alix hasn't heard from Fred for 10 days which is very unusual so he must be very busy or following the Germans.

Churchill's report of the buzz bombs sure makes you boiling mad at our enemies. Hope they find someway of squashing the whole bloody lot of them soon for good and all. Them's my sentiments.

Joan just said "Da da" so guess that means "send along my love and also I'm hungry" which is her continual complaint. Loads of hugs and kissed from both of us. All my love, dear – Peg

#37-July 7, 1944

Dear Peg,

Well, nothing much to report but quite a bit at that. Last night I went into Leeds to a "do" at the Leeds school of Medicine. The blood donor service has a floor there and the unit rolls around the various stations taking blood and to meet the MOs. The chap in charge is a fellow Dr. Stamberg and he invited us in for the evening which was in honour of one of the MOs there who was posted to Ceylon. Charlie Burgess came down in the afternoon with Jim Bailey, who was up here on leave (remember Jim from Claresholm). We asked if it would be OK for them to come and so Doug and I and Jim and Charlie all went in. It was a very nice evening in which we all had a lot of beer and scotches. However the party quit at 12 midnight and our train left Leeds at 2:30 AM. Charlie, Doug, Jim and I stayed on to about 1:00 and then went over to the station where we waited for over an hour and then got on the train to York and got there at 3:30 AM and then got another train to Thirsk at 4:00 AM. We didn't arrive home until 5:30 and then had 2 hours sleep and got up and took sick parade – quite a lot of foolishness but we all claimed we had a good time. I didn't see very much of Leeds except from the train on the way in – bare acres of chimney pots and have no desire to go there and look the place over – it looks very dirty.

After sick parade this morning I went into York to get some supplies – blood sedimentation tubes, etc – Stafford went with me. We ate lunch there and then went to see the York Minster Cathedral. It is one of the oldest cathedrals in England I believe (6 hundred and something). It is a huge old building with a tremendous amount of stonework of various kinds – I was too dopey to really appreciate it but was impressed. I think I like Gloucester Cathedral better however. Came home at 4:30 this afternoon from York and I have now eaten and am going to go to bed and sleep till morning.

Got no mail from you today – only the one letter this week, but should get a stack of it any day now.

Imagine you are really enjoying summer weather now and I wish I were there to enjoy it with you – however honey there will be many more of them in our married life for us to spend together. Bags of love and kisses for yourself from me. All my love, Hamp

35-July 8, 1944

Dearest Hamp,

Two more letters yesterday from my wonderful husband. Life is really sunny. That made 15 letters last week. The letter of your trip to Horome was really a masterpiece. I phoned Margaret and we laughed ourselves almost sick. The last letter was dated June 30 so the mail service is really excellent and it makes you seem not so very, very far away.

Went to a show Friday night with Kay Bartleman. Saw Humphrey Bogart in "Passage to Marseilles" – quite a gruesome show on the whole. All about the Free French and their air force in England. It ended after an hour and a half of awful catastrophes with Bogart's death and over his grave his CO read a letter written to Bogart's 4 year old son whom he had never seen. Very pathetic and I of course turned on the water works like I haven't done since Claresholm episodes. The water just rolled off my chin like a miniature Niagara. Guess that was the wrong show for that night. Have decided that from now on I stick to comedies.

176

Yesterday it rained again so stayed in all day. Joan was just a perfect baby – more so than usual – & played all day in her pen. She laughed to herself and also gave out with a grin when anyone entered the room. She's off her 10 PM bottle now. She gets her bath at night and her bottle saved from supper at 6:30 PM. She sleeps from then all night with some nights waking at 4 AM for a bottle and going right back to sleep or else sleeping right through until 7 AM when she gets her breakfast on those days. So we are getting to be a big girl now.

Saturday night I went to Alix's, Roberta Collins dropped in and we had several drinks of Scotch from my 13 oz. So we got feeling quite jolly but only in a quiet way. Frankie Layton has been picked to go to a staff course at Kingston. He had his picture in the paper and made the radio news – Camrose boy makes good I guess.

Today was another fine day again so Alix, Sandra, Joan and I went for quite a walk and got rather suntanned. Alix has got a high school girl to come every afternoon and twice a week at night to look after Sandra. It's a good thing as Alix was not able to get out much because Mrs. Robertson is still at the Coast. Mother is really wonderful as far as I'm concerned and looks after Joan any time. Of course we have an agreement that if we were both asked out on the same night that I should be the one to stay home. I insisted on that as it is only fair for Joan after all is my responsibility. So far we have had no trouble or had to cancel dates so it's really wonderful.

Margaret was down to Dr. Vant's on Saturday and she's coming along OK, is still nursing David and hates to think of putting him on formula.

2 hours later.

Hi! Have been out for a ride with Marg, Bill and David – their usual night ride to spoil the infant. We drove to the hill overlooking Keeler's farm – towards Whitemud and sat drinking beer, eating peanuts and smoking. It was very pretty with the sun on the river. Reminded me of old times and I sure wished you were along. The mosquitoes are very bad now due to all the rain we are having so we were rather pestered with the beasts flying in and out the windows in swarms.

The war news is still very good and makes one more hopeful for a not too distant end for Germany. Wish they could find a means of wiping out the buzz bombs. They must be quite awful. Please don't sightsee down there, dear, unless you are moved south. Last night Walter Winchell said over the air that he would give $1000 to war charities for each day the war lasted after July 18. Seems very optimistic doesn't it. He may find himself a poor man soon.

That seems to be all the room for this time but I'll write again real soon. All my love, my darling and heaps of hugs and kisses. It can't be too long now. Joan joins me too. More love, Peg

#38-July 9, 1944

Dear Peg,

Today it is raining as usual. I am over at a nearby clinic relieving the medical officer who is taking the day off. I came here yesterday morning and will go back tonight. It is a very quiet spot and I do nothing but sit and read and talk to anybody who will sit down.

Last night I was eating at the mess and looked up and who should I see but Eddie Oldring[7]. He is up at this unit waiting for a posting into a squadron. It was quite a surprise to see him since I had never anticipated running into him in this part of the world. He is looking very fit as he has been doing a PT course for about a month. We had quite a chat today and discussed things in general. I had never talked to him before – he is a darn good chap – very popular in the mess here. Tell Aunty Lena that I saw him – will you – eh honey?

Well darling, I wish you had been with me yesterday. As I drove over here I stopped off at that place with the greenhouses and showed it to the NCO in charge of the air crew mess so he could scrounge some supplies and also I picked myself a pound of raspberries. Lovely sunny morning after a rain and it was beautiful. The only thing lacking in the scenery was your own beautiful self.

It is pretty grim here compared to the place I am – this is what is called a dispersed station and all the units are at least a half a mile from each other. For instance you cycle a mile from sick quarters to the officers' mess and may have to go 2 miles to another part of camp. The exercise is good for the figure but I miss my pig farm outside the window – no company.

178

By the way didn't tell you I saw the birthplace of General Wolf (of Quebec fame) in York – wasn't much interested in it so didn't go in. Also the streets in York – some of them only about 8 feet wide with the houses overhanging so that their windows in spots are only about 3 feet apart – I'd hate to live there.

Well, goodbye for now. Say hello to the daughter. All my love, Hamp

#36-July 10, 1944

Dearest Hamp,

Another good day. Got a letter dated July 2nd – really wonderful service I must say. There isn't anything new to report as we stayed at home today. Margaret was downtown however and got a new dress – red – & hat – white – for Helen Magee's wedding this Saturday.

Joan is really a going concern and we are having a few battles over daytime sleeping. Joan seems to want to play all day and no matter how tired she looks she won't lie down and sleep without putting in her two cents worth of objections. Have her in splints again. I hope I didn't wait too long before I tackled this thumb sucking business. After you left and some of her teeth came in, she forgot about her thumb unless she was hungry – which I could check up on – or unless she couldn't go right to sleep which times she would quietly such her thumb. I kept a pretty good watch on her I think and hope but now that her molars are beginning to germinate she's really gone on the thumb. So back to splints we go – and the funny part of it is she doesn't fuss about it when she can't get her thumb. I only have to splint her for sleeping in case she should waken up so it isn't so very bad. Her present teeth are straight and I sure hope her permanent set will be OK.

Joan's hair is trying to be curly. It is a lighter shade than yours dear and is about two inches long on top and shortens as it goes down to the neck. Everybody comments on her big blue eyes and dark eyelashes. Her brows are fair, however. I think her nose belongs to me and her mouth tends to resemble yours. You know rather large – Ha! Ha! She is built on a small scale really. She isn't underweight and yet is 4 pounds lighter than Marie Collin's baby which is a day younger. However I

179

don't worry about Joan because she's just right. I can see her when she starts to walk. She'll look just like a wee doll and oh so cute! Don't think for one moment that she's fragile or anything. One look at her dressed in her overalls with her face and hands all dirty and an impish grin on her face would make you say "Toughie".

I took two pictures of Joan yesterday standing by her buggy. I hope they turn out. Also Mother took one of Joan and I. Guess what I wore. Yes! My blue velveteen suit! I don't know why everyone wants to take my picture when I have it on. However the first sunny day I've a date with the camera and my bathing suit. I can't quite figure how I'm going to pose this pin-up picture but we'll find a way.

Hope you are completely over your cold. Tell the boys that the next time you snore all they have to do is say "Honey, please turn on your side, you're snoring!" It works like a charm darling, and after all, I should know. Heaps of hugs and bags of kisses from Joan and I. All my love, dearest – Peg

#39-July 11, 1944

Dear Peg,

Well another two days have drifted by and not much to report. Yesterday and today were very quiet and the usual round of sick parades etc. Last night I saw a show which I'd seen before – forget the name of it but it was quite good.

Tonight Doug, Bill Scott and Blair Purvis and myself dashed into Harrogate. We played 10 holes of golf and then dashed madly for the train and came home arriving here at about 11:30. It is funny what you do to amuse yourself. I would never think of a 2 1/2 hour train ride for 9 holes of golf back home.

There is a slight distraction while I am writing – I am in my pyjamas and Ritchie is lying in bed complaining bitterly that my feet smell – I guess I had better dash out to the bath and correct the situation. While I am writing I am also drinking a glass of noodle soup – which my wonderful, thoughtful, much adored wife sent me. We missed our supper tonight and so are nearly starved. We ate the last of the cookies yesterday and so have finished the parcel except for 2 glasses of hot chocolate and one batch of soup. There has been no mail for some time now (about a week or 9 days) but I expect some tomorrow, I generally get it on Wednesday, for some reason or other.

I kicked myself tonight that I didn't get some pictures of the golf course for you – it was very beautiful. I am going back and will try to correct that.

Well honey, will sign off and write tomorrow. Sure wish I had more to write about besides the fact that I love you. Say hello to Joan. All my love, Hamp

37-July 12, 1944

Dearest Hamp,

Good morning, dear. It looks like rain today so it is very silly to be up and around now as it's only 7:30 AM. the daughter wakened at 6:30 and wouldn't go back to sleep – not even when I moved her to my bed – so after an hour of fuss which was as good or even better than saying "I wanna get up now Mummy" I gave in and staggered out of me warm bed. I'm sure looking forward to a holiday and anyone that wakens me before noon is asking for trouble.

Yesterday I had my usual trouble getting Joan to take a nap. She can be dead on her feet but won't give in. Put Joan in her buggy and stayed beside it so I could put her down when she offered to sit up but she just lay back quietly and no movement so I stood for five minutes and then looked under the hood thinking she'd be asleep. I saw two bright eyes looking at me and then heard a chuckle and up Joan sat. She thinks it's a game, I guess. Will have to bring out the iron glove again the near future it looks like.

Didn't write you yesterday as I was busy all day puttering around. Mother is painting up the place – verandas, doors etc so I looked after the household angle. At night Alix, Roberta Layton and Betty Stark came down. We just sat around and knit and talked.

Speaking of knitting do you want long sleeves or sleeves of any kind on your sweater? How about a long sleeved button-to-neck sweater if I can get enough wool? If not, I'll make a sleeveless pullover to put under your tunic. I think that would be warm for winter if you are allowed to wear them – if not you could always put it under your shirt. People would just think you had fleas.

The pictures arrived yesterday and I was very glad to get them and see how my husband looks without my tender care. And believe me it's not bad. I must say you and Johnny look as though the food agreed with you anyway. In a couple of the pictures your face looked very much like Mac's. I'd sure like to be around and run my fingers up and down your ribs on the spare tire but will have to content myself with adding that item to "My Torment List For Future Use". However it's a good insulation and anyway darling you can go on a diet while I learn to cook again. Maybe I'd better shut up before you get sore. But all kidding aside, dear, it was really grand to get the pictures.

Joan has discovered a new trick. She's standing up, hanging on to the sides of her play pen and shaking them for all she is worth. Guess the pen won't last very much longer now. She's stopped that racket now and is playing with "Old Man" – the name I gave her little red soldier.

Helen Campbell comes home from the hospital today so I'll be a bit busy in the mornings bathing Lorne for a few days. Hope he isn't the crying type as they will call me in just like they have done several times for different things all ready.

Am going to Camrose next week so will try and get some film for you.

Alix finally heard from Fred and he's very busy and very tired. Surgery, 24 hrs of the day, etc

That's all for now. Heaps of love and barrels of hugs and kisses, All my love, darling – Peg

38-July 13, 1944

Dearest Hamp,

I got two letters yesterday dated the 3rd and 5th of July so the mail service is really wonderful. The pictures arrived in good time too – post marked June 26 and arrived July 11th so we can't complain about that. I didn't mention yesterday that I thought your wedgy was cute – real becoming to you old man!

Was over at Margaret's last night so took along the snaps. They were amazed at how you had changed – meaning that you look more like Mac now. Marg had some cheese she was saving for Mac's diet but she's considering sending it to you instead. I really don't think you've changed much in weight but rather blame it on the wedgy hat. However I really don't care how fat or skinny you get over there just as long as you come home soon.

Margaret was busy baking 9 dozen cookies for Helen Magee's wedding on Saturday when I went over. I do think Margaret does too much for people at her own expense. David doesn't seem to be getting very much fatter but then he is gaining quite rapidly. He is on the bottle part time now and I think is going to cause a bit of a fuss from what Margaret says. I offered her 3 months supply of SMA but she didn't seem very interested so looks like we save it for our David.

Helen Campbell came home today with the wee boy. He sure is cute – reminds me of Joan very, very much but his hair is dark and his eyes brown. Of course he's not as cute as Joan, *of course*, but he is her type – sort of cuddly if you know what I mean.

Tonight Joan stood up in the big bath and hung on to the taps, threw back her head and let out a yell like Tarzan. She really loves the water and it looks like we're going to have a swimmer by the way she kicks around. Once in awhile she rolls over so quickly that I can't grab her and water rushes up her nose but she just snorts and goes on playing. I'm trying to train her not to swing on the fire rail by the front room radiant. She loves to grab that and shake it. So now I have to take her away and tap her hands (tenderly) and "No, no, Joan." Today when I lifted her away she clasped her hands together and buried her face. It looked so darn cute that she missed out on her punishment. Joan's hair really curls when its damp – just after her bath. It's quite thick on top but dwindles at the sides. It has grown longer that last few days and now seems to be about 2 inches long. Her eight teeth are really up and showing and it sure looks cute when she grins.

I have finally got wise and now take a sleep in the afternoon when Joan does. Today we slept for 2 hours and I must say I feel much better for it. Now all I have to do is go to bed about an hour earlier each night and I should be on the road to gaining some extra pounds. My appetite is good though so guess I'm just the skinny type – but rugged. Have got the directions for your sleeveless pullover and am going to start it in Camrose. There's nothing I'd like better than to spend all my time knitting for you – not just my spare time. Hugs & kisses from Joan and me. All my love, Peg

#40-July 13, 1944

Dearest Peg,

A banner day today. Four letters from you and one from my daughter Joan. The pictures of Joan were really swell honey. It's hard to realize that our family is growing so fast – Makes me feel old, eh old girl? I'm certainly counting the days until we are together again – it'll soon be 3 months and I don't know where the time has gone. I expect it will be another 18 mos. or so before we can count on anything settled. Right now I don't want to come back until I can stay awhile – couldn't part from you a second time. Would refuse.

I wish you had included yourself in a few of the snaps – have only about half a dozen pictures of you and it isn't enough.

Have been quite busy running around on my bike the last two days. Last night Bill Scott and myself went out to take pictures of each other to send to our respective wives. We came on one place with a beautiful rose garden so we marched in and started to take some snaps. An old couple came out and invited us in for a beer and we had a chat for about an hour – they had a lovely home – they were both over 70 but quite bright. After that we rode around for a couple of hours and got some more snaps.

Tonight Bill and I finished our rolls and I should have some films in a week or so – if they turn out. We rode about 20 miles tonight – went down to Ripon. It is quite a pretty town. There was quite a nice old cathedral but it was closed so we had a couple of beers in the pub and then started dusting back. After we got back we made toast in sick quarters and had some of the tea you sent me and it is now 12:00 PM and I'm writing.

The last letter of yours was July 2. I suppose you are in Camrose by now. I'm sorry the mail isn't coming through better but it should start improving now. Well honey, will now hit the hay and dream about you.

By the way don't let Joan take too many liberties with those "rosebuds". They seem to have a fatal attraction for your family, don't they honey. All my love, Hamp

July 14, 1945

Dearest Peggy,

Another couple of days have gone by with little to report except that the weather is really hot with the occasional scattered shower just to keep things about right. Last night went down to the local with Mac about 8:30 and had a couple of beers and trudged home. We met a young chap and his wife and they invited us out to dine on Sunday, so we have something to do tomorrow night.

Tonight there is a big dance in the mess with all attending. There is no want of partners what with all the nurses attending who want to come. Am not too impressed because my dancing isn't a thing for my enjoyment or anyone else's, but will go soak up a few scotches. The bar is closing early tonight however because two mess members, who departed for Canada today, had a party last night. The finale was that they lined all the glasses up on the mantle place and threw billiard balls at them until there was quite a pile of broken glass. Also one of the balls went through the wall and is lodged in sight behind the wall board but can't be obtained without cutting quite a chunk out of the wall. This little do didn't impress the Colonel (O.C. hospital) very much (or anyone else for that matter), so the bar is closing early to curb any high spirits. I thought Air Force messes were the only places where people rode motorcycles up and down the halls shooting off their revolvers, but I guess the army messes have an equal quota of irresponsible characters – which makes life interesting if nothing more.

Manage to keep fairly busy with one thing or another. We are doing a survey of about 1000 fresh cases of NSU and it will take about 6 weeks or more to complete at our present rate of admission. I'm tabulating clinical finds and although it's only routine, it keeps one occupied.

Well darling, hope you got by Friday 13th without anything in particular to disturb you. Will get in such a rut here in a few weeks that it'll take an earthquake to stir me. Miss you very much. Am not impressed with the Canadian sisters except it's kind of nice to hear the accent. All my love, Hamp

July 15, 1944

Dearest Peg,

Another two days marked on the wall. Very little to report. Last night was on duty – there was very little doing except for a few stitches. Played bridge most of the evening and lost about 8 shillings so there wasn't much profit. Tonight cycled about 6 miles down the road to a little pub. Went with F/O Stafford (accounts) and we sat around for about half an hour and listened to the Yorkshire dialect. I am practically getting so I can understand them – hope I don't come home talking like that though – you'll disown me and that would break my heart.

Doug is away on a 48 and Perverseff goes tomorrow on one so I'm more or less holding the fort. Pev – is going to London and so will get some gen on buzz bombs, etc

The weather here has been grand in the evening lately so we make the most of it and try to get out on our bikes as much as possible. As soon as the rain starts it will be pretty dead – the blackout starts about 5 in the afternoon in winter time and it's pretty hard to get around then. Now it is light until 11 at night.

The pictures of the daughter are really grand and – I'm repeating – have practically worn them out showing them off. It was good news to hear that your Dad and Mother had bought the house – it kind of takes a load off my mind wondering if you would get a place that was OK and not too far away from your friends etc

The money situation doesn't matter and I wouldn't worry if you wrote that money off as contribution to my peace of mind. I haven't said much about your Mother and Dad – actually we owe them a very great deal and I have been intending to write them and express my gratitude a little better. Will do so in the near future. The war news is good these days and I hope it continues so. Hope you are getting the mail OK now – it's not very easy to keep writing regularly when you don't get letters. I feel guilty sometimes that I haven't written more often but actually there isn't much to write about since we can't tell you a great deal about what goes on here.

Well, will close now and will write tomorrow night and more or less catch up. Give my love and kisses to Joan and tell her to triple them and return them to you for me. All my love, Hamp

#42-July 16, 1944

Dearest Peg,

Had a very lovely letter from you today. Quite a surprise since I generally don't expect mail on Sunday. It was dated July 5 (written on July 4) so 12 days isn't bad. You made remarks about me being "good" when get home. I am warning you now – I won't be good, but I'll be careful. I occasionally take quite a beating from Ritchie – about how wonderful it is to travel through the mountains in a compartment and how invigorating that mountain air is – however I still think that we have the right idea – don't you dear?? or do you.

Give my regards to Mrs. Lawton by the way – tell her that I'm very sorry her bladder and uterus are in such a bad way and that I hope she doesn't have to go through such tortures getting a new pessary in.

Mother's trip to see Margaret must have really been a schmozzle. Mother wrote me about it but didn't overstress the highlights – guess Margaret is a little temperamental or something – eh honey.

It will be good to get a few films although there isn't much to photograph except Yorkshire countryside. I'm looking foreword to the parcels – they are a real treat – not that we are underfed but it's kind of nice to have an "ice box" to go to.

The cigarettes will also be welcome – have not yet reached the stage where I have any reserves. Have finished the MacDonald's and somebody gave me a carton of Camels so am doing OK.

It's a perfect day today – sun is shining and the pig farm is steaming – if I ever get any property I'm going to make sure that there isn't any pork on the hoof there.

Joan's molar should be there by now – hope she didn't have too much trouble with it.

That idea of Banff in September seems pretty nice. It won't take long for September to roll around. Funny how the time slips away isn't it – each day seems 24 hours to look forward to and nothing to look back.

Well, all my love and kisses to you. Hamp

39-July 18, 1944

Dearest Hamp,

Received another letter from you today dated July 7. You had had a busy social night and really must have been very tired after your night out. It must have been quite an experience traveling around on trains all night and waiting at stations. You won't want to settle down when you come home you wanderer or will you?

Yesterday and today have been pretty hectic affairs. Bathed Helen Campbell's baby in the morning and was pretty busy all day as Mother wasn't feeling very well. She had been going as usual and got too tired and had her spring attack – like she had when we arrived home one day from Claresholm if you remember – and so had to stay in bed most of yesterday. Mother is no trouble when sick because she doesn't want to be bothered and won't eat etc so she was left rather alone.

Today started out as a good day at 7:30 AM and Mother got up but was very tired and looks a wreck. I bathed Helen's baby again and for the last time now as Helen is able to look after him now. Mother called me to come just as I was finishing. Joan was out in the backyard playing and Mother called me to come and look after my daughter so I went around to the back and got quite a surprise. Joan had messed her pants while standing up and it had run down her legs and nice thick sticky goo and unto the playpen mattress. Then she must have sat it and played around as all her toys were covered and she was coated from head to foot – in her hair, ears and around her mouth (at which thought I stop my imagination) her hands and arms were covered and most of the bars of the playpen. Cousin Frankie had nothing on Joan and to make matters worse the sun had dried it on. It was into the tub for Joan – lock, stock & barrel. She was quite pleased with all the fuss and a bath in the middle of the day and so grinned and chattered all through the mopping up exercise.

In the afternoon we went down to se Dr. Leitch and Joan was all agog at a ride on the streetcar and a free tongue blade plus an inoculation. Joan weighs 18½ pounds and is so active that Dr. Leitch just sits back and watches her with a big grin on her face. Joan was pretty tired when we got home so she was bathed, fed and put to bed but wakened up at 7 PM and cried her heart out for some reason and wouldn't go back to sleep so I had to rock her to quiet her. Ahem! She slept for another hour and is now awake again playing. You should hear the mutterings and squeals. Was just in to see the wee dynamo and she was standing up shaking the sides of the crib. What a child!

Margaret and Bill were over on their way to the Magee wedding and left David with me so he is lying quietly in his buggy in the front room with a bottle of water propped in his mouth – as Margaret left him. So for now all is peaceful.

Alix phoned tonight and is worried about Sandra as she has been very listless for the last two days and tonight her temperature was 100. Alix phoned Dr. Leitch but I haven't heard yet if it's anything very serious.

#3 Manning Pool is closing on August 15th. They are keeping on a skeleton staff so that they can reopen it as a demobilizing centre after # 2 AOS was taken over by the North West Staging route today and there is a rumour that ITS is to be closed too. Recruiting for the RCAF has been stopped until fall so the town is beginning to quiet down.

Met Isobel Goodall yesterday and Hugh has been posted to Vancouver from #3 Recruiting at last. Mrs. Lawton said he was more than disgusted with life in general.

Haven't heard from Claresholm since May. I guess they are down at Waterton Lakes right now so maybe I'll hear from them soon.

Got 3 more rolls of film today. I got one, Mother got one and a little kid we didn't know got one for us so if they haven't saved any for you at Camrose, I'll send one of these. Have been lucky so far in getting several at a time as I haven't got any since June. Took in another roll today and they should be finished by Tuesday. If they turn out your pin-up gals are looking at you in their swimsuits.

Joan wants to go to sleep at last so bye for now. Heaps of hugs and kisses from Joan and I.

All my love, darling – Peg

Dear Peg,

Another two days have drifted by and very little to report. Today I went off for the afternoon to a conference of medical officers of this area. Had quite a nice drive going and coming but the meeting itself didn't amount to very much. Didn't see anybody I knew down there except recent casual acquaintances.

Last night Bill Scott and I got on our bikes and went scrounging eggs. We got a dozen and then went into the village of Topcliffe. They are having a fair there today. On the common beside the R. Swale there were a collection of about 50 caravans. They belonged to gypsies who apparently go from place to place as the fairs move. Their wagons were all painted and decorated and it was quite a sight to see them. They are apparently a shiftless lot and spend their time horse trading and lifting things that one leaves about carelessly and telling fortunes. The airmen from the station have had several arguments with them in the local pubs so we didn't hang around very long. There were no amusements of any kind at the fair and it looks rather queer to Canadians to see them gathered for what appeared to be social reasons.

Stafford was up at Harrow yesterday and dropped into the old pub where we enquired as the whereabouts of the Smith ancestors. Apparently the old girl I saw was a little crazy and the man of the house was anxious to see me some time and get my genealogy straightened out – I plan on going up there sometime next week and looking around.

This weekend Bill Scott and I are making tentative arrangements to go to Edinburgh. Don't know if we can wrangle two days but we are going to try. We will take our bikes and then see how much we can cover in a day and a half. Bill has been there before and so I will have a guide of sorts.

Last night we had an aircraft go down near us – one of ours – fortunately no fatalities – a few minor fractures which will come along. Doug was on duty and went and I dozed off when some drunk came in and said "for God's sake get up Doc". He was wandering the halls in his shorts. He fell into Ritchie's bed and promptly went to sleep. I got up and went over to sick quarters. There was nothing to do till morning so

Doug and I came back and carried this bloke down to the first empty bed we saw and finally got to sleep.

I hope I get some mail tomorrow but won't be alarmed if I don't – it all gets here eventually and I know you are writing. Well honey, goodbye for now. Bags of love to the daughter. All my love, Hamp

40-July 18, 1944

Dearest Hamp,

Yesterday was my day to write but as you will see I had a couple more busy days so am writing now. Sunday morning I went to church with Dad and then spent the afternoon sleeping. Spent a quiet night too – reading.

Yesterday went downtown in the afternoon to get some money for my trip to Camrose and also do some shopping. I tried to find some white shoes to fit me but as that was impossible I had to settle for a pair of brown suede pumps with no toe, a suede bow on the front (small) and a high heel – for dress up occasions. Also found that my alligator shoes were 6 1/4 triple A – no wonder I have trouble keeping them on as I really wear 5 1/2 A so figure I got the wrong end of the deal in Calgary. They seemed to fit at first too. Bought the wool for your sweater so am going to start it while in Camrose. Also ordered 300 cigarettes for you and they should arrive some day.

Went out to Margaret's from town, had supper, a couple of ryes and came home at 9:30. Margaret looks robust but quite tired. The Magee wedding on Saturday night took a lot out of her but she won't admit it. She was to Dr. Vant last week and had to be cauterized. David is growing in length but is not putting on much fat so far however he is a different type than Joan and so its not fair to compare babies. By the way Joan was 9 months old yesterday and I didn't buy her anything. How awful!

Was up at 7:30 this morning as I had our stuff to pack so I could send it all express instead of having to bother about suitcases. Am taking Joan's carriage and play pen too. Just got my last bag packed when the express man arrived so that was pretty close. Then turned around and helped Mother prepare lunch for twelve – Aunty Lena, Cousin Winnie and her daughter Maxine, Cousin Netta and her two daughters, Loraine and Donna. These cousins are Aunt Lena's daughters. Then Cousin Ethel – Uncles Jim's girl from Calgary and her daughter Phyllis. Also Elaine Oldring – who married Eddy's brother Ronny this spring – and our family. Fortunately it was a beautiful day so we ate in the backyard and everyone seemed to have a good time.

When the mail arrived there were two letters from you – didn't get any yesterday. In one you had met Eddy Oldring. It was quite a coincidence to get that when Aunty Lena was here. In the other letter you'd been playing golf. It certainly was a long train ride for a game of golf but just think darling we'd be able to belong to a Club in Edmonton and come up from Camrose. Almost the same idea although the distances will be greater here.

Joan certainly enjoyed the "do". Her pen had been shipped so she was on the loose and really gave her Ma the run around.

We took some pictures of Joan yesterday in the back yard. I hope they turn out because they appeared to be very good.

The McDonald's who lived in Claresholm at Yokums' had a son yesterday called Graeme.

Betty Bell is leaving on Friday for Winnipeg to join Gordon who is posted there.

Alix just phoned and Sandra has an abscess in her ear so that explains her temperature and malaise. A fling back from her measles no doubt. The abscess broke today so Sandra should feel better.

Joan is turning into a regular little miss. This morning when she was put down for her nap she lay in her crib and screamed and I mean screamed at the top of her voice and kicked her heels. So I sure left her to herself. She's getting to the stage where she's trying to get along with only one sleep a day but she does get awfully tired on only one nap. However will probably have a few scenes before we get straightened out.

Must go to bed now as it will be and early morning tomorrow to get the train.

I hope your parcels of cigarettes weren't burned on that mail car fire in England honey. Joan sends hugs and kisses to "Da Da"! and so do I also.

All my love dearest – Peg

Dearest Peg,

Three letters from you today – the last one dated July 10. It is good to hear that we are finally getting connected on our mail – makes me feel that you aren't so far away after all.

Glad to hear that Margaret is getting along well with her son and her sitter. Sure am envious of you sitting on the river but I'm glad to hear that you can get there (with Marg and Bill) even if I'm not around. I'm really looking forward to that parcel you are sending – it will really be a treat. You asked about my clothing supply – it is good for the present but by Christmas time will be dwindling and I would appreciate a sweater or two and some socks. I would appreciate a tube of shaving cream – I am just about out and have only the bars of shaving soap which aren't quite as nice.

Doug is going to London this weekend to spend a couple of weeks taking a course in tropical medicine – we will eventually all get the course so you can figure it out for yourself. No matter how optimistic we get honey I can't see myself home for another 18 months – I keep telling myself that so that I will become a little more philosophical. If I stay away twice that long you need never worry that I'll ever be any different than I left you and will always be yours only – want to keep reassuring you of that because I know.

Don't go to a lot of trouble knitting a sweater honey – anything that I can hang around me will be 100%.

I got your picture reframed today – the glass was broken and sent into town for a new glass for it – now you are sitting on the dresser without a frame.

Today Jack Perverseff and myself went down to one of the neighbouring units and got "genned" up on penicillin. We now have it at the station for treatment of serious infections, sulfa resistant GCs and GCs in air crew. We will have little occasion to use it but it is nice to have.

Last night Doug and Bill Scott and I went into Harrogate and played about 16 holes of golf – it's quite a rush to get there about 6:30, get a cab to the course, and then get around and get back in time to get the train home at 10:30. You really are ready for bed by the time you get home. I am on duty tonight but not very busy except for a couple of "bicycle prangs". There certainly are a lot of minor injuries resulting from people falling off their bicycles. The Readers Digests haven't started to come yet but it generally takes about 2 months – will let you know when they arrive.

I'm glad to hear that Joan has your nose – she may be quite good looking if she takes after her mother. Well honey, will say goodbye for now. Loads of love to the daughter and kisses to yourself.

All my love, Hamp

41-July 20, 1944 Camrose

Dearest Hamp,

As you can see Joan and I are in Camrose. We had a good trip down and Joan was true to form – perfect. She sat on the side and played with her 'old man' or else stood up and looked out of the window and chattered all the time saying "Da da" and "Ugh"! Then she had a sleep for 1/2 an hour so we got along fine. Dad met us at the train and was very pleased to see us – especially Joan. She walked right into his heart so to speak and she makes a great fuss of him whenever he is around. Crawls up to his chair stands on her feet and begs to be lifted onto his knee. She thinks his moustache is something especially for her and so they have a gay old time together. Have discovered that our "we un" has an eye for men because whenever anyone comes around in trousers Joan drops all and hikes for them. She makes a bee line for Mac too and also scurried after the express man. She is quite a chore though as she hates to be alone and is continually looking around to see if her mummy is in sight. However we are having a good quiet time and eating like hogs on the good Smith food. I should be putting on a few pounds what with a couple bottles of beer per day – taken for my health ahem! which is perfect and all the food.

Dad has been busy with an inquest over a railway and car accident and Mac is on the go as usual. I must say Dad looks a bit thinner than when I last saw him and tires very quickly but doesn't seem to stop any however.

Mother is the same with her usual ups and downs and is kept busy cooking and training the new girl who is only 13 years old. All in all we are very happy and getting along "par excellence".

It seems very strange however to be in your home for the first time without you being around some place. In fact, I keep expecting you to pop through the door any minute, darling, with some joke or teasing word. On the other hand it would be a tragedy if I didn't miss you so awfully wouldn't it honey?

Got a letter for you today dear written on the 13th of July. Really wonderful service for if I'd been home it would have arrived in 6 days. It was post marked the 14th so that would make it only 5 days. Really a good show.

Started on your sweater today and Joan helps me by pulling at the needles and grabbing the wool so if you find a dropped stitch you will know it is the daughter's handiwork.

The enlarged picture of the 3 of us is really much better than the small ones we got. It seems to bring out the people in it ahem!

Mother wrote to you on Sunday and is rather worried in case it won't arrive as she only put a 5 cent stamp on it. However you will probably get it before this arrives.

That's all for this letter as I'm going to write one with Dad right now.

All my love dearest and bags of hugs and kisses from Joan and I. Bye for now, Peg

July 21, 1944

Dear Peg,

Another day by the board. Nothing much to report today. Our Edinburgh trip is off because Bill Scott couldn't get a 48 and also our PMO is coming up for the day so we all want to see him and get the gen. We are leaving at noon and going to Thirsk and then on to Scarborough to spend the day. It is supposed to be quite a nice town and should make a pleasant day.

Tonight Bill Scott and I took a quick whirl on our bikes and won half a dozen eggs. We came back to sick quarters and poached them and then Bill produced a tin of peaches and Doug produced some sardines, so we had quite a spread.

Just thought of something else I would like – some after shaving talc – am just about out and need something to take the shine off my scars. If you happen to think of it – it would be welcome. I am getting to be quite a scrounger from my beloved wife – don't think that I take everything for granted – I realize how much work goes into the parcels and certainly appreciate it – someday I hope to be able to reciprocate.

A little interruption, Doug came in and we are both writing letters and talking – one subject was a case of beer and the river bank – I got to think of the number of evenings we enjoyed together there and can hardly wait to repeat them with you again honey. They certainly were glorious days to look back on (and forward to). I probably won't write tomorrow or the next night because I will be away. Plan to spend Sunday in Scarborough but may have to come back because the hotels are pretty crowded and we may not be able to get a place to stay. Should have quite a bit to tell you since it is supposed to be quite a nice seaside town. The next time I get I'm going down to Blackburn but want to write there first. Eddie Oldring said that he had a very nice time there and he was sure that I would be welcome if I went.

Hope that I can scrounge some of these forms somewhere – this is the last I have and have to start using English forms which I am not certain will go by air without any hold-up – they should do so, so don't worry about not getting mail.

Well honey, certainly love my wife. Give the big hello to Joan from me. All my love, Hamp

42-July 23, 1944 Camrose

My dearest Hamp,

Are you as hot as we are? It's too bad we can't mix a bit of our different weather together. It's 8:15 PM and I'm still in lather. Have just got Joan to bed so that may account for some of the extra warmth.

Mother sent me the enclosed picture to Camrose so that I could send them right on to you. I tossed the envelope right into the fire and incidentally the negatives – so hang on to the pictures for us darling so that we can put them in Joan's album when you come home.

#1.   Joan in her Sunday best showing you how well she can stand up. She has on her blue poke bonnet, the blue and white sweater I knit in Claresholm which took so long to do as you can perhaps recall, her pink dress and her new white boots. She was between 8 1/2 and 9 months of ages when all the pictures were taken.

#2.   Hi ya pop! Aren't I pretty clever?

#3.   The pink dress once touched her knees. She has grown as you can see. It's now her play dress and crawling outfit when the trousers are dirty. Notice that she's only using one hand.

#4.   Joan as she looks when she's growling like Bud[6] – a slap happy mood.

#5.   Your wife and daughter. Recognize us? Actually not a good picture but it shows up my new hair do. How do you like it?

#6.   Mother was so anxious to get the picture of Joan that she forgot to see where I was consequently I'm the headless wonder. A good picture of my bow legs though don't you think? It's really a good picture of Joan. The shoes I'm wearing are the Italian sandals Fred sent to Alix.

#7.   Your pin-up gals in our sun suits.

#8.   Ditto.

Hope you like the pictures. We are taking more every day. It was lucky that Dad got all these films for you. Hope they arrive safely. I managed to get 3 more rolls a couple of weeks ago so we are very well off.

The war news is sure good now – maybe you'll lose your bet to Ritchie. That's all for now my darling as I'm going to write a blue form too. All my love, dearest – Peg

42-July 23, 1944 Camrose

Dearest Hamp,

Well we didn't write our combined letter on Thursday night as Dad was too tired and couldn't think of anything to write about and we haven't got around to it yet.

It is very quiet here and I haven't been outside of the yard except on Saturday when Dad and I went into town for eggs and bread. We were up in the office and Mac's room and the waiting room are all freshened up with white paint, Venetian blinds etc. It is very bright and quite a cheery place now. Dad's rooms are still to be done. They didn't get the kind of furniture they wanted and will have to wait until the war is over now. But is really quite an improvement.

The weather has been frightfully hot – clear sunny skies and no breeze. Joan gets a bit trying at times as she doesn't sleep well in the day time and so gets over tired. She doesn't like to be alone very long and so her mother is quite busy.

The little school girl that was working here was called home on Saturday but we have hopes of getting another one tomorrow.

Had a letter from Doris Bothwell and Bill was posted on a course to Toronto in June so they didn't get to Waterton Lakes but went to Norwich instead. Counting their travelling time the course, and two weeks leave, they will be away from Claresholm a month all told. Lucky people eh? I wonder if Bill complains about working hard still?

The Lantet's had a little boy but they lost it when he was 3 weeks old so they are rather browned off on this baby business. He is hoping for a posting to Boundary Bay.

Doris wants me to go to Claresholm for the anniversary dance which invitation I will consider but I have the feeling that it would bring back too many happy memories. However we shall see.

Joan is certainly about the toughest child I know and Dad raves about her being so active for 9 months. He doesn't know the half of it however. She had to have two baths today to keep clean. After supper tonight she upset the coal pail in the kitchen and crawled around among the coal dust and was she ever a mess.

She got hold of a hand mirror today too and it was funny to watch her laughing at herself. Then to top it off she leaned over and kissed the baby in the mirror.

Dad just came in the door and is going to write on the last flap. Fortunately I'm all talked out this time.

Am sending some more pictures of Joan and I to you tonight too. Hope you get them soon.

That seems to be all for now, dear. Must listen to the good war news now. Bags of hugs and kisses from Joan and I.

All my love, dearest – Peg

[Written on flap]

[Written on flap]

Just Cheerio Hamp,

Peggy is nicer than she used to be and you know that that just means that we are glad to have her here. Joan is just Joan. Prowls all over the lot principally on her own power. A natural wonder, no fooling, lots of fun. More film going through soon. Allen is at Banff and not sure yet about camera. Love, Dad

Sunday July 23, 1944

Dear Peg,

Well here it is Sunday night and I have returned from my sightseeing just about done out. I am not sure of the date and have no calendar but believe it is the 23rd. It seems about a week since we left – actually it was only yesterday.

Slept in until 10 yesterday morning and then had a leisurely bath and then Bill Scott and I started – laugh – the train from Thirsk to York and stood up all the way – it only took 45 minutes but we were in a compartment – 6 of us standing between the slats and there were 4 or 5 people in each seat so we were really packed in. We got established at the Dominion Officers Club in York. It's run by the Canadians for Dominion officers – it is an old home taken over and we were in a large room with five others. We were going out to Scarborough but the station was so packed that you couldn't take a deep breath – also it was an hour before train time and the queue was already a block long, so we gave it up. We spent Saturday afternoon wandering around York getting some shoes and a pair of flannels for Bill. We finally got the pants but we couldn't find any shoes that he liked – we even had to queue up outside the shoe store and wait our turn to get in. I certainly would hate to drive a car in York – most of the streets are so narrow that they are one way traffic only and the sidewalks are also so narrow that half the time you have to walk on the road. We took another look through York Minster Cathedral – it really is a magnificent edifice. By that time it was 5 o'clock so we had tea and by then it was 6 o'clock so we had a beer and then went back to the officers club.

We sat around the bar there and played cribbage and drank beer and then had supper – had rabbit pie – it was really good and at first we thought we were eating chicken and then realized that the bones didn't look quite right and also it had a flavour which was halfway between chicken and tame duck.

After supper we had no place to go and since York hauls in its sidewalks about 11:00 PM, we just sat in the bar and chatted with various blokes as they came in and by that time it was 11:00 PM and we had sandwiches and rolled into bed feeling quite merry.

We got up at 7:30 this morning and had breakfast (porridge, fried tomatoes, a slice of bacon, toast and tea) and then dashed down to the station to get the train to Scarborough. Will tell you tomorrow about Scarborough. Wish you were here with me to see these spots. Miss you. All my love, Hamp

July 24, 1944

Dearest Peg,

Two letters today dated 12th and 13th – pretty good I call it. You asked about sleeves on the sweater – would like long sleeves and a button up front – kind of a tall order eh honey – also it is only 2 months until winter starts so don't spoil your summer knitting – anything you can get will be OK. The daughter is a full time job and I really don't expect you to do nothing but knit in your spare time. Was glad you got the pictures – as you can see the potatoes, beans and bread don't make me lose much weight. However, I am 6 pounds lighter than when I left you so I guess it was the battle dress and wedge that did it. Reading your next letter over I see you are knitting a sleeveless pullover – actually that is more practical and would be 100%.

Today I got a chit for a registered parcel but the post office was closed by the time I got it so will let you know tomorrow what gives. The mail service is so good now that registering isn't necessary unless it is extra valuable.

Was shopping around York to see if I could pick up something for you – couldn't see anything I thought you would like. If you can think of anything please let me know – Scotch tweed for a suit seems popular however mention anything you might have your mind on.

Was going to tell you about Scarborough. We left from York at 7:30

AM and got on a train – managed to grab a seat and then pretend we were asleep so we didn't feel guilty about the women standing on our feet. Arrived there about 10:30 and then went to the best hotel in town and checked our luggage (coat and knapsack) and then had tea in the lounge. After that we walked down to the sea shore. The sun was shining and it was really very beautiful. There is kind of a bay with cliffs rising on each side with the harbour in the middle with fishing boats, sea gulls and bags of people. On one side is a very old castle. We climbed up to that and Bill got some pictures. Unfortunately he had colour film that you project so I can't get any prints. We walked around for about 3 hours and then had a pint and some lunch. Then we got a taxi and got a 20 mile ride taking 1 1/2 hours for a pound – quite cheap and then caught the bus home. We are getting to be real tourists. Well honey, will write tomorrow. All my love and kisses, Hamp

43-July 25, 1944 Camrose

Dearest Hamp,

Got two always welcome letters today dated July 16 & 18 to your mother – about intended trip to Edinburgh but the one written on the 16th I kept to myself and chuckled over Ritchie commenting on our trip to Vancouver. Poor old Ritchie doesn't know a quarter of it, does he dear? But I agree with you – we did the right thing and I'm going on a trip with you again as the last one was really wonderful don't you agree?

I got a real thrill out of the idea that you "won't be good – but careful' and I can hardly wait for you to come home. I don't quite mean I can hardly wait but I'm sure excited about the idea and will wait but very impatiently. Also I don't want you to be careful all your life when you return as Joan needs some competition but don't you think it would be nice to have at least a year just to ourselves before you have to adjust to a fussy temperamental pregnant woman again. This of course all depends on how long you are away because I'm slowly getting to be an old woman – all of 25 in November.

Am still having a quiet but restful time and it is usually peaceful but the odd flare-up creeps in as you can imagine. Am still drinking 3 to 4 bottles of beer a day – just for my health (?) and also with the idea to use up the supply but that seems a hopeless situation as the supply doesn't seem to dwindle.

Dad brought home $2.00 worth of 10 cent stamps and blue forms yesterday. Maybe he thinks I don't write up enough but then he lectured one on crowding the mails but I retaliated that I didn't care how crowded the mails got just as long as you received your mail.

Mrs. Williams[8] who looks after the Isolation Hospital comes in each day as Dad didn't want me to be doing the housework, which was rather nice of him although I didn't mind for awhile.

Irene came in from the lake on Sunday and went out again tonight, I only saw her twice so guess she was busy doing the washing and ironing. She sent you some cigarettes two weeks ago and so when they catch up with you should have a reserve. It is almost time for me to send you more too as I intend to send you 300 every week.

Have made arrangements to take my Mom & Pop to Pigeon for 2 weeks the end of August so that Dad can have a good rest. He really needs it.

Perhaps by now you will have been to Edinburgh and have seen the "Lochs" and the Scottish countryside. It is really pretty isn't it dear?

Joan is growing like a bad weed and by the end of the day I'm thankful that I'm not 5 months pregnant right now as Joan is so strong that it's all I can do to handle her in my present healthy condition.

Dad had condescended to scribble a wee note again so I'd better not start on a new theme and take up his allotted space.

That seems to be all for now so will sign off until Thursday.

Joan sends you barrels of wet kisses and big greasy hugs.

All my love, dearest, Peg

[Written by PF – partly illegible]

Dear Hamp,

The water passes under the bridge rapidly. You sound pessimistic but I am more or less optimistic. Mostly now trying to doll up the offices for you to come home to. We watch the 8 PM news, we watch 10 PM news and we listen for next 11 PM news when Elwen Phillpot does a good fool job as commentator. Please atril?? above cage. Come up and see me sometime, Love Dad

Just anessed up Hamp arul pyed Sh e me sometime b llu hurry. Dad

Dearest Peg,

Have nothing much to write about but am on duty tonight and it's raining as usual and I feel like talking to you. Got the parcel today – it was 4 films from Dad – the customs declaration was $1.35 and the postage on them was $4.70. It practically floored me to realize that each picture I snap costs 20 cents the way my photography goes – the estimate is conservative. Tell Paw not to throw his money around so much but I sure appreciate the films.

Today was quiet as usual. Received some new identification pictures today – they are the worst I have had so far and the ones I got at Lachine were really bad. Down there we passed through a room and on the way through somebody shouted "take off your hat" and while you were looking to see what was up, our picture was taken. In that one you could see a big ring around my forehead where my hat was – in this one there is a big smudge.

Am going to get the rolls of film developed this week – hope I get 2 or 3 good pictures out of them. Dad wrote today that he and Mac were too busy to take time to write letters – was tempted to tell him that it only takes 5 minutes but didn't. By the time this arrives you will probably be back from Camrose – hope you had a good time (and not too good with Mac and Irene – I don't approve of their parties). Ask your Mother is there is anything she might like over here that I could pick up and send – have still not written to her but will do so shortly (shame).

Didn't tell you (or did I) that Readers' Digest is coming and the first copy came 2 days ago – the July number – have read it once and put it away for rereading.

Sure wish I had the films for the York-Scarborough trip but will get more pictures from here on.

Well honey will close for tonight – all my love to yourself and share a little with our wonderful child. You had better start putting on a little weight and I'll try to lose a little. More love and kisses, Hamp

Dearest Peg,

As I sit here munching a "Sweet Marie" bar, I think what a wonderful wife is mine. Yes – today I got the parcel with 3 whodunits, candy, air mail forms, cookies, cheese and crackers, fruit juice, sliced oranges, peanuts, and coffee with all the fixings. Thanks very much again honey – it's really swell. I have now a fairly adequate stock of air mail forms so can discharge a few of my obligations re mail.

Have been fairly busy today with routine stuff keeping me going and the usual evening bicycle "prang" to keep me up with my needlework. It's a dull evening when somebody doesn't come in after falling off his bike or running into a doorway in the dark, etc Generally minor and nothing more serious than minor fractures – nose, radius, etc Tonight we are having a thunder storm with lightning and bags of rain – was going to go golfing tonight but glad that I didn't now because some of the boys came back soaked to the skin.

Doug is still away of course and won't be back for at least another week. I imagine he is enjoying himself as usual and Interruption: "Broadcast control calling! Broadcast control Calling! – It is now blackout time! It is now Blackout time! Message ends." That is the message that comes over the tannoy every night just about the time I write you. That is the loudspeaker system which is fitted up all over the camp (all buildings and outside) so that you can hear it no matter where you are. There are generally several messages over it every day and you more or less take it for granted now.

Jack Perverseff may be moved shortly. The PMO for our bomber group was through with a lot of ideas which Jack disagreed with and said so very loudly and firmly so it was intimated to him that he might be given the shove. However he and I have both decided that we have given up the idea of kissing anybody's (will say fanny adams) for the duration.

Well honey think I will stir me up some hot water and have a cup of good coffee with condensed milk (instead of powdered milk) in it and then retire and do a little bit of reading. Wish you were here so I could annoy you by eating crackers in bed. All my love to you, Hamp

Dearest Hamp,

Last night was my night to write but my routine was shattered by the wee daughter. Just when I thought I was free for the night she wakened up and no matter what I did she wouldn't go back to sleep. Even rocking didn't perform its magic trick so she was finally left to fight it out by herself after I worked an hour. She finally fell asleep at 10:30 PM so there wasn't much time to write particularly the way I felt when the ordeal was over. However today has been good and so we are on the best of terms again.

Dad took Joan and I down town today to buy Joan some toys. She ended up with a wooden duck, a horn and a weighted man that can't be knocked over because it springs right up again. It was a good haul for the wee tyke.

She has certainly got Dad where she wants him. She loves to crawl on his bed and climbs all over him – pulling his eye brows and moustache. At meal time she fusses until he takes her up on his knee and if she's crawling on the floor she stands up beside his chair and begs to be picked up. It's a good way to get the tasty bits and chew on the odd bone. So you see our daughter is really spoiled now.

I am quite sure she will have curly hair. Tonight it gives the idea that it is going to be curly. I hope so coz she looks more like a girl then. So many people stop me and say, "My isn't *he* sweet? How old is *he?* even when Joan is wearing a dress. Silly aren't they darling.

Dad has some more films to send you and we should get them off tomorrow. I think they will be sent by ordinary mail.

Perhaps by now you will have been to Edinburgh. Haven't had mail for 3 days now so I kind of think you may be in bonny Scotland. Of course that is nothing to go by but its fun trying to figure out where you might be.

Your sweater is coming along by leaps and bounds and is now 21 inches in length. Am almost at the neck – just 2 more inches – and then just have the front to do. Pretty good for 1 night's work eh darling?

Mrs. Laird and Mrs. Hannah are coming over for Bridge tonight and you can imagine how I'm looking forward to it, eh? However I'm beginning to see a wee speck of light about the game so there's hope yet. Bidding doesn't stump me now as much as it used to do. Still have a long way to go though!

It's very hot again and Joan is really getting quite a tan – looks funny with her blond hair.

Mrs. Norton is visiting Marg and Bill so guess they are busy.

That's all for now darling and will write tomorrow. Joan sends hugs and kisses. All my love, Peg

July 29, 1944

Dearest Peg,

Had a good day yesterday. Two letters from you and one from Mother. You seemed to be dashing pretty madly in preparation for your trip to Camrose – hope your stay there will be a pleasant change. Mother said that she had things more or less in shape to receive you.

Missed writing you last and night and am sorry. Last night Jack Watt (W/C in charge of accounts section here) got on our bikes and went up to see Merlin Hicks at the hospital at North Allerton. We rode about 12 miles up and 12 back. Imagine going that far and not thinking anything of it – my bicycling ability is beginning to amaze me. We had a few pints in the local pub and then went up to the mess at the hospital and sat around and met a few of the blokes there and had lunch and then came home. That is the place that handles most of our surgery, x-rays etc, so it is kind of nice to get in and see it occasionally. On the way back it was very dark and we had no lights and were feeling quite happy and had numerous prangs. But weren't travelling very fast so we only have minor bruises to show for it. Jack missed one corner and went flying through a hedge and his hat went off and we never did find it – also he ruined a pair of pants – all good fun though.

I have another head cold but not a bad one – just stuffy.

We have been very busy lately and have scarcely time to stop for lunch and have to spend most evenings puttering around sick quarters here. We are using penicillin for some of our cases now and that takes a little time since the injections are every 3 hours.

Got a parcel chit tonight and will collect it tomorrow if possible. Am out of cigarettes again but still have lots of tobacco so am doing OK.

Had quite a little party a couple of nights ago with the box. Started out with oranges, cheese and crackers, coffee with cream and sugar, cookies and a chocolate bar – quite a spread.

Well honey will sign off and write tomorrow and tell you what goes on. All my love, Hamp

45-July 30, 1944 Camrose

Dearest Hamp,

We're still in Camrose and still have a good rest. It has been raining almost continually since Friday night but that hasn't stopped us from doing anything.

Yesterday afternoon Mother, Joan and I were invited to Eileen Duggan's for tea and she called for us in Marg Hall's car. Marg is still in the East incidentally. It was quite a "do" and turned out to be a birthday party for Eileen's sister-in-law's son, D'Arcy, who was two. Just to side track for a moment Edna Scott – Eileen's sister-in-law – lost her husband awhile ago. They had been married 3 months when he went overseas in the RCAF so he never saw the baby. Besides Eileen, Edna and ourselves there were Gladys Duggan and her daughter, Mary Ellen, Edna Pratt (who is married to Jack Pratt – almost obviously but I understand Jack has a sister Edna too). Edna's mother, Mrs. Pearson, Mrs. Joe Duggan and her 9 month daughter a day older than Joan. She is hydrocephalic and really pitiful to see especially with Joan there bouncing around. However we had a good time and lots to eat – ice cream and angel food etc Joan behaved remarkably well and was *the* model child as usual.

Last night I worked on your sweater until 11 o'clock and now have only 11 inches to do until it's finished so we're getting along very well indeed – if I do say so myself.

We had roast chicken, potatoes, cabbage and custard today and as I've nearly starved since I've been here – in the usual Smith custom, I had two helpings and then went to bed with Joan at 2 PM and slept until 5.

Mac phoned then as he had just returned from the lake with family and Doris Johnson. They invited me for a steak at the York so went along and ate almost as much as the rest of them. Couldn't beat Mac and his 3 bowls of creamed onion soup, however.

I don't believe I told you of my episode with the bat – did I? It happened about 3 AM on my second night here that I was awakened by a swoosh and rapid fluttering followed by more swooshes. I lay on my back and listened for awhile and tried to figure out what it was. It came to my mind it was a bat so I pulled the covers tighter around me and lay listening intently. After 15 minutes of bat soaring over my head and me breaking out in a sweat whenever it skimmed my nose I mustered up enough courage to get up and put on a light and sure enough there was the ugly thing doing nose dives in my direction so I dove for the covers. This commotion aroused Joan and she sat up and grinned at me. So I mustered more courage and grabbed a towel to catch the beast and toss it out the window. I never did get the courage to really catch it, which I could have done, I'm ashamed to say. It finally flew in the closet so I slammed the door in a hurry. Thank goodness I'd left it open. Went back to bed and sweated for a few more minutes. How I hate bats! The funny thing is we couldn't find it next day so maybe it was a nightmare but I'd swear it was too realistic. I still love you an awful lot even though the bat took up all of this letter. All my love, darling – Peg

July 31, 1944

Dearest Peg,

Two things from you today – got a parcel of 1000 cigarettes which were extremely welcome and also got a very swell letter from you.

You and Joan had arrived in Camrose and seemed to be more or less getting settled own to the place. Hope that you enjoy it because I know Mother and Dad dote on yourself and the daughter and are more than happy when you come and sad when you leave. Hope you do gain a little weight – the beer won't do you any harm and Father enjoys having someone who keeps him company so you both are doing OK. (I guess you will be home again by the time you get this letter – yours was July 20).

I am certainly looking forward to getting the picture – I finally got a new glass on yours so you are restored to your place of honour again on the dresser.

Yesterday was a usual day so didn't have anything to write about. Went to bed about 7:30 with aspirins etc for my cold and read a whodunit and feel much better today. Really caught a honey of a cold coming back from North Allerton Friday night but it is practically gone now.

We are busy as usual – take lectures 2 hours a day now – have a bloke through who is organizing us and have a mountain rescue party. We have a lot of snap reading, navigation, evacuation of casualties etc. It is quite interesting but Jack Perverseff and I feel that we have quite enough to do without bothering about that – also we haven't any mountains about here to rescue people from. However the moors are pretty desolate so it may be of value. Also we have a bright yellow jeep to ride around in so that's one consolation.

Well honey, sure wish we were at home together. Miss you very much – keep remembering every little bit of you – how you look, talk etc. I don't get morbid about it but "you'll be so nice to come home to".

Well, all my love and kisses, Hamp

AUGUST 1944

46-August 1, 1944, Camrose

Dearest Hamp,

Well here it is – August, how time slips away and what I've done in the past months is hard to find. Am sort of existing and watching the time go by while I wait for you to come home. As I've said before having Joan was about one of the smartest things we've done as she certainly fills my days and gives me something to do continually.

Was down at Mac & Irene's last night for a change of scene. Mal and Doris Johnson dropped in after closing the store so we all played crazy eights, drank beer and had a good time – even if I was a gooseberry. Got home about 1 AM and found I had quite a "buzz" on but managed to get to bed and sleep it off. Today was rather lazy as Joan and I slept for 3 hours again this afternoon.

Did Joan's washing at Smith Jr's today as the Calgary Power were installing an electric-coal stove which Pa bought for the house so he wouldn't have to fuss with the fires in the mornings. Ha! Ha! Ma of course is very pleased but is worried about cooking 20 pound turkeys without cutting off the legs so she talked until the old stove was set up in the basement. She'll give that idea up though when she gets used to the new stove.

Dad is seriously considering going to the Coast for a week or so to get away from things and Mac can hardly wait for him to go so that he can sneak off for a couple of days or so.

Mac had an interesting case today – an old man with a mesenteric thrombosis so Mac removed 10 feet of bowel and gives the fellow 1 chance in 100 to recover. Second case this year of same nature.

Was speaking about bonds to Dad today and it reminded him of a letter he had received from some place – Claresholm I guess – about sending your bond to him. I said you had written to them to send it to me so Dad told me to keep hands off but to remind him to write. He says he'll put it in his safety deposit box so I guess its six of one and half a dozen of another. As long as he writes it makes no matter to me but for the moment I saw red through green eyes of the monster – jealousy I guess.

Margaret wrote Ma a very funny letter today I thought, about how she was a heathen princess for doing David's washing on Sunday and picking peas from the garden. Mrs. Norton is visiting her as I've told you before I think. Marg says she's really a swell person but you and I know how ma-in-laws can rile us up the wrong way at times.

Have kind of slowed down on your sweater the last two days and have only done 2 inches which leaves 9" to do which isn't so very bad. It however is far from a perfect GI issue but it should be warm and is definitely something for you to wrap around yourself – as you put it.

Joan has at last cut her molar. It hasn't bothered her of late but she's very proud of her effort. She looks as though she's gained quite a bit since coming here and your skinny wife has gained six pounds so guess I'll continue my rest period when I go home. It must be the real McCoy.

The war news is very good but am not overly optimistic and no matter how long you're away, I'll still be awaiting and a' loving you. All my love, Peg

P.F. writes on top – Cheerio, Dad

Dearest Hamp,

Such a very good day after 1 letter last week – 5 today such luxury I calls it. They were written on July 21, 23, 24, 25 & 26. You rather excelled yourself there honey and such interesting letters too. I read parts of them to Dad and almost all of them to Mother. We certainly think a lot of "our Hampie".

Was glad you got another parcel as I was worried for fear it was in the carload of mail that was burned the middle of June but Lady Luck seems to be on our side. The cookies in that box were terrible and I kick myself for sending them every time I think of it. If you can't eat them darling feed them to the pigs. They seem to be close enough so you could toss them (the cookies) from your window.

Scarborough sounds like a pretty place the way you described it and I certainly wish I could have seen it with you. That is one place I didn't see – also nearly all the towns you write about.

Was down at Mac and Irene's last night and we were invited over to Gus and Grace's. We went but had made up our minds to come home early. Had two beers apiece and then came home. Quite good I thought from all the rumors I've heard about them.

Today went downtown with Irene while she paid her bills. Bought Joan a new pair of white boots – leather this time. She won't be able to wear them for a few months but they'll be swell for when she is walking on her own and I couldn't find any in Edmonton that were any good. Also bought three large tubes of Palmolive Shaving Cream and a tin of Yardley's Talc for my dear husband. Got it at Camrose Drug – cheap with the discount.

About buying something for me-can't think what it would be, but if you saw some cute things made from brass or pewter – like small kettles or beer mugs – that we could have in our home it would be swell. You couldn't risk sending china but would be good too. Any old thing even a book of scenes as long as it's from you dear would be just the thing.

Am going to start making covers for dressers and tables etc. this

211

winter as we haven't any really decent ones and we'll be needing them some day soon I hope when we have our wee home. Eh honey?

Dad couldn't find the letter he received from Claresholm so I told him to write to Kennedy so he did – today.

Had a letter from Doris B. and they are anxious for me to go to Claresholm soon as Doris is afraid Bill may be posted. Granville, Lantel Harris (both of them) and Apperly have been posted overseas. Larry had the measles while they were in the East. I think I'll work in five days with them before going to Banff. Figure I could leave Edmonton on a Wednesday and stay in Claresholm to Monday and then meet Kay in Calgary on Monday and go to Banff. Sounds OK to me and like a real good holiday.

Joan is certainly growing into a regular demon. She sits in the high chair borrowed from Mrs. Laird between Dad and me and watches him while he eats as he occasionally slips her a spoonful of egg or fruit juice etc. She just follows the spoon from plate to mouth and it's funny to watch her mouth open and close. She's also very noisy now and jabbers away at the top of her lungs as though she were talking – but it must be Chinese. She emphasizes things at times with Tarzan yells and a real good old raspberry which I taught her. What a mother eh? Everyone within 10 feet gets sprayed. Today she stood up by herself for a couple of minutes without touching anything and when she discovered she was on her own she just stood there and howled, too scared to bend her knees and sit down. She's sure a cute little trick and as I've said before we'll have to have others so you can see for yourself how cute they can be. Here's hoping all the rest are like Joan as she is one in a million. That seems to be all for now. Joan sends bas (as you would say) of hugs and kisses.

All my love, darling – Peg

August 3, 1944

Dearest Peg,

Another two days have slipped by and very little to report.

Have been quite busy and manage to keep my days pretty well filled. Yesterday afternoon took an hour off and got out in the jeep. An army bloke was up from London supervising our mountain rescue business and wanted some eggs so we ran out about 5 miles and back and managed to scrounge a couple of dozen for him, and incidentally I got a little fresh air. Last night Bill Scott and I took a whirl on our bikes for about half an hour and scrounged a dozen for ourselves and so we are doing OK. Haven't had any eggs for almost 10 days now so it will be a change.

Jack Perverseff went to London today for a 48 so I'm kind of stuck for the next couple of days. It isn't so bad except for the paper work. On the average day you see 60 or 80 people and answer the phone a hundred times and can cope with that but the trouble is that nearly everyone you see has to have about 3 forms filled out on him, so it keeps you occupied.

The weekend I may go to a nearby station and relieve the MO there and since it is generally quiet over there I will get caught up on correspondence etc. The weekend after that I hope to go to Edinburgh but won't make any definite plans until I see how things pan out.

Haven't taken any more pictures but have some being developed and should get them away some time next week – hope they turn out OK.

We had sunshine this afternoon for about 4 hours and it was very lovely. Haven't seen the sun for about 4 days now.

The writing is very bad in this letter but the ink is poor and I have a hard job making it flow (ahem!).

When I left home I thought I was through with air cadets but it was a fond hope too good to be true – over here we have ATC Cadets who visit the stations in the summer. So we have just as many bellyaches etc. to worry about from a bunch of young buggers. Time out. A bicycle prang just arrived. Probably a fracture, in the wrist but nothing serious – nobody every gets hurt but they provide amusement for the evening.

Well honey, goodbye for now. Pardon the drivel but am not doing anything to write about. Give my love to the daughter and bags of kisses to yourself. All my love, Hamp

Dear Peg,

Another two days have drifted by and nothing to report. Have been quite busy since Jack is not back from London yet. I imagine he is having trouble with trains since they are so crowded these days. Quite frequently you go to the station and are unable to get on. That is, unless he has been bombed. Doug should be back this weekend and I'll be glad to have him do some of the bumph for awhile.

Have had to stick pretty close lately and so haven't been able to enjoy the beautiful sunshine today. It is really a perfect summer's day. There is a big cleanup campaign on the station and everyone in their spare time is out cutting grass and digging etc. It's making a big improvement in the appearance of the place but it won't last long.

Hope to get some more mail tomorrow but haven't much to base my hope on.

Had a little trouble in the mess a couple of weeks ago but have finally gotten it straightened out. One of the boys got drunk and decided somebody had stolen something of his. So he went and got a revolver and loaded it and started to look for the guilty party. Since he was waving it about a bit I figured that as duty M.O. I didn't want to see anyone shot. Took it away from him after a bit and was quite unpopular for awhile but finally got things squared away and the person affected decided it was rather dangerous and returned the gun to the armament station. He had a couple of nights previously, fired off a few shots at nothing in particular so was open for court martial if anyone saw him, so my creating a scene didn't help him much. However we got it hushed up so it's OK now.

The war news in W.E. is certainly looking good these days. Hope it lasts – eh honey! This thing might wind up sooner than one might expect – certainly hope so. I think it likely though that Jerry will give quite a decisive last gasp, so we won't be too optimistic as to time.

Have still got some letters to write to get caught upon my mail – Margaret, Mother, your Mother – will get caught up over the weekend I hope.

Imagine that you are complaining of the heat over there now – wish we were together at the beach for a few days with Joan – it would certainly be grand. Am curious to know how things are going in Camrose – about Mac and Irene and the nephews and Pa's garden and the neighbors – be sure to send me all the gossip.

Well honey, will sign off and write you tomorrow and try to say a little more. Sure miss you – you are the star actor in my dreams. Well give the very best to daughter Joan from her old man. All my love, Hamp

Postcard of cathedral – Boorham Bar, York

Dear Peg,

York Minster is in the background. Very picturesque city but I'll trade you for Edmonton and throw in London to balance the deal. Forgot to mail this from York.

Love, Hamp

August 5, 1944

Dearest Peg,

Two letters from you today and they were both more than welcome – both were written on July 23 and one was blue mail and the other ordinary – pretty good service. The pictures of you and Joan were really swell. I had almost lost the ability to picture in my mind how beautiful my wife was – the pictures certainly were good. Certainly think a lot of you honey and as time goes by it seems hard to realize that anyone like yourself could be my own wife – I don't deserve the good fortune – but accept it.

After I wrote you last night was quite busy for awhile – had a bicycle prang who lit on both knees, both hands and then on his face. By the time I got through with my needlework it was quite late. Jack Peverseff got back from London last night – was glad to get back to the quiet of Yorkshire after the buzzers.

Today I am over relieving Bill Carter while he is on a 48 – it's a beautiful sunshiny day and I have nothing to do over here so am just taking it easy. Am looking foreword to next weekend for I really intent to go to Edinburgh and hope to have a good time sightseeing and will try to get some pictures – hope the weather will be good.

On the way over here today stopped at a farm and got a bag of apples – some are pretty green and they will probably be productive of quite a bellyache but they certainly taste good.

Was just comparing your present pictures of one I have of you and Doris walking down the wood in Claresholm in your slacks – you look a lot thinner (and that's not because you were having a slight touch of pregnancy in Claresholm) – you'll have to start building yourself up honey. Don't stay too long in Camrose Peg if they haven't got help – you don't want to be magnanimous and stay to help because they'll always get someone and you have quite enough to do, looking after that tornado of ours. Joan looks cuter every day. Would certainly like to hold her just for a minute (if she'd stay still that long).

Mac is as busy as usual I suppose – wish he would write sometime but I guess I can't expect letters if I don't write them.

Well honey that is about all I have to report for the present. Am going outside and sit and soak up the sunshine – had a very unusual case today (the first in 71 years in Yorkshire) – a bad case of sunburn.

Well goodbye for now. All my love, Hamp

48-August 5, 1944, Camrose

Dearest Hamp,

Another two days has gone since I wrote and haven't very much to write about but will start and see what the mind can produce.

We had a very quiet day yesterday after Dad got away to Edmonton – for the day. Mac and he had a ligation of the ileum, four tonsils and 2 emergency appendices, the last one at 1 P.M. so dad was quite peeved as he had planned to leave for the big city with Jack Moxness. Dad's car was being checked over so that's why he took a lift. Was quite busy getting Dad off – brushing his hat, removing spots from his suit and generally standing by while he kept Mac waiting in the yard for him. Everyone was quite disturbed for awhile especially me as I had started dinner of round steaks and hash brown potatoes. They were quite cold

216

when I got time to eat. However we all did what we wanted in the afternoon and evening and quite enjoyed ourselves. Knit on your sweater in the afternoon and then sat with Irene while Mac went to Roundhill and Armena.

Dad picked up a black and white Springer spaniel which Irene had asked for before it was born and brought it home for Frankie and Allen. It is a cute little thing. Someday I hope we can have a dog too.

Joan is still cutting the same molars one on each side at the top. The right one got a head of the left but the gum caught up with it so we had to cut the tooth all over again. Now both are just breaking through the surface but Joan has been good – a slight diarrhea and slightly sleepy but otherwise OK and she still eats like a Smith so she can't be very upset. She seems to be changing quite a lot lately and to me she isn't a wee baby anymore. When I look at her now I wonder why she isn't walking and talking as she almost looks about the size that do. However she's trying hard and yesterday looked right at me when she wanted her supper and said "Ma ma". It sure gives you a queer feeling. She's really a person now and she reacts the way you do. She gets lonesome every once in a while and if she is crawling she comes up to my chair stands on her feet and tries to get up in my lap so she can have a bit of loving and believe me she gets it. She pulls off her wanting to love act at night sometimes so she can sleep with me. Hope she grows out of that eh honey?

Interruption – Have been down town with Irene and then had supper. Mother got the postcard of the Abbey today and Dad had a letter yesterday so everyone is happy.

Flash from the Smith Jrs. The little pup is call "Bill" after Bill Norton because he chose him from the litter. Wonder if Bill will be flattered. The pup is cute though with long floppy ears and dark sorrowful eyes.

There isn't much news. I could write reams about my impressions and ideas I've formed while being here but less said the better. It has been quite difficult at times. But less said about that the better so forget I mentioned anything. All our love, kisses and hugs, darling, Peg

August 6, 1944

Dearest Peg,

A very quiet day so am just writing to let you know I am still around. Have done nothing at my relief station since I arrived. Slept in until 9:00 this morning and then saw 9 on sick parade and finished for the day. After that I fried an egg on the hot plate here and had a cup of tea and then sat for two hours waiting for dinner. It was very misty until about 11:00 and then the sun has come out producing a gorgeous summer day. I looked about for Eddie Oldring but he had been posted to a flying unit for training. He may end back up in bomber command but wants to fly something different from heavy bombers so may not.

Find that this is quite a station – there are two parks within its limits. The airfield itself is build near a village and then the rest of the buildings all dispersed up to a mile in all directions – so that there is a village inside, farms etc. – some of the airmen even complain that it annoys them to have the farmers chasing their chickens through the barrack blocks. I'm surprised that the hens survive with the meat supply what it is.One of the boys ended up at sick quarters with a bunch of green pears. They were quite soft so between them and the green apples I finally did manage to achieve the belly ache I was afraid was impending.

Imagine that you are complaining of the heat still and am just beginning to imagine what it must be like.

The war news is wonderful with Brest falling etc. – we may be home sooner than we think – but I am not being too optimistic.

Well honey, goodbye for now. Give my love to Joan – don't let her forget she has an old man.

All my love, Hamp

Camrose, Alberta, August 8, 1944

My Dearest Hamp,

Just a wee note in the parcel. I haven't written to you for four days now, but will have had all my explanations and apologies by the time you receive this.

The parcel is from all of us as we all had a share in it. Ma baked the

218

short-bread and cookies (don't see how they'll be whole on arrival) –
and sent the lobster; Dad sent the tomato juice and cheese; Joan
fingerprinted the shortbread (look for one marked "Dad" and wrapped
separately); and I sent the rest and packed the box but Dad is paying for
it. So you see we are all united in one purpose whether Ma and Pa realize
it or not. Guess we have one on them eh honey?

Have had 3 beers and am quite groggy as its 11:30 P.M. but am
going down to the office to weigh it and then finish the wrapping so
will say "Goodnight", my dearest, dearest one. (And it isn't the beer).

All my love, Peg

48-August 9, 1944

Dearest Hamp,

Joan and I are again at home and how we arrived and what we've
done for the past few days will be disclosed as you read. A silly letter
form don't you think, honey?

Monday was my night to write to you but I didn't get a chance as I
was on the run in the afternoon and had been in bed all morning and at
night sat with Irene while Mac was at Kinsmen's. Also I was not in the
right mood to write as I might have written the wrong things about
Camrose. Spent all day Sunday pretty close to bed as I got the curse in
the morning and had terrific cramps so retired and slept most of the day
and Mrs. Williams – matron at Isolation who was looking after us during
the day – looked after Joan. It was quite a luxury to rest and read, or
smoke, or sleep. It's wonderful and I can recommend it. Sunday night
the new maid arrived. She seems as though she'd suit Ma but she's a
Catholic so she may not last long.

Tuesday afternoon Irene, Joan and I went over to Doris Johnson's
(Mal's wife) for tea. The Johnson's all asked to be remembered to you.
We had a nice quiet time and Joan behaved par excellence and only wet
on the rug once. Not bad, eh honey? Tuesday night went down to Mac's
to listen for the phone while Irene was out for an hour and when I got
home Joan was crying her heart out and Ma and the maid couldn't
handle her. She stopped as soon as I came home but wouldn't go to
sleep until 10:30 P.M. so felt as though I couldn't write a witty letter so

packed a box for you instead. It was election day yesterday and Social Credit went in and CCF got left far behind. Dad was quite merry and insisted that he drive me to the office to weigh the parcel. I didn't think it was such a good idea but went along anyhow. It took us 15 minutes to get out on the lane in the right angle and then dad drove on the wrong side of the road. Just in front of the office he almost clipped out a couple of cars parked on the west side of the road – we were going north – but managed to turn in time and just about hit a car traveling south which had to go way over to the east curb as dad did not slow down. When we finally parked at the curb Dad exclaimed "Crazy fool, driving on the wrong side of the road. You can never tell what's going to happen on election night." – talking about the other fellow of course. Well I thought I'd die laughing – it was just too funny. But got your parcel weighed, packed and weighed again and away so there' more eats for you honey and a couple of "whodunits". Parcel supplied by Ma, Pa and me.

Happy and Mildred Hailes have bought a house on Main Street. The people who owned it before apparently thought they were some one – so Mac & Irene say. Maybe you can figure out who they were, the name has slipped away from me. John Hills has been discharged from the RCAF due to sinus trouble and was home for a couple of days over the weekend. Talked to him for quite a while when he was at the house and he is down on the RCAF and talks loudly of his treatment while in the Force. He is waiting for his discharge papers from #4 Training Command. I rather gathered he liked to talk and thought quite a lot of Johnnie Hills. Perhaps I'm wrong but you would know.

Got a drive up this afternoon with Mal and Doris as they were going to the races. Figured it would be better than the train and also delivery right to the door which was what I really wanted instead of traveling by street car. Joan stood the car ride very well and squealed most of the way at the cows and horses. Then she became tired and fell asleep. She doesn't remember anything about our place at all so I'll have to break her in again. That's the worst of moving about. Got two letters from you today – the last one written on August 4th. That's wonderful isn't it – only five days. Hope your cold has gone honey.

All my love, dearest – Peg

August 9, 1944

Dear Peg,

Am away behind in my correspondence and will now apologize and explain. I didn't write Monday night because I had nothing to write about and last night was unable to do so – so am writing tonight.

Doug came back from London on Monday night and in the meantime his posting came and he was to leave yesterday. He was delayed and got away this morning. Last night I helped him pack and then we went down to the bar and had quite a few beers and then came over to sick quarters and had some eggs and a can of spam. By then it was quite late so I rolled into bed. Doug's posting should take him out of the country in a week or two. He had a very good course in London and I imagine that it will stand him in good stead.

Have had very good luck with mail – got 3 letters on Monday and one today – all from Camrose. (one of them from you was a kind of P.S. you tacked on Ma's letter). The one today was July 30 – so that's pretty good.

You seem to be having a quiet time at home what with drinking beer and so on – hope Father isn't too much of a trial to you – you'll have to go some to keep ahead of him in the consumption of fluids. Hope your D.T.'s settle down honey and you don't get too many more bats flying around the room in the middle of the night.

Am really looking forward to the 48 this weekend. Johnnie Hunt is going to come so it should be very nice. I haven't been off the station for some days so am getting a little fed up – periodically you get brassed off and fed up but fortunately it doesn't last. I hope the war news continues to be good.

There is a new M.O. coming tonight – will let you know who he is tomorrow. I hope that he's easy to get along with because I am becoming more difficult to please and he will be rooming with me.

Well honey that's about all there is to write about except that I miss you an awful lot. You're going to find me sticking very close to your apron strings when we get together again – Joan will no doubt get quite jealous. Will write tomorrow for sure. All my love, Hamp

221

Dear Peg,

Another day gone and very little to report. Not too busy these days but manage to keep puddling along. Am leaving tomorrow morning (Friday) and won't be back until Sunday night late so may get behind in my letter writing. Will write in Edinburgh and mail on Sunday morning and may keep up that way.

Our new M.O. arrived – an F/O – a strange creature in the RCAF these days. He just enlisted over in England. He went to school in Edinburgh and has been over here since 1937. He finished about 18 months interning and then joined the Air Force for some unknown reason. Very nice chap called Hugh McKay – his home is in Vancouver.

I'm certainly looking forward to the trip tomorrow. Have been a little browned off lately and the trip should be a pleasant change. Johnnie Hunt is going with the dentist from his station and is taking a later train and we will meet him there.

We should have quite a nice weekend since Bill Scott is the only one who has been there before and we others will be real tourists. I'm going to try to get a number of pictures and hope they turn out OK. Am getting the others back from Harrogate this weekend and I hope that they were successful.

I'm curious to know when Doug Ritchie leaves the country – it should be fairly soon but he may hang around for weeks. It would be a nice trip to fly.

Hugh McKay is rooming with me now and I imagine we will get along well if he can stand me.

As I look in front of me cogitating I see a calendar of Hugh's showing a scene – Bow River Valley, Canadian Rockies – with a portion of the Banff Golf course shown. I can just see us chugging through it now – in old Alice – with both of us wondering if it will get us home and me wondering if it is too rough for Junior. Happy days we will have to repeat sometime (with Junior beside us next time).

Well honey will sign off and get this in the mail and then start getting ready for the big trip. Sure wish we were doing it together. Give my love to our charming daughter and bags of love to yourself from your ever loving husband. All my love, Hamp

Dearest Peg,

Well, have arrived in Edinburgh and have spent about 9 hours walking in it.

We got on the train at Thirsk about 9:20 and got in Edinburgh about 1:45. We immediately proceeded to find a place to eat and after waiting half an hour we managed to set some sausages and mashed and scones with jam on them. Bill and I are along incidentally – Johnnie Hunt was held up and couldn't come because the other M.O. developed an attack of renal colic early this morning and was laid up.

After eating we started down Princess Street to the Officers' Club which was making our arrangements for accommodations. The sun came out and it was a gorgeous afternoon and the castle really showed up in all its glory and the park below it. We decided to do some shopping on the way because Bill wanted some golf clothes. We got him a nice jacket for about 2L 10s and then looked for a sports shirt – finally found a checked woolen shirt for the reasonable sum (this will slay you) of 48 shillings – what is more, he bought it.

We then proceeded to the club and found that they had arranged that we stay in a small hotel – got our bags in there and then proceeded to do more shopping. We shopped for an hour and a half and didn't see much – have got one or two things lined up to get for you tomorrow – then went and had tea and then it being 6:00 we went to the Club and had 2 beers and then it was 7:00 so we had dinner and then we went for a walk.

Walked through the park below the castle – in one part of it there was a military dance band playing and open air dancing and in the other side was a bunch of girls doing the Highland fling. Walked up out of there past the flower clock – it was quite interesting to see the dial and hands made of flowers and the correct time being told by it. I imagine that you saw it when you were here. We then walked up the hill to the Royal Mill. There was a guide talking to a bunch of people and was on the street just leading to the esplanade of the castle. We tagged along and it was very interesting – Bobbie Burns Home, the cannon balls embedded in the wall of the old building facing the castle. It was quite interesting to stand on a bit of Nova Scotia outside the gates of the

Castle and hear the history of how one of the Scottish Kings sprinkled a bit of Nova Scotian soil there and then made people Barons of Nova Scotia for a price and so kept his finances more or less square. We had to beat it to see if Hunt came on the train – he didn't – so we had 2 more beers at the Club and walked home and I am writing this in the hotel. Will start out early tomorrow again and will write about what we do. All my love, Hamp

51 (?)

Dearest Hamp,

Well we are back to our old routine now with Joan as usual cock of the roost.

I forgot to tell you last time (and how could I forget?) I wrote that last Tuesday while I was still in Camrose I got a letter from Arbroath, Scotland from a lawyer stating that I had been left £100 pounds sterling free of government tax "in a will by a great aunt of mine on Dad's side. My great aunt died on June 30th and all Dad's sisters got £200 and the daughters (grand nieces like myself) all got £100 (that is Elaine at the coast, Winnie and Netta here – & Ethel in Calgary) so guess we did all right. The money will arrive when the estate is settled. A nice little nest egg, eh darling? It will certainly help my bank account which doesn't leap ahead very quickly. On the other hand however and thinking it over I guess we're doing OK. By the end of next month we'll have 3 more $50 bonds making a total of $400 in bonds as Dad insists on giving me back the equivalent that he borrowed.

In the savings account we have $157. This is not so very good but then we're paying out each month on bonds some of the money which will be going into the account later and too there is always something to pay for which I hadn't counted on. So all in all I think we are doing pretty well – if I do say so myself.

Maw has sure been busy around the house. The bathroom has a new coat of paint and new linoleum and Ma's bedroom has been kalsomined; the verandah has been painted and the outside doors varnished so we fairly glisten in the sun. Quite an improvement however.

Alix and Betty Starke came over last night and we had a so called lesson in "bridge" from a book of Alix's. It was a three-handed game and so a little bit difficult although I taught them the 3 handed method.

Sandra was in the hospital for a week with an abscess in her ear so Alix got a good rest as she was beginning to look as though she didn't sleep nights which was quite true. However Sandy wasn't very sick and is home now.

Got a letter from you yesterday dated July 31st. It must have been held up somewhere for I got 2 letters on Wednesday dated Aug. 2 and 4th. Was glad you got your cigarettes when you were needing them. There are 4 – 300 orders on the way too. Three orders from me and one from Mac and Irene – all ordered about a week apart so when they start you can rely on a fairly continuous stream of cigarettes. Also glad you are getting the Readers' Digest at last. It will be something to read and look forward to.

So far we haven't lost a letter, parcel or order so guess we're doing OK eh honey?

Your sweater is finished so will get it off next week after I've been down town and shopped around. This is your birthday present but as you may need it long before October 28 I'm sending it along as soon as it is ready. It won't arrive until the end of September I don't think. Sure hope you don't freeze before it arrives.

Sent some shaving cream and talc from Camrose or did I tell you, dear? Any how it's on the way.

Went to see "The Lodger" tonight with Alix. It was very good and quite a thriller. I had read the book though and that rather spoiled the show for me.

Joan goes to see Dr. Leitch tomorrow for her last inoculation so will write you all about it then.

Sure hope your cold has subsided, darling. I hate to think of you in that damp country so finish off the war and come home fast. I sure love you and miss you terribly. All my love, dearest Peg

Letter from Arbroath, July 15 6:45 P.M: Addressed to Edmonton and readdressed to Camrose, from the firm of Clark Oliver, Dewar & Webster dated July 14, 1944

Dear Madam,

Trust of Mrs. Georgina B. Bell and Mrs. Annie H. McTaggart

We regret to inform that Mrs. Georgina Balfour Bell, sometime of 3 Dalhousie Place, Arbroath, and late of 1 Rose Street, Arbroath, died on 30th June.

We are instructed by the trustees acting under her sister Mrs. Annie Hood McTaggart, who resided at 3 Dalhousie Place, Arbroath, and who died on 5th January 1933, to intimate to you that there is bequeathed to you by the Trust Disposition and Settlement a legacy of £100 sterling free of government duties.

We shall communicate with you again when the trustees are in a position to make payment of your legacy.

We are,

Yours faithfully,

Clark, Oliver, Dewar, Webster

51 (?)-August 13, 1944

Dearest Hamp,

Am all confused as to the number of the letter as I gave mother two stamps and that rather throws out my count. You see I keep track of the number of the letter by counting my stamps. Easily done as I always buy 10 at a time and I can remember the letters are in the thirties or forties or fifties so I just count the number of stamps used from the 10 and that give me the number of the letter. Very simply, don't you think, darling? A £100 reward for the right answer. All you have to do is solve the problem write a rhyme and send in the entry form. "— – Pardon me while I change the daughter's pants. Interruptions do happen sometimes but we are back again. – My last letter was written on Friday, August 11th. Didn't know the date at time writing and forgot to put it on.

Yesterday Joan went to see Dr. Leitch for her last dose of W.C. and Dip. She is 29 inches long and weighs 19 1/2 lb. – a gain of 1 pound in 4 weeks so we're doing OK. Dr. Leitch callers her "The Streamliner" because 29" is what she should be at 13 months of age. Do you think

226

we could have an amazon in our midst, honey? But Joan is 100% healthy so we have nothing to worry about so far.

Margaret phoned yesterday and invited us over for tea so Bill picked Ma, Joan and I up at Dr. Leitch's office and we went out. Mrs. Norton was still there but leaves on Monday for Seattle much to Margaret's relief. Didn't really get to know Mrs. Norton but my opinion is that she is rather narrow-minded and definitely for good old Ontario. This however is just between you and me. David is at last on formula. He wasn't doing very well but you couldn't tell Margaret that. She has changed a lot since David arrived and has to be handled with gloves on. I imagine she will recover now as she really didn't have much of a chance what with visitors and all. Don't be too shocked when I say that David has only gained 1 pound since he left the hospital. He now weighs 7 lb. 15 oz. but should pick up rapidly. The whole affair has been rather unfortunate and left Margaret a trifle bitter but I think all will change now if Margaret can get a rest. I'm all for bottle fed babies believe me, darling! Margaret really does look a whole lot more rested than before I went to Camrose so when Ma Norton goes she'll be able to have a good rest.

Ma phoned Margaret from Camrose this morning to say that Dad had left for Vancouver with Allen and Frankie at 6 A.M. Mal Johnson drove them to Edmonton to catch the 8:45 A.M. CNR. train. We haven't heard from them so guess they caught it. I'll bet the boys are two excited kids eh honey?

Finished up a roll of film today so will get it developed and sent to you before we leave for the lake. We are going to Pigeon some time towards the weekend for two weeks depending on the weather. It has been wet and cold the last week and the nights almost feel frosty. The Northern Lights were out last night so maybe we are in for a long cold winter. At any rate it is heading for a cold two weeks at Banff come the end of September but the good bracing air should do me good. Kay and I are going alone now as the other girl had to take her holidays sooner than planned. However we should have a good time biking, swimming and canoeing besides eating and sleeping.

Joan is getting to be a very determined young lady. As Dad says "Between the Smith will and the Smalley won't, Joan definitely will do or won't which is uppermost in her mind". If you take her away from something she wants to do she doesn't hesitate to show her disapproval by letting out a yell. It's really quite funny but me thinks it will lead to trouble some day. That's all for now as it's time for Joan's bath. Big hugs and kisses from Joan and I. All my love, dearest – Peg

August 13, 1944

Dearest Peg,

Am now returning from Edinburgh and really had a glorious weekend – as you can guess we kind of stretched our 48 from Fri. AM to Sun PM making 2 1/2 days in Edinburgh. On Saturday morning we got up by 8:00 and got on our way – went shopping first and I managed to get something for you and hope that I can get it to you OK.

About 10:00 AM we headed for the Castle and spent until 12:30 wandering through it. It was really very interesting to see and I managed to get quite a number of pictures of the city from it. The war memorial at the castle was really impressive. After "doing" the castle we went to lunch at the Officers Club and then dashed over to the university area. Went around the Friars Abbey and to the Royal Infirmary etc. and then it was tea time so we went back to the Officers Club and Bill phoned some people who had befriended him when he was there on leave 6 mos. ago. The invited us up for tea – they were a medical student and his wife – he is finishing this year. They were a grand couple and live in a flat with her parents. Their name is Mather. We had a lovely tea and then Mrs. Mather's brother arrived. His name is Noel and he is a Captain in the Royal Scots who was with the 8th Army all the way across North Africa and finally sent home from Sicily with a leg full of shrapnel. He was an awful lot of fun – quite young and very dashing. After tea they took us on the tram (double-decker) to a golf course on the edge of the city and we climbed a high hill and could see the whole city with the First of Forth and the Forth Bridge – took more pictures. After that Bill and I took the two Mathers and Noel Littlefair to dinner at the Officers Club. After that we had a few drinks and sat around and then broke up and went to our homes since we arranged to start out early today (Sunday).

This morning we got up at 7 AM and got going by 8:00. Went down to the Officers Club where we had left our cameras and then went out and got some more pictures. At 10:00 we met the Mathers and Noel and got the bus and after half an hour ride arrived at the Forth Bridge. It was a glorious morning. So we got on the ferry and went across the Forth and back below the bridge – it really is quite a structure.

After that we came back to Hawes' Inn which is beneath the bridge and had lunch. A very good lunch too with good lager to go with it. After lunch we started on our travels again.

Well honey will continue in my next letter. Certainly wish you were with me and miss you. I envy the Mathers but not too much because they aren't us (in other words you are better looking). All my love, Hamp

52-August 15, 1944

Dearest Hamp,

The summer is certainly going very quickly. It's quite cold and rainy and miserable most days and so because of this I've decided not to go to the lake as it would be no fun for Joan or myself. Mother and Dad are going so it will really be a holiday for both of us. My holidays don't really start until the 10th of September when Kay and I are going Banff. We have decided to go there for a week or 10 days depending on the weather and then Kay wants to go to Nanton for a few days and I want to go to Claresholm to Doris and Bill so everything seems to be working out just right. Had Kay over for supper last night and we got all excited about where to stay, what clothes to take etc. & etc. It will be the first time either of us have gone with another girl. Kay has always gone with her family and me too until we were married. Bet this holiday won't measure up to the one we had last year, eh honey? No holiday could unless we were both together.

Got two letters for you today – August 9 & 10 and you were all pepped up about your Edinburgh jaunt. Hope you had a nice time and good weather but I'll know all about it before you get this letter.

Was rather surprised at Doug's posting and yet nothing is a surprise any more. I would gather that Doug is heading for warmer climes and if he goes in the right direction he should meet Fred Day – who by the way is still in the same place and working hard. He had an opportunity to be an anesthetist and got his majority but after considering decided he liked what he was doing even if he was the only Captain around.

Went downtown today to do my banking and shop around. Managed to save $80 plus $27 on the bonds last month. Pretty good eh? Should go to Camrose more often. Oh yes paid my board and room at home too – figured I could afford it and anyway if I were in a rented room I'd have to pay whether we were there or not. Bought 10 pounds of sugar to show my appreciation to your Ma and Pa – just so we wouldn't appear to be scrounging all the time.

While downtown I saw some flannelette pajamas and so pounced on them for you. Hope they keep you warm. Am sending off your sweater and stuff tomorrow. It is really your birthday present but felt you wouldn't mind if it arrived a month early as it is something you can use. The sweater is a trifle big – a bit long I think but then your shoulders may take it up. Mac thinks I should knit a detachable crotch to go with it. Let me know if you want one honey and I'll start a-knitting again.

That seems to be all for now. The war news sure is good and do we hope it will be over soon!

Notice you took aspirin for your cold. Can you get 222 or 292? If not let me know, honey.

We send great hugs and kisses. All my love, dearest – Peg

Monday August 15, 1944

Dearest Peg,

Well have gotten back to the station but have not done a great deal of work. Didn't get back until 6:00 Am today so am not too ambitious. Wrote on the train last night so I hope you could read the letter OK. Was telling you that we spent Sun. morning (yesterday) at the Forth Bridge. After lunch we went down to a naval hospital where this medical student knew a bloke. He showed us around the place we were quite interested. After that we went back to town for tea – Mrs. Mather's mother (Mrs. Littlefair) had spent the afternoon cooking. The previous afternoon I had made a remark about Scottish shortbread – so she made some and used up some (a lot) of her precious butter – it was really delicious but I felt quite guilty. Also she made scones on the griddle and they also were something to write home about with red current jelly etc. After that we left and went down to the train with Noel – the Captain in the Royal Scots and saw him away and then got our bags and got on the train at 7:30 PM. Changed at York at 1:30 AM and got the train out of there at 4:00 AM. We were really exhausted when we got back and I don't expect that I will suffer from insomnia tonight.

Edinburgh was really wonderful and I'm certainly looking forward to the time when we can go there together and see the place. We would have had a wonderful time. The Scotch people seem much more like Canadians and the city itself seems to resemble a Canadian city very much.

In our compartment coming back we had Bill Scott and myself, a Polish Paratrooper, a Scotchman going on holiday and an old man supported by another old chap. We felt very sorry for the oldest one because he couldn't see and had to be led along and had to get up to the toilet every 30 minutes. Finally discovered that he was drinking "medicinal" whiskey and consumed about 20 oz. in the course of 3 hours, so our pity diminished somewhat. We all had a lunch box (we got ours at the Officers Club) so we pooled them and had quite a picnic. The Pole couldn't speak English very well but we learned quite a bit of Polish – he left occupied France via Portugal 9 months ago and was quite a character. I asked him when he would be home – he said 2 months and that he was going straight through – hope he's right.

Well honey loads of love – sure miss you. All my love, Hamp

August 15, 1944

Dearest Peg,

Another day gone by and 3 letters from my beloved wife dated August 1, 3 & 5. Pa and the bond seem to be causing a little trouble – would sooner that you got it but I guess it doesn't matter a great deal as long as it ends up with us in the end. You seem to be having a quiet time – imagine that you are ready to leave by now if you haven't already done so. Imagine that you have had your difficulties in Camrose as you said – I know I always did and never went down without getting in a major argument in which somebody got told off (by me). Glad to hear that you are gaining weight though. The Claresholm gang seem to be moving out – imagine that Bill will be leaving soon too. You should go down – it would be fun for a change. The Banff holiday sounds like a swell idea but remember honey – don't drink with any service men because they all have the same idea and no scruples and it can be embarrassing (talk about a green-eyed monster – eh honey? but I speak from knowing them over here).

Also got a letter from Margaret dated June 9 – quite a delay for a blue mail and I can't imagine what held it up.

Last night I wrote early and was going to hit the hay when Bill Scott came in and wanted to go for a quick bike ride for some eggs. We went to our favorite farm and got invited in for supper. They are a very nice elderly couple and have a lovely home – quite old but beautifully furnished and a lovely garden. We had baked ham, egg salad, cakes etc. and it was all delicious. After that we stayed and talked until 11:00. We certainly collapsed when we got home since we had been up most of the previous night.

I am on duty tonight and writing from sick quarters. The last 7 or 8 days have been perfect summer weather – warm and bright with very few clouds – I didn't think it possible.

The war news is still good with the new opening into Southern France today. We can keep our fingers crossed – certainly look forward to the day when I get of that train and have you in my arms – you're liable to get a rib broken honey.

The sweater sounds good – the nights are beginning to get a bit chilly – hope that we don't have to spend too many winters in the rain here.

Well, all my love to yourself and share it with our delightful daughter. Don't teach her to give her old man the raspberry. Hamp

August 16 1944

Dearest Hamp
This parcel will probably reach you the last of September about a month before your birthday but I wanted you to have the sweater. It is

a bit on the big side but you said you wanted something to wrap around you – so here it is darling!

Came across the panamas in Woodward's yesterday so bought a couple of pairs. Was very pleased as they were off the market for a couple of years and it was just luck that I got them – hope they're OK.

The parcel may be early but I sure wish you a very happy birthday on Oct 28th. Maybe by that time the war will be over – it is a pleasant prospect anyway and that would be a real present.

Heaps of love my darling and its my turn to say I sure wish you were sight seeing with me – I'll probably be in Banff when you read this and do wish you were here.

Have a happy birthday dear, and loads of best wishes All my love, honey – Peggy

Thursday August 17? 1944

Dear Peg,

Am a little vague as to the date but anyway it is Thursday. Received the parcel today with the Journals and they were certainly welcome additions to my reading material. The food was also welcome. Tonight Bill Scott and Jamie (Jamieson – the new Dental Officer) came down to the room and the three of us played knock rummy, drank beer and ate cheese and crackers with a brief pause while I dashed over for the usual nightly stitching job from the bicycles.

Last night Bill and I went down and played golf. We took our bikes with us and cycled to and from the deed – it isn't very far but you can't get taxis and that way it gives you time for a couple of more holes. It's just a matter of sticking them in the baggage car and hauling them out when you arrive. We got rained on a bit but had the exercise anyway – my golf gets worse instead of better though.

I don't know if I told you – I got 4 more films from Dad. Developing is very slow though but should have more to send this weekend.

Monday Bill and I are invited to the home of the local Doctor for dinner and to see some home movies of the Calgary Stampede – some fun eh? It will be something to do but am not to enthusiastic as far as the movies are concerned.

Our good weather still holds out but it won't be many weeks before fall is here with its rain. I hope that the war news continues as good as it is now.

Some night next week Bill and I are going up the road about 7 miles to see an old bloke who is a cabinet maker. We may find something to send home re carrier air take and peculiarly enough his trade mark is a mouse. At the farm house the other night we saw chairs etc. done by him and each had a mouse on it somewhere – running up a leg or on a border.

Am going to enquire at the PO tomorrow about getting my Edinburgh purchase home to you. It is a sweater – cashmere – and quite soft although not too bright. May have trouble sending clothes out of the country.

Well honey, goodbye for now. Will probably write bags of letters over the weekend since I am probably going to relieve again. All my love, Hamp

#53 – August 18 1944

Dearest Hamp

Should have written to you last night but didn't do it so am writing this morning. The letter will get the same plane however as I'll have it mailed over town.

Went over to see Margaret Wednesday night and we sat and talked. David is picking up now and looks ever so much fatter. Margaret can't figure out how she could have been so dumb as not to see that David wasn't gaining – but she couldn't be told as you can imagine. That was the reason for all the trouble with Ma because she spoke her mind about how sick David looked. It's all cleared up now and although David is 3 months old and weighs 7 lbs 11 oz I think he'll grow by leaps and bounds now.

Our wee? Daughter was 10 months old yesterday and you've been away 4 months so we celebrated by taking pictures of ourselves for you. We had Mrs Henderson[9] and Clare and the two children over for tea on the lawn in the afternoon so it was kind of a party.

Last night went to bed early as I felt though I were coming down

234

with something – you know awfully tired, terrific back ache, feeling of nausea and sudden chills which made my teeth chatter – so had a hot bath, put on a pair of my new flannelette pyjamas – yes sir, I got some too – and went to bed. Joan only wakened twice during the night so I had a good sleep and feel almost wonderful this morning.

Ma and Pa are going to the lake today. – that is if the weather clears up. It was rainy this morning and is quite cold. I'm glad I decided not to go as it's a lot of work getting Joan's things and my own ready. Anyway I figured Ma should have a rest. Joan wakens up any time after 6AM and the house is awake for the day so it wouldn't be a rest for the old folks and I'm going to have mine at Banff. Joan tries to put things on her head now – like old rags and paper bags. She thinks she's quite clever. A new trick is to shake her head form side to side and snort – quite intelligent to watch eh?. She has learned how to blow the horn that Grandpa Smith bought her so from morning to night there's quite a din from the Smalley house. Have to take the horn away for peace and quiet once and a while.

Your sweater parcel is on the way now. Also ordered some more cigarettes which makes 4 orders of 300s on the way I hope. Don't know whether I mentioned it or not but your Dad mailed a second parcel of 4 films to you while I was in Camrose – cost 27 cents. There are also 4 more to be sent.

That's all for now. When are you coming home? – As if you know eh honey?

Well, our love dearest, as always, Peg

August 19, 1944

Dearest Peg,

Saturday afternoon and I'm sitting over at our nearby station relieving Carter. Got another parcel yesterday and it was just like Christmas to unpack it. It was really swell and thanks a lot honey – you certainly get a lot of stuff in a small space and I realize that it isn't easy to get all these things together. You're wonderful! Opened the olives and ate them non-stop – a real treat. Last night Bill Scott, Jamie Jamieson and Stafford road into Thirsk on our bikes and had several beers and then road home again.

Bill's bike broke down on the way out and mine on the way back – but you get so you just take it for granted. After we came home we had a banquet at sick quarters with coffee, chicken and tinned meat – all supplied by Mrs. Smith – that's yourself. Friday it is raining steadily and it looks like we have had our summer – hope not though.

Leaves are back in force now – you get 7 days and a 48 (9 days) every 3 months and in addition can get a day off a week. That makes quite a bit of time off when you figure it all out.

When I first came over I thought I was going to save quite a bit of money but find that every time you go away pounds are spent like dollars – am gradually getting a little in the bank but not as much as I had anticipated.

Today I got a letter from Alex Mather, the chap who showed us Edinburgh. He sent me some literature on the university so I may turn into a student this winter if we are still around this part of the country.

Four hours later – haven't done anything but eat a chocolate bar and a package of gumdrops and read 2 American Medicals (plus the Tonics and Sedatives out of the other 3). It's nice to have something to read. Over here there is nothing to read and nothing to do so a day and a half drags by pretty slowly.

Am standing in the dentists' room here and he has a radio – it's kind of nice to listen to for a change – heard Jack Benny tonight – reminds me of Claresholm when we used to collapse on the chesterfield and listen to him before we got the energy to get up and do the dishes.

Don't know where I'm going to go on leave – am going to spend a couple of days down through Blackburn and will look up all the folks of your people.

Well honey, will close and write tomorrow. Can't mail these letters until Monday so just let them accumulate and will get them in together. All my love & kisses, Hamp

#54-August 20, 1944

Dearest Hamp.

How are you old dear? Are you on your trip to Edinburgh yet? There should be a letter tomorrow telling me all about it. Haven't heard from you since last Monday but didn't expect any as you wouldn't be able to mail any letters off the station. Sure hope there's mail tomorrow though as you are so much closer when we were able to talk to each other though letters.

Am sitting out in our new garden chair – green and white wood – enjoying the sunshine after two days of cloudy cold weather which has kept us more or less c.b.'d. I must say it is pretty lonely around here without Ma and Pa and Alix is at the lake so there aren't many people left to phone and invite over. Kay stayed Friday night but didn't arrive until bedtime and had to leave by 8AM for work so have been alone since. That days are busy what with our daughter and the house so they pass all too soon in some respects. Was out shopping for groceries yesterday and it seemed like old times pushing a buggy full of food home – old times except that I bought 2 lamb shops instead of a roast for Sunday dinner. Interruption please dear while I haul Joan out of the flower garden. She's picking all the heads off the plants.

Saw Doris (Marsh) Fleming the other day for the first time in months. They are expecting a family in October although Dr Vant thinks they miscalculated as Doris doesn't show very much.

AOS here closed in July and #3 Manning closed last Tuesday so the city is settling down to its old self especially as a lot of American firms that worked on the Alaska Highway have moved out too. It is still busy however and the population is about 104,000 – about 1000 increase each year since the war started. There doesn't seem to be any decrease in the amount of plane traffic overhead however as the Americans are still flying planes to Russia.

A Chinese diplomat said over the air last night that Japan would probably fall about a year after the defeat of Germany. We are certainly doing fine as far as Germany goes and Japan is having tough going but it is going to be hard to wait another year or so for you to come home – but I'm reconciled to the fact.

Joan just fell into the lettuce bed and is going through a lot of antics to get out. She managed it at last with a lot of grunting and groaning. She's got quite a stomach o her so guess it was hard shunting it around.

Meant to ask you before if you had bought a bike. You wrote about "our bikes" etc. so I gathered you had bought one. Have you and what's it like? A free-wheeler or what?

Joan is sitting up watching the airplanes overhead. She's quite taken with them. Must know her Dad's in the Air Force, eh honey? It's hard to realise that she's almost a year old isn't it? How I hate to see time going by and us not together. But on the other hand it's a good thing time is going for we'll be together that much sooner. Joan just climbed up on a box at my feet – and just fell off again. She's sharpening her teeth on a stone now so I guess I'd better go and look after her. All our love darling, Peg

August 20, 1944

Dearest Peg,

Raining cats and dogs and nothing to write about but hate to get out of practice now that I have a new supply of air mail forms. Haven't done anything today except see about 4 people and then sit and listen to the radio and wait to go back to my own station tonight.

Have just about finished the journals and found them all very interesting.

I imagine that you have left Camrose by now and are getting organized for Claresholm and Banff – suppose that the mail won't catch up with you while you are away but won't let that deter me from writing.

I'm glad that I don't have every weekend off like the Dentists do. Bill Scott is in Harrogate today and supposed to be playing golf – since he can't do that it leaves very little to do.

The war news is certainly wonderful and I hope they aren't getting too much of this weather to slow down their advances. If they continue at their present rate it won't be long before they have occupied all France. Doug should be on his way by now. Imagine that we'll all join him some day but of course everything is full of rumors when the air force or army is concerned.

Have been considering my future a little more seriously lately and don't know just what to do. I had contemplated contacting Johnnie Owen and spending about 4 or 6 mos. in the Path lab. In that way I could regain contact with a lot of lost knowledge in anatomy and biochemistry etc. and also have an "in" at the University Hospital and more or less get some ideas of hospital routines, anesthesia etc. It may or may not be a good idea – don't say anything about it but let me know your opinion.

I was going to finish off a role of film today but it has been too bleak – will do so tomorrow regardless and then get them developed and send them along. Hope that a few turn out OK.

Interruption – the dental orderly just came back from his night off. He got in a fight with some civilians and now has a black eye, 3 sutures in his forehead and a fractured mandible. Pretty strenuous weekend I'd say.

Well, will close and go back home now – my ambulance just arrived to pick me up. Hope to have a couple of letters from you when I get there. Sure miss you honey. All my love, Hamp

#54-August 21, 1944

Dearest Hamp

Have just got the daughter tucked away in bed, cleaned her shoes, folded the washing and fed the dog. The rest of the evening is mine – I hope – so am doing the thing I like to do most first – and that is writing to you.

Didn't get a letter today as I had expected but there's always tomorrow. Did get a letter from Mother and Dad at the lake, however, and they seemed to be enjoying themselves even if the weather is cold and slightly rainy. Dad seems to be taking everything in because and I quote-"All shapes and sizes of women here. This morning we saved a dime as we saw a fat lady without having to pay". Some boy eh? Also had a letter from the American Medical Association wanting such information as permanent address, rank and organisation and date active duty began – for their permanent records of doctors at war – or some such thing – so will fill out the form and return it to them for what it's worth. They even have a Canadian 2 cent stamp on the card so figure if they were that obliging I'd best cooperate.

Yesterday afternoon Joan and I went for a long ride with Marg and Bill and David out to Whitemud and beyond to our most sacred and hallowed spot on the hill overlooking the river – remember darling all those pleasant times we've spent there? And then beyond still further on a road south until we came to the end of the trail at a most unusual farm home made of stones with bright awnings at the windows. Turned back and drove east on roads sided with ripe August grain, some of it stoked too, and came out at the Calgary highway at Ellerslie. Crossed the highway and east for a few miles and then turned north and came out at the Cooking Lake road and so into town. Ended up at the Norton's for supper and stayed until 8.30 as Joan had slept some of the home stretch.

Today did a wash as it was Monday and then phoned Doris Fleming inviting her over for tea which we had on the back lawn. Sandy is now at AOS or I should say the north west staging route at a fairly permanent posting. Doris looks well and about 5 months pregnant although she supposed to be 7 months on the way. There are rumours of ITS closing so the MOs there are expecting a posting – Waddell among them.

Was just thinking Doug won't see Fred or be in the same country. He may see Sid Bridges who by the way is a Fl/Lt but unable to put up his second stripe as he is attached to the RAF and they won't sanction it even if the RCAF will.

Joan is growing up more each day and laughs out loud now when she's pleased with herself. She's a very happy child, seldom cries and is on the whole quite easy to discipline – when the need arises – but as Dad says "with her Smith will and her Smalley won't you can't expect too much". Which may or may not be true. She surprised me this AM by giving me a kiss when I picked her up – and needless to say I was very, very pleased. She now waves bye-bye now when you ask her to – anytime too – and plays pat-a cake. Joan sends you a big fat juicy kiss – which they are – and a great big hug as does your ever loving wife and also all my love my darling. As ever and always, Peg

August 22, 1944

Dearest Peg,

Two more cold wet days have gone by and little to report. Last night we went over to Dr. Swanston's – he is the local doctor in the village nearby and is in the Air Force having just returned from 2 weeks in India and is recuperating from amoebic dysentery. He wasn't at home at the time and we were more or less invited by his father-in-law. Five of us went – we had quite a nice buffet supper and then saw a bunch of home movies which they had taken – one very good reel of the Canadian Rockies and the Calgary Stampede. Made one kind of remember spots. The Swanstons have 3 nice children – twin girls and a boy.

About 11:00 we cycled home – it was pitch dark and we had no lights whatsoever. Your night vision is better than you think and we found our way home without any major accidents.

Today haven't been busy. Sat around all evening reading and no business from the bicycle front as yet – have been munching marshmallows. They are certainly delicious and didn't get moist as you might expect.

Haven't had any mail for 2 whole days now but am being brave about it. Bert Swann – used to be at U of A and who is in aerodrome control here – is going home next week on leave. He had been over here over two years.

Today picked up some green apples. They vary from the size of crab apples to twice as big and are still quite sour but they taste good.

Johnnie Hunt should be back from his course this weekend and I'm curious to know if he will be posted shortly – it is quite likely.

Glad to hear you are back home now (or at least when you wrote). Was afraid you were getting just a bit fed up with Camrose. Well honey, goodbye for now. Sure love you. All my love, Hamp

#56-August 23 1944

Dearest Hamp

Four wonderful letters from my wonderful husband today – all about your Edinburgh escapade. You seem to have had a very good time and bet it was fun just to be away from the station for a day or so.

You great big darling boy, telling me you'd got me something and not mentioning what it is. That is terrible on my curiosity darling but fortunately Margaret read me her letter so now I know – a cashmere sweater. I'll bet it's wonderful. Many, many thanks honey. I can hardly wait to see it and it was sweet of you to spend your precious time looking for something for me.

Joan and I were over at the Flemings last night for supper, we had a nice time but I must say I don't quite know what I ate as Joan was continuously getting into things – not being bad but slightly annoying to the Flemings, I imagine. Into the garage pail, into the soap chips, disconnected the refrigerator, pulled doilies off the tables, tried to take out the radiators, etc & etc. Joan got quite excited and I got quite tired but it was fun anyway except that Joan got sick at her stomach most of the night. She had her own food so guess she must have got too excited but she's fine today although slightly off her food but that will remedy itself in time.

Tonight Kay's sister is coming over to stay with Joan and Kay and I are going to the show. Kay's idea and a very good one I must say.

Had another letter from Mother and Dad and they seem to be having a good time and a rest and are enjoying their stay at the lake.

The Waddells have been posted to St Thomas and had 2 days notice so they have left our fair city. Elliot Cohen was made W/C at North West Air Command. Not bad if you like the kind of work it entails – eh honey?

Got some more pictures back today of Joan and I so will be sending them to you shortly. Joan is certainly growing and is about 2 inches below the top of the dining room table. Today she was hanging on to the top and pulled herself off the floor to wee if there was anything of interest on the table. She hung there for a few minutes and then lowered herself very carefully down to then floor. Pretty good eh honey?

Wee David is coming along just fine now and has gained over two pounds already so Margaret is feeling very happy. Pa Smith is returning from Vancouver on Friday. They went to Victoria too so guess the boys have had a pretty good time. Dad was hoping to fly back but guess they couldn't get reservations.

The war news keeps on being very wonderful. It makes one almost admit that people are right by saying Germany will be out of it by October or there about. Maybe some of the other countries will follow Russia's example. Here's hoping.

Don't worry about me and my trip to Banff honey coz I certainly don't intend to be celebrating when you aren't along and what I want more than anything on our trip is lots of rest, good food and a gain of 10 pounds.

Bye for now. Hugs and kisses from Joan and I. Love always, Peg

August 24 1944

Dearest Peg,

Four not very good pictures. Two were taken outside of Thirsk, Yorks in a rose garden. We were cycling by and went into to take some pictures because the flowers were really lovely. The old bloke invited us into the house and we had quite a nice hour over a pint of beer.

Topcliffe village is one of our local villages which we cycle through. The one with the donkey was taken one evening when we were cycling to Ripon to see Fountain Abby which is one of the oldest in England and supposed to be very beautiful. As we had to cycle home before dark we found we couldn't quite make it – we had 11 miles to go home and it was 4 mile from Ripon so we had a quick beer and beat it home with only brief pauses for a quick pint a 2 other little pubs on the way – quite a country to cycle through because every 3 or 4 miles or so there is a village with a dozen houses or so and a pub and no apparent reason for its existence.

Well hope these arrive

Much love, Hamp

PS They don't match the pictures of my pin up girls which a periodically bring out and stare and wonder how a bloke like myself got such a beautiful wife. More love, Hamp

August 24, 1944

Dearest Peg,

Another couple of days have slid by and not much to write about. Got a letter from you today dated August 13. The way the daughter is growing, she will soon be taller than her old lady (which isn't very tall). Margaret's difficulties will take care of themselves I trust.

Hope your stay at Pigeon is good – be careful in the water honey. Sure wish we could "do" the lake together.

Last night played knock rummy again and made $.30 or 1s3d. Bill Scott lost $.75 so it was a pretty big game. Tonight it is raining and I am sitting in sick quarters on duty writing a letter, giving penicillin at 9 and 12 MN and talking to everyone who stop and gas. Quite a life eh honey. Yesterday afternoon I was told to give VD lectures all afternoon after a film. Ran the film 4 times and then bawled hell out of the erks after it each time – because the last time we showed this particular film was in May and in June we had one of our highest monthly V.D. rates. Am getting a little cheesed with this business of being an RCAF medical officer but guess that it won't last forever. Am not too popular with some of our medical shots around here because lately I have adopted the principal of saying what I think – won't get along too well with that.

Today I got some more films – only 4 and not very good but am sending them along. Also got the ones from Edinburgh on the way to being developed so should have some more shots for you shortly.

Bill Scott and myself will probably take our annual leave together and don't know just where to go – are considering Devon and Cornwall, the Lake District or Scotland.

The war news continues excellent and we may be through with Europe sooner than we thought a few months ago – certainly hope so.

Surely miss you and the daughter – but think that it won't be so awfully long. Give the daughter a bear hug for me. All my love, Hamp

August 25 1944

Dearest Hamp

Have just finished a blue form to you so won't have any news in this letter – just commentary on the pictures.

They are not the best as you can see. We all seem to be squinting into the sun. However, we can't be at our best all the time can we darling?

#1. 9 months old to the day and have I come to get you Daddy, so you'd better watch out.

#2. Pretty busy looking for dandelions and Granny all dressed up for work. She wasn't supposed to be in it.

#3. Thinking up some mischief. Always look like this, Papa, when I'm speculating will I or won't I?

#4. Guess I'll attack the chair – it seems pretty flimsy. How do you like my trousers? Am I a daughter or a son? – sometimes I try to be both!!

#5. Mama thinks I'm going to sleep. Ha! Ha! But not me! Isn't it awful the way I'm strapped in? Please note my teeth. Quite a mouthful eh? – And don't I look tough?

#6. Granny and I on the front lawn August 13th –just 4 days before my 10th month birthday.

#7&8. Mommy and I on the front lawn next day. The sun's in my eyes and Mommy has on your identification bracelet. That isn't my tongue in #7 it's a piece of leaf or some such thing.

That's all for now. Am going to start on some needle point for a foot stool to be used in our "own wee house" All our love, my darling, Peg.

August 25, 1944

To my daddy-xxxxxxxxxx To my husband
    ooooooooooo All my love, dearest
    JMS MCS

Dearest Hamp,

Well, how are you old boy? We are fine thank you very much and hope you are likewise very well. Have just got the "wee datter" to bed and was she tired. We were out to Bartleman's for supper and had a very good time and a very good meal – trout from Cold Lake – simple delicious.

Kay and I enjoyed the show Wednesday night. It was "Christmas Holiday" with Dianna Durbin in the role of a murderer's wife – real melodrama if you can imagine Durbin in anything but a goody-goody role – very different and very good.

Wednesday afternoon went for a walk with Doris Fleming to their victory garden back of the University Hospital, then went up to their apartment for a beer and Sandy came home before we left and insisted that "Mrs Smith and her hoodlum" stay for supper again and so we did.

Sandy thinks Joan is quite a girl. Did I tell you that when he saw Joan in action he said to Doris "I think we made a mistake. We should nave been good." I assured him that it was really worthwhile and that I could think of nothing else but the day you came home so that we could be bad again. He seemed quite pleased with my frankness and hopes you'll be home in the not too distant future.

Alice Greenleese – Eleanor's oldest sister – is very low with bacterial endocarditis. Norris is up from Lethbridge and the doctor advised Irene to prolong her vacation for another week so it doesn't sound very good. They will certainly miss Alice as she was the mainstay of the family.

I hope you can read this as I'm writing it on my knee using the coronet as a desk. Am in the front room with the heat on as the nights are quite chilly now. It almost feels like frost – winter must be just around the corner.

Margaret phoned last night to say that Irene had phoned from Camrose as they wouldn't be able to meet Dad and the boys. It seems that Mac, Irene and some other persons unknown to us at present drove off the road at the Battle River last Wednesday and turned over several times completely wrecking the car. No one was seriously hurt – bruises and shock as far as we know. Irene was very uninforming in her conversation and quite upset. Fortunately for Mac his new car had arrived from the East and was being assembled in Edmonton. As Margaret says, "It must have been quite a stink". We are of course speculating on what happened and will let you know if we ever find out any more details.

Joan has discovered that she has a tummy button and holes in her ears and is kept quite busy exploring her new treasures. It is time I took her to Dr Orr again for another shot of radium, her birth mark is just beginning to show signs of irritation again but her first treatment helped a whole lot. She still has 3 small patches of eczema on her right leg but they don't trouble her much and they are easily kept in check. It has disappeared from the other parts of her body. All for now my darling. Hugs and kisses from Joan and I.

All my love, Peg

Dearest Peg,

Nothing startling to report. On duty the last couple of nights with Jack Perverseff away on a 48 – not too busy at present.

Got a letter from Doug Ritchie today. He's still in London and quite happy about it – he says he expects to leave sometime but in the meantime is doing nothing and liking it. Johnnie Hunt is still away but should be back this weekend.

You are probably basking at Pigeon by now. I hope you have good weather because that place is a little dull if it rains for a few days.

The weather has brightened here today and we are again getting the aroma from our pig farm. I'm not sure but what I'd just as soon have it raining.

Yesterday I buggered the watch Mac sent me. Was winding it when something snapped and it stopped. Have still got my old Gruen so will have something until the other can be fixed – it will take quite a while though I'm afraid.

Am getting train connections worked out for Blackburn and may try to get down there this coming weekend if I can make it. Trains are so crowded these days that it's quite a chore to travel and you are never positive of getting home – so I may not go.

Monday the mobile blood clinic is coming here. Fortunately we only have to provide the space for them and so it won't be too bad. The blood is flown from here to France, so it's quite a worthwhile venture actually. The fellow in charge of the unit is Dr. Stambury and he is the MO who invited us to Leeds one night and we took Charlie Burgess along.

The Edinburgh pictures should be ready tomorrow – will forward them if they turn out.

Remember Tommy Reeves – from Claresholm – student F/O – his pilot who flew with him is stationed at this station. Another chap named MacKay who was at Claresholm for about 4 mos. showed up here the other day. He is ground crew – an F/O.

Well honey, will sign off – good war news don't you think? Give the daughter my love & kisses – wish I could deliver yours in person but it looks as though it won't be long now. All my love, Hamp

Dearest Hamp

This past week has really been a week of good news – news coming so fast that it is hard to keep track of all Allied gains leading to Germany's downfall. It just goes to show you that once a mighty structure starts to crumble and decay its destruction is rapid and complete – we hope eh honey?

Had a very lovely letter from you yesterday and gathered that you are back in the old swing of things again. Glad you liked the parcel and hope you get as much fun out of unpacking them as I do packing them full of surprises for you. It pleased me to see you had to break down and tell about the sweater. Whatsa matter buggerlugs, can't you keep a secret? –even if I did know the answer! The thought that you may all follow Ritchie is a thrilling one even if the country-to-be is hot as hell. I'm quite content to have you where you are for the duration at least – but it would be fun to see how the Eastern hemisphere really lives. Or do you disagree? I think it's a good idea to become a student next winter if you get the chance. 'Tis an opportunity one should not overlook. What would you study? It would be all on your own hook though but I bet you could carry on a lively correspondence at any rate. As for J. Ower and the Path Lab and the future – that too is a sound thought and one in which I very heartily approve. It's not as though you'd forgotten anatomy etc it just that from lack of use of the science one grows hazy on the subject. I know with myself I've forgotten – so called – an awful lot of the ins and outs of nursing. But as I say it's a very sound idea but them darling all your ideas are sound as is your judgement – otherwise I should not have married you my dear. Remember this though, whatever your plans for you're an incidentally our future maybe you'll find Joan and I right beside you just a pitching in to help carry them out. We can think out ideas and then when we get together really discuss and decide what is best for us to do. Please write me your plans my dearest as they turn up from time to time for it's almost the only ray of light cast on our future and into this dull world. When you tell me some of your plans it really gives me something to think about.

Yesterday Joan and I went down to Mrs Lawton's for tea. She said I was to tell you that she thinks Joan is very remarkable for her age and shows a lot of brains and intelligence. Heaven forbid darling – just imagine a quiz kid in our family? However I do agree that Joan is very remarkable. Tonight she discovered that the bath plug is used to let the water out of the tub so it took twice as long for our bath because we had to stop very few minutes and let out a little more of the water.

Was going to do our ironing last night but Kay phoned and asked if I'd mind some company so she arrived with three other girls and we sat around and knit. Have almost finished a pink sweater for Joan for the winter.

This afternoon we went for a ride with Bill and Margaret and David to our own plot of hallowed ground but some other party was trespassing on our land so we moved on for a ways and then stopped for a beer. Very good too.

Tonight after supper I put Joan out in the play pen to enjoy the last rays of the sun. She did have a wonderful time yelling and talking but then all was silent so I went to investigate and there was Arthur Carlyle from next door (Henderson's) putting dirt on Joan's head. It was ½ and inch thick on top and 2 inches thick all around her and goodness only knows how thick in her stomach as she'd been eating it too. So scolded him and hauled Joan in for a tubbing and my was the water black.

Margaret read in the Camrose Canadian about the Smith's accident. It seems that Mac was going to another accident hear Edberg and was going down the Battle River hill when the car got out of control and turned over several times. The top was badly smashed up. The paper days that if Mac had not slowed to 10 mph at the top the accident would have been a very serious one. How they knew he slowed down to 10 mph was not disclosed. There were no other passengers apparently. Mac and Irene got a ride to the other accident and brought their patients back to Camrose suffering from internal injuries. They were certainly lucky I'd say, Mac and Irene I mean.

Charlie Burgess' name was mentioned over the CBC news tonight as being made the new commander of the Thunder Bird Squadron. You probably know all about it but it gave me quite a thrill to hear of someone I know and someone you have seen recently – in the past 2 months anyhow. In some round about way it made you seem very close.

Mother and Dad are still at the lake and the weather has improved a lot. So far Dad has not caught any fish – only weeds. Guess he must use the wrong line – Ha! Ha!

That's all for now dearest. More news from the home front in the next letter. Joan sends bags of love and kisses to her Daddy and your wife still loves you dear and always. Peg

PS Hope you can read this. It's to save using 2 forms. All my love – PS (just a postscript-that's me!)

#59 August 29, 1944

Dearest Hamp

Goodness, it's almost September! Where does the time go? It is ages since we were together – months that seem like years. But you know all about that too. It's getting fallish now – days are much shorter, almost dark by 9PM and not very light at 6AM. Noticed on Sunday how the leaves were starting to change colour. It should be very pretty at Banff if we are not too late for all the magnificent splash of fall in the mountains.

Had a letter from you yesterday and you'd been out visiting again and seeing home movies. You certainly seem to get around a lot and have a change of cooks. Guess I'll have to learn several different ways of cooking to keep you from going to the York Café for a change eh honey?

Speaking of Camrose, Mac and Irene are going on a holiday next week-guess they need one after the accident. Had a letter from Mother today and she said the car turned end for end four times before Irene gave up counting. Mac had several bad cuts on his face but Irene got away without any. As Mother says, "Only a miracle saved them." And the more I hear about it the more I'm inclined to agree.

Dad and the boys are back from the Coast and had a very good time. Dad is said to look very much better that before. I sure hope so as he was really getting down. His chest is quite a bother to him and he's lost 30 pounds since spring. I hate to write things like this but feel you would rather be kept up to the minute. However, I don't think there's very much to worry about for a few years yet but then one never knows.

Had Helen Gun and Doris Marshall Fleming over for tea today.

Made a 7 minute frosting for a cake I baked which turned out to require an hours cooking instead of 7 minutes. It tasted wonderful but was rather hard from so much cooking. Helen is working from 9 to 1 in the Examining Room at UAH now and is happy to have something to occupy her time. She still gets a pneumo each month, however. After they had gone I found Joan in the bathroom stirring the water in the toilet with a fly swatter and having a wonderful time. Wonder where she inherits such ideas. She sure is full of the 'old Nick' so guess she comes by it honestly as we've both been said to have our share of it too. Tonight when I tiptoed in to see if she was asleep she just grinned at me and rolled over as if to say 'OK Ma, if you insist.' She is really such a dear that I'd be lost without her as I've said before. If it should be our fate that you only come home for leave when you return, I sure want another one just like Joan – to keep me busy you know. However, if you come to stay I want a years grace to devote to you. How's that for a future plan? Joan sends a great big kiss and wicked toothy grin and I send all my love darling. –Peg

August 29, 1944

Dearest Peg,

Nothing much to report lately – got behind in my letter writing last night because of the blood clinic. The clinic arrived here about 10:30 and worked through to about 8:30 last night and during the day took 720 pints of blood which was a pretty good effort. Dr. Stambury who is a Canadian was in charge, so after we rounded up the staff and got them fed it was about 9:30. He and I proceeded to the bar and stayed there until it closed at 11:30 and had numerous Scotches and beers and got quite a glow on. He is a very nice chap and is certainly doing a lot of good work. The blood will be flown to France tomorrow morning so is well used.

Today I took the afternoon off and went up and saw Johnnie Hunt. He is getting fatter and happier every day. He is just back from London and full of data on stoolology as he calls it. He says he has finally found what his niche in life has been – he discovered that there was one caste in India which does nothing but clean sheets, dispose of manure, etc.

and he has found by introspection that he belongs to it since he spends all his time getting toilets cleaned up, messes scrubbed, manure hauled etc. I think he's got something.

We had a wonderful afternoon for a ride and Jean MacIntyre, our nursing sister, went along with 2 other officers – RAF men and both good types. We collected a few eggs and I got some pictures of the various places and will send them along. Went to Hawne again and got some pictures of the old Smith farmhouse but didn't have time to try to locate any more of the relatives. The farm has apparently been sold but we went through the old place and looked it over. It's kind of a quaint old stone house with a thatched roof and the usual cooking arrangement – no stove but the fireplace with the oven built in on the side.

On the way home we got lost and really enjoyed it because it was very pretty country that we were riding through.

Jean MacIntyre our nursing sister is quite a good egg. She's getting a little fed up with it all though since she's been 4 years in the Air Force. She doesn't know how lucky she is though – having her husband only 12 miles away and being able to see him 2 or 3 times a week and having a 48 together every 2 weeks. I keep telling her how wonderful a family can be but they haven't produced much as yet (as far as I can see).

I hope to get leave in the next two weeks but may not be able to arrange it. Still don't know where to go and don't much care.

The Edinburgh films haven't shown up yet but expect them shortly.

The war news is still too good almost and hope that it continues. Our future after the European war is settled is very indefinite but I guess we will just wait to see.

Well honey, sure miss you still and wish you were with me or I with you but can wait with some patience now when we realize that when we are together again there won't be an Air Force uniform to contend with. All my love, Hamp

August 30, 1944

Dearest Peg,

Two letters from you today dated August 20 & 21. You seem to be having a kind of a nice quiet time being your own boss. Glad that your Maw and Pa are liking Pigeon and hope thy have had some decent weather by now. You asked who Doug might see. He should be seeing Sid Brydges by now since he left over last weekend. Sure wish I could see the daughter and share one of those juicy smacks but will have to wait. About the bike – they are issued by the Air Force. These stations are very dispersed and so personnel have to be provided with some means of transportation, so they are given bikes on issue. Some of the boys work a good 2 miles from the messes so you need one. Actually I don't need it very badly because we always have 3 ambulances outside the door and a jeep on call – but it's nice to have. We have a lot of transport because these are large aircraft and you may get 7 or so casualties from a flight if it's in trouble.

We keep having the odd minor prang – ground loops etc. but somebody always gets tossed around.

It's funny how you look forward to things. When I get home I'm going to take a holiday of at least 3 weeks and grab my beautiful wife and have a holiday and second honeymoon – don't care if I can't afford it. Will be very glad to feel free again. I am not counting on being home for at least a year but will wait 5 if necessary for only you for a lifetime.

Got a letter from Dad today from Vancouver. He was apparently having quite a time with the boys. He says quote "have had a hell of time to keep them wrecking the hotel and rebuilding it to their satisfaction. Nursemaid to a couple of zoo specimens!" However he seemed to enjoy them and himself and was seeing a lot of old friends, so I guess he got along all right. Also Mother wrote a newsy letter – they really think that you are wonderful (and so do I) and so they should. Apparently things were a little hectic before Father got away to the Coast but OK in the long run.

Got my other films that I took yesterday away today and should have them back in a few days and will send them. By the way – ahem – I am posted on a course out of London – subject is Tropical Medicine. I won't be exposed to buzz bombs so you don't have to worry. I leave next Sunday and it lasts 2 weeks. In that time the mail will be a little delayed because these blue forms don't travel well unless mailed on the station. However will write them regularly and mail them when I can. In the meantime is about 4 days before I lave so I will keep up the news.

Sure miss you. Sure miss Joan. Am quite cheerful however and not morbid so I guess I haven't changed. I weigh 185 pounds dressed. Too much eh honey. All my love, CH Smith

From force of habit I signed my name. More love, Hamp

#60-August 31, 1944

Dearest Hamp

Got another letter from you today dated August 24. When do you figure you'll be getting your leave? Hope it's soon coz you sound as though you might cause a 'ruckus' if you don't have a change of scene and air. Is there something worrying you or is it just a case of real old 'fed up to the teeth' condition? There's nothing to worry about at this end of the line, I can assure you, darling.

By the way was there a picture of the 3 of us in the last parcel? It just came to me last night that I had sent one to you, I thought, but you didn't mention getting it. Guess it just slipped your mind, eh honey?

Wednesday morning Joan, Doris and I went shopping. Do you like ripe olives? I've a feeling you don't but can't quite remember. They are in tins in the store and I thought they might be a nice change if you like them. Let me know so I can send them for Christmas. The Christmas parcels have to go by Oct 25th which seems awfully early. It will seem like two in one year.

Yesterday was up to Doris' for dinner. Sandy has gone north for a week visiting various posts up to Whitehorse on their run so Doris had Betty Eggan and Ruth Fodham for dinner too. Joan as usual kept every one highly amused. Very easy entertainment but possibly not so good for the 'datter'.

Mother and Dad came back from the lake today looking very brown and healthy. They said it was quite cold on the whole with only one or two warm days so Joan and I are quite happy that we stayed home. Alix is back from the lake too as Sandy got a GI upset. Poor Sandy! Fred is still in Rome and had an attack of malaria but is some better now and very busy.

Tonight went downtown with Doris to meet Betty Eggan at the Blood Donor Clinic at 10PM. We also met a Betty Hanna whose husband is an armament officer in the RCAF somewhere in Yorkshire. He has been to York City too. Of course I realize that there are many stations around but you may run into him some day. He like you talks of moving to a warmer climate in the country where Sid Bridges is so we are all prepared for the inevitable over here.

After meeting the girls we went to the Mandarin Café – a Chinese place on Jasper Avenue about 99th street. On the edge of the poor district but a very good place – table cloths snowy white and serviettes. It is quite new and serves mostly Chinese food, steaks and sandwiches. I had a shrimp salad sandwich – about 2 shrimps cross-sectioned several times and a lot of lettuce but really very good. Am now writing you on my return home.

Discovered today that the 'datter' is cutting her upper cuspid teeth – which according to books don't appear until 16 months. She all ready has her first upper molars completely through on both sides and her lower ones are on the way. But that's Joan – always does things in a big way if she does anything at all. Hope you have a good leave when you get it. Joan sends a big band of kisses and a great bear hug and I send all my love – Peg

PS Don't tell a soul – but I love my husband. That's you buggerlugs, so throw out your chest.

SEPTEMBER 1944

September 1, 1944

Dearest Peg,

Another two days have slipped by. It's amazing to me when I look at the date. The time seems to drag along from day to day but the months seem to slip away. I hope that the next few months don't drag too much.

Was going to write last night but we had a prang and we were busy until the middle of the night. Kite crashed on take off and one fatal injury and 7 with severe burns, fractures, shock etc. and was quite hectic for awhile but we eventually got them straightened away and full of plasma and O2 and then sent them to our general hospital. I took our

255

jeep and went up to see them today and they are still plugging along.

By the way our jeep is quite an affair. It's part of our mountain rescue unit of which I am a not too leading light. It is painted bright yellow with big red crosses fore and aft and on the roof. You can't exactly sneak along the road quietly in it.

Earlier in the evening I went into the village to the local pub with F/O Stafford (Accounts). his boys have a get together after each payday and I went along. Had several beers and someone played the piano. We were in one corner and the room was about 25 x 35 feet with about a hundred boys in it drinking beer and singing dubious songs and having a nice quiet time. Quite enjoyed myself but just as I got back to camp the kite crashed and I saw it burning and my evening was kind of spoiled.

I certainly hand it to these boys. Some of them with hands and faces burnt beyond recognition and the first things they ask about is "how is the skipper and the rest of the crew".

I leave Sunday for London and am looking forward to my stay in the South – glad to get away from the place for a few days and not see our routine (colds & V.D.).

Well honey, hope the cigarettes arrive. Have been smoking Limey efforts for about 2 weeks and they aren't too good.

Give my love to Joan. All my love to you, Hamp

September 2, 1944

Dearest Peg,

Another day by the board. I leave tomorrow morning and for the next 2 weeks the mail may be a little sporadic depending on how successful I am in finding a place to mail them from. I think I shall stay at the Royal Army Medical College but do not know for sure that I can get accommodation.

Had another late night last night. About an hour after I wrote you we had another prang and had to go dashing out. Fortunately there were only 6 in the kite and they just had minor bruises. After that I had an erk in with a fractured skull, so we were active for another little while. (By the way. my roommate is a chap named Martin Albers from Mirror.

Knows Aunt Lena and Eddie. He has finished his tour – a Bomb Aimer).

Today it has been raining and blowing and feels about like the middle of November back home. It seems hard to realize that fall is approaching so close. I am going to get the pictures tomorrow if at all possible and will send them along to you tomorrow. The chap who developed them said they turned out quite well but they weren't dry enough to deliver.

It will be quite awhile before I get any mail and should have quite a nice collection by 2 weeks from now. Sure miss hearing from you when it's held up. Your letters practically put me beside you and can practically hear you talking. Miss you more than you can put down in words but don't worry about me getting morbid about it like Ted Slack. (Dentist here who was repatriated and used to break down periodically because he couldn't stand being away from his home and wife). We all feel the same way but there's no use letting it get you down.

You should be down south by now and hope that you have a good holiday because the daughter is apparently not inducive to restful relaxation – night or day.

Well honey, will stop nattering (pardon my good English) and sign off. All my love. Say hello to your Maw and Paw for me and I really will write shortly to them. Hamp

#61 September 2

Dearest Hamp

Well, September has arrived and with it beautiful sunny days and quite chilly nights, though. But it's hard to realize that it is September though isn't it honey?

Last night was over at Eleanor's with Kay to see her and also to pay our respects as Alice died last Saturday. I don't think I mentioned it before. Eleanor looks well as all pregnant women do. Guess I'll have to get out my knitting needles and knit some little things for Norrie and Doris.

Am going over to Betty Stark's tonight with Alix to play bridge. We are at various stages of learning and so help each other over the rough spots. If I do say so myself I'm improving somewhat and enjoy playing now so maybe we'll be able to go out for an evening without my slugging you, like old times, eh dear?

Got a letter from you today written last Saturday and wonder if you went to Blackburn. The thought just struck me that you probably went to church if you were there on Sunday. Or did you?

Am writing this on my knees so hope you can read it without any trouble. Joan is getting to be quite a little miss and certainly knows her own mind. She raises quite a yell when I take something away from her or want her to sit down in her high chair when she wants to stand up. It's the kind of yell that requires a little pant warming to handle as its not very funny but I think we'll overcome that in a few days. She's really growing up quickly now though and is trying very hard to talk. She jabbers more that ever and it sounds as though she were forming words or sentences. I can understand 'Da Da' and 'Mum-mum' but that's about all. However I pretend to understand and we carry on a lively conversation.

The war news is still very good but somehow I'm not very optimistic yet although more so than a few months ago. If only those damn little yellow bodies weren't in the mess I might get a little more excited. However, I won't really get excited until I know you're on your way home. Boy, what a day that will be eh darling? I dreamt about it last night and it was really *the* thing but what a let down when I wakened up. I felt robbed. However one of these days the missing link – that's you BoBo, will be turning up and everything will be hunky dunk again.

As you can gather there isn't much new but it's fun just talking to you. Have you thought of anything you might be needing? What do you want for Christmas? Let me know honey. It's time to feed the hoodlum so must away. Heaps of love and kisses from Joan and I. All my love – Peg

Sept 5 1944

Dearest Hamp

Got two letters from you today. One with the pictures and the other written on Aug 29. The pictures were swell. The garden certainly looked very lovely. I certainly thought the picture of you and the donkey was super. A very good picture of you. It was a great thrill to see that you still look the same and now I know why you ask for pictures of me as well as Joan. Thanks for them, darling, and please keep them coming if you can.

I'm a day behind schedule on my letter writing as I should have written last night but went to a show with Alix. It was Labor Day so we had to go early and when I got home went straight to bed as it was that time of the month again! We saw 'Stormy Weather' with Lena Horne and Bill Robinson in the leads. The cast was entirely negro and was very good – as good as musical s are.

Sunday afternoon, which seems to be days away now, was spent with a two hour sleep in the afternoon and a walk with Alix and Betty Stark. Stayed home Sunday night and read – also had a cigarette. Not bad eh and Ma was home but in bed. Still can't bring myself to smoke in front of Ma and Pa although they know I smoke. Silly isn't it eh dear?[10]

Was downtown most of the day with Doris Fleming – doing the town. We visited all the stores I'm sure, looking for a wool dress for me – but they don't have any in my size that I like. A good thing as I save $20 and use up my old clothes. Managed to buy over $5.00 of groceries for your birthday and Xmas boxes so everything is in full swing. Also ordered 300 more cigarettes. You should be getting some of these soon as I've about 6 orders in now since June but they may be slow as they were starting a new system.

Have one more payment of $24 to make on our bonds and 3 more are ours, actually one is Joan's and one is yours and one is mine. Also have hit the $250 mark in our bank account but it will be less than that after my trip to Banff – considerably less. I don't intend to throw my money away but on the other hand don't want to have to skimp as I think I've earned a holiday – but that's just my humble opinion. Kay and I are going on the CPR midnight on the 16th which will be exactly 20 months and 24 hours after we left to start on our trip together, remember?

Will have some more pictures of Joan and I to send you before I go to Banff. Mother will send mail on to me and I'll have lots to write to you. Sure wish you were here I sure do. Big kisses from Joan and all my love – Peg

September 6, 1944

Dearest Peg,

Pretty far behind in my letter writing but have kind of been on the move. Came down to London on Sunday and had quite a good trip – even managed to get a seat on the train although it was terribly crowded as usual. Am staying at the Royal Army Medical College which is in Millbank overlooking the Thames. It is an old place and loaded with the tradition of the British Army. It has a beautiful mess and the food is excellent so it is really quite a nice place to stay. It is full of brigadiers and colonels but they aren't too stuffy. It's quite a change to sit down and have your meal served to you and even have a linen serviette. Back in Yorks. we have a cafeteria style and it's quite a lot more free.

There are 4 RCAF on the course and we are quite a clique since the others are all RAMC lads. The first night Neil Gorden and myself (he is an M.O. from a nearby station and on the course) wandered around sightseeing and had a few beers. Monday night the four of us went out to walk around and ended up at some club – a bottle club – we all got very happy and Neil passed out so I picked him up and we came home in a taxi and were in bed fairly early again. We have seen all we want of London night life and are going to concentrate on sightseeing from here on.

Last night (Tuesday) we walked down to the Abbey (about 4 blocks up the street) and looked around the Houses of Parliament and watched Big Ben and then went down and located #10 Downing Street and from there to Trafalgar Square where we saw a movie for an hour and came home. It's lovely down here now. The sun shines and it's fairly warm and there are no buzz bombs now of course.

Well honey, sure miss your letters. Will keep you posted a little better now. Am sending the Edinburgh pictures.

All my love, Hamp

Readdressed to Banff.

September 6, 1944

Dearest Peg,

Finally getting these pictures off and hope that they arrive OK.

These are all taken in Edinburgh when we were up for the weekend-end.

The photography is anything but good, but am sending them because you will probably recall most of the scenes.

There are several shots of the Mathees who were the young couple who took us around and of Nel Littlefair who is Mrs. Mathee's brother.

I'm certainly looking forward to the dim distant future when you and I can see the place together. I would make a grand holiday if you were there.

The course here is going well – quite intensive but we have Saturday afternoon and Sunday off and will do our sightseeing then. Gray McClaren is stationed somewhere near here and I am going to look him up if possible. Don't know if any of the other boys are around here or not.

Well honey, am going to dash out and mail these from a Canadian Officers' Club which is a tuppenny bus ride from here. Also we must have tea first ahem? – since it is 4:30 and dinner isn't until 7:30.

Well goodbye for now honey – all my love to yourself and share a little with Joan. Hamp

September 8, 1944

Dearest Peg,

Well, another two days have slipped away. We have managed to soak up quite a bit more knowledge. The course is quite intensive while it lasts and we go from 9 to 1 and then 2 to 4:30 each day and hear an awful lot about tropical medicine in that time. We have an exam at the end of the course and I don't expect to particularly distinguish myself.

To tell you what we have been doing. Wednesday night the four of us decided to go for a walk. We went down to Leicester Square that figures so prominently in the song Tipperary and were not impressed. We sat on a bench for an hour and watched the crowd stream by. Thousands of Americans with every other kind of uniform sprinkled in. Across the street were four old blokes providing music – one was playing a saw and accompanied by a concertina. Piccadilly is notorious for its prostitutes – they throng the area in the late evening and are a source of considerable concern to the American authorities. We are gradually getting our boys trained. After watching the crowd we had a beer at a pub just off Trafalgar Square and came home.

Last night 2 royal navy MO's here on the course took us to a little pub called Shepherd's Pie. It was terrifically crowded and you were never sure that you were getting your glass to your own mouth or some other bloke's as you stood in the crowd and had a beer. We went from there to an officers' service club and had a beer and some sandwiches and then got a taxi and came home.

Tomorrow we are going to try to get to Madame Tussauds and next week we study.

Well honey, sure miss my mail but will have something to go back to Yorkshire for. all my love. Miss you. Never worry about me and any English female, they don't compare. Hamp

#63 September 8, 1944

Dearest Hamp

Was all set to write you last night before going to a show with Alix but when I got there my cupboard was bare of blue forms. I usually have such a stock on hand that I don't worry about them but I got caught out this time. And please darling forgive me and I'll try to do better next time.

Wednesday afternoon was a scorcher so Alix, Sandy, Joan and I went down to the Gyro Park – a block south of Whyte Avenue on 108th Street. Sandra went paddling in the pool but Joan was too little –she just sat and watched. – anyhow the water was quite dirty so I didn't feel the least bit sorry for Joan sitting in her buggy. However Joan got a ride on the swing and played in the sand pile so she had a good time if dirt on the hands face and clothes are any significance.

Yesterday afternoon Joan and I went down to Days for tea on the back lawn. Mrs. Robertson passed a plate of cookies around to all of us – even Joan. Joan was a little amazed at first at the sight of all those cookies but she soon rallied and helped herself with her right hand and was just going to do the same with her left hand when I arrived to save her manners. She had another later on though. She's really quite a gal!

Went to a show with Alix and Betty Stark and realized we'd seen some of it that I'd already seen it at Claresholm with you. It was Edward G Robinson in 'Larceny Inc'. But I enjoyed it again anyway.

Betty Stark is going to the coast on Monday to be with Bill. He at last wrote her to come. Some guys are sure queer. He's in Canada but doesn't seem to want his wife within miles. He's the type that should be sent away – the lug – Growl, Growl.

Phoned Margaret last night and David weighs 10 pounds now and is turning into a good looking 'Porky'. Am going out there in a day or 2 to visit so will have more news then I think.

Kay and I have decided to fly to Calgary on Sunday the 17th and then are taking a bus to Banff. It will cost us only $1.60 more that if we went by the night train in a lower. We are quite thrilled as we have never flown before. We have our reservations booked both ways and am quite sure of a seat as Sundays are not very busy. We also have our reservations at the King Edward in Banff and plan to stay there for a few days while we look for a cabin in town with an open fire place – if we can find one. We figure it will cost less if we can get at least one meal in the cabin as we are hoping to do it for about $75 each which should be quite easily done but as I've never paid for a holiday before I don't really know. However, we may have to settle on $100 – all depends on how extravagant we are.

Am going to start packing your birthday food box tonight so that I can get it off before the 15th and then I must go to bed for by night I feel as though I needed some support in the perineum to keep me all intact – its ever since I got the fairies this time and so believe it or not I've made an appointment to see Dr Vant in October – the first appointment I could get. However don't be alarmed as I feel fine and it's only for a check up. As we don't want anything to go wrong with those particular treasures-eh honey? Joan sends big hugs and kisses and I all my love.- Peg

#64 Sept 9, 1944

Dearest Hamp

Well you old gad about – so its to London now is it. Of course you are just about ready to go back to Yorkshire now or is it India?

Just got your letters today telling of your trip to London. I gather it is for a course in Tropical Medicine although you did not say so in so many words. Where is Johnnie Hunt now? How long have you known you were going to London? Is there anything else you are holding back darling? I'd kind of like to know as one's mind tends to get over active some days and it is easier on me to know all than to imagine so don't hesitate to tell me if there are any changes in the offing – which by the way – I do expect.

It's too bad your course finishes before the black out is lifted or are you staying on another day or night to see some of the lights of London? I'm sure glad the Robombs were knocked out before you got there except for one attack if I remember correctly.

By the way dear I couldn't register your birthday parcel with the sweater etc in it as it weighed too much so I hope no one will swipe the parcel on you. You should have the one sent from Camrose by now. Hope the shortbread wasn't too crushed. I'm sorry about the cigarettes darling but they say this new system is holding up orders but they should be along real soon – we hope.

Alix, Sandy and Joan and I went down to the Gyro Park again this afternoon and the children had a great time in the sand pile. Will have to get one for Joan for next spring.

Our weather now is really wonderful particularly for the harvest. It is actually the best weather we've had all summer.

Fred is still in Rome but expects to move up again any day now. He has had malaria again but is now fine or did I tell you that before? It seems to ring a bell.

Mrs. Umbach is in town from Sexsmith – haven't seen her yet but we had a long chat on the phone. She asked about you. One of her boys is in Yorkshire too – her boy by her first marriage – George Cameron by name. Speak of the devil and Mrs. Umbach has just come in the front door. Have said my 'Hellos' and am now going to say 'G'bye' as I'm on my way to Alix's.

Am keeping my fingers crossed about our future but it kind of looks like you're going to be a world traveler at 27 eh honey?

Joan says 'G'night Pa' and heaps of hugs and kisses from all of us. All my love darling.-Peg

Dearest Hamp

I must apologize for my last letter. It was written on Saturday after I'd received your letters of Sept 1 and 2nd. In them you wrote of going to London but never mentioned why and I thought you were holding back on me for some reason or other – which was a very unjust thought on my part my darling. Those letters arrived after a week spent in 'building up' a tropical country – to myself so I could get used to an almost certain fact about your future posting. I'm very sure you will be joining Doug soon. Also last Wednesday the thought suddenly came that you were on course in London and I know it to be true so it was no surprise to me to get your letter. Guess I'm psychic eh honey? However as I say I was not in a very good mood so that's why the letter back. But the answer to all of this lies in the fact that on Monday (today) I got two more letters from you and one dated Aug 30th which told all about your posting. It must have been held up somewhere so hence the apology. Is it accepted honey?

The other letter was written on Sept 6th and arrived on Sept 11th – very good service eh dear? You seem to be having a good time in London; Hope the course is very interesting too.

Had a letter from Doris Bothwell also and she had been in the hospital with asthma but is better now. She can hardly wait for me to go down there and has planned lots of things for us to do. Sounds very interesting and am kind of excited myself. The Burgman's have a son and the Reid's are expecting. Woodhouse is in quarantine because they had one case of polio which is quite prevalent in the south of Canada and northern US.

Was downtown this afternoon and bought my air ticket and a few odds and ends. Then went out to the Norton's' for supper and the evening. David is certainly fat now –I wouldn't have recognized him if Margaret hadn't been along. He's not over fat but has certainly changed. Bill has some skin condition on his chest and stomach which looks like ringworm but isn't. He was kept quite busy scratching.

Mailed your birthday parcel to you today and sure hope you are around to receive it instead of having to send it on for another few thousand miles. Sure hope your cigarettes have arrived by the time you get back from London but I haven't got any slip saying they have been sent to you and I have five receipts so they'd better start sending them along and right soon too.

Are you staying long enough to see the blackout lifted in London or have I asked you that before?

The TCA serves breakfast on the plane so Kay and I are going to shoot the works and have everything. Hope we can keep it down.

Haven't really started to get my things ready yet and have half of my clothes at the cleaners so hope I'm not left holding an empty suitcase.

Joan is going down to see Dr Ou tomorrow almost a month behind time but it doesn't really matter. Hold yourself honey – I've at last made an appointment to see Dr Vant for Oct 20th or have I mentioned that before? Joan sends you hugs and kisses. All my love darling – Peg

September 10, 1944

Dearest Peg,

Nothing very much to report except extracurricular activities. We have managed to do something every night and not study. Neil Gorden – the M.O. who is my room mate here, is a very nice chap and quite a poor influence as far as serious study is concerned.

Friday evening we went to a show – a burlesque I'd guess you'd call it – the jokes were very corny and quite English but we enjoyed it nevertheless. Quite a funny arrangement – all the theaters have bars in them and there are about 4 intermissions so we kept whipping out for a quick beer and so the show got better as it went along.

Saturday afternoon we were off so we came to Madam Tussauds. It really was amazing – the figures at first rather embarrassed you and you felt that you were kind of out of place. They certainly were lifelike. The chamber of horrors didn't impress us unduly because the worst of them weren't quite as bad as the victims of a minor aircraft crash.

Saturday evening we met Chick Stogdill – he's a S/L and a member of the RCAF Medical Board here – the neuro-psychiatrist. He had been up at our station visiting and we got to know him quite well. We went to numerous pubs and got feeling quite merry and then went to a place called the Exhibition Club to which Chick belonged. It had bars on 3 floors and crowds of people in all of them. By then it was midnight so we got a taxi and volunteered to take Chick home. By the time we delivered him and then drove to Millbank the bill was 30 shillings and we were no longer impressed with the cheapness of English taxis.

We slept in until noon today and now it is a lovely afternoon and we are going to wander out and see some more places – St. Paul's etc.

Sure miss you here Peggy. The more I see of English life the more I long for you and the life at home. All my love, Hamp

September 12, 1944

Dearest Peg,

Not much to report again. No mail from home of course so don't know how things are with you. Didn't mail my last letter so it will come with this one. I take them up to the Beaver Club which is near the Admiralty Arch of Trafalgar Square and little out of the way but the only box for Canadian mail that I know of.

Sunday Neil Gorden and I, after I wrote, wandered down by the Abbey and across the Westminster Bridge and then ended up at a little pub where we sat and drank beer and then came home.

The weather has been wonderful for the past few days. Right now I am looking out my bedroom window across the Thames with its barges and tugs and so forth. The traffic isn't as heavy as it would be in peace time – I imagine. Very pretty along the bank here but spots are quite badly blitzed. Yesterday noon we dashed up to Neil's Bank and by St. Paul's – that area was very heavily damaged and the destruction is terrific in places.

By the way at times now you can hear heavy explosions and on Sunday they were quite plain and are supposed to be from the bombing of Le Havre – quite a distance for it to carry.

Last night we were going to study but Pete – a navy bloke with a scruffy beard from Edinburgh who is on course with us – persuaded us to a show with him and we went and saw a show about an American aircraft carrier dodging through the Pacific – it was quite good.

Friday is our exam and I imagine we had better do a little work because we have had a lot of stuff thrown at us.

This has been quite a holiday and I hate the thought of Yorkshire again. Neil and I are quite a congenial pair because our families are the same age and we both produce pictures of them at the slightest provocation. Mine of course are quite a lot more attractive but I haven't been rude enough to make an issue of it.

Well honey, goodbye for now. All my love, Hamp

#66 Sept 13 1944

Dearest Hamp

You should know something of tropical diseases and their remedies by now – pardon me. Am back again – Hi! There was a big bang from the kitchen as Joan pulled the toaster from the cabinet to the floor! Ah me! What a darling child! (Not that I don't love her). You seemed to have had a good time in London. Bet it was a nice break. I wish I could have been there to do the town with you – it would be such fun.

It is quite common talk over here about the Air Force and India – especially since the Churchill and Roosevelt conference – it is surprising the number of boys that have gone already. Official word came through last night that ITS here is closing on Nov 20th or 10th – anyhow sometime in November so this part of town will become more normal again. But the airport is busy as the RCAF has taken over many of the northern fields from the Americans and expect to take over more.

Dandy Fleming was up to Grand Prairie and Whitehorse last week supposedly doing dental work but managed to get some shooting in – six of them bagged 8 ducks – and hopes to go up again soon.

Am knitting a pair of short stockings for Joan and Just managed to rescue my work in time. She sure finds the things you forget to put away. The house looks different since she started to crawl as all the knick-knacks have been moved away and all breakable things put out of reach. We are going to have one room completely stripped except for toys for the rest of our brood darling. I'm convinced it's the only way for peace of mind and the only thing for a play room. Joan is real good and knows by now the things she shouldn't touch like the radiant and

268

tri-light but every once and while she goes berserk and runs from one thing to another just to torment us.

Had Joan to Dr Ou yesterday and he seemed to think she was doing OK. Her birthmark is not as red as before and the tissue is level with the surrounding area – also the blood vessels which were noticeable before have disappeared. It still gets irritated at times from the diaper though. Her eczema is good but flares up on her right leg every once in a while so we still use coal tar. However I know when it's coming back as Joan goes off her food temporarily. We are to go back within a month so guess he was busy as I kind of got that impression. Didn't know Drs were such important people in my life before – ahem! But we've been to at least one – Dr Leitch or Dr Ou – every month since you went away and have appointments on into November. Not bad eh? And then it's time for the dentist. Joan says to tell you she's trying to stand up under the table but keeps bumping her head. All my love dearest – Peg

Sept 16 1944

Dearest Hamp

Am rather a day behind in my letter writing and no real excuse other than I've been busy washing, cleaning, pressing and mending. Was out Thursday night to Mary Frizzell Clark's, an old school friend of mine who is up from Calgary on a holiday. There were 8 of us there mostly married with a child and a husband overseas. It was a nice quiet evening and we all did a lot of knitting. We'll all be a quiet home-loving bunch when our husbands come back from their travels eh honey?

Was home all day yesterday packing and cleaning the house to cut down on mother's work while I'm away, then at night washed my hair and went to bed early.

This morning rushed downtown and got some travelers' cheques and did last minute shopping. Then dashed back and finished packing. George and Jim Oldring from Ottawa and Montreal respectively (Aunt Lena's boys) came over in the afternoon to see Joan and myself as we hadn't seen each other for four years or so. They were very impressed with Joan (but of course!) and thought she was the real thing.

I was to have spent the night at Kay's and go out on the 6 AM plane but at 5 PM TCA phoned and said I was deplaned but could go at night. Why they picked on me I don't know. Poor little defenseless gal I guess. Anyhow Kay refused to go too so as plans stand now we are going on the night plane tomorrow – that is if one or both of us don't get bumped in which case we'll go by the midnight train and will have to sit up as its too late to get a berth now. Here's hoping we go by plane though. But we'll get there somehow never fear.

The war news is better and better. Hope the Germans crack soon so that we can get the Jap mess going in full. Then perhaps you can come home to us and believe me we're sure waiting for you, my darling, no matter how long it takes.

Am seriously thinking of taking a part-time job somewhere just to kill the time as Joan doesn't require so much attention now and some days do drag. Guess I could go to Varsity but have no desire to do so, so why go? Would it be alright with you if I did so (job I mean)? I don't need the money you understand – it's just to keep me from becoming an introvert. All my love dearest – will write from Banff. Peg

September 17, 1944

Dearest Peg,

Well, have arrived back and am in the routine again. Got back late yesterday and on duty as soon as I got here and about 10 minutes after I took over there was a prang so it didn't take long to get into the sewing again.

Have some quite good news – I think – as a matter of fact it's a real relief. I won't be seeing Syd Bridges or Freddy Day in the near or distant future unless we have a get together in Alberta. Will stay in these parts for the duration and then be seeing you. Actually it's the best news we have had for sometime.

Sorry my writing has been so sporadic but we had a little difficulty mailing letters and I figured that it was just as quick to wait until the end of the week and send them air mail from here.

Was quite disappointed when I got back. Had no mail from you but I guess Bill Scott was saving it and he has gone away for the weekend but should be back tonight and then I will probably be reading mail far into the night.

I did have a parcel however and it was a good one – candy, cheese and crackers, shortbread, lobster, whodunits etc. and it was really swell. It kind of got battered about a bit but held together well and the laundry bag was as good as new. I pretty nearly did the wrong thing – was going to rip into the end (you know the way I rip into Christmas parcels as if I couldn't wait 2 minutes to unwrap them) when I turned it over and saw the note and then took a second look at the bag.

The last 3 days in London were quite quiet. We studied 2 nights (believe it or not) and then had our exams on Friday and went out to dinner Friday evening and came home Saturday morning. The trains were packed as usual but we managed to get a seat to York.

It's kind of nice to be back. London was a pleasant change but Yorkshire is OK too. Sure wish you were here honey. Miss you more as time goes by and love you more. As I have said before there will never by anybody but you and the conviction gets firmer and firmer as time goes by. (if it were possible). Give Joan a big hug and a kiss for me. All my love, Hamp

September 17, 1944 (Evening)

Dearest Peg,

Two letters in one day to my gal but had to tell you about getting 6 letters from you today. Your first was Aug. 23 and you had apparently had quite a hectic time with our tornado at Flemmings. Sure wished I could have seen it. Nice for Elliott Cohen but hope he gets a little time in elsewhere than there and you know where – the boys from Canada can take over and will come home – in due course and don't imagine that will be too soon – but it's sure something to look forward to.

By the way honey, I met Frank Apperley on the way back from London. He had just arrived back and was proceeding to Scotland on leave. Got "genned up" on Claresholm and felt quite homesick for all the good times we had there. Also as I was standing in the station in York a train went through and I saw Harry Glanville and Gordy Loretet sitting inside – small world isn't it?

Mac and Irene seem to really have done a job of the Battle River Hill – that 10 m.p.h. is quite a laugh. I hope they had had a few beers so it will teach them a lesson. Probably they were quite sober though so there won't be any lesson. Have been curious about Joan's eczema but didn't like to mention it without being able to touch wood as you read the letter. You tell Sandy Flemming that if he ever has any regrets about not being good, that he is crazy and I will tell him so in person sometime in the future.

Listen buggerlugs – I can keep a secret – but not from you. I fortunately have a wife to whom I can tell all so out of force of habit I did.

The war news is certainly good these days – Holland today and I hope that it sticks. If they continue at their current rate one of these days I'm going to get awful drunk – probably won't however because everybody else will and we will be busy picking up the bikes and stitching up the casualties.

Saw a wonderful sight tonight – *street* lights – *lit* – Houses with light showing through their windows and nobody worrying about having the blackouts. Saw a bus going down the road with its blackouts not drawn. Really looked cheerful. Had a nice afternoon today and will write tomorrow and tell you about. Quite an outing with the padre and heard him preach a sermon. (Pardon me if I appear to sound quite virtuous.

Sorry I didn't mention getting the picture of us three. It now adorns the dresser and bookcase alternately – depending on where the batman puts it when dusting. Very proud of you both. Also I do like ripe olives.

Well honey good night and will dream about you. Bags of love, hugs, kisses and what have you.

All my love, Hamp

Hotel Palliser, Calgary, Sept 17 1944

Dearest Hamp

Well here we are back in the banana belt which feels like the Arctic. We had a very enjoyable flight – much like a roller coaster as there was a strong wind and for half the trip couldn't see a thing but clouds. They started to break up over Red Deer and then we were able to see the mountains and some of the countryside underneath us. Had a cup of coffee which was quite a struggle to get down as every time I took a mouthful we either dropped a few miles or climbed a few thousand feet which didn't exactly help my appetite. I don't think I could stand up to a nose dive or a tail spin. But anyhow it was more fun than a smooth ride. It sure is the way to travel. We arrived in Calgary at 7 PM just ¾ of an hour after leaving Edmonton.

Having been bumped from the morning plane holds us up 24 hours as we don't leave Calgary until tomorrow morning's train. My baggage just weighed 40 pounds so I didn't have to pay. Kay's weighed 42 pounds and it sure had her Scotch pride a bit hurt to pay the extra 10 cents. Joan was eleven months old today. Just imagine at this rate we'll soon be grand parents or is that rushing it a bit too much?

Joan discovered how to unlock her playpen today so poor Ma will have quite a time. It was swell of her to offer to look after 'the tornado'. I'm not worried about Joan but am wondering what shape Ma will be in when I get home.

The lights went on in London tonight. Did you see them? I'll bet it was a thrill for the people.

We are going out to see Mary Frizzell Clark now who left Edmonton yesterday so must away. It's only 8.15 now just imagine! Ain't science wonderful? All my love dearest and do I wish you were here. Always, Peg

September 18, 1944

Dearest Peg,

Well one more day nearer to my wife and daughter. The time is certainly slipping away. Forgot to tell you last night – I'm really enjoying shaving with Palmolive again after using the cake soap.

Also had a card from Doug Ritchie yesterday. He was in Casablanca at the time and said it was as cosmopolitan a spot as the movie seemed to indicate and that he was enjoying it. Also said our pig farm was a bed of roses compared to it – so guess I'm quite pleased to sit here in Yorkshire.

Yesterday afternoon I didn't feel like waking and working and went off with Ross Cameron, our protestant padre. He was in Edmonton for a couple of years – Presbyterian – and knew your Dad by name. He was invited to preach a sermon at a place called Patley Bridge. There they have the ruins of an old church dating back to about 1100 AD and every year they have a procession up the hill to it, in revival of a yearly pilgrimage that was made there. Since it was Battle of Britain Sunday he was invited. A very picturesque spot on a hill top overlooking a beautiful valley – ruins of a church actually with no roof and the procession inside. The old vicar led it and he kept calling out "mind the dirt, mind the dirt" as they came to spots where cattle crossed the road and left their landmarks – I found it quite amusing.

After the service we were invited to tea to the local manor – a wonderful old place the main hall of which was built in 1629 and parts of it are the cloisters of the monks who quarried stone for Fountain Abbey which is 6 miles away. They even had a secret panel with a skeleton behind it (a skull). They gave us a very nice tea which included baked ham and this was 6 weeks bacon ration for them so we were quite in their debt when we left.

On the way home we stopped at a country inn for dinner and had roast duck – quite a meal. After that we came home and made coffee and gassed until past midnight. So it was a very pleasant day.

The war new continues good. The weather here is perfect at present and I hope it lasts so that the operations in Europe aren't obstructed.

Well honey, will sign off. all my love to yourself. Miss you. Love you.–Hamp

#68 King Edward Hotel, Banff 3PM, Sept 19 1944

Dearest Hamp

You will be pleased to know that already your wee wife feels 100% better and like a rejuvenated woman. It is fairly cold up here, cloudy and scattered showers but so far it hasn't kept us hotel bound.

We had a noisy night Sunday at the Palliser. Our room was on the east side overlooking the station entrance and the trains came through the window on an average of one every 15 minutes all night. At least it seemed so. Then there were parties going on, on each side of us and at one thirty AM came a knock on the door and a key rattling in the lock. Kay and I were in bed at that hour and so roared 'Who's there?' Nobody answered but the door was opened and a man boomed, 'Who's in here?' So I says 'Miss B and Mrs. S and this is our room. What do you want?' So he says 'I'm the house detective looking for a party.' And goes out locking the door. So Kay and I settled down to a nice *quiet* rest but sleep didn't come until after 3 AM for me. We left Calgary at 10.30 AM by coach and arrived here at 1 PM, got settled in our room, had lunch, changed into skirts, sweaters, ankle socks and sport shoes and walked to the Cave and Basin and back. Then around the streets in town looking for a cabin but decided it was just as cheap for two to stay at the hotel so here we are until next Monday. Last night we went for a short walk and then turned in to read in bed. It was another noisy night as there were a couple of drunks across the hall talking at the top of their voices – old ranchers so their laughing was rare and raw. They quieted down at midnight so we had a wonderful sleep until 10 AM. Had a big breakfast, donned our wooly pants plus skirts and sweaters and walked to the Bow Falls and about half way around the golf course. It was not too cold but very invigorating. We also have warm gloves so you see we came prepared. On the way back it started to rain – a slight drizzle but it feels like snow is in the air. We got back to town about 2 PM and am now writing to you before we start out again. One of these days we'll break down and have a swim but I can't quite see myself in a bathing suit with snow falling even if the water is hot. We took some pictures of ourselves today so will be sending you some. If only there weren't honeymoon couples around it would be ideal but I can't help watching them and envying them a great deal. However, our days will come again and with much more joy because of the waiting which doesn't improve my missing you very much. I imagine you are back at the old grind again. Read in the paper where London wasn't very bright and not without its bomb excitement. Had a letter from mother today and she and Joan are getting along very well so I'm not even thinking of them. All my love dearest – Peg

Dearest Peg,

Another good day yesterday – three letters from you. You are really spoiling me and I love it. The pictures were swell and the ones of you really hit the spot – could practically reach out and touch you and boy how I like to just be able to look at you for a minute even if I couldn't say anything – would be wonderful. Guess there is no use talking though – it may not be too long but don't think we can count on it very soon.

I have big plans when I get back – am going to grab you and go away for at least two weeks and monopolize your time completely and forget about post-war rehabilitation for that length of time anyway.

Actually got 4 letters – dated Sept 5, 8, & 9 and the one with the pictures. The daughter really looks like a toughie in some of them – must be wonderful to see her but I can see that she is really a handful.

I have quite a good stock of blue forms now, thanks to you. So you don't need to worry about sending any for a time. It must be rather difficult to get them for the both of us.

I hope you got your plane reservation – it would make quite an interesting trip and much better than the train we used to spend so much time on. Hope Ross Vant doesn't find anything too radically wrong. Johnnie Hunt is on leave.

By now you should be riding horses and climbing mountains in Banff. I hope you have nice weather.

Last night Bill Scott and I went out egg gathering with Ross Cameron, the Padre. We got half a dozen each and then came home to Ross's place and had lunch and sat around. Later on some more people dropped in and we had quite a pleasant evening all told.

Met Bill Hales today – he left Claresholm about the time we arrived. We have quite a common bond because Dad officiated at his arrival in Camrose. He wanted news of everybody. Errol Shaw, used to be at Claresholm, arrived on the station yesterday and Dave Hunter is nearby although I haven't seen him yet.

Well Peg, goodbye for now. Loads of love and kisses. Give the stinker my fondest greetings.

All my love, Hamp

Dearest Hamp

Today was a wonderful day and although the sun didn't shine it was very sunny for me. The reason? Well I got 3 letters from my dear husband and were they welcome! One had the Edinburgh pictures in it and they were good, honey. Although you still haven't lost your worried look. What was troubling you chum or is that the way you look now? Apart from that frown you still look the same and very wonderful to me. The other letters were written on the 10th and 12th and you were still buzzing around London. I'll bet it was a might drier after you folks left but still very wet eh dear?

Today we got up real early – 9.30 to be exact – had breakfast and went riding for 2 hours up the Spray Valley and around the golf course on the bridle paths. It was really super and our nags didn't go fast enough to make us stiff in fact our trouble when we first started was to get them to move but we finally persuaded them to shift a few feet forward and then with that we were away. Finished our first roll of film so will have some pictures for you tomorrow night but there won't be any of Joan in this lot.

After our ride we had a sandwich and cup of coffee and by the way the tea and coffee ration is lifted now so the war must be on the wane. After our snack we walked – yes sir, we walked and not because we couldn't sit down either – to the Cave and Basin for a swim. The water was lovely but the air was cold so after you'd been in a while you started to feel cold or rather chilly. It didn't make us sleepy at all which was a good thing as we had to walk home again. We are now drying out our hair by a roaring fire in the lounge and waiting impatiently for 6 PM so that we can eat. Got weighed at the pool in my bathing suit and I top 98 pounds – quite a figure eh honey? Can you imagine my sylph-like form? Am trying to fatten up my torso but without any results. Guess I need my honey. I feel swell however and still wish awfully that you were here. All my love always – Peg

September 23, 1944

Dearest Peg,

Didn't write yesterday and it's quite a long story – hope you'll forgive me. Thursday night Neil Gorden phoned me from his station and asked me to come over because the squadrons were not flying and they were having a party. Went over and had quite a large evening – met a lot of people I knew including Charlie Burgess and his navigator Fergie, Sam Franklyn who used to be at Claresholm in our house (he is just about through his tour now and has his S/L) and a lot of other chaps who have been here at some time or other. Also met someone named Stan Paulson who is the armament officer there and comes from Camrose. He had mickey of rum which he and I drank. Neil Gorden had a mickey of rye – which he and I tasted until it was gone and then I had numerous drinks with everyone else. Got a ride home at 3:00 A.M. and arrived here at 4:00 and in bed by 4:30. So last night I had really had it (since I took sick parade at 8:30 and carried on all day). Fell asleep on the bed and didn't wake up until 7:30 the next morning – 13 hours sleep. So maybe you won't forgive me for not writing but at least you'll understand.

The weather is now becoming like fall – the nights are cold and blackout is nearly complete by 7:30 in the evening. There is not heat for another month so I've a lot of chilly evenings ahead.

I'm now thinking about leave and will try to get away in a couple of weeks time. Don't know where to go but Bill Scott and myself will go together possibly to Northern Ireland – depending on how good our finances are since it is supposed to be expensive.

Well honey, I suddenly remembered that the Daughter has a birthday coming up – her first and the 6 month anniversary of when I left home. Haven't gotten her anything yet but will try to correct it. I think I miss you a little more every day and look forward to our reunion much more as the days go by (if that were possible). Give the stinker my love. All my love, Hamp

Dearest Hamp

The weather is improving more and more each day and today the sun is shining and the clouds are high above the mountains. It is really grand.

We went canoeing again yesterday. – This time up the Echo Creek where we canoed together last year – remember? The water is very shallow this year due to the scarcity of snow during the winter so we made good time standing up and using the paddles as poles. We fooled around splashing each other almost tipping but it was great sport.

At night – 6 PM – we bought a case of beer on my permit and made a night of it and by ourselves. That was really silly to see us propped up in bed reading and drinking the case between us and then feeling so good that we got very wise-cracky and hooted and howled at each other. We finally settled down at 2 AM and slept until noon today. The reason we laughed so hard was that we were mimicking these insurance men who came up to us at dinner trying to date us up for a drink in their room after dinner and a lot of big talk about golf and riding. If they only knew how we joked about them they'd be very embarrassed. Men on the prowl are quite funny as they all use the same line just as though they had rehearsed their speeches. Don't worry about me darling as we don't trust any body but keep strictly to ourselves. It is the best way as no one has a chance to get any ideas. Am really being good which is no trouble as I don't want to be otherwise – and heading your very wise words of 'Don't drink with servicemen'. I've changed it slightly and my motto is 'Don't drink with men'.

Have had several letters from mother and Joan is doing alright by herself but mother is beginning to feel the strain. It's amazing how Joan can wear everyone down so. We are leaving for Calgary on Monday and then for Claresholm on Wednesday. It seems ages since I left home but the change is good for me.

Hope you are liking Yorkshire again honey if you are still there. All my love dearest one – Peg

Dearest Peg,

I imagine that your holidays are just about over and you are reaching the stage where you don't want to go back but you will still be glad to get home. Should get a letter tomorrow and hear something of what you are doing. The mail is beginning to come a little better, some people are getting cigarettes so I expect that mine will be coming shortly – have practically gotten accustomed to the Limey efforts though.

Johnnie Hunt phoned tonight. He's back from leave and had a letter from Doug. Doug is apparently liking it but told Johnnie to tell me to forget about it and look after my wife and family – that advice isn't very hard to follow.

Yesterday being Sunday it was quite quiet. Went out to a pub called the Blackmoor (guess it was really an Inn) and had quite a good meal and sat around and had several beers and rather enjoyed it. Went with Jack Watts who is the W/C in accounts here.

I expect to be going to a nearby station to relieve for a week. Should leave tomorrow or the next day if Jack Peverseff comes back from leave. Macphee, the other M.O. and myself get along very well. Don't remember if I told you about him. He has been overseas for 3 1/2 years and is back from Italy and N Africa. Is single and doesn't care if he goes home or not – surprisingly enough he acts quite sanely so I can't figure it out.

The war news is good but I hope they don't develop into a static state. Am really looking forward to home (which is you). Got some more films so must start taking some more pictures. Should get a few tomorrow of Harome and must send Dad some of the old Smith Mansion (that thatched house).

Well honey will sign off – wish you were with me. Give the daughter a hug and a kiss for me – don't know how you will convey the same to yourself from me but anyway – All my love, kisses, etc. Hamp

Palliser Hotel, Calgary, Sept 25 1944

Dearest Hamp

Here we are again and right over the railway tracks. Why I patronize this hotel is more than I'll ever know.

We had a very lovely weekend as far as the weather was concerned and have sunburned faces and dried out hair but feel very wonderful whether we look it or not.

Saturday night we dropped in at the dance about 10.30 PM and had a few dances with some blokes – as you would say – and then returned to the hotel by midnight and were very glad to get to bed. We were going to be up early Sunday morning but didn't waken up until 10.30. However we got up and by the time we had dressed and had breakfast it was almost noon. We got a couple of horses and went on a trail back of the Post Office and over the edge of a mountain down into Sundance Canyon road. It was very pretty and not without its thrills as we had to descend from the heights by way of a rocky trail which zigzagged down the shoulder of the mountain and being on a horse made you feel insecure. In future I'll do my mountain climbing on my own two feet. After riding we went canoeing again as far up the Echo Creek as it is possible to go – only some rapids stopped us from proceeding. We certainly go in for strenuous exercise, don't you think? Saturday afternoon we were biking but that is not for me – I was glad to turn the bike in at the end of an hour for I got tired of looking for walks that went down hill all the way. Guess I'm getting too old. Last night we strolled up to the Banff Springs and then turned in. Up at the crack of dawn today again – 10 AM this time – and out on the horses again. Quite a horsewoman your wife is and do I love it but I had enough of the horse I was on today for it kept eating on my time and no matter what I did it wouldn't go. It took 2 hours for a one hour ride. However we told the owner and he took off 50 cents and showed us pictures of his wee nephews. Too bad I didn't have some pictures of Joan handy to compare but I wouldn't want to spoil his enthusiasm for his relatives. We are going down to Claresholm on Wednesday after a bit of shopping and hair-doing here. I'm really glad I was able to take this holiday as it's been almost perfect – as perfect as it could be without you – and I feel ready for the wintry blasts. Hope there's mail from you at Claresholm. All my love always – Peg

September 27, 1944

Dearest Peg,

Well, am in new quarters for the next 4 to 6 days relieving John MacIntyre who is on leave with his wife (our nursing sister). Am rooming with Stan Hurd the M.O. in charge here – a very good sort. No mail today but got three letters yesterday. In one you were asking to be forgiven (as if you ever need to ask that) about the misunderstanding about India and the course. At the time I wrote the letter I was going to repeat it in the next, just in case the one didn't arrive, but didn't do it, so it was my fault. Do you forgive me honey? Had better repeat – the boys from Canada are going to get the tan and we from here will be coming home if the show over here ever finishes. News isn't very good today with the British paratroopers taking a step back – hope there isn't much more news like that.

Had a swell day today – took the afternoon off – since I'm not feeling very conscientious these days. Went down to Ripon by train with Bill Scott (only about a 20 minute ride) and then rode our bikes to Fountains Abbey. It was constructed in 1000 and was quite interesting. It is set in a valley with a stream running through it. The abbey itself was in ruins but was well kept up with green lawns etc. around it. The stream had been dammed to make a succession of small lakes for about half a mile. It was the most beautiful spot I have seen in England so far. Bill and I took bags of pictures – I took about 2 1/2 rolls – a lot of them with me in the foreground and bits of the scenery behind me. They should be developed in a few days and will send them. By the way I haven't got the other pictures yet because the chap who is looking after them is on leave – back today but I am away this evening before he arrived.

We cycled back to Ripon by various country lanes most of which had gates on them with sign saying "private road – no admittance" and had supper in Ripon (fried spam, chips, fried onions and a jam tart) and then came home by train again. All in all it was very pleasant – hope the pictures turn out OK because I think you will like the spot.

Rode over about 8 PM to the station here. Bright, brisk moonlight night – sure wished I had my honey beside me but imagine there will be a lot of full moons in the future.

The daughter will be quite spoiled while you are on holiday, no doubt. Am anxious to hear how Banff is and all about Claresholm etc.

Give my regards to the Bothwells when you write them on return and tell bugger legs (Bill) not be so damned lazy and drop me a line.

Well honey, good night – all my love, Hamp

Palliser Hotel, Calgary, Sept 27 1944 11.30 AM

Dearest Hamp

I have just finished the big struggle of packing and shutting my suitcases and figure a letter to you would be a good thing while Kay struggles with her bags. She has a harder time than I do as she brought everything but the kitchen sink and is more as we go along.

My money is getting low and it looks as though I'll be writing a wee cheque in Claresholm. It is very lucky I have a ticket home. Time out to laugh at Kay as she sits on her bag and struggles away without much result.

Yesterday we had our hair done. I went downstairs and Kay was in the street as we couldn't get appointments at the same time – got soaked $1.50 for a shampoo and fingerwave – ain't it awful? Then we went shopping which was a mistake as I bought a 2 piece wool dress for $16.95 – very pretty though. The skirt is a dark plum shade and the jacket light tan with plum and green panels – sounds awful doesn't it but it's really very pretty as you will see when you come home. It's a size 11 by the way as I'm just a little girl but there was a time when I took a size 14. That was when you first knew me. See what you do to me! Also bought a dress for Joan and a fancy bib that fits over the shoulders for Larry Bothwell and Joan, a pair of earrings for mother, and a 12 inch cigar and 2 tins of stew (one beef and one lamb) for your next parcel. So far Dad is left out. Also couldn't see anything for Doris and Bill. After shopping we met Mary Frizzell and had lunch in the Oak Room. I had cracked crab and very good too. After lunch we toured the stores again but I hung on to what money I had as there's a hotel bill to face and bus fare to Claresholm. Then we went to Mary's for dinner and the evening. I phoned Doris from there. My it was good to hear her voice and she sounds the same as ever. By the way I remembered to pay for the call.

News Flash –S/L and Mrs. McKeichan are now the proud parents of a daughter born Sept 17 (gleaned from the Herald). Jack Day is also the proud Poppy of a daughter – Sherryl Louise born Sept 22nd (gleaned from the Journal). #4 and #2 HQ of RCAF are combining in December and moving to Moose Jaw so that means more postings for some people.

We are leaving on the 2.15 bus for Claresholm and so I thought I'd best write now as I may not get a chance at it tonight. Sure hope there's mail in the old town for me. All my love my dearest and I do miss you terribly. I can't say how much. Always – Peg

September 29, 1944

Dearest Peg,

Took a run today back to the station and picked up three letters from you. You had flown to Calgary and spent one day in Banff. The trip to Calgary sounded quite rough but I imagine you got more of a kick out of it than you would have it if had been plain sailing. Flying is a wonderful method of getting around but I still think it is dangerous at times.

The dentist over here is Charlie Duke – he married Grace Vikers and he took his dentistry at Alberta. He is a darn good egg. He showed me a letter he had gotten from Lorne Oatway who is in India (you probably remember Lorne who went to U of A). Lorne seemed to be enjoying the experience but didn't say one good word for the climate. He said that there was a small ant that covered the whole surface of the country and everybody in it and between the bugs and the heat – he would just as soon be home.

Look at the date – one more day and then we start winter. In 19 more days (today included) I'll have been away from you 6 months. It seems like 6 years at times but I repeat honey – you never have to worry about me – I'll be just the same as when I left and you never have to harbor any deep thoughts of me chasing around. You are my only gal and always will be. Shouldn't keep repeating this but we see so many people who worry about home and their homes worry about them and the main thing always seems to be – is he being faithful – funny world isn't it with so much depending on the sexual function – but I guess that's how it is – anyway I repeat, Hampton will never be a source of concern to you.

You asked about a part time job – as far as I'm concerned honey – you are your own boss and you couldn't find a better one. However I would sooner that you didn't tie yourself up in something that dragged out and set hours and you couldn't take a day off or sleep in if you wanted to (guess that one wishes someone else to do the things they can't). If you took an occasional job of specialling or something of that nature it would be a break for you. Don't work in a store or an office. Don't go on the staff of a hospital. A third don't – don't listen to me and do as you please dear.

Well "luv" – as they say in Yorkshire and it takes a bit of getting used to because you get on a bus etc. and they "tickets please luv, go right on through luv etc." – will sign off and quit trying to back seat drive.

All my love and kisses, Hamp

Bothwell Hotel, Claresholm, 1ˢᵗ Installment, Sept 29, 1944

Dearest Hamp

Here I am back at the old stomping ground and the place looks the same except for a few new coats of paint and minor alterations. Dr Carroll has built another house between Palmers and the lane. I didn't think there was room for one but there it is and the same size as the Glanville's too. Scofields are to move in it but Scofield smashed a plane beyond repair while landing the other day and is grounded now so he may not be needing the place.

Was over at Lawson's yesterday for a small get together with Hughie, Doris, June Olson, Marj Hutchison and Mrs. Carroll. Dr Lawson is no longer in the RCAF-he was discharged 2 weeks ago. Quite a surprise. Yes? No? He is at present at Mayo's USA on a course – Physical Medicine – and then returns to the Col. Belcher where he has a position with the Civil Service. Rehabilitation, maybe – I don't really know. However it was quite a surprise to me.

June Olson is the same as ever. I haven't seen Penny yet but I hear she is a big girl and walking all over the place. Our old home doesn't look the same place at all. The walls are painted a cream color, the ceiling white and it really looks a new place altogether and quite bigger. The furniture is arranged differently too. The dining table is across the front window, the chesterfield across the corner where we had the cabinet and the cabinet by the phone with an easy chair and radio by the stairs and the other chair where we used to have it. I preferred our way of course! And was very glad the place did not look the same as I don't think I could stand to stay for afternoon tea this afternoon if it were exactly as we left it. The Hutchinson's are expecting a baby in a few months – it seems funny to see Marj so fat. Mrs. Carroll is much the same and paid you quite a compliment. They had the Blood Clinic down a while ago and apparently things didn't go as smoothly as when you handled it. Mrs. Carroll said that she and the doctor had been talking about how well the clinic had gone when you were here and they couldn't say the same for the last one. So I guess you're quite a boy especially when I remember how some of the local gals raved about you after you'd done your wee bit for the Red Cross.

Kennedy is down at McLeod as CO here with Leverimore as CI. TP is adjutant. Bill and Harry Pateman are flight commanders of SBA and still grousing away about this and that and that and this. Bill claims he's lost weight. Now weighs 190 but I fail to see the difference and Doris still kids him about his plush seat spread. This is only the first installment of the letter and so will continue on another form. Everybody wants to be remembered to you. All my love dearest and miss you – Peg

2nd Installment, Sept 29 1944

Dearest Hamp

You'll never guess what it's doing outside – a real gale with snow – yes snow – flying fast and furiously. Good old Claresholm and yesterday was such a perfect day. Kay and I came down by bus on Wednesday – stood up until High River and then got a seat. We are sure traveling in every conceivable way. Kay is at Nanton visiting her brother's in-law.

Doris is still the same old Doris but not as slim as she used to be before Larry got on the way. She has been quite lonely without us as she doesn't get out as much as she used to do. Bill wishes 'old doc' was here so you could have good arguments about our families. He's really quite taken with 'the boy' and rightly so as he's a cute fellow. Larry has Doris' eyes and hair coloring but it is hard to tell just who he looks like. He's a good baby and is busy all the time sitting up and trying to crawl. Says 'Dada' too so he's doing all right. Bill built Larry's crib and it's really quite an affair as it's made to fold up and fit in the trunk you boys made. It's all smoothed off and varnished with stencils of little horses on it. A real job. Larry sleeps in a corner of the front room and I sleep on the couch so we are quite chummy. I'm sleeping with a man in my room – aren't you jealous honey?

Last night Harry and Etta Pateman, Doris, Bill and I got in Miranda and went for a steak roast out to the creek where the instructors had their party when you got Alice all beered up. We had a real good feed and sat around talking until 11 PM. Then drove back to King's to pick up Larry and I drove Miranda back here. She's a good car and Bill got synthetics for her and a 'B' ration so they are all set. The old car really purrs along.

This afternoon Doris and I are going to Olson's for tea and tonight over to Godley's for a beer party. Saturday night the Patemans are coming over for supper and then we are going out to the Mess. I sure wish you were here honey as I miss you more than ever down here. It brings back such happy memories but I'm being brave – yes siree!

Got 3 letters from you upon arrival here and was very, very pleased to know you will be around there for the duration – what ever that may be. But it sure sounds better than other countries I can think of. Glad there was a parcel for you when you got back. You should have your birthday present by now – hope everything fits.

My next letter will probably be from Edmonton as we fly from Calgary Sunday night provided the storm stops a blowing around. I'll be glad to see little Joan again for although I've had a good holiday away from her I kind of miss her. All my love dearest, Peg

OCTOBER 1944

October 1, 1944

Dearest Peg,

Sunday and very little doing and have done nothing since I last wrote except sit around and drink tea. The Medial Officer here is Stan Heard – he doesn't like England, he doesn't like the English, he isn't fussy about being overseas. Not very good company because he keeps mentioning his dislikes in no uncertain terms. I get great delight in being the Pollyanna of the crowd and sitting back and saying it isn't good but if you've got to fight a war, it's not a bad spot to fight one from with tea twice a day. Don't think he appreciates me however.

Have been busy at nights writing up my course on Tropical Medicine – had it copied on bits and pieces of paper and since some of it may someday be useful out on the prairies, I'm kind of consolidating it in a half decent manner. Don't go back to Topcliffe until Tuesday night and will be kind of glad to get back to where I know someone.

The sick quarters here are the same as ours – all the permanent RAF stations are built on identical plans – even have the same bottles in them practically – so it's no effort to find your way around.

Am curious to hear how your holiday went. Sure wished I could have been along but really count on doing some day with you when we can go and do as we want e.g. mountains and horses etc. without worrying how "Junior" is getting along.

By the way honey, you may notice that my writing is not very good – kind of buggered up my pen by dropping it point down on the floor. If war news isn't too good will ask you about January to try get me a new nib – a broad brush one.

Don't plan to go on leave now until Nov. because want to go to Northern Ireland and hear it is expensive so will save some money. It's amazing where the money goes although lately have been buying cigarettes and that costs about a pound every 8 or 10 days. However the tobacco pool is beginning to operate so it won't be long now.

Have procrastinated (as usual) so long on Joan's birthday present that I will probably not get one in time we will leave it to you and send her something not so personal by wire.

Well honey, sure miss you as usual. Would like to deliver love and kisses in person but guess it's not feasible just now. All my love, Hamp

At Home, Oct 2 1944

Dearest Hamp
    Wrote you last Friday and am a bit behind with this letter but didn't

have time to write. To continue from the last letter-

Friday afternoon Doris and I went to Olson's for tea. Dorothy Burton and Myrna were there. Penny has grown but still looks the same, not very much hair and her funny wee face. Myrna is quite and girl and quite spoiled as you can imagine. Bruce came in before I left and asked all kinds of questions as he expects to go overseas this month. At night, Bill was Orderly Officer much to his disgust, so Doris and I went on a spree as Patemans asked us to a beer party. The Godleys and the Burtons were there and we had a lot of fun with that screwy Harry. We played '7 Up' – of course – and I made $1.50 so you see I didn't let your reputation as a card shark down. Also drank my share of beer as Harry didn't want me to let you down on that score either. However I didn't get any where near to being blitzed so Harry had to give up his effort when the beer ran out. Then we had bacon and eggs, bread, coffee and really had a good feed. Pat Burton as usual had to be wakened up for food – I guess 5 cents a cards is a pretty low stake for him. Billy came in about midnight talking his usual cowboy lingo and generally letting himself be heard. Myrna was up until after midnight but nearly dropped in her tracks before she was put on the chesterfield. We stayed until 2.30 AM and them scrambled home and into bed real fast.

Doris and I had a real long talk the next morning and then got cracking on a roast beef dinner as Ettie and Harry were coming over for dinner. The meat was cooked far too long for our liking dear so you really didn't miss much on that score. We went out to the Mess after and it was the Atkinson's 8th wedding anniversary so Marjorie and Derek had a small party so there were more people out there than usual. Talked to the CO and Walt said they hadn't found anyone who could beat your record for downing the potion. That really must have been something! The Livermores, TP's, Kennedys, Atkinsons, Flowers, Featherstones, Clarksons were there and all asked to be remembered to you. Also saw Kirkland, Ernie Watson, Puffer, Doc Simpson and one or two others whose names I've forgotten. I drank my favorite – rye and ginger all night – but Etta started out on a mixture of scotch and gin due to a barman's mistake instead of scotch and water. That drink was really something! I had a sample and it made my drink taste like water. Left Sunday on the 1.25 bus and arrived in Calgary at 4.15. Discovered at 9PM that the plane was an hour late so I could have taken the late bus and stayed five hours longer in Claresholm. However, we sat around the Palliser and eventually got home after an uneventful but beautiful moonlit plane ride and our holiday was over. It was really a grand change and we had a lot of fun but I still wish you had been along. All my love dear and more about home now – Peg

October 3, 1944

Dearest Peggy,

Tonight I go back to Topcliffe. Expect to get some mail when I arrive. Really something to look forward to. By the way, I'm still waiting for the pictures to be developed and should have them tomorrow (how many times have I said that now!).

Sunday night after I wrote you we had quite a panic. I got called about 2:30 AM Mon. I went dashing off with the ambulance to a spot about 15 miles away. It was a brilliant moonlight night and was quite a nice ride except for the fact that I knew we weren't going to have much fun when we got there. We saw the fire when we were about half a mile away and it was quite a sight with ammunition going off and flares exploding with all their colors. The aircraft was pretty well burnt and after it cooled a bit I had to go in and fish out 4 bodies. Three chaps baled out without injury and one baled out but too low so he got killed. Then we got home about 5:00 AM and to bed by 6 after I had gotten all them identified – quite a job and only possible by bits of letters etc.

Yesterday and today have been quiet however and tomorrow I get back on the old routine at home station. Things are quite quiet at present since the days are clear but cool. The mornings have brilliant sunshine which lasts until about 1:00 PM and then it clouds with scattered showers. At evening it clears and with the full moon at present, it is really quite nice. Wish you were here honey and we could give that moonlight some reason for shining. However it may not be long.

There is going to some kind of a shake up in our clutch shortly and our establishments are being altered. I may be posted to a neighboring RCAF station but don't know yet.

I have tried to get into a General Hospital treating nothing but G.M. patients and mainly V.D. Haven't had much success. It would be dull work but I hope to get a G.M. practice some day. Well honey, that's about all the chatter for now. Will write tomorrow when I get the mail (I hope). All my love to you and pass some along to Joan from her old man. Hamp

Dearest Hamp

Well it's good to be home and was I glad to see the daughter. I didn't think I missed her but when I was almost home I could hardly wait to see her. I knew she had blue eyes and blond hair but beyond that I didn't recognize her. She certainly has changed – seems much fatter and has learned lots of new tricks. When an airplane goes over the house or a train goes on the bridge Joan sticks her hand in the air and goes 'Oh! Oh!'. If you say to her 'Where's Daddy?' she points to the picture of the three of us and goes 'Dada'. When she gets in the bedroom she immediately crawls to the bedside table and takes our picture in her hands and sits down and points at you as says 'Dada'. The closes it up and turns it around and around and then opens it up quickly and burst into peals of laughter as she sees the picture again. She's really quite a girl. She's trying awfully hard to master the art of walking and has done 3 steps so far but she's well on the way to tottling by herself. She's really the cutest she has ever been and do I wish you could see her now.

Gus garrison phoned last night wanting your number. He's been posted overseas and leaves on Thursday. Claire will be living in Edmonton so I'll have to see her sometime.

Miss Peters phoned when I was away and also last Monday offering me a part time job if I cared to help them out so after talking if over with mother I accepted and started work today. It is really super. I work form 9 to 1 every day but Sunday and am in the examining room on the ground floor. I'm my own boss and just do what I like. The examining room now handles small cases like injecting veins, some types of suturing, ambulatory dressings, examinations, accidents etc. I get my lunch, my laundry and $42 a month which isn't bad at all. This is more or less an experiment as I took it on condition that if I found it too heavy or if Mother did then I could quit. I intend to pay Ma another $20 a month so I'll just be making pin money but it's better than half sitting around all day. Today I had one of the staff who cut his finger, two examinations and an infected hand. Yes – you're right – Alexander presided.

Yesterday afternoon I was downtown rounding up some more things for our Christmas box. Also ordered some more cigarettes. By the way I got 3 receipts so you should have at least 900 by now. Also made the last payment on our bonds and deposited $90. to our account so our account is back to $200 again after my trip. We now have 3 more bonds to our name too so if you stay away long enough I may get $500 saved but please don't stay away on that account.

The war has seemingly slowed up again – which was to be expected but I sure hope we get the breaks from now on. Joan is in the midst of the magazines and having a wonderful time but it's rather risky as she still loves to tear up the paper. Am going to Flemings for a goose dinner at 9 PM tonight when Sandy returns from shooting. Fortunately Doris has the goose now so we won't be disappointed. Joan sends big kisses and hugs and I send all my love – as ever and always-Peg

October 4, 1944

Dearest Peg,

Really had luck yesterday – got 3 letters from you – one with the picture and they were really good. Have received nothing but favorable comment from the 50 people I have shown them to so far. You are getting more beautiful every day and the daughter is becoming as charming as her mother. Really give you a homesick pang to see who I am so far away from – however honey – you'll be so nice to come hone to. Two letters were air mail and dated Sept 21 and 22 and they came at the same time as the ordinary mail dated Sept. 21 – so you just can't tell these days. That 98 pounds doesn't sound so good skinny – you had better start eating potatoes and macaroni or drinking beer or something.

I got some pictures today finally and am sending them along to you. They are actually very poor but the best effort I can produce. The most are snaps of Fountains Abbey and the pictures of me are very poor (ahem). However there are some others taken with a New Zealand pilot and his girl with Neil Gorden and myself. We snapped them when we were going through a park in London and they got talking to us since she was a Canadian. Don't know their names but they are quite harmless. Also took pictures of Harowe Yorks but they didn't turn out so will have to go back and try again.

Was not very busy today – did buggar all to put it crudely and hope it doesn't last that way. Tonight I did a little dicing as the saying goes (dicing with death). Went flying for about an hour just to see how night flying went. Enjoyed it a lot but will not be doing any more. Have flown about all I want to for awhile – a good crash robs you of a lot of your enthusiasm for awhile.

Well honey, I miss you very much. Your pictures are wonderful. Wish we were together but will be all the more wonderful when we are – absence really does make you realize how lucky you are to be able to be with one. All my love, Hamp

October 4, 1944

Dearest Peg,

Enclosed are a whole bunch of pictures and none of them any good. Part of the fault is that they are poorly printed but can't do much about that just at present.

There are endless pictures of us and Fountains Abbey and you'll not find them very interesting but am sending them along so you can kind a keep them for the family album so I can look back on the Battle of Yorkshire.

The three of London are fairly good except the girl – she's not with us, I repeat again. We all look quite pleased with everything – namely because the sun was shining. Also Neil and I had just had a couple of beers and were strolling along and got chatting with these people. On the same roll I had a shot of Westminster and the Houses of Parliament – taken on the fly. They didn't turn out – suspect that my photography is no good and neither is the guy who develops them for me.

Well will sign off – am writing a blue form tonight also. All my love, Hamp

Dearest Hamp

I'm a day behind schedule again but I've really got a good reason this time. Was going to write you last night after getting Joan settled and before going out to Alix's but lo and behold (or is that the right thing to say now? On second thought it doesn't sound very good!) the little visitor's arrived for this month two days early and caught me unprepared as they gave no warning so I had to dash out to the drugstore before it closed and then kept right on to the Day's. So you see it was a case of Mother Nature first and you next. Sorry honey but I'll try not to let *anything* interfere again.

I'm very pleased with my job as it isn't much work at all in fact the last two days has been almost no work – two patients yesterday and two today. The room is sure spotless if I do say so myself as I've scrubbed everything in it – in my own time in my own way – and I sterilize the instruments for something to do. Took inventory yesterday and got replacements for all the missing articles so the place is all stocked up and ready for anything. Hope some activity starts soon as I would like to think that I learned more than how to clean things when training. However as I've said it's really a super job and I'm really glad to be back in the swing of things at old UAH while I'm 'a-waitin for ma man'. Joan does OK under this split care and isn't spoiled at all – yet – as far as I can tell.

We get up at 7A.M. – which is when Joan arises anyway – and I dress her and feed her and then have my breakfast and get dressed and then work by 9. Joan stays inside until a little after 10 as the mornings are chilly and then goes outside in the playpen where she plays until lunch time. Mother feeds her and puts her to bed so I actually don't miss much of her at all as I'm home to get her up. I get out of house work though and some days the washing too as mother does it if she has time as before and I really feel much happier having my days filled and if you can believe it I've gained a pound already. Had a chest x-ray done on Thursday and all is well as we knew anyway – or did we?

Was over at Flemings on Wednesday night as I mentioned for a goose dinner. Doris had to retire to bed as she was starting into labor a few weeks early as the baby is supposed to be very small Dr Vant put her to bed. She seems to be OK so far. Speaking of babies, Jack Day's daughter died from hemorrhage and his wife Connie is very ill with puerperal sepsis and apparently she can't take sulpha drugs. She was in labor from Monday to Saturday and I mean Monday to Saturday and has had nearly all the complications in the book. Some people have all the breaks don't they? They think Jack is on his way back now. Henderson next door is on his way home – forced down at sea etc and now getting leave. By the way Echo Tetzloff is wearing Sammy Epstein's ring – you remember Sam, Sam the wonder man? – Well him in 'poison'.

Marg and Bill are down in Camrose for Thanksgiving. Irene phoned and invited Joan and I down but didn't think it fair for Margaret as they do make more fuss of Joan – if I do say so – so had my job as an excuse but actually could have gotten away. We'll go down some other time.

Joan walked five steps to me tonight but is still pretty scared at being on her own two feet and wouldn't try again but she's getting there. We bought her a Toidy chair in blue for the toilet and a blue padded seat so she sits on the 'big doings' now like a king on the throne and has a whale of a time but won't do her business in the lap of such luxury so will have to retrain the gal to the super model. You're quite an important guy for 'Dada' is all she's been able to say for the last two days and I can hardly get your picture away from her so maybe you'd better come back and look after her as I seem to be of no account. All my love, luv, Peg

October 7, 1944

Dearest Peg,

Well, 3 more days gone by. Sorry I didn't keep up my writing routine yesterday but it is a long story. Last night (Friday) was in the start of writing my letter to you when we had a panic – somebody riding a motorcycle ran into the front of a truck – took his right leg off just above the knee, gashed himself up pretty badly. We poured in plasma and blood, etc. tied off some vessels and shipped him out, but he isn't in very good shape. The chap with him had a compound fracture of the femur – so it was quite a flap. Earlier in the evening I went over to G/C

295

Verner – the engineering officers place and played knock rummy in front of a fireplace (he lives in a house of his own on the station) and won 47 shillings – quite a profitable evening.

The night before Jack Watt and I got a ride up to Charlie Burgess' squadron where they were having a party. Charlie and I (I am ashamed to admit) both were very intoxicated since he had a bottle of Scotch and then Jack and I came home without hitting anything in the car he borrowed – sure do foolish things though and am going to reform. Can't see any point in going out any more because there is nothing to do but sit around with the blokes and drink and when you do that you invariably get squiffed. The next morning I wasn't feeling too bright so I rode up to see Johnnie Hunt since George Elliott (the chap in charge of V.D. control for the RCAF Overseas) was here and going up. Had a very pleasant morning. Johnnie's brother, Bill was up there with him for a few days.

Got a letter from you yesterday dated Sept. 25. You were back in Calgary and seemed to have had a good holiday. I'm certainly glad you got away on it because you seemed to be getting a little brassed with your daily routine – hope you can put on some weight honey.

Well dear – the war news doesn't encourage one to expect an early cessation but am more cheerful about waiting when I realize that I won't be getting that sunburn. Sure miss you and love you.

All my love, Hamp

October 8, 1944

Dearest Peggy,

Nothing much to write about since yesterday Sunday is generally a quiet day with us sitting around all afternoon talking and complaining and guessing when the war is going to end. By the way, our discussion group decided that things are a little more hopeful for an earlier ending than they were a few days ago.

Jim Bailey just phoned up from a nearby station and is coming over to eat and discuss the situation over a pint. He is just nearing the end of his training and in about 6 or 8 weeks will be in operations in a heavy bomber group – hope he gets along all right.

By the way honey – I finally got my leave straightened out. I am going to leave this coming Friday and am going to Ireland. Will go to Belfast first then have borrowed a few civilian clothes and will go south to Dublin. Bill Scott and I are going – will go as far as Cork I expect and then more or less wander back and try to see as much of the country as possible. Don't expect to see many of the O'Smith's but should have quite a nice holiday.

Apparently food isn't rationed and you can get steaks and also the streets are lighted with neon signs etc. so it will be quite a treat.

Few hours' interruption. Jim came over and we had several pints and he has gone and I'm about ready for bed. We chatted about Claresholm and got it pretty well discussed.

Well honey, will sign off. Sure wish we could take this trip together but –.

Give my love to Joan. Didn't send her anything for her birthday except a few posies – hope they got there on the right day. All my love, Hamp

Oct 9 1944

Dearest Hamp

Happy Thanksgiving Day to you my darling.

We have had a very quiet day here – just like a Sunday except that I went to work for 4 hours and didn't do a darnn thing. There were no patients for the Examining Room and I didn't see any doctors but heard Dr Vant in the hall. Not bad getting paid 43 ¾ cents an hour for doing nothing and a full course dinner on top of that eh honey? And do I make the most of my dinner too! Where my appetite has finally sprung from is a mystery but now I can't eat enough. Food is a real treat now after not caring whether I ate or not for so long. I'm going to be so full of energy when you come home and so darn fat that you won't recognize me for a few minutes. Before I went to Banff I didn't have much energy to do anything. Everything was such an effort that I put off doing lots of things that needed doing and I was getting pretty depressed and hard to live with too, I think, but that's all changed now. Just what the answer is I'm not quite sure for I'm doing more in a day now than before. Could be that's the answer.

Got your cute 'don't' letter on Saturday and am taking some of your advice chiefly not listening to you very much. However darling, I won't go on to a full time job because Joan is my main and first responsibility and anyway I want to be around her as much as possible because she's so cute and ¾ you. Also won't do general duty even for 4 hours and the hours in a doctor's office are not suitable as it's afternoon work. I'm really just on this job temporarily as the woman who really has it is on sick leave and Miss Peters doesn't know when she is coming back. She's been away 3 months now so it may not last long. If they want to keep me at the hospital they'll have to offer me something about the same or I'll just come home.

The new Soldier's hospital is almost ready for use – two wings 3 stories high and with a big auditorium and projection room. It is connected to the main hospital by an underground tunnel.

Took some pictures of Joan today but she's a real hellion so don't know how many will turn out. When she gets annoyed at anything she goes beet red in the face and waves her arms around. If I'm holding her up on her feet and she wants to go one way and I want to go the other there's an awful fuss with bouncing up and down on the feet. So it looks, darling, as though we're going to have fun training our child eh honey? And Joan doesn't get her own way all the time believe me but she sure likes to try and show us who should be boss. She's developed a lot in the past few days and can bend down and get up without hanging on to anything. By the time you get this she should be walking and in a few weeks she'll have four more teeth at the bottom to correspond with the top. She has 12 teeth now.

The buzz bombs are around again so the news has it. I sure hope this bloody war doesn't last so very much longer, everyone is getting tired of it all but still carrying on. You should have your sweater by now. Again I sure hope it fits. All my love dearest and Joan sends love too – Peg

October 10, 1944

Dearest Peg,
Winter is coming and the weather is slowly getting worse with the

fog and rain beginning to appear. The heat has now been turned on however, so it's not so bad. Am gradually getting things lined up for leave – will go to Belfast and then to Dublin and then to Cork. Am kind of looking forward to it although traveling is a damn nuisance – makes you appreciate home though.

Yesterday got a chance to have a flip in a new aircraft and went to a nearby station and back. Sat in the mid upper turret and amused myself whirling around and shooting down imaginary people. Was quite a nice ride although it was a bit misty and a lot of the time we were in cloud – am definitely not going up again however. Last night went into Thirsk with the pilot who took me – a kid named Stu Black, along with two others – Jim Dunlop and Dave Graham and we had a steak dinner and then came home by 9:15 and went to bed. Rather an enjoyable evening.

It looks bad for the moment – just had a panic for the ambulance to pick up a bicycle prang so will sign off for the moment.

Minor prang with a few stitches in his head and nothing serious.

The mail is quite slow at present over the station but should get a letter or so, one of these days.

Don't know if I told you – I scrounged some cigarettes from Johnnie Hunt and hope to pay him back one of these days.

The victory bonds on and I don't know whether to buy a hundred or 150. Am going to have it sent to you and registered in your name – so we should get it. Also honey – we are all caught up with our bonds now, aren't we? If not, let me know. I think Father kind of grabbed our last effort but guess it is OK.

Well dear, guess I will hit the hay and will write you tomorrow. After Friday there won't be any letters for about 8 days while I'm away. I will continue to write however and will mail then all in a bunch when I get back. Miss you an awful lot and love you more every day. All my love, Hamp

Oct 11 1944

Dearest Hamp

Got 3 letters from you yesterday after the weekend and Monday holiday. It sure is grand to hear from you and know you are still wanting to come home. Ha! Ha! Those crashes must be awful I'd sure hate to do your work my darling. I hope you won't get too hard.

Am glad you got the pictures so soon. It's kind of silly the way they go airmail on a four cent stamp but very nice though.

Alix and I went to the show last night. It wasn't very good but I enjoyed it as I was in the mood for a show. It was that little punk of a Robinson in 'Destroyed' and another silly comedy. That is the extent of my night life in over a week.

Now that I have some place to go every day i.e. the hospital I don't have the urge to go on the tear every afternoon and night. I'm more settled now so I guess that's why I'm gaining a little weight. Before Banff it seemed I just had to be on my way somewhere all the time.

Was up seeing Doris Fleming today. She's still sticking around and not very happy as Dr Vant won't let her up. Connie Day went home yesterday so it almost sounds like a lot of heavy talking – meaning that it couldn't have been as serious as at first suspected.

Haven't had any news from Camrose for over a month but hear they are alright. Guess I'd better drop them a line soon. Joan is sure growing up. She's a wee girl now and not a baby any longer or have I mentioned that before?

Today at Flemings she was on her best behavior and Sandy was making quite a fuss of her so she kept going at him. Sure wish you were here so Joan would know her Dada. She sure raves about you and your picture though from early morning to early night.

The weather is swell now – real Indian summer days and awfully good for hiking. Maybe next fall we can be going up the river I hope. I don't want to seem too anxious but what about my cashmere sweater Honey? All our love dearest – Peg. Joan sends a big juicy kiss.

October 12, 1944

Dearest Peg,

Didn't write last night because there was nothing to write about. The day was quiet and we sat around and watched it rain and listened to the wind blow. In the evening Neil Gorden came over and we sat around with MacPhee and had a pint and talked and then I went to bed.

Today I got three letters from you and it was wonderful to hear from you and all about Claresholm. The news about the MacKeichren was really something – it just shows how few clues nature has doesn't it honey. Bob Lawson's discharge was rather a surprise – guess he is in an ideal situation for him and it kind of takes care of any worries he might have had for his future. The description of the old place in Claresholm certainly fills me with nostalgia or some such stuff – could weep when we recollect all the good times we had there together but – will be repeating before long I hope. Bill and Harry will probably be coming overseas one of these days and I will be seeing them.

Tomorrow Bill Scott and I set out on our travels. We are going in civilian clothes since you can't cross the border in uniform without being interned. I got a pair of tropical (summer uniform) pants from Jack Peverseff and a coat from Johnnie Hunt. The pants have room for me and a sack of flour and the coat is built to include Johnnie's stomach, so I've got lots of room but will be quite comfortable.

We will probably stay a day or two in Belfast, then go to Dublin and then to Cork and then home again. It should be a good trip but I don't care one way or another about seeing Ireland except to say I have been there.

Had a letter from Dad and one from Mother. Dad writes a whole page and tells me buggar all about what's going on and I couldn't read it even if he did – but it's sure good to hear from them. Mother's letter was dated Aug. 27 so most of the news was old stuff about David (Marg's infant) and so on.

Well honey, miss you very much – love you very much – give the daughter a hug and a kiss on her birthday from me and tell her that next birthday she has, I'll send her a real present and hope I can deliver it in person. Don't be too anxious about getting a job Peg unless you really get fed up with things. All my love, Hamp

October 13 1944

Dearest Peg

Friday the thirteenth – a fine day to be setting out on leave. At present I am in a Salvation Army hostel in Newcastle waiting for a train to Carlisle. We got here about 3.30 this afternoon and after checking baggage and getting the gen from the RTO we went out to tea. I had a lobster salad that was very good. Then we went to a show that was just mediocre and then after wondering around in the rain came to a hotel and went in and got a chicken dinner – quite a pleasant surprise for us even if the chicken was boiled. Then we sat in the George until 9.30 and drank a couple of beers and now we are waiting for our train to leave at 12.30. Get to Carlisle at 2.05 – catch the boat train at 2.35 and get on the boat at 7 AM tomorrow. Quite a night yet but we aren't very busy and are very philosophical about it.

Today I finally got your birthday present away – it isn't very fancy and not much of a surprise but it's the best I could do at the moment. Hope it gets to you on time. Say by the way (the scrounging starts again) I'm down to my second last tube of Pepsodent tooth paste – could you send a couple of tubes with the next box (I'm confidently assuming there will be one). Bought a $100 bond yesterday, was going to get $150 but weakened at the last minute. Didn't get one at Lachine and by the time I finish this leave I'll be broke so you can see I've wasted $100 I ought to have put into a bond. I will try to rectify it though.

By the way, our Flight Sergeant at the hospital, Jack Maddox, is posted home after 3½ years overseas. He and his wife are going to the coast on holiday and I gave him your address and telephone number and asked him to give you a buzz as he went through Edmonton. He is a very good chap and has a very nice wife apparently for he is even better correspondent than I am and that's pretty hard after 3½ years away. He will be able to tell you all about how your other half is getting along and I hope you get this letter before he gets there. He may not go west but promised to phone you if he did.

Well honey, will sign off for the present and add to the epistle as we go along.

Saturday October 14 – Well honey, Bill and I are now in Belfast and we still have scarcely recovered enough to give a damn. Got about 2 hours sleep last night and then got on the boat. Sat down to breakfast and then we started to get out in the Channel so I stopped eating because I suddenly lost my appetite. It was very rough and I stood leaning over tossing my cookies. I felt much better because there was a Royal Naval bloke one each side of me doing the same. Will continue on another form. All my love, Hamp

October 13 1944

Dearest Hamp

Friday the 13th old thing – are you superstitious? Nothing has happened to us today as far as I can figure out. Was at work (?) again this morning and had one patient at 9.00 for an examination by Dr Anderson. The rest of the morning was my own to scrub enamelware and sterilize things and then sit and try to look busy when anyone came around. Have thought it would be a good time to write you but on the other hand I'd be afraid Dr McGugan or someone would come in and my letter would not be its usual masterpiece (ahem!)

Last night Joan was really off the beam for the first time in her life. She wakened up at midnight and couldn't get off to sleep again and so rutted around for an hour and then started to cry. .She howled and howled and nothing would please her. I gave her your picture to try and stop her crying but she said a tearful 'Dada' and threw it on the floor. Next I offered her a drink of water and she splashed that around her bed so I got real big hearted and took her in bed with me – as usual. She stopped after another 15 minutes for about an hour and then started up again. We finally got to sleep at 5 AM and Joan was sawing off little wooden blocks when it was time to get up. Still can't figure out what got into her. However she's OK now and quite the wee miss with her trying to get her own way all the time and not succeeding.

Got the first of your Christmas parcels off today. It has been ready almost a week but no one went downtown. However 10lbs 7oz of it got off today – thanks to mother. It is full of food. Mother says the church have sent you a box too containing a box of chocolates and other goodies. Don't forget to write and thank them this time, buggerlugs, whether you know the people or not. Write to Mr. Daniel Young. He married us you know honey and as how you were as near to your right mind as possible at the time, you should remember him. Enough of this twaddle but don't forget just the same.

This is my third consecutive night at home. Not bad for a change eh? If I don't make a date with Alix I never see her as she never phones me. Wonder how long it would last if I didn't break down. That seems to be all for now so will sign off for another time. Joan sends great hugs and kisses. All my love dearest, Peg

Dearest Peg

Saturday's letter continued.

As I was saying the trip was very rough and if I had felt any worse I wouldn't be living to write about it. Bill and I were eating and I got a bit green – Bill laughed and continued his breakfast and told me that my mistake was you shouldn't take fluids. About half an hour later his skin got the color of a shamrock and he proceeded to feed fishes. Made me feel a little better.

Just about everybody aboard was sick including navy and airforce so I admit I'm a bum traveler but it was partly the fact that it was a very rough sea and a small flat boat.

When we got there the sun was shining and we were really beginning to feel that it was worth it after all. Came by train to Belfast and got a double room with bath at the Grad Central Hotel – just luck since we had no reservation. Then we had dinner and came up and slept until 6 PM – went for an hour's walk saw the town hall and a few places, bought the paper and some apples, had dinner and have now collapsed in our room again.

Gee whiz honey sure wouldn't wish this morning's trip onto anyone I love such as yourself but still it would be wonderful to see this emerald isle together. Tomorrow we are going sightseeing and the next day will leave for Dublin. Will sign off and add to this tomorrow.

Sunday Oct 15/44

Here we are again honey. Today we got up at 0900 after having had 10 ½ hours sleep and set out to see Dublin. Took a tram out to Bellevue Gardens which is on the side of Belfast Lough with County Down in the distance. It was a clear sunny day and warm so we are lucky. The gardens are very pretty and we got several pictures with Cave Hill in the background. This is a rock promontory which dominates Belfast. After exploring this area we came back by Belfast Castle. Couldn't go in because the navy has taken over. Then came back to the hotel for lunch, looked at our guide books and decided that we'd seen just about all of Belfast. Walked down and took a picture of the town hall and then went to a show – really corny – Dorothy Lamore in 'Her Jungle Love' and are now back at the hotel.

Belfast is certainly crowded with service people of all descriptions with navy predominating. I'm glad I haven't got my uniform with me – too good to stroll along the street and act like an Irishman. Sure got mad at Bill – he is trying to develop an Irish accent and keeps practicing it on the natives much to their disgust.

Well honey, will sign off and tomorrow we go to Dublin – hope we won't have any difficulty crossing the border (coming back anyway). All my love, Hamp

October 16 1944

Dearest Hamp

I'm a day late writing again and have no good excuse except that when I was through my daily routine – which is usually about 8.30 PM – I was not in a very good mood and figured I'd write the wrong type of letter – you know, one in which I'd blow my top and crab and complain etc. – so read for a while and then went to bed.

Saturday Alix and I went for a long walk around Garneau and yesterday I took Joan over to see Doris and Sandy. Really a very exciting weekend don't you think honey? It wasn't a very quiet Sunday afternoon at Fleming's as Joan always goes berserk when she gets near Sandy. I practically tidied their whole apartment cleaning up after Joan before we left. Was going to leave her at home for a change but mother was down with one of her tired spells again and stayed in bed until supper time. She's some better today.

You won't know the old house when you come back as we've had it insulated and on Wednesday are going to have the living room, dining room and halls papered. Real snooty, eh?

Scandal at the hospital has it that Dr Ellis was named correspondent in a divorce case and is going to marry the lady concerned – Mrs. Louis Hyndman. This will be her 3rd marriage, 2nd divorce. Sounds like Ellis got himself hooked but then one never knows.

Had a blood count taken today and tomorrow am going down to Dr Anderson's office for a check-up. Just routine hospital stuff. Then on Friday I go to see Dr Vant. I should visit a dentist and Joan should be vaccinated so again we are having our little tours.

Joan will be a year old tomorrow. It really doesn't seem possible. When I look at her I wonder where the time has gone. I hate to realize that the days aren't waiting for us, as we are for each other, but are gliding by. I hate to think of getting older without you beside me to watch me graciously age. I'll try not to have gray hair when you come back and will promise not to dye it. How's that you old BB?

Joan is sure cute as a button and if I do say so myself has the loveliest cornflower blue eyes. Her hair is platinum – not a yellowy color but real white and her little teeth are so pearly white. She' got a good tan and her cheeks are rosy so all in all she's the spittin' image of health – and you I must add. Guess our boy will look like me the poor handicapped soul.

This letter should reach you just about your birthday so here's hoping you have a very lovely time and happy returns of the 28th my darling. Don't get too drunk but do have fun. I hope your birthday presents and food arrived in time – they aren't much but I can't get or send the things I'd really like to.

I'll say goodnight my dearest and all our best. We all hope you'll be home for your next birthday. Bags and bags of hugs and kisses and loads and loads of love – always – Peg

Oct 17/44

Dearest Peg

Well, here we are in Dublin. 365 days ago I was the proudest man that ever walked as I looked at my wife and realized that she had produced a daughter for us and was well. Still remember how blue your eyes were as you opened them up and looked at me as I came into your room. You grow more wonderful with each passing day.

We got into Dublin yesterday about 4 PM and had a nice journey down lasting about 3 hours. The train had a diner on it and it was quite something to have a meal on the train again. None of the English trains have diners on them since war began. When we got here we couldn't get a taxi so we got a (trotting??) cart. It's drawn by one horse and is a tow wheeled cart for 4 people. You sit with your feet hanging over the sides with nothing over your head but the sky. We sure felt a bright looking pair as we went wheeling down the main drag with the rain coming down and a rug over our knees and stopped outside a very nice hotel on O'Connell Street. We eventually got a room at the Shelbourne Hotel – it is one of the oldest hotels and very nice. – Say a funny thing happened on the way down. In our compartment were an Irish couple and an old priest. They kept boasting about Ireland and really gave us an interesting travelogue on the way down. The old priest was a friendly old fellow and seemed to know every one on the train. I asked him when the Irish sweepstakes was being run and could we get tickets. He said he would look it up since he had just happened to buy a ticket. So he pulled out his bible and opened it up and pulled out his sweepstake ticket. I thought Bill and I would explode at that point.

After getting settled at the hotel Bill and I took a stroll around. The first thing we saw was an ice cream parlor so we went in and ordered the fanciest ice cream sundae on the menu. – dripping with fruit. They have an ice cream parlor about every 5th store. It certainly is a wonderful country. We followed that up with a glass of milk – my second glass since I've been over here. After that we went to a restaurant and ordered a steak. We had a wonderful steak with all the trimmings in a very posh French restaurant – paid through the nose for it but it was a pleasure.

After that we went to a show – Bing Crosby in 'Going My Way'. Certainly enjoyed it – when we came out of the show the trams were all brightly lit, the street lights were brilliant and the store windows were lit. It was just like home. After that we had another fancy ice cream sundae and came home and collapsed into bed.

As you can see we did very little but eat – we even went by a place and saw some cream puffs and went in and bought one each and ate them in the shop.

I won't lose any weight here but certainly enjoy the place. Things England doesn't have are expensive but plentiful. Well honey, Happy Birthday to our daughter. All my love, Hamp (continuing on another form)

(Continued) Oct 17, 1944

Dearest Peg

To continue with my Dublin Diary, got up today and had sausages and eggs for breakfast then bout 11.30 proceeded to do the town. Were just going out the door when the doorman said 'Why don't you get passes to go through the Guinness' Brewery and John Powers Distillery?'. So we did. Guinness has a huge plant and we had several excellent samples and when the sightseers went through they stopped us because we were Canadians and gave us a sample of their extra special export stout – very good. We went out and had a steak dinner and took a few shots of historic spots and then went back to John Powers Distillery. We saw the plant and then the assistant assistant manager got us in an office and brought us a bottle of Irish whiskey. I drank about a tumbler full and then whizzed out feeling wonderful. We then went down to O'Connell Street and had dinner (steak of course) and had some ice cream and are now at home. Tomorrow we have to see a couple of churches, Trinity College Library etc.

Dublin is really an excellent city and I think one of the nicest I have seen (even without the steaks etc). You would really like it Peg, we must try to see it sometime together. O'Connell Street was pretty much destroyed during the fighting in 1916 and again in 1921-22. It is all rebuilt with new buildings and is very attractive. Well, will sign off for the night and continue tomorrow.

Oct 18, 1944

We are now on our way to Monaghan which is in Monaghan County in the north of Eire. Bill's relatives come from some kind of estate there a couple of hundred years ago so we have to be off to see about it. This morning we went down and saw about connections and then on the way back to the hotel we dropped into the Bank of Ireland which used to be the old houses of parliament. The only chamber which is intact is the old House of Lords. Then we went over to Trinity College and went through the library and now we are on the train and going via Dunkalk and Clones to Monaghan. In our compartment is an elderly lady name Mrs. Dalgety from near Dublin (Leixlip). We have been talking to her and she has invited us to spend a leave at her place – she apparently has a country house and it may be quite civil. However I don't suppose we'll ever get there. Well honey, will sign off and tell you what we find in Monaghan. All my love, Hamp

October 18, 1944

Dearest Hamp

And how's Mr. O' Smith today after his fair trip to the Emerald Isle.? Is it as green as they say? And are their girls as pretty as the songs and stories make out? You see, honey, I've never been there so you're one up on me – darn it all!

Yesterday was a banner day for us. First it is exactly half a year since you went away; second it was Joan's first birthday and third I had my physical exam at Dr Anderson's office and in the evening I joined a girl's club so we really were quite busy all in all.

It seems like many a year had gone by since we were together and I'm sure looking forward to the day when you'll be coming home again. Guess I just wasn't made to be married and then forcibly separated from my husband. However one of these days the waiting will end.

Joan was certainly queen for a day yesterday. At 8AM just to start the day she got a wire from Toronto from Dad. Then about noon the parcel post brought her the cutest winter outfit from Grandpa Smith. It's a blue bonnet, coat and leggings – the same material that Doris Bothwell used to make a bunny bag if you remember, and the same color. The coat is trimmed with white fur and Joan is really a doll in the outfit. Wish I could get a color film to take some pictures for you. Grandpa and Grandma Smalley gave her a one-piece snowsuit for outside every-day-in the winter wear and Granny Smith sent $5 to get her something. I knit her a sweater but as far as something from the both of us – it hasn't arrived yet – whatever it will be I don't know. Maybe I'll wait until she walks and then give her a kiddy car. Joan got a card from the church Cradle Club and Aunty Marg Norton who is knitting her a sweater and a pair of shoes from Sandy Day – so all in all she made quite a haul.

I got 2 letters from you (Oct 8 & 10) and you mentioned posies. Guess they're on the way as they haven't arrived as yet.

Dr Anderson has me taking hematimics as my hemoglobin is 89% – he says I'm a way too thin and need fattening up and so advises a snack in the mid PM and one at bedtime – bread, honey, milk etc. So it kind of looks like I'm going to be fat – or fatter at any rate. He wrote 'thin but well enough for part-time work' (ha! Ha!).

Last night I was out past Margaret's to the Junior White Circle – a club that Kay belongs to – I joined it I might add. We packed 2 ditty bags and we're going to provide books and stuff for the new hospital. It's a girl's club – some of them married, most of them business girls and all my age. I felt I didn't know many people anymore so this will help.

Today we had the decorator so the house is a shambles but what is done looks very nice. More about it in the next letter or when activity is more or less in a standstill. Marg is still in Camrose. Hope you had a marvelous holiday darling. It's sure wonderful to get away from routine for a while. All my love dearest, Peg

Oct 19/44

Dearest Peg

Am writing form the Western Arms Hotel in Monaghan. It is an old place and we wash in a basin and someone comes and knocks on the door and leaves a pitcher of hot water. It is quite a nice place though and the meals are good. After we got settled last night we went down and had a beer and sat beside a peat fire. By the way, we saw a lot of peat bogs yesterday and I got a picture of them if they turn out – it was raining. Then we went and asked our landlady about this Anketill Hall (the name of Bill's original homestead). She said she didn't know much about it but she could get an old gentleman in to tell us about it. We went to a movie and afterwards went to her sitting room and this old bloke gave us a lot of gen and we had a drink of very good scotch and some ham sandwiches and went to bed very pleased with ourselves.

It's funny how ashamed so many of the Irish from Eire are of not being actively in the war in spite of the fact that they have 200,000 volunteers in the British Forces (which isn't bad out of a population of 200,000). So many people we have talked to would appear to be wishing to be more actively in the British Empire. This old gentleman told us last night that the feeling was that England had 'sold out' to loyal Irish by granting complete independence to a bunch of rebels who are not entirely the majority. They wanted home rule but were proud to be British – guess one shouldn't discuss politics over here though.

This morning was bright and cloudless – we tried to get bikes but couldn't so we hired a car and drove out to Anketill Grove. It was quite a fine place at one time but is in a state of disrepair at present although still retaining an outward semblance of past glory (ahem!). We got a lot of pictures and are now back at the hotel sitting around waiting to eat. It seems that we do little else but that.

It has really been a grand trip even though we have seen little of Ireland. We were going to Cork but it took nearly a whole day to get there – the train burns sod down there because they can't get coal, so it runs in fits and starts. We will have to do that one ourselves I guess honey. Well, all my love again and again. Sure miss you. Love and kisses to Joan. Hamp

Letterhead of Western Arms Hotel, Monaghan, October 19, 1944

Dearest Peg,

Just a line to use up a little of this free stationary and find out how long a letter will take from here to Edmonton – or if it gets there at all.

We are having a very enjoyable time being real tourists. I really look like one with my tropical worsted trousers that don't fit and my tweed jacket that's too big and my green zipper sweater underneath.

We are fortunate in having another nice day with the sun shining. It's rather like home in late September because the leaves are turning and it's quite cool. However at home you don't see hawthorn with its red berries etc. I would trade it all for a bit of poplar and would trade the universe for a look at you – but there's no use reaching for the moon just at present.

Looking out the window here you see all kinds of horse drawn carts – most of them with two wheels. Quite a rural setting. Our taxi today when we went out to Aucketell Grove (correct spelling this time) was a Model A Ford and we were traveling in class.

The farmers who now inhabit the old place were quite untidy but very friendly. I got talking with an incredibly sloppy elderly woman and she asked me if Canada were in the war too. I assured that that was very much the case and she then remarked how awful it must be to have all that fighting right at your own home. She didn't seem to realize that the war was mainly in Europe – she probably couldn't have read a paper even if she did manage to acquire one.

This is quite a change from Dublin – more of a country atmosphere. Dublin is what I would imagine a continental city to be like in peace time – the people very smartly dressed and quite a friendly atmosphere. However, it was funny to see barefooted, ragged children playing on the streets. The poor are very poor indeed. Prices in Dublin are quite high for some things – fruit, for example – pears ranged in price from 6D to 10S and cantaloupe were 10 to 15 S – cheaper than London but still expensive.

Bill and I haven't wasted any money but have managed to spend a fair amount and are getting progressively more broke. I had hoped to get some linen but won't be able to afford a great deal.

We pass through the customs going from Ulster to Eire and they are very strict. The reason being the rationing I guess – the tea ration is generous in the north but very scrimpy in the south and sugar is the opposite. Also they have the 100% purchase tax on ceramics in the north and this is not on things down here.

I mentioned Mrs. Dalgety of Leixlip wanting us to stay there if we came again. She was quite a spry old lady and she and her husband moved to England in the last war and opened a convalescent home as their war effort since her husband was physically unfit for service. They specialize in fishing, shooting etc. and it sounds quite attractive.

Eire is quite a nice change because you get away from uniforms etc. Americans are not allowed down here at all (at least American Armed Forces are not). It is their own ruling and not the Irish – the reason being that some of their men caused some trouble with some of the soldiers from here.

Tonight we have had an invitation to play bridge. The lady who operates the hotel and the old gentleman who gave us the gen on the places around and then she is inviting 4 of the local townspeople in – they are all about 60 so it is quite OK honey. It should be a pleasant evening.

Tomorrow morning we go back to Belfast and catch the boat tomorrow afternoon. We will then be seasick and feel like hell all night as we ride back sitting up. However, c'est la guerre or some damn thing or other.

I hope Joan got her flowers to her and she is OK! I will hear from you long before you get this probably. Well honey, better quit my chatter.

All my love. I am letting the kisses accrue with compound interest until I get back – so prepare yourself. Hamp

Oct 20/44

Dearest Peg

Now we have seen everything. After I wrote you yesterday we went downstairs and had lunch and then enquired what there was to do for the rest of the day in the way of sightseeing. The woman running the hotel then phoned Lord Rossmere the local baron and asked him if it would be OK if we went over his estate. He said OK and invited us out to tea! We walked out about 2 miles and then came to his estate. It was a mile from the gatekeepers house to the castle and the scenery was the most beautiful I have seen in the British Isles to date. The estate's purely for pleasure and covered with old trees which were just changing colors and interspersed with grassy hills. There were 2 or 3 little streams running through it and about 7 lakes on it although we only saw 5 of them. It was really beautiful and covered miles! We arrived at the castle and the old boy showed us through it. It is a huge old place and it was quite interesting. Lady Rossmere then arrived and we had tea and then she showed us the gardens etc. The old bloke himself was very friendly and nice. They were quite wound up in the tradition of themselves but I guess you can't hold that against them. He is connected with the air ministry but on leave for 3 months and she was a driver in London throughout the blitz from 1939 to the end of 1943. After seeing the place we walked back to Monaghan – very tired but quite pleased with ourselves. We had a quick steak dinner and then played bridge for the evening. There were 2 tables and we had a lot of fun – my partner was quite an old lady and a very keen player. She had a good sense of humor and a beautiful Irish accent (so had they all) – most enjoyable.

We are now on the train to Belfast – we will have a few hours there and then catch the boat train and be on our way. We have cleared the customs now so our worries are over – not that we bought anything. Well honey, goodbye for now again. All my love, Hamp

(continued), Oct 20/44

Dearest Peg

We are in Belfast and just sitting so I thought I'd write you a line. We got in and after getting around in a taxi we had exactly five shillings each with which to buy two meals on the way home and to get some linen – so I guess I don't get any linen this time – I'm sorry honey but money just doesn't seem to last long here and we can't cash a cheque. We have just eaten lunch for 2/6 and have about 2 hours to sit around before we catch the boat train. We found an officer's club that is very nice and so cheapness recommends it if nothing else – will sign off and continue later.

Oct 21/44

Well we have arrived back at starting base and are glad to be here. We had to stand up in the corridor of trains from Stranraer to Leeds, i.e. from 10 PM to 5.30 AM the next morning and then caught a train from Leeds that got us here at 7.30 AM. Just collapsed in bed and didn't get up this afternoon until it was too late to get my parcels (have two of them) so now will have to wait until Monday.

However I got 4 letters from you and you seemed very pleased with things in general and your new job in particular. It sounds like an ideal set up for a married gal with an infant and am really glad that you have got something that you like. Glad that your chest plate was taken and you are gaining weight. Didn't realize that it was getting you down and am really happy that things are a little better. I'm not much of a help but hope to make it all up with interest some day. The daughter is beginning to talk and that business about her old man really makes me stick out my chest. Hope that we can start her conversing ourselves (you and me) – not that you won't do a good job without my help. Well, honey, will sign off and write on Monday after I get the parcel. All my love, Hamp.

Dearest Hamp

You will be thinking I'm an awful so & so coz here I am a day behind again but honest 'injun' this week has been quite the busy week. We had a woman papering the walls. Don't laugh you bum for she did a good job of all the rooms – did everyone but the kitchen and bathroom. The hall dining and living room are done in a light paper embossed with a flower pattern. Mother's bedroom is a pink vertical striped affair and mine the same done in green. Real classy I must say. This 'gal' that did the hanging earns her living that way and is 78. If I'm as spry at that age life will be worthwhile.

Thursday afternoon I wrapped your Christmas presents up in fancy doings and are you going to have fun with the unwrapping! I've already sent off a food box and as your mother is making your cake I decided to withhold mine and send it in November so that you won't have too much at one time. Thought I'd mention this fact so you won't think I've neglected your stomach. Ha! Ha! Thursday night Ma and I were busy trying to straighten up the place and get the next rooms ready to be done. Friday morning went to work as usual and in the PM had my wee date with Dr Vant. Am very glad to report that everything is ship shape and I'm in A1 condition all set for your home coming and ready for another blessed event – yes really! Got a prescription for vitamin pills and Benzedrine sulphate to tide me over the rocky monthly periods so as for my health I guess I gotta say I'm a perfect specimen. Friday night was spent in more cleaning up.

Today went to work again if you can call it that – for I'm not very busy in fact am lucky if I get one patient a day. Was downtown just for the ride with Alix and Sandy this afternoon and tonight we are going to a show.

Am very sorry that I have to write the following sad news. Doris Fleming went into the hospital yesterday and this morning her baby was stillborn. It was a hydrocephalic so it's really a blessing it didn't live however that doesn't help Doris and Sandy very much as they were looking forward to the baby so much. I haven't seen Doris yet as she isn't allowed visitors and it won't be exactly easy when I go.

Marion MacKay – from my class – had a daughter born today so at least some people are happy. Doris Bothwell sent Joan a cute pair of pink mittens for her birthday. There was no letter so I don't know any more news of Claresholm.

Got your last letter before your leave today. I'll bet you made quite a picturesque sight in your borrowed clothes. Wish I could have been around to heckle you and get a few laughs. You should be on your way back to camp now and I hope you had a wonderful time darling.

Joan is still growing and has 16 teeth now. She's a real little miss now and each day is full of wonderful new things for her to do and discover. She still isn't walking as her crawling gets her around much faster and besides I think she's a wee bit lazy. But there'll come a day.

Winter is on its way for the nights are quite frosty. However the days are perfect Indian summer so we manage to get out a lot.

Am going to the dentist on Monday and will mail your parcel then. It will seem funny waiting for Christmas now after getting all your things lined up.

Hope you have a happy birthday dearest. Am rather worried about your parcel as it was mailed in August. Sure hope it gets there OK. Ordered some more cigarettes – some should be there by now. Must away to the show. Joan sends you bags of love and kisses. All my love my darling, Peg

Oct 23/44

Dearest Peg

Thanks for the birthday greetings and box. It was really swell – all of it. The sweater fits just right – not too form fitting but not too big. The pajamas were perfect also – have just finished tearing the back of two pajama coats so am now up to strength again – also these are warmer. The tie, books, candy and etc were also swell. Give the daughter my thanks and a huge kiss for her card – makes one feel pretty important to get a personal message from each of the family. Have another parcel in hock but didn't get it out today since it's registered and I couldn't get over that far. Imagine that it is film from Dad.

Today went to a conference at our Group Headquarters – all the statures were represented and our DMS for overseas gave us all sorts of

316

duff and gen about our futures. The only thing that seems certain is that we won't go east from here but beyond that nothing is sure. The boys that have been over for 2 years will gradually be sent back but the rest of us will just carry on. How long depends on how long this phase of the war lasts.

Our post war rehabilitation – looks like it's up to us to scratch for ourselves and the devil take the hindmost. That's about all we learned but that's some consolation at least.

By the way, on the way back from Ireland I didn't get ill so my self confidence is restored but also the sea scarcely had a ripple which may explain it. The holiday in Ireland was nice but the journey too and from was exhausting – did nothing yesterday but sleep since I still had a day left of my leave. Got up at noon and then collapsed again for the afternoon and went to bed early after a couple of pints.

Well honey, thanks again for my birthday present and your good wishes. Missed you and love you an awful lot. All my love, Hamp

Oct 23 1944

Dearest Hamp

Today was really a red-lettered day for Joan and I. Didn't work all that hard in the morning but was kept busy cutting adhesive tape for Dr Alexander while he strapped an ankle. I don't mind his puddling along when I have nothing to do but when you're busy it's another matter. However I eventually got home from work and got dressed to go downtown to visit the dentist and incidentally mail your Christmas presents. Was just going out the door when the postman arrived and asked me to sign for registered mail. Yes siree! My darling the lovely sweater has arrived and it must have come by air for it only took 10 days. Guess you're surprised at that eh honey? The sweater is really a dream and so soft! I love the color too as I'm very partial to grays and guess what? It fits perfectly. I'm the real sweater girl now – just wait until you get a picture of your pin-up gal. All in all I'm very tickled at my marvelous husband. Again many thanks my dearest it will be my best birthday present this year.

After getting all excited about my sweater I went to the dentist. Just have two old fillings that need replacing – no new cavities – pretty good eh old thing? – as it's a year since I paid the old boy a visit. Have to have an x-ray of my mouth as he thinks 3 of my wisdom teeth are impacted, for only one has come through. Oh me! Sure hope I ain't got any more in 'ma head'.

Well when I returned from town there was a box of flowers waiting for 'Joan Smith' so I promptly fell on it and opened it. Again my dearest you deserve a medal for they are the loveliest flowers I've ever seen. 6 beautiful pink roses and white baby mums with a bunch of fern. The roses are really super and should open up beautifully. You are without a doubt the world's best husband. Many thanks and hugs and kisses from Joan and I.

Am going to have a BMR as Marg Hutton wants to know why I don't weigh more than 99 pound stripped. So far she can't find anything wrong and neither can Dr Anderson. A fine thing eh honey? But as long as I'm OK I don't mind being 99 pounds coz I've really got a flat stomach now. Have some pictures to send but am waiting for some reprints of the Banff trip. Many thanks again darling and bags of love, hugs and kisses always, Peg

October 24, 1944

Dearest Peg,

Some more of my poor photography. These pictures got lost when I had the last developed and finally showed up. They were taken about 5 or 6 weeks ago when I drove up with our M.T. officer – George Kelly, to visit Johnnie Hunt. Our N/S Jean MacIntyre was along and also S/L Hooke, one of the intelligence officers here. I also got two pictures of the old Smith place at Haunce and am sending them along to Dad.

#1. Johnnie and myself standing outside sick facilities discussing things in general. In the background, you see their air raid shelter and the Red Cross flag above it.

#2. Two of the medical officers – one a familiar face – the other is Hugh MacKay – a kid from Vancouver who just completed his medical training in this country.

#3. The nursing sisters – taken in sick quarters at Johnnie's station – not a good picture.

#4. Outside sick quarters again – wonderful structures these mission huts.

#5. Taken on the top of Suitenbank – Hooke in the foreground and the countryside behind. This is a beautiful bit of country on a sunny day – it's a high bank with the moors on the top of it stretching off to the north and farmlands below. Hooke and myself were off trying to scrounge a few eggs and got the picture (& no eggs incidentally). You can see the field divided by hedges.

Am in the process of getting my pictures from Ireland developed and hope they turn out OK.

Sorry these pictures aren't very interesting to you but it gives you an idea of the people we have to associate with.

Well honey will sign off and am writing a blue mail. All my love, Hamp

Oct 24./44

Dearest Peg

Well another night and am just sitting around. Had quite a panic after I wrote you yesterday – had a lad in who had gotten hit by a truck outside camp. Did the usual act with plasma, 02 etc but he died about 3 hours later in sick quarters – about 0200 today. He had a fractured pelvis, humerus, laceration of his lung – so guess the MO didn't kill him. I'm thinking that I'm afraid – interruption – I was going to say I was afraid that I wasn't going to get on these roads at night on my bike any more – when the phone rang.

Have just finished dashing off madly in the ambulance about half a mile from camp with the sky lit up by an aircraft burning. Those Halifax's can really produce a glow. I expected to wait around and then produce several bodies. Was pleasantly surprised to find the crew standing around waiting for me – 9 of them – and no major injuries and no burns – was a real relief. The kite started to burn as soon as they hit but they were out of it and half a mile across a field before they knew what they were doing.

That is our panic for the night I hope. Am not on duty but was over at sick quarters writing my gal a letter – it's warmer over there. Have a nice warm sweater now but it still isn't quite enough for these Yorkshire winter evenings.

Say honey – have an apology – I got 900 cigarettes yesterday also but forgot to mention it because I was so impressed with my birthday box. I owe 300 of them but have enough to smoke for a while now. I tried out the new pajamas last night and they were really the genuine McCoy – warm and they fit. Must tell you again – really a wonderful wife that I have.

Am curious to know if you got the flowers OK – hope that you did. Must apologize for your birthday present when you get it. But had a little trouble finding anything and kind of pushed the sweater off on you.

Give my love to the daughter again. Keep gaining weight. Hope the job keeps good. Sent some pictures today. All my love, Hamp

Oct 25 1944

Dearest Hamp

Well how are you old thing? I've kind of lost touch with you this week but guess the mail will come a rolling in next week and all about your trip to Ireland.

Had my Basal Met on Friday morning – yesterday and its normal (+8) so ha! ha! again. Did some cleaning out of drawers in the PM and tied up all the letters you have written and placed them in a box. 92 blue forms to date and several ordinary mail. You sure are setting a record dearly beloved. We'll take an evening off some future night and go through them together. That should be entertainment well into the night.

Was busy again this morning cutting adhesive tape for Dr Alex. – my how I love that man! Met Dr Levey in the hall and we had along chat. Hadn't seen him before as he was away. He asked all about you and wanted to be remembered to 'Hamie' – that's you dear! Went out to Mat to visit 'Marsh' – she's getting along fine and seems quite cheerful but it was a big disappointment as you can imagine. I took her one of our roses and a few of the mums – knew you wouldn't mind my sharing their beauty.

This afternoon we had a 'do' for Joan – to celebrate her birthday. Margaret, David, Aunt Lena, Cousin Netta and her daughter Donna – age 3 ½ years – Mrs. Robertson, Alix, Sandra, Mum, Joan and I made up the party. It was quite something and a cake with a candle. Joan's second as she had one on her birthday. Joan enjoyed the crowd, Sandra and Donna the food, David the new environment and the rest of us the children so we all had a good time. David is sure a real porky now – weighs 17 pounds and just rolling in fat. His cheeks look as though he were hoarding his supper but he's good and solid however.

Am going to the Varscona with Alix tonight to see 'King's Row' – supposedly a good picture. Mother was to have gone out but Dad is coming home from Toronto. He had to get off the train at Winnipeg as he had a bad cold which settled on his chest. Guess he's some better or he wouldn't be coming home tonight.

Art Henderson – next door – is coming home tomorrow after two years overseas so Mrs. Henderson is awfully excited. I wonder what the feeling is like. I'm sure I'll be up on the roof top yelling when I get word you're on your way. The war news is improving again so perhaps one of these years we'll see the end. That seems to be all for now. Joan still says 'Da Da' all day long. Heaps of love my darling always – Peg

Oct 26/44

Dearest Peg

Another couple of days have more or less disappeared. Yesterday afternoon I went to the inquest of the lad who was killed on the road the other night. Sat in a freezing court room for 3 hours without my coat on and when it was over the coroner asked me if I were going to demand professional fees and I chattered out that I was and collected 1½ guineas which made the cold easier to bear. However I came home and I bought everybody a drink and I'm no further ahead. By the way, the lad who got killed – we received a note the next day that he had been treated for syphilis and would we please contact him and get blood. Since I had a hang nail and had his blood all over my hands I dashed out and took a Wasserman from the body and am waiting for the answer with considerable interest – should be OK though.

Today Hugh MacIntyre arrived from Canada – he is going to a nearby station. He came over with Gus Garrison and Gus was to have come up with him but had his posting changed at the last minute.

Should see him sometime though. I feel practically like a veteran after talking about #4 Command.

Mac MacPhee the other MO and myself have decided to adopt the policy of making all new MOs that arrive believe we are 'around the bend' and about to be discharged on medical grounds. Mac did everything but bite Hugh so we have gotten off to a good start.

I got another parcel this afternoon but haven't had a chance to pick it up yet. Imagine it is from home but will let you know tomorrow.

Am writing early tonight because I am on duty and it is pay day so we can expect our usual run of minor (or major) accidents.

Yesterday our DMS (big medical boss) was up from London to see us. Made no rash statements but handed us the usual line. Am getting used to hear people getting things promised to them and getting nothing out of it (e.g. Mac is going to a hospital). Well honey, all my love and kisses. Hamp

PS Have managed to get a good supply of blue forms so won't keep calling on your supply (except with writing to me then) More love, Hamp

Oct 27 1944

Dearest Hamp

Tomorrow is your birthday so many happy returns you old dear. Hope you had quite a nice time.

Wednesday night Alix and I went to see 'King's Row' – like I said. It was a heavy melodrama about a sadistic doctor who took his revenge on people by operating without and authentic reason and always without an anaesthetic. It was away back in the 1890s when operations were done at home. He really must have been quite marvelous though for no one developed an infection. Remarkable – eh?

Last night Mother and Dad went to the Corona for dinner and then to a show so I was alone for most of the day. Haven't got much to write about as you can probably gather. Did buy $300 worth of bonds yesterday though. 2 for cash and 4 on time. I figure I can pay up on a bond a month but may change my mind and let the bank account increase somewhat. When the last bonds are paid up we'll have $900 in bonds that I know of and about $400 in the bank. I hope I'm not being foolish about the bonds but somehow I don't think so. However as I said last time I'll work on the bank account now. Just as always when I get it up around $250 something happens – holidays or bonds. But bonds are really money saved so I guess it's the same thing.

You should have seen Joan last night. She took all her toys out of their box and then sat in it and was so pleased with herself she laughed for 5 minutes. I have some pictures of her I must get away to you – also the Banff ones. You've probably heard that last sentence before. Did you take pictures in Ireland? – or weren't you allowed to. Must write Doris soon and thank her for Joan's mittens. Guess I'd better do it now eh honey? Joan says Dada and heaps of hugs and kisses. All my love dearest, Peg

Oct 29 1944

Dearest Peg

I survived my birthday as you can see and am older but no wiser. There was a party in the mess last night and I was right in the thick of it. It just happened to fall on the right day and was quite a lot of fun. I got quite squiffed but didn't make too much of a fool of myself – so that's it for another year. The other parcel I spoke of was 300 cigarettes – that makes 1200 I have gotten from you in the past week. Am now 600 ahead and that is ideal because there are always people who have run out and you have to give them away here and there.

Have not been too busy lately but managed to keep occupied. Mac MacPhee is posted home and leaves tomorrow for the repat pool – he is pretty happy about it after 3 years overseas and I can't say that I blame him. He is going east so won't lave an opportunity to get in touch with you.

Johnnie Hunt came down last night. He had another letter from Doug Ritchie and Doug isn't too pleased with his set up. He apparently has buggar all to work with and doesn't particularly like it. Guess we can't grumble too much after all.

It seems funny to think that November is approaching and Christmas is just around the corner. The weather here is cool but the last two days have been sunshiny and bright – hope it lasts just a while longer. In winter there is nothing to do here since it gets dark so early and you haven't any chance to see the countryside by bike during the day – am rather looking for a move in the next month or so but it isn't definite. The work will be the same but the faces will be different and that's some help.

Don't know if I told you about the CO here – a kid age 22 with DSO and DFC and 4 (or 41) trips and a GC – a nice chap but just a little junior to be in charge of a large station – doing OK though.

I suppose Joan is still tearing around and giving you the usual trouble. Miss you both an awful lot when I'm just sitting around like now and thinking about you. Give my love to her and my kisses. All my love to you, Hamp

Oct 29 1944

Dearest Hamp

Yesterday was really quite the day, darling, for I got 6 letters from you. You must have been kept quite busy on your trip writing as often as you did. Ireland sure sounds like a swell place the way you write about it and must be quite the place for gaining weight. What were you trying to do honey, fit into your borrowed clothes? About the toothpaste – there's some Pepsodent already on its way in your Christmas box and it will carry you along until the next box when I'll send you some more. Also some razor blades as I forgot to put them in the box. No kidding honey it was really swell to get your letters and so soon too, didn't expect any until next week. It was only a week ago I heard from you and then last Monday your flowers and sweater arrived so I hadn't really much time to miss you. Not much – ha ha that's a laugh when every fiber of my being screams to have you back here again. Sometimes I think this separation just can't go on, but it seems to doesn't it honey? But at least we know it's not forever.

Today was quite a hectic one with the wee daughter. Went to church this AM with Dad and left Joan with Mother so don't know how she behaved but this afternoon she was into everything. Pushed her buggy out on the veranda beside the playpen while I got ready to take her out.

324

When I went to get Joan she had pulled everything out of the buggy into the playpen and was sitting sucking on one of the metal caps from the wheels which she had pulled off. She was covered with grease and having a wonderful time. Guess I'm just born to learn the hard way eh? Finally got all cleaned up again and away Joan, Mother and I went. We toured the streets and then went around to see Marsh as she went home from the hospital yesterday. She feels a lot better. While we were there our dear daughter had to wet on the front room rug. How mortifying! This training business is quite a chore for when you think they're house broken they suddenly revert again and the cycle is repeated. When we got home Joan tore around shaking the trilight, pulling over a bunch of Dad's books and screaming 'Bad Bad' at the top of her voice all the time. I'm telling you she's quite a hellion when she goes on one of these tears but don't worry we get along OK. All our love dearest, Peg

Oct 30 1944

Dearest Hamp

Am writing again tonight as I'm going to club tomorrow night and wouldn't have time between my chores to drop you a line.

Another very good day for me – got 3 airmail letters and the pictures of Fountain Abbey. The pictures were very good on the whole and it sure looks like a very beautiful place. Take a tip from Bill Scott darling and stand a wee bit closer to the camera so we can get a good look at you eh honey, please honey? You seem to have more room in your uniform now. What's the matter – got a bit thin before going to Ireland?

Was very pleased you got your birthday box in time and in good shape. It has been on the way since August and I had visions of a fish wearing your pajamas and sweater. I hope the sweater is really OK for it isn't a masterpiece by a long shot. Don't you belittle the perfect sweater you sent me. It's really a dream as I've said before.

Joan is really quite a destructive child. Dad bought her a little toy which you push along like a lawn mower sort of. It was yellow and red made of wood with colored beads strung between the wheels. She really loved it and got a lot of fun pushing it along – for about 4 hours – and then she stood on it like she does with all her things. But this toy couldn't stand it and so folded up into pieces. Guess we'll have to buy her stuff made from cast iron or some such stuff.

Tonight she just went to bed in her first pair of sleepers with leggings and a drop door at the back – not that she'll bother using that but I can dream can't I?

By the news tonight it looks like the Zombies are going to see a bit of action whether they like it or not. It's about time they did something with the reserve army and home army to keep hard feelings down.

Got Fred Day's address from Alix so that I can write him a Christmas note. Am sending it to you in case you want to write him too. Here it is – Capt. Fred G Day, RCAMA, #5 CGH, CA, CMF. Glad our cigarettes finally arrived. There should be another 900 on the way, someplace or other. That's all for now dearest. Big heaps and kisses from Joan and all my love my darling. Peg

More love and I sure miss you heaps, more love again.

Oct 31 1944

Dearest Peg

Two letters from my love today and very welcome things for a lonely bachelor (temporary only due to there being a war on). You seem to be a pretty busy gal what with working for a living and joining girls' clubs and so forth. Sorry that the flowers did not arrive and can't imagine what happened – guess the daughter will think me kind of a bum but will try to do better.

It was bad about Sandy and Doris' baby. Convey my sympathy and condolences. They were certainly lucky to lose it though since it was hydrocephalic. Hope they have better luck next time. We don't appreciate our good fortune until you see someone else's tough luck.

Have been fairly busy the last few days since I have been alone – but not too rushed – have still time to sit for half an hour or more morning and afternoon and discuss the war over tea. We always manage to accumulate 3 or 4 visitors at tea time and have a bull session. We came to the conclusion today that the war won't end this winter and probably early next summer. However we can't be quoted as reliable authorities since the people we see here are a little eccentric. For instance someone came in with a great worry today because he had a red spot on the end of his nose and said, 'Say, Doc, my red corpuscle is coming out – will I die?' That constitutes a fair amount of our practice so we don't have to be very astute. However I did pick up one kid today with an early pulmonary tuberculosis so that's something.

Have not yet gotten my Ireland pictures developed but will do so this week. Happy to hear that you have no complaints inside or out except being skinny. That statement about being ready for a blessed event when I get back was pretty daring – may have to save your letter and show it to you in writing. I'm ready to do my part but we won't be too hasty – will do our honeymoon over again and make it last for several months this time. It's kind of nice to make our plans even if they are so very indefinite at the moment – isn't it darling? Look forward to coming home more and more but mustn't dwell too much on that sort of thing because you merely beat your head against the wall and can't do anything about it. Well honey, all my love and kisses. Hamp

NOVEMBER 1944

Nov 1 1944

Dearest Hamp

The 1st of November today and winter is really setting in – cold north winds and scattered snow flurries and poor wee Joan hasn't been out for 3 days coz no one was going to take her for a buggy ride.

Really had a busy day yesterday. A car went off the highway north of Leduc and the four occupants were brought in for medical treatment so we really ran around for a couple of hours – Dr Anderson, an intern and myself. One woman had a long deep cut down to the skull and a bad cut on the leg. She was really in a gory mess – cleaned her up somewhat and admitted her to iiN. Another woman had a broken clavicle and a third had the right side of her face scraped clean of skin. The man had a small scratch on his nose and a skinned knuckle. By the time I got my little room back to order and instruments left sterilized it was 3 PM so figure I'd done my duty for the day. Today was quiet again except for a little boy who pulled a table over and crushed his hand a bit.

Joan is beginning to get the walking idea at last and is managing slowly but surely to maneuver on her own. She says 'ta-ta' now when you give her something and it seems funny to hear the wee mite saying 'thanks' so to speak. As I've said before Joan isn't really very big but big enough to look healthy and small enough to look like a doll. She is also starting to feed herself now but it is quite a messy ordeal as we have to take the food from the dish and spread it around the tray on the high chair before eating it. However I'm ashamed to say she's still on the bottle – one before an afternoon nap and one at bedtime. It's my own fault however as I haven't tried to take it away yet but really must do so this weekend when I have the time to fuss with Joan all day. I don't think it will be too hard but Joan sure loves her bottle. Got my check from the hospital today for October minus 4 days before I started. It came to $37.94. Am going to pay more room and board money from it and put the rest into bonds – payment on my last ones that is. That's all for now dearest, Heaps of love my darling, Peg

Nov 2 1944

Dearest Peg

Had a very nice letter from my wonderful wife today dated Oct 25th. Am glad the sweater was OK and that it arrived in time for your birthday. Was afraid that Joan's flowers had gone down the drain but since they arrived and were OK then I'm very happy. We hear stories that the flowers sent by cable wire are generally rather scruffy and not up to much and was hoping that the daughter's would not live up to the rumors.

Have had a very quiet 2 days of November to start with. Last night Mac MacPhee called a conference in the bar because he was going away. Mac is a short fellow with curly hair and glasses and one eye that was a little cock-eyed and looks the picture of innocence – but he has a passion for beer and stories and has a wonderful habit of getting to know people. By the time he got through he was beautifully corned and had challenged two Group Captains to a game of high cock-a-horse – 2 teams riding piggyback and each trying to dump the other on the floor. Mac and his 'horse were quite drunk so the Groupers won 2 falls out of

3. Mac had a black eye this morning and we have his 'horse' in the hospital today with a foot injury – so Mac's leaving party was quite good. I stayed relatively sober and didn't put up any 'blacks' as the saying goes.

Today I paid back 300 cigarettes I owed a bloke and now have 300 left out of the 1200 I got from you – it's amazing where they go but that long cigarette drought rather got me into debt but am now clear and hope to keep even.

Christmas time is just around the corner but I haven't gotten your Christmas present yet – was going to get something in Ireland but ran out of money. Will try to rectify the situation shortly if I can get away for a day.

Well, guess I will amble back to the mess and read for a while or play with our latest animal – a wooly pup that belonged to the skipper of a crew that got killed the other night and whom the mess have adopted. The one before this was a Scotty but some clot ran over him on his motor bike a couple of weeks ago – a real nice dog in spite of his habit of urinating in the corridor just outside my door. Well honey, thanks for your thanks in your letter – made me feel very good. All my love and kisses – Hamp

Nov 3 1944

Dearest Hamp

How goes your Yorkshire winter old dear? Ours seems to be slowly setting in – a wee bit colder each day and more scattered snow flurries. However we haven't much snow on the ground and the river has only started to freeze around the edge.

I took Joan out for a ride this afternoon while I went shopping and she got a big thrill out of snow flakes falling around her and when the wind blew her face she held her breath and then laughed. The fresh air sure whips a rosy color in her cheeks and she looks a perfect picture of health. It's really wonderful to have a healthy child-over a year old and not even a slight cold – touch wood! Just goes to show you that if the parents are perfect their children will be something super special eh honey? Oh! Brag brag on my part about Joan, you and I (or me which ever fits in here – am too lazy to be bothered with grammar right now).

Had Joan Vaccinated yesterday. Alix, Sandy, Joan and I went downtown in Day's car to the Inoculation Clinic in the Civic Block. It is run by the city – free inoculations for anyone who cares to go. It turned out to be a good thing. A nurse gives all the stuff as that's all she does you get out in half an hour compared to waiting an hour or so in Dr Leitch's office. Sandy is getting scarlet fever shots. Joan will have to get these sometime and then she'll be all immunized I guess. She'll probably come down with measles or some such thing but what am I saying?

Am making a pair of sleepers for Joan. I like sewing now but am no whiz at it yet but I'm a-learning. Looks like you'll have the expense of a sewing machine when you come home. Aren't a wife and a family an expense – eh darling? Come now tell us the truth.

As you can gather there's not much to write about but it's fun just sending you a scribble. Joan says love to Dada. All my love dearest, Peg

Nov 4 1944

Dearest Peg

Nothing to report as usual. It's amazing how little there is to write about as you probably have concluded after 6 months of my letters. Everything is pretty well routine and doesn't vary much from day to day. Last night just sat around and had a pint of beer and played a game of billiards and was in bed by 10.30. Tomorrow is Sunday and is not any different from any week day.

No excitement today – spent the afternoon telling somebody that he was wrong – a pilot came in and announced that he refused to fly any more. Couldn't be talked out of it and in a little while he'll be paraded and stripped of his wings and commission. Didn't blame the kid but it is hard to be sympathetic because the rest that fly are as afraid as he is but carry on and a lot get killed. Most of them know their chances but carry on and don't let it get them down.

Today was windy and cold and must admit that my new sweater is a welcome addition to my wardrobe. We had a bunch of ground crew posted here today – a couple were fresh over from Claresholm and said the place is pretty well broken up and they seemed glad to be away.

Maybe we left at the right time – before Marjorie Atkinson took over the station.

We are expecting a new medical officer in tonight – a chap named Thorne. Hope we can get along with him and if not it doesn't matter anyway. Say honey if you can get me a couple of nail files and send them over they are nearly impossible to get over here. I guess that covers my scrounging from you for the time being.

If you see Margaret tell her that Ken Creighton (Camrose school teacher) is here for the time going and will be going on operatives at a nearby station shortly. He looks and acts about the same and has dropped into sick quarters a couple of time to look me up.

The war news doesn't change a great deal these days. I don't envy the boys sleeping in slit trenches now that winter comes and still agree with Ritchie 'If you've got to fight a war this is a pretty comfortable place to fight it.'

Well honey, give Joan my hugs and kisses. Suppose she will be walking by Christmas – it will be quite an event to have a Christmas tree this year with her around to pull it to pieces. All my love to you – Hamp

Nov 5 1944

Dearest Hamp

Have just got Joan to bed and you no doubt will be pleased to know she came off the bottle today and with no fuss. Was over at Margaret's last night with Marg Hall and the conversation got on to babies. How queer eh? Marg H made a remark about you telling her to take Ann off the bottle when she was 8 months old. So I thought, 'Boy, if Hamp were home now he'd sure be annoyed with me for not having Joan off it long ago. So now my old dear spouse you can relax and rest easy coz our daughter won't be walking around with the milk bottle in her hand. I gave her 'Raggy Anne' the doll your Dad gave her to take to bed and she toddled off to the bedroom hugging the doll as tightly as she could. It looked real cute.

I walked into the living room today to see what Joan was up to as she was very quiet. She looked at me with a funny twinkle in her eye as if to say 'What are you going to do about it?' – but I couldn't find out what she'd been up to. A little while later I went back with a piece of raw apple for her. She took the piece and sat down and promptly took 3 small screws from her mouth so she could eat the apple. The screws came from the play pen and she'd shaken them loose and managed to get them out. Just can't leave her for a second!

Got two letters from you yesterday and one had the pictures taken on Hunt's station. You look quite skinny beside Johnny, darling, in fact almost gaunt enough to demand a few worries. You sounded pretty disgusted at the 'higher ups' in your airmail one. Guess on really can't expect much from the air force though. By the way, have you syphilitic chancres on your finger? You're always getting mixed up with someone's blood you old buggerlugs.

Heard an address on rehabilitation the other night and here are some points which should apply to you. 1. A grant of $7.50 for each month served in Canada and $15.00 for each month served overseas. 2. A grant of 7 days pay in lieu of leaves for those overseas. 3. A clothing allowance of $100 – I think this applies to officers as well. 4. Something to do with $80 a month for a married man plus dependents allowance while doing something or other. Education, I think, very definite eh? 5. Free traveling to place of enlistment or any desired destination if mileage the same. A man who has a profession may use the grant for further studies or for setting himself up in his profession or for establishing a house or for furnishing a home. It sounds pretty good if they can work it but it is actually small compensation for your sacrifice and in some case disabilities. Of course the disabled get other grants as well. Thought you might be a bit interested in the above.

The war news sounds good again so maybe we'll have you home by next fall. I'm counting on it but can't figure out if I'm an optimist or a pessimist. What do you think? All our love dearest, Joan and Peg

PS Eleanor and Bill – of Lethbridge – are the proud parents of a son – William Robert – born yesterday – don't know what he weighed.

Nov 8 1944

Dearest Peg

My letter writing has slipped and I'm sorry. No good reason except that there just wasn't anything to say and I couldn't fill a page. Have been pretty quiet lately. Night before last was on duty and sat around and saw a show in the mess – Mickey Rooney in 'Babes on Broadway' and it really was terrible. The got a call from sick quarters and saw a chap brought in-in coma. I finally diagnosed a rupture cerebral aneurysm and it was correct. Was going to go to bed early but went into the bar and drank beer with the boys and then went to bed.

There's nothing doing tonight and will probably end up playing cribbage in sick quarters with Cpl. MacFarlane. He is one of our orderlies and quite a character. He has been overseas 4 years and is getting ready to go home. He is a great big man who used to be a hard rock miner in civilian life and got talked into being a nursing orderly while waiting to get trained as an air gunner. He's still an orderly and good one but quite a rough and ready character. I enjoy making ward rounds with him because he goes in and bellows 'Turn off the radio and stand by your beds.' If you start to examine someone's chest he rips down the bedclothes with one hand and practically tears their pajamas off them with the other one – never a dull moment.

Ted Thorpe our new MO arrived today. He has been here about 28 months and is pending repatriation and so won't be a keen worker. Seems a nice fellow however. Tomorrow our station comes under the RAF and won't be in the Canadian Bomber Group anymore. Don't know how it will affect us but it actually shouldn't be any different.

Imagine you are snowed in for the winter by now. Our days alternate between wind and rain and wind and sun and we can't grumble very much except the Nisson Hut which is our ward is colder that our refrigerator. If they haven't got pneumonia when we get them we give it to them.

Well honey, will sign off and write again on schedule. All my love, Hamp

Nov 8 1944

Dearest Hamp

Should have written to you last night but just as I was sitting down some company called on Mother and Dad so I got eats and by the time we ate it was time to go to bed being midnight so here I an a day late again. Monday was my day for the dentist so went down and had 2 x-rays taken to see if there were any cavities under the enamel which are just starting. Have only had 2 small ones filled in 2 years and he thinks it's too wonderful I guess. The x-rays only took 5 minutes and I was dismissed so went to the bank and collected my paid up bonds, put $120 in the bank, gave ma $60 and kept the rest myself. My monthly income is now $208 so looks like I'll be paying a small income tax this year if I'm taxed on your allowance. However I don't mind coz the government needs it I guess. Had all our bonds, $350 worth put in the bank and I'm paying them a quarter a year for safe keeping and clipping off coupons to put in my account. Quite reasonable and it saves me a lot of trouble. Also bought you 300 cigarettes. Yesterday went out for a walk with Sandy, Alix and Joan and collected some developed pictures taken at Banff. There are some real good ones of me and I think you'll like them.

Started some embroidery last night – covers for our bedroom dresser when we get them. Rather late to be starting a hope chest eh honey? – But better late than never.

Got two letters from you today. Guess your birthday was quite a stink from your report but fun eh? Am glad you're all set to do your part on a new member for our family but I don't think I said just when I'd be willing. But you know me – always ready, willing and able. The second honeymoon sure sounds wonderful and I'm all for it. Maybe we'll be surprised again and have a second honeymoon baby, darling. The honeymoon ones are the best I think but then we haven't had a chance to really prove otherwise have we?

Joan is walking all over the place and is so pleased with herself that she won't sit down for more than a second unless she's eating. Her vaccination 'took' so that's over with. She still has a touch of eczema on her leg but I hope that it will clear up someday. That's all for now. Will try and write again tomorrow and get caught up. All my love dearest – Peg

Nov 9 1944

Dear Peg

Another night. Had quite a good day – got two parcels – one from

Margaret and some more films from Dad. No Canadian mail in though so haven't heard from my beloved wife for over a week now. Also today I got some more pictures – these were taken by Bill Scott in Ireland and down at Fountains Abbey and I asked him to get duplicates of mine and many of them aren't very interesting but am sending them all along and you can kind of hold onto them.

Things are fairly busy at present – at least there is enough to keep me occupied for the day. Merlin Hicks (medical officer who used to be here and managed to get in a hospital) was here to night. He has finished his hospital appointment and in now on his way to the continent. He tried his FRCS this month and I hope he made it.

Tonight Cpl MacKinnon (chap from Saskatchewan who is one of our orderlies) and I played cribbage and I beat him 6 games in a row – ahem! He will reciprocate tomorrow probably. He is a fairly well to do bachelor who owns some farms in Saskatchewan and a very nice chap – about 45.

The wind gets colder every day and I have now got my sweater for the winter. The American elections came to a very popular conclusion. The English papers made no secret of the fact that they wanted him back and it's quite a relief to realize that things won't be upset too much.

Interruption. Just had a lad come in who said he was getting a little nervous about flying. He was a tail gunner of a crashed aircraft who was trapped in the tail as the bombs went up. The CO of the station helped chop him out (not this station) and got a hand blown off in doing so and the rest of the crew were nearly all involved. He is now going back to complete his tour and is flying here. I can certainly see the kids view point and felt sorry for him.

Well honey, all my love and kisses to you and share them with Joan. Miss you. Hamp

Nov 10 1944

Dearest Hamp

Here we are back to the old forms again. I had run out but managed to get some from the drug store.

Mother and Dad are out again tonight at a meeting – some special ones have been on at the church all week so I've been a homebody except for working in the mornings.

Last night we had Dr and Mrs. Cooper the minister of the first Calgary for dinner. They came from Atlanta, Georgia last year and it was fun listening to them talk. The daughter is an 'awful sweet queen' and a 'wee sugar' and I'm a very 'charming girl'. My such flattery eh dear? After everybody had gone I spent the night doing the dishes. Mother said to leave them till she came home but I knew we'd be doing them far into the night so kept myself busy for an hour or so doing them.

I was talking to Babs MacRae today. You may remember her from the hospital – graduated a year or so before me and was in charge of A&B for a while. She married an RAF chap – Patton – who was a patient at the wing. He has arrived back in England 10 days ago and Babs has received word from Ottawa that she can go to England in two weeks or so. Is she ever excited. Can't say I blame her a bit do you? She's going to Sheffield, Yorkshire so I told her to keep her eyes open as you can never tell when she might run into you or some of the other boys. However Sheffield is quite a way from where you are I think.

There has been no word from Maddox so I guess he didn't come west or if he did he didn't phone here at any rate.

Today Joan climbed up in the armchair by the radio, hauled a magazine off the table by the chair and settled down like an old timer to look at the pictures. She's a bit hard on them though and she's apt to tear them for no reason at all. She is crying now so guess I'll have to go and settle her down again. See you in a minute I hope.

Hello again! It sure makes Joan mad when she can't get off to sleep so she rustles around, grunts and groans until she's wide awake and then she howls for a bit of sympathy which she usually gets. She's certainly got Dad's number for she runs to him as soon as he gets home and he's always letting her have his paper or magazine so I guess she's a bit spoiled – but in the right way. She goes for anything in long pants so you don't have to worry about her being afraid of you when you come home. She'll soon grow to know and love you just like her old lady does. How could she resist the old Hampton charm?[11]

There goes the daughter again – guess her vaccination is bothering her so had better run along and tend to our daughter. A salty kiss from Joan this time and all my love dearest, Peg

336

Dearest Peg

Things are improving wonderfully – two letters yesterday and one today. Things seem to be going along and you manage to keep pretty busy. Certainly wish I could help you – miss you more each day and love you more – but I guess we'll get together one of these days eh honey?

Yesterday I was quite active – night before last Jack Watt and I went up to see Merlin Hicks off to France. We packed him off about 7 o'clock and then did a pub crawl on the town until about 10 PM when the pubs close and then went back to the mess at the hospital and sat around and talked until 1.30 with Merlin and a bunch of the other MOs. Actually it was quite nice because we don't get a great deal of opportunity to meet those fellows and they do most of our work. We slept in the quarters at the hospital and then got Merlin away on the train yesterday noon. Jan and I then drank several beers and a double rum (for tis cold) and went to a show and went to sleep until 5PM when we got our train home again. A very pleasant day off except it cost me about 4 quid which I couldn't afford.

We didn't get into any trouble except I got in an argument with the medical specialist at the hospital (who nobody likes) and more or less told him off.

Also as we were going along the street back to the hospital we all developed the urge to relieve our bladders so we adjourned to a handy dark passage way. Suddenly the wall in front of me opened and a bloke cam out waving his fist and yelling 'Jesus Christ they're even pissing in the keyholes now' and apparently it was just an unlucky shot for me. We didn't tarry to discover the situation – quite amusing at the time and a complete accident because we didn't know there was a door there in the modified blackout.

Jack Watt is quite a good type – he has 2 kids and quite a nice wife – doesn't compare with mine however and his family is pretty homely. One of them he hasn't seen yet. Give Joan my love, hugs and kisses and get her to pass some back for me. All my love, Hamp

Dearest Hamp

Another two days by the board and as you would say 'not much to report'. Let's talk about the weather, that's a good opener or are you fed up with it too? Our days are quite frosty but all the snow, the little we had, has gone. Had Joan out yesterday with Sandy and Alix but we came home after ¾ hour as I was too cold. Today I got really wrapped up with a hat and mittens and we were out with Sandy and Alix for an hour and a half. Joan really had rosy cheeks this time and with her pink mittens and blue suit really looked a picture. Wish I could get a color film just to show you how pretty we are. Ahem.

Yesterday was Saturday so I spent the night embroidering and have now finished one piece – 3 more to go and then I'll start on something new.

Mother has gone to church tonight and Dad is in Calgary so this week has been a record breaker as I've been in every night but still don't seem to get to bed any earlier. However, I'm more rested. It's a funny thing but the more you stay home the less you want to go out. However it's not good to stay in all the time so must make an effort to go out next week.

I guess I should tell you that I'm working general duty on i-N for four hours – 9 to 1 – 6 days a week. Have been since the first of the month. Mrs. Brown, who had the examining room before, came back and as they're 50 nurses short I said I'd try it for a while. Don't find it heavy and there's really more going on than in the Ex-room and so much more interesting. By the time I get to work the beds are made so there's not much of the hard work left. Also as the charge nurse Helen Fife and I are the only grads on the floor I get the office 3 times a week so I really enjoy it. If it does get too hard or I get too tired I can always quit but I don't think that will happen. Also that extra money a month means that I can buy more bonds – not that I was in any need of the money – let me repeat! Don't want you to get the wrong idea about my working.

Here's something to think about darling, for the future. If you are able to let me know when you'd be coming home – that's when you get your orders sometime in the year I mean, I could go east and meet you. It sounds like a good idea to me but it may be too complicated. However you can let me know what you think eh honey? It's kind of fun planning though isn't it?

I see from the papers where they're not sending anymore air crew overseas and are demobilizing all new grads forming a reserve exempt from army call up. Seems you have all you can handle over there. Don't volunteer for the Far East service old bean unless you want to coz I want to see you sometime. All my love, Peg

PS Did I ever tell you that I love you very much? If I didn't I should have coz I do. This letter seems full of 'Is', please forgive.

Nov 13 1944

Dearest Peg

Another night has me in its clutches and it feels the same. A clear cold night with the usual stream of aircraft heading out overhead with their four motors and navigation lights – quite a nice sight to we chair-borne soldiers.

Didn't do very much today but sit around and watch Horne try to sell some slippers. He went into Harrogate to buy his wife something for Christmas and all he could get was a pair of red bedroom slippers lined with wool. When he got back with them we all decided that they were so horrible he decided not to send them off so he tried to get rid of them. Fine morale builders we are eh honey?

Things are quiet. We are gradually accumulating a sick quarters full of upper respiratory infections and the block resonates with coughing and sneezing. There is a little more interest in things than war at least.

We alternate 2 weeks about with sick parade and our parades now will begin to amount over 30 with our problem children coming in all day. It's funny why everyone here runs to the MO and you see them with poorly fitting shoes, sick worries, homesickness, and they even come in if their uniforms don't fit in order to get a chit to get them changed. It will be strange to start seeing people again who are ill.

There is a huge shipment of parcels in and I'm counting on getting a supply of cigarettes out of it – sure hope so as these limey efforts are beginning to pall again. Have acquired a cigarette holder as my hands looked like those of a busy proctologist before the age of rubber gloves

– also what's good enough for Franklin D is good enough for me.

Well honey, will stop my drivel. All my love, loads of kisses and everything else to my darling wife. Hamp

Nov 13 1944

Dearest Hamp

A month ago you were on your way to Ireland to feed the fishes, remember? Or how could you forget eh? Time is certainly slipping by but still none too fast for me – or you either I'll bet.

Mother and Dad are renewing your Readers Digest subscription for your Christmas present. Are you still getting them OK? There are some medical journals in one of your Xmas boxes. I'm not renewing the subscription for it if that's OK by you. If you want to keep on just say the word.

Helen Campbell the girl on the east side of us got a wire today that her husband would be home on Thursday after a year in the Royal Navy. Bet she's excited as they have a 5 month old son. Art Henderson is still home on a months leave too after 2 years overseas so maybe you'll be coming home in another six months shall we say and hope it's true?

Went to the dentist this PM and got a glimpse at my x-rays – four cavities under old fillings and one impacted wisdom tooth. Had two of the fillings done today and my jaw feels like a mountain and looks like a hill. Just took a 292 and feel slightly woozy so thought if I scribbled a wee note to you I might feel slightly improved. So please forgive the writing.

Got 2 letters from you today – Nov 2 & 4. You mentioned that your letters weren't very interesting but darling how would you know? You don't read them or wait for your own letters. I'd hate to read the ones I write but I know you enjoy them so that's all that matters. PS – your letters are very interesting and amusing too in spite of what you think.

Mother was talking to Mrs. Barbara Smith and her daughter Jessamy Arthur of Claresholm – remember? – lost her second baby last week. Little Freddy is only 3 months older than Joan so they didn't waste much time. Now we know what they do for entertainment. Ha! Ha! Catty eh dear? But who are we to talk?

Joan is a going concern these days. She has outgrown her playpen

– so to speak – and it limits her activities. Found her today with a package of my cigarettes stirring up the water in the toilet bowl. What a child. She trips up to the table now and the dishes and silverware get pulled off if she can reach them and she keeps her eyes on the kitchen cupboards hoping that someone will leave one unfastened sometime no doubt. I hate to think of the mess if she gets into the soap chips or the spices. [Almost missed this space so will send more love and kisses. Bye again, I mean it this time darling!]

I'll send you some nail files in your next parcel. Had planned to put one in your Xmas box but couldn't find any in the stores. Joan sends a big kiss – me too. All my love Peg.

[Guess all this foolishness must be my 292 – I want to keep on writing to you but hate to fork out another 10 cents stamp I guess. Heaps and heaps of love and kisses. This is definitely bye for now.]

Nov 14, 1944

Dearest Peg

Got another birthday parcel from you today and thanks very much. You certainly went all out on my birthday with a box of gifts and a box of food – it is all swell and thanks an awful lot to a wonderful wife. Think more and more of you and realize more and more how much too good you are for me. I haven't got anything away for Christmas for you yet and at my current rate won't get anything in time. To tell you the truth I just don't know what there is except antique silver and linen and that doesn't seem like a very good gift.

How do you like my pen nib now? I just took it in and ground it down on the dentist's drill and then loosened up the nib with a pair of pliers. I couldn't get this limey ink to flow out of it but it seems to be fairly loosened up now.

Today was a typical English winter day I guess – a cold rain all day that was half sleet at times. Really would like to hear a radiator surging again or even hear our old gas stove roaring.

Got my two pairs of Dack's back from repair today. Had worn through both pairs that I got shortly before leaving home – guess this sight seeing is hard on shoe leather.

Ross Cameron, the padre, came today and presented me with four packages of Buckingham's so I guess I will smoke Canadian cigarettes for a few more days. Am trying to keep out of debt with my smokes so that the next bunch I get will be all mine.

Well honey, not much to write about except that I love you and miss you. Am sending along some of our Ireland pictures tonight – there are quite a number so will split them into about 3 or 4 envelopes and just drop them in the mail without much communication on them.

Hugs and kisses to Joan. All my love to you, Hamp

November 15, 1944

Dearest Peg,

Here are a collection of pictures. A lot of them are not very good or very interesting but am sending the works anyway. They are pictures Bill Scott took with his camera and I gave him a blanket order for duplicates and so got a number that aren't of very much interest to us. The ones of Ankletell Greene are rather pretty but we haven't very much in common with the place. It was his old family house. The ones of Fountains Abbey are, to a large extent, repeats of the ones I sent along previously but some are fairly good shots. The rest were snapped as we went through Belfast and Dublin.

Hope you get them in good order. Sure wish there were a few of you and I together included amongst them. Love you and miss you, Hamp

Nov 15 1944

Dearest Hamp

It was a beautiful day today – real warm and sunny – 48 above. Pretty good for the middle of November so our winter hasn't arrived yet. The river was frozen over yesterday but I'll bet the ice has broken up again today.

Last night I went to club at Kay's and got a lot of our embroidery done. I should finish the third piece tonight and then have one big one left to do.

We had quite a busy day yesterday – a gastrostomy and exploratory lap. Both patients arrived from the OR at the same time with blood transfusions and orders for Wangenstein drainage and only two nurses on the floor as it was noon. You should have seen all the red lights that blazed for an hour before someone answered them but it couldn't be helped. Today I was in charge from 10 to 1 and managed to keep very busy and the patients in a good mood too so figured I earned my $250 or whatever my pay is. But as I always said, it's more interesting when you're busy.

Dr Gillespie talked to me for quite a while and wanted to know all about you. He said I'd certainly married one of the best boys they'd turned out in many years and I fully agreed with him. I married you honey remember? Aren't you proud? I sure am.

Saw Dr Tucker touring the halls with Dr Ellis so guess Tucker is out of the army now as is Ken Hamilton.

Alix phoned today and wanted to know your number as she is sending you some cigarettes. I can't send any to Fred as he has more than he can use. He sent Alix 6 packages of '333's' that they get in Italy. He's still in Rome and slightly fed up with 'this getting a lot of work'.

Aunty Lena had a letter from Eddy today and it appears he does a lot of visiting in Blackburn as there's a girl around there somewhere. Trust Eddy.

I renovated a stuffed teddy bear and rooster that I played with when I was three and Joan has had a wonderful time carrying them around and trying to hug them both at the same time. She seems to understand what is said to her now and puts some things back in place when told. It depends on how she feels at the time though coz she's really an independent person and has been known to sit on the floor and shuffle her feet when annoyed – but not for long I might add. That's all for now as life is quiet. All our love and kisses dearest. Peg

Nov 17 1944

Dearest Hamp

Seven months today you left for parts unknown but my doesn't seem like years ago? However it can't be for much longer with all the

343

new shuffling and discharging etc going on in the Air Force. Too bad you haven't been over for 3 years or so and then you might get home eh? Oh well only 2 ½ more years to go – but what am I saying? Sure hope this new drive on the Western Front will smash the Germans for good.

Has a letter from Doris Bothwell yesterday and Claresholm is closing on April 1st. Surprise eh? Also all the boys who have something to go back to can get a discharge 8 weeks after sending in a resignation so Doris says Bill will probably stay in the Force until April. They got a notice to vacate their place then anyway. The Olson's have been posted. June and Penny are in Calgary with Flora Appleby but don't know where Bruce went. Had a letter from Jean Palmer They are fine and Bruce is in a RCAF hospital at Yarmouth NS. Jean and Nancy are with him.

Miranda has been sold and for $250 too, to some farmer around Claresholm. Doris says they still have the defrosters and heater in case you are interested.

Ray Burnap was mentioned in a King's list recently because he rescued a woman due for maternity from the Pembina River flood area. Ray, a nursing sister and a pilot were along. The pilot got an AFC and the nursing sister got mentioned like Ray. Amazing isn't it? He probably just went along for the ride. Meow!

Doris Fleming just phoned. She's feeling very much better. Haven't seen her for a couple of weeks but may go over this weekend.

Bill Norton is on the night shift again. They got a letter from you yesterday. I got two. Wonder how you're liking being under the RAF or are you still attached to the RCAF?

Today Joan got shut out in the hall accidentally and after about 5 minutes out there she started to knock on the door. Where she learned that is something I don't know but it looked funny to answer the knocking and have one year old come walking in. The other day Dad came home and Joan struggled in, found his hat, gave it to him and said 'Bye bye'. Just a gentle hint I calls it.

That seems to be all for now. Heaps of love and hugs and kisses and all my love darling – as ever – Peg

Dearest Peg

Missed writing last night and have a feeble excuse. Started playing knock rummy at 7 PM and we were going to quit early. By 10.30 I was so far ahead that they said to hell with Smith – we're going to sit here till his luck breaks. At 3 AM this morning we quit and my luck was still holding so I made a little money – we haven't figured it out yet however.

I really hit the jackpot today – got 5 letters from you and last was written Nov 8 which is just about as close together as we can get via the mails. The Banff snaps also arrived.

The daughter is certainly growing up all of a sudden – talking, feeding herself and now walking all over the place. Wonderful child even if she does wet on other peoples rugs occasionally.

You talk about a wife being an expense – if it weren't for yourself I don't think I'd have a cent. Also about income tax – none of my income is taxable and that includes your allowance and Joan's allowance. Therefore I guess you can forget about paying tax on that $37.50. I asked Jack Watt our accounts officer here about it and that's correct gen I'm sure.

The pictures of you at Banff really are swell – you get better looking everyday – don't know how you do it honey but you do – very proud of and very much in love with my wife – and my daughter. Glad the daughter is vaccinated and what not now – kind of takes care of her for a while. Am also pleased to say that you didn't mention any wisdom teeth. I wasn't very pleased to hear that you might have to go through the discomfort of their removal and am relieved to hear nothing about them.

Tonight is another foggy night but not so bad as last night when it was so thick that they couldn't run cars on the roads without someone walking ahead of them.

Well goodbye for now and it's now my turn to write tomorrow and get caught up.

All my love, Hamp

Dearest Hamp

Three days since I last wrote to you and where the time is going I cannot say. The weeks are really rolling away from me as the days are full since I started working. The mornings are the same old hospital routine and very busy and taking the daughter out most afternoons does away with the hours too. At night I try to get caught up on many things such as writing letters, sewing etc. As Joan usually doesn't settle until 8 PM – although she's in bed around 7 – the evenings go fast too.

Was out walking with Alix and Sandra on Saturday and Sunday afternoons. Saturday night Alix and I went to the Garneau – saw Frank Sinatra in 'Step Lively' – why I don't know. Don't see it unless you want to be bored to tears. Joan's eczema is up again – not weeping but very itchy and on her stomach and legs so she's a bit hard to handle and so she wore me out last night before I got her to settle. That's why I'm writing tonight.

Got the photograph album up to date and most of your pictures with writing underneath so we will know what they are all about. You're filling up an album you know but keep up the good work old dear.

Visited the dentist again today and got another tooth filled. One more to go and then I visit Scott Hamilton to see about my impacted wisdom tooth. Dr Gemeroy says he won't touch it as it looks as though it will have to be slit and pried from the bone. I get a tooth ache at the thought. Don't expect to get it done before December so I have time to really think up a big ache. Wish you were here to hold my hand or my jaw or something. But maybe it's as well you are not then you won't see your wife turn on the waterworks.

Bought Joan a pair of blue bedroom slippers – like rabbits with ears and eyes and she's so proud of them she sits down every once in a while to get a good look at them. Had her in Joan's Coffee Shop yesterday and she embarrassed me by running up to a man, throwing her arms around his knees and saying 'Dada!' Looks like she needs you to take her in hand. We should get a letter tomorrow as we haven't had one from you for four days. Got a letter from Ma Smith and she sent me $5 for my birthday. What to get is a problem. I know some things I'd like but am waiting until after the war. Patriotic eh? I wonder! All my love and Joan's kisses – mine too. Peg

Nov 20 1944

Dearest Peg

Another letter from you today! You are really distinguishing yourself and it is quite a treat to make my daily pilgrimage to the mail bag and get rewarded with such regularity. The daughter is her usual mischievous self. It must be kind of nice to see her toddling about even if she's a little harder to keep track of. By the way my chancre didn't materialize and the sample of blood I took from the body was decided as negative so I guess all is OK. However at the moment I have an infected thumb of my right hand – some erk's boil got into it I guess and I have to have a prick stuck in it tomorrow. Not a very major operation however and shouldn't incapacitate me for more than the 10 seconds it takes to do it. At the moment it makes writing a little difficult – gives me an excuse for my scrawl.

You wanted to know if I thought I'd be home next fall. I don't know but it seems possible. My personal opinion is that Germany can't last past next June or July and the after 3 or 4 months we should be on our way. However you never can tell – sure hope so honey – miss you more and more but will wait for the day of our reunion and you never have to worry about me going astray.

Today I got a parcel from Mac and Irene – very nice but no note enclosed. Have got your parcel at sick quarters and every afternoon we have a sandwich or a piece of cake or an olive or some hot chocolate. Makes quite an occasion of it these days.

Tonight have just sat around and played cribbage and chewed the fat with our medical corporals. Last night drank several pints of beer and chatted with the boys. The time goes by fairly quickly but it doesn't pay to sit back and think about how I wish I were with you – just makes it harder. Well honey, will write tomorrow.

All my love, Hamp

Dearest Peg

Another day gone by and very little to report. Today had my surgery done. Tooled up to the hospital about noon and had a squirt of Pentothal and got my thumb incised. Lay around for about an hour and a half and my affliction so sore that I couldn't sleep so I wandered around and checked up on a bunch of patients I had sent in and then came back here about 4.30 and rolled into bed and now after 3 hours sleep I feel like a new man. The thumb is 100% better and should be cleared up in a day or so. Doesn't make writing very convenient but gives an excuse for my illegible scrawl.

No mail today but certainly have no cause for grumbling – you certainly outdid yourself honey and I love it. I wrote Mac and Irene last night and thanked them for the parcel. Also I did a little scrounging – asked them to send some cigs also – hope you aren't offended honey, if you are I'll cancel the request. But Johnnie Hunt told me he was having trouble with his in spite of the fact that he was getting 300 a week from his mother so he got a couple of other people to send some and mix up the brands. Some brands come through faster than others. I told then to send anything but Sweet Caps for although I prefer them, they are a little sporadic. So even if I don't like the brands they will form a reserve to fall back on and when I get in debt I cam pay them back with the other brands and have your Sweet Caps to smoke.

Another 4 days and it will be your birthday – wonder how you are going to celebrate. It's going to be quite a stack of candles to blow out eh old dear? Not very many at that for an old married woman with a grown daughter.

Speaking of my operation – ahem! If you ever need any minor surgery get Ernie Watts to give you some pentothal – I had a wonderful joy on for about 2 minutes as I was recovering and felt beautifully and happily drunk and no hangover. Now I realize how the other chap feels.

The sky tonight is full of our aircraft coming back – like to hear it and hear the sound. The wars news is good and I hope that the weather stays good – it's a long tough struggle yet but if the present rate continues it won't be so bad.

Didn't send flowers for your birthday and am sorry – didn't start the wire burning soon enough and was told that the situation was hopeless when I got to it. Hope you have a happy birthday dear and hope I can come myself for the next. All my love, Hamp

Nov 22/44

Dearest Peg

Three letters from you today – the last one Nov 13/44. So you finally broke down and confessed that you were doing general duties on i-N. Hope you like it and glad you are doing it if it makes you more pleased with life. Please honey though, don't take a full time nursing job because I don't want my wife to be continuously worn down physically and also if you feel like taking a week off at intervals on your 9-1 job please do so. Nursing is not a life which I would pick for you – at least hospital nursing isn't. Don't get the idea that I'm criticizing because I'm not – anything you do is perfect and everything you do – as a matter of fact you are the most wonderful thing that ever existed – and I love you.

You are being pretty ambitious with your embroidery and all. Should have quite a collection if you keep up at your current rate. (Excuse writing, thumb still bundled up)

Today was a lazy day – last night I felt a little dopey so I stayed in sick quarters and then had breakfast in bed here and slept until 10 AM before getting up to make ward rounds and start my day. Pretty soft life I lead darling but will try not to make it a habit.

You told me not to volunteer for the East. Don't worry about that! If I go east it won't be as a volunteer and if I go I'll probably go under guard. No chance however, I hope.

Old John Archer is a pretty busy man – pretty near up to our speed – eh old girl? The weather (ahem!) keeps fine – clear and cold and hope it lasts.

Had quite a fancy tea this afternoon – meat sandwiches (courtesy of Dr Smith's thoughtful wife) and cake. Gradually eliminating the parcel.

Tomorrow I go to relieve at a nearby station for the day. Tomorrow night the staff is having a party for Cpl MacFarlane who is going home.

I will have to attend and so probably will not write. Will no doubt consume gallons of beer and sing songs. It is in one of the local pubs and preceded by a meal. Should be kind of fun. Well love and kisses and a lot more I can't send with this mail. All my love, Hamp

Dearest Hamp

What goes on over there? Or is the air mail grounded? We haven't heard from you for over a week. It's probably that the weather has closed in or you may have been posted since the RAF took over your station. However I'm not worried about you yet as the mails are held up every once in a while. By the time you get this I'll be relieving my mind so forget about it.

Haven't done very much but stay in bed since I wrote you on Monday. I picked up a cold and sore throat last week and Monday night it really started to head up. Just the typical flu which develops into a bronchial cough which stage I'm in now. Am cured but am not going back to work until Monday as I still feel like I'd fought the battle of Britain and Normandy. Joan has developed a bit of coryza but I don't think it will head up. Hope not as I've tried to be careful.

Her eczema is improving again although it does get very itchy at times. Got some more pictures yesterday and am sending them along ordinary mail.

Sent a subscription of the Readers Digest to Fred as a Christmas present. He is getting lots of cigarettes so figured I'd better think of something else consequently the Digest.

Got the letter you mailed form Ireland today written on October 19th, opened and examined by censor of course. It was a good letter darling – you should take up writing as a hobby. The letter arrived in a little over a month's time so that wasn't too bad.

Got Mac and Irene and Marg and Bill their Christmas presents. Crystal cigarette boxes with four crystal ash trays all set in a rack of crystal – handy and compact – if they don't break. Thought you might like to know what you were sending. Have you any ideas re gifts for the family and friends etc. Let me know honey if you have eh honey please huh?

We have conscription at last so the boys in the army should be happy. It's about time though. Don't know when Canada has been so worked up about anything before. The war in Europe is doing alright again. It sure must be hard sledding for those fellows. I don't envy them at all but sure wish I could help.

We had our first real snow today and it looks as though it would stay this time. Has been snowing for 6 hours – maybe we're in for another big fall of snow. Heaps of love my darling, Peg

At Home (as usual), Nov 23 1944

Dearest Hamp

Enclosed please find some 'pittures'. Hope the last bunch arrived OK. I was a little doubtful about the envelope.

The ones in the case are a collection of our better (ahem) pictures taken over a period of two months.

On opening up the case, and of course having a peek at them all first, we are ready to start a detailed description of where, when, why and who. So draw up a chair, settle down and here goes. Quiet please as we must concentrate on the subject at hand. As has been said we have opened up the case and:

Picture #1 reveals the 'little woman' sitting on a log the banks of the Bow River below Bow Falls at Banff, of course! Not bad eh?

Picture # 2 – The 'little woman' again all decked out in jodhpurs and boots leaning on the parapet of the Banff Bridge with Mt Rundle in the background. There has been a considerable warming in the climate since the first picture was taken. Not bad weather for late September in the mountains and again a pretty good picture. Please take particular notice of that sylph-like form. No whistling please.

Picture #3 – Grandma behind the hat and Joan definitely on her own – for a second. Taken in early September. Quite a gal eh honey? – meaning Joan, Grandma too if you like.

Picture #4 – Joan in her buggy – mid-September. Can you see the curls? They are there anyway. Quite fair too don't you think?

Picture #5 – Joan really on her own. Taken mid November at 13 months. She has been walking for two weeks and is wearing the

351

snowsuit Grandpa and Grandma Smalley gave her. Again I say quite a gal!

Pictue #6 – Joan and I taken on her year old birthday. Joan is wearing the outfit Grandpa Smith sent – no leggings on as it wasn't cold enough. The coat and bonnet are pale blue trimmed with bunny fur which you can't see in the picture.

Picture #7 – The 'old lady' again trying to look like a horse woman but can't quite hid the air of expecting a fall. In case you are wondering who was on the other horse, Kay was. She took the picture.

Picture #8 – The 'little woman' again – this time as a yachtsman. Taken late afternoon on Echo Creek so not very clear but on the other hand pretty good considering the subject material.

The other pictures have writing on the back and more or less speak for themselves. Hope you liked them. All our love dearest, Peg

PS A Merry Christmas and a Happy New Year if you get this in time – if not a very happy second wedding anniversary dearest. More love, Peg

PS Am sending the pictures in the billfold under separate cover as the easiest way to send them since if I send them parcel post I can't send the letter and it's questionable if I can send the case letter post. This letter will sound funny if you don't get them at the same time. Guess you'd best wave the letter en honey? Bye again and more love, Peg

Nov 24/44

Dearest Peg

Well I didn't write last night as I said I wouldn't. Last night was quite an effort – the whole section moved out in a bus to the Blackamoore, a pub down at Ripon. There we took over and had a piano. Drank innumerable glasses of beer between 7 & 10 and then at 10.30 came home. Got lost on the way and didn't get back until midnight. Then Sgt Hopper and Cpl Mackinnon and MacFarlane and myself dropped the party and sneaked back to sick quarters where we consumed a bottle of scotch and Cpl MacFarlane regaled us with stories of MOs he had seen. I think the prize was an RAF MO who had bad feet and used to

352

soak them each morning and when sick parade started would take them out of the water and put them on the desk to dry and sit back and smoke his pipe and get the sick to parade by. However we finally got to bed about 4AM and now I am just ready to hit the hay – wasn't very keen on sick parade this morning at 9AM.

Tomorrow is your birthday – guess it is your turn to have innumerable beers. I still have an excise for the writing as the thumb is still under cover. However it is pretty nearly cured so won't have any good reason for my scribble.

There are a huge number of parcels in the station and expect that one of these days I'll be turning up with several hundred cigarettes etc.

Well honey will sign off and hit the hay – sure miss you – thin you would have enjoyed the affair last night. All my love to you and Joan, Hamp

Nov 25/44

Dearest Peg

Many happy returns of today! – a little late but better than never. Hope your celebration is a good one and apologize again for not sending flowers.

A very quiet day today with the usual run of sick and afflicted – none of which were terribly serious. On duty tonight but a very quiet night – provided the boys keep their planes going. The writing is a special effort tonight because I now have my thumb out in the open again and nearly as good as new.

The war news continues good and our time keeps slipping away fairly quickly and we'll be together again before we know it. At least the MOs have a definite plan of duty – two years overseas at a maximum. The poor erks are now being repatriated after 3 years and some stay nearly four so we can't grumble too much – although we have no reason to be too cheerful.

Guess I was just lucky after our section party the other night. Jack Perverseff went over to the sergeants' mess and got in a crap game. He lost sixty quid which is quite a severe loss even in these crap games. He has been quite quiet since but we'll organize another game one of

353

these nights and try to get it back. I don't play the game myself anymore – I was going to be one of the boys one night and lost 10 quid which I couldn't afford and have been trying to save up ever since. Never again! Figure that confession is good for the soul so finally broke down.

What are you going to get Joan for Christmas – a pair of skis or a tricycle? I have come to the conclusion that I won't buy anything for her here and will leave it up to you – there just isn't anything decent to get here.

Well honey – you get more beautiful with your passing years so each birthday is going to be a more important event in my life. Will make up current deficiencies with interest as we celebrate your natal day in years to come and may eventually convince you that you are the most wonderful creature in my world. Love you an awful lot. All my love, Hamp.

Nov 26, 1944

Dearest Hamp

Well, old dear, your wife is now 25 – passing the quarter of a century mark. Yes sir, that's me getting on I'd say but no grey hairs as yet – I hope. Really had quite a nice birthday though considering. Mother and Dad gave me a hand carved wooden dish shaped like a leg about 12 inches long and 8 inches wide – for sandwiches, fruit or junk. It really is quite nice and another thing to store for our home. I think I mentioned that your mother gave me $5 but haven't got anything yet. Then came the mailman with three letters from you so it really turned out to be a sunny day. You seem to be having quite a time getting caught in dark alleys with your breeches down, so to speak. You always get caught in some kind of situation don't you honey? Reminds me of the time you and I and a case of beer got involved in a mess on the river bank and we had to come home and change our clothes accompanied by a very unpleasant smell – remember dear? It seems very funny now. To get back to my topic I was very glad to get your letters and know everything is OK and that you're getting your parcels OK too. While I think of it – don't worry about Christmas presents for us. It won't really be Christmas to us anyway until you are with us and we can wait for all the good things in store for us. I'll look after the families too and although it won't really be the same as you sending something it will have to do I guess.

Last night went over to Margaret's for a chicken dinner. Ann Robertson – Marg's neighbor and Willard Prierson's wife and sister – a vet friend of Bill's dropped in for the evening. We drank beer and played poker and all in all it was a good time – even an angel cake with 'Happy Birthday' on it. Lost 10 cents at poker though but that really wasn't too bad I guess.

My cold has almost disappeared so guess I'll go back to work tomorrow. Joan's nose is still running and it seems to bother her more at night as she's quite restless. She thinks it's a great joke for someone to blow their nose so she's been going around all day blowing down her nose into her hands. She is really learning things very quickly. When I say to her 'Joanie want to go-go?' she hikes right into the bathroom. And if you say 'Drink of water, Joan?' she smacks her lips. Pretty clever eh honey?

Here are some jokes for you. Ollie and Olga were going to get married at last so they went together to get their marriage license. The Registrar took all the required information from Ollie and then turning to Olga said 'I suppose there's a little Swede in you too?' and Olga replied 'Ja, Ollie couldn't wait.' Ha! Ha! This next one was gleaned from 'Tonics and Scoratives'. A big burley male patient was getting heat treatments in the cabinet. He became hard to handle and was strapped down and eventually quieted down. A nurse came in to take his temp from the rectal thermometer which had previously been inserted. She proceeded to the proper location but – no thermometer. On walking around the cabinet to speak to the patient she saw the thermometer in his mouth so asked, 'How did the thermometer get in your mouth?' To which question came the abrupt reply, 'I burped'. Again – Ha! Ha!

That seems to be all for now. Sure hope you're not freezing stiff over there honey. Big hugs and kisses from Joan and all my love dearest. Peg

Dearest Peg

Got a letter today dated Nov 15. Pretty good traveling. You seem to be keeping busy what with your work and your club etc. Things here are getting a little more wintry – had quite a heavy fall of snow last night but tonight is clear and cold. The snow looked almost like home but it is much wetter and doesn't last very long and there aren't any Christmas carols on the radio.

Johnnie Hunt got posted today – he is going to the continent and leaves shortly. He should have quite a cold and damp Christmas and can't say that I envy him a great deal. I may move up to his station but won't know for a while – seem to be pretty well rooted here.

Ted Thorne – the MO-went down to London today. He has been quite browned off since he came here because he was led to believe that he would be repatriated shortly since he has been over about 2 ½ years but the time gets closer to Christmas and he still hasn't heard anything. I hope he gets a little 'gen' down there.

Yesterday afternoon being cold and wet about 6 of us decided to take the afternoon off. We sat around and drank beer and then collected a variety of food from all our parcels and ate practically all afternoon. By that time we weren't hungry so we went down the local pub in the village and had a few more beers. Then home and so to bed with another Sunday behind us and another week in the foreground. Quite a nice bunch of boys here and I have made a number of friends since coming here – would be almost sorry to leave the place for that reason.

Have been sitting around tonight reading. Got caught up on my letter writing on Saturday – wrote 5 (correction 4) letters to all at home so have felt quite righteous ever since.

Wrote away to a medical correspondence college yesterday to get a little gen on how to get an education – just to have something to do in my winter evenings. Don't anticipate that I'll get any scholastic records but may be able to learn something and at the same time cut down on my beer drinking.

Progress report on the thumb – it is now healed and nearly as good as new.

Well honey, will sign off. Love you an awful lot and miss you an awful lot. Will wait patiently until we get together again and lead our normal existence. Give Joan hugs and kisses from me. All my love, Hamp

Nov 28 1944

Dearest Hamp

Our winter has really set in now with a good 6 inches of snow and 5° below. I bought Joan a sleigh last week, the kind with a railing around the back and sides. Joan is tucked in a blanket and away we go. She thinks it's a lot of fun as she's near enough to the ground to reach our and touch the snow. Yesterday we tipped and rolled out into a snow bank. I expected to hear quite a howl but Joan just sat up and laughed. Mother takes Joan out for a walk every morning before lunch. They walk up to the corner and back which takes about 20 minutes as Joan has to walk up everybody's sidewalk. I gather she's quite independent as she's always waving goodbye hoping to be left alone.

I got two nice letters from you yesterday and you seem to be right in there getting letters and parcels. It's funny how they arrive in bunches when they're mailed one at a time. I usually write 3 in a week and you get 5 at one time. Silly isn't it. You remember the parcel Margaret sent you and the birthday food box I sent? Well Margaret sent hers about 10 days after mine and arrived to you a week or so before mine. That's crazy too. However as long as you get them that's all that matters.

You should see our front room right now. Joan is out of her playpen and on the tear. The magazines are scattered across the room and Joan is carrying one of the pillows from the chesterfield around. Right now she's got it on the floor and is rolling around on it. The cover from the piano bench is on the floor and Dad's books are pushed on the chair and floor. I just caught the table lamp as it was falling and she's shaken the trilight 3 times with a scolding each time. In other words the place looks kind of blitzed. Interruption while we play 'ride a cock horse'. I was sitting on the chesterfield with my knees crossed and Joan came and sat on my extended foot. If the latter is rather crushed blame it on Joan as she makes a grab for it every now and then. Right now she's tormenting Bud by crawling after him behind the chesterfield – and now I'm out of ink.

It's my club night tonight so I may get our dresser set finished. Spent last night doing some smocking on a dress mother is helping me make for Joan. I hope to get four done for Christmas.

i-N is without a charge nurse until December – just two more days fortunately, so I'm having quite the time being acting charge nurse and only on duty four hours a day. This morning I turned on the pressure and 3 of us finished up the 6 remaining unmade beds in 10 minutes. The morning was long gone when I clamped down but believe me we really got some work done. But tomorrow it will have to be done again so you almost say to hell with it.

It's time to get the daughter's supper ready so had better get cracking as she's getting wilder than ever and almost had the letter torn up. Haven't any more jokes and no news but bye for now and all our love. Big hugs and kisses form Joan and I. More love dearest – Peg

Nov 30 1944

Dearest Peg

Quite an eventful three days have slipped away. Missed writing you last night but will explain later.

Got 3 parcels in the last 3 days, the first one was from the First Baptist Church in Edmonton and consisted of a box of candy, shaving cream etc and was very nice. Then your parcel came and it was really something extra – from soup to nuts and including the shoe polish and laces. Thanks very much again honey and sorry I am not reciprocating a little better. Yesterday I got a parcel from the Women's League in Camrose and it was also quite nice but didn't compare with yours of course. Today I got a parcel from the Camrose Eastern Star – a pair of socks, a handkerchief and a bar of soap. All in all I've done very well.

Got 2 letters from you on the 28th dated Nov 17 & 20. That news about Claresholm was quite a surprise and the story about the boys being able to get out an even bigger one. It's quite a surprise because there are an awful lot of boys just going through their second tour and it doesn't seem quite fair when there are so many that haven't done one yet. You can only live so long on operatives and they know it and feel that they don't mind taking a chance – but why press your luck. Bill Davis did well by Miranda – better than I thought possible. Too bad about Joan's eczema – hope this is a minor siege this time and doesn't cause you too many sleepless nights. That wisdom tooth is not much to look forward too and I would dearly love to be there and hold your hand and your head and have you shed a few moist tears on my neck – don't save it for that though honey. Tell the daughter to be careful who she calls "Da Da" – her old man is a green eyed monster at times.

Had quite a panic the day before yesterday – a minor explosion at our bomb dump and 7 airmen got badly burned. Bags of plasma etc and one died later on but the others will be OK except for scarred hands and face. Pretty well shows that you can only get so careless with explosives and then you develop regrets. However I guess those things have to be expected.

Now to explain about last night – ten of us piled into two taxis and went down to a pub called The Checkers near Harrogate – nine of them instructors and myself. We had several drinks and then had a chicken dinner. Then we stood around and drank beer and played darts until 11.00 and came home. The boys brought back a dozen quarts of beer and a bottle of gin and then we came down to my room and made lunch. Everybody contributed and we had soup, which we cooked in an alcohol sterilizer from sick quarters, then canned corn, then tongue, then your cheese and crackers and then beer. All in all it was quite an effort. The room was quite messy what with spilled beer and food. About 30 people in the same wing of the mess didn't enjoy the noise but we did. The pay off was when 5 of them started to play cards. The dealer dealt a game called 'Switch' two of the others thought it was another game and the other two wouldn't agree on the rules. It ended up in a terrific argument with everybody shouting and finally they quit and finished the beer and went to bed. Afraid I am not a good influence as far as consuming their beer – the trouble is the expense. However honey, it's harmless – I don't get into trouble and the parties are all stag. You will never have to worry about me. Miss you. Love you an awful lot. Give hugs and kisses to Joan. All my love, Hamp

Dearest Hamp

Got two letters from you today dated Nov 21ˢᵗ &22ⁿᵈ. It doesn't seem possible that you are answering letters which I feel I wrote only a few days ago. Really a remarkable mail service eh old dear? Your fingers will be all healed up by now I suppose. I'll sure remember about that pentothal – sure wouldn't mind going on a jig especially when I could blame it on an anaesthetic. Trust you to find out about it you old drunkard you!

The work at the hospital has quietened down somewhat – today at least – as Fyfe is back so I no longer have the responsibility of the floor. Enough happened while I was in charge to last quite a while. May have mentioned that one of the students came down with chickenpox after being in bed for 3 days with a sore throat. Then 2 days later another nurse patient blossomed out with scarlet fever. I discovered the rashes first so was right in there with Dr McGugan which doesn't mean very much other than it's best to be on the same side of the fence when he's involved.

I've taken Joan out walking the last two afternoons and I mean walking. Of course it takes us a long time to get anywhere as there's a lot of stopping and starting, falling and getting up etc. but we have our fun. Joan's eczema is more or less under control again. The coal tar Dr Ou gave us seemed to have run its course and wasn't helping at all so I switched to the preparation you had made up in Claresholm – oil of coal tar, zinc etc and it's done the trick this time. It's oilier of course and I think that is the reason. Sure wish it would clear up as it keeps her awake several hours some nights and myself included. Nothing seems to relieve the irritation at times and when I say I've used everything I really mean it – calamine with phenol, coal tar, Vaseline, nivea cream, zinc, lanolin and a last resort tangel which does seem to sooth the skin at any rate. Have you any further ideas? Dr Ou just say "Carry on with the treatment" but as I say it's cleared now but for how long I can't say. But we're not too down hearted as yet just feel so sorry for Joan who has to put up with it all.

Last week I mailed you some snaps in an envelope and also a wallet with some pictures. The wallet is going parcel post and will take quite a while to get there and the letter pertains to the wallet and will seem rather silly by itself so hang on to it until the parcel arrives eh honey?

I'm glad you asked Mac and Irene for cigs as I don't get downtown very often but manage to send them to you every 2 weeks at least. I'll feel better about it all as I know you can use all you get. Anyway I think the least Mac & Irene can do is send some to you oftener than they have. I think you're pretty important and so can't see why they don't write oftener. I'm pretty sensitive about things where you're concerned anyway and feel that there isn't such a thing as too much where you're concerned. Now, don't you feel spoiled? All for now. Hugs and kisses from Joan and I. All my love, Peg.

DECEMBER 1944

Dec 2 1944

Dearest Peg

Well here I sit relieving at a nearby station and very little to report. Came over here this morning after dashing through sick parade and I have little or nothing to do now that I've arrived. This place is the one I generally go to and it is not a very active place.

Yesterday took the afternoon and went up to the hospital where we send most of our stuff and gave some more evidence in the preliminary hearing of the inquest of the kid who got burned to death. These inquests always strike me as kind of funny since the chaps are killed in the course of a prosecution of a war and you couldn't have an investigation in the field – but that's the way things run and all our casualties are released via the coroner.

Last night was asleep in the mess after supper when Jack Watt came in and took me off to the Blackamorre – our pub down at Ripon. We sat around and drank beer and sang. Five of us went – the two Wing COs in charge of the squadron operating nearby and an intelligence officer. We were the only ones in the place so we had a nice quiet time singing doubtful songs at the top of our lungs. They tell me that Charlie Burgess is now screened – that is he did his last trip on his tour about 4-5 days ago and is now on the way off operations. I was certainly glad to hear that he had made it. After 10 o'clock we proceeded home and went to bed early for a change.

I'm going to have to stop making such a good fellow of myself. It is harmless and I don't get into trouble but it is expensive and if I continue I'll have to write home for money. Every time you go out a pound is equivalent to a dollar and you buy a round of drinks and so forth and never spend less that 2 or 3 pounds. However, I'm going to reform (ahem!).

Well honey, Christmas is just around the corner – imagine that the Christmas lights will be turned on soon in Edmonton. Hope we will see them together next Christmas. Miss you and love you more and more.

All my love, Hamp

December 3 1944

Dearest Hamp

Here it is December all ready. It just doesn't seem possible. I sure wish there was a way of living over the past months again with you the perhaps they wouldn't seem quite so meaningless – but each month passing brings you one month nearer to us. Wonder how many more months lie ahead of us? It may be sooner than I plan as I'm still counting on another year. That way it doesn't seem so long. Who do I think I'm kidding?

Friday and Saturday afternoon the quartet went on its usual walk and Friday night Alix and I went to a show at the Garneau-"Two Gals and a Sailor". Saturday night I went over to see the Flemings. Sandy was in bed with a reaction from some "shots" so Doris and I sat down with a bottle of scotch. Mixed our first drinks with Montserrat lime juice and it was terrible but we drank it anyway. Took our other drinks with water and although we made several weird faces we enjoyed our scotch. As the night was warm and we were well warmed we walked to the skating rink to look on and finally wound up at Joan's for a sandwich and coffee and then came home by 11 PM so that was another Saturday night chalked up.

Doris tells me that Dr Scott Hamilton charges $25 per impacted extraction so it looks as though I'll have quite a small sized bill from him. Haven't seen him as yet but will know more about it tomorrow when I see my dentist. Dental surgery must be quite a racket eh honey?

We were out with Sandy and Alix again this afternoon and ended up at Robertson's for a spot of tea. Sandy and Joan had a great time playing together. It doesn't seem possible that Joan is old enough to play with other children but she seems to be able to stick up for her own rights to a certain extent.

She had a bad fall yesterday. Tripped over her feet and fell headlong against the foot rest of her high chair. She got a nasty crack on her forehead and the sharp edge of the chair made a half inch cut. It looked pretty bad for a while as it bled quite a bit but it turned out to be a clean cut with the edges together so it will be all right. She may have a scar but it won't show very much. Right now there's quite a bump.

I must start on the Christmas shopping in earnest this week but wish I knew what to get every body – it might make it easier.

Fred Day has been in the hospital again – this time with sinusitis but he's OK now. He told Alix the German prisoners gave him some flowers for some reason or other and he thought it quite a joke.

We're sure having fun with the 'zombies' over here but guess the situation will right itself in time. The very thought of them makes me furious. Guess that's all for now. Joan sends big hugs and kisses and I miss you all ways and always. All my love dearest, Peg

Dec 3 1944

Dearest Peg

Well have got quite a bit to report. Seems I said I had a lot of good intentions but my company is bad. After I was through yesterday with my relief job the 2 MOs returned and one of them (Bill Carter) persuaded me to go into Harrogate for the evening with the Dental Officer (Jack Day).

We went in and after checking in at the room went down to the American Bar – a very nice spot. Sat around getting pleasantly squiffed and then 3 pilots came in from my station – they proceeded to buy 2 or 3 cognacs for me and by then I got into a conversation with a guy named Frank Toas – an English chap and very nice. He had his wife with him

363

and we got to talking and they said why don't you drive out to our place and spend tomorrow. I was very agreeable – Bill Carter wanted to go to a dance and the upshot was that I went out with these people.

I immediately rolled into bed and died until 9.00 the next morning and then Frank brought me up a cup of tea and I went down to see what I had gotten in to. They have a lovely home and three perfect children. The boy is 14 months and just the same age as Joan and really wonderful to see and hold. There is a little girl age 4 and another 7. We had lunch and then sat around by the fire while I gave my life history and showed off my wife and family.

I can truthfully say it was the nicest day I have spent in England. They can't get a maid of course so washed dishes and did all the things one misses – playing with the kids, sitting by the fire in an easy chair, etc wishing I had my wife with me.

At noon time we wandered down to the local pub and all had a pint of beer – it was a lovely old pub and seemed to be a kind of club where all the neighbours make a point of going on Sunday to see each other. They mostly seemed to work in Leeds and commute from there. Frank is an electrical engineer who deals with the power supply for this part of the country.

Caught a bus at 5.30 and came home. They invited me back to spend any weekend – say it's their work to entertain Canadians and apparently have a regular bunch of customers. Well honey, so you can see I enjoyed it – think the kids made it so likeable and they really are nice people.

Well honey, will sign off. With love and kisses to you and Joan. All my love Hamp.

PS – I didn't get my yesterday's letter mailed so you have a double header

Dec 4 1944

Dearest Peg

Another day away. Quite busy today what with sick parades and so forth. Managed to see quite a fair collection of head colds, influenza and odd and sundry aches without getting too impatient.

Tonight I went to a movie and saw "The Great Waltz". That's about the third time I've seen it. Remember the first time when we were a-courting and had passes to the Garneau and we sat in a double seat and held hands and had to leave early to get you home in time. Those were the days and I practically broke down and wept for thinking of them. Funny what incidents provoke an overwhelming wave of homesickness and missing one's wife. Nothing serious or morbid however honey and we'll speak again some day.

Tomorrow I go up to Johnnie Hunt's old station to relieve for a while. Don't know how long I'll be there – it may be permanent or it may before a few days only. Won't get my mail until Saturday next so guess I'll miss out completely this week.

This Saturday all the Canadian MOs are having a big get together to listen to A/C Tice, our chief MO from home. Don't imagine that he'll have a great deal to tell us but will go and listen to his line at least and do a little beefing. I've been a bit cheesed off lately and maybe the change for a week will do me good – hope so anyway. Don't get the idea that your husband is grumbling but one gets a little tired of the same people and change is stimulating to your desire to work.

May go down and look up this family that looked after me over the weekend – spend Sunday. Get a little domesticated playing with Godfrey who is the baby boy of Joan's age and a lovely child. The home is very nice – right over a golf course and a river and they have a boat. Would kind of like to develop an invitation there because they are such nice people.

Well honey, will sign off for another day. Christmas is just around the corner and have done nothing about it for you but will try to correct my evil ways.

Miss you, love you an awful lot. Hugs and kisses to Joan and swing her once for me.

All my love, Hamp

Dec 5 1944

Dearest Hamp

Well old bean, how're you doing these days? We've kind of temporarily lost touch as we haven't had a letter for 6 days now. But even if the postman called everyday it still wouldn't be enough. Isn't it awful to have such a demanding wife, eh buggerlugs?

Well sir, to start on my doings, yesterday I went to the dentist for the last time until I visit Scott Hamilton in January. Had a tooth filled and the scale chipped off my teeth. Ever had it done? I think it would be good treatment for Hitler. When old Doc Gemery was through scraping my teeth he practically had to scrape me from the ceiling. No kidding darling the next time anybody puts one of those curly picks between my teeth and under the gum line I'm just going to beat it. As I was leaving the office the old boy said I had better not make an appointment with Hamilton until I had 10 days to 2 weeks with nothing to do. Cheerful eh? My I'm so glad you're not a dentist – they're the most depressing creatures. Or do you disagree honey?

Last night I went to a new club that's being formed. It is for young married girls and is in connection with the church. We meet in private homes however. There was quite a number of the old gang of gals I used to know years ago and they go to church about as often as I do – real good Baptist types. I was voted in as secretary – absolutely refused to be president – so guess what I got stuck eh?

Had a letter from Ma Smith yesterday and Irene is in Macklin as her brother Leo died in the East of a heart condition so the grandparents are feeding the boys. Everyone seems to be fine and Dad is busy keeping the Isolation Hospital full of scarlet fever.

We went out for a walk with Sandy and Alix today and had them back for tea. Needless to say the house was quite a mess after the two scamps had been loose in it.

Tonight I did Joan's washing and some ironing and then cleaned Joan's and my white shoes. Of course bugger me has to upset the white polish all over the bathroom. It splashed on two walls, on the underneath side of the basin and bath, on the hot water heater and tank, coated Joan's toilet seat and all around the floor. It was under the window and a few spots managed to get to the west wall. So I really did a good spring clean washing walls etc. However I don't seem to be as tired and manage to keep on the go from 7.30 AM until 10.30 PM and by the way, I've gained a pound. Now weight the colossal sum of 96 pounds stripped naked yessiree! That's all for now my darling. Heaps of hugs and kisses. All my love, Peg

Dearest Peg

Another two days away and a very good one today – got this letter from you today and it was wonderful to hear from you (as usual). Sorry to hear that you had the flu and hope that you are well over it by now. Don't go dashing back to work when you don't feel like it. Remember you are your own boss except for a little heckling from the man who loves the ground you walk on. The daughter still continues to be a ball of fire – wish I could see her in action some time – will do!

After I wrote you night before last I had quite a hectic do. About 12.30 got aroused for a crash. I thought it was on the drome so just pulled my pants on over my pajamas and stuck on my jacket and shoes – no socks. Got a pin point and found out it was about 15 miles away. We located it by luck up in the hills and had to climb up 2 miles where I found a crashed aircraft with 3 dead and one died just after I got there. There were 3 with serious injuries, multiple fractures etc The ambulance in the meantime came up within about ¾ of a mile and we evacuated the casualties by stretcher over the roughest kind of country. Got them to hospital alive but just and then figured I'd just about had it – mud all over since it was raining and needed to walk the rough boggy areas with about 6 inches of mud in them. Went back the next day and extricated the bodies. It was quite a hectic night and I got about 1 hours sleep and so collapsed last night and slept.

Tonight I have been playing knock rummy – lost about 15 shillings in a three-handed game while we were waiting to get started and then made 25 shillings so made a net profit on the deal.

The air is thick with rumours of what is going to happen to the airforce boys and everybody is getting newspaper clippings of being able to get out and others contradicting them. Guess it will all simmer down eventually – hope the war here continues well.

Sorry have not sent my Ireland pictures – have a good many and finally decided to parcel them and send them by registered mail. Had quite a shock today. As well as 3 letters from you got one from Mac and one from Dad. Mac's is just about impossible to read but have managed to decipher most of it. Dad wrote an excellent letter for a change – didn't' actually mean that but he put more news in it rather than just talking. Must write Dad and Mother tonight.

Dad keeps enquiring about you in a subtle way wondering if you'll be down over the Christmas season. Should take a day or three and go down and see the place (providing they have a maid).

Well honey, guess I've about run out for the night – will write tomorrow night and tell you the events of the day (which will be nil probably). All my love to you and share it with our precocious infant. Hugs and kisses, Hamp

Dec 7 1944

Dearest Peg

Pearl Harbour Day – & so what eh?

Nothing much doing to report. I feel terribly conscientious – I just wrote a letter to each of Mother, Dad and Mac. I owed them each one and now caught up for another week at least. That was Mac's first communication but Mother and Dad write regularly about every 2 or 3 weeks. It's funny how hard it is to write letters when you don't receive them. Our existence is so humdrum here that you just can't fill up a form about what you have done.

The boys are a little brassed at present – we have been told that there is now a shortage of RCAF MOs in Canada and that there is no longer a 2 year tour over here but we are here until the European war is over. It doesn't bother me because I believe it will be over before the next 18 months are up but some who have just finished their 2 years aren't so happy. However they can't complain because the army certainly doesn't hand out any set tour of duty. We ought to get a little definite gen on Saturday when Tice holds forth and will keep you posted.

That business of moving up to Johnnie's station fell through (with a little pushing from myself). I wasn't too keen to go and another MO arrived so he went up. It's a nice spot up there in summer but an awful hole in the winter time.

Interruption – somebody walked in and wanted some sleeping pills – our MT Officer – guess his vehicles can't be running too well.

Got new stoves in our Nissen huts today so finally will be able to keep our patients from freezing to death. The other ones burned for about half an hour and you spent half your time bawling out ambulatory patients for not keeping the fires going. Speaking of fires, rather liked Mac's story of some carefree youth lighting the huge bonfire on Halloween that Camrose had built as part of it's celebration for V-day when it came. I think their preparations were a little premature.

Well darling, will sign off – if you hear any more about Ollie and Olga drop me a line. Give your Ma and Pa my regards and Joan a kiss for me. All my love, Hamp

Dec 8 1944

Dearest Hamp

So Santa Claus came early to you this year. Ain't it wonderful? You should gain a few more pounds with all that food plus the beer (ahem!). I knew you were getting all those parcels and it's sure swell that others are thinking of you. It really must have been quite a week.

I got 3 letters from you on Wednesday and one today and so am all caught up again and quite the happy gal. You seem to have been quite busy lately what with your parties and panics etc. Guess I have to get in practice so I can keep up with you glass for glass when you come home or else you'll have to cut down a bit to my level, old sot – but we can thresh this out when you come home. I realize that there's not much else to do when you have time off but I hope it won't be too chronic. And just while I'm in a prattling vein – don't forget to thank the people for their boxes *soon* eh honey? That's all from the naggy wife and now I'll turn into my old sweet self.

Thursday afternoon went Christmas shopping with Doris Fleming but didn't seem to accomplish very much. Got towels for Alix, and picked up the cigarette racks for brother and sister. That was all that day. However I took in 25 negatives of Joan – pictures that you have – to be developed and am going to stick them in a small album to send to your Dad – just as one gift. He thinks the world of Joan and I thought he'd get quite a bang out of some of her pictures. I was going to take her downtown to Housey to get a good picture taken but somehow never got around to it and as they wouldn't be finished before Christmas now I'll really make a point of getting one done just after.

369

Don't quite know what to get Joan for Christmas as there aren't any substantial toys anymore and she's sure a destructive little so and so. Today she pulled two of the elements out of the radiant and kind of crumbled them up. She tries so hard to talk but so far can't get much further than "Da-Da" and "Mum-Mum". We are slowly getting into the climbing stage and one of these days I'll find her sitting on the piano or some such elevated place. She's sure full of old nick and that's easy to understand when you consider who her parents are and all they used to get away with in the good old days eh honey? I often think of the things we used to do and it's really a marvel that we survived isn't it? But by jiminy I'd sure be in there pitching again given the chance with you. What say old bean?

By the way my excuse for not writing last night – got busy with Joan's washing and ironing coz when one is out all day the work kind of piles up and poor Ma just can't do everything. Ordered some British Consuls for you yesterday and will really make an effort in the future to send 300 a week and no kidding. Guess I should start wishing you a Merry Christmas from now on so that you'll have a Merry Christmas. All our love darling and we sure miss you. Bags of hugs and kisses, Peg

December 10 1944

Dearest Peg

Nothing much to report. Yesterday was my day to write but missed last night. Was wandering down to my room to write when I passed Murray Talmudge's room. He said "Come in Doc". So I went in and he gave me 300 cigarettes which he had promised to give me. We sat and talked and he brought out a bottle of rum. We had a couple of rums and pepsi colas and then Hap Hewitt (another instructor) came in and we chatted away and drank the rum. So Hap then produced one and we talked on and by the time the 2nd one was gone we weren't very coherent and went to bed. Excellent rum. I had good intentions but I got led astray.

Yesterday we went to Group and saw A/C Tice. He didn't tell us much we didn't already know. Repeated that we were not going east from here, that MOs are frozen into service and can't get out and that we are here for the duration of this phase of the war. – so there isn't very much in that.

Today had a very good mail day. Got two letters from you. One was a blue form written November 30 and was very nice to hear that I rank so importantly in your life. It's kind of nice to hear it again and again – even if you do know someone loves you, you like to hear them say it. Also got a bunch of snaps – will more or less save the letter on top of my pile and re-read it when the wallet with picture arrives.

I hope poor old Joan's eczema improves. If it isn't any better and Harold Orr isn't very helpful then the best advice I can give you is for you to take her down to see Mac in Camrose. He is quite a good all round medical man you know.

Also got a cheque from Dad today – $100.00. That really puts my bank account in shape and will try not to spend it in riotous living, honey. You need never worry about that though dear (I repeat). My friends are all male.

Today it's looking like Canada – snowing very hard and assuming that white Christmas look. Say, I'm a bum. I got my Christmas box form you yesterday honey. It looks swell and it's better than that. I opened it up but that last warning note inside stopped me cold. I didn't open anything (so help me). Love you an awful lot. All my love, Hamp

December 11 1944

Dearest Hamp

I'm a day behind in my letter writing but can kind of blame it on Joan. She developed another cold just after getting rid of one and this makes her restless in the evenings. Her nose runs so fast that I practically have to stay right beside her to keep it clean and so when she goes to bed she gets kind of mad because she can't breathe properly and keeps herself awake. That's what happened last night and by the time and by the time she got to sleep I was ready for bed too. However her cold is breaking up and she's much better today. Her appetite isn't hindered any so she can't be very ill.

Saturday night I went over to Alix's and have now almost finished my embroidery and thinking about the next pieces I'll do. We talked over every conceivable problem and topic of the day. We have decided to take up bridge in earnest and we are going to have a foursome in January and play each week so maybe we'll know a bit about it when you come home. Sunday I spent quietly at home and took Joan for a walk in the afternoon. She was well bundled up so she wouldn't get more cold.

Today I really cleaned up on the Christmas shopping. Was downtown for 2½ hours and bought presents for 14 people. How's that honey? These gifts are from you too so here's what I've bought so you'll know what the family and friends are getting. Bought your mother a slip, shirt and bloomers. Yes sir, bloomers, and some notepaper called "Hampton". Your Dad a book by a war correspondent called "I Won't Forget" and the album of pictures of Joan. Mac & Irene this hostess set I've told you about – for cigarettes – and a model aircraft for the boys – Frigate Hurricanes. Marg and Bill – hostess set and rompers for David – real dressy ones. Doris and Bill Bothwell – fancy table mats and bedroom slippers for Larry. Eleanor and Bill Skelton – fancy table mats and new super duper waterproof lap pad for Bobby. Alix – linen guest towels and crayon book and crayons for Sandra, Kay Bartleman – collar and cuff set, Doris Fleming – bath salts, Aunty Lena – notepaper, Mother – purse and Joan – picture books, blocks and sleigh which she's using already and a few more things to buy. I think that's everyone. What do you think of the list? Then of course there are the cards and I'll try to remember everybody. It's been quite a job and I'm glad it's all finished but the wrapping.

Coming home our streetcar ran into another one and all the passengers were thrown from their seats and onto the floor if they had been standing. I hit the seat in front and banged my knees and skinned my nose. It was just like a good bang on the ice. No one was really hurt however which was really lucky. All the way from town the car kept dropping the cow catcher and we finally had to stop at the High Level for about 20 minutes. Some people were really nervous and just got out and walked but not me. I decided to stick with the ship – was too tired to walk across the bridge anyway.

Got two letters from you today and you seem to have spent a nice weekend in Harrogate. Anytime you need any money old bean just say the word and I'll gather the sheckles together. It's your money remember so write anytime. I've spent some of it so don't write for all you should have coz it ain't there – anywhere up to $50 is OK honey. Maybe I should have sent some anyway or wasn't that a hint darling? But as I say don't get too broke coz you've money here. That seems to be all for now. Alix is writing you tonight too and I'm going to write Fred. Big hugs and kisses and all my love dearest, always, Peg

December 12 1944

Dearest Peg,

More water under the bridge and it's pretty chilly water in these parts at the moment. We are having our cold wet days with slush on the ground and cold damp air. Am gradually getting hardened to it.

Not much to report. Had a real good panic today. An aircraft caught fire in a hangar. A Halifax makes quite a blaze and it's even more magnificent when it's in an enclosed hangar with gas tanks going off and ammunition and flares exploding. Nobody got hurt and although one half a hangar and a Halifax were written off it wasn't too bad. Everybody had a marvelous time watching the blaze (your husband probably got the most enjoyment except for wondering who was going to get blown up). All in all I was quite pleased with it because I managed to get out of giving 3 V.D. lectures to a few hundred erks.

So far I have managed to resist opening my Christmas parcels except for one – the cigar. My curiosity got the better of me so I opened it up. Quite a major effort in cigar construction. If you don't hear from me for about a week you'll know that I have smoked it and haven't recovered.

Jack Perverseff is away at the moment in London on a course in war surgery. I hope to get a week's course in February.

Am at last getting my pictures bundled for mailing and will get them away tomorrow. Sorry that I have procrastinated on them so much honey. Will try to correct my shiftless ways. Don't do anything but keep occupied somehow. Last night went to a show in the mess – Moonlight something or other. It wasn't very good and took time off between rolls to have a couple of beers. After the show about ten of us retired to my room and ate out of our collective boxes. I have pretty well finished my stock.

By the way – just opened my birthday cake two days ago and have now finished it with tea. It was delicious!

Well honey, will sign off. Miss you an awful lot – wish you were with me – not in Yorkshire but in Alberta. Give hugs, love and kisses to Joan. All my love, Hamp

December 13 1944

Dearest Hamp

A Merry Christmas to you darling and many many hopes for your homing coming by Christmas 1945. I figure that this letter should just about reach you around the 25th and so wish you the very very best from the bottom of my heart and here's luck for all your wishes in the new year and may they all come true. Along with all this goes my assurance of an everlasting love for the man I married. At times it's been very hard going without you to help but such times fortunately have been few and far between. When you stop to consider we have been so fortunate in all the things we've done together and I know it will be the same after the war. What has passed in the last 8 months has gone and as far as I concerned just a blank space in my life. Perhaps you won't be able to forget them as easily as I can but we can at least say quite truthfully, "It can't go on forever" and having said it take new hope for 1945. And too, we have our faith in each other so we can stand the absence quite tolerably for a while yet. I seemed to have digressed considerably from my opening sentence, to get back to the subject – a merry Christmas dearest and all the best in the new year.

I haven't been anywhere this week so news is quite scarce, however I'm busy getting things ready for Christmas. Wrapping parcels, sending cards, writing letters and doing embroidery on some dresses mother made for Joan. Decide to work through the holidays from 9 to 1 except on the 25th as I don't expect to be doing much of note. The only two parties I've been invited to are on the same night – Dec 19th – isn't that always the way? The hospital party and our club "do" – stagette of course. Have decided to go to the club do as it seems to head up to a merrier time. Haven't seen Alix this week as she's been busy with her in-laws.

Fred has moved further north from Rome to some place like Reggia. Some Italian who entertained Allied officers was lynched and thrown in the Tiber a few months ago and Fred was quite shocked at the brutality of the people. It seems the Italian was a collaborationist or something. Fred sent Alix an Italian revolver and several other interesting curios he was able to pick up and they are quite amazing – swastika armbands, etc. You'll have to see them some day.

Joan was to go to a Christmas party at the Church today but as her nose is still running away with her I kept her home. She's sure the cute trick. When she makes a puddle on the floor she says "Ba Ba" and tries to wipe it up with her hands. Today she put a magazine on a puddle in her play pen and then started to chew pieces of it – very appetizing I'll bet eh honey? Really we do feed her enough you know! She weighs 25 pounds now – still just a little girl and dainty in a clumsy way. Just her Ma talking. Merry Christmas again dearest and all my love always. Hugs and kisses from Joan, As ever Peg

December 14 1944

Dearest Peg,

Two more days nearer the arrival of the old man in the red coat. Nothing doing in the past 2 days except the usual long line of people with coughs and colds. The weather has been quite cold with damp fog and a wind that goes through you, so that kind of encourages our practice.

Had an invitation to spend Christmas in Liverpool. George Kelly, our M.T. officer, invited me down but since I've been invited to take other people's place if I leave the station, I guess I had better go there (if I leave). Don't want to stay here particularly because you have a good time but it's all liquid.

Got very conscientious the last time I wrote to you and got away 5 letters – one to Mr. Young for the Christmas parcel and also for the other parcels from Camrose and one to Dad. So now I'm caught up.

Got another parcel today but haven't collected it – hope it's cigarettes.

Played knock rummy last night and lost 15 shillings – not very good eh honey? Made 8 shillings playing cribbage with the sister though so helped out. She is still 4 shillings up on me though since she skunked me twice awhile back for 12 shillings.

Today one of our erks who has been in Holland and broke his leg and came back here to complete convalescence, gave me German wings with swastika on them – will send them along one of these days. Also donated some Dutch money.

Suppose you are swinging into high for Christmas. Hope you quit and don't work in the hospital on Christmas day.

Had quite a dull afternoon – gave 3 V.D. lectures to the erks following a film. If I ever see the film again I'll go screaming mad since I've seen it alt least 6 times all the way through and it lasts 45 minutes. This one is an American one called "Pick Up" and it goes into all the gory details of chancres, GPI, Fakes and even shows congenital syphilis, so the erks are quite impressed. You always have some say though "Gee that wasn't as bad as the last one I saw where 6 guys passed out". However they get the idea a bit.

Well honey this should be the letter to wish you a Merry Christmas and all that goes with it and will try to improve on future ones a bit. Give the daughter heaps of love. All my love to you. Hamp

December 16, 1944

Dearest Peg,

Another Saturday night but a very good one. Got two letters from you. Like yourself, I have been looking in the mail box twice a day for about a week and drawing blanks, so it's really a swell evening after all. Yours were dated Dec. 3 & 5 so can't grumble. Glad to hear that all is going well and you aren't having your molar removed until after Christmas. Money is no object honey when it's yourself we have to worry about.

Joan must have given herself quite a bump. – Good thing I wasn't around to have to dash in and treat the casualty. Would no doubt have panicked when it was our own darling daughter who was the victim.

About Christmas – I got Margaret to get some things for me and was going to send the cards to enclose – being careless as usual left it too late for the cards so will say now that the gifts are from your very loving and adoring husband with best wishes for a very Merry Christmas (and strict instructions to take on an overload of turkey for me and start increasing that one pound gain to ten. You must weigh 110 pounds by the time I get home to protect your ribs from that first bear hug.

My Christmas plans are still indefinite. I may have to go to a nearby station to relieve and won't know definitely until next week.

Has been quiet here in the past two days with no major panics to report. Last night I went out with B Flight instructors to The Checkers – the inn near Ripon – had a very good meal and then stood around and played darts and drank beer and scotch. We were the only ones in the place and quite enjoyed ourselves. Came home at 11:00 quite squiffed and at peace with the world. They are a nice bunch of fellows – all pilots – all with DFC – one with a bar to his – and very good company even if their idea of a quiet beer is a bit strenuous for one's stomach. However it's quite harmless and another evening gets put away.

The weather has really been cold for the past two days. The wind and drizzle blows right through you. When the room gets to 55, it's comfortably warm and when it's up to 60, the heat is practically unbearable. A hardy race these English.

Got letters from Mother and Marg today. All are well. Surely is wonderful to hear from you and then hear from them and have them say how lucky I am to have such a perfect wife – as if I didn't know it. Also got a parcel from the Camrose Baptist Church today – chocolate bars mainly and will save them for the children at that place if I go there. Also yesterday got the one from home with cake in it – very good cake and practically all gone what with having it twice a day for two days.

You are quite ambitious being secretary of your new club and attempting to redecorate the bathroom with white shoe polish – no wonder you don't gain more weight what with your days work and all the etceteras added.

Well honey, will repeat my wish that you have a really good Christmas and holiday season with the same for Joan and all at home. All my love and kisses and thoughts. Hamp

Dearest Hamp

Please, darling, do forgive the long silence that has slipped between us. My only excuse is that I've really been too busy to write – that really sounds awful I know. I could have written on Thursday but I'd just written on Wednesday. Friday afternoon Alix and Sandy dropped in for tea after our walk and Friday night Alix and I went to the show. Saturday afternoon we went out walking again and Saturday night I fancy wrapped all the presents.

Today I started in again and wrapped them for mailing and then mother decided I did such a good job that she asked me to do hers so I did 20 parcels all told, then took Joan for a walk and tonight finished tying the parcels and then started on the cards and now at 11 pm I am writing to you then really must have a bath and wash my hair as I'm going to Marg Howson Craig's for tea tomorrow. So please darling forgive me!

It is mother's birthday today and Joan and I got her a necklace and dad wired flowers form the East. We expect him home for Christmas and think he'll just about make it.

We had a snowstorm yesterday so everything is lovely and white and the weather still hasn't reached zero. Really a wonderful climate so far.

The orderlies at the hospital gave me a $ to buy Joan a present from them. The money was raised for all children whose parents are on the staff by the Orderlies' dance. They made more money this year so gave to the temporary staff too. It was quite a surprise. Joan has learned to climb on and off the chairs in the front room and so has spent a very busy day getting up and down besides trying to help me do the presents by pulling everything off the table and scattering it around the room. She is really on the go these days and hates to stay in her playpen for any length of time so consequently the house is always up side down.

Got a letter from you on Friday. Hope your mail catches up to you soon coz it's awful being without. When are you going to get to Lancashire – do you know? Mother keeps asking if you've been. Personally I think you'll have more fun if you go to Pickup's as they have more of a family – you know not widowed aunts etc.

Well darling, have a Merry Xmas and very Happy New Year's eve and best of everything in the New Year. Big hugs and kisses from Joan and me and please forgive again! All my love dearest, always, Peg

Dec 19, 1944

Dearest Hamp

Have just finished the last of the cards and got all the parcels away yesterday so I think I can relax again. In my past letter I mentioned what a hectic Sunday I'd had well sir, when I was having my bath I started to figure out when my last bath had been and darling you'll never believe me when I say it was two weeks ago but that's a fact – apart from a sponge down every day I hadn't been in the tub. Oh my! Ain't life busy and my it's nice to be dirty – or should I say clean.

Went to Marg Dowson Craig's for tea yesterday and Effie Dunn Gain, Marg McFadgeon Fowler, Pearl Fowler, Alix and myself were there. Pearl Fowler talked about how well thought of you were in the RCAF. It seems Cpl. M – pharmacist W.D. who used to be at Claresholm and to whom you taught blood smears etc. – talks about you all the time – so Pearl says. How do you feel wonderful person? That's my husband!

Last night it was our club party so I'm free to go to the hospital party tonight. We had a nice quiet time last night and I got a very pretty apron form the Christmas tree from Ray B – made by her lily-white hands.

So far we've got two Christmas cards – one from June, Bruce and Penny Olson. Bruce is out at the coast and June is in Calgary. She hopes to be able to join Bruce if they can get a place. The other card was from S/L and Mrs Wilf Barrell. It was sent to Claresholm. I wrote them today to bring them up to date.

Joan is quite busy these days working herself up for Christmas. We got a parcel from your mother today but didn't open it. Joan of course was all for tearing right through, just like her old man. I don't know just where on the ceiling to hang the tree but figure that would be the safest place.

Phoned Margaret tonight and they are getting ready to go down in January some time. Don't know yet what I'm going to do on New Year's Eve – probably go to bed. Oh well, sleep is good for one.

379

Am on my way to the nurses' party so had better get a move on. It is starting to snow again and the wind is quite cold. Dr Anderson drove me home from the hospital today so we talked about you ahem!

Haven't had any more mail since last Friday but due to the busy season the mails are tied up. How are you doing on your new station or are you back on your old stamping ground? By the way, got my dentist's bill yesterday for my fillings – $30 – for 5 fillings and 3 x-rays. Ouch! Oh to be a dentist. Heaps of love, hugs and kisses from Joan and I. Always. Peg

Weds. Dec 20

Dear Hamp

If you should get this before New Year's eve say Happy New Year! If later – all the best to you in the new year. I got Peggy's present from you – a topaz pendant (her birthstone). Very plain and cost 20 dollars plus $5 tax made $25 (good math. that). Then spent $3.95 on a very nice peach embroidered nightgown. Pendant from Younge's (Birks, Lady's and even Irving Kline offered little but gold wash costume jewelry). Nightie from Thomson and Dine's. Surely hope Peggy likes them the way I've squandered your money. Decided Peggy would get your presents from Joan anyway. Know Peggy will be surprised to get the presents. Hope your card arrives in the next few days. Will wait until we're on our way out of town on Saturday at the latest. Worry not about the money – took it out of a reserve and goes back into it so doesn't figure in our spending for a long time. Should have written days ago but life goes on – not much Christmas spirit but plodding just to get things done. David surely isn't getting much – we get him things all the time so not much but duplicates to get him now.

Betty Laird and family arrived today. Had them and parents and Jack to dinner – very good dinner too. Her husband is a swell egg – American self – assurance but not too pushy and very interesting. Nice little girls too. Wish Peggy and Joan were coming to Camrose with us but a I guess they should stay with the Smalley's. We could make our own way if it got tough at home. Dad phoned today to say that they had no maid but we're taking our butler and our chamber, parlor, and scrubbing maid personified in ourselves so should be able to get along. I'm looking forward to going and it'll take a lot to dampen or dry my enthusiasm. Peggy and I are going together or separately later. Better I should mail this. No.

Gonna phone Peggy first and see if she's clean – she said last night she had her first bath in two weeks. The squalor and I thought it was me I smelt on accounta our hot water tank was bust. She won't pay me anything not to tell you on accounta she has written. She's trimming the house and tomorrow she's coming to eat supper with Helen and Phillip and me – Helen tending David while I scurry down town. Bill and I are invited to Hasties' Friday to see the tree while David has a drink. She and Jessie MacKennon will be sorry for that when they see our tree and watch us drink our very good Christmas stock. Golly, Jingle Bells on the radio has me leaping – to turn it off. Love, Margaret

December 19, 1944

Dearest Peg,

My apologies for not writing last night. Was invited to a nearby station for the Sick Quarters Christmas party. This is the place I have relieved on a number of occasions and so that was the reason for the invitation. Went with our nursing sister, Jean MacIntyre, since she had worked with most of the staff. Was quite a nice party with one ward cleared out and a large dinner table and Christmas tree and so forth. Had a bag of beer and after the meal brought in a record player and everybody danced. The beer ran out at 11:00 and we were about to proceed home when we discovered it was so foggy that you couldn't see 2 feet in front of you so we had to stay. I was delegated to a bed in an unheated ward not in use and damn near froze but was brought 2 eggs for breakfast and ate them in bed so it more or less compensated. The fog lasted and we crept home his morning about 5 m.p.h. Tonight it is thicker than ever so things are quite quiet.

No mail today but all mail is slow – guess the flying weather is poor for air mail. Hope my letters are coming OK now but don't imagine they will be too regular. Am writing every other day (with the odd lapse which I will be careful to explain away).

Have a confession. Night before last was sitting around with nothing to so I opened my parcels from you. Everything was really wonderful honey and thanks for everything from cigar to shirts. It will all come in handy. Have not yet built my aeroplane but will keep you informed as to progress.

381

Jack Peverseff came back from London last night full of war surgery. He had quite a good course with a few "incidents" to explode him out of his net.

Things are quiet here as usual. Have been behind all day since didn't get back here until nearly noon. Sure doesn't seem like it will be Christmas in 5 days time, but will probably get the idea when the turkey appears.

Well honey, again – have a good holiday. All my love, Hamp. Miss you an awful lot

December 20, 1944

Dearest Peg,

Haven't done a great deal of note, since writing you last night but feel in the mood to talk to you. Have sat around the past two evenings reading my Christmas "Who done its" that you sent in the parcel. Still have one yet.

Our fog still persisting and hope that it lifts since things on the continent aren't going so well at the moment and a little air support would help an awful lot. Sure hope that Jerry doesn't push on any further and that his recent advance gets the complete chop.

Mail seems very slow these days and guess it is the same on your side of the water. Guess one just getting impatient since it's only 4 or 5 days since I last heard from you.

This afternoon the Christmas decoration committee took over the mess. We made endless chains of kind of aluminum foil and draped them around and cut down a few holly trees. The place is gradually beginning to improve but it will take quite a little more creative effort since Christmas decorations are just about impossible to obtain.

I'm staying here over Christmas. Ted Thorne and I flipped to see who would go up to relieve at Wimbledon and he lost. I may try to take leave over New Year's but don't know for sure if I can get away.

Christmas will be social here with officers helping to serve the dinner etc. and then returning to the mess to drink up the Scotch supply that has been saved up and then eating and that's that. You kind of look forward to it though.

Say I forgot to mention how nicely the Christmas presents were wrapped. Didn't tear into them as usual but carefully undid them and

382

then saved all the stickers and tinsel for one of the RAF who works in our orderly room and they were re-used on Christmas parcels. That kind of stuff is hard to get also and was much appreciated.

Didn't sleep well last night so am retiring early. Last evening went over to Sick Quarters and one of our orderlies, a Jewish lad, had some salami. He fried it up with a couple of eggs, opened some dill pickles and produced some good mustard. I really like salami (garlic sausage) but it *was* almost more than my stomach could stand. That's the second time I've done that and should know better.

Well honey, all my love and kisses, Hamp

December 21, 1944

Dearest Peg,

The sun shone today but not from the sky – get two letters from you and was wonderful, written Dec 8 & 11, so we aren't doing so badly. Have taken your advice and signed the pledge – funny how things go in bunches – one week you seem to get all sorts of opportunity to join convivial friends and the next, there is nothing to do but sit in the mess and re-read the papers and listen to the BBC (which is not very entertaining). However honey, am not a chronic alcoholic and don't you worry about it. Also my dearest, was well of you to offer your hard earned cash but actually have more than I need and find that if I need more, I am spending too much and therefore I just settle down. Get another nice thing today 300 – British Consols and that breaks the cigarette famine finally and can stop buying these gaspers. Apparently you got them just before you wrote on Dec. 8th, so the service was pretty good.

Got a nice letter from Alix Day and are writing her and Fred. By the way, watch those Edmonton street cars and don't get that nose of yours skinned again – it's too perfect to risk on those dangerous vehicles.

You seem to have had quite a busy shopping bee and to have done pretty well by everybody. Sorry again that I'm not more help but don't feel that you need any because I always claimed that you (my wonderful) have perfect taste and wouldn't forget anyone either.

I put in for my leave today and go from the 24th to Jan. 4th. Would have let it slide but I was told today that I may be posted to a Coastal

Command Squadron in Ireland and so want to get it in. I am going to Blackburn for 2 or 3 days and then I think I'll just bum around and see parts of the country that I have missed. Hope all your relatives will know who I am. Will take a chance.

This Ireland thing may not come off because I seem to be pretty stationary here but if it comes it will be a 6 or 8 mo. tour of duty and it will probably be in a rather isolated spot. Will try not to get bushed. However, won't count any chickens until the eggs are at least laid.

All our erks are having a wonderful time decorating the hospital and our supply of cotton is really getting the large and hairy chop, as the saying goes. Got 3 little Christmas trees and the YMCA came through with some red and green rope and we gathered some holly and with lots of aluminum foil, things are looking up.

Well honey – miss you an awful lot as you probably know. Miss my daughter and would like to have the opportunity to teach her to talk. All things come to they who wait. So will just wait eh honey? Love you an awful lot. Even like having you kind of bawl me out. All my love, Hamp

Dec 21 1944

My very dearest Hamp

Certainly am bubbling over with joy today coz I got five letters from you dated Dec 6 to 16 so you can see that they've been held up somewhere. That bit about the 2 year rotary system is pretty grim especially since the German counter-attacks but the war can't possibly last two more years – or can it? You're wonderful writing all those thank you letters darling. – yes sir a very good boy and just imagine getting a Christmas box and not opening it! Of course the letter was dated Dec 12 and anything can have happened since then – like yielding to temptation and opening a few of them. The idea of not opening them was so you would have something to look forward to on the 25th. Sure hope that Churchill cigar doesn't knock you for a loop, or make you sick or something.

Speaking of being sick – wee wifey is ailing again in a temporary way. Last night suddenly felt a drawing sensation on the left side of my perineum and by midnight there was quite a lump. Figure I had developed Bartholinitis (?) so went to see Dr Hutton at the hospital. I was right so now Dr Proctor is giving me x-ray treatment every morning for a few days. I figured I developed it from using Tampax – yeah I know what you've said about them honey but I'm the type that has to learn the hard way you know – and believe me I sure am. It is really quite painful and uncomfortable but I guess I asked for it. Have sure taken a ribbing about my condition from people in the know. Dr Hutton remarked "Yeh you and your nun's life" and Dr Vant looked at me with a gleam in his eye and said "Remind me to write a letter overseas". That's what I get for not taking the time to have a bath for a couple of weeks.

Was over a Margaret's yesterday to take presents and she really gave me a surprise or rather you did. Darling you are without a doubt the most wonderful husband in the world. Don't know what my present is but I'll bet it's something very super. The card you mentioned hasn't arrived but that doesn't matter. It was really a surprise as I had got quite resigned to not getting a present – in fact really didn't expect one. My but I sure love my husband!!! Yes siree!!!!

Am going over to Doris and Sandy's in a few minutes to help them open a bottle of wine.

Here's another *joke*. Two British sailors were walking down a street in the slummy district of New York when some babe stuck her head out of a window and says "Hi boys – come on up and I'll give you something you've never had." "Blimey", says one to the other. "She must have leprosy!" Ha Ha. That's all for now.

Again, many thanks for the letters and the big surprise honey. It was really swell. Joan joins me in sending our love, hugs and kisses. All my love dearest. Peg

December 23, 1944

Dearest Peg,

Got your Christmas letter today and thanks very much for the good wishes. The sentiments are reciprocated with interest. The last 8 months has been a long time but as you say we have our complete faith in each other to make the waiting less intolerable than it might otherwise. The next 8 months will go as quickly and by then we can start looking forward to a family re-union.

Things here are as usual. Had a small panic yesterday. Hugh McIntyre phoned for help in the afternoon and went over but it was just an erk with a broken leg and I stood around while he ferried him to the hospital. Nothing to break the monotony except a well fire which didn't provide any excitement.

Christmas is here – all our decorations are out and things are beginning to look brighter and more cheerful. Don't expect much activity but I'm on duty on Christmas Day and will have the usual line-up of drunks I suppose. Hope the war news gives us a little more cause to celebrate in the next few days.

Today got 300 cigarettes from John Madden – our flight sergeant who used to be here. Quite a pleasant surprise and must write tonight and thank him.

Things were quiet this afternoon and made 27 shillings playing cribbage – 9 from a patient, 11 from the dentist (Art Kalfos) and 7 from the nursing sister – pretty good day's work eh honey? (am not boasting).

Last night somebody gave me a 26 oz. of Scotch. Quite a nice Christmas present – too bad you made me take the pledge honey – but maybe I'll get a sore throat and be able to use it as a gargle.

Have been trying to clear Sick Quarters for Christmas but still have about 15 who will have to stay. However we have a turkey and the Airmen's Mess could only get geese, so they can't grumble.

Don't know any more about Ireland and won't talk about it until something definite develops. It may or may not come. Everyone says I won't like it, so that's no help but in the winter it doesn't matter because you can't get away from the station anyway and all stations are much alike. Well honey, miss you, love you and think only of you. Give the daughter a squeeze for me. All my love, Hamp.

Dec 24, 1944

Dearest Hamp

A merry Christmas to you tomorrow. Here it is Christmas eve and it seems like any other Sunday night. Have to keep reminding myself that tomorrow is the 25th.

Friday night finished up the Christmas wrapping and them spent the rest of the time till bedtime sitting in a bath of MgSO$_4$ to which I kept adding hot water. Really felt like a boiled kippered herring by the time I got out. My condition doesn't seem to be improving very quickly – but then I don't give it much of a chance. Get x-ray treatment every morning somewhere between 9 and 1 so put in an appearance on the floor while waiting – can't say I do my work however as I have to keep sitting down every 10 minutes or so. It isn't spreading so I guess it will just have to run its course.

Yesterday afternoon I decorated the tree. Its not very big and it is put on two apple boxes. The idea being to keep Joan from messing it up. However I discovered her walking around with one of the glass balls. She is kept pretty busy untying the bows on the gifts and the parcel Marg and Bill gave me – which I think is perfume – is carried around the house. Joan keeps handing it to Dad saying "Ta-ta". She's really quite the excited girl. The decorations all get a big "Oh!" and Joan's eyes are fairly popping. Wonder what she'll do tomorrow?

Saturday night Alix and I were going to a show but I didn't feel like going so Alix and Jack Day's wife's sister Eileen Watt came over for the evening. Alix was busy making doll clothes for Christmas and I worked on my embroidery – yes it's almost done and about time eh honey? Marg and Bill left for Camrose today. I've got two snaps of David along with some of Joan to send to you.

Am just back from Alix's – 11 pm – after taking over their Christmas presents and feel very gay after two tall scotches with ginger ale. Carm. Kehoe from Toronto was there and spoke of meeting you and the boys when you were East. She asked to be remembered to you. That seems to bring us up to date again. The war news is improving slightly again thank goodness. Those silly old Germans!!!! Must away to have another Sitz bath. Here's hoping you have a good Christmas. Big hugs and kisses from Joan and me. All my love dearest, Peg.

Dec 26, 1944

Dearest Hamp

Happy Boxing Day, Merry Christmas and Happy New Year to a very very wonderful husband. Your present to me was very lovely indeed

– a pendant topaz, my birthstone mounted on a 10 K gold base with a gold chain – it really is pretty my darling – and a peach satin nightie (which I'm going to save for your homecoming). Many, many thanks honey. Also got a letter from you wishing us a merry Christmas written on the 16th. It couldn't have been timed better.

We had a very exciting day. Got up at 8 and fed Joan then placed her in the playpen while we ate but she wasn't very pleased and her lower lip stuck out a good inch while she simpered and twisted the hem of her dress around her hand. I've never seen her pout before but she certainly put on an act so I finally broke down and let her out. We had the doors shut between the dining room and living room but Joan pulled the curtains aside and saw a doll sitting in a wheel barrow. Well darling as you can imagine there was no holding her back from then on her tempo of excitement increased until she was wild. She untied all the presents and got them unwrapped for me between times playing with the doll and the barrow. When everything was unwrapped she tossed the papers around the room. Joan really had a haul – 2 dresses from mother, barrow from dad, dresses from Lucy Bothwell, Alix and your dad, sleepers from Marg and Bill, shoes and gloves from Mac and Irene, 3 nighties, 2 chocolate bars, mittens, toothbrush and fancy coat hangers from your Ma, Panda bear from Mrs Umbach, cleaning set (broom, mop, duster and apron) from Kay B, kimono from Doris and Sandy, necklace and bracelet from Jean Brumwell, picture books, doll, blocks from you and I, mittens from Mrs Underwood, bib and soap from Auntie Lena. That's about all and quite enough for a 14 month old. I did just as well as Joan – your gift, Tweed perfume from Marg and Bill, perfume and talc from Alix, 2 pairs stockings from your Mother, 1 pair stockings and white satin nightie from your Dad, lovely linen tablecloth from Mac and Irene, soap from Auntie Lena, set of dishes for baking apples, stockings and pink satin nightie bath oil and powder from Ma and Pa, notepaper from Eleanor, tray cloth of cutwork and Kay's picture from Kay so me thinks I did very well. All the nighties sure tickle me as I'm building up another trousseau as well as a hope chest. Mother and Dad did equally as well so we really got far more than we deserved. Sure hope you had a good day too darling – maybe next year we'll be celebrating together.

About that turkey dinner – in the 1st place ours was a goose and in

388

the 2nd place I didn't have any dinner as I was admitted to the hospital. At 4 pm started to run a temp with pain in my left groin as well as a very sore fanny so am now in bed in 308. Have had 75 gms of sulphathiazide and am getting compresses which I put on from a stove by my bed. I spent a fairly comfortable night and my temp is just about normal so don't worry about me coz by the time you get this I'll be home and all cured. Dr Vant hasn't seen me yet but it was his idea to come in when I talked to him. The rest will do me good as I just won't stay in bed at home. But darling don't worry about me coz I had a good Christmas even if I did miss my dinner. I sure won't be using Tampax again. All my love dearest, Kisses from Joan and I. Peg

December 27, 1944

Dearest Peg,

Have nothing but apologies for being so many days over in my writing. Christmas is finally over and we managed to survive the season without any major casualties and very few minor ones.

To give you a blow by blow description of all that goes on. Christmas eve was quite quiet for awhile since I was on duty for a part of it. (ahem!) In the afternoon before Christmas I was invited down to the C.I.'s office for a drink. All the instructors were in and since I was the only non-flying type there I felt quite honored. So I invited the C.I. and CGC back to sick quarters for a drink out of a bottle whiskey I had acquired. About eight of us assembled and drank it and then 2 more bottles of Teacher's Highland Cream appeared which we drank and then proceeded to the bar where we sang Christmas Carols for a couple of hours. At 9:30 I brought over a cereal jug of beer to the night staff and we had a chicken dinner. By that time it was 10:30 so went over to the Sergeants' Mess for a couple of hours and then over to the WAAF Officers' Mess for an hour and then back to our mess where more carols were produced and so to bed at about 3:30.

Up for sick parade on Sunday morning and then the sergeants came to our mess for beer in the A.M. Took time out to come over and carve the sick quarter's turkey. Didn't think that the opportunity to carve one would show up this year but it did.

389

Then proceeded to the Airmen's Mess where we served the airmen. That took about 3 hours and actually was a lot of work (with time out for the odd erk to pour you a prescription out of his bottle). Then to the Sergeants' Mess for a couple of hours and then back to our mess to dress for dinner.

Had a few drinks and part of Christmas dinner and then Art Kalfos (dentist) and I proceeded to the Airmen's Mess where we served free beer for about 3 hours. Then to the Airmen's' dance for an hour and then back to our mess to complete the evening singing carols. As you can see – Christmas day was busy.

Will continue on letter #2. All my love, Hamp.

December27, 1944
#2 (Continuation)

Dearest Peg,

Last letter carried us through Christmas Eve and Christmas day until about 3:30 AM of Boxing Day. Boxing day (yesterday) woke up at 10:00 AM and said good morning to Ted Thorne and no sound came out. I had laryngitis and emitted nothing but a few hoarse squeaks all day. Fortunately the voice is somewhat improved today but it still breaks at inopportune intervals. Don Easton (used to be P.M.O. of #4 T.C.) came in yesterday. He is just over from Canada and hasn't a job yet and is touring the various stations looking over the situation. He and I sat around all last evening and talked about everyone that we knew mutually in #4 and am more or less up to date on everyone's activities. Retired at 9:30 last night because I felt pretty well beaten. Had to get up at midnight to see an erk who got pretty badly pranged on his bike. He was wearing glasses which broke, to the detriment of face – fortunately his eyes weren't damaged. I was rather in a poor mood and had to take time out to tear a great hairy strip off the orderly for letting him sit in a chair and bleed all over the floor while I was coming over, rather than applying a little common sense first aid. That was the only casualty over the holiday, so we can't grumble too much.

Today was business as usual except took an hour and a half this morning and showed Don Easten parts of the station that were of interest. The radar set up is quite interesting to see and he got quite a kick out of it.

Tonight am on duty again because tomorrow I go on leave. Don't expect to leave the station for a day or so though and then am going to visit those people down at Linton (near Harrogate) for a couple of days and then go up to Blackburn and look up your folks.

Heard today that I should be leaving for Ireland about the middle of January but will believe it when it comes.

Well honey, now you know how I spent Christmas. Had a good time being an extrovert, didn't get into any trouble and passed the time. Hope you had a good time. Wished that I could join you a little more closely but hope to sometime in the not too distant future. Give my fondest regards to our daughter. Miss you and love you more & more. All my love, Hamp

December 28, 1944

Dearest Peg,

Well tomorrow I go on leave. Don't know what the itinerary will be yet but have a ride to Renden if I want to use it. Am going down to these people's place at Harrogate for 2 or 3 days, then to Blackburn for a day or so and Fleetwood and then am going to go down to Renden for a weekend possibly. I don't know anyone there at present so haven't much to go down for except to look around and do a little sightseeing.

Suppose you are well into the Christmas season by now and it will be the middle January when you get this letter. Wonder how you will spend New Year's. I am going to spend it just putting. Have just about reached the limit of my celebrating ability and don't look forward to any New Year's celebration. Would be nice to be at home with yourself though and repeat our New Year's efforts. Hope that next year's will be better for the two of us.

The war news is looking a little better now and sure am praying that it steadily improves. The weather seems better – today we had our first bright and clear day for weeks and dashed out with camera and got a few snaps of one in front of a Halifax. Hope it turns out OK and will try to be a little more prompt in getting them to you. It's quite a struggle getting them developed in these parts now that the photo section can't do them for us.

Am going to take my aeroplane down on leave and will let you know what progress I make constructing it.

Well honey I better get busy and tell you how much I love you because there will be a blank of nine days before I can tell you again! Will keep writing though and mail the letters on return. Will have you with me on leave as always and keep thinking how much fun we could have done it together – not much consolation but we will work overtime to make up for it.

Give my love to the daughter again. Miss you both very much. All my love, Hamp

Dec 29 1944

Dear Hamp

You may be surprised to get this not from me but don't worry. Peggy will have told you that she is in the hospital and also what she thinks is her trouble. She is in good hands and Dr Vant is looking after her and has decided to drain the spot tomorrow. Peggy is anxious to let you have a letter but will probably be writing herself tomorrow or the day after. Mrs Smalley is looking after Joan as well as going to the hospital every day. Really there is nothing to worry about as Peggy will likely be up and around by the time this arrives. Joan is a good kid. You would not know her if you were to see her now. She runs about all over the place and of course gets into all kinds of mischief. She has the usual tumbles but hardly ever cries. She is a real sport. She has not begun to form words yet but chatters in her own way and laughs a great deal. She surely is interested in life and takes a great deal of notice of anything new. She is very fond of outdoors and is neither afraid of the snow nor the cold. Like most youngsters she likes to go off on her own and walks down the street waving good-bye. We had a quiet Christmas. We had breakfast and then opened our Christmas parcels. There were lots for every one. Peggy and Joan came in for a full share. Joan got a little cart, two or three dolls, four dresses and lots of other things. She was particularly taken with the two dolls one of which squeaked when a certain place in its back was pushed. Joan has not solved the mystery yet but keeps on trying to make it squeak. She plays so hard all day except for her sleeping time in the afternoon that when she is put to bed in the evening she sleeps all through the night. She is healthy, happy and a real treat.

Peggy keeps us informed of your activities and we are glad to know that you are getting along so well and have been able to see so much of England, Scotland and even Ireland. I am sure that you will find it all interesting but I don't doubt that you would rather be on this side. Peggy said that there is a possibility of your getting four days leave at New Year and that you might go to Blackburn. I hope that you were able to do this and that you met my sister. If you did I hope she told you of Mrs Smalley's cousins who live at Darwen about four miles from Blackburn. These two men would be able to show you around and give you a good time. If you did not get there this time go there before you come back as we would like you to meet them. Their names are Sidney and William Pickup, address Sudall Rd, Darwen.

It is like old times to have a baby in the house. It reminds me of the time when Peggy was a baby. Joan wakes up early and of course demands a good deal of attention but she is in good hands. Margaret and Bill went home to Camrose for a few days at Christmas and seemed to have a good time. Margaret sent some flowers to the hospital today.

I had a long trip which took me to St John, Monckton, Fredericton, Amherst etc. I was away for about a month and in that month all our birthdays, Peggy's, Mrs S and mine, took place so that we saved the celebration until Christmas as I did not get back until two days before. Then Peggy felt that she could keep on no longer and went to the hospital before we had our Christmas dinner so that it is not with eating too much that she was taken ill. Of course going to hospital did not mean as much to Peggy as it would have done to someone who does not know so much about it. She knows what to ask for and she was able to get a private ward. I suppose if I were able to tell you the floor and the number of her room you would be able to call it to mind. Perhaps Peggy has done this already. Peggy is of course among friends and the nurses and even Miss Peters call on her. I have not been able to do so as yet but will do soon. Peggy will be writing you herself soon. She got two letters from you today and they did much to cheer her up.

Well cheerio. A happy New Year and God bless you Hamp is the sincere wish of your Edmonton Mother and Dad.

PS – Will send roses to Peggy in your name

393

(This is quite detailed but I figured you'd like to know all. Will keep you informed darling. More love and kisses)

Dearest Hamp

Well here I am still in my wee bed and it looks like I'll be spending New Year's Eve here too. Oh well, hadn't anything planned anyway!! Sure hope you have a good leave though honey and aren't too bored with the relatives. This Ireland business sounds pretty bleak though. Hope if you do go you won't be in too lonely a spot. I didn't think you'd be able to wait until Christmas before you opened your presents old buggerlugs. However I think you did very well to wait as long as you did. Sure hope everything was OK and just what you wanted. *In reading this through it sounds pretty grim (which it was) but kinda put a bit of salt on it for your sake honey.*

I hear Dad wrote you the other night. I'll bet it was quite a shock to find his writing inside. Hope you've recovered by now my darling. Am sorry you've had to worry about me but everything is pretty good now. Today is the first day in a week I've been able to move without any pain at all. It really got pretty bad dearest. I was so swollen and tender that all I could do was lie flat on my back and look at the ceiling. Pretty grim yes siree! Had $MgSO_4$ compresses at first but they got so irritating that I couldn't put them on without crying so we switched to a perineal lamp that was quite a comfort. However by Thursday I couldn't void because the area was so painful that the muscles wouldn't relax so Dr Vant decided to aspirate it the next day. So yesterday at 1.30 pm I got taken into the Ex. Room 3rd floor and had a local put in which I might say almost finished me off. I thought I could stand any amount of pain but after that bout have changed my mind. Guess I made quite the fool of myself in a mild way. However Dr Vant opened the abscess with a scalpel and a Kelly forcep and about 2 ounces of purulent sanguineous gunk came out. The swelling deflated like a balloon. Some dettol was then injected and the incision left to drain. It felt wonderful to be able to walk again and void etc. Today I feel wonderful and no pain of any kind. It's simply amazing. All the nurses say I look wonderful – no drawn look to my face. Can it be true? Miss Peters even admitted I looked very tired and as though I was in pain a few days. Guess I must have looked terrible eh honey? However it's all over with but still don't know quite how it developed as Dr Vant says Tampax could be an irritating factor but he doesn't think it could be the cause. It's a mystery to me cause I've been a very good girl, honest my darling. Am still on Sulphathiazol – have now swallowed 345 grains of it. Oh me!

Marg and Bill were up to see me Tuesday and told all about Camrose. It seems Mac got drunk this time – not Dad. Marg will tell you all in a letter. The next day I got 3 roses and 4 mums from them. Alix has been very good too. She brought up a radio and cigarettes etc. She got the letter you wrote her. Mr Young was up yesterday and he too has got a letter from you. Gee you sure are a wonderful person and my husband too! Oh my!!

Joan is getting along OK but wearing mother ragged as she's on the go from morn to night. Dad left last night for a funeral of an old friend in Manitoba so it will be a quiet New Years for our family. However we aren't complaining yet. Heaps of love my dearest and don't worry as I'm OK again.

Joan sends big hugs and kisses and all my love, Peg

1945

In January 1945 Hamp was posted to Castle Archdale, Lough Erne, Northern Ireland with Coastal Command at the Royal Air Force flying boat base. In June 1945 after V-E Day he was posted to Number 22 Canadian General Hospital in Bramshott, England as a Medical Officer in the venereal diseases unit. He was repatriated in December 1945.

JANUARY 1945

(Letters from Hamp to Peggy were addressed to Mrs. C.H. Smith, 11024 – 89 Avenue, Edmonton, Alberta Canada and post marked, Field Post Office, On Active Service, 10858 RCAF Overseas. Letters from Peggy to Hamp were addressed to F/L C.H.Smith, C 10858, R.C.A.F Overseas and written in pencil on envelope, 423 Sqdn.)

Jan 3, 1945

Happy New Year, darling!

Dearest Hamp

Cheer up old boy I ain't dead yet and far from it altho' I'll bet you've been wondering what the score is. Well I didn't have any blue forms and no one has been out until I went for a stroll today and got some so that's the main reason for the delay. I got out of the hospital on New Year's Day at 3 pm and have been taking it rather easy since then. I feel very much better although tired but that's a general complaint and also lost a couple more pounds which I shall pick up real quick later.

Dr Vant says the culture from the abscess was E Coli and he doesn't know how I got it. Also if the gland doesn't work because the duct is plugged or if it forms a cyst I'll have to have the darned thing removed so don't know yet just what is going to happen. However it's no cause for real concern so don't worry your perfect blond head about it, darling. Of course I've quit working and am not going back until I'm darn good and ready if at all. Am going domestic again and really go all out on looking after the daughter and trying my hand at cooking etc.

On New Year's Eve Alix and Eileen Watt came up to the hospital about 9 pm with a small bottle of rum, so we celebrated by drinking rum and Imperial drink – not a very good combination but better than nothing. Marg and Bill came over to the house on New Years day after I got home. They looked as though they'd had a good time the night before. They went to some dance or other.

Joan has certainly changed. I hardly knew her. She's grown a couple of inches I'm sure and really looked cute as she had just wakened up and her hair was curling every which way on her head and her cheeks were as rosy as an apple. She's certainly into everything and Ma sure did the extra super job of looking after her. Today she noticed a spot of water on the floor and first felt her pants but they were dry so she got the dish cloth off its rack and wiped the floor. At lunch time she had her new doll with her and a spoon and put the spoon to the doll's mouth while she smacked her own lips. Pretty cute stuff eh honey?

Your letters are coming through but we haven't got beyond December 23 yet which really isn't very far away but seems like years ago to me. Sure hope you had a good time both at Christmas and New Year's. On the King's New Year's honor list Fl/Lt J L Lewis, Claresholm got the AFC and Duff Davies a recommendation – don't know what for, the paper didn't say. Had a phone call from Etta Pateman yesterday and Harry is getting a discharge because he's 34. Ollie Rostrup's husband is posted to the new hospital here when it opens. Had a letter form Doris B and she's got a sinus condition and also under treatment by a Calgary gynaecologist for some reason or other – periods every 2 weeks I think. The Lawsons have now moved to Calgary. The George Stewarts (or Stuarts) who were at Claresholm in our house had a daughter on Dec 17th. I knew something would come out of those visits. Chuck Rainsforth is back in Canada – he phoned from Montreal last week so guess Harriet is happy now. Frankie Layton left for Calgary last night to go overseas so Berta is back again to join our circle. I guess that seems to be all the news and doings up to date, darling. As I've said don't worry as everything is OK now. All our love and everything as always, Peg.

Dearest Hamp,

You old dear. Many, many thanks for the wonderful cable for our anniversary and all the love that went with it. It was phoned to me today at 11:55 AM and came in the afternoon mail. I don't know when you sent it but the date on it was Jan. 4 and if that was the case you sure had the priority rating, old chum. Sure appreciated it and think it was grand of you to remember so far ahead when you were married. I would gather that Jan. 15 means just as much to you as it does to me and believe me dearest, I intend to keep it as a very special time in all our years together. I hope this letter reaches you in time to send all my love to you for our Anniversary too, my darling.

Yesterday we had quite an exciting day as Joan went to her first birthday party – apart from her own. Sandra was two years old yesterday and we were invited along with Mrs. Day Sr., Helen Day Cairns and daughter Gail, Marie and Roberta Collins, and Marie's daughter Irene (who is a day younger than Joan), Carmon MacRae Dunlop and Mother. So you see it was quite a do. Alix gave all the children toy carpet sweepers so they really had fun trying to brain each other with the handles and we had fun refereeing the game. At tea time Joan got the high chair and Sandra and Gail sat at a small table and Irene on her mother's knee. They had ice cream and cookies and you would have died laughing at Joan feeding herself ice cream. At home she pretends to feed herself but I have to keep the spoon filled as she can't manage to get the food on the spoon. But at the party she wouldn't have any help and really made short order of the ice cream. Alix had made paper hats for the kids and Joan's was like an Empire Loyalist bonnet and was she proud of herself. She really looked so darn cute and everybody made a big fuss of her. She wore a white silk dress and pink sweater, pink sox, white shoes and a pink bow in her hair and with her blue eyes and pink and white complexion she really was a picture – if I do say so myself. Mrs. Day had never seen her and really raved about her. Oh my! We had sandwiches, ice cream, angel cake and tea so it really was quite the affair. I wore my new necklace that my very good husband gave me and it was greatly admired, too.

Got two letters from you today too and you really were an extrovert as you say. It must have been a very busy time. No wonder you got laryngitis with all that carol singing you did.

I'm feeling much better although I tire easily. Was back for a check up this morning and things have cleared up fine so far although there was no word about whether the gland was functioning or not. I'm to go back in 3 weeks so may know more about it then. Joan is trying to climb up on my lap. Just a minute.

Hi Pop. How are you? H TJJJjj look foooow oooooo. Joan

Sure hope you can figure out the message. She let me help at first but the rest is a secret and 'writ by hand' by Joan M. Smith in person. Joan is saying car and bow wow and just plain Bye and baby – so guess we're picking up. These are on top of her old vocabulary of Da Da and Ma Ma etc. She's sure a going concern. Am going to get her picture taken at Housen this month so will sure send you one. Again all my love on our anniversary and always. Hugs and kisses from Joan too. More love, Peg

January 6, 1945

Dearest Peg,

On our second anniversary I want to take a little time to tell you again how much I think of you. We had 15 months together which were the happiest time I have ever spent and I think that they are only a tantalizing taste of what happiness is in store for us in the future. The past 9 months have been very difficult to endure at times and I have felt that the separation was something which couldn't go on. Fortunately your letters and pictures and all the little things you have said, have kept us very close together and at times I almost feel I can turn around and talk to you.

In the time I have been away I have never been unfaithful to you and I swear before all that we hold dear, that I never shall be – in action or in thought. People, such as ourselves, who are separated by the war seem to fear nothing except that their partners will not be absolutely true. That is something you need never fear as far as I am concerned and I'm sure that you don't – but a little re-assurance occasionally doesn't do any harm and I felt that you don't mind me mentioning it once again.

It will be grand to be together again and start on our own home at last, but I don't believe that either of us wants to be together and then go through the trial of separation again. Therefore I can look forward to my stay here with considerable calm because we know that when I come home it will be to stay. Therefore even if there are a few added months it will not be too long a time out of a life-time.

Well honey, will stop my drivel. Give our daughter my love on our anniversary and to you all my love and thoughts. Hamp

January 6, 1945
Letter #1

Dearest Peg,

Have arrived back from leave and am away behind in my letter writing since I didn't keep up to date as I went along. My apologies honey – was thinking of you but just got too shiftless.

To tell you all that I did. Leave started on the 29th and I slept in until noon and then caught a train to Harrogate and by bus to Weatherby and then walked a mile and a half to Linton. Arrived at the Toa's about 5:00 PM and there was nobody home but the kids and their grandfather, Mr. Dodgson. He is a nice old bloke who used to be a cartoonist and used the pen name of Kester and was apparently quite well known and did fairly well by himself. Frank and Margot – the Toa's arrived home about 6:00 P.M. and I got more or less settled. That evening Frank and I went down to the Windmill which is their local pub. It's a quaint old place and I met a lot of the people there abouts. They are all well to do business people who commute from Leeds and now that they can't operate their cars to go out in the evening, they all come down to the pub. It's more like a club than anything else and they are all fairly young couples and very sociable. I met a lot of nice people and really enjoyed it. Managed to accumulate several invitations for weekends but won't be able to take them up on it since my posting is supposed to be on the 8th. I stayed with the Toa's until the morning of the 4th of January. Intended to get away sooner but was made so welcome and the weather was so miserable that I didn't leave. While there I slept in every morning until noon – in spite of the noise the kids kicked up. The day after I arrived – the 30th – the Toas' had a party and it was a costume affair. Some very weird costumes appeared and some rather nice ones. I didn't do anything except masquerade as an RCAF M.O. and get quite cheerful on the liquor.

The next night we were invited to a New Year's party by some people called Meller. They had a lovely home and a wonderful cellar – ahem! It was quite a sedate party but I got quite morbidly cheerful with a bottle of rum. We came home about 2:00 A.M. and that more or less looked after New Year's celebration.

Well will stop temporarily and continue on the next letter. All my love, Hamp

January 6, 1945
Letter #2

Dearest Peg, To continue where I left off.

The next 3 days I did nothing but sleep until noon and then get up for lunch and bum around with the kids all afternoon. They are lovely children and I got quite a kick out of them. The oldest is a girl about 7 – kind of a brat but quite nice. The middle one – Veronica – is four and really a beautiful child and she completely won me over. The youngest – Godfrey – age 10 months – about Joan's age and really a fine baby but don't think he comes close to our marvelous infant. It certainly is a treat to be in a home like that and see the kids and all – makes you a little homesick though because you more or less see what you're missing. However we'll make up for it in time darling and until then might just as well be patient.

Each evening Frank (Toas) and I took a stroll to the local and had a few pints and gossiped with the neighbors. Frank is an interesting fellow – spent several years in Shanghai and has traveled over most of the Far East. He is an electrical engineer and has quite a responsible position in the power system for this part of the country. He is a little hard of hearing however but I more or less got used to talking a little louder. It was a bit difficult for the first couple of days with my laryngitis but that cleared up in short order.

Finally I got my ambition up and set out for Blackburn on the morning of the 4th. Frank drove me to Leeds and then caught the train to Manchester. Wandered around Manchester for an hour and then went to catch my train for Blackburn. Went dashing madly down the platform just as it was leaving and missed it. Caught the next train to Bolton and then to Blackburn. Wasted a couple of hours and got thoroughly chilled waiting around station platforms for trains. Got to Blackburn and then proceeded by taxi to Aunt Maggie's. She was out and I was preparing to wait on the doorstep when a neighbor sent me across the street to Mrs. Sweetings. She is a sister-in-law and a very nice person. We talked for an hour or so in front of her fire and felt quite at home. More love, Hamp

January 6, 1945
Letter #3

Dearest Peg,

Aunt Maggie (Mrs. Horsfall) arrived home and I went across and introduced myself. Merely said my name was Smith and from then on I was one of the family. She is a wonderful old lady and it scarcely seems fair to call her old – she is as active as anyone half her age and her mind is also very young. She immediately sent me to my bedroom and got settled – she keeps a bed made up all the time for anyone who might come in. The house is very comfortable and I believe she has altered it considerably since you were there. A bathroom opens off the bedrooms and she has added a kitchen at the back of the house. Very comfortable indeed and what impressed me most favorably was the warmth of the rooms and unlimited genuine hot water.

We talked until midnight in front of the fire and covered just about every angle. She was properly impressed with pictures of you and Joan and produced several pictures of you in your youth. One in particular was good – you and your Dad and Mother – a candid-camera shot which looked to have been taken in downtown Edmonton.

Really enjoyed the evening. Was ashamed that I hadn't taken her more – gave her a pound of tea which Mother sent and some tea bags which you sent, and she seemed glad to get them since she is a great tea drinker. She showed me a cake holder she is giving you[12]. It is a lovely old piece and I am to go and pick it up before going back. It's rather quaint and I imagine your Mother knows it well.

I was really impressed with Blackburn. It's a very pretty town and the park right near Aunt Maggie's is really beautiful. Also the view of the countryside from the back of her place was a surprise after seeing little but factory chimneys between Manchester and Leeds.

I was going on to Blackpool the next day but decided not to since traveling is such a nuisance and it would only give me a few hours there since I had to be back tonight. So got up at ten and took the tram down the hill and got my train time and then came back for dinner and left at 3:00 P.M. for home Will close and continue. All my love, Hamp

January 6, 1945
Letter #4

Dearest Peggy, to continue

Your (our) Aunt Maggie really is a grand person and I hope to spend a couple of days there on my next leave and also to get to Fleetwood for sure next time. Would have gone there but it takes a whole day traveling and I had to get back today and start to get organized for my move to Ireland.

Got into Leeds about 6:00 P.M. (changed at Halifax) and then came home. In the station at Leeds I met our station adjutant – Wallie Colley – we had a compartment to ourselves and he produced a bottle of Scotch. We kept nipping at it until we got to Thirsk and found then that it was gone and we were in no pain whatsoever. So we slipped into the Golden Fleece (the inn in Thirsk) and had a couple more for the road and then came home. It kept out the cold a bit for there is snow and ice on the road and the weather really feels wintry. (However we actually didn't need that for an excuse.)

All in all it was a very nice leave and a good rest. Didn't do anything very exciting but enjoyed it all.

Got home and had 3 letters from you. You seemed to be pretty busy. Sorry to hear about your Bartholinitis – hope your sitter is a little more comfortable by now. It all goes to show you honey that you need me to keep you in shape. That gland probably just flared up out of spite from not being used for the purpose which nature intended it. You had better get that all fixed up before the return of your ever loving husband. Also stop using Tampax. Well, will quit ordering you around. Hope you are better now, honey.

The Christmas presents weren't very original I guess but you know that I meant well and wanted to do something for you – will do better next time. Sure hope your condition didn't spoil your Christmas.

Well honey, miss you terribly. Think of you a lot and wish that I could get a peek at the daughter for only a minute sometime. However time is flying and it won't be too long. All my love, Hamp

January 7, 1945

Dearest Peggy,

Got two letters from you today and was really glad to hear from you but sorry that you had such a bum Christmas (by the way, that isn't meant to be a witticism). Hope that you are all over your condition by now and more or less back to normal with no ugly operation scars to mar your beauty.

The daughter really made a haul at Christmas time – she got nearly as many things from everyone as I got from you and her in my box. That Christmas dinner you missed nearly made me break down and weep but will make up for it on the next one we have together. Hope you managed to get under way again before New Year's rolled around.

I still have gotten no word on my posting. I was supposed to leave tomorrow but as yet there has been no confirmation by mail, so I just sit and wait – will probably hang around here for weeks. I have no idea what station it is but it will be Coastal Command and probably quite dull but the change will do me good.

After writing you last night we had a small party. Three of the boys were posted home and with my posting imminent, it provided an excuse. We drank innumerable beers and got quite cheerful about it all. We were all duly registered in the hall of fame – got one shoe taken off and the sole of your foot covered with lamp black and then you are up-ended and leave your footprint on the roof of the Bar and then sign your name to it. My flat feet were no drawback at all. (P.S. I need some soap

– toilet soap.)

The M.O. who replaces me came in last night. He is a French Canadian named Andre Leduc and seems OK in spite of his broken English. Ted Thorne left this morning on a week course and Jack Peverseff is on a weekend in London and Jean MacIntyre is on leave so I had the place more or less to myself today.

Jack Peverseff had a little tough luck – was going somewhere by transport and the vehicle hit an old man and killed him. Frightful nuisance although it wasn't Jack's fault, it kind of worried him.

Lost two very good friends two nights ago – left here on their second tour so they could go home for good – they went down over Hanover. Most unfortunate because they were good blokes who I had gotten to know quite well.

Ted Thorne is a little disgusted – his posting home has been delayed another two months – looks like he's going to put in his 3 years in full.

Well honey, sure hope you have your health back. Between bum and thumb trouble we have quite a time – my condition was a little easier to discuss though when it came to showing people your operation.

Well darling, will sign off. Say hello to the hurricane for me. All my love, Hamp

January 8, 1945

Dearest Hamp,

You will be just back from your leave time. The days seem to be slipping away again so fast that I can't keep track of them. I wrote you last night – ordinary mail – and sent some pictures and intended to write you on the blue form too but Alix came over for the evening so didn't get around to it.

Friday – late afternoon – I went to a show with Kay Bartleman. It was "Frenchman's Creek" very pretty Technicolor etc. and it stuck to the book but it was frothy and when the end came I thought "So what!". Guess I'm just hard to please. After the show we had hot cakes, pork sausage, maple syrup and coffee. Very good too, I might add. Was home by 8:30 and went to bed almost right away. Sure keep very respectable hours sometimes.

Saturday "the quartet" went for our usual stroll and came back to our house for milk and cookies. At night I went to Day's and Alix and I did needlework. We are well past the point where we feel that Saturday night is a big night. To us it's just another night, guess it's about the same way with you. Isn't it funny how you can do what you have to do each day and then put in time each night and to outward appearances quite quietly while all the time something inside of you keeps beating "One day nearer to the day (you Hamp) come home." At least that's the way with me. Sometimes I get so restless that I feel that another day like the last one and I'll scream. But so far I haven't done so. Maybe if we could all let our pent up emotions go we'd feel much better. However we on this side of the world can't complain, as things are much the same as in peacetime. I sure slipped off the walk there for awhile. Time out honey while I kick myself back on again.

Chuck Rainsforth is back home but in a body cast as he fractured a vertebrae in a jeep accident. Mr. Young was around to visit me today and he was talking about Chuck. He says he's a very sober and serious young man now and who wouldn't be eh darling? Am going around to see him one of these days and see if I can't cheer him up somewhat.

Was also downtown for awhile this P.M. and sent you 900 cigarettes. Hope they arrive soon as I'm rather behind in sending them to you. Also put $100 in the bank and find that after Xmas spending, dentist's bill and victory bonds I've $20 more in the bank this month than at the same time last month. (Me thinks that's pretty good. Am still around the $250 mark though and I've got my hospital bill $28 to pay out yet.)

Joan is getting more active each day – if that is possible. We were building up blocks tonight but she couldn't stand to see them piled up and so scattered them all over the front room every time I stacked them. However we had fun and got quite excited. She isn't housebroken yet but we're sure working on it. Say honey would you do me a favor? Would you write Mother and Dad sometime and thank them for looking after Joan and me. I try to but feel that a note from you would carry more weight. Just when you get time honey. All my love for now dearest. Hugs & kisses from Joan and all my love again. As ever, Peg

Dearest Peggy,

This is the first letter I have written you while under the influence of alcohol (Etc)

I must tell you before I sober up that I *love* you one (hell)!! ! ! of a lot. As a matter of fact I love you more than anyone that ever has or will exist. As a matter of fact (to repeat myself) I love you just the same as if you were about 2" (inches) away and I could reach out and talk to you.

Therefore honey that is the reason that you are the only

PS Pardon the horrible letter

star that ever shines around

PS Do me love my wife

here, even when the fog is not

PS Your are wonderful woman

around. As a matter of fact

(hang around)

If I wait 18 years, or about

which is

36 years, too quick to wait for

P.S. You are my wife and boy am I lucky!!!!

the most wonderful person who ever existed in all the world for me or anyone else.

P.S. Dearest Peg – Love & kisses to you & ours

Pardon me for being so fried but I bet a lot of people in the mess who wished me god speed and thought I have a very wonderful wife in looks and everything else.

Your ever loving husband.

All my love, wishes and affection. Hamp

My darling wife,

Pardon me for writing such a horrible letter but I must take time out to tell you that you are the one I am waiting for (for the next 10 years).

Dear Peg,

Sure is a terrible letter but I had to write to you because you are the only subject of thoughts and conversation that appeals to me.

January 9, 1945

Dearest Peg,

I owe you an apology so here it is. Last night I wrote and mailed you quite a terrible letter. I'm awfully sorry. No excuses except I was quite stewed and thinking of yourself, so figured that it was a good time to drop you a line, which I did. The worst of it was that it was promptly mailed and was then too late to retrieve. Hope you will forgive me honey and it won't happen again. Love you more than anything else and when I'm a little fried, it is just twice as much, so maybe you can see the reason for wanting to talk to you. Now the because! Went into the bar about 7:00 PM to have a double whiskey and then have a hot bath and try to get rid of my cold – which I picked up returning from Blackburn. One thing led to another and everything was a whiskey – consequently the schnozzle developed. Sorry again.

Had a good parcel day today in cigarettes. Got 1200 – 600 from Alix Day, 300 from you and 300 from Mac. All in all it was quite good and now I can pay Thorne 300 and still have 900 as clear profit. Your boy friend here will have quite a cough by the time he gets through these.

My posting did not come through today but London phoned and said it was in the mail. I am going to Castle Archdale in Ireland. It is a Coastal Command Squadron #423. Quite an isolated spot but from all accounts is not a bad station for awhile (about 6 months).

I should be here tomorrow and probably I will leave the following day.

It has been snowing all day in large damp flakes and it looks and feels quite wintry – but nothing like home for all that. The station has been graveled and all available erks and air crew are out shoveling off runways and dispersal's so that the boys can start dicing when it clears. (dicing is an air expression meaning – "dicing with death" – which they figure they are doing whenever they take one of our crates aloft).

Well honey will close now and say – sorry again. Love you very much. Say hello to our tornado from me. All my love, Hamp.

Dearest Hamp,

Wonder where my wandering husband is tonight – England, Scotland, Ireland or Wales? It's rather hard to speculate with the Air Force but my guess is you're still in England at this date. I had a letter from you today dated Dec. 28 but a lot of water has flowed under the bridge since then as you were just getting ready for your 9 days leave. I'd sure like to be going on leave with you honey but such pleasant things will have to wait awhile it would seem.

Haven't much to report since my last epistle as life moves on the same each day. Went to Mrs. Lawton's for tea yesterday and heard a lot of talk most of which is forgotten. Her nephew Wally got the D.F.C. so she's quite proud of him. She wanted to be remembered to you and sends you greetings and best wishes for the New Year. That is all I remember.

Had a phone call from your mother this morning wanting to know when I was going to Camrose. I'm planning to go down sometime in February and Margaret and David may go down at the same time for a few days. It will make a full house but more interesting as far as I'm concerned.

Went to a show with Alix last night. Deanna Durbin in "His Butler's Sister". It was quite funny but the love scenes made us both very lonesome. However Alix consoled us by saying that she's more optimistic now about the end of the war than she has been since Fred went away. I sure hope it's a good sign and the war news is finally picking up again so here's hoping it won't be too long now. I'm still counting on seeing you next fall sometime – that's the time I set when you first went away but I'll take it in stride if I'm wrong.

Am doing a new piece of embroidery now – a chair back set (for the back and arms of a chair and chesterfield). It's in a cross stitch xxxxx – and each one done is a kiss for you. Quite a game and I'm sure going at top speed. There must be about 6000 in the 3 pieces so don't forget to collect them some day. Alix bought a chair for her needlepoint for $49.50 – not bad for one chair eh honey? It's real furniture. Yours truly is too busy paying hospital bills to buy a chair. Anyway I'm saving our money to furnish a whole house or go on a trip or something. Sure hope the mail service improves again soon but the weather is bad in the East. All my love for now. Joan sends hugs & kisses. As ever, Peg

January 11, 1945

Dearest Peg,

Well, I'm on my way. Leave this morning for my Coastal Squadron in Northern Ireland. The nearest place is Enniskillen in case you should be curious about looking it up on the map.

I don't look forward to the journey with any pleasure since I leave this afternoon at 2.00 and will arrive there tomorrow evening sometime and will be changing trains and packing luggage about every 3 hours until I arrive.

No mail for the last few days and suppose it will get here by the time I leave. I don't know how the mail service will be there but it will probably be a little slower than our present system since this new place is a bit isolated. Well honey, I am in the midst of packing and clearing – had to do it all this morning because the posting was this morning and when it came in today it had me leaving here last Monday.

Will sign off and write as soon as I arrive there. All my love to you & Joan, Hamp

January 12, 1944

Dearest Hamp

Two more days by the board and not very much to report – as you would say. We are having the most wonderful weather – it was 39° above today and yesterday it rained. Ontario isn't as lucky however. They have about 40° below so it looks like the banana belt has moved north a few hundred miles.

I went shopping yesterday to the local stores and bought some food for a food box for you and also managed to get two nail files. They have been off the market for a while. These aren't very good but the best I could do.

You are getting mail over here – physicians samples from Smith,

French and Kline Labs. Yesterday you got two 6 ozs. of Eskay's Neurophosphates – one with vitamin B and one without so your dear wife is robbing the mail and drinking your tonics – as of yesterday. Today you got Paredrine Sulphathiazole suspension – about 3 oz for nasal and sinus infections. "The fundamental reason for its striking success is the fact that it is not a solution but a suspension of microform crystals of free Sulphathiazole." Unquote. If you would care to have a sample sent in a plain wrapper address your request to Mrs C H Smith and it will be sent to you by return mail. Ahem!

The wee daughter is getting cuter every day. She has developed the trick of wrinkling her nose when she laughs. It really looks silly. She follows dad around all the time and today I heard him say from the back of the house, "Can't a fellow have a moment to himself once in a while?" after she found him in the bathroom. When I scold her for such things as emptying drawers or playing with the elements from the radiant she just looks at me, opens her mouth wide and growls like a mad dog and the look you get is enough to day "you touch me and I'll bite." And I for one don't want it for the world. However she doesn't get away with very much as I believe in a slight tender spank once in a while. But with Joan it only works once in a while. If she's made up her mind to do something all the spanking in the world doesn't stop her. So you can see our 'datter' has a strong will which has to be handled carefully or she'll be the boss – as if she wasn't already. She takes the rag doll (your dad sent her when she was a month old) to bed with her every night. That is the pet and is called Raggy Ann. Marg is the doll she got from us for Christmas and Pandy is the bear Mrs Umbach sent, so you can see our family is growing all the time. By the way I'm feeling ever so much better and looking more like my old self and I do mean old. Really felt like 90 at one point but am down to about 30 years now. By the time you get back I'll be a gay young thing.

All my love as always dearest. Hugs and kisses from Joan. More love, Peg.

January 13, 1945

Dearest Peg,

Taking you up to date after that last note I scribbled in the midst of my departure. I am now in Northern Ireland and can't say just how it will be in the long run. However honey, I think it will be a nice station in which to spend a few months.

Had a hell of a journey over. Managed to get all my junk into my trunk and a kit bag and they both weighed plenty. Left Topcliffe at 2:00 PM changed my luggage at Harrogate and got a train to Leeds & changed to Carlisle! Got there at 6:00 PM and my train left at 2:30 AM. Went and saw a good show – "The Seventh Cross" with Spencer Tracey and then waited in the station for four hours. No heated waiting rooms so hung around and drank innumerable cups of tea. For the last hour, one of the porters took pity on me and took me into his fire – it was as good as a suite at the Hotel Vancouver to me at that moment. Caught the train to Stranraer and got my luggage off on the boat and off at Laine and on the train for Belfast and off at Belfast and across the city to another station. Stayed in Belfast 4 hours and then to Omagh where I changed again and then again at B. junction and finally arrived here and got a transport to the station. I just related all this so I could get a little sympathy because as you remember, war here now, porters are scarce and at each change you have to dash madly down to the baggage coach and have your luggage out and then see that it gets into the next.

By the time I arrived here last night I was really beaten. The M.O. I am replacing is a chap named Kester – he came over seas with me and has been here ever since. There is an old Irish chap named Pierce who is Sr. M.O. of the station – he was a flyer in the last war and doesn't seem too "genned up" medically but is a nice old bloke and should prove pleasant to work around. My squadron is quite a good one and there are a lot of nice chaps in it. I will be rooming with one – a pilot – forget his name at the moment. Swell fellow though. My quarters are a Nissen hut. There are two to a room and eight to a hut. Wash basins are camp style and there is a place outside with a pail in it for use as a urinal only. The bath house is about half a mile away!

An old castle on a hill forms the nucleus of the station and the station fades away down the hill all around it. The mess is about 1/2 a mile from it and my quarters about the same, so I will get a little more exercise.

We have an M.I. room for sick parades in the castle but our sick quarters is another old country house about 4 1/2 miles away. That is not very convenient but it seems to have a fairly good set up. Two other stations use it but only one of them has an M.O. We all look after our own patients.

All in all, I think it will be quite nice here. The weather and billets are cold unless you keep stoking your fire. Each room has a small coal stove in it and there seems to be a fair supply of coke.

Well honey, am not getting any closer to home but will probably get closer to you because there isn't much to do but sit and look at your wife's picture and keep writing. Miss you a lot. Give my love to the daughter. All my love, Hamp

January 14, 1944

Dearest Hamp

Well, darling, our second anniversary is tomorrow and as I think about it all I can hardly remember that there was a time when we didn't know each other. It seems as thought you've been with me all my life so far. Things that happened to me that have no connection with you just don't count. In fact I'm so wrapped in you and anything pertaining to you that nothing else matters and I must say it's truly a wonderful feeling. Guess this is a bad case eh honey? I'm certainly praying, wishing and hoping that we'll be together again this time next year. Do you remember a letter I wrote the night before we were married? Well darling the theme is still the same and always will be so thinking of that letter I send all my love to you as a starter for a third year together.

Last night Alix and I went to the Princess Theatre to see "See Here Private Hargrove". We enjoyed it very much as the lines were really witty.

This afternoon Chuck Rainsforth came over to see Joan and I. He rather beat me in my good intentions to call on him. He doesn't look very robust but says he feels fine although he is a much more serious young man than when we knew him. He is on a two months leave and then thinks a four or five month's convalescence duty at the coast. It seems he fractured a vertebra, wedged two together and tore a flap of tissue from his skull requiring 26 stitches. Harriet is stationed at a convalescent hospital at Niagara but Chuck, after saying just that,

416

informed me that they have decided to call the whole thing off. Just what that means I don't know as I didn't care to ask. All I could think of was "Just what I thought would happen!" and so didn't open my mouth knowing me! I guess it is the best solution to a rather unsatisfactory match but I do feel a bit sorry for Harriet. You probably don't agree on that account but it's too bad never the less.

Joan of course showed off very nicely for Chuck and he thinks she's real cute and is quite willing to sit down for 17 years and wait for her – so maybe won't have much trouble marrying her off. Me thinks it will be the other way around darling. I must say she really went too far in showing off though' as she sat on a cold air register and wet right into it. Our daughter sure shows off in a most peculiar way eh honey?

Flash from the British Front – Eddy got himself engaged to some girl in southern England. Boy am I sure glad you're a married man honey! But Eddy of all people – Oh me! Aunty Lena is really bursting with the news let me tell you!

That seems to be all for now honey. Am looking for mail now as it should be through soon. All my love my darling. Hugs and kisses from Joan. Love, Peg.

January 15, 1945

Dearest Peg,

Two days have gone by very quickly since I last wrote you. Have been quite busy since every one else buggered off as soon as I arrived and I was more or less left to struggle along alone.

Am now sitting beside my fire in the Nissen hut and stoking with one hand and writing with the other. It's quite an art to keep them going with coke. I have discovered after spending 2 hours relighting it after it went out when I was unpacking.

Have gotten quite settled in the routine here and seems as though I had been here for weeks already. It's a very beautiful spot in summer but is very damp. It rains every day without fail and you can't walk anywhere without having to go through mud.

Spent the evening in the mess last night and met a lot of the boys. They are a very nice bunch – seem a bit more mature and settled than the lads in bomber command. My roommate is Bob Bartlett – a pilot and a captain of a crew. Swell fellow, doesn't smoke or drink and goes to church twice on Sundays and says he figures a little religion won't do any harm in helping him through a tour of ops. He will be a very good influence and also seems a hell of a lot of fun.

There are 3 M.O.s here – sold S/c Pierce and a chap named Galdener – a Jew – who is M.O. for one of the other squadrons. Haven't met him yet because he is away burying his father.

Have had a few minor panics since arriving here but nothing serious.

Seems funny to dash off to a crash in a power launch rather in an ambulance like before.

Sick parades are large here because it's so damned cold and everyone seems to have a perennial head cold.

By the way honey, write to me now as 423 Squadron, RCAF Overseas the mail will get here a little more quickly. The service is apparently as good as that in England and possibly only a day longer – so we have nothing to grumble about.

Well dear, this is a nice spot but would trade 50 of it for Edmonton. Miss you and Joan. Bob Bartlett has a daughter a few mos. older than Joan. Well darling, All my love, Hamp

January 16, 1945

Dearest Peg,

Had quite a surprise today. Got your letter. I didn't expect them to arrive so soon. First one I opened was from your Dad and my heart was beating on the soles of my boots when I read the start of it. I immediately opened yours, which was dated two days later and things began to look a little better again. You had quite a poor time of the Christmas season and I'm sorry honey. Hope you are 100% again by the time you get this letter. Would have liked to be around and give you a little helpful sympathy but give it to you now and surely hope and pray that you are OK now. Don't go back to work too soon – take at least a month off and get kind of caught up on yourself darling. Maybe it's just as well I wasn't around – can just imagine the nurses looking at me when

I came in and whispering behind their hands that there was the villain of the piece. It all goes to show you that you can get a boil on your "private parts" without me there to make it worse. If was sweet of your Dad to drop a line. Got a letter from Margaret and one from Mother today. All is well at home and it was apparently a damp Christmas – maybe you were better off in 208 compared to Camrose.

Have been quite busy for the past two days with sick parades and one thing and another that right after writing you I collapsed on the bed and slept until 11:00 and then made my trek outside and got into bed.

Tonight have sat around stoking the fire and reading a paperback named 'Claudia'. Really enjoyed it because it was a story of a completely happy married couple and it kind of seemed like us in a way – except you are a lot smarter than Claudia.

My roommate was away last night and tonight. He was out on an operation and got diverted to another station down south because we had duff weather. He made an attack on a submarine yesterday and I'm anxious to hear about it.

Had a flip today in a Sunderland. It's a huge boat – used to think the Halifaxes and Lancasters were big but this really makes them look small. You can move around in it like in a small bungalow. Really enjoyed myself dashing in and out in motor launches – quite a novelty at present but damned cold. Didn't brave the weather for supper but made some tea on the stove and stole a can of meat from Bob. Well honey hope you are well. Love you terrifically. All my love, Hamp

P.S. More love and kisses and pass some to the daughter.

January 16, 1945

Dearest Hamp

You certainly were a busy boy on Jan 6th & 7th writing all those letters that have found their way to your ever anticipating literary public. Yes siree they certainly were welcome and well worth waiting for. You seem to have had a very nice leave visiting here and there. Mother and dad were very pleased you managed to get to see Aunt Maggie and were also glad to get your letter.

Just ignore my request that you write Ma and Pa. You beat me to it wonderful husband! And as for the very lovely anniversary letter, many thanks. We must be psychic. Isn't it funny how our letters to each other for our anniversary were almost parallel in thought and word? You couldn't have received mine when you wrote so it's very amazing. When I started to read yours I thought I was reading my own again. We certainly are quite an amazing couple if I do say so myself. What say you old boy? Our wonderful daughter is more surprising every day. Today she came running out of our bedroom with my summer hat cocked on her head (you may remember the white straw affair I bought in Claresholm) and my mirror in her hand. She was certainly very proud of herself and proceeded to show off in her usual manner. Yesterday she managed to sneak the bread knife from the kitchen cabinet and when I went to get it back she waved it around in the air and hit me accidentally in the face just to the right of an eye. By the time you get here you may not recognize your wife from all the new scars she is acquiring in your absence. Joan's birthmark has entirely disappeared now and her eczema is quiescent at present (touch wood) as it may disappear now that she is older – I hope.

I have a parcel almost ready to send. It only requires packing and wrapping which takes the most time I find. However I hope to get it all finished tonight. Am sending you piece of our wedding cake-part of the last layer. It is really better now after 2 years than it was when we were married. I think I'd better send you several cakes of soap in a separate parcel as I'm sure the soap must taint the food. Will also send more toilet articles at the same time such as nail files and razor blades. Will try to get it off by tomorrow or Thursday.

The war news is certainly very good now but I'm not overly optimistic yet. Guess I hate to be disappointed by reverses etc. However I do feel you'll be home by next Christmas – at least I'm a-hoping.

Am planning on having a tea some time next week as I owe several people. But more of that when it is more definite.

Guess you'll be in the Shamrock Isle by now. Hope it isn't as bad as people have made out for you. Must go and do some cross-stitch now and think about you. All our love my darling from Joan and I. More love – Peg

January 18, 1945

Dearest Peg,

Another two days gone by and very little to report. The rain continues and at times there is hail that beats down on our tin house like machine gun fire. That came about 7:30 this morning and it was quite a struggle to drag myself out of bed and up the hill to take sick parade.

Bob Bartlett came home last night. Glad to have him back and stoking the fire – save a lot of swearing and confusion to have him light it since I haven't gotten accustomed to it yet. It's a wonderful heater though.

Sat around the billet last night and made hot chocolate and tea and toast and jam and honey and cheese and opened a can of peaches. All Bob's food but very good. I left everything I had acquired in that line because it was too heavy to carry.

Spent an hour down on the dock this morning watching things. Tearing rain and wind and spray and the boats ploughing through. Flying was as usual and I certainly hand it to the boys in Coastal – they haven't got any picnic because they fly all hours and all weathers.

Usual run of sick parade today with innumerable coughs and colds and backaches. Not very interesting but it keeps one occupied. The M.O. of the other squadron is back – a chap named Goldenring – an Irishman and a Jew. He is about as talkative as anything I have ever seen but is a very nice little chap, very obliging and will be good company.

Say, forgot to mention our anniversary but wrote a letter for it so guess it will be OK – hope the flowers arrived in time.

Say by the way honey – if you send me parcels – don't enumerate on the customs declaration what is inside them but just put "Soldiers Comforts". That saves anybody being tempted with what is inside and pinching them and they get here OK.

Well goodbye for now again. Miss you. Give Joan my love and kisses. All my love, Hamp

January 18, 1945

Dearest Hamp

You become more amazing as time goes by. Guess what arrived

421

today? Yes that's right – the most beautiful flowers I've ever seen – outside of my bridal bouquet – and a very lovely card. I can't express just what the flowers mean to me. All I can do is thank you very much darling and really thank you in person when we get together.

No fooling darling the flowers really are lovely. Maybe you said what flowers you wanted – I don't know, but at any rate they are perfect for our anniversary as they are the same kind you sent for the wedding – 3 roses, 6 carnations (3 pink and 3 white), 8 daffodils, 3 iris, 3 snapdragons and some green laurel. Really they are perfect and I only wish you were here to enjoy them with me. Maybe some of the boys have been gypped on that flower service but I can truthfully say that you couldn't have done much better if you'd have seen what you were getting.

Now that the flowers have arrived I've decided to have a tea on Saturday afternoon to show off my flowers of course. I phoned Claire Garrison but she's going to Vegreville. Gus is stationed in Lincoln. Carol Young is in town for the duration she thinks and so is coming over. Mac is in Montreal taking a course in Psychiatry. He's just finished a course in Neurology in Toronto. Carol came home until Mac is definitely posted and anyway me thinks they're expecting another member to the family. The gals that are coming are Marg Howson Craig, Roberta and Marie Collins, Alix Day, Kay B., Helen Green, Helen Day Cairns and Jean Brunwell so it should be quite a chattery "do". Marg Norton can't come as she is going skiing I think. Anyway Ma Smith came up from Camrose last night due to the maid situation and she felt she had nowhere to go so up she came. It's a good idea though as a change is good for everyone at times. Bill is still working night shift so it will make a busy time for Margaret.

I mailed your parcel today so it's on the way. Also ordered more cigarettes. Saw some very nice embroidery – stamped on linen – 4 pieces for $1.00 so bought it. I'm really going to be a busy girl. Mother gave us a piece of needle point for a chair. It is almost finished so will get that done. PS – I asked for the needlepoint. Kind of robbery, I'd say. Well must away to bed. That's all for now. All our love dearest always, Peg.

Dearest Peg,

Midnight of another day and very little to report. Went to a show tonight and saw a double feature – one of them Dagwood & Blondie – quite enjoyed it even if it was a bit stupid. Came home about 10:30 and for the past hour have been trying to coax the fire back into life with no success so am writing this from bed.

It has been snowy and cold for the past 2 days with everything dry and frosty and about 2 inches of snow on the ground. Moonlight tonight and it looks kind of like home. The erks around here are slipping all over the place though, up and down the hills, and limping into sick quarters with assorted injuries.

Didn't do anything but sit around last night and read. Bob and a chap named Roy Pender and myself – stoking the fire about every 15 minutes and listening to the radio. Made toast and had hot chocolate and jam and peanut butter. Don't know if I told you or not – when Kester left I bought his half of the radio for 4 quid. An awful price when you figure it out in dollars and cents since it isn't much good. However Honey the quid is about a dollar and when you have spent it, it is gone – so what the hell! (poor attitude, eh darling?)

Am alone over the weekend again and will have 4 nights running on duty again. Have nothing to do though so it doesn't matter a damn.

Bob is out again tonight on the water more or less in charge of night traffic. These chaps certainly put in long hours – work a lot harder than the boys in bunker command and it's all cold, wet work. Good bunch here and I like it better as the days go by. Absolutely nothing to do but the work keeps one quite busy all day so the time goes well.

Well honey that's about all there is – no more mail yet.

Miss you a lot. Thinking of you and the daughter more than I can say. Will drop you a line tomorrow and see if I can be a little more interesting. All my love, Hamp

January 21, 1945

Dearest Hamp

This had been quite a busy weekend. Friday night I was busy baking etc. for my tea. I made rolled sandwiches and square ones, then a chocolate cake and an orange sponge cake. Yes sir and all by myself too. The sponge cake was about 6 inches tall and really very light. I was certainly surprised at the results.

Saturday morning went very quickly as we put the finishing touches on the house and of course Joan followed us around and undid our work as fast as she could. She knew something was happening so only slept ½ an hour in the afternoon much to our disgust. I dressed her up in white and put a pink bow in her hair and she showed off as usual until mother took her out. I guess the tea went off OK but don't really know as I was pretty busy keeping people fed etc. Jean Bramwell helped me a lot and Kay B poured – or should I say presided at the tea urns? At any rate that's over for a while.

At night Alix and I were invited to Lila Watts – Jack Day's wife's sister. We took our needlework but it turned out that several other girls were invited and we had a bar party, more or less, and played a game called "Nertz". Rather a noisy game and a combination of solitaire and Margaret's "Spoon". Really enjoyed myself as it was my first real night out for quite a while. Alix and I came home quite heady at 1 AM after 4 bottles a piece. Because I was out late last night the daughter wakened at 6 AM. My I was annoyed. Me thinks she's cutting more teeth as she sucks her whole fist almost up to the elbow. Makes her rather a stick and wet mess.

Today mother and Joan and I went over to Margaret's and Bill's to see Ma Smith. She looks very well indeed. Joan and David had a big time together in their own way and got very excited. David sure is a cute big fellow and very happy. He weighs 20 pounds now and has rolls of fat around his thighs. We had a very good turkey dinner with all the trimmings and I'm afraid I rather made up for Christmas Day by having a second serving of everything. So you can see we had a very busy time of it. Ma is going home tomorrow. She was just up between maids to do some shopping. That's all for now dearest. All our love as ever and always – Peg

PS The war news is certainly very encouraging these days. I sure hope it's the last round up. Are you in Ireland now? I kind of got carried away with my own doings in this letter. More hugs and kisses!

January 22, 1945

Dearest Peg,

Got a letter from you today and it really is good to hear from you again. Seems like more than a week. This one was Jan. 5, was certainly relieved to hear that your condition had subsided and that you were home again and back into your old routine. The mail should start coming faster when you start addressing mine to #423 Squadron – Bob's letters are up to Jan. 11 now – so it saves almost a week in transit.

Things here continue – have been quite busy the past two days. Sick parade at 8:30 and busy until about 11:30 then out to our sick operations at Necarne and make rounds which take a couple of hours, then lunch and then back for afternoon sick parade, medical rounds etc. until 5:00. The day keeps well filled up and really enjoy it because you haven't any time to sit around and wonder what to do.

Last night saw another show – an old one of about 1930 vintage with Jimmy Cagney. Kind of stunk but filled up the evening. Tonight Bob and I aren't going over to the mess to eat liver but are heating a can of chicken and having cheese and toast etc, – the life of luxury eh honey? All the comforts of home except home and you – so I guess there is an awful lot lacking but shouldn't grumble.

Bob is one of the better correspondents – he writes his wife about every night and does nothing but boast about his family and wish he were home. He's an awful lot of fun and I couldn't have been luckier in getting a room mate.

The weather is crisp still with snow on the ground and erks still falling over themselves. Nothing today but a cut head and a broken wrist though. We have a portable x-ray over at the sick quarters so it helps a bit. Can take our own chest plates etc. but must confess that I'm no expert at reading them – better get a book I guess.

Goldenring – the other M.O. comes back tomorrow and I will be relieved of sick parade for a week which is a help.

Will be glad when spring comes – the mornings are too cold. It's really a major exertion of will power getting up these mornings since the room is like an iceberg. Nothing serious however.

Tell Joan I got her note on your letter and that I'll be seeing her sometime before not too long. Old Joe Stalin is certainly helping out towards that trip home – hope the good news continues.

Well honey, will sign off. Loads of love and kisses to yourself and Joan. All my love, Hamp

January 23, 1945

Dearest Peg,

Wrote last night and nothing much to write about but wanted to tell you that I got the album of snapshots today and really appreciated it. The pictures of you were wonderful and wanted to reach out and grab you from that horse and carry you through the portals of Castle Archdale. Just a little jealous of the horse but nothing serious.

No other mail today but spent a couple of hours looking at the pictures. Am sending you some more pictures tonight – they aren't very good and don't mean very much but you can add them to the collection. Will try to get some more pictures here when the weather improves – today it was foggy all day and cold but not a bad day.

Slept in until 9:00 this morning because Goldring took sick parade and then ambled up and saw a few sick and afflicted and then went to sick quarters at Necarne. Came home early this afternoon and sat around and gassed with Bob Bartlett. He had his wireless operators in discussing the situation with them and so after an hour or so we had tea and cake and then Ray Pender came over with some bread and cheese so we ate on. Don't think I'm going to lose much weight here. Went over for the evening meal at 8:30 and am now back stoking the fire again.

The old squadron leader M.O. is quite a character. He does buggar-all work and appears at sick quarters for about half an hour a day and then goes out scrounging. He has the reputation of being the world's best scrounger and it's a full time job for him. He lives nearby and runs a car so his car needs gas, repairs, or he needs something for the house. It sounds like exaggeration but I can truthfully say that every day since I've been here he's taken at least half a day to scrounge something – and that's been going on for over a year, so the flight sergeant tells me. I like him though.

Well honey. Loads of kisses and all my love. Hamp

January 23, 1945

Dearest Peg,

Am sending these pictures very belatedly. They aren't very good and don't mean really much. All those of me show me with one hand in my pocket. That way I kind of hid the fact that Johnnie Hunt's coat came down to my knees and went around me twice.

There are a bunch more on the way from Yorkshire. I had them all packaged for sending for about 6 weeks and kept forgetting them and finally left them in a drawer. Most of them duplicate these pictures but will send them along.

Should have some more snaps before long and will try to be more faithful in sending them to you. Well honey, just a note so will sign off. Love you an awful lot. All my love, Hamp

Included in envelope. Cartoon aerograph addressed to F.L. C.H. Smith, Medical Officer, R.C.A.F., Topcliffe, Yorkshire, England from D. G. Ritchie, 11418, RCAF # 35 Squadron, India dated Oct. 31/44 showing a fellow sitting in a room on a suitcase sweating with palm trees and mosque scene out window. Radio is playing "And the snow lay round about". Written on it – arrow pointing to man "Too bloody true" and at bottom "What's the latest gen. – The Anglo Indians look blonde!!

Written on back of card by Hamp: This is the Christmas card I got from India. Not very informative but quite typical.

Also in envelope pictures – woman and young girl – Alix and Sandra Day????, – Peggy and Joan on steps at Day's Joan holding a Raggedy Ann doll.

427

Dearest Hamp,

So you're in the land o' the Shamrock eh? And how are you liking it now? I got three letters from you on Monday written before you left England. I must say the one you wrote while under the influence of alcohol was quite something, you old dear. It took me two days to decipher every word in it. The sentiment sure is wonderful though and I'm keeping this letter very carefully to hold over your head if need be in the future. You may be sorry you wrote it darling. Ha! Ha! But no kidding I enjoyed it very very much – only don't repeat the performance under those circumstances – like walking into ladies bedrooms like you have done before or some such thing (I'm just fooling). Got another letter yesterday describing your journey and the new station. Yes siree! I do sympathize with you for all that baggage changing you did. You should have worked up quite a muscle by now old bean. It looks as though you'll be doing a lot of walking on the new station too. My oh my what an athletic husband I'll have. Eh honey?

I must break down and confess that I've spent a bit of money. It happened this way. I went downtown yesterday to buy a new hat. Got one too – brown with green trimming. Cost $4.50 regular $8.95. But that's not all. Walked through the fur department at Woodward's and saw this very cute seal coat – Russian Seal which is really dyed rabbit. I tried it on and just had to have it. The ticket said $195.00 so decided to put it back when the saleslady came along and said "That's a real bargain. Can you wear it?" The coat was a size 11 and the only one in the store so was marked down and as it was a stock taking and January Sale it was marked down further. I got quite a shock when she said it was selling for $59.50. I couldn't believe it and said there must be something wrong with it. But no sir. The size was too small for most people so they had marked it down to get rid of it so miracles do happen. It is really not an expensive fur as coats go but when I stopped to figure that my old winter coat really is quite cold and a decent cloth coat these days costs $50 up and that I can get at least a couple of years wear out of this coat it's really quite a bargain. So I'm very very pleased with myself. So that's one thing off your shopping list for a few years at least. Ain't I wonderful or am I? I'll probably get so fat that I can't wear it next year. As I was walking

428

down the street with my new hat and coat, a Candid Camera fellow took my picture so if it's any good I'll send it to you.

Our club went on a sleigh ride last night – strictly female. There were 12 of us and we had a very good time. Am going to a post-nuptial tea tonight. One of the older girls of the church Helen Reid married her boss a Jew so it should be quite a to-do. As I have to get Joan to bed and get myself all spruced up I'd better toddle along. Will write about the sleigh ride and the tea tomorrow and tell you all about it.

Joan has reached the stage where she wants to help us. She has her own little mop and duster and follows us around. Looks like I'll have her all trained to look after the house when you come home. Child labor you know. Oh yes – sent you 900 cigs. yesterday too. That's all for or now honey.

Heaps of love darling with hugs & kisses. Peg

January 25, 1945

Dearest Peg,

Two more days laid away beside the others. Not very busy doing much but keep warm. It still stays cold and snowy. Everything is very beautiful and got a couple of snaps today and will get more tomorrow. It got so cold that it froze some milk that Goldring had in a carton and it amazed him – he dashed around showing it to everyone because he had never seen frozen milk before – afraid I couldn't be properly impressed.

Got 3 letters from you yesterday the last one Jan. 12 – so we are gradually getting caught up. Hope my letters are arriving more regularly now. Glad I got a letter away to your Paw and Maw before your gentle reminder came – sorry that I had not done so before honey and will try to improve in the future. In that same letter you seemed just a little low – darling – hope you don't get too browned off with your daily routine. Things look a little better every day and maybe it won't be long.

The grease spot is just a bit of a snack – genuine margarine. Also got a letter from Mother – things seem to be going fairly well at home. Hope you go down with Margaret – the two of you might have a better stay with each other for moral support.

429

Quite a problem in camp for the past week – most of the plumbing is frozen and the available ones produce quite a queue with no priority unless you have an M.O.'s chit showing that you have diarrhea (not quite that bad but pretty nearly).

Had a phone call from a chap named Arthur Ireland. He is a Camrose kid and is stationed nearby and will be coming over for an evening one of these times.

Well had better start writing a letter faster. Bob is preparing for bed and since he is operative tomorrow and has to be up at 5:00 AM, I had better get ready to retire also.

Bob MacCraig was just in complaining about the food in the mess tonight. I didn't go over for dinner because I had a big tea at 5:00 o'clock. Still haven't got used to that extra meal. Bob lives beside us and is a very nice chap – he has a spaniel named Smokey who spends his time sleeping on his bed and smelling very doggy – very friendly animal and makes the place kind of homelike. Would like to have my own but guess I won't be here long enough.

To describe our Nissen hut – 4 rooms with two in each room and divided by such partitions. You can hear everybody else's radios – the programs aren't synchronized so you have bags of variety.

Al was just in and offered me a pint of milk. We can buy milk over the bar here and it's quite a treat after the last place.

Well honey, miss you and love you an awful lot. All my love, Hamp

January 25, 1945

Dearest Hamp

Hope you've got over your wife's extravagance old bean. I'll bet you're glad I don't go down town every day eh? I'm really just fooling coz I know you don't mind and anyhow I ain't afraid of you!

As was mentioned in yesterday's letter I went on a sleigh ride Tuesday night with the girls in the business girl's club. We met at 124th St and 102nd Ave at 8 PM and took the bus to the end of the line where our sleigh was waiting. It was one of those perfect nights that we get here – somewhere between 10° & 20° above with a full moon and a clear starry sky. We rode and ran behind the sleigh at intervals for an hour when we arrived at our destination – a little log cottage about half way on the road to the Country Club. Perhaps you can remember the tea room sign we saw when we went driving one afternoon at your graduation? I remember that day very well. It was a warm sunny spring day and we zoomed out on the Jasper Highway with never a care, just wanting to go on and on and never turn back. To get back to the other night – the cabin, a 3 roomed affair, is simply a dream – what I'd plan for a cottage if possible – the inside walls were stained and varnished logs and a big stone fireplace with green dry wood burning – ah! The scent of that wood! There were deer horns etc hanging amongst the Indian beadwork on the walls and Indian rugs on the floor. The entire house was lit by candle light – big 8-day candles and smaller ones in silver candelabra. We'll have to go out there some day eh honey? To eat we had spaghetti and hot rolls, angel cake, devils food cake and coffee. Very good too for we starving girls. Speaking of starving makes me think just how lucky we are to be in Canada not in Europe or the Far East somewhere. Anyhow we had a wonderful time at least I enjoyed myself but wouldn't it have been fun if you had been along. I must remember a sleigh ride for forms of future entertainment. The war news is much better. Oh darling I do hope it's almost over.

Last night I went to this post-nuptial tea and enjoyed myself again talking to people I haven't seen for a long time. Also had more good food. In the afternoon I went down to Irving and Lacey's as the stones on the side of my ring were quite loose and turning around in the setting. Boy was I glad I discovered it before I lost them. My watch also needs cleaning. Oh me! Just one thing after another.

Joan is so darn cute these days that I can't remember all she does. She is beginning to catch on about this training business. She comes up to you with a lovely smile on her face and looking right in your eyes says Go! Go! So you promptly drop everything and rush her to the back of the house only to find she had wet pants all the time. She laughs gleefully as it's quite a joke to her. By the way dearest I hope there's bush country near your station. I'm rather worried about your constitution. As you only mentioned the "watering pails". Are you the sanitary inspector?

Had better sign off now as I've run out of paper. All my love dearest. Big hugs and kisses darling. As ever – Peg

Dearest Hamp,

By now you should really be settled to your new routine. I wonder though if you'll really get used to all the exercise. But you'll find a way to get a ride if at all possible. Eh you cute thing? P.S. you can get even for that last remark when you return.

Last night Margaret and I went to a show – the first time we've really gone out together since you went away. After the show we went into Picardy's for coffee. We were home by 10 PM as Helen McGee was looking after David. I'm going to Alix's tonight for a small stagette party so you see I've really been stepping out this week. (The reason for all this is because Ma & Pa are going to the coast for a couple of weeks or so on Tuesday. Dad is going to a convention for a week and will then take a week's holiday so we persuaded Mother to go along. She wanted to go in March sometime but maybe she will stay on after Dad comes home and really have a good rest as she is quite tired. Guess I'll have to postpone the Camrose trip for another month at least.

Had a letter from Doris yesterday. There is quite a lot of shifting going on down there so everyone is living from day to day. Don't know if that rumor about discharges from there is fact or fiction but I guess I'll get to know sooner or later. Derek Atkinson has accepted an office position with the Pan American Airlines in New York so they have gone and as Doris says "Can't you just see Marjorie in New York?" My! Yes! The baby front is still active in Claresholm I would gather as the Reids' and Merritts' had sons. And ha! ha! the Clarkson's are expecting twins according to the doctor's report. Finally had a letter from Eleanor and of course wee Bobby is the only baby – to them anyway. Norrie has not been well and is getting liver injections. This baby business isn't too easy anytime I guess. Also had a letter from Irene. Mac and the boys have had the flu but are better again. The office seems to keep Dad and Mac both busy

I see from tonight's paper where Ray Burnap has been sent to Montreal on a course in Anesthesia. His wife and two children are going to follow shortly. Enough said about it as things like that don't sit on my stomach very well. Maybe I'm just being silly.

Our weather has been simply beautiful lately but colder with hoar frost lasting all day with the trees and shrubs lacy white. It is getting colder though so I guess we are in for a cold spell.

Joan has taken it into her head to waken up for a couple of hours just as I'm going to bed. My it makes me annoyed. If I lay down the law she starts to howl and wakens everyone up in the house. Yes I really think she's a mite spoiled but it's my own fault as she's so cute. If you were here she'd really be spoiled you old buggerlugs you!

Mr. Woodard phoned me tonight to say you had written a thank you letter. Gee you're wonderful simply marvelous. He seemed quite pleased too. His son was with the Army in Ireland and got lousy so you be careful darling. That's all the local gossip for now. Heaps of hugs and kisses and barrels of love from Joan and I. More love.

P.S. The Bothwells and Skeltons want to be remembered to you. Me too! More love.

January 27, 1945

Dearest Peg,

Another letter yesterday. You are really distinguishing yourself these days. I guess it seems that none are coming because they are arriving one or two at a time instead of a week's mail all at once. Thanks for the anniversary sentiments darling and you know I reciprocate them all completely.

Things here continue very cold for theses parts with a good many degrees of frost and the huts like ice bergs in the mornings. You certainly don't stand still very long after you get up. That record you hung up of 2 weeks without a bath will soon be broken by your husband unless our cold snap abates.

Got a letter from one of the nursing orderlies at my last station and he sent me 4 snaps which we took one afternoon. I'm in all of them and some aren't very good but am sending them along tonight and hope they arrive in good order.

Haven't done a thing unusual for the past 2 days and so there is nothing to write about. Spent a couple of hours in the mess last night and then came over and stoked for an hour and then was called up to sick quarters for an hour or so and then returned and read a book for a couple of hours.

The dentist here is Jerry LeBouef – a French Canadian and a very nice chap. He has a wife and baby at home too and is just as anxious to get home as the rest of us but talks more about. He is waiting with a bottle of champagne to open when Joe Stalin enters Berlin. His current slogan is "Joe for king" and, after the news from the Russian front is over, doesn't even hang around to listen to Western front news. We all get quite a kick out of him.

Goldring is away again today but we aren't busy. The old S/C comes in every morning for an hour and sits and then buggers off. At the moment he's scrounging a new cylinder head for his car since his got cracked by freezing. That fills up his days pretty well so he keeps out of the way.

Doesn't seem that I'm going into my 3rd week here – the time certainly slips away.

Hope to have a steak tonight – Jack Ross – one of the navigators – went into town and said he'd bring one back for me. Am not counting on it but it would be a nice change from our current run of spam and bully. Meals are good here but not as good as the last station – not losing weight though. Well honey will sign off. Give the daughter a hug and kiss and tell her to keep away from the cold air register. All my love, Hamp

January 27, 1945

Dearest Peg,

Four pictures from Yorkshire.

1. Myself and four of our orderlies outside sick quarters soaking up a little sunshine.
2. It's hard to say whether the firing squad is just about to start or just finished. Actually things probably weren't as bad as I look – probably that direct sunshine was more than I could stand.
3. Art Kalfas acting the fool in his usual cheerful fashion. He generally didn't go around with his hat over his ears.
4. Myself looking pensive and Art looking pleased with all and sundry. I was probably staring over at the field at some Halifax wobbling its

way in and wondering if the day was going to stay good.

Well darling that's all the snaps for now. Have some more in the process of manufacture and will send then alone. All my love, Hamp.

January 29, 1945

Dearest Hamp,

Today was a red letter day again as I got four letters from you. By all accounts you seem to be enjoying your new station. At least it is a change of scene and that business of riding on a crash launch sounds quite thrilling. Had a letter from Dad Smith today and he thinks I'm very wise to quit working. He says quote "I am sure that Hamp would much rather come finding you the warm healthy little girl that he left behind him than a more or less bedraggled hag whom he doesn't expect to see." Unquote. So guess I'd better start putting on more weight or I'll be a 'bedraggled hag' for sure.

I see from your mail that you are censoring letters. Had to laugh at one letter where you described Bartlett to me and incidentally praised him quite highly. He was the one that censored the letter – at least his name was on the outside.

Joan and I were down visiting Mrs. Lawton this afternoon as it was 10 below and too cold to stay out very long so we dropped in there for tea. She hadn't any news but thinks Joan is looking more like me, however. Poor child.

Forgot to mention that I saw Dr. Hutton on Friday morning at the Hospital and she says everything has cleared up beautifully and that I look much better than before. So guess I'm OK now.

Was at a small party at Alix's the other night. Helen Day Cairns, Leila Watt, Mazie Wheatley, Alix and I were there. We played a card game called "Thirty" – think I mentioned it to you before. I made $.20 so it wasn't too bad.

Went to Church with Mother Sunday morning. First time since last spring. But I'm up on you even at that eh old bean?

You spoke of reading "Claudia". I saw the show. Believe me I'm sure glad you said I was a lot smarter than Claudia coz I thought she was pretty stupid. However it was a pretty good show.

Guess I'll have to be sending you some food so you can pay Bartlett back or you two won't be speaking to each other.

Things are pretty hectic here as Ma & Pa are getting ready to go away. However I think I'll survive their departure. The war news sure is swell these days, eh honey. All our love, hugs and kisses from Joan and I. All my love darling, Peg

January 30, 1945

Dearest Peg,

Wonderful day today – four letters and the last dated Jan. 21. You seem to have been having quite a busy time. Hope my letters are coming through a little better now. One of them was Jan. 3 and had gone to Yorkshire first and then been delayed in catching up to me. It contained a lot of news with Joe Levee and Duff Davies. Glad to hear old Harry Pateman is going back to peace time. Be interested to hear the progress of your Bartholin. Read Bob that piece about Joan trying on your hat with the mirror and he was positively amazed since his infant isn't as precocious. Glad the flowers arrived and were all right – they couldn't have been as good as you said but it really made me pleased with myself to have you say it. Hope to deliver same in person next time or at least fairly soon.

Today got a Christmas card from Mr. Young. It was quite impersonal so don't think I'll answer it because it's quite a struggle to write to him and really don't expect an answer from him.

The weather is wonderful today – just like spring with water rushing everywhere and the sun quite warm – managed to acquire quite a head cold yesterday and feel that a little wifely sympathy should help a lot since I'm not ill and yet feel sorry for myself. Am really going to try to soak it up when I return to you darling.

Didn't go over to the mess tonight – sat around and heated a tin of meatballs and had bread and marg and jam – quite a good bit of scrounging and very good. Saves plodding over to the mess.

Got the pictures today in the mail – the ones I forgot at Topcliffe. Am picking out a few and sending them along and will send the others in a bunch. They are the ones from my leave over here and there is a letter in them dated Nov. 15 and never sent – so you see what a hell of a husband you have darling.

Sat around the mess until about 10:30 last night and then came home and went to bed for an early night. About midnight "sea lowe" rolled in drunk – that's Bob MacCraig the short little navigator who rooms next door. He kept us awake until 2:00 AM – made us toast and jam and bothered us generally.

Well darling that's all there is to write about except that I love you more every day. Had a haircut today – thought I would remind you of it since I always had to dramatize my hair cuts so you would notice them – remember buggereyes.

Give Joan love and kisses from me and my regards to your Maw & Paw. All my love, Hamp

FEBRUARY 1945

February 1, 1945

Dearest Peggy,

A little behind in my date – time goes on thank goodness. Have nothing to report of interest except that our snow is now gone and everything is back to its usual green. I really enjoy the rain now since it's warm again and seems almost like spring at home.

Last night the squadron held a party for several departing members – the adjutant and a couple of pilots. It was just a drunk pure and simple, and not intended to be anything else. There were two full jugs of punch to start with – the punch contained rum, scotch, gin and assorted flavoring and was quite good in spite of the mixture. We all got quite cheerful. The bodies started to fall about midnight and after I helped carry a couple home I decided it was time to go to bed. Was awakened at 7:00 by Bob MacCraig – he had passed out in the mess and then recovered and filled up a 3 gallon cereal jug with beer and brought it over to give us all drink – it was turned down without thanks.

Wakened at 1:00 today (took a day off) and then Dave Stewart who rooms next door – came in and we cooked 3 steaks which we had acquired in town by devious means. They with onions and toast proved quite a banquet. About 2:00 PM the casualties wandered over to the room – sprained wrists etc. and I went back to work again. Going out to sick quarters to take x-rays and wandering around the billets seeing the ill.

This letter is just a description of a typical party at these Air Force Units so when I write you and say the boys had a party – you'll know just what the procedure was.

Well honey, will sign off and try to write a better letter tomorrow. Miss you and love you an awful lot. Give Joan my love. All my love, Hamp

February 1, 1945

Dearest Hamp,

So it's now February. As usual time is slipping by and I'm a day behind schedule again. Finally got my family away to the coast but it was quite a hectic time what with them both packing at the same time, loosing things and not getting a taxi until the last minute etc & etc. Fortunately Joan slept until nine the next morning so I got a good sleep.

It is wonderful for a change to do things or not do them – just as you choose – and to work out my own routine – not fitting in with anyone else's program so we are get a change and a rest.

Joan is a real darling too. She follows me around all day – helps to dust and tidy up. But she's a real demon at times when I take something away from her that she shouldn't have. Sits right down on the floor and screams, muttering foreign gibberish at me. So I stand her up and dust her seat with a sharp clip and she stops so suddenly that I wonder just what I did to her. Today she got into my purse and before I knew what was going on she had my registration card, street car tickets and wallet floating in the soapy dish water. While I was cleaning this up she got into the cupboard and rearranged the pots and pans. As you can see my time does not drag.

Was over at Robertson's yesterday with Joan. We were invited for dinner and really had a very good time. Sandy and Joan are beginning to play well together although Joan still gets the rough end of things – like getting pushed over. Poor Sandra gets put in another room for a few minutes "just to straighten her out" as Alix says.

438

Had a letter from Fred today – rather short and a trifle grim. It didn't sound like Fred at all. He was either very busy or else has changed to a more serious person.

Saw from the paper last night were Peter Voloshin had received a commendation for "meritous service" signed by General Montgomery so guess he's busy on the West Front.

The Russians at this point are 39 miles from Berlin. It can't be too long now but I'm not very optimistic yet – don't trust the old Germans at all though they really are taking a beating. However the war won't be over for me until you're home for good. Then and only then will I really get excited. Have kept my feelings more or less hidden for so long now that it will take something like your home coming to really rouse me.

We're having a bit of 20 below weather now but can't complain as our winter has been wonderful. Sure hope you aren't shivering too much over there. You'd better learn how to keep a fire going so that when we get to Camrose you can carry on with your chores. Ha!Ha!

That's all for now. Joan sends her daddy hugs and kisses. All my love darling, Peg

February 3, 1945

Dearest Hamp,

Two more days gone by but nothing to report as we are quite the home bodies now. Got two letters from you yesterday and one today so am all caught up. Today's letter was dated Jan. 25 so that really isn't bad. Was very glad you have at last got the album of pictures as it's been on the way for three months and I'd almost given it up. Guess it got caught in the Christmas mail. Speaking of pictures I haven't got those Irish pictures of your leave last October. Perhaps you didn't mail them. Can't remember if you were mailing or just talking about them.

Had a letter from Mother and Dad too. They had arrived at the coast and it was foggy but they have hopes for better weather soon.

Alix, Sandra, Joan and I went shopping today on Whyte Avenue. Joan was very good and got a big bang out of walking down the street and hanging on to my hand – it was really vice verse.

Our daughter is really taken with herself. Every time I brush her hair I have to hold her up to the mirror so she can see what she looks like. And when she passes the open French doors she can see herself and does she preen. Excuse please honey while I go settle the "datter" – she's weeping and wailing in her bed. Back again. She wanted a drink of water – the regular excuse – and a bit of loving both of which she got. P.S. She's still crying. Some nights she's a regular heller to put to bed coz first she doesn't want to go and second she doesn't want to be alone. Dr. Leitch says children can cry for 2 hours without any ill effects but so far Joan's mummy hasn't been able to stand it longer than 20 minutes. She really puts on the broken heart act and sobs from the soles of her feet. Speaking of feet reminds me of our expensive 16 months old child. I got her a pair of white Packar boots for $3.50. Don't we hope the price of shoes doesn't rise in direct ratio with her age eh honey?

Got my candid camera pictures back. Real good one of my new coat and hat but I look very grim – as though I ate nails regularly. Honestly I hope I don't look like that all the time. I'll send it to you next week when I get some pictures of Joan and Sandy which are being reprinted.

Have I mentioned that Alix got your second letter? Well she did. Are you feeling OK old bean? You sure are a changed person as far as correspondence goes – and still more wonderful every day. Am I glad we're not living in Berlin right now. Just think of 1000 bombers. That I can't imagine. All for now, my love. Heaps of love, hugs & kisses from Joan and I. As always, Peg

February 3, 1945

Dearest Peggy,

Another two days with not a great deal to report. Have been quite busy with our usual routine and nothing very exciting to write about. Haven't had any mail from you but got a letter from Mother today dated Jan. 23/45 – she said that she had been in Edmonton and reassured me that I still had a wonderful family.

Had a letter from Gus Garrison today – he is still near Lincoln and not doing anything but managing to keep quite happy. He had heard from Dave Moffat in Holland – Dave is about the same as the rest of us! Gus had seen Al Elliott and Gardener Craig and spent an enjoyable weekend with them. Gardener was back convalescing from a fractured ankle and was out of plaster but not back to normal yet.

The weather continues wet with solid sheets of water keeping every ditch running like a small river. It amazes me why this country wasn't washed away long before my time.

The last two nights have had an egg and toast in the hut for supper. Pretty luxurious this war is getting – we aren't starving to death by any means – and manage to keep ourselves amused a bit.

Time out – had to go up and see the usual erk with a black eye and a fracture into a sinus – quite a common complaint unfortunately. They are all very surprised to see their cheek inflate when they blow their nose.

Goldring has been away for the past 2 days but will be functioning again tomorrow. The old S/C was in again for his usual half an hour and then buggered off on the scrounge. He managed a chicken, 18 eggs and 3 pounds of butter today, which was a pretty good day's work.

Got a reply from my medical correspondence college today – 11 pounds to get a tutor to write the M.R.C.P. – think I'll possibly contemplate the effort as soon as my finances seem sound. Will have to put in a little concentrated effort and may learn something. The idea of this is that they send out a syllabus of work and then you write periodic exams to check your progress and all in all kind of go back to school. Will keep you posted honey about my education.

Well darling, will sign off and will write again as usual. Miss you and love you. All my love, Hamp

February 5, 1945

Dearest Peggy,

Four letters from you today constituted a record level. The last one was January 31 and addressed to me in the squadron, so it also set up a record. I hope my mail is arriving as well. I'm glad you got that fur coat – you needed a warmer winter coat and even if it only lasts a year its money well spent. Quite an eye you have for a bargain honey. Got a letter with pictures of you and the daughter and David. You and Joan look better every day but you looked a little thin honey – you'll have to do something about that or I'll come home and put back your weight the hard way (a miserable male is your husband with these dirty threats of throwing his genes around). Am pleased that you saw Marg Hutton and that all was OK and you "looked much better than before". Guess you meant in general and not the particular area of your affliction.

Dad also wrote today. He was in excellent form and really wrote a good letter. Sounded as if he was more or less working and keeping on the straight and narrow. You spoke of your Dad and Mother going away. Too bad its winter time – you could have gotten organized and taken our dynamo down to Camrose for a spell.

Things here carry on as usual. It was a beautiful morning today. Sunshine, green grass, warm wind, all manner of birds singing – too good to be true. At noon it suddenly clouded, started to thunder and there was a heavy rain squall. Cleared again but repeated at hourly intervals throughout the day. Very unpredictable and I guess one will automatically take a trench coat wherever you go – winter and summer. Snowdrops are out here and that's supposed to a sign of spring.

Got up at 6:30 this morning and helped Jerry LeBoeuf with his trunk, he flew to the mainland and had to be organized by 7:00 AM. As he was packing last night he called me in, and he and I and Freddy Weir (Jerry's roommate) opened and drank his bottle of champagne – out of a beer mug, a jam jar and an olive jar. Pretty ritzy, eh darling, this Nissen hut life. It tasted pretty good but Jerry kept moaning about no champagne glasses.

That's a pretty smart daughter we have – getting housebroken and helping with the housework. I guess she'll go! go! in the right place as soon as she has to worry about cleaning up her own puddles.

Well honey, miss you and awful lot and love you very much. All my love, Hamp

February 7, 1945

Dearest Peggy,

Two more days put beside with the others and not a great deal to report as usual. Am in the midst of trying to get the damn fire to burn and if this letter is a little more disjointed than usual, you'll know I've been up stoking.

Yesterday was Mother's birthday and I wrote a letter on the day but am afraid my greetings will be a trifle belated. (Am pleased to report that the fire is blazing merrily away temporarily – after me dumping half a bottle of lighter fluid on it).

Have been anything but busy today. Got up at 9:00 and ambled up to sick quarters and saw 8 or 10 people and then out to sick quarters to see the 2 or so that we have in at the moment, ate lunch out there and then back this afternoon to do absolutely nothing. Went down and got two parcels – 300 British Consuls' from you – mailed around the first week in January – and four films from Dad. A pretty good haul for one day and thanks very much honey – I have been smoking limeys for the past week to the detriment of my health and pocket book. By the way darling – we can now order 200 cigarettes a month from over here – I'm sending my first order in today – they should come all right. Would appreciate if you would keep on as usual though because you never seem to have a stock on hand and they just evaporate – 1200 seems to last about 2 weeks instead of four. I would like to get to the prosperous stage where I have a couple of thousand laid away but guess I never will.

Last night Bob and I held a house cleaning – cleaned up a mound of useless stuff and chucked it out – such as good tins that might be useful and never are, old magazines, etc. We discovered the meeting grounds of several families of mice so things are a little better. The batman even went so far as to wash the floor today, so our effort didn't go unnoticed. (Pleased to report the fire is now away – if the bloody coke will burn)

This evening promises to be quiet as usual. Change your clothes and go to the mess and have a couple of beers before dinner, eat, sit around awhile and then back to the billet and read and listen to the radio. The war news is pretty good these days darling so our cloud may produce that silver lining sooner than one might have dared to hope – keep praying honey.

Well, give my hug and kisses to our daughter and look after yourself. I think of yourself as being a little closer every day. All my love, Hamp.

Dearest Hamp,

Just keeping up with the snaps. I really haven't many this time but started another roll today.

These pictures by the way are quite terrible. The ones of Joan are as usual quite good but I'm awfully sorry to say I just had to cut myself out of one as it was more than terrible. And as for the candid shot I look as though I was mad clean through. However it's a good picture of my new hat and coat.

The one of Pete speaks for itself.

The days are going so quickly now that I'm chief of the domain and have to cook and clean. But I don't mind how quickly time passes right now I only hope it slows down when you come home so I can enjoy your company to the utmost.

The war news is very good and it looks like the "grand finale" now so perhaps it won't be too long before we see each other again.

That is all for now. For recent and up-to-date news read your blue forms.

Bye honey and bags of love. Sure hope you've recovered from looking at the pictures.

All my love, dearest, Peg

P.S. On second thought decided not cut myself out of the picture. You have my permission to laugh and howl but for goodness sake's don't show either one of me to any one. More love, Peg

Included in envelope:
1. Picture of Peg walking down street in new hat and coat.
2. Picture of Peg and Joan on steps at Day's.
3. Picture of Joan and Sandra.
4. Newspaper clipping with picture captioned:

Capt. P.C. Voloshin, who has received from Field Marshal Montgomery a personally-signed certificate lauding his work. The certificate said: "It has been brought to my notice that you have performed outstanding good service and shown great devotion to duty during the campaign in France. I award you this certificate as a token of my appreciation and I have given instructions that this shall be noted in your record of service." The officer's wife lives at 11531 86 Street. A graduate of the University of Alberta, he was a practicing physician in Saskatoon when he enlisted.

February 7, 1945

Dearest Hamp,

Several days have gone by the board and we've been quite busy. Sunday was a very mixed day as I had bought a prime rib roast (small) on Saturday so invited Jean Bromwell for dinner. Started to bake an apple pie and found the dough wouldn't roll out. I was quite disgusted so crumbled it all up again and added more water and then decided it was flour it needed so added more flour. My unorthodox and shocking procedure was decided upon because I figured the pastry wasn't much good anyway. However as fate would have it, it was one of the lightest pie crusts I've ever made. You try and figure that one out darling, it's too deep for me. While I was messing about in the kitchen Joan was entertaining Jean by showing her your picture and every time Jean laid it aside to try and write a few letters Joan came out with quite a line of gibberish and handed the picture back. So poor Jean spent quite a miserable afternoon and said the only saving feature was that you are her secret passion so she really didn't mind looking at the picture. Now I'm jealous to think that anyone else can have loving thoughts about you.

Monday morning I did a wash and Monday afternoon baked a cake and cookies as the Club was coming over Tuesday night. At night I went out to the Church Club and Jean stayed with Joan.

Tuesday I cleaned the house, waxed the floors and swept the snow from the walks. By the way darling, am I boring you with this household routine? In the afternoon after finishing cleaning I made sandwiches and got the finishing touches to things. In and out of all the routine was Joan. She has to help wash the dishes now and then I wash the floor.

She helped me peel her potatoes and then threw all the garbage out of the sink. My fault I know as she shouldn't have been sitting on the kitchen stool. Now she has learned to climb on the breakfast nook table. I found her up there yesterday mixing salt, pepper and sugar and then eating the concoction. Goodness knows what she'll be into next.

Kay B. slept here last night after club and today has been very quiet for a change. Got your pictures of Ireland on Monday and I think they're very good. Why don't you come nearer to the camera so I can see you better. The one of you and your "lady friend" was very very good. You haven't changed a bit. In fact you don't look as old either. How does it feel to be young and with the boys again, *old thing?* I'll be writing again tomorrow to make up for the lost time.

All our love my darling with big hugs and kisses from Joan and I.
Peg

February 8 1945

Dearest Hamp,

A very good day today – 3 letters from my fond husband and the last dated Feb. 1st so we are not so very far away from each other. It certainly must have been cold over there you poor thing while we swelter at 38 above today. That sounded like some party old boy, and then you try to tell me they sell milk over the bar. Oh Ha! ha! I'll bet very few buy it.

Well sir to report my activities – did the heap big wash today – sheets et al and then baked some cookies for the Club to take to the boys in the Wing. Then as it was such a gorgeous day Alix and Sandy, Joan and I went for a long walk. Alix and I are in the same boat as Mrs. Robertson left for the Coast on Tuesday so we just see each other in the day time.

Joan started right out this AM full of the devil. She got into my jar of Arrid and when I found her she was covered – hands, arms, face and legs and having a wonderful time. How we got the cookies made is a mystery as she kept sneaking away with things from the table and I'd tear around and retrieve them. Then she wanted a drink of water so I gave it to her and as she's so independent these days had to hold it all by herself consequently the water spilled on the floor and when I scolded her and was cleaning up the mess she looked me straight in the eye and spat on the floor. How she thinks up such nice ladylike things to do is beyond me.

Chuck Rainsforth phoned me last night as he had just returned from Claresholm and had to tell me the latest news. Kennedy has been posted to an Eastern O.T.O. and then overseas. They held his posting party while Chuck was there and the boys mixed Kennedy 2 oz. each of run, scotch, rye, gin, wine filled up with beer and bitters but the old soak was still on his feet at 5 AM. The mess has slipped a great deal I would gather. Some of the boys have been posted. Brown and few others I can't recall.

Jean had some beer at the house last night and I must confess that on one bottle I got quite stinky. Was very tired and had been doing cross-stitch all night so that may account for it. Am doing a picture now of roses and delphiniums in cross stitch in different shades of rose, blue and green. – it will be like a tapestry when it's finished – I hope. More stuff for our hope chest eh honey.

Mother is sending a breakfast set she got for us in Vancouver. I gave her the money to buy one if she saw a nice one. They are having a good time it would seem. That's all for now honey. Joan sends you big hugs and kisses.

February 9 1945

Dearest Peggy,

Another letter yesterday in 6 days (Feb. 2). Pretty good service we're getting honey and I hope that mine are arriving nearly as well. So you are a real bachelor now with your family at the coast. It's kind of nice to be by oneself for awhile but I imagine you'll be glad to see them back again. Envy their trip – will have to do the same one of these days and pray that there aren't 18 inches of snow to keep us bed bound – might produce a David before we anticipated.

Things have kept in their usual rut for the past two days and not much to report. A little busier today and going from 9 to 6 for a change. Goldring is away tomorrow and the S/C is off as usual.

Am just in the midst of making toast with bread and margarine I managed to scrounge in town on the way to sick quarters this morning. That with a cup of tea and so to bed to prepare for the next 24 hrs. as per usual.

To continue after a piece of toast and hot chocolate and after listening to the last act of Julius Caesar over the BBC. Got another letter from Dad yesterday. I asked him to pick up a couple of flash lights for me which he has sent – figured he could get them in Camrose and also honey I think he kind of likes to send something that he knows you want – maybe I'm wrong. Anyway he also said that he sent you instructions to stop work quote "Told her that you would rather see her as the girl you used to know rather than a crock". Think he was making it a little strong but his sentiments are sound and well meant I'm sure. Think you'll have to slip awful far before you end up looking like a crock darling and am not greatly perturbed about the possibility.

Say, will you be my valentine? Didn't send you an official one because they only had about 3 in Irvinestown and none were really appropriate.

Well buggerlugs – give the daughter a hug and a kiss for me – and a kick in the pants if she has a tantrum. All my love, Hamp

February 10, 1945

Dearest Hamp,

Well my dear hubby how are you and that terrific cold you acquired after your last party? That sure was a shame such a great big cold for such a great big man. Oh you poor dear. How's that for sympathy? Now I can get out of role and say it serves you right you old buggerlugs you but I sure hope you don't get pneumonia.

Did bugger all yesterday except go for a walk with Sandra and Alix. Kay and two of the girls from club came over for the evening again. They were here Thursday night too after visiting the Wing or did I mention that before? Anyhow we played bridge and then ate and Kay stayed the night. Didn't hear her get up this morning so she made her own breakfast and left me a wee note.

Your radio stopped working this morning so guess another tube has gone. Very annoying to say the least as the big radio blew a tube last

448

Sunday so now I can't keep up on the news and the nights are lonely but will get them fixed on Monday.

Joan was impish again this morning. Got busy covered head to foot with Dutch Cleanser and then a few minutes after I had cleaned her up she had hand lotion all over her. The only solution I can see to all this is to get everything away in cupboards and I mean everything. She can even get the perfume from the back of my dresser some way or other. She is simply busy all day. Sometimes you can almost see her little mind in action. And eat! My goodness. Tonight for supper she did away with 1 slice of bread, small glass of tomato juice, 1 carrot, 1 potato, 1 egg 1 1/2 peaches and 1/2 glass milk. Needles to say she has a bit of a potbelly but that'd OK if her mother *had* – eh honey? But her Pop has one too plus a spare tire or so.

Mother sent me a breakfast set (dishes) from the Coast They arrived this morning. 32 pces. Cream background with a green flower spray on them. Also two large cut glass ashtrays, 4 small ones and a cigarette dish. They are all very, very nice. Sure am collecting a lot of things for our home, darling so all we'll have to get is the furniture – ha! ha! and a car for you.

The latest cute sayings of Sandra. – Alix put her on the toilet turned on the tap and said "Sandy go-go like the tap." and Sandy – big smile on her face says "Hot or Cold Mommy?" Joan doesn't talk sense yet but she's really feeding herself now. That's all for now. More love etc, Peg

February 11, 1945

Dearest Peggy,

Another two days gone by and they have been fairly eventful. Got a letter from you yesterday that was written on the 29th of Jan and so preceded the last one I had gotten from you. You seemed quite busy getting your last fling in before the isolation period with the daughter started while your family was away at the Coast. Would certainly like to be there doing my bit to spoil the daughter but guess my time will come and will certainly make the most of it.

Was in Beleek yesterday – the home of the china – did not get a chance to go through the pottery but intend to do it sometime in the future. Apparently they are not turning out much of their best china at the moment but will try to pick up some little thing if I see what I think you will like. Also went out yesterday and picked up 4 survivors from a ditching. They were rescued by a life boat but had spent 3 1/2 hrs. in the sea and were pretty well exposed. Two of the crew were swept away and the boys were a little despondent. Gave them each about 2 oz of issue rum and it's amazing what a cheerful glow they got out of it.

One of our aircraft crashed on land today and 11 of the boys were killed. I knew them all well even after my short stay here. The kite blew up after she hit and it's not very pleasant trying to fit your friends' arms and legs onto a body without a face so that you can bury them. Managed to dig out enough to identify and so that was the extent of the medical treatment that they required. Was out from noon until 7:30 tonight trotting around the bog they crashed in so I am about ready for the hay. Sat around the mess for a couple of hours and helped one of the boys get drunk who had lost his roommate who was his inseparable companion and had been with him for over two years. Feel quite sorry for some of these kids. They're all pretty good types.

This letter is a little morbid. Had better start talking about you now – my wonderful wife weighing about 98 pounds and gaining every day and growing more beautiful each day I'm away. Give my love and kisses to the darling daughter.

Miss you a lot. By the way – the other MO, Goldering, got posted overseas (east) today and will leave shortly. All my love, Hamp

Happy Valentine's Day tomorrow & all my love. *Double heart with arrow through it drawn with initials CHS MCS*
February 13, 1945

Dearest Hamp,

We are still basking in a balmy sun with water running in the streets and the temperature is around 43 above, but I fear it won't last long as it is 30 below in the far North – the coldest for them all winter so it looks as though we may be in for a cold spree. Really can't complain though as we've had a marvelous winter.

Sunday Joan and I were out for dinner at a friend of Jean

Bromwell's – another nurse at the University. Yesterday Marg and David were to come over for supper but David got inoculated instead. Wonder how he liked the switch of plans? They were to come today but as Bill can drive them tomorrow they are coming over then.

Joan and I went for a walk this afternoon and took the radio to the radio shop and Joan's blue outfit to the cleaners as she fell in the mud. We waved bye bye to everyone she met and generously passed out a friendly neighborly feeling of good will. We called on Alix and Sandy and got a ride in the car to the post office and then an invitation to supper so we are just home. Joan was really tired as she tries to do everything Sandy does – with quite drastic results sometimes as you can well imagine. We also finished a roll of film today on the front veranda. Hope they turn out as they should be quite cute. Took some in the house on Sunday – Joan running around with only her panties on. It was quite sunny in the front room so they may, with a bit of luck, turn out OK.

Mother and Dad are leaving for Victoria tomorrow so it will be almost another week before Dad gets home and almost 2 weeks or so before Mother comes and then Joan and I leave for Camrose. Goodness it's almost a year since you went away all I can say is "it's a hell of a long time."

Bob Zender's father was killed in a railyard accident last weekend. He was to have retired in April. Art Beauchamp is with a Hospital Unit in England. Jack Day is with a Graves Corps in Holland burying the dead and Fred is still in Rome so that's the news so far.

Now for a joke! 1. A young married couple were at the desk in a hotel and the clerk asked "Would you like a bridal suite?" So the groom asked the bride "Would you like a bridal suite?" and she replied "It's not necessary, dear, I can hold on to your ears!" – Ah me! 2. Q. What are the reasons men get up in the night? A. 5% get up for a drink. 10% get up to go to the toilet and 85% get up to go home. —— – Ain't it awful? I got these from Jean in case you are wondering about it.

Then there's the one about the knitting needles but it's too long for now so if I should forget to sent it to you remind me some day, eh honey? I may not write it as it's not very nice. P.S. Don't think I'm being undermined coz I'm not. That's all for now. MCS signing off. Tune in next time same place. Heaps of love, hugs and kisses. As always my darling Peg

Dearest Peggy,

Another letter from you today. This mail service here is too good to be true – a letter every 2nd or 3rd day instead of 3 once a week is a real break. (I'm not putting the bite on you to keep writing but just expressing satisfaction).

Things have been quite busy in the past two days. Old Goldring leaves in a flat spin yesterday and running around with his head under his arm – talking his head off as usual without getting anywhere. He finally got cleared from the station on embarkation leave – he's going to get married on Friday before he leaves so it's going to be quite hectic. About a week ago I asked him when he was getting married and he said the middle March because "it takes about 2 months to plan a bit of a do" – can imagine his troubles now.

Finished up about 5 o'clock yesterday and hopped into the ambulance to run out to sick quarters to do some work. Going down the hill from the castle we went around the corner and ran head on into a truck. A patient in the back I was taking out to x-ray his chest pranged his head and I had to put several stitches in him and admit him – quite a good effort for a routine chest plate I thought. The ambulance was pretty well unserviceable so it was a little perturbing.

Today the sun actually shone for about 5 hours and amazed everybody including the met people – however a mild gale with showers is on tap now so things are normal again.

About the leave pictures from October – haven't sent them yet honey but will do so shortly. I have a roll of film being developed now and should have them in a couple of days – will send them.

Got a long and newsy letter from Margaret yesterday. The family all distinguishing themselves with their letter writing these days.

The old squadron leader is working a little harder these days – he comes along for an hour in the morning instead of 15 minutes. He's in the midst of moving to a new house and tried to take furniture from the nurse's quarters at Necarne but was told they were leaving if he did so he scrounged some elsewhere. Well darling, love you just as much & more. Give to daughter my fatherly regards. All my love, Hamp

Dearest Hamp,

You are without a doubt the most wonderful and most thoughtful husband in the world. You really spoil me. Gosh I even got flowers on Valentine's Day. Many, many thanks my darling. You can never imagine just what a thrill it is to be remembered so often. Really honey without a word of doubt all the flowers you have sent have been beautiful and this last bouquet is even better still. There are four daffodils, 4 tulips, 1 carnation and 1 iris and I'm sure they are the pick of the crop. I forgot the pussywillow and laurel branches, they are in it too. To the tune of "Oh what a beautiful morning" I now sing "Oh what a wonderful husband". That's you old boy and many many thanks.

Also got two letters from you today. You seen quite cheerful in spite of the wind and rain etc. I sure think it's a good idea for you to get your M.R.C.P. The more I think about it the better it sounds. If you need some financial assistance I'll be glad to send it to you at your first request so please don't hold back because of the financial angle. You have a fair amount here. So don't forget.

You old buggerlugs you! What's the idea getting me all excited about you tossing your genes around when you come home. Don't threaten me so! Gee whiz. I've done nothing but eat since I read that line. Pardon me while I dash out and get me a diaphragm – not that I don't want to get pregnant again but please give me time to have fun again. I'm really not worried you old son of a gun but try to control those emotions you great big brute of a male you. Ha! Ha! Come on home and let's see what we can do this time. Thems me true sentiments sent with much love.

Had a letter from Mother too and my favorite cousin Bob one of the Vancouver Smalley's was killed in a raid over Germany last week. Aunt Maggie in Blackburn had a letter from him on Jan. 28 and at that time he had been on 13 bombing raids and had 17 to go. He was a bombardier. The family got a wire on Saturday to say he was missing and one on Sunday to say his body had been found but there were no further particulars. Pretty grim I would say.

Jean and her escort have just left for a Valentine's dance at the hospital so I'm alone finishing my second bottle of beer – Jean's rations.

This is the life – smoking when I want to too. Only one thing lacking to make a perfect homey setting and that's your great big beautiful self. However with the war news as is we may be doing just that in the fall. Have decided not to take a holiday until September and by that time you may be here. Who knows! What a lovely idea eh honey?

Margaret and David were over for supper tonight. David sure is a cute guy and weighs 23 lb. 15 oz. almost a pound more than Joan. That's all for now honey. All our love hugs and kisses. Forever and always yours, Peg

February 15, 1945

Dearest Peggy,

Another quite busy day laid away. Am actually quite rushed these days with routine bumph and can't say that I mind it. Keep going to about 11:30 each morning and then go to sick quarters for rounds and finish about 1:00 and then am busy from 1:30 until 5:00 or 5:30 and then on call every night. Actually would sooner that it continued that way but guess another M.O. will be showing up in a week or two.

Tomorrow the squadron parades for the funeral of the boys who crashed and it won't be a very good day. It's funny how quickly those things are passed over though – more or less ignored I guess. Tomorrow night there is an unofficial going away party for one of the squadron commanders so everyone will get quite squiffed and the funeral will be forgotten for good.

Had a letter from one of my orderlies back in Yorkshire today. Everyone seems a little browned off and unhappy so I guess I remained there long enough.

Today acquired a desk lighter made out of a 0.5 machine gun bullet. It stands about 6 inches high and is quite a good effort. Will try to get a crest of some sort bronzed onto it and then will send it along as a souvenir of these parts. Also borrowed 300 cigarettes pending arrival of some – now over 600 so hope they start rolling in soon.

Bob is away tonight and it's kind of nice to just be able to sit around and read by yourself and not have to worry about talking to anyone or doing what someone else wants (not getting to be a hermit darling, but gives time for meditating about home and loved ones). By the way, had the most wonderful dream about you last night. It wasn't very decent but I guess it was all right since we are so thoroughly married to each other.

Well dear will sign off again and write you the gen of the next couple of days. Give the daughter my very best. Hope you are not too tired of being alone with family away. All my love, Hamp

February 16 1945

Dearest Hamp,

Another letter today dated Feb. 7 so we are not very far apart. Looks as though we finally have got straightened out with the mail as your letters are arriving one at a time now.

Today was quite cold – at 3 PM it was 10 below but as were getting low on food we just had to brave the elements so out we went. It wasn't too bad as the sun was shining so we decided to visit Sandy and Alix. Had a good time too. Joan and Sandy had their milk and cookies at Sandra's little table and quoting Sandy "It was a real party."

This morning we did some of the house cleaning and Joan helped me wash the kitchen floor. It was my idea and I found out the hard way that it wasn't very good. I had ideas that Joan would just play in the soapy water but no sir I mopped up almost more water than we started with. Joan must have added a few ounces to the flood on the floor. It was really hard to tell though as Joan was soaked from top to bottom and had put everything in the water she could lay her hands on – even Pandy – her little bear. He sure looked like a drowned rat when I hauled him out of the bucket. Guess he'll be drying for weeks.

Wednesday night after writing you and after Jean left for the dance I sure felt like the old stay at home. Then when I got to bed Joan wakened up and stayed awake until 4 AM for some reason or other. At 3 Jean and her escort came back for a beer and I sure felt lonely but virtuous listening to the long silences between muffled conversations and wondering first what they were up to. Guess that's what being old does to me. Remind me not to worry too much when Joan starts coming home with her beau friends. Silly isn't it when you think of the things we used to do and then start wondering about our grown up children at some future date.

Mother is in Victoria now and Dad is due in Calgary next Tuesday and Wednesday so guess he won't be home until next weekend. Don't know when Mother will be home.

I now weigh 98 pounds – almost a gain of a pound a week. Pretty good eh honey? If I should keep on at this rate I should weigh almost as much as you do in four months time. Gee I'd sure look worse than Aunty Lena and then if I got pregnant on top of that – oh my goodness! However I don't expect to keep on gaining but your threat is a good incentive to eat and eat and eat.

The flowers look simply wonderful and each time I look at them I think "What a perfect husband!" I sure love you honey and miss you a hell of a lot but the war news is good so maybe soon. All my love. Joan sends a big wet kiss. As always darling, Peg

February 17, 1945

Dearest Peggy,

Two letters from you yesterday. Guess the speed of the mail service will cease to amaze me after awhile but yesterday broke a record. Post marked noon of Feb. 10 and since it arrived here late of Feb. 15 it took only 5 1/2 days – not bad eh darling.

Things here progress. We had a funeral yesterday and 10 of the boys were buried here. It was a beautiful sunny and warm day for a change. I was busy and couldn't get down and was just as happy.

Got the two flashlights from Dad today – they are actually quite good and will light the path to and from the "house" quite nicely.

Didn't do very much last night. Had half a dozen small Guinness and then came home and had toast and cocoa and went to bed. Bob has a friend coming tonight or tomorrow – he is a private in the army so we are getting our food stock built up so he can eat here and not have to worry about going to the mess. We have managed to acquire some steak and eggs, bread and margarine – so he won't starve to death unless he's a strict vegetarian.

The daughter sounds to be developing into quite a determined

456

character what with spilling water on the floor and then spitting – she seems to have quite a definite mind of her own – hope she approves of her old man when he comes home or else he's really going to lead a dog's life. This being "young and gay with the boys again" honey is beginning to pall a little and I would give anything to become just a little hen-pecked by none other than yourself. However your inning will come soon I hope. News gets better every day and hope it lasts.

Mother wrote yesterday but didn't have very much to say – glad to hear from her though now mind.

Chuck Rainsforth won't go back to Harriet I suppose. Don't know whether I blame Harriette or not. Chuck according to all reports was anything but faithful to her and she knew it. Also his medical records before they were married weren't so hot in one or two spots, so don't imagine that lead to a great deal of confidence in him. However, Chuck is quite a nice fellow and now that he's older should make a good husband for anyone and probably much too good for Harriette.

Tonight there is another party in the mess but since I'm duty Joe, I'll have to forego the pleasure – and just as well. Next week there is a mess dinner for the squadron in honor of the W/C who is posted. It should be a major brawl and must be sure not to be working that night.

Have been busy the past two days – rushed with a lot of routine but at least it puts the days behind a little more quickly.

Well honey – will sign off. Love you very much and miss you and the daughter. Give her a kick in the pants for me. All my love, Hamp

February 19, 1945

Dearest Hamp,

The mail is extremely good. Got two letters Thursday, one Friday, the Yorkshire pictures Saturday and two letters today dated 9th and 11th so really I can't complain at all. The pictures were very good and I'm glad to see you are looking so well. I always get quite a shock when I see pictures of you because you look exactly the same as the last time I saw you. Somehow I feel you must have changed a lot and sometimes I think I won't know you when you return but the pictures belie all my thoughts and oh happy day you're still the same, old Hamp – to look at any rate. Your last letter was pretty grim but it gives a good idea just how trying your work can be on your morale etc. Not pleasant work at all looking for missing parts. Something like that really must affect the station for several weeks. I always said war is a grim business without any glamour and even if the plane crash was an accident it doesn't help matters does it? But enough of this depressing topic.

We sent you some pictures of Joan on Saturday night and I hope they arrive all right as they are just like Joan is all the time. You'll be able to see what a glamour child we have.

Yesterday Sandra and Alix were over for dinner. We had roast beef, baked potatoes, beets and beans and home made ice-cream. If I do say so myself it was all very good. Joan and Sandra really went wild running back and forth screaming and laughing. For the first time Joan objected to Sandra having a certain pet toy – just an empty hand lotion bottle with a red cap. Any how it led to a small fight and I was kind of glad to see Joan sticking up for her rights at last as Sandra has always had her own way around Joan. But that was once it didn't work out and so Joan grows up a bit more.

Had a time getting the daughter to sleep after they left as she was too wound up to settle for the night so she howled for about an hour and just screamed every time I left her.

Today we did the weekly wash and then this afternoon we walked to the Safeway store. Joan made friends with the butcher and he showed her all the meat in the refrigerator. Then she helped the manager put bread on the shelves and he put her mitt back on after she showed him that it was off. Quite a gal our daughter – always after the men. Yes I know honey – just like her old lady *used* to be. You old buggerlugs. And by the way when we go to the Coast again I hope there is 18 inches of snow so we will be bed bound so there! Do you know what storks live on honey? You don't? Well green pears of course! The Air Force are no longer called wolves, they're called hounds now coz they're always looking for someplace to bury a bone! Ugh! It must be the erks again! Aren't I awful. That's all for now. Joan can kiss people now if she's in the mood so a big juicy kiss from Joan and all my love my darling. Always and forever, Peg

Dearest Peggy,

Nothing much to report. Have been quite busy with the usual. Was up most of last night – had to see someone at midnight and then got a message at 4 AM that someone "was acting queer" up at sick quarters. I wandered up and found a drunken Canadian sergeant with a big cut in his lip where someone had hit him smartly. Sewed him up and he staggered out saying – "Get ready for a patient with a fractured skull, I'm going back and bust that guy on the nose". I was a little skeptical but sure enough 2 hours later another sergeant wandered in and I had to put a few stitches in his lip where his teeth had gone through them. I wasn't very grateful for the business but found it kind of amusing.

The night before there was a party in the officers' mess and I left early because I was on duty. The casualties rolled into my room until 3:00 AM. However one of the boys who fell off a table and cracked some ribs insisted that I get up and play cribbage with him. I did so and won two pounds – so maybe it was worth it.

Last night we cooked steak and eggs – very good too except the meat was a little high. Stan Glaze, Bob's friend is here and we laid in more steaks than he could fry so we had to eat up the extras so they didn't spoil completely. Tonight we have just had 2 eggs, toast and tea. Much better meal than the mess provided since they had liver and sausages (boiled liver & ersatz sausages).

The old squadron leader is kind of in the deep stuff at present. He got caught trying to get someone to smuggle a bottle of ~~champagne~~ sherry across the border and now the police are snooping and the Air Force are wondering what the score is. However he'll blarney his way out of it somehow. Guess I won't see him for about a week though, while he's going around seeing everyone.

Am just in the midst of taking a beating – someone came in and is accusing me of rolling a patient of mine the other night for two pounds when he was in no condition to defend himself in cribbage – what with being a bit squiffed and having 2 broken ribs. However the bloke is just a bit bitter because he now owes me 6 pints of Guinness lost over cribbage.

Well darling, my activities aren't very exciting but keep me busy.

All my love, Hamp Miss you. Give Joan my love.

Dearest Hampton,

That was a lovely Birthday letter – reached me exactly ten days later. Nothing warms one's heart more than – just to be remembered. Thanks a thousand times.

Note am answering on George Washington's birthday.

Happy memories center around the anniversary. Gone are those days. Am happy to be writing to my boy and the best is yet to come – when our boys come home. All well here. We still stoke to keep warm too. A mild spell again but it will not last. I went out this afternoon – ground slick – was so glad to hail the taxi to bring me home. Will not try that again soon.

Have not seen Mac and family since I last wrote. Not such a rush of work. There is usually a slack time after the holidays are over. Am still hoping to see Peggy and Joan.

Peggy is really an exceptionally good letter writer. She certainly loves you. A lucky boy to be so well mated – and at the right time in life. She does well being an only child. The other girl has lots of good points too – but her principles are not as high as your wife's and sister's. Sent Margaret the prettiest dress. Got it last week. No new goods in that I wanted for myself. Put my cheque in the bank. Am enjoying it more though. Can always spend money. So nice to have some though. Want to see my mother once more. She wants to return to Sheridan in April. Rather hope she does. Pearl will arrange. That druggist aunt is rated at $75 thousand dollars to her credit. Made it mostly in the drug business. Still at it. Russell is better. I want to go to Sheridan but rather wait until this German war is over. So many restrictions and I want you to be home first.

Told Mrs. Ireland that Arthur had grown up since she saw him. I hope you get your box in good condition. Not much in it to make you fat. Must get you off some more tea etc. in March. Mrs. Ireland says send less than the 11 lb. and send often. If Peggy comes for a visit she will help me.

Hattie spent this Monday with me. Her man did not send the money for the house Monday so she laid off packing, ate noon lunch with us and we had a foursome in the afternoon. Real good fun. A coincidence both of our right hands are lame, hers in a cast from a strain last summer and mine from a fall in the yard last September. My hand swells from writing and beating a cake. Dish washing really keeps the swelling go down. So I do all of it. Our house work is not great chore. Margaret is the one who has work. She seems to work all the time. Keeps David up to all the new "quirks" in baby raising (not text book language). Feeds *every one well. Keeps her house spotless. Does all those big washings daily. She does not have time to get pretty things to wear like she used to. I am hoping Dad will give her a new sewing machine for her birthday – think he can get one from the Co. in Red Deer. I have just written a letter of inquiry. Peggy made David the nicest rompers for his Xmas gift. Am sure she is going to be a good seamstress – Marg too, for she does wonders by hand. Well this is not much to write to one so far way. Not much news to write. Tom Williams got his eye put out at a hockey game last week. Bad news – his mother is Dad's Isolation Hosp. nurse. Mrs. W. came and helped out when Peg was down in the summer. Think I will ask her to go and see Tommy in the U. Hosp. Had his operation last Saturday.*

Will sign off for tonight and write again soon. Much love, Mother

February 22, 1945

Dearest Peg,

Got a very swell letter from you that made me feel like a million dollars. My conscience bothered me a bit about your Valentine flowers – I didn't actually wire those but gave Margaret some extra money in January and she did the actual deed – would have wired them otherwise. Glad you liked them darling and my sentiments on sending them, are the same that you expressed on receiving them. You really are a wonderful person you know and I'm sorry I can't do more to show my feelings – the time will come.

You don't have to take my sentiments about the genes too seriously honey – we will take the usual precautions to procrastinate on the remainder of our family.

Too bad about Bob Smalley, when I was visiting your Aunt Maggie she got out a letter from him in which he told how many trips he had made and how many he had to go – one of those tough breaks.

Missed writing you last night because of the squadron party. I was supposed to be off duty and so got quite squiffed. Phoned sick quarters about 10 PM to see how the old S/C was getting along and found he had buggered off to get tight somewhere. Came home mad and went to bed immediately. It was just as well because I probably would have passed out later on anyway. He rolled in about 7:00 A.M. this morning and woke up all the staff who sleep at the M.I.R. with a cup of tea half full of whiskey, towel over his arm and quite squiffed. They all enjoyed their tea in bed and then he sent a "fog lifter" down to me via an orderly – a glass of milk with and egg, an oz. of whiskey, an ounce of rum, sal volatile, salt and pepper. Actually it was very good. It's hard to get mad at the old coot because he is actually very likable.

Have been standing around the pier head all evening waiting for a couple of kites with engine trouble to land. No panic resulted and all I did was shed considerable rain. Went out on the loch the other afternoon in a launch – beautiful day and really enjoyed it. The launch beats along about 20 knots and it's a very comfortable craft. Wouldn't mind owning one myself.

Got a letter from Mother yesterday – things are the usual at home and she seemed to be a little inactive and wanting a little more social life.

Well dearest will sign off and hit the hay listening to the rain on the roof – don't mind it actually and kind of like it. Miss you very much as usual. Give Joan my love & kisses. All my love, Hamp

February 23 1945

Dearest Hamp,

I'm days behind in my letter writing but as you may have guessed Dad is home so I'm a bit busier than before. Can't really use that excuse as I went to a show last night with Alix and Helen Cairns. We saw Abbot & Costello in "Lost in a Harem". It was not particularly good but we laughed a lot anyway.

Dad came in Wednesday night with a cold and bronchitis so I've been doing the odd bit of nursing care. He's much better however so I think he'll survive my care and cooking. Today Joan and I did a wash – Dad's clothes etc. Then I washed the kitchen floor and tidied up the house. Alix phoned so Joan and I got ready and went over town just for the ride. We got home at 5 PM so I put the dinner on and whipped up a sponge cake and then we ate and were all finished by 6:30 – potatoes, carrots, asparagus, round steak, peaches and tea. Joan and Dad played around while I got the washing in. Then Joan had a bath and went to bed. I did the dishes and made some cookies so have just sat down at

9:45 PM. I don't know where I've got all the sudden overwhelming energy from. If it's because I'm gaining weight I hate to think what I'll be doing when I've added on 10 more pounds. But it's wonderful to have the energy again and not feel tired out all the time. Joan's been sleeping until 9 AM so I get about 10 hours sleep a night. It's a wonderful tonic I guess eh honey?

Mother is still in Victoria and having a wonderful time – luncheons, teas, dinners etc. That's just what she needed and I'm very glad she finally decided to go for a holiday. When she gets back it looks as though I'll have to get my impacted wisdom teeth out as they are beginning to sprout in the wrong places. Maybe I'll get down to Camrose one of these days.

The new hospital was opened yesterday and I'm sending some clippings so you can see what it looks like now that it's finished.

Cousin Bob who went missing on Feb. 8th was in the Pathfinder Squadron so Dad says. His position was in dispatches in December after a raid on Dusseldorf. I'm sorry that you never had the chance to meet him as he certainly was a grand fellow.

Joan was very glad to see Dad. Guess she was tired of looking at my face only. However she has a very exciting time and Dad doesn't have a minute of peace. That's all for now as we haven't been doing anything spectacular. How's your studying coming along or is it? All my love darling with heaps of hugs and kisses. As ever and always, Peg

February 24, 1945

Dearest Peg,

Three letters today created a little sunshine that more than made up for the omission of it by our weather. You seem to fill up your days without too much trouble – guess you are like myself and have the occasional big gap that just has to be filled in somehow. (Better get off that talk eh darling before I start getting homesick).

That was one of the better cute sayings of Sandra's – pretty smart. When is Joan going to start writing letters – I'm getting a bit self conscious about my daughter being a young lady of 16 mos. and still not corresponding.

There was a "do" in the mess last night for the departing C.O. of the station – a very nice party with free drinks flowing briskly – proud to announce that I stood around and sipped Guinness mug slowly and watched everybody get stinking drunk and then came home and in bed by 11:30 – quite sober. Ain't I to be congratulated darling.

Bob goes on leave next week and I'll be alone for 18 days. Kind of a pleasant change in a way and look forward to doing what I want to do.

Having a little trouble getting my sleep these nights – two nights ago some of the boys wandered in about 2:00 AM and kept me awake until I got mad and got up to throw all of them (the smallest) into the creek that runs outside the hut. Last night they came about 3:00 AM next door and kept bellowing for a can opener and it took about half an hour to locate one. Then at 4 o'clock the duty officer came in to use my phone to make sure the crews were getting up OK for ops.

Have made tentative arrangements to go on leave at the end of March. Plan to go to London and look in at headquarters and then visit on the old station for a day or so.

Dad wrote today also. I told him about my post war plans (immediate) of taking a holiday with you. He announced "In spite of what you say you are coming here for a week first and let Mac have a few days". I'm afraid that they've had that – it made me mad to see it and I'm still mad but won't say anything and just carry on with usual ideas. It's funny how short a year or two seems when you talk about other people being separated but when it's yourself it works out to a hell of a lot of long days and dull evenings. Heard an old joke today – One girl says to another, "Do you get a nervous feeling when you are out with your boy friend alone?" Reply, "No, my boyfriend's not nervous!". Not very new but will find something to reply to yours so I get to hear the one about the knitting needles. Well darling, miss you very much and love you very much. All my love, Hamp

February 25 1945

Dearest Hamp,

Goodness me it's almost March. Time is certainly flitting by. What have you been doing lately I wonder. No mail for a week so that puts me two weeks behind in your activities again. Tomorrow really should be a good day for heaps and heaps of mail – I hope.

Yesterday Joan and I were pretty busy cleaning house – vacuuming, dusting, waxing, etc. Then we all – Dad, Joan and I – went to the Safeway for our weekend rations. At night Alix, Roberta and I went to the Varscona to see "Lassie Come Home". Have you seen it? It's all about a collie dog and Yorkshire people – the story was light, no real plot but very entertaining and the scenes (of California) taken in color were very beautiful. If you haven't seen it and get the chance it would be 2 hours enjoyably spent anyway.

Today we just loafed around but it wasn't a very good day as far as Joan was concerned. Everything was against her from the time she got up – just couldn't seem to keep out of trouble and the final blow fell at 3 PM when Joan tumbled off a chair and fell on her face with her lower lip between her teeth. So, consequently her lip is quite messy. There are four teeth marks inside and one deep one outside with several scratches. Her chin is quite swollen and quite blue even after cold compresses. From then on she kept falling and bumping herself and couldn't eat any supper as her mouth was too sore. The poor wee tyke was really glad to get into bed where she was safe and secure from this cruel world.

Ollie Rostrup is in town now as the Col Mewburn Pavilion has been opened and of course he's looking for a house but so far no luck as places are very scarce here.

Mother won't be home for a week or more as she just left Victoria today and then is going to stop off in Vancouver and again in Calgary. So she's having a wonderful time.

Guess what darling? I now weigh 100 lbs. Yes siree! Aren't you proud of me and the way I'm gaining? You really must have scared me into action with your well timed threats. And how I love them!

That's all for now as we certainly aren't doing anything very lively these days but are quite contented to sit but God! How I wish this war would end. The boys are doing a good job but the waiting sure is hard. Isn't it honey?

All my love my dearest. Forever and always. Yours, Peg

Dearest Peg,

Two letters from you today – one with the pictures. That candid camera shot is good of your coat and hat but you look as if you are looking around for something to throw at the photographer. Still mighty pretty though, darling.

Things have been as usual. Got some cigarettes today from my overseas order (900) and since I now owe 900 I'm not really much ahead of the game as yet – should be able to declare a profit next month.

The daughter is looking a little more grown up with each set of pictures and is soon going to be quite a young lady with long hair and everything.

Have had quite a varied practice today terminating with a miscarriage. Went out about 8 miles and rescued the wife of one our C.O.'s who was about 3 months and bleeding quite profusely. Then picked up a civilian off the road who had been riding in a service vehicle and fallen out as the door flew open when it rounded a corner – she had a broken arm and a nice collection of cuts and bruises.

Finished up by helping eat a chicken one of the chaps had acquired and had cooked. It is now 1 PM and I'm quite comfortably full of chicken and dressing. It really was a treat. When I get home I'm going to get you to roast a couple of them, sit down and eat a whole one myself – what a hog! – no wonder I have a spare tire.

The old S/C was going to take over in the morning while I slept in but now he has to appear in connection with his sherry smuggling so I guess I've had my day off for this week.

He goes on leave in a week's time so I hope a replacement arrives for him. Not that he does anything but he helps fill in and takes off some of the odd jobs which are a bind.

Bob is flying tomorrow and so is sound asleep (I hope). He goes on leave in a few days and is beginning to show the need for it.

Well darling will sign off. Still love you more than ever and miss you. Give Joan a great big kiss from me. The war news is good and I hope to deliver them in person before too damn long. All my love,
Hamp

Dearest Peg,

Well, that last day of the month and soon spring will begin in earnest. In two more days I'll pass into my 4th year in this outfit – what a waste of time, eh darling? Actually it has gone by very quickly but I hope that we are well past the half way mark of our service career.

Tonight there was another small do for the departing S/C and to welcome the new squadron C.O. – A W/C Stan MacMillan. He used to be an old bush pilot out of Edmonton and you probably remember his name. He seems a very good type and should get along very well here.

Slept in this morning until 11:00 AM – with 3 phone calls between 9 and 11 and a couple of people coming in and our Batman clattering about. Art Ireland, a chap from Camrose who is posted home, phoned me to see if there was any message. Couldn't think of anything in particular however but certainly envy him.

Tonight it's raining and blowing again but the wind is getting much warmer and things are getting a bit more summery. Another month and maybe Ireland won't be so bad after all.

Had quite an unpleasant surprise today – my mess bill was 18 pounds – pretty awful eh honey. Thirteen pounds worth of tickets, and 5 for laundry, squadron funds, messing, and assessments for going away presents etc. Am going to economize next month because 18 from 22 is 4 pounds and you don't save very much to go on leave at that rate of expenditure.

Have just finished a banquet – toast, Prem and ovaltine – courtesy of Shepherd and his roommate who now live next door. Shepherd is a heck of a nice chap – a pilot – about 30 – a wonderful pianist and organist and quite an all round chap. Used to teach music and play a church organ in Toronto and seemed to do quite well by it. He and I both enjoy annoying Bob and his horror of drinking and not going to church. – so are quite bad influences – quite harmless actually.

Well darling signing off as usual and love you an awful lot still (more & more). The war news still looks awful good and sure hope that it lasts. At current rate maybe we'll see each before too long. By the way – this W/C MacMillan was with Ritchie in India and they came back together and Ritchie is now in England. All my love, Hamp.

Dearest Hamp,

No darling you haven't missed a couple of letters it's just that your wife hasn't written you since Sunday. I'm really ashamed of myself and apologize to the fullest of my capacity which doesn't change the situation does it honey? To explain though I've been gallivanting at night since Dad is home. So I'll write a long letter and it may run to two forms this time. Sure hope you'll forgive me, darling.

Joan's lip is almost better now although she was quite fussy for a few days, wouldn't eat much and was hard to put to bed at night. On Monday as I was putting out the wash Joan walked down the back steps and ran down the back walk until she slipped on the ice and skinned her knee. That set her off for the day so I spent two hours at night trying to get her to settle down to sleep. In exasperation I asked Dad to go in and settle her – a change of face and all that sort of thing so Joan went to sleep and now Dad tells me how to put Joan to bed. I sure get a big bang out of Dad and the daughter. They are seldom separated and I can't do a thing with Joan while Dad is around. It's not Dad's fault – just that Joan likes to show off.

The days are pretty hectic as our daughter is into everything. Tuesday she found out how to open the bread drawer and the cake drawer so we spent the day putting bread and cake back in the drawers. At night she tripped over the rug and banged her eye on Dad's shoe and so developed a slight case of a black eye. She really looks a mess but it won't be forever – I hope. So Tuesday night I felt like a change of scene so went to a show with Carol Young. Mac is coming home on Saturday for two weeks leave – between courses I think. Their second baby is expected in April some time.

Wednesday was quite a quiet day for a change and things went fairly well. Only lifted Joan away from the bread box twice but I found her sitting on the dining room table picking artificial posies from a vase. Me thinks I'll have a few gray hairs when you return my darling. In the afternoon Margaret phoned as she had a letter from you. Bill is working days now so they are the happy couple again and stepping out – supper dance and stuff like that. I went over to see them Wednesday night for a couple of hours and left Dad to experiment and improve on his technique of putting babies to bed.

The days are busy what with routine work, Joan and meals for Dad so if I go out at night you're minus a letter. However I hope you won't be too severe with me. That's all on this form more on the next. Heaps of love, dearest, as always, Peg

2 Cont'd – March 2, 1945

Dearest Hamp,

We are up to Thursday now. That was the day the storm really broke over my head. A wicker rocking chair for Joan arrived from Mother and we had a lot of fun unpacking it and then rocking in it. That was good for an hour so while I'm busy cleaning the rugs what happens but Joan gets at the bread box and I find her sitting on the kitchen floor with a box of brown sugar having a wonderful feast and scattering the sugar around like an old fashioned farmer seeding his land. We got that cleaned up – Joan's help being to track it around a bit more – and it's time for lunch and then the afternoon sleep. All is quiet on the bedroom front and Dad and I are enjoying a good meal cooked by me ahem! when I hear a sound from the back of the house so in I tiptoe and what meets my eyes but Joan sitting at the foot of her crib with the desk drawer open – 4 decks of cards, envelopes, paper and pencils scattered all around and 'her Highness' eating a sulphonamide tablet that I had forgotten was in the drawer. Honestly sometimes I think I'm not fit to be a mother and this was a good day for such thoughts. But I got everything straightened out and Joan settled for a couple of hours so I defrosted the refrigerator. I put all the food on the cabinet and well away from the edge but nor far enough however for at 5:00 PM as I came up from the basement – only went down for potatoes – there was Joan as happy as a chicken with a dozen eggs around her. Yes sir I really mean it – 4 smashed with yolk running all around, 6 cracked and 2 OK. The dog was hanging around and it wasn't until I started to wash the floor after washing Joan that I missed the bacon. Bud had eaten about a quarter pound of bacon. That was definitely the last straw so I phoned

469

Alix and we went to a show at 8 o'clock. Today was wonderful so I'm staying home – too tired to go out anyway.

Got two letters yesterday – the only bright spot in the story. They were dated the 15th and the 17th so my mail service isn't quite as rapid as yours. The old S/C must be quite a character. Sure hope you don't learn any of his tricks for I must have someone in my family I can handle and as I can't manage Joan very well it looks like you are the victim – you poor *hen-pecked-to-be* husband you! Hadn't realized you were hen-pecked before you old buggerlugs! Why didn't you tell me? Just wait till you get home! *A threat!* Ha! Ha!

The news is on and the 9th is across the Rhine. Yippar! I hope we're away on the last lap now.

Got my legacy of £100 on Tuesday – $444 and some odd cents in Canadian money. You never commented last July when I wrote you about your heiress wife. What'sa matter honey are you jealous? I've been thinking I'll put it in bonds and later use it to buy electrical equipment for our home – washing machine, refrig. etc. or a silver tea service. What do you think?

Mother is still in Vancouver and Dad leaves tomorrow for Calgary and Winnipeg so we'll be alone again. Sure hope Ma comes home soon as I'm getting just a wee bit tired of being alone. That's all for now my darling.

Heaps of hugs and kisses from Joan and all my love. As always, Peg

March 2, 1945

Dearest Peg,

Yesterday I hit the jack pot – your parcel arrived and was most welcome. Thanks for everything from soup to nuts and nail files. The soap didn't smell like cheese or visa versa, thanks to the wrappings around the soap. All in all it is quite a good effort – a very good one. Ate the olives last night without any pause but there is still enough left to keep the wolf away for a while.

Today was a gorgeous day. Quite brisk but scarcely a cloud in the sky and brilliant sunshine. Too good to be true actually. Went out to Necame and snapped some x-rays of a wrist and on the way back stopped off at Mrs. Rockwell's. She is the local eating place which seems to cater to Canadians in particular. Had a steak with 2 eggs and fried onions and toast – boy was it good. Must do again sometime but find it a little difficult to get away most of the time.

Bob Bartlett given leave tomorrow. He's been getting a little hard to get along with lately and it's a good thing for him that he's going. He takes life and his flying quite seriously and worries a great deal about little things. I'm glad to see him finishing his tour now or else I might have had to finish it for him (i.e. ground him).

Have just finished playing about 8 games of darts in the mess and getting beaten in about 7 of them. My aim doesn't seem to improve but it's something to do at least.

Tomorrow night one of the RAF squadrons here has challenged 423 to a mess competition – i.e. a tournament involving every game that can be played in the mess including beer drinking. It should be quite a hectic evening and since there are a few of the Canadians who don't see eye to eye with some of the English boys – it should be even more interesting.

Am getting to the stage where I'm looking foreword to getting away for a few days. Only one more month. If my finances don't look any rosier I may S.O.S. for some money. It takes about 30 pounds for 12 days and I'm riding a little close to the line. That sounds extravagant but pounds unfortunately don't stretch very much. However darling I won't S.O.S. unless absolutely have to and will apologize profusely if I do.

Well honey, thanks again for the parcel. Hope to get some mail tomorrow from you. Give Joan my love and kisses. All my love, Hamp

March 4, 1945

Dearest Hamp,

How are you old dear? It seems ages since I heard from you but it's actually only 3 days. However even if I got a letter a day I'm sure I'd still look for more.

We have been very quiet the past two days. Dad left for Calgary yesterday and Joan snapped right back into her old routine of going to bed quietly and not causing much of a rumpus during the day. I guess like me a man around is just too much as we really aren't used to males in the house. However darling you need have no worry as I'm sure we'll fall into the routine very readily when you return.

When you return! What a lovely phrase! It's like music to our ears. I read once a description of what war is but the phrase that stuck in my mind was "War is like a woman sleeping on a lonely bed." Guess I remember that line because it applied to me more than the others. However my bed is not lonely. You are not actually there but I can dream can't I? and reminisce of the times we spent together, of our honeymoon – how we tried to fit into the same tub, the supper dance etc. & etc; of Claresholm and all the intimate memories that the mention of the name revives; of our last two weeks together, the night you left – seeing you disappear to far horizons as the train left Marg and I behind; even days before we married, before we really knew each other when we'd walk blocks in a somehow understanding silence. No darling my bed is not lonely but you're not there in person. Like the hit song "I dream of you more than you dream I do".

No, dearest, I'm not drunk, but one more drink of rum and coke would have lifted me into a gayer mood but as there was no more rum in Jean's bottle I'm left in a cloud of memories which are rather bitter sweet. Sweet because they are of you and bitter – slightly – because we are apart. But maybe it won't be too awfully long now before you're home. This isn't the letter I started to write. It's not exactly a lift for your morale but perhaps you can take heart by reading between the lines and seeing that I'm wearing my heart on my sleeve and if you look closer you'll see the name "Hamp" engraved so deeply that time and distance will never erase it.

I'd better change my tone or the tears will be blotting the ink as I write.

The weather is 20 below so Joan and I haven't been out for two days. Jean and her friend Greta were here for supper and the early evening and have just left. Dad should be home tomorrow night but where Mother is I'm not just sure – Vancouver or points east to Calgary maybe.

I didn't do very well by this letter darling but let's blame it on the rum. Shall we? Haven't any real news anyway and maybe you won't mind reminiscing with me. Isn't the war news good? Everyone is so hopeful and I sure trust it's time this time.

All my love, my dearest. As ever, Peg

March 5, 1945

Dearest Peg,

Three letters from home today. Two from yourself that made our spring day seem even better that it was and one from Mother.

The pictures of Joan were really good – she is getting to be quite the young lady and it seems hard to realize that our infant is beginning to grow up a little. She gets better looking and more like you as she grows – hope it continues.

Sorry the mail doesn't come better; I'm slipping in my g-d writing again and missed yesterday. Had fully intended to sit down and write you a good letter for a change but here's my excuse.

Yesterday morning I promised to take the new W/C McMillan out to see our sick quarters at Necame. He and Hoop Cunningham and Jack Gorden (2 flight commanders) piled in with me and we rustled. I sat them down to wait for me while I made rounds and left a bottle of our issue rum for them to try. They made huge inroads in it and we then left to visit S/L Pearce at Ballynamadad because I promised to have a Guinness with him in the local at noon. We had a Guinness and the gang had several Irish and we went towards camp. They dropped off at Irvinestown and I came home and did my afternoon's work and went out at 4 PM and picked them up. They brought back 2 bottles of rum to my room and then sent out a general call and about 20 people came in for a drink. They ran out of rum again and got 2 more bottles from town. The party continued until midnight so I didn't write (and didn't get tight either darling) because the congestion in the room kind of stopped me. (Boy! what an excuse – half a page.) It was very cheerful afternoon though and everybody had a very good time.

Say, I made an awful faux pas. I didn't mention the laundry bag around my parcel. It was and is quite an effort and I don't know whether to hang it in the room or keep it in the drawer and just bring it out occasionally for inspiration. Need a laundry bag however so it will probably be the former.

Today was a nice quiet day and did my minimum without many qualms of conscience. It is really warming up here now and spring is in the air. Wish we could collaborate a little on this atmosphere but will settle for good old Alberta in the spring of '46 (I hope). Miss you very

473

much Peggy but am waiting with considerable patience for the time when we can kind of settle down together and not worry about the Air Force and all its annoyances. Shouldn't be too long.

Mac send me 300 more cigarettes today so now I have my debts paid off and am 600 ahead of the game. An unprecedented state of cigarette prosperity and hope that it continues.

Imagine that you will be starting to get in the lookout for an Easter Bonnet and a few spring clothes about now. When I come back you are going to really have to put your foot down to keep me from getting a loud checked suit in any color but blue. That hundred pounds is wonderful – keep it up or else! (Snarled the villain of the piece). All my love, Hamp

March 5 (?), 1945

Dearest Peg,

Things go on without a great deal to report. Manage to keep busy with routine and very little extra curricular activity of interest on which I can report. Have shown the daughter's latest pictures to just about everyone on the camp now and they all are forced to admit that she is without a doubt, the most wonderful infant they have had the pleasure of viewing.

Last night was the inter-squadron do. The RAF boys won all the games requiring much finesse and the Canadians won all those involving enthusiasm such as beer drinking relays etc. The beer relays were quite amusing although a little damp. Ten men a side lined up on each side of a long table and each with a pint of beer in front of him and then proceeding to each follow the next man as he downed his pint. Bob MacCraig thought that it was such a good game that he challenged anyone to a race on a second pint. It was declared a draw so they drank another one. He won and after he came back from being sick, he was quite proud of himself.

A patient has just come in but I'm ignoring him. He sprained a wrist badly and after it was nearly better he went on leave. He came back yesterday worse than ever. But one of my spies saw him crawling on his hands and knees across a square in London, chasing a pigeon. He isn't getting a hell of a lot of sympathy for some reason or other.

I have been instrumental in getting a pilot named Jack Gorden (F/L) repatriated. He may go west and if he does will give you a ring if he goes through Banff while on holiday with his wife. He's a very nice chap. Also he's taking some pictures home for me and will mail them to you (I hope) – if his good intentions persist.

This evening sat around with the M.O. from a nearby station and had the odd pint. He's a very nice chap, and RAF man – very pleasant.

I'm having a lot of trouble – there are 3 people heckling me. Bud Powell told me to tell you that his dog is going to have pups. He has a floppy eared mongrel bitch (on whom he dotes and visa versa) and her confinement will be quite an event.

Have had suggestions that I ask you for food etc. etc. and I replied that I have everything I need but you. The next suggestion is that you dehydrate yourself and dispatch yourself by next mail. Quite a good idea if you regenerate OK but don't think we can take the chance. Well will sign off, all my love and kisses. Give the daughter my fondest regards and etceteras. More of all my love, Hamp

March 6, 1945

Dearest Hamp,

Spring is here again. It was 40 above today. We just don't seem to be able to keep winter with us. Not that we actually mind, anyhow it looks as though the climate has warmed up considerably since we were married as this is the second mild winter in a row. Guess ole mother nature approves of our marital bliss!

Dad was to have come home last night and I stayed up until 12:30 and no Dad appeared. He didn't arrive on the morning train either but I got a letter from Mother from Calgary so that explains Dad's absence from home. They are both arriving tomorrow night if they stick to their plans and I can assure you I'll be glad to have them home as I'm just a little fed up trying to keep up my interest in food. Guess I was just born lazy as I can cook potatoes for Joan and me but I can't seem to eat them. Maybe it's my cooking eh honey?

I put a harness and leash on Joan this afternoon and we walked to the store through streets that had turned to running streams. My Joan enjoyed herself splashing through the water and even with the leash on she got a lot of her own way as she practically pulled me along. This is not good weather for walking. It would be easier swimming which Joan tries when she falls into a puddle.

As I wrote before I sent you 1800 cigs. in January and they should arrive soon as I've received the card saying they were on their way. Bet you could use a few hundred fags about now. It's time I got another parcel off too. February seemed to go so fast that I missed sending you one so will have to make the next a super duper one so you can repay Bob for all or some of the food you've scrounged from him.

Alix, Helen Day Cairns, Connie Day and her sister Lela and I are going to a show tonight "The Thin Man Goes Home". We are going to be quite snooty as Alix is taking the car. Jean is studying for exams so she's going to be the "sitter" for tonight.

The war news is certainly very good these days. I hope Monty can fulfill his mother's prophecy and have the war over on the 23rd of this month. But even I can tell that is impossibility.

Am feeling kind of cold so guess I'd better go and eat a bite of something or other. This is really a boring letter if I'd thought sooner I'd have written up the knitting needle joke. It's too late now but I'll remember some day to tell you or write it to you. How goes the studying student? Or are you? Big hugs and kisses from Joan and she says she's trying to be good now. All my love darling, Peg

March 8, 1945

Dearest Hamp,

Well old thing Ma & Pa have finally arrived home. I was very glad to see them and so was Joan but now I definitely can't do anything with her. Neither can Mother. I've never seen any child with such a determined will of her own and sometimes I'm at a loss just how to manage her. However with an equal determination and a lot of strenuous work I may be able to round her back into shape again. She just seemed to go berserk all of a sudden two weeks ago. Guess she discovered how to exert herself and is going "all out".

Mother and Dad had a good holiday and Mother looks quite rested. However we'll take that out of her in a few days.

Tuesday night we had a very good time. The five of us (Alix, Helen, Connie and Lela) went to see the "Thin Man Goes Home". It was good entertainment but didn't seem quite as good as other "Thin Man" shows. After the picture we went to our newest cafe the "Shangri-La" next door but one to Nye's Stationery. They advertised it a lot but it's not much different from the other cafes – just new and clean so far. Anyhow we had our tea cups read but the reader was a way off the beam as far as I was concerned – there was a dark man in my cup etc. and all the time I was thinking "She's crazy she means a blonde!" However she did say I was going to get some mail and sure enough today I got 3 – dated Feb. 22, 24 & 26. You seem to be busy as usual. Like you I was kind of mad at your Dad's remark because I feel Mac could get a holiday if he tried. I hope life in Camrose won't be like that all the time with you getting what's left after Mac has his innings. That's kind of a mean thing to say but I'm afraid darling that if you don't look out you'll just be a second fiddle to Mac when actually you've got brains and guts enough to stand on your own two feet. But it always makes me mad when they say "It'll be swell when Hamp is back so Mac can get this and that" etc. & etc. This is just being a green eyed monster and shooting off my mouth-you can bawl me out when you get home.

I hear the Air Force is putting the finger on some of the boys overseas to volunteer for the Far East. Sure hope they leave you alone as there are enough chaps around here to choose from. That's all for now honey and another h— of a letter. All my love, always – Peg

March 9, 1945

Dearest Peg,

Another warm spring day (without the sunshine) and time proceeds. The war news is certainly good these days and I hope that it continues. One of these days we may find the war over (I still say about July and hope that I'm not to optimistic).

Afraid that my last letter was a little more disoriented than usual but I had quite a little bet of heckling while in the throes of composition.

Tomorrow is my big day – have got a day off and am going to usefully employ myself by doing a bit of flying. It won't be too interesting but one occasionally has to expose oneself to the jobs of those with whom you have to deal. It's quite a routine in a way but kind of enjoyable too except you see an awful lot of water after 1 to 15 hours over it. I'll probably be elected to the job of cook – could be worse eh darling – If I don't get airsick.

Have been playing darts in the mess for the past 3 hours and don't seem to improve but manage to have quite a bit of fun one way or another. Another chap, Bill Potter, a navigator, and myself have elected ourselves a team to challenge all comers. It's a toss up as to whether Bill or myself has the least clues about the game – but we haven't any pride in it anyway.

The mail is a little slow these days but should get some tomorrow night when I get back. We have been informed that some of the mail between Jan 19 and 23 has been lost, so if there was a lapse there, it is explained.

Was just in the midst of writing you this afternoon when an English officer turned up to consult me about a shiner he had acquired. Sopil, a Canadian had come in this morning with a fractured metacarpal acquired by a sheepish "bicycle prang". I put two and two together and got the right answer. Wonderful thing, this constant cementing of Empire relations.

Well honey have told you all that has happened except for my latest dream. Remember our last night in Camrose when I was devouring (visually) the naked lady in my arms, who told me "Yes darling, it's all yours!" Well anyway you came back to me just as if you were there again. What a wonderful dream. You are quite the psychologist honey. You must have known that that would be the way. All my love, Hamp

March 11, 1945

Dearest Hamp,

It is now Sunday and I haven't written you since Thursday and also I must apologize for that last letter. It was terrible and not at all the letter I set out to write and on top of that Dad forgot to mail it on Friday

478

morning so it didn't go out until yesterday which was very awful too. Guess Dad and I are just a couple of buggers eh honey?

The last two days have been fairly entertaining. Eleanor Greenleese Skelton is in town from Lethbridge so she had some girls for tea on Friday to see her son Bobby – and herself of course. As it was Mother's Red Cross day I took Joan. All the way to the West End by street car. She enjoyed the ride very much and had a wonderful time exploring a different house. Eleanor's little boy is four months old and a good little tyke with scads of brown hair – almost as much and as long as Joan's. He was very much taken with the company and refused to go outside so Joan entertained him by almost squeezing him to death and annoyed him by playing with his rattles. In the evening Alix and I went to the Garneau so that was a day well spent.

Yesterday was quite a lazy day as we just did the house work and then went to the store in the afternoon. At night I was invited to Helen Day Cairns along with the rest of the fivesome – namely Alix, Connie, Lula and of course Helen. We played a new gamed called Nertz until we were just that and then ate. In Nertz everyone has a deck of cards and deals himself 13 cards face down. That's the Nertz pile. Then you deal five cards face up and at the word go you play a modified solitaire, everyone playing at the same time, putting your aces in the center of the table and keeping your five cards stocked from your Nertz pile, while you turn the cards up in the last of the deck 3 at a time. Everyone plays on everyone else's aces and the person to get rid of their Nertz pile first says "Nertz" and everyone quits playing. The cards left in the Nertz pile count 2 against you and the cards you've played on the aces count one for you 100 is game. Do you get it? When 5 people play and all at the same time, on the same stack of aces, you sure go crazy in a hurry. Then too it's quite noisy. My score for the first game was 25. That's your wife honey! But I won the second game. You ought to try it sometime if you can savvy the above description. We play for the grand sum of 5 cents a game and a lot of hard work for 5 cents.

Today was a good spring day so Mother, Joan and I went for a long walk. Joan in her buggy now as most of the snow has gone.

I hope to get downtown soon to buy myself some new clothes for spring. I feel a spending mood coming on and that's not good as I usually forget myself and get carried away. Mrs. Day Sr. is all enthused about the end of the European War and had dresses made for the grandchildren to wear to meet their daddies. I'm not that bad yet but the news is truly hopeful. All for now honey. Heaps of love and kisses from Joan and I. All my love dearest, Peg.

March 11, 1945

Dearest Peggy,

No mail for nearly a week now from you. I should hit the jack pot tomorrow or the next and have quite a haul of news. Yesterday I kind of jogged myself out of my usual routine and had a heck of a pleasant day as a result. Love flying. Will give you a blow by blow description so you know what it's like at times where the trip is routine.

Got up at 4:30 and dressed and went down with the crew and ate poached eggs and beans – the first real breakfast I have had since coming here – and then got briefed with the crew for the trip and then into the launch and out to the aircraft and take off. For the first couple of hours just stood around on the upper deck behind the pilots and looked around. It was a cloudy day but very bright and absolutely no wind so the whole trip was smoother than riding on a train. After walking around and bothering everybody went down to the galley and peeled potatoes with one of the crew who was the official cook for the trip (between duties). Started dinner about noon and went on until about 1:30. The crew spelled each other off and ate in turn. The Sunderland is really huge. There is a galley about midships – about 8 feet square and then forward of that is the wardroom with twin bunks and a folding table in it where you eat and sleep (a little larger than the galley). Then you go forward to the deck where it is only about five feet high and you have to stoop a little. (By the way there is an airborne toilet and wash basin in a little room up there). Then you climb some stairs to the upper deck where pilots, navigator, wireless op, engineer etc. hold out. Had a steak and egg, beans, boiled potatoes, coffee for dinner so didn't suffer at all. After lunch took a spell of watch in the front turret and fired the guns at sundry sea gulls, floating wood etc. (Very lenient is the front gunner at that point) didn't hit anything but the tracers are kind of pretty. After that retired to the ward room and slept for 2 hours

480

(operating fatigue set in). Then spent an hour in the rear turret looking out at nothing but water and the odd convoy to break the monotony. Then had afternoon tea and went up on top and took over one of the pilot's seats and flew the thing for an hour. Not quite like an Anson but managed to keep on course with the odd correction by the navigator who developed a few gray hairs, then back and chatted with off-watches in the wardroom until return. No panics so didn't have the opportunity to see the boys drop any depth charges but had a very good day and got in 12 airborne hours. It wasn't a particularly long trip so you can imagine that the long trips can be a little fatiguing flying over water and keeping on looking for something that doesn't often appear.

Flew over part of N. Ireland and it was really beautiful from the distance with its green fields separated by hedges. There isn't one square inch that hasn't got a field hedged in, unless it's a road or a small plot around a farm house.

Tonight saw a show in the mess – 'The hit parade of 1943' and kind of enjoyed it. Not a bad picture at least.

Well darling that brings you up to date. Wonder if you are in Camrose now and if you are liking it at all. Miss you. Love you very much. All my love, Hamp.

March 13, 1945

Dearest Hamp

Today was one of those beautiful spring days with a blue cloudless sky and very warm sun. Nearly all the snow has disappeared – that is all the snow on the southern exposures so the north bank of the river is beginning to get a bit greener every day. To add to this beautiful weather I got 3 letters from you today – my weeks ration, the last letter was written on the 5th. Margaret phoned me this morning and read me the letter you wrote her.

They (Camrose I mean) are without a maid at present as Ann's mother had a stroke so Margaret is going down on Thursday. I may follow shortly but as has been mentioned before I must get my wisdom teeth out first as they are beginning to bother me now. One has broken through the gum so I think it won't have to be touched but the lower one has turned sideways and now that it's starting to grow my face and ear are aching so guess it calls for prompt action. I thought I was going to hold out until you came home so you could hang on to my hand or vice verse but fate is against me. Lucky you eh honey?

Went downtown yesterday to spend some money on a suit and dress etc for myself. Bought you 900 cigs and came home with a pair of shoes for Joan and a pair of stockings for myself. The extent of my shopping! Didn't see anything I really liked so that was money saved for that day.

However I spent $5 on a small go-cart for Joan today so she can use it instead of that big buggy as it's pretty heavy to move around. Got the go-cart through the wanted adds and it is in real good shape. Figure on selling the buggy and should get from $20 to $25 for it. Don't worry darling we can always get another one when we need it.

The news analysts on this side of the pond are quite optimistic about the end of the war. Some say 6 weeks but the more conservative say it should be over by June. The first one is preferable but the second will be very good too. However if it should all be over in April you'd probably finish up your 6-8 months posting in Ireland before you'd get the "go" sign for home. I'm still plugging for September or October but you can come home before that you know. What are the signs of the time over there and your own opinion about homecoming etc? You've never written about it and I can't say I blame you but just this once honey what do you think about it all?

Joan is a wonderful child again and quite happy. She's recovered from the arrival of Ma & Pa and is back in the groove. Glad you've got your parcel. I've another one almost ready to send. Joan says "Hi ya" and sends hugs and kisses. All my love dearest, Peg

March 14, 1945

Dearest Peggy,

I'm a day behind in my writing and must apologize. Monday and Tuesday I hit the jack pot on mail and got four letters from you, Feb. 23, Mar. 4 and a double letter for Mar 2 full of apologies. You actually don't have to apologize for not writing daily because when you do, it compensates for any that might have been missed. Also if you are busy letter writing is kind of a chore and one's better to wait until the opportunity presents itself for leisurely compensation of an epistle. You must have had quite a busy time when your Dad got back from the Coast what with washings etc. I hope I am as successful as he is at soothing the infant. It certainly is wonderful having a rich wife as I'm in the need of 15 pounds. Am going to wire you for it and hope it is on its way back by the time you get this letter. Find I can't finance leave and my life here. Haven't been off the camp since arriving but still manage to get nil of my 22 quid a month and have none left for leave. Your reminiscing in your letter brought back or at least renewed an awful lot of happy memories – truly we will repeat in the not too distant future – even our compartment to Vancouver and all that went with our first holiday together.

Yesterday I got a letter from William Pickup at Darwen. He invited me to come and stay and visit with them at Darwen and sent a very cordial letter. I will reply darling and am going to try to get there and to Fleetwood on my next leave. I am very anxious to go to London this leave because I want to and must get into RCAF overseas headquarters and tell them that I'm still in existence over here or else I might spend an awful lot of months without relief. I've got no one to replace me on leave yet and if one doesn't arrive I shan't be able to go – got my fingers crossed.

Have been quite busy during the day for the past 3 days. Was going to write you last night but started playing darts in the mess and about 4 hours and 4 pints later I quit and came home and went to sleep. Tuesday I took a patient out 20 miles to convalesce at home after a couple of months in hospital. Went to a place called Fenton – where they have one of the few horse drawn railways left in our modern world. Had tea at his farm house (homemade bread and country butter) and then came home via a few local pubs at Fivemiletown, McBrides Bridge and Irvinestown. Quite a nice afternoon and the first time I've been off the station actually.

Interruption – have just been to sick quarters to see a dying erk who was bleeding to death per annum. Arrived to find him quite smug in the possession of now found hemorrhoids and after inserting a finger and following it with my boot, I'm now back in the hut. The problems of air force medicine!

We lost another crew today from one of the RAF squadrons – crashed about 90 miles away and a wash out – we don't have to worry about picking up the remains in that one – which is a relief.

Am getting to be quite a psychiatrist, about every new erk that comes in the unit now is holding his head and hollering about a headache or nerves or insomnia. See at least 4 people a day on sick parade like that and they are quite a problem. Am beginning to lose my patience with the weak sisters – that's why I figure leave won't do any harm – you get a little cheesed with seeing them 7 days a week and half the nights and doing endless paper work on them.

Well darling had better quit me binding. Give my love and kisses to the daughter and keep on dreaming – I'll do the best I can with your dreams.

All my love, Hamp

March 16, 1945

Dearest Hamp

Got a very nice surprise today – two letters from you which raises my quota this week to 5 – a very good show darling, a very good show.

Before it slips my mind again as it has on several occasions lately I want to ask – what are you going to Headquarters in London for? Or is it any of my business? Or is that where you're apt to meet old friends unexpectedly? Heard on the news today that the V-2 bombs are hitting London again or still so do be careful darling if you must go. Those bombs don't seem to make things very healthy when they're around. Also buggerlugs you are in the dog house. Do you realize you made another "faux pas" besides the one about the laundry bag? You never mentioned the wedding cake in your box. Oh my you shameful boy. Was it moldy or something when it got there? I'm just henpecking you a bit so the shock of it when you get home won't be too great.

You seem to be having quite a time in your dreams. It's funny though I'm dreaming more as the nights go by and like your dreams most are not always decent – in fact they are very seldom decent – but I like them. This seems an awful thing to say but sometimes when I waken up I feel completely content and satisfied. Boy you sure must

484

have had what it takes for a dream to be so real. Then too spring is in the air again and my yearning for you is increasing more each day but the war can't last much longer now which is a very comforting thought – but enough of this for now.

Wednesday night Alix and I went out to Margaret's and sat and talked. Rod Burgar is a poppy now. Can't remember whether it is a boy or girl. He is still stationed at Haigersville.

Yesterday Mother and Dad had company in for lunch, Mr and Mrs Young and Mrs Young's brother, so we were quite busy. In the late afternoon mother took Joan for walk so I did all the dishes. At night Eleanor, Kay and I went to the Capital to see "30 Seconds Over Tokyo". I enjoyed it very much as it didn't seem to be too much of a war show. We got out at 11.45 and then had milk shakes so it was around 1 AM when I got home so today I'm slightly tired.

Joan is full of the "old mick" the last few days. She's not bad, just full of life and teasing us all the time. Her eyes just sparkle when she's up to something. She sneaks up behind me and tickles my knees and then runs away bursting into peals of laughter.

You may be pleased to know that I finished my cross stitch tapestry today – the roses and delphiniums. It measures 14" by 19" and really took quite a lot of work – about 4 weeks of 2 hours each day. So you better remember to comment on it when you return. The next step is to frame it. I'm going to try to do it myself but if I don't succeed I'll have to get it done for me.

How about applying some of that instrumental stuff on your own repatriation honey? How was that 14 hour trip? Bet you won't want to be doing that everyday eh? Do take care of yourself if and when you get to London darling. I'll be wondering about your welfare all the time you're there. That's all for now dearest. Joan with a gleam in her eye says "Hi Pa, heaps of love and kisses". All my love darling, Peg

March 18, 1945

Dearest Hamp

And a happy St Patrick's Day of yesterday to you! And did you celebrate appropriately honey? I don't know if you'll get the letter I wrote to you on Friday night as Dad phoned from town yesterday on his way to Calgary to say that he couldn't find the letter. I know he took it with him so it will turn up and he'll mail it. There was really nothing of importance in it but I will repeat my pleas – look after yourself in London darling and stay away from the V-2 bombs. They're not healthy.

Aunty Lena came over for supper yesterday and brought several letters from Eddy and his wife Joy which told about their wedding. He is stationed in Bromley, Kent. At night Alix and I went to a show. Yes, again, and I'm getting to like them. Alix finally got some mail from Fred so she's happy again. Although he wrote that if there was a lapse in the mail it would be because their unit was expecting to be moved to Europe and he hoped to see Jack if at all possible so now Alix doesn't quite know where Fred is as everybody's mail seems to be held up lately.

You really had quite a struggle writing your last letter. You might tell Bud Powell's pooch that I wish her luck in her coming ordeal. And whoever asked for food, (jokingly I think) can rest assured that a parcel for *you* will be on the way shortly if that is any consolation for he'll have to keep in your good books.

Joan has been the perfect child all week – as happy as a lark running about and singing and chattering to herself all day. She's getting her second molars too but so far they don't seem to be bothering her. She really goes to bed at night quite tired out and has got over that fussy streak – for a while at any rate. She only makes puddles in the house accidentally now and usually tells us when she needs a bit of help.

Today was a grand day so Alix, Sandy, Joan and I went for a walk. We'll soon be able to go down to the park and back in the sunlight. How is Lock Erne for swimming? Or weren't you near enough to it? Maybe it's too cold anyway. I think Joan and I will go down to the lake for a week or so this summer as she's much easier to look after now – no special foods and only 2 washings a week – pretty soft eh darling?

I think tomorrow would be a good day to see about my teeth and get that out of the way. Then Joan should be done for scarlet fever but think I'll get it done in Camrose.

That's all for now dearest. Nothing very important but I love you as always only each day it burns in me more deeply. All my love darling, as ever, Peg

Dearest Peg,

In case you didn't already know it – your husband is a bum – for not writing you for about four days. No good excuse but just a combination of circumstances. Friday was my night to write but went to a party at Killadeos, a nearby station. Since there is no mail out of here on Sunday I didn't write last night so now you have the whole story.

Friday night was a most enjoyable evening – it was a mess party and although I didn't do anything but soak up Scotch and Irish whiskey – I enjoyed it. Their mess is in a huge old house and is quite a nice place. Met the local doctors and dignitaries and thoroughly enjoyed myself.

Yesterday was Saint Patrick's Day. The old squadron leader started in at noon. Offered me a beer and I settled for a coke and when it came it was half full of gin and ruined my stomach for the rest of the day since I was still a little dyspeptic from the previous evening. Last night had a few minor casualties and a couple more troublesome ones – one was a nun with a broken nose and the other an erk who was dining in a pub and somebody broke a glass in his face and then tried to hit him over the head with a bottle. Fortunately all he required was a little needlework and warning about March 17.

Don't know if I told you that I had acquired an Irvine jacket – fleece lined leather coat – nice and warm and if I get posted elsewhere may find it useful. Snagged one from a crash and then had one of the boys who was posted give me his and he turned it in.

Haven't heard anything about my leave yet and Friday is fast approaching. Am wiring for money from you tomorrow since I won't be able to finance leave and my mess bill too. Will promise to economize later darling and try to repay the loan.

Am getting a little cheesed with life. My days are very busy from 8 to 5 with about half an hour for lunch. It's all routine and paper work and therefore gets to be quite exasperating after awhile.

Have a temporary new roommate – a chap named Dave Bircomb who is just here on the way while waiting for a room.

Well honey this isn't a very good letter for waiting 4 days for. Must apologize but nothing really ever happens of much interest. Have got some films developing. I must go and collect them soon. Will sign off and will write tomorrow and bring you up to date with my routine. Give Joan a hug for me. Miss you.

All my love, Hamp.

DEAR PEG PLEASE WIRE HUNDRED DOLLARS TO ME SOON AS POSSIBLE TO ROYAL BANK OF CANADA TO COCKSPUR LONDON LOVE. HAMP SMITH

Tuesday, March 20, 1945

Dearest Peg,

Two letters from you today and really good to hear from you as usual. Things seem to be going as per usual. You must get that wisdom tooth out before it starts to bother you too much. If Scott Hamilton does it, it won't bother you too much. Either have a local or go into the U.A.H. and get Orville Watts to give you the shot. Your Nertz game sounds kind of hectic – we don't play cards very much around here though and have a hard time scraping up one deck when the spirit moves us to have a cribbage game.

Things here are as usual – am bogged down in routine. Won't be able to get away on leave for awhile because can't get a replacement. May go next week. Had a letter from Doug Ritchie. He is in London working for the medical board – doing routine physicals and is thoroughly cheesed already. He has a room of sorts near Knightsbridge and asked me to stay there on leave if I wanted to – so may do and save hotel bill – if I get down there. He heard from Johnnie Hunt – said he was doing Sweet Fanny Adams and not very happy but managing to maintain a little sporadic euphoria.

Wired yesterday for 20 quid from you. Will probably be able to repay it shortly and will try to do so anyway. It's just that I have no reserve and can't seem to keep a shill in my pocket – which is embarrassing at times. The chap who sent the wire for me said he changed the twenty pounds to 100 dollars – if so will try to remit some of it again shortly so it doesn't interfere with your Easter spending.

You asked for my considered opinion as to when the war would end – well honey, you got me. I don't think it will end before fall and there aren't many betting otherwise. Hope I am not too optimistic. They are asking for volunteers for occupation but Mrs. Smith's husband is not among them and never will be if he can help it. The war news is certainly good and I think May and June will see major activity. (It took 56 days to buildup the Normandy bridgehead and hope the Rhine one isn't any longer).

Spring is still sneaking up on us. Last night and tonight have been lovely evenings. Funny country though – looked out last night (on my evening trek to the place) and the moon was shining in a cloudless, starlit sky. Twenty minutes after I came back a squall came up and the rain on the tin roof and wind were practically deafening.

Sunday night after I wrote you we had a small panic. A truck coming back from the railway station with about 40 erks in it tipped over. Nobody was hurt by a miracle. One kid was convinced he had a broken leg and I ruined a bit of rest x-raying him just to be sure and got back about 3:00 PM. Am getting to be quite the radiologist with our little portable machine. Must get a book and find out what I'm looking for.

Have quite a problem these days with our Air Force erks that are being drafted into the army. Most of them aren't very happy about it and are getting a little hard to convince when people present their complaints.

Tomorrow have to go to a funeral of the bunch that crashed in the Free State last week. Unfortunately 6 can't be identified and have to be buried together – tough break since they are English and a couple have wives at the ceremony.

The buds are beginning to break into leaf here – are you jealous darling? – can't say I am enjoying the spring a great deal though.

Well dearest had better quit my chatter. Do you realize that we are now into our 12th month and the year is at hand – not an anniversary we can celebrate but a good one in the fact that that's one year of separation we can have put behind and are that much closer.

Well, will sign off. Get the daughter cracking on her reading and writing so that I can convey my love to her in person.

All my love, Hamp.

Dearest Hamp

I'm a day out again as it was club night last night. However I've a lot of news so that may make up for it.

Monday I went downtown and bought a new pair of black suede shoes, material to make my spring hat (which by the way is now made. Just a bunch of blue flowers & veil, really quite silly) & a picture frame for my embroidery (which is now framed as of today). It's a big picture about 30" by 24" when framed so that will fill up space in our home.

Joan is running a slightly elevated temperature & is slightly ratty to deal with. I think she's cutting more teeth but I'm watching her closely as I've developed a cold. Not a bad one but it makes me really dopey. Next Tuesday I go to see Dr Hamilton about my teeth. Oh my!

Got your cable today – this afternoon – so will go downtown tomorrow and send the money to you. Hope it arrives in time – I think it should. Sure hope you have a good time on your leave. Wish I could dehydrate myself and then come over and help you "do England". Don't forget to send your IOU to the house fund for $100. Cheer up honey I'm just kidding as the money is really yours anyway, so have fun darling. I don't just know what method of the several ways I'll send the money but will enquire at the bank and use the fastest service. It'll be on its way tomorrow.

Yesterday was quite an exciting day for us. Can you keep a secret for s couple of months? That is from folks back here. Dad got a letter yesterday asking him if he'd accept the honorary degree of doctor of divinity from a theological college in Chicago at their spring convocation. Naturally he accepted and is giving the Baccalaureate address as well. Mother is very excited and has decided to go with Dad and as he's on his way to Toronto and Ottawa mother will go east too and visit old friends. She also has an old aunt in Massachusetts whom she hasn't seen for 30 years or so and I guess she'll see her too. This all happens in May so yours truly will be alone again. How about finishing up the war and coming home? Eh honey? The war news is very good though and it can't last much longer as had been said before.

Got an Easter card from Doris Bothwell yesterday and Bill has got his discharge so they are leaving for Ontario tomorrow. Nice work if you can get it, eh honey? Etta Putsman phoned me tonight to ask me to tea next week with some of the girls from Claresholm – Mrs Dave Hunter etc. Harry got his discharge in January as you may recall. Etta says that George Stuart or Stewart has his discharge and also Ron Edmonds so the war is over for some people which makes it more hopeful for the rest of us I guess.

See from the paper today that Jean Gilchrist had a son yesterday. Also to switch subjects Dave Hunter made the headlines as a S/L & squadron leader of the Moose squadron and quote "succeeded to that responsible post with only ten trips over enemy territory behind him."

Joan and I are going to Camrose in April – yes really – so that we can then be free to live alone in May. If we didn't have the dog I could stay on in Camrose but that can't be so we'll enjoy ourselves in our own way. That's all for now darling. Again' I hope you have a good leave. Heaps of love hugs and kisses from Joan and I. As always – Peg P.S. I love you very much.

March 22, 1945

Dearest Peg,

Two more days. Have been quite busy but not much to report. No mail service last writing but got 900 Sweet Caps from yesterday and 900 British Consuls today so my cigarette larder is well stocked. Thanks very much honey. That's the best reserve I've had and I'm going to try to keep it up to that so not be too generous with my hand outs unless a further surplus comes.

Night before last had a busy evening – with an erk with the usual fractured metacarpal and one who fell off a top bunk into an iron bucket and pranged a few ribs and vertebral processes.

Yesterday afternoon went to the funeral in Irvinestown – not a very pleasant afternoon but the ceremony was brief and quite nice. There were seven buried in the Farotetac ceremony and one in the R.C.A. parade, lots of flares and a firing party and all quite in order. After the ceremony picked up the old S/L and then went to one of the pubs and had a couple of Guinness and then had tea in town.

Last night spent an hour and some racing over the lough in a motor launch. It was a lovely evening and dashing along in the moonlight at 20 knots was really enjoyable. Finally located an aircraft on some rocks. No one was injured so it was a pure pleasure trip.

About a couple of hours later went out and picked a drunk erk off the road with a broken clavicle. Got him laid away and then had to stand by while an aircraft in trouble landed. Quite a busy evening but nothing very major. Today our only panic was a civilian who had a caterpillar tractor run over his chest and abdomen. Fortunately it was a boggy area so managed to get him off our hands alive although he had a real traumatic asphyxia.

Yesterday got a letter from Dad dated Jan. 9. It had been out to Naples and hung around there for awhile. The reason I guess was that it was labeled Med. services so they sent it to the Mediterranean.

The old S/L told me a good one about his home town newspaper when he was living in S. Ireland. The Screamer Eagle had quite a reputation for reporting. Writing up a funeral they stated "However following the ceremony Alderman McCormack fell over the grave and broke his leg, which cast an air of gloom over the whole proceedings". Couldn't help thinking about it while at the ceremony yesterday because a while before I came here one of the pall bearers at an Air Force funeral fell in the grave and bruised himself pretty badly. Well the room is beginning to fill up a bit – asked for jokes but all I got were: One old man said "I don't smoke and I don't drink and I don't run around with women and tomorrow I celebrate my 90th birthday." And the other old man said "How?" Or the girl who said "I don't smoke and I don't drink and I don't f-f-f-find fault with those that do" (with stuttering).

Well no more contributions except long and dirty ones. Well darling will sign off. Miss you very much but the news is still good. My leave is very indefinite so the money I wired for will stay in the bank (probably). Give Joan loads of love and kisses from me. All my love, Hamp

March 23, 1945

Dearest Hamp

Well, old boy, your money is on the way as of yesterday. I went downtown in the morning and discussed the ways and means with the bank. I could have had the money in the bank in London today but I hope you don't need it quite so soon. It should be there on Monday however as it goes by airmail from here to Montreal and from there by cable. The exchange is $4.47 to the £ so sent you £22/10 1/d which is $100.57 so you can buy me something with the 57 cents eh honey?

From the bank I walked into Morton's Ladies' ready-to-wear and bought a dress. It's a 2 piece outfit in gold gabardine (a yellow shade) something like this *(small drawing)* – 3 ties instead of buttons and white embroidery around the neck. It's a size 11 and fits perfectly – too long of course – so with alterations cost $20.20. Oh my, the price of vanity or something. And just by the way of change I'm wearing my hair up on top – swept up you know! Everyone says it looks swell that way but anyhow it's a change. It goes something like this *(another small drawing)*. Doesn't it look awful the way I draw it. Guess I'd better get a snap taken so you can see for yourself.

Got a letter from you today written on March 14th – guess you're getting just a trifle fed up with no real change of scene. But don't forget to handle the higher ups with gloves darling – no more letters like you wrote to Easton eh?

We were glad to know that Cousin Bill wrote you a letter. Hope you get a chance to see them as they are our more prosperous relatives – they own a cotton mill in Lancashire. They are church goers and would expect you to go to church on Sunday. Thought I'd better drop a word off warning to you – but church once in a while won't hurt you, you know. Who am I to talk though as I've only been two or three times since you went away. Uncle Herbert on the other hand would be only to glad to take you to the local pub – so mother says. He lives in Fleetwood and is a veteran of the last war and was with the army of occupation in Mesopotamia for 3 years after the last war so you'd probably have a jolly time rolling home.

Margaret is expected back from Camrose this weekend. Bill was to drive down and get her but he's home with the flu. So far my cold hasn't developed into anything serious – just a dull ache in my left maxillary sinus which may be due to my wisdom teeth. Joan is still a demon in the day time but has been going to sleep as soon as she's in bed – both afternoon and night. It is definitely her 2 year molars that are bothering her and she occasionally gets quite feverish and goes off her food but nothing really serious. We have been trying to teach her to bow her head when we say grace before meals. Tonight she watched us with eyes large as saucers and when we started to eat she put her head down and mumbled away to herself and then burst into a hearty laugh. We just about killed ourselves laughing and Dad said, "So that's what it looks like eh?" and Joan wrinkled up her nose and nodded her head quite vigorously. Quite an accomplished child eh darling, and what a tease. Just like her old man I'd say! Alix was over for a while tonight when Mother and Dad were out and now it's bedtime so must away to dream and reminisce of better days to come and happier days gone by. Have a good leave if you get this in time. All my love darling, forever and always yours, Peg

March 23, 1945 Friday

Dearest Peg,

Actually I haven't anything to write about tonight since I wrote last night but tomorrow is the last mail day for the weekend so I'll chat a wee bit with you.

Have just finished a big steak and 2 fried eggs and a tin of cherries so am quite at peace with the world. Went into Kesh today with the old S/L and we had a couple of Guinness and then went on the scrounge. I acquired some steak and a dozen eggs and he scrounged about everything in town but the main road. Am getting quite attached to the old boy and in spite of the fact that I bitch at times about him, still think he's all right.

No panics today except the usual stand bys as aircraft come in with engine trouble.

Am having quite a few distractions in writing what is a corny letter at best – bagpipes are playing on the radio and Bartlett's standing over my shoulder rubbing in his smelly hair tonic and giving me his usual list of hypochondriacal symptoms – have finally discouraged him by poking him once gently in the stomach with my fist – now the radio is on Achtung! Achtung! warnings so I guess I can't win.

Has been a gorgeous day today – warm and cloudless – spring fever has me firmly in its grasp but guess I'll survive.

Another interruption – am now drinking tea and eating cookies –

the padre is next door and brought in tea and cookies – Shepherd who lives next door and the Padre keep collaborating because Shep is a very fine organist and musician and plays the church organ and organizes the choir.

Probably forgot to tell you. Bob got back from leave on Wednesday and has only about 5 more trips before he finishes and he's about as cheerful as I've seen him. Another interruption – Darcey Stewart just came back from the show and is in the midst of describing how Lassie came home. Lassie is now home and this letter is getting steadily worse.

Got a letter from the Canadian RCAF Medical Director today giving the brief on demob. It didn't say anything and just asked what our desires were. I am in the process of writing and saying I don't want to go east and I don't want to stay in the RCAF any longer than I can help and that I'm cheesed with the way they run our part of the RCAF. Guess that is about all there is to tell them.

Well honey will sign off. Sorry the epistle is scrummy. Love you very much. All my love, Hamp

Letter to Royal Canadian Air Force – Overseas

RAF Station
Castle Archdale
Nr Enniskillen N.I.
24ᵗʰ March 1945

Air Commodore JW Yice
Director of medical Services (Air)
Ottawa, Canada

Dear Sir

In reply to your most welcome letter of 12/3/45 I am forwarding information necessary to complete the card indexing of myself.

Name: Smith, Christopher Hampton   AF No C10858
1. 2/3/42[14]   2. 28/10/17[15]   3. Married   4. One dependent child
5. N.A. – will practice at Camrose Alberta
6. G.P.   7. N.A. 8. After demobilization, intern and spec. training.

I have no desire to remain in the RCAF any longer than is absolutely necessary and will not volunteer to go to the Far East from this theatre of operations.

My aims on demobilization are to get further hospital training prior to proceeding to Camrose, where I hope to engage in general practice with my brother. If no openings for hospital training present themselves on release from the RCAF I will proceed at once to Camrose and work with my brother until a hospital appointment becomes available. After two years of general practice it is my intention to obtain special qualifications in Genito-Urinary surgery.

Prior to enlistment I had completed ten months of graduate and twelve months of undergraduate internship. After this inadequate training and three years as a station Medical Officer, (with more to follow), one does not feel competent to impose his services on the general public.

Admittedly the service doesn't owe us a damn thing as far as training goes, but it is most annoying to sit and stare at your aspirin bottle day after day and hear encouraging reports of rotation for RCAF in D.P. and N.H. hospitals and to compare our lot with the R.C.A.M.C. The staff of our Caduceus now represents the fountain pen used to refer one's patients to General Hospitals which you never hope to see or which you visit apologetically as a "poor relation".

You will gather from the above that things are normal here in Northern Ireland.

Thanking you again for your letter, I remain, yours faithfully,
C H Smith
Flight Lieutenant,
Medical officer, 423 Sqdn.

March 25, 1945

Dearest Peg,

Another two days gone by with very little to report of interest. Yesterday and today were perfect spring days with only scattered showers. Primroses and butter cups are out all over the grounds of the castle and the place is as beautiful as any spot could be, without yourself to grace it.

Tonight saw a movie in the mess, 'Lifeboat', and drank a couple of Guinness and then went to the hut across the way and had a piece of toast and am now in for the night.

Today I got some pictures. They aren't very good but will send them along. Those of me look a little two tonnish but I guess I am, so what the hell. They were taken at the end of January with snow on the ground and it looks quite wintry.

This evening before the show I was base umpire at a baseball game. Was no hell and got quite a lot of discussion from the respective sides. The sergeants and officers were playing and the officers won. The ball field is down by the Lough and a very pretty spot except that it is right by the sewage farm and a bit smelly if the wind is in the wrong direction.

At tea time today the band played in the mess. Every Sunday the band plays from 4 to 5 during tea in the anteroom and we have sandwiches instead of bread and jam. Kind of pleasant change and it gives you an excuse to quit work early.

Was kind of amused yesterday. I was sitting around chatting with one of our orderlies and the conversation turned to movies. He mentioned a bunch of shows and then Gone With The Wind came up and he announced that he had seen it 173 times – "A damn good show but after a while, Christ!" Discovered then that he was a motion picture operator in peacetime. "Gone with the Wind" never struck me that way before.

Well darling the news is certainly good these past 2 days with Montgomery over the Rhine. Hope all goes well and we'll keep our fingers crossed and start praying. Tell Joan her old man thinks she's just about as wonderful as his wife, which is quite something. All my love, Hamp

March 25, 1945 – March 26, 1945

Dearest Hamp

Thought I was going to write you yesterday afternoon (Sunday) but every time I picked up the pen Joan was right at my elbow waiting to annoy me – managed to get the date and salutation down but that's all. However today is another day so maybe I'll get this letter finished.

497

Saturday I bought some insurance for Joan and I – a mother and child policy for $1000 ($500 each). It costs me this year $4.78 a month or a 5% discount if paid yearly. At the end of 20 years we both get $500 which will fall on Joan's 21st birthday year; or if we should be disabled before that time we can draw on that; or if we die the benefactors would receive the money. And you incidentally darling are the benefactor. I figured it was time I started something or other on Joan so enquired about policies etc.

At night I went to Linda and Connie's with Alix and Helen Day – our foursome again. We played Nertz until we could hardly see. Just managed one game the whole evening which I won. Then we ate and told jokes or funny stories. Do you know the difference between a super nurse and a super duper nurse? Well, a super nurse can make a bed without disturbing the patient but a super duper nurse can make a patient without disturbing the bed. Ha! Ha! and be careful which one you call me!

Yesterday stayed in all day as Joan had slightly swollen glands and there was an awful wind outside with occasional rain. At night a big fatigue came over me so I went to bed.

This afternoon was out to tea with Esther Pateman, Pat Hunter and Avis Lewis (they were in Claresholm after we left but were good friends of Bothwells). We talked over old times and where everyone was and I found out that the night before Doris and Bill were to go East with two other couples a cancellation for all their discharges came through so for as far as I know they are still in Claresholm. Can't you just see Bill stomping and swearing at the RCAF particularly as they had everything packed and they had to leave Wannamaker's by April 1st so Margaret and Michel can move in. Alix finally got some up-to-date mail from Fred written from an American steamship and postmarked Marseilles March 14th so looks like Fred will see Jack. He got a letter from Bunny Michalyshin and he is in Germany now.

It has been raining nearly all day so most of our snow is gone. Spring is definitely here. How about there?

Isn't the wars news wonderful? It is good to know this is the last round for the Germans.

Am going to a show tonight and Dr Hamilton's tomorrow about my tooth. Yoi! Yoi! Yoi! Or something.

Mother is still talking about going East in May. It's too bad you couldn't be home by then eh honey? Well old darling thing (Ha! Ha!) That's all for now. Joan sends you heaps of love and kisses. She's almost talking now. All my love darling, as ever, Peg

27th March 1945 Ireland
(Posted Edmonton 17th April 1945)

Dearest Peg

Well how are you darling? Did you get your Easter wardrobe fixed up? Are you going to Camrose? How is daughter's eczema? Things here are normal. Yesterday was a gorgeous spring day and took the camera out and took a roll of film and am getting it developed today. I'm more or less organised in the photography section now so will try to be a little more prompt on getting snaps away to you.

Yesterday morning the PMO phoned and asked when I wanted to go on leave – I said any time so relief was arranged for this Thursday. However four hours later he phoned again and said there was no relief so I guess I'll go at the end of April – am certainly not suffering but a change is as good as a rest.

I still haven't gotten down to Beleek yet to see the pottery. Want to acquire some bits of china there just for the sake of having been through the place. One officer went yesterday and got some nice stuff although they are making very little fine china at the moment.

Last night had a domestic evening-sat home and darned a few socks and read and listened to the radio and ate a can of beef stew you sent in the last parcel. You occasionally get fed up with sitting around the mess doing nothing but talking to familiar faces and playing darts or pool or ping pong. It will be quite a luxury to be able to sit at home some day and have a pleasant evening just admiring my beautiful wife. Time out to go to the mail.

Two letters from yourself dated Mar 12 & 18. One was the one you had misplaced and warned me about London. With the status of my leave as it is at present you won't have to worry about me straying away from my lough here. By the way you wondered how far from the lough

499

we were, we're practically in the water here and it's very pretty at times. The wedding cake was a faux pas-wasn't it?? Not mentioning it at least. Ate it all by myself in divided doses as it was better than candy-delicious! Had a bit each evening for over a week and quite a luxury. Forgive me darling – your dreams must be nearly as good as mine and mine are something to write home about (to you only). You certainly are a brazen picture in my nocturnal associations and reunions with you from time to time – you might even blush to see yourself.

What can the daughter say now? Am curious to know how her vocabulary is progressing and if she is getting to the stage where she can swear back to her old lady.

Well evening is here now and it has been a nice quiet day. About 5 o'clock the old S/L and myself went into Irvinestown and had a couple of Guinness and then I went out to sick quarters and had tea and then back to the mess and fell asleep in a chair by the fire and woke up and ate and am now back in my room. Quite an ambitious programme. Am sending some pictures along to you. They are not very good but will give you an idea of how things are around here. Two were taken while the snow was on and things look pretty wintery.

Tomorrow am having a visit from George Elliot. He's the VD controller for RCAF overseas whom I got to know in Yorkshire and in the course of official correspondence I mentioned how good our steaks were over here so he's really coming over for the trip as we haven't any problems for him in this area.

Well Peggy, the war news brings us a little closer each day – I hope things continue to go well. Should be over by midsummer if they do we may see each other in the fall if all goes well. Will close now with heaps of love and kisses. All my love Hamp.

March 30, 1945

Dearest Hamp

This week has been another of those funny weeks in which a couple of days are missing. Tuesday I had one wisdom tooth out. Went to Scott Hamilton's at 3 PM had 2 x-rays taken, my tooth out and was walking down First Street at 3.45 PM. Pretty fast work eh honey? It really wasn't bad at all. The local was very good and in spite of the fact that the chisel and mallet reminded me of Hank and Huckell[16] and sounded like a good amputation too, everything was OK. Wednesday I felt quite dopey – a hangover from 292's and novocaine – my head felt like a good hangover too. Feel OK now though. There are two sutures which will come out on Monday and then there's the upper tooth to be removed some time shortly. Wednesday night I crawled into bed really early and slept like a drunk until morning.

Last night I went out to see Margaret and Bill and hear all about Camrose. Bill took Dad to the United Church on his birthday. Yes siree, really set the town back on their heals and Bill has earned the name of "Mission Bill". However I guess everything is as wet as usual with Mac & Irene giving their usual parties. I'm planning to go down next Friday provided my teeth are all fixed up.

Today Alix, Sandy, Joan and I went for a walk and came back to our house in time to have tea and cakes with Margaret, David and Bill. They came over with an Easter parcel from Mother. Real cute aprons for Joan, some of Dad's birthday cake, chocolates for me and a dozen eggs for mother. Really a nice parcel and quite a surprise too. Tomorrow night the fivesome are coming here for a change so I've finished baking a spice cake and a batch of brownies. Mother and Dad were out to the Garneau Theatre.

Joan is really a demon these days. She's got big eyes and rabbit ears and doesn't miss a thing. Yesterday she upset a bottle of ink on the dining room table that mother had just put down and today she pulled a dozen eggs on the floor. They were all smashed this time but thank goodness mother had not put them far enough on the table so we went scot-free. You can come home any time darling and look after this whirlwind for a while.

Do you know you've written 175 blue forms up to March 14th? Aren't you really wonderful honey?!! I counted them today as I was making up another bundle. Isn't the war news very very good? It can't be much longer now and as Matthew Hutton has just said, "It's all over but some of the fighting", which seems to sum up the situation in a nutshell. Are you on your leave now? Haven't heard for a week. That's all for now. Hugs and kisses from Joan and all my love my darling for ever and always. Sure miss you. Love again, Peg

April 2, 1945

Dearest Peg

I'm certainly away behind in my mail and must apologize darling. No good excuse.

Wrote you last Thursday night because I thought the next day was Saturday and it was Friday.

Friday I entertained George Elliot. In the morning we went down and scrounged a motor launch and took quite a little run on the lough. It was a windy day and quite rough but it was fun banging along over the waves. In the afternoon went out to Necarne and looked the place over and then had a few Guinness in Irvinestown and then steak and eggs. On return I went back to the usual routine of repairing erks who had fallen from their bikes.

George got away Saturday morning and was busy on Saturday afternoon and evening. Sunday noon went out to visit the old S/L at Ballinamallard and we drifted down to the local and had a Guinness and incidentally annoyed his wife tremendously by making him late for dinner. He came in and announced this morning that a pall of gloom was hanging over his head at home but didn't get too down-hearted about it. Last night played darts in the mess until midnight and then Frank Grant and I came back and fried eggs and had snacks until 2.30 (with Robert lying in bed screaming about the noise at 5 minute intervals). Suddenly we realized that this morning we went on double British Summer Time and so had to set the clocks ahead an hour. Got very fatigued all at once when the time changed from 2.30 to 3.30 so abruptly and so my excuse for not writing last night.

Got a nice long letter from you today. Thanks for sending the money. Should get confirmation shortly from the bank. Glad to hear you started on your spring wardrobe. Don't know whether I approve of your change of hair do (not that you aren't beautiful any way you wear your hair) – just throwing in my two cents worth to try to boss the little woman around. Wonder how all the boys – Bill Bothwell, Ron Edmonds etc, like their civilian clothes – lucky fellows. Don't envy them too much until this phase of the war is over but after that I'm going to do my best to do likewise.

Don't worry about me doing anything rash to annoy the clots who manage my business for me. I'm going to be most cooperative until I get back to the loving arms of my wife.

Well honey, am just about ready to hit the hay. The pay off was today – a sanitary inspector came about 5 PM and Hampton had to play the genial host. He wanted to see the camp and so have spent 2½ hours walking him through the various messes and sewage plants (actually we walked *by* the latter). Will sign off – news is awful good. Miss you very much. All my love, Hamp

April 3, 1945

Dearest Hamp

Yes siree! Your wife is just as big a bum as you are. Here it is Tuesday and I wrote to you last on Friday. Well not much has happened since then. Saturday night the gang came over and we played this Nertz game and then ate. No one had any news as no one had had mail for a week or so.

Sunday being Easter I was appointed to represent our family at the morning service so donned my fur coat and winter hat and went on my way. It was quite cold and anyway my new outfit wasn't ready (alterations not finished at the store). Some of the vainer members of my sex braved the cold winds in spring suits anyway. PS – I think they froze. The service was quite good but I lost the trend of the sermon after the first few minutes as I was wondering just what you'd be doing at that particular time. Stayed home the rest of the day and night as I was tired from our strenuous Nertz game of the night before. Monday morning I went down town and had my sutures removed and a good thing too coz something tasted like a dead herring.

By the way Ernie Watt is a Lieut Commander in the RCNVR and hasn't been at the hospital for about 9 months or so – don't know where he's stationed. I meant to tell you that but it slipped my mind. Effie Dunn Gain and Ethel Liebermann Fried (she's been divorced and remarried again to a USAAF doctor) are the anaesthetists now. After getting my sutures out (and again by the way that extraction cost me $15) I went shopping for lingerie – slips etc. – as my trousseau is wearing out now. Got 2 slips, 1 brassiere and no pants – but don't worry I still have some I can wear honey. Lingerie and stockings are very scarce and about as hard to get as the moon!

In the afternoon I got 2 letters from you which were very welcome indeed. Glad your cigs arrived OK and that reminds me that I sent 900 more yesterday. Last night was our church group so I put in a few boring hours. Have done the wash today and am now writing you while Joan is asleep. Pardon me she just woke up but is playing so I won't bother her. Interruption while I read two letters from my husband that have just arrived. Spring in Ireland sounds very pretty. Our spring is just marked so far by the disappearance of the snow so it's much like late October before a snow storm. The hospital phoned me this afternoon and are absolutely stuck for nurses – none on the registry etc – so as I've already turned them down before I agreed to work from 7 to 11 for a couple of nights – on iiN I think. However as I'm going to Camrose on Saturday they can't work me for too long. Nurses are very scarce all over the Dominion and there's some talk of taking drastic steps about it – like conscription or something I guess. However I'm not worried.

The war news is very good these days and the way things are shaping up is very surprising but it will take them a while to clear up all the rat's nests though. Must go as Joan is beginning to assert herself. She learns a new word everyday but her pet phrase is 'More!' usually said at mealtime. All for now my darling. Joan sends big hugs and kisses. All my love as always, Peg

April 5, 1945

Dearest Peg

Late again – practically as usual in the past 10 days. Have not been doing anything of note and have no good excuses or otherwise – except laziness and lack of subject matter.

Got a nice long letter from you today. You seem to be getting around to that wisdom tooth and by now I hope it is just a memory. Hope it didn't cause you too much annoyance and sorry again honey that I couldn't attend and hold your hand. Very glad to hear about the honors being bestowed upon your Dad – he certainly deserves them. Your mother and he should have a very pleasant holiday in May.

A new medical officer came in on Monday. A Scotch lad who has been in India for the past three years. He just settled with his wife and child in Liverpool and then got sent here to relieve. Naturally he is not too pleased with the posting and I can certainly appreciate his feeling. He is an excellent type though and I think we will get along very well while he is here with me – for 2 weeks. The old S/L is away on leave and will be back in about 18 days – not much change while he is away and things go on about as usual.

Got a notice from the bank yesterday that 22 quid plus some shillings had been deposited in my account. Thanks again darling and will try to reform and save money.

Yesterday Bob Bartlett and I went to Irvinestown and had steak and eggs at 6 o'clock and the sat around and I had the odd pint while Bob grumbled about getting home. We arrived back at 8 PM and then played darts and consumed Guinness in the mess until midnight and then went over and ate onion sandwiches. Very good onion but I can taste them better right now that I could last night – they don't improve with age.

The war news is very wonderful these days and it looks like Jerry is down on his knees with the knockout blow coming at any time. Hope he doesn't stave off the inevitable too long.

Bob has 3 more trips to do and then is screened from the squadron and will go to a conversion unit to instruct several months before going home – not a very bright future I'd say.

Got 4 more films from Dad yesterday and also have some more developed. They don't include me very much and when they do I look like a real farmer. My battle dress is beginning to get just a little sloppy and the crotch of my pants hangs around my knees.

Well honey, miss you more and more and look forward to our reunion more every day. Give Joan my love, Hamp

April 7, 1945

Dearest Peggy

Another 2 days and not much to write about. Am sitting here

listening to a corny English comedian on the radio – their jokes and songs are identical with those of American vaudeville 20 years ago and I don't think I'll ever become sufficiently English to appreciate them.

Last night was the squadron party for all ranks. They had about 150 gallons of beer and more – it was a fair amount but the Canadian erks have acquired a tremendous capacity and can drink a gallon to quench their thirst and then wonder when the beer comes on. They heard that the beer was going to be short and so spent time in all the locals on the way and arrived quite high. The dance was held in a hall about 6 miles from here and air women were invited. It was quite a brawl and the WAAFS were chauffeured home about 11 PM which was a good thing. The erks careened about until 1200 and then I beat a strategic retreat with the CO and managed to avoid any casualties.

My new helper, Porter, my Scotch MO looks like he's going to fold and leave me holding the bag. He had amoebic dysentery in India and now feels that vague abdominal unrest presages a recurrence. Think he's more or less building up a case so he can get the hell out of here. Can't say that I blame him and I won't do anything to hold him up if he wants to wangle it.

We have been having a little trouble with our station CO lately and I had to go up and get a strip torn off me by him yesterday. Some of the boys were a little vivacious in the mess the other night and I volunteered to look after them. A couple strayed out of my care though so Hampton was left holding the bag. Didn't worry me at all but its annoying to have someone you have no liking for and who you would have nothing to do with in civilian life telling you what you should be doing along those lines. However it's water under the bridge and the boys are all happy now so things proceed without much worry.

The weather here is warm but remains wet. Am not too cheesed with all as yet but a change would be welcome for a few days. Ike and his boys are certainly rolling us nearer home everyday and hope all continues well.

Miss you a lot darling and think of you very often. Give Joan love and kisses. All my love, Hamp

Dearest Hamp

I am many days behind in my writing again so will see what I can do to make up for it.

We are now in Camrose – came down yesterday. Joan is a good little traveler and amused herself all the trip without wanting to get down off the seat and run around. She had a man in the seat behind us picking up 'Raggy Ann' for her for quite a while – seemed to think he was there just to amuse her so she'd laugh and squeal as she gleefully tossed her doll down again. It's a good thing the trip wasn't any longer though as she was beginning to get a bit restless just as the Camrose water tower came in to sight.

I had a busy week what with getting our things all ready and then working on 3 nights from 7 to 11. I was glad I was coming down though as I would sure hate to work many nights – doesn't appeal to me like it used to even if the night shift isn't as busy as the day shift. I packed up a box to send to you and took it down town Friday afternoon but horror of horrors it was one ounce over 11 pounds so they wouldn't take it so had to bring it home and didn't have time to reduce the ounce. However I'll round up a parcel from here and send you the other when I get home.

Alix and Sandra drove us down to the train and for a wonder it left on the dot so we just made it. Dad met us at the station here – between operations. He had quite a shiner as he had fallen against his bed on Wednesday – but we don't talk about that. He's been in bed all day today as it's too big an effort to move around and his right chest is bothering him again. Joan has made herself right at home but misses me if I disappear for a second – mama's girl you know. Dad had some new toys waiting for her and Mother had Margaret's doll carriage and cradle brought down from the attic so Joan is doing all right for herself.

Last night Joan and I had supper at Mac's and them I came back and put Joan to bed. When she went to sleep Mac and Irene and I did the town. We visited McNulty(?) at the Arlington and picked up a dozen beer then went to Happy Hailes' and had a beer and lunch then on to Gladys and Fred Duggan's and had another beer and then on to Mofitts. It was after 12 by this time but the Groves, Byers (one pair of them) and a few more people dropped in so it turned out to be quite a 'do' and we came home at 4AM. I was the soberest one there and we'd had several scotches and beer before dinner but oh my, what a hangover today. Had morning sickness (from drinking, my love) for the first time since you went away but felt considerably improved after. Just a typical Camrose evening but I certainly couldn't keep up the pace indefinitely. Mac is much thinner, weighs about 185 pounds and Irene is very thin – 114 pounds – so I'm not the only one darling. Joan took to Uncle Mac and made quite a fuss of him and she had a wonderful time playing with Alan and Frank. Today has been quiet fortunately and quite cold as our winter returned again on Thursday. Am continuing on another form. All my love my dearest, Peg

April 8, 1945 – #2

Dearest Hamp

How goes the struggle with you? You are now up to date on all our doings but Mac has asked me to present a certain matter to you so I will. I don't know just what your reaction will be to the idea but Mac said he'd write you too.

It seems that Mac is getting just a little browned off with Dad's tactics. He's never really sober and in poor health generally and makes usual mistakes insulting patients etc. However this is all old stuff to you but just increased in tempo. This is Mac's idea. He wonders if you could apply for a compassionate discharge on the grounds that your Dad's health is very poor and his practice needs you as the war in Europe is almost over this would be the opportune time to start the ball rolling. Mac wants to know just what papers you would need and he can get a letter to the Hon. McKinnon, MP for Edmonton, through Frank Mohler. It seems Mrs Mohler suggested this to Mac. Mac threatened at Christmas time to get another doctor to help him and kind of retire Dad so Dad straightened up for a while but has slipped again. That's the situation and idea in a nutshell. Mac wants you back as soon as possible.

I don't feel that it is my entire responsibility to get into this so I've bound Mac to write you in detail. As I say I don't know just how you'll react to the suggestion. However don't get too het up about it until you hear more about it. Of course the whole thing really rests in your hands, that is, the results if any and I am only going to take one side and that is your side. Whatever you decide to do I'm right with you. Right now my feelings are kind of mixed up as I don't know what your thoughts will be. Sure I'd like you home soon but you will be home soon as the war can't last forever but please my darling for our sake don't jump into something without first considering all the angles and if you'll be doing right by yourself for after all you are really the only one that counts. It seems to me other people are only looking at their side of the picture and not entirely looking at your position. However, I may be wrong. So there it is – make of it what you can.

Arthur Ireland is back but we haven't seen him yet. Rumor has it he was married last night. You may be interested to know that Pete Patrick is in Iceland. Fred Day is in Belgium – some big city. They set up their hospital unit and have nice quarters but the only catch is it's right on 'Robot Row oo Alley'. However with the Canadian advance that may quiet down. Jack Day is with the Canadian Army in Holland.

Mother is fine and Mac and Irene just dropped in on their way home after making rounds.

That seems to be all for now. I hope this letter isn't too disturbing. Perhaps tomorrow will see a letter from you again so another week has gone by again. Am wondering if you've got your leave yet. What's this about you expecting a posting to Europe? Dad was asking me if I'd heard anything further. You'd probably get more activity over there eh honey? Well dearest buggerlugs, here we are at the end of the paper again. Bye for now. All my love, always and forever, Peg

April 9, 1945

Dearest Peg

Today was mail day and got your letter of Mar 30. Glad to hear you are minus a wisdom tooth without too much trouble and hope the other one has gone by the board by the time you get this letter. The daughter seems to be more of a going concern every time you write and would certainly like to be around to help you manage her. Hope your stay in Camrose isn't too wet and hectic.

Am writing this at noon from my little cubby hole off the courtyard of the castle where sick quarters is billeted. It was an awful struggle to get to work today – beautiful warm sunshine and as you wander through the castle grounds on the way to work spring seems to have arrived all at once. The leaves are all out, birds singing, primroses all over the place and the rhododendrons in blossom. Ah spring! –with no Peggy to share it with – the day will come though.

Last night the MO at a nearby station developed a pleurisy so had to lease lend Porter to the unit since the chap who is ill was there by himself. That leaves me here alone again so have to keep the nose to the grindstone. It seems funny to think that we used to have 3 MOs at Claresholm and now don't think much of being here alone on an operational unit with twice as many personnel. Guess the war must be tapering off. The news is certainly good and I'm just waiting for the Russians to start rolling again across the Oder on the Berlin front. That should quite finish them and we can look ahead a bit and start estimating when we'll get home.

Got a letter from Margaret today. She says Joan is a real girl child and quite an infant. Margaret didn't seem to have had a very hilarious time in Camrose – it certainly amazed me to hear of Bill carting Paw off to church on Easter Sunday. I'm ashamed to say that I didn't realize that Sunday was here almost for the days go on without much change on the 7th day.

Don't care much about leave now and certainly don't look forward to it with any great anticipation. Hope to bum around London and take some pictures of the spots one wants to remember but have no ambition apart from that.

Have just finished perusing the book 'The Sun is My Undoing'. About 1200 pages and I got through it in about 5 hours – you can imagine how much was read – about ½ a page in 10 kept the continuity of the plot.

Bob is flying again today and then has only one more trip before becoming tour expired.

Have just finished my afternoon's routine and am about to go down to the launch and visit one of our satellite camps across the lough. The weather holds so it should be a pleasant trip with bags of sunshine for a change.

Well, honey, will sign off with love and kisses. Tell the daughter not to get too bad before her old man returns. All my love, Hamp

Dearest Hamp,

No mail as yet but may be in tomorrow. I wonder what you are doing – the same old stuff or have you got your leave yet?

It is Mac's birthday today but haven't seen any of them. Irene was cooking a roast of beef at Mac's request for noon dinner but at 1.30 PM he hadn't arrived home. However he had a free afternoon and several crocks so I guess they are pretty busy.

Last night was Irene's bridge club at her place so I was invited to sub. It was the first time I'd played duplicate bridge and I really enjoyed it. However I'm still no whiz at the game but am catching on more each time I play.

Monday afternoon Mother and I and Joan went up to Irene's for coffee as Mother had not seen the house since the woodwork was painted white. It makes quite a difference-the rooms look much bigger and brighter. Monday night I went out on a country call with Mac and Irene.

Today Dad took Joan and me for a ride to the hospital and we met the Sisters. Joan didn't take to their outfits and although she didn't actually cry she certainly showed them that they couldn't rush her[17]. She climbed up to Dad and clung to him so tightly that no one could have pried her away.

I told Mac I had written to you and he says he won't be writing until he gets your reaction as he doesn't want you to think that he's making or wanting you to do anything you don't want to do. His idea is mainly to eliminate a long wait after the war before your discharge.

I spoke to your mother about our holiday when you get back and she doesn't think it's a good idea as its not necessary and just sentimental rot. She too thinks you should come right home and let Mac have a holiday before he cracks up. So looks like we'll have to wait a while for our second honeymoon eh darling? However we'll get it in someday.

The war news is getting better all the time and makes everything look brighter. People over here are getting optimistic again but with some restraint as they don't want to be let down as they were in the fall by the turn of events.

Joan is learning more words each day and knows which is the goat head in the den.[18] She is quite intrigued with the heads on the wall and the bird in the cage. She fell down over her own feet tonight and cut her lip again – only inside this time but it is kind of swollen so she looks a bit queer.

That seems to be all for now. Hope to get mail soon so I can gossip with you. Hugs and kisses from Joan. All my love darling, forever and always yours, Peg

April 11, 1945

Dearest Peg

A long letter from you today of April 3rd – things seem to be going as per usual with you and you manage to get your days filled in. It's amazing how the time passes, isn't it? The days seem to disappear surprisingly rapidly although one isn't occupied normally the time doesn't actually drag. Don't go back to nursing Peggy – I really wish you wouldn't unless you really want to and are bored with life. It's not a good life and the daughter is enough of an individual now that she needs her mom to kind of overlap and make up for the lack of male parentage. Do as you please but I'd really be much happier if you didn't return to the routine at the UAH.

Your Easter parade seemed to be a little subdued. Mine was more so as I told you and have already confessed that I didn't go to church.

The old S/L came back from his few days in England and will be on leave around here for the next 10 days. Tomorrow night I'm going out to dinner there and will probably roll home at some late hour after retiring to the local for a few after dinner. Am looking forward to it for a change.

Today woke up with a head cold but am not suffering overly. Spent the morning on the lough waiting for an aircraft in trouble to come in. It was too foggy to see it and it finally got down with no incidents.

Tuesday afternoon went out with the CO in his launch to visit one of our satellite units across the water. It was a beautiful day a thoroughly enjoyed the run. He and I are quite sociable again so all is OK.

The war news is wonderful these days and maybe I'd better give you these instructions that some crude bugger is reputed to have written his wife. 'I'm coming home soon. Take a good look at the floor because you won't be seeing it for a while after I get there.' Disgusting what-Spring must have had him in her clutches.

Robert isn't waterborne yet from his days flying. Hope he lands OK in the midst of our scattered showers.

Well darling, love you more and more (keep saying it because I do). Miss you. Give Joan the big hello from her old man. Love, Hamp

April 13, 1945

Dearest Peg

Midnight of Friday 13th and nothing of note has happened. Went flying today with Bob on his last trip. It was quite interesting with shipping and [illegible]. It was very rough in our area however with high winds and sporadic squalls. I wasn't very enthusiastic about the noon meal however and then the galley stove went up in flames and we grabbed an extinguisher and squirted carbon tetrachloride all over the place. That finished me completely and immediately proceeded to have a small ill. Recovered without incident and carried on but the appetite fell off a little. About 11 hours out and Bob as happy as hell to be all through – don't blame him.

The Air Commodore in medical charge of coastal command visited yesterday. Showed him around the place and got him away. He made me quite pleased with Hampton by handing out bouquets on work and cooperation in handling the RAF squadrons here – in other words – 'keep it up'.

President Roosevelt's death was really a shock and hope it doesn't affect the course of events at all – it shouldn't but one never knows.

The war news is really wonderful – things look better every day.

This is a poor letter as usual. Four people are in the room listening to the midnight news and making rude comments and rubbing it in about me shooting a bird today. It isn't much consolation to have a couple of others ill with you – it doesn't make you feel any better. Can sympathize with the lack of appetite provoked by our cyclone's gestation.

Bob is in the midst of cursing at Stewart who is the navigator of the crew. Dave Stewart is very young in a way but very blasé – Dave's moaning about having a damp dream last night and having the object of his affection in the dream to be a very homely acquaintance when it might as well have been Hedy Lamar or someone similar – quite an educating discussion don't you think?

Well darling will sign off and hit the hay and hope to see you one of these days before long. Give my regards to your Mother and Dad. Much love. Many kisses. All my thoughts, Hamp

April 14, 1945

Dearest Hamp

Today was really a wonderful day. Got a letter from you. The 12 days without mail has been like 12 years – it almost seemed as though you weren't even in existence – which is just a plain dumb thing to think. The last few nights I've been dreaming all kinds of mixed up silly dreams about you – the kind of dreams that leave you a wreck in the morning – so I figured mail or some news from you would be coming soon.

Glad to hear you're getting or rather thinking about the days when you can get out of the service – perhaps you won't mind getting the letter re Mac's idea. Have been kind of worried about that as I wrote some things I shouldn't have about Mac. Am just getting to know him and he's a swell guy. From the way Margaret talked one would think he was starting to follow in Dad's footsteps and I was beginning to feel I didn't want to come down here to live for fear we'd end up the same way – one thing leading to another was the idea. But now I see I was wrong. Mac does drink quite heavily when he gets started but he can lay off it for weeks at a time and then too he doesn't get much sleep – called out about 3 times on Wednesday night and answering the phone 6 or 7 times from midnight until 7 AM which is quite common I gather. After Mac's birthday Dad got after him for being drunk and made him drink 3 glasses of water. Mac was mad as he claims he was sober so he threatened to leave as soon as you come home but he told me he really didn't mean it. McNulty was just too good to Mac I guess. Mac sure hopes you'll get a discharge as soon as you can so he can get back to a more normal existence and Dad is very willing to obtain any certificates necessary regarding his health so that's that I guess.

Thursday night Joan wouldn't go to sleep for 2 hours and as I can't leave her without a big fuss and as she can climb out of bed, I sat in the dark. She sleeps in the single bed without the bars as she would probably fall over them. I put two straight-backed chairs up to the bed so she can't roll out but that doesn't stop her from climbing down if she's awake so she usually ends up in bed with me. After getting Joan to bed I went down to Mac's and out in the country with them to bring in a patient. Then came home myself. Yesterday was a quiet day and as it took 2 hours to get her settled for bed again I stayed home and went to bed early – 10 PM. This afternoon Joan and I are going to Ann Schloss's for coffee. Have you ever had rum and milk? I had some last night it it's very, very smooth. Try it sometime honey.

Terrible news about Roosevelt wasn't it? His death couldn't have come at a worse time. It's too bad he couldn't live to see the end of this.

Well darling I feel much happier today thanks to your letter. Sure miss you a hell of a lot. Camrose doesn't seem right without you. All my love dearest, Peg

April 16, 1945

Dearest Peg,

Two long letters from you today – of April 8th from Camrose. You sound as if things are normal there with Paw making a fool of himself and the Smith Juniors proceeding in their usual fashion. Don't know what to do about that question of trying to get home to help Mac. Am going to sit and think about it for a couple of days and then will write and let you know what is to do. I'm going on leave a week today and will go up to London and then will feel out the situation and see how the land lies. It's pretty hard to know what to do isn't it darling? Figure on going in and talking it over with Noble who is the man in charge of

515

our RCAF overseas and getting his ideas on the actual potentiality of anything I might attempt to do. Am not fussy about going home on those grounds at this phase of the war but we do have our future to contend with.

Was to have written you last night but was too lazy – went to bed early and tried to give my cold some considerate treatment for a change – no avail however so will just cough along until it goes by itself.

Yesterday afternoon went out to tea with the local gentry. These are some of the local land owners (who incidentally own the castle where we have our sick quarters). I got backed into a corner where I couldn't refuse to give some lectures to the local Red Cross which Mrs Herman sponsors. They have a lovely home and it will be very pleasant to establish their acquaintance. Unfortunately my time is so tied up that I can't get out and have had to turn down a couple of dinner invitations there – much to my regret. They are a nice couple and have traveled widely over the world and are very interesting – except Mrs Herman talks too much.

Tomorrow is the anniversary of our day of parting. In a way it seems difficult to believe that one year ago I looked at you from the platform of the sleeping car as you stood beside the train and tried not to weep. The year is now easy to look back on – but almost unbearable to look forward to. I hope the next months are not long and also not too bad to look back on.

The daughter's 18 months old tomorrow. Amazing that our infant gets up the world isn't it? Well honey, the midnight news is on and I hope the new Russian offensive goes forward well. Keep our fingers crossed. If they break through the war will be over before this letter arrives.

Miss you very much these days. Love you more and more. All my love, Hamp

Written in pencil on envelope: Bramshot Military Hospital

April 16, 1945

Dearest Hamp,

Tomorrow you will have been gone a year. Just imagine that. It's quite easy isn't it darling. And tomorrow Joan will be 18 months old. It should be some kind of an anniversary I guess, but just exactly what kind is hard to decide. Much better to celebrate the anniversaries of your home coming for that will be something. Right honey?

Saturday afternoon Joan and I went with Dad inspecting dairies – milk producing farms I should say and Joan was quite taken with the cows, horses, dogs and chickens – also the ride. At night I went down to Irene and Mac's and we had rum and milk and rye and water and then Mac and I decided it would be fun to ship up a new recipe so after much discussion we finally made some kind of goulash. This "har" is the recipe old thing: 1 can of clams, 1 can of mushroom soup. First simmer the clam juice and add 4 celery stalks chopped, 4 strips of bacon, 1 small onion chopped. Cook for a few minutes then add the chopped clams, mushroom soup and 1/2 can of milk. Bring to boil and serve to all who think they can take it. It was really quite good but awfully filling. Irene settled for a sandwich so Mac and I finished our own dish. Mac suggests we try mushroom soup and lobster meat next time but I donno. Are you impressed with our culinary tastes?

Sunday was a quiet day. Went for a short ride but stayed close to home and played bridge with Ma at night and she beat me by 50 points. Today has been quite uneventful so far so will wander down to Mac and Irene's and try to drum up some activity.

The new maid arrived on Saturday – about 5 ft. 9 inches and 200 pounds. Awfully huge and Joan is quite impressed with the Amazon. Dad of course got off to a good start by asking her (Jenny) if she wanted to be paid by the week, month or pound. Trust Dad. Everyone held their breath until Jenny laughed so now he calls her Jenny Lind – the Swedish Nightingale. All very well but she's Ukrainian.

Joan certainly takes to Grandpa. He takes her for rides around the block and out walking. He's the only one she'll go with – outside of me – so he's awfully pleased and so far has stuck to beer only – with no signs of falling off the beer wagon to search for whiskey! It has been very pleasant down here this time with only the regular sputters and spats which are just routine anyway.

The weather has been cold this weekend with snow flurries and cold strong winds. Joan has developed a mild case of sniffles but nothing serious.

I plan to stay another 10 days and then must go home as Mother is leaving for the East the 11th of May. That's all for now my darling. Hope the rainy weather is over for you and that you get your leave soon. Hugs and kisses from Joan. With all my love dearest. As always, Peg

April 18, 1945

Dearest Hamp,

A very good day today – two letters from you dated March 27 & 29. Got your IOU just fine and will save the letter (Ha! Ha!) as usual. Mother was glad you got your Easter parcel in time for Easter. The leave business must be pretty hard to wangle, but I guess you'll get it sooner or later, eh honey?

You asked several questions most of which have been answered by now. Joan's eczema is still flaring up but really nothing compared to her first bout. Right now her two year old molars are ready to break through so that may have something to do with it. Mac says she should be over it all by the time she is two. By that time you'll be able to see for yourself I hope, eh darling?

Showed Mac and Irene all your pictures on Monday night – brought them down to show off your photography. Came home early with a box of chocolates sent to me by McNulty of the Arlington Hotel. Very nice thought.

Yesterday Joan and I went to the WCL at Irene's. No we're not turning Catholic – it was more of a tea. Joan enjoyed herself with the other kids but when I left the room to help serve tea her face would pucker up when she missed me. Oh my, what a calamity. Mac came home at 5.30 and Joan promptly started to show off and made a big to do of Mac. She played with Joe the new pup, a setter, and really had a wonderful time. Then Mac took Joan outside to do some movies so you will be able to see what she was like at a year and a half. The pay off came when Joan, with her back to the camera, stooped over and wet her pants with quite a stream. The she turned around and stamped in it. Mac was laughing so hard he could hardly take the picture and Irene and I were having hysterics in the front room. It should be quite a picture but won't Joan be embarrassed when she gets older.

518

Tuesday night I went to Schloss's for bridge subbing for Enid Moffitt but at 10 PM I got called home as Joan had wakened up and Mother and Jenny can't handle her. She just won't be quieted down at times. She was so upset that she even had her shoes ready to put on, to go out and look for me I suppose. So that rather broke up my evening as I couldn't go back. Today Joan hasn't let me out of her sight and tonight I had to lie down beside her before she would go to sleep. Guess I'll go through all this again when I go home. Oh well, it won't be for much longer and then we can all settle down to a normal life.

Mac had 3 majors yesterday and took 3 pennies out of a little kid's stomach today. He's been called out every night that I've been here but things are all a bit slacker I understand.

Another Victory loan on Monday. Each one I hope is the last one. Not that I mind giving or rather investing my money but I always hope the war will be over. Oh well, why should I complain. Really haven't any grounds for it except that you're away and that's enough for me.

Joan isn't swearing at her old lady yet – at least not so I can understand. Another month or so and she should be really talking as each day adds another word to her vocabulary. Oh yes, I must tell you I gained 3 pounds last week due to all the food I've eaten. One just can't get along without an appetite down here. Be sure and remember some of those dreams so you can tell me about them eh honey? That's all for now. Hugs and kisses from Joan. All my love darling. Always – Peg

April 20, 1945

Dearest Peggy

Have again skipped a day in my writing and no good excuses. Things have been going as usual except we had a few days of glorious weather with temperatures of July instead of April. It's the first time I've seen dust in the air since I came here.

Wednesday I took off and drove up to Londonderry with the old man (Pierce). His two daughters came along and we had a grand day. The girls are about 13 & 10 and nice kids. We dropped them with some of his friends and then drove to Limavady where he was stationed for about two years. After arriving we visited all of his cronies who seemed to all possess a bottle of Irish whiskey. We had innumerable social rounds, s delicious dinner, visited at the local hospital and drove off for the evening with the doctor. It was a grand day and I enjoyed all of it. About 11 PM we started for home and the old boy had just about had it so I drove home. I won't say in very good shape but we came home in fine style and screamed along up and down the Irish hills via Castleclerg and then Omagh and home to Irvinestown. Spent yesterday trying to recover and at the same time introduce F/L Miller to the station. He is the new MO who finally came in to take over one of the other squadrons. Porter who he's relieving is leaving tomorrow.

Monday I go on leave and am really looking forward to it. So far have scrounged a trip to Belfast but hope to possibly fly to England. It is a hell of a journey across the Irish Sea because it takes about 36 hours to get to London and is a very tiresome journey. If you can fly to southern England it is about 4 hours so the difference is considerable.

Pardon the writing but Bob is using the table so I am writing this on my bed. Also about half ways through Bill Porter and Frank Grant and Hoop Cunningham wandered in very drunk and just back from leave so it's taken about an hour to disperse them. Well darling, will sign off with all my love. Not a good letter but will try to improve tomorrow. Hamp

Sunday April 22, 1945

Dearest Hamp,

Well sir, according to the news V day is almost upon us but somehow I don't feel too elated. I suppose I just can't grasp the full significance of such a thing but it really will be terrific. It is hard to believe though isn't it darling?

Got more letters from you on Thursday and Friday so those were exceptionally happy days. Was glad you got a new MO and hope you can get your leave before he develops a good case of dysentery for himself. It must be pretty grim to have it at that.

We haven't been doing anything very exciting but manage to keep busy. Have been up to Mac and Irene's the last two or three nights for a while as everyone retires to bed so early and I am just wakening up about that time. Mac got hold of some fresh crab on Friday so that put in a good hour or so as we nibbled crab and guzzled beer. Last night we went to Gladys and Fred Duggan's (they're expecting again any day now). Happy and Mildred Hailes were there so we all played poker. I sat between Mac and Fred so had real good advice and came home with $1.06 up. Don't know how the others made out as I was called home again at 11 PM because Joan had wakened up. However I really didn't mind as I was getting tired anyway.

Yesterday afternoon Mother had Irene, Eileen Duggan and Isobel Brown in for tea and bridge – just for me. It was a rainy day so it proved to be a very good idea.

Joan is getting her picture taken tomorrow – sure hope she behaves this time. She gets cuter every day and has acquired new words – 'bisc' means biscuit, 'Dick' means canary, 'Dick's ba' means Dick's bath, 'Dick's be' means Dick's in bed, 'Toot-too go' means train gone and so forth. She's starting to repeat what you say to her now but so far just in the voice inflection but no real words. However it's all a good sign I guess. Joan sure has Dad around her little finger although he claims she hasn't got him cornered. All she has to do is pull at his trouser leg and say 'coat-go' two or three times and off they go even if it's only around the block. He bought her an ice cream cone but as she'd never had it in a cone before she didn't know quite how to manage it. But she learns quickly.

My ma & pa are going east a week Wednesday so I'll be going back to the city on Friday. As I've said before it's been a real good stay this time and here's hoping I won't have to make many more visits without you. That's all for now. Sure miss you a lot and as usual wish you were here, but it *can't* be long now. All my love my darling and hugs and kisses from Joan. Always, Peg

April 22, 1945

Dearest Peggy

Well, I'm now off on leave and really looking forward to leaving the place. Have been busy cleaning up my odds and ends and they seem to be quite numerous. It's a lovely sunny day and I hope the weather lasts.

Plan to go to London for a few days and see Ritchie and drop in to headquarters and talk to Noble re the situation in Camrose. After that I'm going to meander – may go up to Yorkshire or Lancashire and bum around for two or three days. I have eleven days but will be traveling for nearly three of them so it actually doesn't leave a great deal of time for ordinary perambulating around the area.

Bob Bartlett is going with me as far as London and then is going on to Bristol to stay with relatives. If my time is sufficient I will go up to Blackburn and Darwen – will see how time sorts itself out.

This note is kind of a scrawl but am hustling to get off and the padre who is here listening to the news is going to take it down and mail it for me. (Our post office is about 1/3 of a mile from here, on the other side of the hill).

Well darling, wish you were coming with me but with the current news it may not be too long.

Give Joan hugs and kisses for me. All my love, Hamp

April 26, 1945

Dearest Hamp

Joan is having her afternoon nap so I'm sitting on the bed writing an overdue letter to you. The last few days have been quite busy and the weather has been awful. We have an inch and a half of snow on the ground and the temperature is around 30° so it's not much like spring. I got Joan's picture taken at Langbell's on Monday afternoon and the proofs are quite good so it should make a good picture. She is smiling and showing her teeth in the both of them – one is kind of wistful and the other real happy so am having both developed. Will be sending you one of each when they are done. Monday night Mac phoned and invited me down for crab so down I went and then home to bed. Tuesday went quite quickly but didn't do much – Irene came over for coffee in the afternoon. It was bridge club at Verna Byers at night and everyone had to dress up in something old so I wore one of Mama's old evening dresses – flowered chiffon about 1928 style and made quite a sensation as I really looked quite stupid. However it didn't interfere with my game for in one hand the first table went down – 1000 and the second – 700 and I went down – 50. Pretty good for me I figured. It was duplicate bridge and each table plays the same hand as you no doubt know. And yes sir, I played the hand all by myself with no help too! I'm gradually getting the drift of the game but I'll freely admit I'm no whiz – just lucky at times. Yesterday afternoon Irene Byers had a tea for me which was very nice. After meeting the same people so many times this visit I feel as though I know a few people in Camrose now so it won't be too bad when we come to stay. Last night Mac and Irene invited me down to meet John and Alice Bill (Alice Majaky ?spelling). The Schlosses were there and we saw home movies. One role had the pictures of us taken last year. It's hard to believe that Joan was ever that small. The pictures were good though and it was swell to see you in action again old dear. Made me quite homesick for you. It was quite a wet night inside with Mac having himself quite a time with the women – all except me as I was a relative or so Mac said as he more or less apologized for ignoring me so Irene and I made lunch and were more or less the solitary drinkers. Being ignored didn't worry me at all though. It will seen funny when you come home and I've a man again to look after me at parties instead of me playing solitaire all the time. I'm going to be awfully mad if you look at another woman the way Mac does some times – so take warning dear buggerlugs you!

Joan is really quite a toughie. We were out the other afternoon where another little girl was – about 4 years – and Joan pulled her hair and pushed her around considerably before I could stop an undeclared war. And this morning in a store down town she walked up to a little boy and grabbed his coat and the two stood glaring at each other. Wonder where she gets all these tricks?

We are going back to Edmonton tomorrow and sure hope there's mail. Have had 5 letters from you since coming down which is quite good but they are about 3 weeks old or so by the time they arrive. Dad sent you 4 more films today and has 4 more to send. Flash – I now weigh 105 pounds. Good eh honey? The war news is really good now so we should be seeing you in a few more months. Hugs and kisses from Joan and all my love as always, Peg

PS The Mac Young's now have a daughter as of April 22nd.

Langbell's picture of Joan, April 1945

April 29, 1945

Dearest Hamp

Here we are back in Edmonton. Had a pleasant surprise waiting for us. The pictures you packed up away back in November arrived and in good shape and were the pictures of Ireland under the snow. It looks as though it was really cold but very pretty if you were in the mood to look at nature's handiwork. All the pictures were very good and I was thrilled to get them. Thanks a lot honey and sure I'll put them in your album. Must say you look as though you're thriving – Ha! Ha!

Margaret and Bill met us at the train for which we were grateful as it was nearly 7 PM when we arrived. The most astounding news from the home front was the surprise that Mrs Norton (Bill's mother) had remarried. Bill was still slightly baffled but Margaret seemed quite pleased about the whole thing.

Joan hadn't forgotten the old home here and so slipped back into the old routine, that is all except for going to bed without me being in the room. She got rather spoiled at Camrose as she could get out of bed easily down there. The first night at home she cried for over two hours and hung tightly to me when I went in the room. And last night the same thing started again only she didn't cry quite so hard. About half an hour of that and she stopped so I thought 'Good! The ordeal is over', but I was wrong. The next minute Joan was running into the dining room. Yes, Daddy, she had climbed out of her crib. That's our daughter darling. Nothing stumps her. She climbed out 3 times and then I got real mad and finally stayed in the room until she went to sleep. Tonight I decided to leave the side of the crib down so she won't kill herself and now after putting her gently back to bed 8 times she's finally asleep with 2 dolls, 2 teddy bears and a string of beads – for comfort I guess. Joan is a funny one to handle. Getting cross or spanking her has no effect on her other than making her twice as determined not to cooperate. I usually warn her 3 times and then spank her which usually has the required effect but this business of not going to sleep required different tactics as she was afraid I would leave her. So every time she appeared tonight I would say, 'Why hello, how are you?' Isn't it time you were in bed?' At which she would shake her head so I took her by the hand and led her back to bed. And after 8 times she finally got the idea. This child training sure requires a lot of patience which I don't always have so the training works both ways I guess.

Thursday at Camrose was Joan's bad day. She fell off her toilet seat which she was using to help her reach something and scraped the skin off her back. Then we went to Irene's to a tea and Paddy Groves pushed her down the stairs and she skinned her forehead and got a big bump. Then during the night she fell out of bed so it was quite a time. I'll try to keep her in one piece until you get back but it's a job darling.

The war news is too hopeful these days with all the rumors flying about. I'll probably drag on for a few more weeks but there's no question as to the outcome now. Alix has gone to the coast with Sandra so it will be quite lonely when Ma & Pa go East on Wednesday. The mail is sure punk these days. I'm a month behind on your activities. Sure miss you. All my love and hugs and kisses from Joan, as always – Peg

Letters to Hamp were addressed to 'F/L Smith CH, C10858, # 423 Squadron, R.C.A.F Overseas'. Letters to Peggy were addressed to 'Mrs C H Smith, 11024-89th Ave, Edmonton, Alberta, Canada'. Most of Peggy's letters to Hamp had 'Bramshott Military Hospital' hand scribbled in pencil across the front of the envelope.

May 2, 1945

Dearest Hamp

So you're almost finished your leave now honey. I hope you had a good time doing what you wanted to do and when and where. Yes I finally got mail and am up to date again. It seems the English mail wasn't getting through at all – the weather I guess – and when it did arrive I got your latest letters one day –April 20 & 22 – and the forerunners – April 9-16 – the next day. I knew you were OK but it's a relief to be absolutely certain and assured isn't it old dear. V day should be almost any day now. So many things have happened this week that it is hard to keep up with the times but it looks like a grand finale this time. And what a grand finale eh?

This past few days have been busy for me. Monday afternoon I went over to see Margaret and family and keep them up to date on Camrose. David is a big boy but too fat to crawl yet – he is trying to though and he has a tooth – an upper one. Margaret told Dad off when she was down so she's not exactly the loved daughter right now but she claims she doesn't care anyway. Time is a great healer they say so this will take its course and everything will probably be the same again. In the evening we drove out to the Highlands to look at some lots that Margaret and Bill seem interested in. They're talking of building etc. Oh yes and it was on Monday that I supported the Victory Loan for $800. Paid $600 cash – $450 of that was my legacy – and $200 on time. I really went too far out on a limb I think as I've $5 in the bank now but have enough for this month and then I get another cheque – I sure hope!

Tuesday afternoon I dug, built and carried sand for Joan's sandbox and is she ever pleased. The days are real hot now and Joan is out all the time even fussing when I bring her in for meals but she is a real tired girl at night and so sleeps like a log. She's getting quite a tan and with her spirit she's a very good Indian – with blond hair. Thank you for that darling! Maybe we'll be able to make a lady of her in time and with due patience. Tuesday night I went over to the hospital to see Carol Young and she's quite pleased with herself for having a girl – then on to the Junior White Circle for our club meeting.

Today I went downtown and paid Joan's and my insurance for this year ($54.49). Then as I was walking through Eaton's I saw two summer wash dresses in the Young Girl's Dept I liked and as they were size 14 I bought them and believe it or not they fit without any alterations. Sure! Imagine your wife buys dresses in the children's department. Don't you feel like a cradle snatcher? Do you still love your child wife Bumbo? Then I went to the bank and deposited part of my cheque and it was then I found out that when the insurance company collects I'll have $5 left. Boy can I spend the money eh honey?

Mother and Dad left for the East tonight so we ate all alone again and Alix is away. Oh my! Dad put up a wire fence between our yard and Henderson's after supper – with my help – and was still packing when the taxi came. That's my Pop with his quiescent ulcer. I gave mother $50 toward her trip as a Mother's Day present so she may have a bit better time.

Joan has just wakened up and is out of bed as I am afraid to leave the side up now that she can climb out so had better go and see what is what. She sure is a Mama's girl now but Mama can't handle her. I guess she's got my number. She is very hard to handle right about now. Yes I'm back out. Joan is still awake and the pitter-patter of little feet means that she's up again. It's a damn nuisance. At one time the crib would keep her in even if she cried but now it doesn't so you get quite annoyed when you have to put her back to bed 8 or 9 times in the evening and then 8 or 9 times if she wakes up during the evening but guess miracles don't happen suddenly so I'm going to have to work on this one. Well dear husband it looks as though with a bit of luck you'll be home by fall. It's something to think about eh honey? Joan sends you more hugs and kisses. You'll have a lot to collect. I sure miss you and love you more and more. Always, my darling – Peg

Dearest Peggy

Things are all back to normal. I'm back from leave in the rain and am in the process of cursing at the bloody fire.

First I must apologize for being such an awful bum and not writing to you while I was on leave. Never seemed to make connections and I was just too shiftless.

I left for London two weeks ago tomorrow. Went down with Bob Bartlett. We spent Sunday night in Belfast at the Canadian Legion and then after stamping around the streets all morning doing a bit of window shopping in the midst of which I thoroughly surprised us both by going in and buying a pair of grey flannels. We went to a show and then dashed for the Larne boat train. On arriving at the barrier we discovered that we were routed via Horsham and the boat didn't leave until 7 PM instead of 4 PM. However it was well worth the wait since we sailed from Belfast itself and although we sat up all night in the lounge of the ship it was better than transferring at Larne and Stranraer. We arrived at Horsham near Liverpool in the early hours and then it was 6 hours to London.

As soon as we arrived I went to Knightsbridge and contacted Ritchie. He informed me that he had a flat with a spare bed so my problem was solved as far as accommodation went. The first evening he and I and 2 dentists named Mac Lien and Tim Ryan went on a pub crawl around the pubs and then home. Wednesday morning I went down to headquarters and saw G/C Noble who is our chief MO in these parts. I asked him his advice and explained the Camrose situation to him quite frankly. He said it was quite likely a large part of the RCAF would be home by summer although it was indefinite as to how many MOs would go. They might go home with the troups on the basis of seniority overseas. With that scheme I would have a 50/50 chance of being home before fall but it's rather vague just what the situation will be. He said that if I felt I should be at home to submit the detail in writing and he would do all he could to push it along. Therefore I'm going to write Mac and tell him to put it in writing and send it along and will proceed from there. More to follow. All my love, Hamp

Dearest Peg

The first letter just about answers the Camrose problem. I want more than any thing else in the world to be home with you and more or less start off in Camrose with Joan. I had hoped to kind of get along with the demob but now feel that we have too much of our future at stake to let things slide along. It's kind of taking the easy way out (or at least trying to) but I "couldn't care less" about what anyone might think of the attempt.

After my first days business at headquarters, hung around where Doug works. It is a base accounts and the M.I. room opens out into a K of C lounge which more or less caters to transient personnel coming in to look after their accounts (which everybody does at some time or other). It has genuine coffee and sandwiches and you could buy two packages of peanuts, 2 chocolate bars and a package of gum per day so it is really a treat for the erks on the way by. That evening we had dinner down town and then visited a couple of local pubs and then went up to the Overseas League – a club which operates even in peacetime. There was a bar and dancing but Tim Ryan and I stayed at the bar (because my feet hurt) while Doug and Mac MacLean went up to the dance where hostesses are a bunch of well-meaning English women who volunteer to entertain the forces. After that closed Tim said "Come on over to a good club I know" so the four of us trudge over and each order a scotch. The four drinks cost 28 shillings so I think maybe it isn't a very good club after it cost me £3. So we go home happy.

The next day I went up to the Medical Board which handles all RCAF repats and browsed around since I know 3 or 4 people on the board. While I'm there I get a chap named Whaley to look at my sinuses and we have an x-ray and decide there are pathological changes but not enough to take me home (damn it – points for trying or E for effort or something). That evening the four of us again – went up to the headquarters mess and got quite merry on a lot of good scotch and glared back at a lot of wing commanders and above who frequent the place. After we left Tim says he knows a good pub (I still hadn't learned enough to suspect Tim's "good" places to have a drink). We go there and it costs about 2 quid to get out and Tim meets two of his female acquaintances and says he knows a good spot to go. Doug and I looked at each other and said "Sure Tim" and evaded him by running up an alley to have a leak and then just kept right on going up the alley. More to follow. All my love, Hamp

Number 3 is missing.

May 5 1945, No.4

Dearest Peg

Every noon I met Tim Ryan at a place called the Trevor Arms – a very delightful pub that set up a good lunch. We had several "bitters" as routine and also managed to acquire a little food. It was very pleasant and one of the customs of the country to which I warmly ascribe. Tim and I got along very well and it was with considerable regret that I said goodbye to him on the Saturday night. He is going to Cairo and was going up for embarkation Sunday. However Monday noon when I appeared to pick up Doug there was Tim again – he had been given a week's leave so turned right back to London.

Monday night we felt we should expand our brand of entertainment so we went to the variety – "Strike It Again". It was just fair – supposed to be the best show in town and although I have grown much more tolerant of English humor I still don't like it very much – at least I didn't laugh enough to even out the quid I put out for a seat. However while there I met the nursing sister form the station here who had come on leave. She's a deadly creature – talks too much and is about 38 and getting desperate for a man – keeps on pestering some of our more mature air crew. Got backed into a corner to take her somewhere the next day and so went out to Kew Gardens. The company kind of spoiled it but it was really lovely – the trees were in blossom and just about as nice a spot as I've seen anywhere. Got home from Kew about 4.30 so went to a show and then had a quick lunch and put the girl on a tube and said I was busy for the next few days and that ended my female companionship for the leave. Honestly honey I just cannot be comfortable with anyone of that type or any other when I'm away from you. No one will compare with yourself and you need never worry about me straying off the beaten track. Really say it to hope you'll believe me because I never looked at anyone since I left you and never will.

On Wednesday afternoon I went down to Services London Library, which lends books. For £3 I got 3 books for 3 months and can exchange them as often as I want in that time. Kind of a good arrangement. Will hurray to improve my mind. Wednesday night we did the usual pub-crawl.

Thursday afternoon Day and I went to a Heart Clinic conducted by one of the best cardiologists in London. It was excellent; they had some really good cases. Really enjoyed it and it was quite stimulating. That evening we came home and cooked a steak each on the gas ring. More to follow. All my love, Hamp

Saturday May, 1945, No.5

Dearest Peg

Well we're near up to date – last thing was cooking steak. We used up 2 weeks meat ration each and had a *fair* sized steak. Amazing this county's ability to survive on what it eats in the way of meat.

Came home Friday – yesterday – got into Belfast this morning from Heysham. Managed to get a berth last night and it was quite a treat to sleep lying down while traveling in this country. The boat journey is quite pleasant and it is one of the few places where you can get regular meals while in transit. This morning wandered around Belfast and met a couple of our erks and had a Guinness or two with them and then came back on the train with 3 of our officers, had a steak in Mrs Bothwell's and have now reached the billet and am cursing at the fire as I said.

Bob Bartlett was recalled from London the day after we got down there and is posted to the repat pool in England in a ground job. It's a real break for him now that he's finished his tour.

Sunday After I got back yesterday I collected my mail – 3 lovely long letters from yourself and a letter each from Mother, Dad and Irene. They all told me what a wonderful, charming, thoughtful, capable wife I had and how lucky I was. Their letters weren't news but it's kind of nice to hear everyone shout your praises even if they didn't use anything but minor superlative. Am certainly looking forward to seeing that picture of Joan doing her stuff. Was going to ask you before to get some movies of Joan in action but didn't quite think of that kind of action. If Mac says anything to Joan when she gets bigger we'll give her an old picture of him to use as black mail. He was using a tree and was quite nonchalant since he didn't suspect the camera.

Well, honey, these aren't very good letters but will try to improve and will promise to be a faithful correspondent. Keep cheerful and keep your fingers crossed. Remember everyday I'm away makes me love you that much more. Give Joan all my hugs and kisses and get her housebroken so that if I do manage to persuade her to sit on my lap she won't make me wonder what's so warm and wet. All my love to you darling, Hamp

7th May 1945

Dearest Hamp

Today is the day! Isn't it wonderful! Such a thrill to waken up in the morning and find the allied world celebrating. I knew that as soon as I wakened up that this was V-day – just an indescribable feeling and then the phone rang and it was Margaret to tell me the news. It came at 7.30 AM so there were many people who didn't know until they had got to work so Edmonton received the news quietly and people began to hang out the good old Union Jack. I couldn't settle down to anything and as we are alone it was too quiet so I bundled Joan up and we came out to Margaret's. That's where we are now and Joan is asleep in their bed.

Am behind in my writing again but have had different girls in at night. Was over here for dinner last night and fully intended to write when we got home but discovered there were no more blue forms. Now I'm glad I didn't write before as today deserves a letter to you. What are you doing? Guess you'll be pretty busy patching up the alcoholic casualties eh?

We hear from Camrose that Mac was driving on the sidewalks this AM – a moving van blocking the road was his excuse. Sure am glad I'm not down there as several people will be meeting their Waterloo – or Abeyloo Ha! Ha!

Joan and I are enjoying our being alone very much. It's fun for a week or so to be on your own. The sand pile turned out to be quite a

532

brainwave as Joan is outside all day and by herself most of the time so I can get my work done much quicker. We were at Auntie Lena's for lunch on Friday with Netta and her youngest and Eileen Oldring (married to Ronnie) with her 6 wk old baby so Joan had a busy time. Eddy has been posted to Scotland now.

Saw Alison Boyd McBride Douglas on the street the other day – on leave from Gander Bay Nfld. She claims she enjoys it there but is very busy doing her own work and cooking in their 5 room apt. Isn't that pretty grim darling? and no possibility of a baby to look after either.

So far we haven't had a drink today and it's 4 PM. Pretty good eh honey? But Kay Archibald and Mary Hall are coming over so then we'll start. But I'm not given to riotous celebration of the day. It's great news but I'm just so thankful that this stage is over that that is enough. And now for the Japs eh? Will be waiting for news from you but I don't expect you'll know any more about homecoming than you did before. However it's grand to be able to say I'll see you in a few months and really mean it. Isn't it darling? All our love my dearest with lots of hugs and kisses. Always and forever Peg.

9th May 1945

Dearest Peg

Well, we've finally got the news we have been hoping for so long. The future now lies before us without too much to raise doubts whether we ever would get down to living a normal existence again. It shouldn't be too long darling but we must try to be patient because it will be several months before the RCAF Overseas starts trucking home. I don't think anyone knows for sure how long it will be in spite of some claims and rumours that the majority will be back before August is passed.

V day was really quite flat here. We had no celebrations of any kind on the station because we are still operational here since the U boats are just in the process of giving themselves up. Our lads are flying as much as ever and are escorting the odd U boat to port. Our V day will be announced sometime in the future and the station will then have a 48 hour stand down.

Miller the other MO went home on Sunday for a 48 but just got there at the right time and won't be back until Thurs or Friday. The old S/L is a dead loss so I was duty Joe yesterday but managed to get quite cheerful in the mess last night. Most of the boys went off to the local towns – all those who weren't flying today. All the villages around had all the pubs going full blast and local farmers in for miles around. Dancing in the streets, bonfires, etc.

Managed to get a few casualties last night early in the evening, before midnight. One fractured maxilla, one jerk who put his fist through a train window, minor cuts etc. and even a drunk who didn't know his name or where he lived so he reported to SSQ (station sick quarters). Two WAAFs got hysterical and all in all it was a good day in spite of our lack of celebrating.

Soaked up considerable whiskey between calls last night and about midnight went up to the station commanders house (he and I are on much better terms now) and four of us drank a bottle of whiskey. I got cheerful but was still coping and went back to the mess about 0300 and picked up a couple of the boys and we came back and made toast and fried eggs and sat around until 430 AM. Needless to say sick parade at 0830 got a rather jaundiced eye.

Got two swell letters from you on Monday. Every time I hear from you convince me you are more wonderful than I ever deserved. Hope your victory celebrations weren't too solitary with all away. We'll have a private celebration of our own one of these days.

Have just listened to the account of VE throughout England. Certainly wish I had happened to hit in London but maybe it's just as well to be kind of tied down. Well honey, will sign off. Love you an awful lot. All my love, Hamp

May 9, 1945

Dearest Hamp

Well old boy, how is the hangover from VE Day – or are you still celebrating? Just remembered that today is a holiday in Britain too. Can't get over it. It's too good to be true.

After I wrote on Monday Marg, Bill and the kids and myself got into the car and drove downtown. Believe me, the city had really wakened up after the first shock. Traffic was 3 lines deep on either side of Jasper and moved west to 109th Street, turned around and went east to 100th Street and turned around again. The loudspeaker and radio sound cars blared band music, people shouted and waved flags and blew horns. The streets were deep in paper and confetti and everyone was very happy. There was no parade though which was a disappointment. We came back and had supper and a bottle of beer and then Joan and I came home. There were even more people in town at night and I heard on the radio that they burned an effigy of Hitler and danced on the street. So guess it was quite hilarious. Marg Hall and Kay didn't arrive so all the Nortons and the Smiths Jr. had was a bottle of beer apiece. Tuesday which was really V-E Day was spent at home by Joan and I. Really very quiet. Mac phoned me from Camrose in the morning but I couldn't get all he said as he mumbled and his voice was quite thick anyway. He was mentioning something about you coming home and maybe getting a course in GU from the Air Force. More than that I couldn't be sure what he said. I wonder if he remembers calling me!

I hear from the grapevine that Bob Zender has just returned on a compassionate leave because of his father's death. Audrey went to Calgary to meet him on Monday. Heard also that Claresholm is now only a 'holding unit' but haven't heard where Bill and Doris are.

Joan is still a tyrant. Kay came over tonight to stay with me so I spent two hours persuading our child to go to sleep. I could really shake her teeth out sometimes she's so stubborn. Oh well, it's probably just a phase of her growing up.

I really can't think of any more news. The only thing I'm waiting for is your home coming as I'm going to Calgary or Winnipeg to meet you – whenever that will be. Sure hope it won't be another year though. I'll be satisfied if it's by fall. Had a letter from your mother today and she's feeling very well. That's all for now darling. Heaps of hugs and kisses from Joan and all my love dearest. Ever and always, Peg

Fri May 11, 1945

Dearest Peggy

Well am pretty well into the old routine again but things are better now. Miller got back last night so now there are two of us and one can have a little leisure and soak up summer sunshine and get around to see some of the beauty spots. Lough Erne really is beautiful in the sunshine and I don't doubt that Castle Archdale is one of the most beautiful locations on the lough. However, it ain't nothing without yourself darling.

Tonight Frank Grant (a pilot) and Doug McKay (a Nav) and myself wandered about 2 miles around the edge of the lough to the ruins of the original old castle – quite a nice walk. We came back and had a can of chicken, toasted sandwiches and I'm now writing this is bed. This afternoon put Miller to work immediately and I went out to Necarne and lay in the sun beside the brook which runs in front of the place. Got quite a good sunburn. Came back at 4.00 and Frank and Doug and Hoop Cunningham (a SL in charge of one of our flights) and myself played four handed cribbage. Doug and myself lost a shilling each. We played all last evening until about 11 PM and lost 11 shillings and four pints of beer so we aren't so hot. After that we came over to my hut and fried eggs, made toast and coffee and opened a tin of stew. All four of us are now out of food completely so guess I can stop worrying about my figure.

Shepherd my new room mate replacing Bob came back from his course at Bristol tonight. He apparently enjoyed V-E Day quite well and overstayed his leave by two days.

Our boys are still doing lots of flying and it doesn't look like our V day stand down will come for quite a while. It will fall kind of flat when it does arrive.

The rumours of what will happen to us are flying thick and fast and nobody knows for sure. I wrote Mac on Wednesday and told him to write to Ottawa and ask for my release if he believed he had adequate grounds and Dad would add to the grounds. Then asked him to send me a copy of the letter or letters. It may or may not speed up something honey – but anyway the deed is done. It looks like we will hang around for some months yet – nobody knows how long. It may be soon or not that some go back. All my love, Hamp

Dearest Hamp

Well old dear how is the old routine going? Much the same I guess as it will be quite a time before the war's end makes any real effect on postings and such like. However I'm sure waiting for news of any kind as it seems ages since I last heard from you. So much has happened since you went on leave. It's too bad your leave didn't last long enough to take in V-day celebrations in London.

I got quite a surprise on Thursday as Mac and Irene drove up to our house so Mac could get a rest. He went right to bed and slept for four hours, then had a bath and ate his first solid food in days. It seems the weekend and V-Day were too much for him so he had a mild case of DTs. I guess Irene said it was the worst session yet and she was quite a wreck herself from worry. Mac tried to pass it off to me as too much work but I'm not fooled and anyway Irene really opened up and told me quite a lot which was pretty grim. I can't ever see you carrying on like Mac does which is quite a comfort. I'm sure I couldn't take it like Irene does so take a warning old buggerlugs dear!

Friday night I had some of the girls in and we had a good stag party so today has been spent in quiet relaxation – as quiet as one can be with Joan around.

She has taken to throwing spoonfuls of food around the kitchen again and what a mess. Buddy got a spoonful of pudding between his eyes today which he didn't appreciate at all. She gets the phone down and talks and laughs in it and has herself a good time. The consonants go something like this: "Dado? Dado? Oh meba, do doe", etc etc with several laughs and then "Bye!" It really sounds quite silly. She has increased her vocabulary to hat and coat, ride, walk, Bud, baby Joan and baby doll. Of course they aren't very clear but I can get the drift of the conversation every once and a while. Today in the store she helped herself to the apples so I had to buy two partially eaten apples.

Alix came back from the coast tonight but I haven't seen her yet of course or talked to her. I hear that Bob Zender has arrived back in Edmonton on a compassionate posting because of his dad's death a couple of months ago. Perhaps you'll be seeing Fred soon as he had talked of going to Ireland on his next leave and hope to get up to see you. That's all we've been doing honey. Marg and Bill are coming for dinner tomorrow. Heaps of love my darling. As ever, Peg

May 13, 1945

Dearest Peggy

Today is Mother's Day and I send love and best wishes to the finest mother that my daughter Joan could ever hope to have and the best wife that any man ever possessed. (I say possessed but actually that is wishful thinking). Sorry that I didn't send you flowers from here but will try to atone for my sins of omission.

Things here have been quietly settling into their usual rut. Heard Churchill tonight and quite enjoyed it. His caustic comments of [??middle ?olera *illegible*] will rouse some of our neighbours.

Plans are gradually shaping on the station for the V Day celebration but no one knows when it will come. It will be a two day holiday and a complete shutdown. Things are still going strong here and the boys are doing quite a fair amount of flying escorting in U boats and looking for more! I'm certainly praying that things come to wind up here before August. If the squadron moves I hope it's before July because I will probably leave here then in any event and if they go to a warm climate I will stay in England but if the unbelievable happened and they went to Canada I might go with them. The last alternative is most unlikely and highly improbable so don't get your hopes raised one little bit.

The weather has been grand until today but now rain, hail etc has returned – hope it doesn't last.

Played cribbage this afternoon with Frank Grant and after two hours effort managed to make six pence – not a bad effort eh honey?

I hope the mail has caught up with you by now and you have forgiven me for not writing while on leave.

Some of the boys have been quite busy lately hanging up blocks. Disregarded instructions not to celebrate V Day and leaving camp to get drunk when they should be on duty – two have been put under house arrest and they may be court martialled. Rather takes the edge off the festive spirit to say the least.

Don't know if I told you about the squadron leaders latest – took

538

my corporal off to the local pubs in Kesh after I had a Guinness with them in Irvinestown after I had made rounds at sick quarters. They got quite stinking with drinking and then went fishing. The squadron leader tried one boat by himself and upset it – in uniform and all. Didn't phase him a bit though – went to a farm and borrowed a tattered old suit and then they retired to the pub and proceeded with their drinking. Quite a character. He hasn't been near here for 7 solid days now. His release group comes up in June and he's worried sick because he doesn't want to leave the service. Well honey, signing off. All my love, Hamp

May 15, 1945

Dearest Hamp

Yesterday was a very good day indeed – got 5 letters all about your leave. You sure had a bang up time and I kinda wish I had been along to pub crawl with you. That news from Noble sure is hopeful and boy will I keep my fingers crossed and really pray that you win on that 50-50 chance. Wouldn't it be wonderful darling to have you back with us again?

Sunday Marg, Bill and David came over for dinner and then we went for a ride to White Mud. Haven't been there for ages and it was good to get down to the river again. Alix came over tonight with a sun bonnet for Joan from the coast. She looks very healthy and is quite plump now but Sandy is sick again running a temperature of 103°. The symptoms sound like a flare up of the old ear trouble after the measles last year so Alix is rather worried.

Jean Brumwell and Jessie Horne called in last night to see me. They are here for Convocation which was today. They are both going out to Victoria to live as both their families are out there now.

Joan and I have spent a very quiet day and have not done much but clean the house and iron. Joan is kind of fussy these days and I think her big molars are beginning to stir around a bit. She is not eating meals very well and then keeps asking for "bics" (biscuits) all day. I can almost make out all she talks about now. Her system is to pronounce the first syllable of a word and let it go at that. For example "ri" is ride and "bu" is bull and "ha & co" is hat and coat and so on. It's not hard to understand most of it when you catch on. And by the way you don't have to worry about her wetting on you as she's quite good at letting you know when she has to go and I have her on a routine that helps a lot. However accidents do happen but she hasn't wet on me for months now so maybe she's growing up a bit. Last night we had a good time playing hide and seek. I'd hide and Joan would come and find me – what a racket we kicked up.

Well old dear that's all we've been doing and it's not very interesting, however we are enjoying doing absolutely nothing. It was sure good to hear from you as I've had mail only 10 days in 2 months. Not your fault though as I always get scads when the mail does get through. Big hugs and kisses from Joan and all my love forever, Peg

May 16, 1945

Dearest Peg

Got your V day letter today and also the news of the 10th. Your celebration seemed rather quiet like my own – we'll have to catch up on that when we get together – whenever that might be.

Things here are back to normal. We're in the midst of our second day of rain and its really pouring down. The creek outside is high again and hope none of our drunks get too submerged if they fall off the bridge outside my door. Fortunately it is only about 3 feet deep at most.

Night before last we had the RCAF show "All Clear" on the station. It was really excellent and I enjoyed it very much. They were touring Bomber Group when I was there but I didn't get a chance to see them. Yesterday noon had steak and eggs in town for lunch and bummed around the station all afternoon dodging work. Last night Doug McKay and myself issued a cribbage challenge and played from 7 to 10 for drinks – a scotch a game and double for skunks. We won six scotches and lost two and had several Guinness and so ended up as drunk as newts about 11.00. The show came over to the mess after performing again last night and were entertained. There was more liquor and so we were even merrier. Came home about midnight to my last inch of bread and margarine with someone produced a tin of fish and some honey so we had toasted fish and honey sandwiches – very good combination.

540

Unfortunately I had a tin of about 2000 vitamin B tablets in the hut – someone ate about half of them because he felt it was good for him and took the rest around adjacent huts and passed them out. All in all the evening went well and for a change no one hung up any blacks.[19]

There is no news of what the squadron will be doing although current rumour is that we will have definite information as to our disposal by the first of next week. Mac seems to have celebrated V Day appropriately – don't blame him a bit. Our celebration won't be for some time yet I suppose and will be more or less anti climax. Everyone has a bottle of rum bought and stored for the occasion so there will be lots of cheer flowing and very little else.

No more news of what is going to happen to the RCAF over here. Probably most will go home soon but no one has any clues. Six Group, which was the Canadian Bomber Group I was at is apparently folding up. My last unit there was a heavy conversion which converted crews from their advanced operational units onto Halifaxes and Lancasters and then we sent them to the various squadrons in the group to replace losses etc. Because they were converting into operational types we had a fair number of training casualties plus what we picked off the moors from flights which pranged returning from ops.

Well honey, will tell you more about things now that we are nearly the most of over the war. Miss you very much and am counting the days until we will re-unite. All my love, Hamp

May 18, 1945

Dearest Peggy,

Another two days and very little to report. Yesterday I took the afternoon off and sat be hind the hut. That was all very well except five people joined me with three bottles of rum and several cokes. It was very pleasant soaking sunshine and rum but after a while we found ourselves quite flushed from one cause or another. We then proceeded to Mrs Bothwell's in Irvinestown (by ambulance of course) and had steak and eggs. Unfortunately someone found a pub with a bottle of rum which we drank and then came home by ambulance. We stood around the mess discussing the general situation when Wing Co

MacMillan came in very worried and asked us if we would disappear because he had a little explaining to do. He and Doug McKay took the station COs car away two days ago and went off and bought several cases of rum for the squadron for V Day. (The station CO was in London and MacMillan was acting CO). Unfortunately they did considerable sampling and on the way home they had the extreme misfortune to hit a tree, which caused considerable havoc to the automobile and rendered it completely unserviceable – so you see that he might have cause for anxiety. So we got in a taxi and went back to Irvinestown and had several Guinness and another steak and then came home. I have taken the pledge completely from here on though because of the fact that I am broke and also have had a very bad case of migraine today.

Got some pictures yesterday and am sending them along. They aren't very good but aren't too bad – hope to get more good ones in the near future.

Well honey, you see that your husband is not a very good type but promises to reform. Sam Miller (the other MO) went off today for the weekend so I'm more or less on my own. He is going on leave in 2 weeks time so I'll be back to normal again. Well honey, will sign off, promise to reform. Love you very much and wish we were together. All my love, Hamp

Loch Erne 1945, Hamp on left

May 19, 1945

Dearest Hamp

I suppose it seems ages ago since you had your leave. To me you've just got back to your station and written your wife 5 beautiful letters all at the same sitting. It must have taken you ages to do them all. I haven't any later news form you yet so that makes us about 3 weeks apart. Is it any wonder I'm living a few weeks behind time? Just so I can be with you in thought when I read your letters. It's no wonder that the time seems to stand still once in awhile is it darling? But really can't complain at the mail service.

As you may have guessed this week has been rather dull – not much activity and the days are chilly with strong winds. Spring is late so there's not much incentive to be about and doing. I must have a low depression this week as there wasn't much ambition around me. Wednesday and Thursday evening just stuck around home – went outside to put Joan in the yard and that was all. Friday was a hectic day – did a washing – mostly Joan's things and cleaned house and got Joan in for lunch and while I was getting it ready she got into my talcum powder and dusted it all over the bedroom and while I cleaned that room again Joan got hold of some of Bud's dog biscuits and scattered them all over the dining and living room rugs so I cleaned those again and finally got her to bed for a nap but the meter man came and wakened her up after ½ an hour. I got her to sleep again and the next thing was screams of 'go-go' coming from the bedroom. I went in and our daughter, yes *our* daughter, had dirtied her diaper, wool blanket, crib and worst of all mother's newly decorated wall. I sort of held her at arm's length and stuck her in the tub and with visions of you doing the same to Frankie, cleaned up the mess. That was the climax for the day. Food throwing at night was a mere trifle however by the end of the day I didn't think much of our charming girl. However we're good friends again and we go into affectionate huddles every once and a while. I've got to admit that she's really quite a gal and you don't need to worry about her not paying any attention to you because I know she will and within a week my nose will be shoved out of it. But I won't be jealous 'cause it's your turn to get her affections now – and mine too please.

543

Dad is now Dr Smalley – sounds queer doesn't it? As of Thursday and now all of Joan's immediate male relatives are decorated. She's really got something to live up to eh darling? Mother and Dad should be home this week and I'll be glad to get out for a change. Sandra had tonsillitis so haven't seen Alix but once since she got back.

I hear from Margaret and Bill that Mac and Irene have torn their permits in pieces – a noble gesture and a step in the right direction but there are still ways and means. Not an interesting letter I'm afraid darling but I'll try to improve next time. All my love always as ever, Peg

May 22, 1945

Dearest Hamp,

Got two letters from you yesterday May 9 & 11 and one today May 13. So I'm right up there. Yes I guess your V day celebrations will seem rather stale but at that I'll bet it won't stop you boys from having a hilarious good time. Am really glad you're getting a bit of a break now that Miller has returned. Sure hope it lasts. That bit about the possible moving of your squadron is very intriguing – leads to a lot of thought doesn't it? It's just so nice to know that the European war is over and that I can think of seeing you sometime. I'm not raising any false hopes though darling – just waiting for something more substantial than rumors. I'll not really believe you're coming home until I see you with my own eyes. What a happy vision that will be eh honey?

Jean B is leaving tonight for Banff. As I think I've said before she has been here since Friday and it sure is good to have someone around even though she has been out a lot. However Mother and Dad are coming home tomorrow morning so we won't be alone long.

Yesterday I washed and then cleaned the house and at night the Missionary Group from the church came over for a meeting – 25 women – what a moo! Sure was tired when they left as I had to feed them. But it's nice to know our house will hold 25 people – I guess.

Today I cleaned thoroughly for Mother and Dad – waxed floors etc. The house really looked clean until Joan got at it – throwing food around. She's in bed crying so guess I'd better go see what's to do. Pardon me for a minute darling.

Well back again! Joan wanted to "go-go" and was sitting on top of the desk. What a child!

Alix says that Fred was going to Ireland the 6th of May or there abouts. But maybe he got waylaid in London around V-day.

Tomorrow Joan and I are going to David's first birthday party. Margaret invited us over for tea with Marg Hall, Kay Jackson and children and never mentioned David's birthday. However we are not so slow. We know it's David's birthday and will make it quite a day for him.

The weather is at last warming up a bit and the cold winds dropped today so I took a sun bath in the backyard this afternoon. It felt really swell to get the good old "sol" near me. But there was no babbling brook by Necarne to lie beside and dream about you. I'm supposing that you were dreaming about me, when you were there, but you were probably sound asleep you old goat! However I still love you and always will. It seems your are my one weakness that I'll never be able to overcome – as if I wanted to do so! Sure wish you were home now – we could have such fun together. But it won't be too long now. All my love, dearest Peg

May 23, 1945

Dearest Peggy

A little lapse in my writing but I have quite a good excuse (as excuses go). Sunday morning we had an aircraft go down on the Isle of Man so the Wing Co and I panicked around all day to fly over but were held down by the weather. We got away on Monday morning in an Oxford borrowed from a nearby drome and arrived at this drome at the north end of the island about noon. We had quite a time landing and damn near pranged. The Wing Co didn't want to fly because he hadn't flown an Oxford for over a year. An Australian volunteered to go with us since he was married to a girl in the WAAF who was stationed on the island. This chap said he could fly the type but when we got out to it he announced that he hadn't been in one for two years. We said the hell with it and went anyway but his landing took about 30 bounces each about 30 feet high and the Wing Co took over to keep us from running

545

down a Wimpy[20] ahead of us. Old Stan MacMillan then resolved to fly home and did so – and damn well of course.

On arriving at the aerodrome we found most of it blown down. Our kite, a Sunderland, had landed on the grass beside the runway in front of the control tower. The crew piled out and then it blew up and ruined the control tower and also blew the walls off two big hangers and kind of made two more into the air jobs. A church a mile and a half away had its stained glass windows ruined so all in all it was a bloody good bang and caused considerable stir on the drome. The kite had a full gas load and all its depth charges so that explains it. The boys really had a miraculous escape. They were breaking cloud and hit a hill in Ireland. The pilot recovered just in time but removed all of the hull of the aircraft on the first impact. The Sunderland really has a stout hull so it was quite a blow. No one was injured there although one fell through the floor when it was ripped out and cut his knee. They then managed to stay airborne to reach the Isle of Man and let down on land. On landing one lad fractured a couple of vertebrae but nothing too serious considering. He and the chap with the lacerated knee were the only injuries and no one on the drome was injured so it was a good show.

After we arrived at this place near Ramsey we got a car and drove 25 miles to Douglas on the north end of the island where they were in hospital. It was a beautiful day and the coast road was really a lovely drive. The Isle of Man is a very nice holiday visit but not very pretty in itself except for the coastline. We drove around Douglas and then on the way back stopped at Ramsey and had a meal and several beers with the rest of the crew (whom we met in town) and then to bed. Yesterday it rained all day so we couldn't get off and hung around the mess reading, eating and drinking beer. Came back this morning in perfect weather except for clouds and back to work again. Well, honey, there's my excuse. Got a letter from you today. Love you more and more. All my love, Hamp

May 25, 1945

Dearest Hamp,

It doesn't take very long to swing back to the old family routine. It hardly seems that Mother and Dad were away at all and they've only been back two days. Dad is just like a little kid with a new toy showing off his hood and new sheepskin. But we're very proud of the new "Doc". Mother brought Joan a sun suit, sox and wool blanket and panties and shirts. I got a new dress – just an afternoon wash dress – an umbrella – as I didn't own one – marmalade dish and salt and pepper shakers for our home – so fared very well I'd say.

Wednesday afternoon Joan and I went out to Margaret's for David's party. It was really quite a "do" – twelve kids and ten adults. So Marg was very busy for days in advance. And like your mother she put on quite a spread. The kids ate at the table and Joan got along fairly well without my help but she wouldn't eat her ice cream and left the table to play in David's playpen. Kind of anti-social but she enjoyed herself. At night I went over to pay Alix a visit as I haven't seen much of her at present. Fred didn't get beyond London on his leave. What's so attractive about the big city eh honey? Jack is writing about volunteering for the Jap War. He figures he'll get home sooner and that the war will be all over before he's through his training. What a hope, the dope. Alix wishes Fred were around Jack to push his teeth down his throat. It's a grim prospect for Jack's wife, Connie.

Yesterday was a holiday and in good old Western fashion it was cold and wet. Mother let me sleep until noon which was greatly appreciated and so the day went very quickly. At night I went out to Glenora to a get-to-gether of our club. We played Rumoli and I was 10 cents up at the end of the evening. Better than you are eh honey? Then we ate and I came home at 12:30. Today has been quiet but was not dull as there was a letter from you. Glad to hear you were forced to go on the wagon you old goat. Maybe you won't suffer from migraine until next payday. Yes siree you'd better before you come home or I'll pin your ears back old boy! Right now I'm just kidding but if I get thinking about it I might do it so take the warning dear! I'm kind of broke myself and waiting for my check so I know how you feel.

Had a letter from Irene today too and Mac is busy in his spare time planting the garden. They are still on the wagon. Pretty dull I guess.

Must wash my hair tonight as you wouldn't recognize me with it combed out straight and a blue ribbon to hold it off my face and no make up on. Really quite a drip that's me but it's good to let one's hair

David Norton's first birthday

down once in awhile. By the way I gave up the Up-sweep for awhile as it took too long to fix so am back to the style you like. Joan's hair is quite curly and how I envy her. Where did she get it I wonder? That's all for now darling. It's wonderful to know you'll be home in a short time. Can hardly wait.

All my love, my darling. As always Peg

May 26. 1945

Dearest Peggy'

More water has passed under the bridge. Got another letter from you yesterday – sorry my letters to you haven't been coming through better. I try to write every second or third day and occasionally (quite) slip a day when there isn't much change in the old routine.

Spent yesterday afternoon wandering over the station taking pictures. Have got quite a little accumulation of snapshots built up and am sending them along. They are not at all good but will add to the collection. It was a beautiful afternoon so went on to the lough with a dingy and got a few snaps of some of the flying boats and then came back through the castle gardens etc. – don't imagine they will turn out very well as usual.

We have had no new rumors as to what happens to us. The squadron will be connecting on to relocators for transport purposes but no body has any clue as to where they will connect or when. The patrols are still going out but there hasn't been much doing for about a week and the boys are starting to get a little brassed off. Guess it will be pretty hard to keep everyone happy for the next month or so. The CO is off down in London now so he may be able to produce some news on return.

Coastal VE Day seems to be approaching and we may have our stand-down in a few days – doesn't matter very much now however.

Say thank you darling – got 900 cigarettes from you today and they

War on U-Boats Was Waged from Lough Erne

Coastal Command's U-boat war in the Atlantic was waged principally with the Sunderland and Catalina flying boats, and one of their main bases was located on picturesque Lough Erne at Castle Archdale, peacetime mecca of anglers and holidaymakers.

From its charming pre-war setting that peaceful wild bird sanctuary grew into a veritable hive of industry. It is a town in itself, composed of Service men and women of many countries whose devotion to duty has saved the lives of countless Allied seamen they have successfully escorted; and just as their toll of enemy U-boats is a formidable one, so also is the number of survivors picked up after their ships had been torpedoed.

The Sunderland is a really remarkable aircraft which has been in operation throughout the entire war. It was responsible for the safety of the ships sailing between Britain and America during the "gap" period, when land-based aircraft could only escort the much-needed convoys part of the way. It was during these operations that Sunderlands fought off many an attack of the long-range Luftwaffe raiders.

This exclusive "Belfast Telegraph" photograph shows a Royal Air Force flying boat base at Castle Archdale, nestled among the islands of Lough Erne. Their crews and aircraft fought out the Battle of the Atlantic with Hitler's U-boats.

were more than welcome since I was finishing my last carton. Thanks very much.

Taffie, Bud Powell's dog, produced last night or a least Bud said she jettisoned which is the term here when anyone drops DC or gas load. She produced 12 pups so it was quite a jack pot.

Got a newspaper yesterday with pictures of our base here and so forth. Am sending the clippings along to you – will give you an idea of the place. Well honey, the days go by and we get just a little closer each time. Miss you a great deal and love you a great deal. Say hello to Joan. All my love, Hamp

May 28, 1945

Dearest Hamp,

The days are most certainly slipping away – means to the day when you'll be coming home to us. It's almost June – isn't it wonderful darling? Our summer has finally arrived now with the trees in leaf and flowers blooming and today it was 84. We need rain very badly as everything is so dry – driest spring in 17 years so perhaps the gardens and crops won't be so good. The East is practically flooded with rain. Silly isn't it.

Haven't done anything of interest lately. Went over to Alix's last night – Sunday – and we went to Mrs. George's to a "do" in dad's honor. Mother got a corsage and Dad a card of congratulations so they were quite pleased.

Joan is so darn cute these days and tries her darndest to talk. It sounds really queer to hear her jabber away with inflections and not know what she is really trying to say. However she pops out with the odd word every once in awhile like this morning when she ran to the door screaming "Milkman Milkman" and pointing at him. He nearly dropped a quart of milk he was so surprised. Her pet phrase though is "More meat!" as she's a real cannibal and likes beef raw or cooked, fat or lean. It should be easy to cook for you two I'd say eh honey? Joan's eczema is all gone now – written touching wood of course – and she's getting quite a tan from playing in the sunshine which looks real classy with her white curly hair. Her pictures arrived from Camrose and are quite good. Am sending one Air Mail to you so you'll get a better idea what our child looks like. Also have a roll of film being developed so will send those along too. I had two of Joan's pictures enlarged and colored – same one I'm sending you. That's for our home when we get one. Also am getting quite enthusiastic about a home of our own so am going to buy things I see in the stores that I like – such as lamps etc. No furniture – unless I should see some small rare piece like a chair – because we don't really know where or when or what kind of a place we'll have at first. Went downtown today all set to buy but didn't get enthusiastic about anything so came back with just 2 loaves of bread. Alix is scouting for a house or an apartment as they have their furniture from before but she really doesn't think she'll be lucky enough to get a place as living quarters are really scarce around these parts.

I hear from Camrose that Mac is pretty busy writing to the powers that be to get you out of the RCAF so whether it works or not he's quite happy with the trying. And me – I'm just happy knowing it won't be too long before you're back again. Sure hope you can stay with us for a long time next time – like forever. That's all for now my darling. Love you more and more each day. As ever and always, Peg

May 29, 1945

Dearest Peg

I'm really behind in my letter writing and have no good excuses. Should have written on Sunday night but didn't and have a fairly good excuse for last night. Since Saturday have been busy killing time without very much constructive work. Saturday afternoon went bicycle riding to Kesh and managed to get a little exercise – damn near burst a blood vessel on some of these Irish hills. Saturday night played four handed cribbage with Doug McKay, Frank Grant and Hoop Cunningham. For a change Doug and I only lost about 3^{20} to them and improved our morale no end. Sunday I worked and Sunday evening there was a show in the mess. Unfortunately the station CO cornered me and we sat and drank beer for about two hours and then cornered someone else and retired to his home on the hill and played liar dice for a penny a throw and six pence was the momentous loss of the evening. Didn't get home until 2 AM so that is the reason I didn't write you. Yesterday afternoon went in to Irvinestown with Frank and Doug and we had two Guinness and then went to Mrs Bothwell's for tea – we had a steak and eggs. I then left them and wandered out and bummed around and went to Mrs Herman's for dinner. Mr and Mrs Herman are the local lords and have a very nice home with butler as major domo etc. Had a fresh trout then lamb chops etc so I didn't do badly on the eating yesterday. We had coffee with genuine cream in it – first time since I left you. They have a lot of land here so don't lack very much in the way of farm food products. After dinner I then proceeded to the Irvinestown Red Cross Society meeting and delivered a first aid lecture. Have been dodging it for weeks but finally was cornered. About 10 PM went and picked up Frank and Doug who were waiting for me in a pub. Unfortunately they had bought a case of Guinness so we came home and drank it – with them very high and me quite sober. I finally went to bed and they went home and that is the reason why I didn't write you yesterday. So now you have all the reasons and apologies. Will swear to do it no more so help me and will be a more regular correspondent from now on darling. Well honey, the days go by and you get nearer and dearer. Miss you both a lot. Give Joan my love. All my love, Hamp

May 31, 1945

Dearest Peggy

Well, the squadron knows its fate more or less. Effective tomorrow we are in Transport Command and no longer under Coastal Command. The last aircraft flew on operations today and we will gradually pack everything up in the next few days. The squadron will probably move for training in a couple of week's time but nobody has a clue whether it will be a station in England or Ireland. We all hope that we will see the last of Ireland shortly.

We pretty nearly finished our last day with a casualty this morning. An aircraft of ours had its starboard outer engine catch fire while it was in the circuit, the engine fell out and knocked off the starboard float as it did so. Fortunately the boys made a good landing and got to hell away from it via dinghy as it started to burn. We had quite a dash over the lough in the process however and thoroughly enjoyed the panic.

The last two evenings have been very busy – Doug McKay and

myself playing cribbage vs. Hoop and Frank and just managing to keep from losing any money. We felt a little self conscious in our game tonight – we were haggling over a shilling when one of the boys came out from the crap game in the next room with a double handful of bills – 75 quid makes a lot of paper. However we will never shoot crap to make ourselves out good fellows and one of the boys.

Sam Miller went on leave today so I am tied down for the next couple of weeks. It will keep me out of mischief and is quite a good thing since the weather is terrible with buckets of rain all day every day.

The future of myself and the squadron is a big question mark and I wish I could give you a little definite information. Some of the big boys of transport are coming here on Tuesday next so we may have a little more gen by then rather than rumours.

Got a parcel from Irene yesterday – food. First food parcel for some time so it really evaporated when all the people I had scrounged from came in and sampled it.

The problem of entertainment for all the squadron for the next couple of weeks will be considerable. No one has any definite job (except myself) since we are not doing any more flying for coastal so they will have lots of opportunity for getting themselves in trouble. An extensive sports and entertainment programme is laid on and that may help a little.

Well honey, miss you very much, think of you very much and don't get much closer to home. Maybe some day before long. Give Joan my love and kisses. All my love, Hamp

JUNE 1945

Letters to Hamp have written on envelope in pencil 416, in ink, 22 Canadian General Hospital, Bramshott; Surrey

June 3, 1945

Dearest Peggy
More water away and nothing to report. The squadron is supposed to be moving in about 2 weeks time and going to southern England to

a reception centre. From there it will probably be broken up and the majority sent home. However those due for repatriation have been told that it will be two months probably three before they get a boat. I have no idea where I fit into the picture and won't raise any false hopes one way or another.

The other squadrons here are folding up also. The sister squadron of our flying Sunderland's (RAF) flew the last trip of coastal command against U boats today. That means that no more flying will take placeò in this theatre in coastal command. They had the news cameras etc on the station taking pictures and held to make it an event with a promotion of Catalina's from the 3rd squadron buzzing around. The RAF squadron is the oldest squadron in Coastal and flew the first trip and the last of this particular phase of the war.

At the above arrow (ò) I have had an interruption. Three people wandered in with a bottle of rum and insisted that I have a drink – and very good too. They each had a new rumor of what was going to happen to the squadron and I gave my latest so we had quite a chat. It's funny how rumors build up at a time like this. These chaps all claim we are going to the reception centre at Torquay and then be repatriated. I still don't know where that leaves me – won't go any further than Torquay probably but speculation is wonderful.

Things have been fairly quiet lately and there is damn little to write about. Nobody is working but myself it seems (poor me – not patting myself on the back but awful close). There will probably be a two day stand down for the station shortly and everyone will do even less than usual. Hope the weather improves. For the last five days it has been showery – which means it rains like hell for 20 minutes then stops for 10 and starts all over again – day and night – just depressing.

Last night we had quite a banquet in the hut. About 8 people brought everything they had to eat. It was quite a variety ranging from soups made of tin of cream of tomato, some chicken noodle and a little Bovril mixed in. It was good in spite of the fact that the chicken noodle spilled on the floor once, fortunately before we had added all the other ingredients.

Gave another lecture to the Irvinestown Red Cross Society on Friday last – hope it is the last one I have to give because they don't hold a hell of a lot of interest for me. Saturday night we played cribbage with

Doug MacKay and myself as partners losing as usual. One of these days we're going to get lucky and beat Hoop and Frank Grant and stop our swearing.

Well darling there isn't much news. Spend more and more time thinking about yourself and the daughter and seem to get quite homesick. Miss you both as much and more than usual. Sorry I'm such a bum correspondent but there just isn't anything to write about around here – will be kind of glad to get back to England. All my love, Hamp

June 5, 1945

Dearest Hamp,

A few days have gone since I last wrote and my only truthful excuse is that I'm a bum. On the other hand the days have been quite full however that is no excuse as it could have been arranged to write – I guess. Well having said all that, my darling, now I'll tell what has happened lately.

Saturday I spent at home all day sewing etc. and at night went to Alix's and played bridge with Helen and Leila. Sunday morning I went to church. Yes siree to church! Dad stayed home to take care of his granddaughter. That's a real good reason! Had a headache all day so stayed home in the afternoon. At night was all set to write but got started pasting your pictures in the album so that took about 3 hours and then it was time for bed.

Etta Pateman phoned on Monday and we met uptown to go shopping. I bought a dress, hat and shoes (my next winter hat), paid $4.00 for watch repairs and have at last got a watch again. Also sent a box of food to you which I've been collecting for a long time – canned chicken etc. It is possible that if you are moved you might not get it but I sure hope you did. Let me know darling if you think I should keep on sending them – not that I've ever been very good about sending them promptly – but if they might get lost in all the shuffle that does on now. I may as well wait for awhile and hope you'll be back soon.

Harry Pateman is working as an architectural draftsman at Muttart's Lumber Co. and they find life quite different from Air Force life – not as much money for one thing. Etta had a letter from someone who had heard that Bill Bothwell had been on the reserve list for a week, got called back and sent overseas. If that is the case I can just hear Doris and Bill talking at the RCAF. Haven't heard from Doris for a long time so this is just rumor.

Monday night I went on a hike with the church group and we played soft ball and had wieners, do-nuts and pop. Today I feel as if a truck had run over me. Sure am stiff and sore. Of course your wife would have to play catcher and do all the moving around but guess I'll live although at this point I wonder if it's worth it. Just joking of course.

Joan is getting more independent each day and I really have to be very firm with her at times as she is the type that tries to make you give up. She sure has a strong mind. Had some pictures developed so will mail them today too. Sure hope your photo of Joan arrives OK so you'll know what you'll be coming home to. That's all for now my darling. All my love as always, Peg

June 5, 1945

Dearest Peggy

Got a long letter from you yesterday. Glad to hear that your dad and mother got back. Give your dad my congratulations and tell him how pleased and proud I am to be his son-in-law. (I was before he got his degree but am glad to see that the remainder of the continent is beginning to show some recognition of his worth.

Things are still floating along here with lots of rumors and no facts. Am managing to keep quite busy with my routine and also am inoculating the squadron to keep them out of mischief and to keep me occupied. There's' very little to do in the station for the personnel so the erks are playing baseball or poker and generally having a lazy time.

Doug MacKay and I have stopped playing cribbage for all time. We got a little fed up with our continued losses and are now losing at horse-shoes. We had sunshine yesterday evening for about 2 hours between showers so we were exercising our athletic abilities on the horse shoe patch. Today the downpour has started again so things are normal.

Tomorrow is the anniversary of the big day and is apparently a holiday for all the troops in the theatre – afraid it doesn't affect me as usual.

Got a rather depressing letter from Dad yesterday dated May 24th. He told me how hard he was working and asked me to please come home. Unfortunately it isn't that easy and unless they start the proceedings as I requested them to I will stay here until I am moved home by the normal course of events. Dad spoke just as if I had never written and I was wondering if the letter went astray.

Well, honey, things aren't very interesting here and I wish to hell we would move – maybe it won't be long now.

A chap named Gordon MacDonald who trained in Edmonton phoned me from Belfast yesterday. He is in Ireland and had heard of my address from George Abott, a chap I know in London. I invited him up to spend a day or so here so he will probably come up this weekend and see the place. Well, will sign off with all my love and kisses, Hamp

June 7, 1945

Dearest Hamp,

Sure got quite a surprise yesterday, darling. Got a letter from you which was really very welcome and also your $100 bond which came by registered mail. I had quite forgotten that you had taken it out and so it came as quite a surprise. That raises our savings to $1600. Wealthy eh, old thing?

There is an Edmonton-Peace River convention on in town this week so Mother and Dad are not home very much. However yesterday my Jr. White Circle Club put on a banquet at the Corona for all our mothers. It was a very nice affair. We had dinner in the small banquet room – the one we had the wedding reception in – and ate grapefruit, tomato soup, fried spring chicken, potatoes, peas, ice cream and coffee. After eating, we played court whist until 11 PM. Mother didn't stay for that as she doesn't play cards and anyway one of us had to put Joan to bed. Dad was elected to look after the daughter while we were away and he says he had a busy time as he did nothing but entertain her and vice versa. When Mother got home Dad was bathing Joan as they had put the hose on the garden and really got quite messy. Some fun that was I'll bet.

The last week of June Mother and Dad are going to Brandon to the

Union Convention and will be away about two weeks traveling around the country. So Joan and I will be on our own again.

Hope you can read this scribble. I'm writing on our – yes, yours and mine – card table and it shakes with each movement.

That was an interesting piece of news about converting the Coastal to Liberators. Just where does that leave you old boy? I suppose that is what you are wondering too. Your mother wants to go to Arizona this summer but is afraid to do so in case you should come home. However it is probably better that she stay home as it is not time to travel now with all the troop movements that are taking place. The boys coming home, the Americans leaving for new postings as they are closing down American bases in the north – all makes the railways very busy.

If the weather is good this weekend, Margaret, David and Bill are going to the lake and I may go along too so if you are minus a letter that will be the reason. The weather is still sompin!? Hope you find out soon what is going to happen to you as the suspense is terrific. Now that you might be coming home soon makes it harder to wait then before the war ended. Guess you feel the same way too.

All my love my darling, always and forever, Peg

June 7, 1945

Dearest Peggy

Things still progress without any movement of note. The newest rumor is that the squadron is going to convert to Lancaster's instead of Liberators for their transport effort and will go to Yorkshire to convert. If that were the case then we would go back to Topcliffe (which I left in January). It is just a rumor fortunately and I hope we keep well away from Yorkshire.

We are now filling our forms to see if we are volunteering for the East. My first choice is retirement from service, second is service in the western hemisphere and 3rd is service over here and I am not even mentioning that warm climate.

Am still in the midst of inoculations. Do about 100 a day so will have a couple more days work to finish the lot. The bloody rain continues and its as cold as February. We had about 3 hours sun yesterday evening and

I was sitting out in the sun reading when 3 drunks came back from town and started to annoy me. When I was no longer useful one started to hurl insults at some English lads who live across the creek from me and finally provoked one S/L so completely that he decided to come over and put him under arrest. However with a little persuasion and jujitsu I got him to bed but it kind of spoiled the sunshine.

Our official VE Days have finally been laid down as next Monday and Tuesday and they will be station Holidays. Miller won't be back until Wednesday so at least that will keep me on the straight and narrow path of sobriety.

Don't know if I told you or not. I was supposed to go to Yorkshire to visit the Toa's on leave. Never got out of London and didn't write them because my leave had been cancelled about 3 times and I had written in disgust and said I would get there if I ever got away. They wrote to headquarters and asked if I were dead and said that the children were wondering where "Uncle Hammie" was and where I was if alive. The letter was passed intact to the station here and since then the adj. has passed the news around and Uncle Hammie is taking a kind of beating. Have hastened to write to prevent a recurrence of same.

Well honey, things don't move very fast do they? One gets pretty cheesed but the only consolation is that the more time I get here then the chances of getting out seem that much better. Love you more than ever. All my love, Hamp

Written on envelope: In pencil 416
In ink: 22 Canadian General Hospital, Bramshott; Surrey

June 9, 1945

Dearest Hamp,

I sure hit the jackpot today. Got last one written on June 3rd [21] to date. You will have moved
you get this and I suppose the
step in the right direction although
to be a long wait. Grim

Read in the paper the other

> *Torn out corner probably due to postage stamp*

pessimistic report on the movement of you boys. It said that by Christmas all the relatively long service men should be home and all the others home by spring. So the fellows that have to wait for 2 or 3 months for a boat are really quite lucky – on the basis of the newspaper report that is. However it's all so uncertain and the unexpected may happen all of a sudden. With that thought in mind I'm really quite busy finishing my embroidery and sewing fall and winter dresses for Joan so that we won't be caught unprepared and anyway it sure keeps me busy.

It looks as though King would get in again by the way the returns are coming along. The soldier vote won't make any difference to the party in power really; it will only decide the close runners in the various ridings. Yes siree! I voted for the Liberals and I'll bet you did too coming from a strong Liberal family eh honey?

Saturday night the gang were over at Days and we played bridge. Nothing really exciting but an evening out at any rate. Last night I went down to Alix's and we did embroidery. Sandy is going to have her tonsils out this month as she is not picking up after her second attach of tonsillitis.

Our daughter is getting to be more of a handful every day as it's a co between us to see who has will. She's forever getting in some today it was a can of oil. She always manages to get into the garage

Torn out corner, as above

somehow and find some real treasure. I wouldn't change her off for a child that sits still all day though even if it does wear me down. Guess what Joan needs is some competition but I'm not weakening yet on my "non-pregnant-for-at-least-a-year" idea. Ha! Ha!

There isn't very much to report as each day is much the same as the last but at that I'll bet we're not as bored as you are over there. I hope you are getting a change of scene though as that will help for awhile. I didn't go to the lake with Marg and Bill as Mother was rather tired after the convention and anyway Helen and her husband were going. A foursome is too much competition for me as I still miss you a hell of a lot and get pretty queer ideas about being a gooseberry. Time is going by quite quickly and another couple of months should decide your future one way or the other. All my love, my darling, Peg

June 11, 1945

Dearest Peggy

Monday morning with a station church parade of all ranks in commemoration of VE Day and all is quiet. Have just finished sick parade and tore a huge strip off everyone who was trying to scrounge out of the parade and am now sitting back and scrounging out of it myself. It is raining as usual so am not even going down to look at it. This is the first parade that has been held here – practically for the duration – so it should be pretty sloppy.

We still don't know what is going to happen to us. The newest rumor is that we will be put on Mark V Sunderlands and start ferrying troops between southern England and Montreal. That is quite a good rumor but about as unreliable as the rest of them. Everyone is quite cheesed off with the whole situation and a move anywhere would be welcome to provide the bunch with a change of scenery. If the squadron did go on ferrying at least I would be able to cross the Atlantic, but the possibility of the rumor being correct is most remote.

Tonight there is a big dance in the station. It is being held in one of the hangars. The floor is concrete and quite rough so it won't bring in much but sore feet.

Someone showed me letter from his wife in which she quoted a rumor "The officers in the air force are all going to be sent home and discharged from the service and the NCOs will be kept in to do the flying. This is to save money since they don't get paid as much." Does that sound sensible to you honey? That is about the payoff as far as ridiculous rumors go. However she also had a joke in the letter which I read. You've probably heard it but I hadn't and so will proceed – An army private went to his officer and asked to be sent home and discharged. On being asked why he said that he was a married man and missed his wife. Well, said the officer, you shouldn't miss the feminine touch so much – look around and you'll see that over here we have WAACs, WAVEs and nurses. Well, said the private, that may be so but I've wacked it, waved it and even nursed it and I still want to go home for an honorable discharge.

Am signing off to get this in the mail. Will write tonight (June 13/45). All my love and kisses, Hamp

Dearest Peggy

Just a bunch of not very good snaps that have gradually accumulated. Am going to get ambitious shortly and start taking a bunch more and will send them along too. Many of these haven't very much interest to you but they kind of give you an idea of the place around here. The bunch is quite convivial as you can see and that is actually the only compensation that the place has.

You can kind of get an idea of what our sick quarters is like. Actually it is a pretty old place and the country in front of it is lovely – an ideal rest home for our erks.

Got your pictures of Joan today and thanks very much. She is certainly growing up and I'm afraid I won't know her when I get home. Hope she recognizes me. It's a good picture.

Well darling, will sign off – started assembling these prints about 2 hours ago but got interrupted to go across to Grant Libby's hut and have an egg. Goodnight and goodbye for now. All my love, Hamp

June 25, 1945

Dearest Peggy,

Just a note. This is the second lot of pictures I have sent you today and hope they all arrive OK.

They were taken about six months ago but the censor held them up at the photographers for about 3 week and then OK'd them.

These have been passed by Censor of Coastal Command

The pictures aren't too good but they give you some ides of the size of a Sunderland and of the general set up of our slip ways and marine craft.

All my love, Hamp

Hamp on starboard wing of a Sunderland

Hamp in front of Necarne Castle sick quarters

June 14/45

Dearest Peggy

Sorry I finished your last letter so abruptly but left the darn thing in my desk drawer and VE Day being shut down as far as mail went (in or out) kind of neglected it and then had to dash down the hill after sick parade Wednesday morning to get it out in the mail.

Monday was quite a day. The sergeants' came over to our mess at noon and got quite squiffed. In the midst of it Gord MacDonald phoned from Irvinestown. He came out immediately and showed him the mess and then seven of us hopped in the ambulance and went into town to our favorite pub. (I pinned the old S/L down and made him work since Miller was away.) We consumed a large quantity of Irish that Tom McKenna the publican had been saving for V Day and got thoroughly squiffed and then went over to Mrs Bothwell's for steak and eggs. Ate our meal and retired to the pub and drank gin until about 8.00 PM. By that time both GR and myself were quite blind – he went up the street and got to know the publican and helped bottle several dozen Guinness in the back yard and ended up with a bottle of rum and a bottle of scotch. We then all assembled and came back to the mess and drank considerable rum and then went down to the dance in the hangar. We mainly concerned ourselves with the bar in army Co MacMillan's office (which was just across the way) and finally emerged to grope our way home.

Wakened on Tuesday with firm resolves never to do it again. After I took sick parade we wandered down below and I showed him the aircraft, the operators block and so forth. Scrounged coffee from the adj. and then back to the mess. Gord went back in the afternoon – don't think he was too impressed with the place because he had a horrible hangover and also lost his hat the night before. It turned up again in the mess the next day with no badge on it and was absolutely soaked – apparently having spent the night in a puddle somewhere.

Tuesday night there was a Squadron party but I just collapsed in my hut and 3 separate parties wandered in and out with bottles of rum but I couldn't even muster the strength to be polite.

Sam Miller came back yesterday and things are more or less normal. Last night however there was a party in the WAAF officers mess and W/C MacMillan and Rod Milne (one of the flight commanders) and myself went over and drank several bottles of gin and wandered home together at 5AM this morning – just a little beaten. Thank goodness that is the end of the VE celebrations on the station – except for a station party tomorrow night (the big one for the officers' mess). I am on duty so will have to stay proper – also have invited three of the local doctors whom we see around occasionally and will have to do a little general hosting. Well darling, will improve my correspondence next week. All my love, Hamp (PS – sending snaps along)

June 15, 1945

Dearest Hamp,

June is half over and I really don't know where the days go to. The days don't mean very much but they sure are being put behind. Guess they are rather long for you if you're not very busy eh honey? But perhaps if you got out of all that eternal rain you may cheer up a bit.

I've been busy again this week and haven't had time to do all I had planned on. In the daytime plus routine and looking after Joan I made her a dress and kept several social affairs at night. Tuesday night was Club meeting and we took pictures as it was our last for the season so it was after 12 when I got home. Wednesday – went to see Doris and Sandy Fleming. They are back in town at last. Sandy was up north so Doris went to Saskatoon. They have moved to the West End so we don't see each other very often. We had a good supper and then I taught them to play "Nertz" and Sandy hopes I never mention it again. Think I told you his mother died last February after a gall bladder op. well his father dropped dead in April so what with the baby and all it's been quite a winter for them.

Thursday night the club went on a hike to "the pines" and took wieners, buns, bacon, cheese and coffee and beer so it was quite a hike. No! This is not the church group and yes! it was strictly feminine company. So today am taking rather easily!!

Joan is certainly getting to be quite tricky. Yesterday I happened to walk into the front room and there was Joan sitting in a big chair, my purse opened and on her knee, my cigarettes in her hand and one dangling out of her mouth and was she peeved when I broke up the show. She's a mimic these days so you have to be careful what you do in front of her. Today she carried her rocking chair to the kitchen sink so that she could play in the water and she had just started to climb up when I came along so she just pretended she was only going to rock anyway and so sat rocking under the sink.

She is learning to be very foxy at an early age but I guess she comes by it quite honestly eh honey?

Was talking to Alix today and Fred is back in Antwerp after his leave but expects to be posted to England soon.

By the way honey now would be a good time to get some P.G. work done on your correspondence course – you know while you have nothing to do! Ahem! I'd advance you the money old bean! Fred is talking of taking some course and having Alix go to England. It's just an idea of Fred's right now. Fred's address is the same as before except for the Mediterranean. It is Capt. F.Y. Day, R.C.A.M.C. #5 C.G.H. CAO. So now you can write to him and get together on a bang up do. That's all for now honey. Joan says "Daddy" quite plainly now instead of "Da Da". Heaps of love and kisses etc. Peg

June 17, 1945

Dearest Peggy

Another Sunday night and nothing unusual to report. The tannoy is going steadily outside my door, calling up crews with a little panic, but nothing major. The squadrons are doing air sea rescue while standing by and there are two liberators down at sea en route to America – one off the coast of Portugal and the other about 800 miles south on the way to the Azores. Our lads go out and drop dinghies etc (if they can find the birds). Creates something to do if nothing more and may save a few lives.

Friday night was my mess "do" and it was quite something. About 500 people milling around drinking scotch and rum and dancing. Import4ed a bunch of local Irish girls for the partners by bus and they were taken away by 3.00 AM so it was a large evening. I drank innumerable rum and cokes and even went so far as to dance about twice until someone pointedly remarked that my wife either had very small feet or very bruised ones (so keep out of the way when I go dancing in Alberta). Had a good time though and it was a good party and a nice one.

Yesterday morning managed to get up a 7.30 as usual and stagger up for sick parade. Then went down and picked up Doug McKay and the Wing Co – they were a little battered still when I dragged them out of bed but they insisted the day before that they wanted to go on the ambulance in the morning and do some business at the bank. Left them in town and then went to sick quarters to do the usual rounds, take some x-rays and what have you. An hour and a half later went back for them and found them in a pub drinking ample scotches. Refused to join them and vice versa so had to go back yesterday afternoon and haul them home to bed about 5 PM – both boiled again. (What a life eh honey?) Hope we leave here soon and hope my chances of getting into #22 Can Gen Hospital keep looking good. Well, honey, goodbye for now and all my love (give Joan some) – Hamp

June 19, 1945

Dearest Hamp

The mail is certainly good these days. Got a letter today written June 11th and 13th so that's pretty good traveling. That must have been some VE Day celebration you had if what is between the lines in you letter as an indication – just a blank space between days. Bet it was a very hectic affair at that eh honey?

The newest rumor is quite exciting although I don't quite see where that leaves you – unless sitting behind in England. You might of course get a flip back when your turn came but I just can't imagine you being stationed on this side and your squadron posted here. However, when you get to England there should be more definite rumors. We hope eh darling?

As you may have guessed from my last letter I was so tired or rather dopey when I wrote it was as I'd been out sunning all day and got very drowsy at night so kept finding myself going to sleep and sentences being left unfinished. Have got a fair tan now as we haven't been doing much of note so sunbath in the afternoon. Joan is getting to be quite an Indian too. Hope you would claim us when you get back even if we look like something scraped off a desert.

Saturday night was over at Alix's with the gang. We have switched to bridge and are beginning to get quite interested in the game. Sandy is going to have her tonsils out in the AM so won't see much of them for a few days. Am going downtown in the morning to look at some bed sheets etc for my hope chest and then on to Margaret's.

The railways are having quite a change take place now as so many of the boys are coming home so over-night accommodation is discontinued, i.e. the sleepers are taken off such runs as Calgary-

Edmonton, Regina-Saskatoon so people have to sit up all night. The diners are for service personnel and the civilians get what is left if any so it is advisable to pack a lunch. That will make a lot of people like myself spend the summer in the back yard. Wouldn't it be nice when you get home if we could take a quick trip to Banff eh honey? I'm just stubborn I guess and hate to give up good ideas like that without fighting a bit. However, am just keeping quiet for the time being. But don't worry darling I'm really quite easy to handle. That's all for now. All my love as always – Peg

June 21, 1945

Dearest Hamp

Guess by now you're in England, or are you? It will be kind of nice to get away from all that rain you write about eh honey? On the other hand you'll probably miss all the good food you get at Mrs Bothwell's not to mention the good old Guinness which is so good for you – unquote. Guess I'd better keep up the food parcels or you may get a bit underweight which would be very bad indeed. Ha! Ha! Speaking of weight I'm still holding my own at just over the 100 mark which was what I weighed when you married me so that must be the way you like me. However I seem to recall that even then you kept talking about building me up – and brother you sure did! Ha! Ha! again. But you should see Thora Magee – she really is a mountain of motherhood or something anyway.

And speaking of mothers and etc. the Flemings are in the family way again – expected Dec 24. Here's hoping they have a happier Christmas than the last time.

Was out to see Margaret, Bill and David yesterday and must say they look very well. Bill is putting on quite a bit of weight and Marg hasn't lost all the pounds she put on When David was on the way and David of course is quite plump so that makes for a healthy family all round! Quite a pun that last remark!

Isabel Barrett phoned today. First time we've talked to each other since our wedding. Wilf has been to Winnipeg and points east but is now in Calgary so they are going down next week. She made the remark that you probably wouldn't be out of the Air Force for some time after you come home as they were recruiting MOs when Wilf was in Winnipeg so I just said, "One never knows". Several officers have been sent from Calgary to Washington so Wilf doesn't know how long he will be staying there. He was posted overseas before Christmas but it was cancelled. Isobel still complains about her lot –just as usual – but personally I can't see that she has very much to beef about.

Sandy had her tonsils out yesterday and is home today with everything OK so maybe in a week or so I'll start seeing Alix again. It certainly is very quiet around here but Joan and I are getting a good tan and getting quite chummy. She calls me 'Mummy' now and gets quite perturbed if I'm absent for very long. Who'd have thought I'd acquire an apron string for someone to hang on to eh? All my love dearest, as always, Peg

June 22, 1945

Dearest Peggy

Sorry I've slipped in the writing. Have big news to report. I am now posted from the squadron and am going to the #22 Canadian General hospital to work. It is quite a break in a way although it will be kind of a routine. Am the RCAF's representative in the GU side of the place – it's a hospital that treats all VD so I'll be up to my ears in Gonorrhea and what not – it'll become pretty tiresome but at least it's a big improvement to my present situation and will be damn good experience in the future, or in that particular line at least. May get a little bit of other GU so can't complain a bit. My address will be (attached – #22 Canadian General Hospital) RCAF overseas first with number etc as usual.

The reason I have not been such a good correspondent in the past 3 days is because I have been in Dublin. On Monday the Wing Co. talked me into going to Dublin with him to get away from the place here. We (Doug Mackay, the Wing Co. and myself) left on Tuesday and came back Thursday evening. Actually we stayed in Don Lough Haire (Kingstown) which is on the sea coast about 6 miles from Dublin. We stayed at an old hotel called the Royal Marine Hotel[22] and had a grand time. Did nothing but sit around in the sun, eat steaks and consume good scotch. Visited local pubs and only went into Dublin for one afternoon. Had kind of a quiet time but it really was a change from this place and a pleasant one. One afternoon we had several scotches and them got 7 lobsters and 2 crabs and hired an open carriage and drove up on top of Killeney Mountain which overlooks the city. Dozed in the sun on the way up and then got out and ate all the shellfish and then went down to the beach and had tea. It was very pleasant but don't know where we put all that lobster. Well honey, will write tomorrow. All my love, Hamp

June 24, 1945

Dearest Hamp

Mother and Dad have gone again and it's been a long day and looks as though it will be a longer 10 days as everyone seems busy or away and Joan manages to keep the days very busy. Had invited Alix, Connie, Leila and Helen over last night but it all fell through at the last minute as Connie and Leila went to the lake and Alix had to stay home as Alix developed a stomach attack so Helen came over and we sat and talked. Margaret went to Pigeon for a week or so with Helen Magee so won't have her to phone to put in time. However as I said Joan keeps me busy. Right first thing this morning she got into a bottle of Liquid Pet and somehow managed to get the top off it and of course poured it all over the floor. She had her slippers off and was sitting in the pool soaking it up. When I first found her I was quite cross but broke down and laughed when she tried to scramble away. Her feet just wouldn't hold on the slippery floor so she slithered around trying to get up and really looked quite silly. Sure got a lot done though for by 9.45 AM and on Sunday morning too Joan had had her breakfast and bath and I had washed the kitchen floor and cleaned a very oily sink. We relaxed for the rest of the day however in the back yard as it was quite hot and anyway all that activity first thing in the morning was more that I'd bargained for.

Joan is really quite a girl as has been said before and everyone that knows her is amazed that she's only 20 months old when they see all the things she does. The other day she was out on the boulevard trying to climb a tree and she really uses her head when it comes to doing things. It's really quite uncanny at times. Last night she had to bath herself – wouldn't have any help – and it was quite funny to see her soap the wash cloth, squeeze out the water and wash her stomach, arms and even under her arms if you please. But when she stood up in the water to wash her seat etc I though I'd laugh myself sick. Of course she had to do it again just to show off because I laughed. She's getting quite bookish now and sits for hours (if I'd let her) looking at the pictures. And I'm beginning to get her lingo, or she's speaking plainer because we hold quite lengthy conversations and she knows the right answers to questions such as, "What does the milkman say to the horse?" A. Milkman says "Wo!" "What does the rooster, cat, dog, lamb, say?" (asked separately of course) A-" Do-le-do, ne-o, bow wow, Ba!" "What does Joan say?" Sometimes it's answered "Mummy" and sometime "N'mo'ning" for "Good Morning". Pretty smart eh daddy? Your little baby milk jug is in my bottom drawer and the other day she found it and said "Daddy's?" She hasn't seen it for two or three months. Oh yes honey we've really got the ninth wonder of the world here. By way of a change from the doting mother, Jack Day has signed up for the Pacific. All for now. Sure miss you honey. All my love forever, always – Peg

June 25

Dearest Peggy.

Some more snaps – am sending two lots of them – more or less split up so that they won't be too bulky. Just a note here because will add the comments on the back of them.

These are our Dublin pictures – most of them taken around the Royal Marine Hotel. We took a few down town in the various parks but they didn't turn out.

Well honey, will sign off – move tomorrow to Surrey. Hope it isn't raining there.

Love – lots of it and all mine – Hamp

June 25, 1945

Dearest Peggy

Well, have finally gotten packed and cleared and am ready to take off in the morning. Certainly don't look forward to the journey because start at 6 AM tomorrow and arrive in London at 11AM the next day – having sat up all night on the train.

This #22CGH[23] is apparently in a lovely setting in Surrey and it should be warm and sunny. The work may prove a little boring after a while but it will certainly provide a pleasant change for the first while. Shouldn't stay more that 2 or 3 months and by that time who knows what will happen. In a way it will be a good thing to get away from the squadron since they will remain in the country (England) in definitely and fly transport to the Far East.

Last night got quite inebriated. Had a few short ones with the boys and was going home to write this letter when the G/C and W/C of my squadron said we must go and see Mrs Gordon (the G/C's wife) so I could wish her goodbye. We ended up by getting two bottles of scotch and getting quite squiffed in a pleasant sort of way. Don't feel so good today though because I acquired a real good head cold yesterday and am no stuffed up and shivery and not sure whether it's coryza or hangover. Not serious at any rate.

Mailed 2 lots of snap shots to you today and hope they arrive OK. Some of then are quite good of the area here and also of our Dublin 48.

Miller came back this noon and I officially threw in the sponge as far as the station goes this AM. My replacement is a chap named Arthur and he is arriving tomorrow. Don't know him but suspect that he has just arrived from Canada (what a future he has eh darling).

Got snaps of Joan on Saturday. The infant is certainly growing up and her mother is more beautiful every time I see her. Wish you had sent more of yourself darling. Have practically worn that snap our – just staring at you makes your husband quite homesick. Maybe it won't be too long – the days seem to vanish all right as you said in the airmail I got from you today. Didn't have blue forms from you all last week but the pictures really compensate.

Well honey will sign off and write to you as soon as I arrive at #22. All my love, Hamp

June 27, 1945

Dearest Hamp

A very good day today – got a letter from my husband. Yes siree! & it sure makes a difference to my morale. The VE Day festivities seem to be lasting a long time on the station but it's a darn good excuse never the less. Hope you won't be beyond the celebrating stage when you arrive home coz I haven't celebrated it as yet. Maybe we could go dancing so I could step all over your feet first just to prove a point to the person who made that uncalled for remark about your dancing. My feet have never been bruised by you and they certainly aren't small. What's all this about #22 CGH? That was a new one to me and really sounds like a good posting if you get the break. Sure hope it comes your way, honey, as it's about time you got out of the bush, so to speak.

The days are going by as usual and it's almost July. How time skips along. Haven't done much of note lately. Monday Joan and I sunbathed and yesterday it rained so we kept indoors which was quite trying on Joan – and myself as the day wore on – but I managed to get another dress made for Joan. I rather like sewing now that I've got the hang of it a bit so looks like you'll be stuck to buy wee wifey a sewing machine. It's quite a necessity in the home I find – just a build up that last remark, darling.

Forgot to mention in my previous letter that I bought a table lamp for our future front room – living room I mean. It has a blue china base set in a small wooden base with a silk rayon shade trimmed with mulberry satin – the exact shade of the satin pillows your mother made us. I think that's why I was tempted to buy it and the colors are just what I wanted so all we need now is you, a house and then a table to put it on. However the best things in life a worth waiting for and brother I'm sure waiting! Ain't it the truth though honey? If it takes a million years for you to get back I'll still be waiting – might look a bit queer but so would you probably so that wouldn't matter.

The daughter is cutting her third two-year molar and was kind of hard to get along with today. You can look forward to all the fun of such things with our second child darling so don't feel left out of things. Must go to bed. Was going to write several letters but haven't the strength. Sure miss you my darling. All my love, Peg

June 30, 1945

Dearest Peggy,

Well, am getting more or less settled into this place and getting to realize the routine. It really is a pleasant change to move form Nisson huts to a more or less permanent setup and have running water near the place and not have to go half a mile for a bath etc. It's a beautiful setting down here in Surrey – I never realized how lovely southern England was, until I traveled through it yesterday coming down from London.

I left Castle Archdale on Wednesday morning and came via Heysham (Liverpool) instead of Stranraer. Managed to acquire a berth so the journey actually wasn't too bad although it wasn't restful. Got into London and went up to headquarters about 3.30PM. Talked the situation over for an hour or so and got checked in and so forth and then found myself invited to the farewell party for G/C Noble, the DMS (PMO) who is going home. MOs had assembled from far and wide and Ritchie, Don Easton etc gathered. We went over to the headquarter's mess and had numerous free drinks and then proceeded home quite merrily. I stayed with Doug and caught the train out to Haselmere the next morning and got in here yesterday noon. Spent the afternoon kind of getting settled with the place and having a bath and then hit the hay about 7.30 last night and read for a while and then went to sleep.

I am rooming with Howard Ellis, a major who had a VD treatment unit on the Continent and I'll be working with him. He's quite a good Joe and very likeable but leads quite a hectic existence. Actually Gord MacDonald is responsible for the unit and has done a damn good job. There are about 400 patients all the time and there will be about six MOs. The work won't keep too interesting but at least will keep us occupied and I'm looking forward to it.

When I was in London I found that RCAF repats are really stalled at the moment and the majority certainly won't be on their way home before late fall and a lot will be luck to be home by Christmas. My priority isn't high and if I have to stay anywhere I want it to be here where the life is good and you have something to keep you occupied. Not a bright future honey, but I'm trying to be philosophical and I hope you will be too. After we have been away from each other for so many months I guess we can tolerate a little more one way or another. The MOs are a good bunch and there are several I know – Ewart Duggan, Jack Tysoe, By Robertson and the others are very friendly.

Well darling, will sign off and will keep you posted well in the future. Remember me to Joan. All my love, Hamp

June 30, 1945

Dearest Hamp,

Got your letter about your posting today and am I ever pleased about it! It sure is swell darling and hope it turns out to be as good as it sounds. I suppose you've left Ireland by now although you didn't mention when you would be leaving and by the way just where is #22 located? I like to look you up on the map so I can tell just where your are.

Hope you can read the scrawl as I'm on my stomach on the back lawn soaking in the good old sun. Joan is asleep as its 1:30 and very hot. Don't know how long I can stand the heat even though I've only my bathing suit on. Looks like it will be nice for the holiday weekend although that doesn't affect us one way or another.

Got your pictures yesterday and enjoyed looking at the Irish locations. Seems to be a pretty spot. The boys look like a good crowd on the whole so guess you really have been lucky. Helen Day's husband got word he was drafted for home and then the powers that be took his name off the list and posted him to Germany. He's in the Education section and didn't volunteer for occupation but looks as though he's kind of in a spot. Helen naturally is quite disgusted. He was stationed with #6 at Middleston-St. George Yorks so they were all quite hopeful for awhile.

Fred and Jack Day have finally met up with each other and apparently had quite a bang up meeting in the Day fashion. Last news from Fred – he was in Dunkirk expecting to go to England shortly. Alix was over last night that's why all the news on the Days.

Doris Fleming came for lunch on Thursday but there's no news from that source other than Sandy wants a discharge – but who doesn't eh honey?

Mother and Dad should be home sometime next week and I hope it's soon as this living alone is not for me – life is too boring this way even though I'm kept busy.

The gang is coming over tonight for bridge and I haven't decided what to feed them yet however I'll scrap something up.

Just how long is your posting for, do you know? and how does it affect your coming home sometime. Don't suppose you know the answer to that one either eh honey? Glad you got Joan's picture OK. She's just like that all the time only quite a bit more active. I honestly don't think she's ever still – even when asleep. Wish I had 1/4 of her energy. That seems to be all for now. Heaps of love darling. Sure miss you and wish you were home, oh well! All my love again. As ever, Peg

JULY 1945

Letters to Hamp addressed to: F/L Smith, C.H, C 10858, #22 Canadian General Hospital, R.C.A.F Overseas. Written on envelope in different handwriting-"Bramshott Military Hospital"

July 2, 1945

Dearest Peggy

Well, have put two days behind and will gradually get to know the routine around here. The mess here provides the best food I have seen in England – Canadian cooking and they have butter or margarine three rimes a day instead of just for breakfast. Also there is not tea at 4.30 and dinner at 7.30 so it's kind of nice to get back to the old routine. At current rate I won't lose much weight unless I acquire a bicycle and start doing a little peddling around these hills.

Toured the hospital this morning. It's built as a rectangular corridor with the wards etc branching from it. It's about a mile around it so it seems quite an area and there are a lot of odd departments tucked away in it.

Our particular VD department is going full blast with over 400 patients and a rapid turnover rate. I don't know what these lads will do when they get home to their small towns and have to associate with decent women once more. A good proportion, majority, are just back from the continent and awaiting repatriation so they don't enjoy their stay in our wards very much.

Got a letter from you today date June 19th so the mail is doing pretty well in catching up. You seem to be leading a quiet existence and I hope you don't get too bored. I don't like to raise your hopes for my very early return but I rather believe that it won't be too many months before we are together again – sure hope so honey with all my heart.

One good thing about this hospital unit – I'm merely attached here and so have no air force responsibilities. With that in mind when things look possible I can pull out and leave without having to worry about an air force replacement having to be provided. But guess I'd better not dwell too much on that. Hope you got the last snaps I sent you. Some were quite good. Have a few more that I will send in the next few days. Will then have to get busy and start taking some pictures of the place around here.

Played knock rummy in the mess tonight and made the huge sum of 2/6. Will never get rich or poor on gambling around here anyway. The inhabitants of the mess are the steadiest lot I have been with since joining the outfit. Well honey, love you miss you very much. All my love
Hamp

July 3, 1945

Dearest Hamp,

So you are now in Surrey old boy! How you do get around but I guess it's kind of nice to see different places and this time you are quite near London so you should have some good 48s. As you can tell I got your last air mail letter from Ireland today. Sorry you haven't been getting any mail from me lately. I'm still writing so it should all catch up with you sooner or later.

Yesterday Joan and I went to the Day's cottage at Cooking Lake with Sandra and Alix. Mr. & Mrs. Day, Helen and her daughter Gail, aged 4, were there too. We had a good day sitting out on the beach and Joan really enjoyed playing in the water and sand. She didn't want to come home and was a very tired girl when she was finally put to bed. Sunday was a cloudy day but awfully sultry so Alix called around and took us for a ride to White Mud. On the way Joan saw a pony and so the last two days I've heard nothing but a story about a "Bomy" as Joan calls it.

Mother and Dad are not home yet but I sure hope they arrive soon as I'd like to go out for an evening once in awhile.

I've started something for you to wear as a civilian – your returning home present – won't say what it is coz it's a surprise and may not even turn out as I've never made any before. However in your spare time you can start guessing and I'll tell you when you're right. Honest I will.

Made Joan a pair of sleepers last night so now I think her wardrobe is complete for a year or two. The sleepers are size 2 but Joan is so small she'll be wearing them when she's 4 I'm sure.

See from the paper tonight where Pat Costigan is back on 30 days leave prior to the Pacific. He as you know is in the Paratroopers and jumped at the Rhine so there is quite a write-up about him. Also Ernie Watt has been promoted in the Navy to eight Surgeon Lt Commander or Commander, forget which. Also Ron Horner has signed up for the Pacific and goes on a course in Tropical Medicine and as Nora can't go with him she will be coming to Edmonton to join the rest of us. It says in the paper tonight that 126,000 men will be home by the end of 1945 – 65% army, 35% RCAF. So you try to be in that 35% eh honey? Here's hoping anyhow! That seems to be all the news for now. Hugs and kisses from Joan and all my love as always, Peg

July 6, 1945

Dearest Peggy,

More water under the bridge and not a bad bridge for a change. Things here are quite pleasant – brilliant sunshine on many days instead of once a year, and a beautiful countryside. It is very hilly here and the hospital is more or less on top of a large hill. Have been out walking a couple of nights. Last night GR Macdonald and myself walked down to Haslemere which is about 2 ½ miles away and then detoured back by the local at the foot of the hill. Had a few beers and came home. The old pub is quite a place – an old woman about 70 operates it and keeps all her beer in the basement. Every time you order one she carries your glass down to the keg and fills it and brings it up. Since the place is quite popular she gets her exercise but it takes some time to get any beer, whish is a good thing.

The VD Department is going full blast. We have about ¾ of hospital admissions now and don't seem to slacken off a great deal. Keep about 350 beds full and the turnover is pretty rapid of course. One of the patients just remarked to me "Gosh the country will be rotten after the war." and I reminded him that Canada would possibly be the place to suffer since they never seem to learn to keep the front of their pants buttoned and all hope to go home.

We have a day off a week. Mine is Sunday but there is no place to go in particular so will probably just hang around.

The riot at Aldershot was apparently fairly minor but unless the repat scheme is hurried up a bit there will be a lot of grumbling. They are way behind schedule on repat and it may take quite a time to get all the boys home.

Well darling, wish you were here in Surrey with me – life would be just about perfect then. However will amalgamate in Alberta one of these times and oh boy! Give Joan my love and tell her that I think she is wonderful even if I don't write her very often. All my love, Hamp

July 6, 1945

Dearest Hamp,

How goes the struggle? Looks as though some of the troops were making Surrey into quite a hot spot right now and really can't say I can blame them. The way rumors fly over here it will take about 2 more years to get everyone home. However maybe the situation will improve somewhat so I'll keep trusting in my lucky star.

Sure feel in a buff mood today. Got all worked up about Ma and Pa coming home tomorrow as it's been quite a lonely time. In two weeks have seen Alix twice, Doris once and had the kids over once and that leaves a lot of nights alone which explains all the sewing etc. I've accomplished. Anyhow to get back to where I started. I cleaned the house, washed and waxed the floors etc. and then got a letter and they won't be home until Tuesday. Got so mad at the idea that I sat down and bawled as it was the only thing left to do. It of course didn't solve any situations but made me feel a hell of a lot better.

To change the tone of my letter now and back on to safe ground. What are your favorite colors in men's clothes? What color of suit do you plan getting and etc? The reason I ask is because men's clothes are hard to get, good quality ones I mean, and thought if I knew what your tastes are now I'd be able to pick up the odd shirt and tie or sox etc when a good shipment comes in. Don't worry darling I won't buy you a suit or anything gigantic like that. How is your dressing gown holding out? I thought I might make you a new one if I can get some nice stuff. As I've said Joan's things are all finished and most of the things for our house so you are next. Aren't you a lucky fellow? Oh boy.

By the way Frank Layton is in Aldershot just in case you have a hankering for old home friends – saw Berta on the street the other day.

Helen Day's husband had his posting cancelled and finally after 6 postings in 2 days was left where he was for a couple of weeks. Some people seem to get pushed around eh honey? That's all for now. Not a very cheerful attempt I'm afraid. All my love as always, Peg

July 8, 1945

Dearest Peggy,

Here are the last snaps that I have from Castle Archdale. They were taken in Irvinestown on V.E. day (that day again) by Hoop Cunningham and I got them from him just as I left. Everyone is quite cheerful about the whole situation and they are actually fairly good snaps. Your may recognize Gord Macdonald in them among others. Am writing a blue form as well so will sign off. All my love, Hamp

Picture in letter of young couple in front of a house.

July 8, 1945

Dearest Peggy,

Another two days have kind of vanished. Had three letters from you today and they were really welcome. That daughter of ours is a real character by the sounds of her – didn't realize that she was a genius but I'm afraid that I'll have to admit it and agree with you that we probably have the smartest infant in the world. Hope that she isn't too sophisticated when I get home to talk to her. Movements here are slow and will continue to be – I think seriously and almost certainly that we won't be home for Christmas – but you never know and we must keep hoping. By now you should have the news that I'm in 22 CGH. Have met a lot of people we know – it's kind of like old home week in a way. You wrote about Thora Magee – her husband Leonard Loveseth is stationed down the road and spent the evening here with Cam Harrison last night. I wish I had had your apt phrase of Thora being a "mountain of motherhood" to pass along to Leonard. Cam has volunteered for the Pacific and expects to go home shortly. Jim Cardy was also down last night to do a PM – he could only stay a few moments to talk but is coming back next Wednesday. We phoned Art Beauchamp last night after everyone got cheerfully talkative and he is also coming down on Wednesday. Have not heard from Fred Day yet but he will be by here one of these days since everyone goes by here on the way home. Frank Christie is in a hospital in Germany as registrar.

Guess by now with your meat rationing a steak is a luxury. When I get home rationing may be off again I hope.

The last two days have been perfect sunshine as usual – we can't have too much of it as far as I'm concerned.

Got a letter from Dad and Mother today. Both are well and seem to think that I have one foot on the gang plank. Little do they know just how little shipping the Canadians have available for repat. The Americans may be 250,000 men ahead of schedule but we are about 50,000 behind which is no drop in the bucket of our total.

Well, honey, the work keeps up – have managed to start delving into a couple of books and everything is good here – except I haven't got you and you are about the only thing I want in life. All my love, Hamp

July 9, 1945

Dearest Hamp

A couple of days have gone by again and I'm in a much better mood

– also got 2 letters from you today (June 30 & July 2) which always improves my outlook considerably. Your new setup sounds OK. Yes siree you'd better acquire a bicycle and keep your figure trim coz you'd sure look funny next to your wife's silhouette if you put on much weight. It's nice too that there are some of the U of A boys around – kind of gives you something in common. Yes, darling, I'm very pleased about the whole thing. As you may have guessed our little bunch here (Alix & etc) are pretty wise old owls. We sit and discuss all angles of the repat situation and have figured out ourselves that we may have our husband's home by Xmas or with a stroke of real luck by October – but knowing the air force and the army we really don't expect much. So you see we are quite philosophical too although I'm sure we all have a secret hope that it won't be very long before our men come home.

Life is still quite quiet here and although I'm not bored – for life is really too interesting at any time for that – yet it is rather dull but we'll survive it all – have no fear honey.

Saw Mac Young Saturday afternoon. Home on holiday to see his new daughter. While here he got word that he was posted to Calgary which is very nice indeed for them if they can get a place to live.

Margaret and David came home from the lake (Sylvan) on Sunday night so Joan and I were invited over for supper today. I took a layer cake I baked yesterday as Marg hadn't time to bake. Joan had a good time with other people to look at instead of her old lady. Everything went fine until Joan tapped David on the head with a hammer found somewhere or other. Don't think David was hurt much as he didn't fuss until Bill started to talk with great disgust and the air was suddenly quite frosty. Joan got a spanking and behaved herself much better and the atmosphere changed. It didn't seem to bother Marg but I've never seen Bill look as mad. He was in kind of a ratty mood anyhow, working hard and the weather hot.

Mother and Dad are must arriving home now so had better welcome them! Excuse. Well they are home at last so guess I'll be able to go out at night for a change.

That's all for now darling. Hope you like your new work and that "You'll be home for Christmas". All my love as ever. Sure do miss you but we'll make up for it eh honey? Joan says "Hi ya Pop!" All my love darling, Peg

July 11, 1945

Dearest Peg,

A day late writing again and have no good excuse because I haven't done anything but sit around and read and look out the window. Yesterday we had a real rainy day that was almost like Castle Archdale, but the sun has taken over again, so things aren't bad. Managed to keep fairly busy throughout the day with routine. Some of it is fairly interesting but I imagine that it will rather fall into a routine after a while. This evening Mac and I walked about 2 miles down to the local and had a few beers and then home again. The old lady doesn't dispense it very quickly so you can't get whistled and you have to walk home 2 miles up hill so it's a fairly harmless past time to go down there.

Guess I have to write Dad soon to tell him why it's so hard to get home. I don't know if he realizes it or not but it's rather annoying to keep getting letters "please come home". God, if he thinks anyone likes sitting around this island marking time and being away from one's wife and child he's mistaken. There is nothing I would sooner do than go home tomorrow (or right now) but it is unfortunately not that easy. However darling, guess that's enough on that subject eh? Our innings will come and we'll make up for it all – not too far away considering all the months we have behind us. Hope you got the pictures I sent by parcel post – about time they arrived.

Well, honey, sure miss you. Am not getting too morbid since am relatively happy in my present job. Hope you can keep cheerful for a little while longer too. Give Joan my love and kisses. Love you an awful lot. All my love, Hamp

July 11, 1945

Dearest Hamp,

Well Ma and Pa are back again and had a wonderful time. The Board gave Dad a gown to wear with his hood on special times so he's all decked out for anything that comes along and Mother got a corsage of roses and a Dominion Life Membership for the Missionary Society which is quite an honor as they are given out sparingly, so everybody is pleased. They

583

brought Joan a pair of sox and 24 chocolate bars and a meat grinder and a bread board cut like a little pig for us so we did all right too. It turns out to be quite profitable when they go away eh honey?

Got your last bunch of pictures from Ireland and they are very good indeed. The Sunderland's certainly are quite a palace – really big stuff. The pictures of you in Dublin are very good. You look very healthy and don't seem to have changed at all. Maybe you have put on some weight but I can't see it in the pictures – though your face does seem a bit fuller in some of them. That was a smart looking outfit you were wearing. Is it your own or did you borrow it? Rather a rude question I'm afraid darling but the outfit looks so smart and fits so nicely that I hope it's yours. Aren't I terrible?

Margaret phoned today to say that Thora had a letter from Leonard and he mentioned seeing you somewhere in Surrey. You'd get caught up on the latest news as Leonard hasn't been over long. Although I haven't seen him for ages.

We are really back in full swing today. Dad brought a man home for lunch today and Mother decided this AM to have a tea this PM for Mrs. McMullen who is visiting from Winnipeg so we really tore around as there wasn't much food in the house. I baked a cake to help out. In the afternoon Aunty Lena phoned and came over for supper so we've really had it for today. Her latest news – Eddie and his English bride are expecting a baby Ha! Ha! So now watch me count the months like Aunty Lena did with us.

Last night Alix and I went to see "National Velvet" at the Garneau and really enjoyed it. Apart from the fact that it was a good show it was our first one in many a week so it was a real night out.

The weather is getting real hot now and doesn't cool off even at night and Joan is getting brown like an Indian. Me too! I'm tired so must to bed. All my love dearest and heaps from Joan too. As always, Peg

Letter redirected to:
C/o Mrs... P. F. Smith, Homeport, Pigeon Lake[24]

July 12, 1945

Dearest Peggy,
You are certainly spoiling me these days, 3 more letters today. Two

were June 8 & 13 and re-routed from Ireland but the other was dated July 1. Don't know how you keep so cheerful darling and hope you can be patient for a while longer. This posting will last until I give it up or get sent home. In other words, if the units kind of become static and all have MOs or there is a reasonable chance of going home then I'll leave here and catch a boat. Not too soon at the present rate but maybe things will gradually step up.

I got a letter from Camrose today nothing in it except the reply from Ottawa on the request that I be released. It merely said that the situation in Camrose was common across Canada, I would go to Canada when the deficiencies of the service over here permitted it and even if I were in Canada I probably wouldn't be released since I didn't have a sufficiently high priority – all which we already know. It rather annoyed me that nobody put any kind of a note in with it and seems to indicate that their attitude was "what a stinker you are!" However, honey, I don't know what the hell I can do about it except write my understanding wife for a little sympathy and try to keep from showing self pity in a situation over here that is unpleasant for me and apparently more so, to the people at home. Wrote Father a letter and told him just what my attitude was and hope that he takes it the right way. Troop movements seem to be going a little better so we can wait a few weeks and have a few statistics and then start figuring out an approximate date for that big reunion.

Art Beauchamp was supposed to have come down last night to visit but was unable to make it and will probably show up over the week end. Today was another sunshiny one and really is as hot as July weather over there in civilization. Will have to get out and get a little more exercise and see if I can reduce this pot belly of mine to a more respectable size – so you won't completely destroy me when I come knocking on your door.

Tomorrow is my day off but don't plan to do very much because I haven't any clothes except my oldest suit – the others are all at the cleaners and this one is beginning to look a trifle disreputable – also tomorrow is Friday the 13th so had better just lie in the sack for most of the day and keep out of harm's way.

Well darling will sign off and cease bitching for the duration. Miss you and our daughter. All my love, Hamp

July 13, 1945

Dearest Hamp,

Friday 13th and meatless Friday. Yes. Meat is rationed again and the weekly amount of 1 1/4 lb. per person. 3/4 lb. less than last time but even so I think we'll manage. Your dad will probably worry about it but he'll survive one way or another no doubt.

Got a letter from you yesterday and it looks as though you were going to be busy if the number of patients is any indication. Surrey is a pretty spot I'm told so you won't lack for scenery at any rate.

Today was a real scorcher. At 7 PM it was 91 so you may guess we are melting away. Joan had a very good day and managed to keep cool in spite of the heat. I put a tub of water out for her and then donned my bathing suit to darken my tan some more but Joan had the right idea she sat in the tub and splashed around, dunking her head under and having a wonderful time. When the water got low she dumped it out and carried the tub to the hose, put the nozzle in it and rank back to me saying "Mummy, mummy, more. More water". So I was kept pretty busy. At one point I was lying on my stomach dozing and – just like her old man would do – she came over to me and threw a wet rag on my back. Sure woke up in a hurry. A great sport yes sir!

Claire Garrison phoned me yesterday. She's back in town again for a little while. Gus is still in Lincolnshire and not very happy as he's with a R.A.F. outfit. His number is C11993 in case you want to write to him sometime.

We haven't done very much these last two days as it's been too hot. However I spent a couple of hours last night putting your newly arrived snaps in your album, then washed my hair and piled it up on top to keep my ears cooler.

The next time you see Leonard you can touch him for a cigar or something as he is now a "pappy" of a 7 lb boy John Eric as of 2 AM this morning.

Uncle Tom and Aunt Jenny from Vancouver are coming to Edmonton next week so we are going to be quite busy for a few days I guess. They are on their way to Winnipeg for a holiday. We have a summer school student here right now so can't see that they will be staying here.

The Exhibition starts next week – first one since the war started. Won't be going myself but couldn't we have fun there eh honey? However there are lots of things we'll be doing together in the future. Is there anything you are needing darling? Just ask, old boy, just ask. Joan sends hugs and kisses. All my love darling, Peg

Redirected C/o Mrs P. F. Smith, Homeport, Mameo Beach, Pigeon Lake[24]

July 16, 1945

Dearest Peggy,

More time gone by and nothing much to write about. Spent a fairly eventful weekend. Saturday night was quite a good affair in that everyone stood around and got very cheerful and some even danced. About 1:00 AM there came the most terrific thunder storm I've ever seen with lightning, a downpour of rain which lasted for about an hour. Just walking from the mess to the quarters I got absolutely saturated and when I arrived I found the roof leaked and my room was flooding. That involved running around and gathering up various pots and wash tubs and gradually cornering the major part of the flood.

Yesterday morning was Sunday and we can sleep in until about 8:30. However Howard Ellis, my room mate, woke me about 7:00 AM and started a conversation and so I got up and was dressed by 8:00. At 8:30 I went over to the mess and asked for breakfast and found out that it was actually 7:30 since Sunday we went off double British Summer Time and wound the clocks ahead an hour. (This is all a little involved but anyway the gist of it was, I got up at 6:00 (instead of 7:00) I was damned annoyed to lose an hour's good sleep.

Last night Mac and I went out to dine at these peoples' place in Haslemere. They are a nice young couple with a couple of boys age 2 and 4. We had a very nice meal and then retired to the local and had a beer and then came home in the rain.

Say – got a parcel from you today and thanks very much for everything from jam to nuts including cheese and crackers, candy and all the fixings. It was mailed on June 8 so delivery was quite rapid.

We keep busy. The psychiatrists have moved over from Basingstoke with all their screwballs so between VD and them this is getting to be quite a place.

Well honey, miss you. Give Joan my love. All my love Hamp

Letter to Hamp from his sister Margaret

July 16, 1945

Hi Hamp

Received your letter today and it really shamed me. I am the slow correspondent. Thought of you even more this last couple of weeks too so dunno why I haven't written. David and I were with Helen Magee Gordon at Sylvan for the first two weeks of July and last in June – sorta mixed up here somehow. The lake life includes you I find. Sylvan's more fun than Pigeon or if the CH Smiths and Nortons ever get cottage minded it's my choice. We went to two dances. Phillip and Bill came down for July 1ˢᵗ and then to take us home. Got the smartest seat for David on the front of my bike and that plus a 25 cent straw hat made a real set-up. Wheeled uptown for mail and groceries and milkshakes alla time. I lost a few pounds in the right places too. Has been either too hot or too rainy since we came home to get beyond Magee's! Really enjoying life since my holiday and Bill gets his after next week so we're going to Sylvan again. Was kind of tired of the routine but Helen's so good to David it was almost like a holiday without him – sounds mean but he and I see each other a lot every day. He's really cute now though a little spoiled. Showing some interest in his feet since we got him army boots that really clomp. Bill's been fishing several times without much luck but figure it's a good outing anyway and one little trout makes us a fashionable fish course with our dinner. He and Mr Heller are down the alley playing horse shoes now. I'm kinda keeping out of Mr H's sight today since I forgot to put in sugar for his cocoa on Saturday and he's the Cocoa King on fishing trips – ale all day and cocoa at night evidently for a sportsman.

We're just back from seeing Thora and John Eric Loveseth – JE weighed 7lb 5oz so beat Davie. Born Friday the 13ᵗʰ too. He's not as nice as David and Joan were but pretty sweet at that. (I sort of forgot in my memoirs that Davie looked like a chipmunk to me at first.) Thora makes me mad as usual being so darned enthusiastic, exaggerating the baby's weak points and being too darned healthy herself for me to watch. After washing and a chocolate cake this afternoon I was in no mood for frivolity and besides figure she oughta be suffering over her lunch counter instead of animated today. Mrs Magee's embroidering nighties and still has to trim the basket (David's at that). Dunno why it makes me mad to see that boy sorta neglected.

July 13th was our hottest day. Shirley and Ann Robinson and David and I went to the south side park via the street car and bus – David in style between times in his red go-cart with Shirley holding Ann's plaid umbrella over him. Had a swim and Bill brought our prepared supper – cherry pie too made by me just to make you envious.

This is some time later – talking to your wife. She and Joan are joining Mother at Pigeon for a few days. I refused same invitation since Davie is too at home in the car to take a bus trip. Feel guilty we aren't planning our holidays around Dad and Mother more but the summer is too short to baby them and Davie too. I'm not quite as sensitive as I used to be and it's to the good. You used to annoy me when you didn't worry with me but I can see your point now. We'll spend a week with them at that probably.

Am using Bill's pen I gave him for Christmas and can surely crowd in the gabble with it. Joe's watching from the chesterfield. He says to tell you the English sun can't beat Alberta for bringing out baby robins at dawn. Glad though that you're in out of the rain – was beginning to worry about your sense! Can't enthuse over your line of work but figures it's very worthwhile. You didn't sound awfully impressed with your meeting with Leonard. Hope he isn't going to make a mutt of himself because he's a very nice chap but can't carry his alcohol very well. Norm Murgatroyd is back. Letter from Helen saying they are coming in from the coast Wednesday on the 1st section – hint to meet them I suppose but we ain'ta gonna. One good supper is the extent of our hospitality. Just not the type we want to know every day for all I like 'em. Irene and Mac can do the honors for all of us. Bill won at horseshoes and is now teasing Joe. Figure a light lunch and bed will finish the day. This is a scrawl alright but there's a lot of it. Lotsa love, Margaret

July 16, 1945

Dearest Hamp,

Got your letter of July 8 today, really good service don't you agree? Margaret got one too and so is writing you tonight too. Sure don't think much about your idea of not being home for Christmas. You may be right old dear but it's too damn far to think you won't be home then. I have the feeling that you'll be back before (one of my feelings again) but it may be that I won't allow myself to even consider any other ideas. However time, as usual, will answer all our questions and in the meantime as you say we must keep hoping.

Saturday night got a phone call from your mother inviting Joan and I to the lake for a week or so and as Mac had offered to drive her out on Sunday we are packing for a week's visit. Mother has a 12 year old girl with her and so wants a bit more company. Margaret refused to go as David is such a problem at a lake – even though she's just back from Sylvan and going again when Bill gets his holidays.

Saturday night went over to Connie Watt Day's for bridge. The regular crowd was there and we had a good game although I didn't win – bad cards I guess.

Sunday Mother and Dad went to Wetaskiwin for the day so Joan and I spent it with the neighbors. Clare Henderson and her two children and husband were over for the day and Joan had a marvelous time playing with the kids in their sand pile. She threw sand by the shovel full on to her own head and it trickled out her panties so she was really quite a dirty girl. At one point Arthur climbed on to his Dad's lap and appeared to be enjoying himself until Joan came along and said, "Down! Down!" tugging and pulling at his sweater so Arthur got down and she promptly scrambled up and sat on Dr Carlyle's knee. My but Arthur was jealous but everyone thought it was darn clever of Joan. Of course I agreed but didn't say anything! When Art Henderson was home on leave prior to going to Calgary for his discharge Joan used to call him "Daddy" because she heard the grandchildren and mistook Art for "daddy". It's just a name to her so don't feel insulted. She is talking in sentences now – can't always understand the words but we get along. When you ask her to call Grandpa she screams "Bull" at the top of her lungs – for "Bill", I hope don't you honey?

Sure hope you're wrong about the time of your trip home. Who knows, luck may be on our side. It's swell the boys are around to keep things going as you say – "old home week". Well that's all for now and next news from Pigeon. Joan sends big hugs and kisses and I – all my love, as ever and always, Peg

Pigeon Lake
July 18 1945

Dearest Hamp

Here we are at the lake having a lovely quiet time and getting lots of sun, sand and water. We had quite a trip down by bus but it really wasn't too bad all told. The Depot of course was mobbed and as it is hard looking after baggage and child in a mob we toured the buses once to see if ours was around and then waited in the shade for it to be called over the loudspeaker. However by 4.10 it hadn't been announced so we toured the buses again as it was supposed to go at 4.15 and sure enough we found it – where it had crept in on us all loaded up and raring to go. However the driver opened up the back and put our stuff in and we climbed aboard and got the last seat. A lady from Winfield had the other half and she was nice enough to give us the window side near Leduc so Joan was kept busy mooing at the cows etc en route and trying to take off her shoes every time she spotted a pond. We arrived at Wetaskiwin at 6PM and what a mob waiting for the Camrose bus and ours. At first it looked as though we might have to wait at Wetaskiwin while our bus made an extra run into Camrose but as the sky looked like rain and our driver was anxious about the dirt road west of the lake they managed to squeeze all east bound traffic into the Camrose bus even though they had to lean on the door from the outside to close it. Poor people! At least we didn't have to wait. Then our bus was loaded and away we went with people standing up to the lake. We arrived at 7.30 and the Buckingham's met us and drove us to the cottage. Your mother had a chicken dinner waiting for us which we finished off in fine style. Joan was so tired she went to sleep without any fuss. The poor kid hadn't gone to the toilet from the time we left home until we got here – which is a record and no wet pants. We just couldn't get out of the bus at Wetaskiwin as I had planned. Don't know how she did it but she did.

She wakened up at 7.30 AM all set for a good day and she had it as the weather was perfect so we spent 2 hours in the morning and all afternoon on the beach. Joan had a wonderful time playing in the sand and running in the water and was really surprised every time she tripped and got a ducking but she's no sissy so came up laughing every time. Sure wish you were here with us as the 3 of us could have such fun.

591

However maybe next year every thing will be changed – sure hope so eh honey?

Your mother is the same although she's still saying she has no sense as she eats more than she should. She brought a 12 year old girl along as a maid and she helps out a lot although you can't expect her to do all the work so we divide the work and get through in good time.

That seems to be all for now. We are getting even blacker out here. Hope not all dirt as I'd like to claim some of it as suntan. Heaps of love my darling. Joan sends barrels of hugs and kisses to her daddy. As ever and always, Peg

July 20, 1945

Dearest Peggy,

Have been a poor correspondent again and no good excuse except laziness. Have been quite busy lately with one thing and another. Tuesday was my day off, worked all morning and slept all afternoon and got caught up on a little reading in the evening. Wednesday was routine with writing from 8:30 to 5:00 PM. Wednesday night went to a dance – quite a big event and have a good story. One of the nurses here named Jackson, works on one of our VD wards. She is engaged to an air force pilot but unfortunately this chap has one leg in plaster since he crashed a while ago. She invited me since I was so respectable. So myself and another chap got quite merry in the mess, what with drinking several double scotches, and then sallied over to the dance. Had quite a good time and came home early so I guess its OK honey I hope. Last night Jack Dickout, another Edmontonian, came over to visit Mac, so Mac and Jack and myself sallied down to the local and had a couple of pints and then came home fairly early (since the pub closes at 10:00).

Today has been a mad rush of writing. Have been filling forms and compiling charts since 8:15 this morning and have just about wound up everything. Now at 8:00 PM we take duty about once a week and cover for the person who is off. Taking their ward with about 60 pts. and then seeing your own and then writing up charts for discharge. Then you see all new admissions and allocate them to various wards and by that time it is noon. Afternoon you take instrumentation parade and pass innumerable sounds and urethroscopics (much to the discomfiture of the boys since a local anesthetic isn't used). Then you repeat the morning's routine. It keeps you busy at times but it is all quite a routine and has a terrific sameness about it. Also I'm the statistician at the moment and spend a couple of hours a day recording treatment results.

Well honey that's about all I've been doing and if you do the same thing every day it doesn't leave much to write about. Doug Ritchie phoned me yesterday – he got to the continent on leave and visited Brussels, Paris and Berlin etc. – scrounged the trip and it was strictly off the record.

Got two swell letters from you yesterday. Will write more often and sorry to be so lazy this week. All my love, Hamp

July 22, 1945

Dearest Hamp

A day or so behind in my correspondence again and no real excuse except that I leave my writing until Joan is asleep and the last few nights it's taken it's taken about 3 hours to her to sleep as its so easy for her to climb out and see what's going on and so keeps her wide awake. Last night Mother and I were playing Honeymoon Bridge and Joan would sneak out and help us play a hand. Then I'd put her back to bed with severe threats but before we could get our hands made up for a new deal she'd be out again so after two hours of that everyone was pretty tired and we all went to bed and a fine thing eh honey, when a not quite two year old can make grown-ups go to bed! If I spanked her your mother would say "Oh she's just a baby – don't spank her she doesn't know any better." However I don't quite agree with that coz Joan sure does know what she's is up to so I spanked her anyway but it had no more effect then water on a duck. That's our daughter – head strong, determined and won't take "no" for an answer.

We have been having a good quiet time on the beach and in the water and Joan just loves it. The Wildman's – next door – are down en masse and Bill Wildman's wife and little girl Bonnie are here too so Joan spends a good deal of her time visiting next door.

Had the Buckingham's in for bridge on Thursday night which was a slight change. We had expected Margaret and family down for the weekend but they didn't arrive and when we got the evening paper we saw that John Magee had died on Thursday and was to be buried in Camrose on Saturday so that accounts for their absence.

There are quite a few Camrosians here – Irene Byers, Jessie Burgess, Irene Hagle, Ann Schloss etc so we may all get together sometime. Alice and John Bill came over today for a few minutes and Joan had a marvelous time with "the man" as she calls John. She sure goes for the men.

Got two letters from you today. Ottawa sure seems definite about not letting you out – which is really what I expected. However, darling, there's one thing about it – they can't keep you forever so one of these days you'll be as free again as a married man can be. Ha! Ha! Poor boy you sure are shackled. I'll try and make your married life as comfortable as I can for you even though you are tied down with a proverbial ball and chain. Guess Mac was pretty mad to find that Ottawa doesn't think Camrose a very important spot – that's the way of the world I guess!

That seems to be all the news. Mother says to tell you she can see you all over the cottage – which doesn't really help a helluva lot! Joan and I sleep with your sun helmet hanging over our heads and Joan says, "Daddy's hat!" She's got red nail polish on today for the first time in her life. All my love dearest, Peg

July 22, 1945

Dearest Peggy,

Another couple of days gone by and soon it will be August. Suppose that you are almost thinking that a holiday and change of scenery might be a good idea. If your Maw and Pa keep running out on you, you had better pack up and take a couple of weeks somewhere and kind of get the place out of your hair. Can imagine that it's a pretty lonely existence at times and last week was the first time you ever admitted that it got you down (when you just sat down and bawled when the parents didn't arrive on schedule). I wish that I could give you any kind of clue as to when I might get home. It will probably be near Christmas, but that is pretty indefinite.

Heard some news of Johnnie Young yesterday. He is back from the continent and is up near Cambridge with a transport squadron. He is quite unhappy as usual and may go home before long. I hope to see him one of these days. Johnnie Hunt and Dave Moffat are still on the continent. Gus Garrison is in England with a squadron and is quite unhappy. Guess nobody is very pleased with things these days eh honey? – However the repats are proceeding, so it may not be too long.

George Elliott came down last night and is here today. He is the RCAF VD controller and quite a good character. Last night played bridge in the mess for about 3 hours and my partner and I made a little over 10,000 points to our opponents 2000 – quite a shellacking but we go rubber after rubber with slam bids – couldn't go wrong.

After I went to bed Howard Ellis, my roommate, came in with Mac MacDonald's pup – a nondescript animal about 2 months old. Howard was a bit corned and figured that the dog was cold outside. It wouldn't get off my bed and wouldn't sleep anywhere but on the pillow so I had rather a restless night. I chucked it on the floor a couple of times but it howled so damn loud between piddling, that had to reclaim it. First bedmate since leaving you honey, but you were never like that. All my love and pass some to Joan from me, Hamp

July 24, 1945

Dearest Peggy,

Another bit of time has slipped away. Have been fairly busy during the day time but the evenings are a little difficult to fill at times. Last night Howard Ellis, Rube Songmen (our bacteriologist) and myself wandered down to the local pub and had about 3 pints and then wandered home again. That last two days have been hot and mid-summerish (for this country) but don't get much opportunity to take in the sun during the day.

Have a few newspaper clippings to send. Was going to push them along sometime ago but it kept slipping my mind. They are pictures of Castle Archdale that appeared in the Irish and English papers and one clipping from an illustrated magazine. They give you some idea of the place and after you receive them I promise not to mention the place again.

Our wards keep full and whenever we feel that the incidence of the disease is dropping off, a new influx more than compensates for those we send out.

You asked me about my civilian clothes, the flannels are mine but I borrowed the coat from one of the boys. Must acquire some kind of tweed jacket sometime however. About civilian clothes – I have no idea what I want but am sure that I don't want it to be any form of blue for awhile.

Thora and Leonard Loveseth did well by themselves but if Thora was a "mountain of motherhood" just imagine what you were honey with your 8 pounds of Joan. Yes sir there just isn't anything that you can't do better than the neighbors.

Well darling, miss you very much, love you more and more. Am getting a real itch to have a close look at that chee-ild of ours. Give her my love and look after both of yourselves. All my love, Hamp

Canadian Red Cross Society Envelope and stationery – logo "Keep in touch with the folks at home"

July 25, 1945

Dearest Peggy,

Just a bunch of clippings of Ireland. I found them in my trunk and forget if I had sent any of them before – so am sticking them in an envelope. They show various shots of the slip-ways and hangars at Castle Archdale. The crew coming in, in the dinghy and the bottom right corner of the clippings is Jerry Allen's – he is the chap who roomed in my hut at Archdale (room beside me).

The solitary clipping shows what the Lough was like when it froze over last January and the erks had to keep the ice chopped away 24 hours a day for about a week.

Will write more on a blue form tomorrow. Excuse the writing – I am on my bed and leaning on an elbow to write this. All my love, Hamp

Dearest Hamp

Got your letter of July 20 today. Pretty good service eh honey? But you don't have to do all that apologizing about not writing for I haven't written since Saturday. Yes I'm the bum this time. Have been busy as you will see but that's not a very good excuse.

Joan and I came back from the lake on Thursday. We had a nice quiet time but were glad to get home. Your mother wanted us to stay until August 15th as she plans on staying that long. However I find when I get away form here I want to come back and when I'm here I want to go away. Just these unsettled times me thinks, but it will be good to get into a place of our own as soon as we can get together. Living with our families is all right for a time but never as good as one's own place.

To go back over last week – the days were spent on the beach and in the water and going to the store. Monday night the Buckingham's took us for a long ride – west along the highway and north almost to Mulhurst. Then Mr Buckingham started to try and fix the pump so Joan was out of bed quite late. Tuesday night the neighbors in the south came over for bridge – Galt and Mary McAllister from Wetaskiwin. He is in the Air Force stationed at Comox. They are a nice couple and as his people own the cottage we may see them again in future years. You will be jealous at the daughter for making up to Galt for she followed him around all the time and kept talking about "the man". He of course was swell with her but wait until you get home – she won't have eyes for any other man.[25] You'll have trouble going to the office without her I bet.

Wednesday Joan wakened with an awful cold. Don't know where she got it but she sure had it. Her nose and eyes ran all day and she was kind of hard to get along with. However at noon we got quite a surprise as Dad (Smalley) came strolling in on us. He had got a ride from Wetaskiwin with the mail. He'd been down on business and intended to go back that night as he didn't know I was going home the next day. We persuaded him to stay overnight and go back with us. It was a rainy day so he didn't get out on the lake as he had hoped he would.[26] It would rain our last day there of course. Was glad of help home though as Joan was not herself and slept most of the way on the bus. She's cutting her last two teeth and with the cold felt quite miserable but is a lot better today. A dose of magnesia, a hot bath and some Vick's rub did the trick. Fred Day is posted to #2 CGH at Wilhelmkhaven – yes on occupation. Temporarily he hopes and is quite disgusted. All for now and all our love, dearest – Peg

July 29, 1945

Dearest Hamp

Yes, as you say it's almost August. Amazing isn't it darling? No I'm not thinking of a holiday as we've just come back from the lake and that was it. Am saving my money in case you do come back sometime and we can manage to get away somewhere. Believe it or not I got a letter form you written last Sunday July 22nd – remarkable service old boy, remarkable service. Makes you seem just next door. Your work seems to keep you pretty busy all day and I hope you are finding it interesting. It's swell that there are so many chaps around that you knew back here.

Can't say that I'm not a bit envious of the nursing sister for taking you to the dance. Really am as I'd love to be taking you myself. However darling I don't object as it's something to do but make this stipulation that you take me to as many dances as you go to – which is about 4 now me thinks – just to keep things even. Just remember I went to a dance in Banff last fall as was mentioned almost a year ago so that cancels one dance and just makes 3 to come. Is it a date old bean?

Went out to see Margaret and Bill last night. We were going on a wiener roast but it started to rain so I went out there for a visit. Irene Smith was in town the first of the week to see a dentist and she went out to see Margaret so we got up to date on Camrose doings. Dad is in the hospital again. It seems he slipped form the wagon again but no worse than usual. Irene also broke the news that Dad has deeded the cottage and contents to Mac. Marg doesn't care as she doesn't want any of it anyway as she's pretty well severed relations with Camrose and only writes when the mood comes on which isn't very often. Mother doesn't know anything about it and that makes me mad as there is a lot of her work in the contents and I think she should have a say as to its future. May be wrong but Marg agrees with me that the least Mac could do is tell Mother – but what the hell anyhow! Eh darling?

Marg Duggan Hall's husband is coming home in August – he's at the repat centre now. Not bad after 4 years eh darling? Jeepers in a couple of years maybe you'll be there too. Ha! Ha! Sure hope that's a joke – sure hope so!

Guess what Joan's new name is? When you ask her name she says, "Doany Mith" – pretty good eh? She repeats everything everyone says so she's kept quite busy. She still has her cold but it hasn't got any worse although she runs a slightly elevated temp at night but she's pretty frisky in the daytime. All for now, heaps of love – Peg

Addressed to Peggy but written to P.F.

July 31, 1945

Dearest Dad,

Time seems to move along over here without leaving very many footprints. We manage to keep quite busy one way or another with a steady flow of patients – keeping about 350 or 400 in all the time. Our VD rate should gradually drop but each new draft of men from the continent brings quite an influx of business to us.

Repatriation seems to be progressing slowly and in a couple of months we may have some vague idea what the score on it is. My old squadron is now down on an airfield near Cambridge and converting to Liberators preparatory to start flying out east. Am quite glad to be away from it because it is liable to be stationed in this country for some time.

Guess the glads[27] are beginning to come into their full glory now. Would like to have a look at them. Have just about had a belly full of these parts but guess it will get fuller.

Hope you and Mac can manage to scrounge a bit of a holiday during the summer months.

Don't know how long I will be here but it may only be until the end of September and after that it's a matter of keeping one's fingers crossed.

Well, will write again soon.

Love – Hamp

P.S. Don't forget I'm still here and like to get the odd letter.

Dearest Peggy,

Well, here it is 8 AM and me, sharp as a tack, am sitting in my office writing my beloved wife a letter. Not much has happened since last writing but have managed to keep occupied sort of and out of trouble. Last week was a very quiet one and did little but sit around or go down to the pub of an evening and soak up a pint or two. Last night Howard and I went down to the "Seven Thorns" and had a couple of quick pints. The trouble was the Howard had sneaked a bottle of Scotch at noon and had retired for the afternoon to sip it. By the time we set out he was in no pain and I was away behind him – however I'm getting pretty philosophical about Howard and manage to keep out of his way. He's a bachelor about 40, a very nice chap, but he believes that there is nothing like a double gin and water to use as an eye opener first thing in the morning and that strikes one as carrying that sort of thing to extremes.

Should get a letter or two from you today. Got two on Saturday and was glad to hear that you and the daughter were at the lake. At least you'll have a change of scenery even if you don't have a very hilarious time.

The daughter should have quite a lot of fun with all that sand to throw around.

Got some news of the squadron this week, the ones who didn't volunteer for the east all went to a repat or air crew holding unit pending going home. The others are now at their air field near Cambridge. Guess I left them at the right time because they are holding the erks to their 3 year overseas term until they can get replacement volunteers.

Well honey, will sign off and write sooner and better. Give Joan love and kisses. All my love, Hamp

July 31, 1945

Dearest Hamp

Here it is the last day of July – midsummer and what rains we have had the last two days. Almost like a monsoon I guess, and wind too. Went over to see Alix last night and couldn't use my umbrella coming home as I was afraid I'd take off in the wind so I really got quite soaked. No ill effects today however so the outing couldn't have done any harm.

Got two letters from you yesterday – one air mail written on the 24th. Service gets better all the time. And one with pictures of May 7th sent on July 8th. The pictures with you in them were really super. They sure made me homesick or something! This waiting is hell – ain't it darling? However some day…!

Fred Day appears to be in the midst of work again. The Hospital – #7 – is well equipped and an old German hospital. He is looking after a ward of chronically infected fractures experimenting with penicillin which hasn't been used on these cases. There's a lot of surgery to be done and as the Colonel who was over Fred all through Italy has been posted to #7 too, Fred is quite happy. Most of his patients are German and likewise all the nurses except an English nursing sister – so he's right in there.

Phoned Doris Fleming today to see how everything was and Sandy is in Winnipeg hoping to be discharged. He was in Calgary the first of the month to get a medical and really got the works – gastric analysis, barium x-rays etc. Dr Vant is in the hospital quite sick and rumor has it he will have to give up his practice. He had a bad skin infection on his hands which has spread all over and to top it off has a heart condition as well. So that looks pretty grim.

Have decided to break down and tell you that I'm knitting sox for you. So you see honey the longer you are kept over there the more sox you will have to come home to. Ha! Ha! Have finished a pair of dark green ones with a fancy raised pattern all through. Am going to start on some diamond ones next – grey, blue and scarlet. Do you think that will be bright enough for your reformed taste? And by the way before I get in this too deep, do you like hand knitted sox? Sure hope so darling coz you're going to be wearing these whether yes or no. That's a threat!!!

Was wondering honey if you would keep your eyes open for a little something for Mother by way of appreciation for all she's done for us. A hunk of cloth or a piece of wood or something to send on or bring with you. I guess things are hard to get but maybe you'll come across something some day if you have the time. How's about it darling? If you've already thought of that please don't get mad at your interfering wife.

601

Joan's cold is almost better so she is getting busier each day and full of the old mick again. You should see her roll her eyes. Gosh, tis bedtime. All my love my darling – Peg

July 31, 1945

Dearest Peggy

Tomorrow we are right in the midst of summer with fall staring us in the face – it amazes one sometimes to wonder just how the time has passed – at least it seems to slip away to me and you can't look back and add very much on the profit side of the ledger.

Had a major event in the ward today. A black and white cat wandered into the nurses' office and gave birth to six very bedraggled kittens – the theatre for her confinement was the floor under the nurse's table. Quite shameless of the old girl I thought but I guess when that sort of thing kind of comes on you very suddenly, the crowd doesn't matter. What made it more funny was the fact that the nurse here apparently dislikes cats very strongly and was actually indignant about the whole situation and wasted gallons of disinfectant cleaning up the mess after the lady had completed her confinement and been moved elsewhere.

Have been up to my ears in figures all night trying to draw conclusions from the mass of material we have been tabulating – no very startling conclusions however but it keeps ones interest alive. Dagenon (?) was supposed to be the drug of choice for the treatment of most cases of non-specific urethritis. At least we have disproved that, thank God, since it is so damned toxic to the average erk.

Had a phone call from Doug McKay yesterday. All the aircrew who didn't volunteer for the east have been moved to Snaithe in Yorkshire and will go to the reception depot at Bournemouth this week for repatriation to Canada (forget when he phoned if I have already told you this).

Have started to think about my next leave. Plan to wait until October and go to Lancashire to visit all the relatives. Had a letter from William Pickup renewing the invitation (I wrote him a little while ago and kind of told him I'd take up his invitation sometime). Well honey, will sign off. Miss you a heck of a lot and love you very much. All my love Hamp

AUGUST 1945

Dearest Peggy,

One of those letters again. Have been down to the local and it is now 10 PM and I want to write the little woman and give her the business about how wonderful she is (because she is you know) so here is Hampton administering the full treatment by air.

Have been golfing today. This afternoon Clarence Schneiderman and Howard Ellis and myself decided that the day was perfect so we all would go golfing. Worked all A.M. quite industriously and got all the "clappy" gang (gonorrhea gigolos) convinced that they would get along without us for a couple of hours and then headed out.

Went down to Lipwick at 1:00 PM and found we had time for a quick beer. So we had one but unfortunately old Howard has a nose like a beagle for bottles and since a bottle had come on in the "Anchor" at noon, he had to hang around until 2:00 PM when it closed. So we stayed and Clare and myself were very cautious but Howard took the full treatment. We went down and got clubs, balls, etc. and were all equipped for about 11 shills per each. Managed to navigate the first hole without any major set back, when this Surrey sun started to sweat a little of the Surrey gin into Howard. On the second hole he drove both balls about half a mile into a wood and then lay down beside the tee and said "golf is good – but not for me". We said "damn the torpedoes full speed ahead" and left him. An hour and a half later we came back and picked him up – in the meantime he had acquired two passing females – both about 45 (35 to 50) and said "come on down and have a meal" (tea). It transpired that one of them was Johnnie Wichen's sister (the English A/G with DFC who went through Claresholm to get his wings). We had tea and left them and retired to the pub but it was a good day for us (but boring for you). Will write tomorrow. All my love, Hamp

Dearest Hamp

Well you old goat, how are you? Say what do you mean for not writing to me for six days you old bugger you? Ha! Ha! No darling, I'm really not annoyed coz the letter arrived yesterday and it was written on Monday, excellent service old chap, excellent service – Monday to Friday. And today the paper clippings of Castle Archdale arrived. They were quite interesting. Have put them in the album with all your snaps so am up to date again and waiting for more.

Went to a show last night with Helen Day Cairns but life is a trifle dull as Alix went to the lake (Sylvan) on Wednesday and Marg & Bill went yesterday to Pigeon and then on to Sylvan. However, I'm sewing again – nightgowns for Joan and myself and a fall coat for Joan from green corduroy – if I ever get it made – and then in between times there are your sox, so you see I manage to keep busy.

May go to Sylvan for a week and stay with Alix. I plan to go without Joan so I'll get a break as it's quite a problem moving around the country. However, Dad gets his holidays now so I'll have to wait and see how the land lies and then too, Joan is getting to be an awful "Mama's girl" and even fusses a bit when left with Mother so if Joan is going to raise too big a stink if I go it won't be worth it. Guess that's what moving around does to Joan as she's afraid I'll leave her. Looks like we've got something tied on our apron strings eh honey? This raising kids in war time is not a perfect set-up but better than in Europe at that.

Went downtown yesterday and bought a pair of sheets and some aluminum pans. Yes sir for use some day. Perhaps they'll have to stay in the cellar for a couple of years but at least I'm cutting down on some of the things we'll have to buy to start a home. Am leaving the big things for you – like living room, dining room and bedroom furniture – it costs money. Ha! Ha! Ain't your wife a meanie?

Joan is really talking now – repeats everything that is said – in her own words of course. She has all her teeth and can really use her head when she wants to do so. Bought her a plastic desk phone yesterday and she's having a wonderful time going around saying "Hello? Ha! Ha! Doany Mith. Mommy phone. Bye!"

Ron Horner is getting his discharge to go back to Vant any time now.

Was talking to Marg Hutton and she said so, so it must be right. Havelock McLennon and Jim Anderson are also out so your time may come one of these days. Let's hope so eh darling? Sure hope it won't be too long, not more than 3 months anyway before you're home even if you don't get out. We can wait though. All our love dearest, always – Peg

August 7, 1945

Dearest Hamp

Oh boy did you ever make a faux pas and will you ever have a lot of explaining to do. Ha! Ha! I've read about exaggerated cases in books but never in my life did I think my husband would join the ranks of the absent minded. Are you considerably worried now my darling? Well this is what your unpardonable sin is. I got two letters today both addressed to Mrs C H Smith etc so opened them. I always look at the date and read the earliest letter first and always the initial reading is just a bare scanning of the lines to satisfy myself everything is OK and that you are in the same place etc so that scanning calls for skipping the salutation until the second reading – which I did on letter of July 29. Everything was fine until my eyes picked up one phrase – "Hope you and Mac can get a holiday…" So I wrinkled my brow and quick turned back to the front and read "Dear Dad". You old buggerlugs you! And there weren't nay secrets in it either. Shucks! If you made the same mistake with Dad I hope your letter to me was clear sailing. Anyhow I'm flattered to know that you write me so often that my address flows automatically from your pen – that is of course if you weren't suffering from a hangover form three pints in the local.

The daughter just roused with wet pants and when I scolded her she kissed me and patted me on the face and made quite a to-do all the time I was scolding. Just a chip off the old man's back (pardon me!). You could *almost* get away with murder with such tactics.

Speaking of visiting the relatives we had a letter from Aunt Maggie and she was wondering where you were as you had promised to write and hadn't. You bad boy! Sure hope that leave of yours is just prior to your leaving England for good. October sounds like a long way off right now but it will be here before we know it!

Haven't done anything of real note. Monday was a civic holiday so celebrated it by making myself a nightgown with 2" lace around the neckline – for my (I mean our) second honeymoon. That makes five I've got hoarded away in my trunk – pretty swoosh eh darling?

Joan is certainly talking these last few days and even tried to dress herself today. So apart from always wanting to be with "Mommy" she is getting very independent – people marvel at her for her age. Oh! We've got quite *"the* che-ild". That seems to all for now. Heaps of love my darling – Peg

August 8, 1945

Dearest Peggy,

My apologies again for being such a bum correspondent. It's been a week since I wrote and I'm sorry. Have received two letters from you the last one was July 31 and post marked Aug. 1 – so we are keeping pretty close to each other. Can hardly wait to get caught up on those dances with you and even to be able to take you down the street for a coke would be worth more than a week holiday anywhere, right now. In the past week I have done absolutely nothing. Had a few drinks last Saturday night in the mess and the other nights have just moped around and read except for last night. Came over there to work but instead played 4 handed cribbage with some of the orderlies (*note well) and then the sister came in with her boy friend named Bill Carsen, whom she is going to marry shortly, and Bill produced a bottle of rum and rye. We had a couple and then Bill and I went over and found him a bed. And we went to it. Now the true confession comes – where the * is above – is 24 hours ago – by the time I got Bill to bed and heard how "wonderful his girl was" (quote), it was M/N – the witching hour – so we hit the hay.

Today at 7:00 P.M. I finally finished and said – well I'm going to write my one and only and to hell with young love. I was just at the point marked with the * when Bill came in and said we all had a wonderful day off and I have a bottle of Canadian rye – let's drink it while my true love changes her clothes to go on night duty. OK says your loving husband – "I've been through it all before myself – I'll help a pal" – so we sat down and drank it. So now it is about 2 hrs. later – and I love you one hell of a lot and I'm twice as sure that you're wonderful because I've just seen ourselves portrayed again – gee whiz Peg I wish I were home and I'll sure as hell wait till I am.

August 10, 1945

Dearest Hamp

Gosh here it is almost the middle of the month and almost the end of the war, at least according to commentators etc the end is near and a good thing too for with all these atomic bombs and so forth we are getting just a bit too smart.

Got your letter of August 2 on Tuesday. That was quite a game of golf you had – sure hope you took all that was coming your way for that price old boy. Talk about inflation eh honey?

Wednesday night I went out to Kay Bartlemen's and knit on your sox. She expects to go in training in Victoria this fall – if accepted – and is quite excited about it. I tried to talk her out of it but no go. Guess people just have to learn the hard way. Was also talking to Doris Frizzell's husband – school friend of mine – who has just returned from overseas after being prisoner of war for a couple of years. He was certainly glad to get back. His son was 10 days old when he went over so it was kind of a shock to him to be met by a grown child – almost that is.

Art Henderson (next door neighbor) is back with his discharge and I've never seen anyone so lost and bored with the town. Thank goodness he's going to University of Manitoba this winter – it may help to fill his time.

See from the paper tonight where Eric Duggan from across the street (and incidentally Ewart Duggan's cousin) arrived home this AM after 3 years in the air force overseas so they are gradually whittling the number of years service down and your turn to come home should arrive any time in the next year or so eh honey? I'm still quite patient about the whole thing but around Christmas time I may get a bit hard to live with if there's no hint as to when you'll be home.

The end of the Pacific war will speed up discharges a great deal but of course I realize the meds are stuck examining etc and will be one of the last group out. However as long as we are together who cares how long it takes or where we are. What say darling?

Joan spent the morning being a "toot-toot" and filled the house with all the noise. Tonight she pretended to kill flies and so busy swatting at us with a rolled paper. She can really talk now and it makes everything so much easier. Dad is called "Pugh"-last syllable of Grandpa. She won't say grand and so just shortens it to "pugh". As you can gather I haven't much news. Will take myself away and get some – I hope. Heaps of love darling from all of us. As ever, Peg

August 10, 1945

Dearest Peggy,

Another couple of days gone by with nil to report good or bad. My last letter kind of finished with a bang. I was quietly writing you when Bill Carsen came in. He is engaged to one of the sisters here and I met him and kind of made him feel that he was not unwelcome. He consequently came in that evening with a bottle of Canadian Rye which we drank, went over to the mess and had a scotch or two and then he went over to the sisters' mess to see his one and only. I showed him the way over but left immediately to finish the letter and get it in the mail – it might have been better if I had postponed the finish for a day.

Things are in quite a turmoil what with rumors of Jap capitulation flying thick and fast. If they are correct then we may get home a little sooner than we first believed not a great deal sooner, but a little I think. Sure hope so darling – keep your fingers crossed. That atomic bomb is certainly demonstrating the terrific power it has for good or for evil – depending on how it is used.

Will look around and try and get something for your Ma and yourself. Sorry I have been so thoughtless. Things are hard to get and are just junk at twice normal prices so I haven't done much shopping. However I will start to concentrate on it a little more.

We still keep busy and I manage to have my 60 patients with me all the time.

Well honey will write sooner. Miss you. All my love, Hamp

Dearest Hamp

Is tomorrow V-J Day or is it not? At the moment that seems to be the $64 question. It probably will be as the whole thing looks like a repetition of the V-E Day rumors – one day the war is on, next day it's off. However it won't be long now eh honey?

Well, don't really know what to say now. Haven't been out since Wednesday so news is nil. Your grey, red and blue sox are coming along remarkably well though however and I've made another nightgown for Joan.

Speaking of Joan, she's turning into a very polite girl – but still a toughie. Today she sneezed and surprised everyone by saying "s'cuse me" and at dinner she said "please" and "ta-ta" at the right time. Yesterday morning she did a "potty dance" in front of the mirror "a la nude" – by that I mean that she was jumping up and down and laughing while she waved her pot around in the air. Quite the dance I must say. Maybe we should change her name to "Gypsy Rose" as she hates to wear clothes.

Was reading a book of anecdotes the other day and the following appealed to me.

A sailor was taking leave from the hard boiled 'girlfriend' of his day pass and he said, "If anything should happen to you in nine months you'll call it Fatima won't you dear, as I like that name." To which the babe replied "If anything happens to you in 3 weeks time you can call it eczema if you prefer." Ha! Ha!

> A buxom woman went to her doctor for a quick method of committing suicide – one with no muss or fuss. The doc was quite concerned but as the woman was having a great deal of trouble with money, husband and children he at last consented and advised her to go home, undress, got to bed and shoot herself below the left breast. She took his advice, followed his directions and shot herself through the kneecap. Ha! Ha! End of joke.

On Tuesday I'm going by bus to Sylvan Lake to spend a week with Alix and Sandy. It will be a good break as Mother has offered to look after

Joan. Awfully decent of the old girl I must say but she'll probably need a rest after the che-ild has gone through her paces.

That seems to be everything up to date except that I miss you a bit more as time goes by – but the one consolation is that the war is over or almost so at least we know you'll be home one of these days eh honey? Keep your chin up old boy and don't let that gang let you down. That's all. Heaps of love as ever and always – Peg

August 12, 1945

Dearest Peggy,

Nothing to report from here that's of any interest. Am duty Joe today and keep puddling along with routine of viewing these diseased male appendages and reflecting what a hell of a state the world is in.

The news of Japan is too good to be true and I'll believe it when it is official. They surely can't go on much longer but they can certainly be a nuisance for a while if they refuse to capitulate. We may make it by Christmas after all and can only keep hoping.

Last night being Saturday night – went down to the pub with Roy Clarke, Mac MacDonald and Leonard Loveseth. Had a few beers and home to the mess where there was a party on – had something to eat and went to bed. Not a very exciting evening but managed to get another 24 hours scrubbed off that calendar.

I wanted to run up to London tomorrow but am afraid of running into V.J. day so am just going to relax on my day off and do nothing. Hope it stays hot. Last week was cold and wintry and we thought that summer had gone but today and yesterday the hot sunshiny days of this part of the country, returned. One certainly can't grumble about the weather down her and at times might be foolish enough to say that it was almost too warm.

Well darling, give the daughter loads of love and lots of kisses from me. Tell her that she might have to claim her old man before too long. All my love, Hamp

Dearest Peggy,

Well, the big day has come and it seems hard to believe after all these months and years. We get a pretty selfish viewpoint over here since the end of the Pacific war doesn't affect our immediate prospects a great deal – but it certainly does affect our future ones. Certainly hope the shipping situation eases in the next very few months.

Wonder what you did on VJ day. We worked in day time till noon and then retired to mess and had a quick toast and then came over here to finish up our work. Len Loveseth arrived at 3 PM with a Jeep and so Mac MacDonald and Roy Clarke and myself piled in and we drove to Brighton. There was nothing doing on the way and Brighton was just a mass of people we went on to Eastbourne and had tea and then the pubs opened and we had a beer or two. We then did a pub crawl by Jeep (had a driver named Ben) and met about a million people who were really enjoying themselves. Every pub had a piano in it and we thoroughly enjoyed ourselves until about 10 PM and then we shook off a couple of Aussies and some Englishmen and set out for home. It was about a hundred mile drive home and every town we came to had the pubs going full blast and dancing in the streets to the music of mouth organs, accordions etc. We stopped about half an hour in four places and joined the locals and then forged on. Ran out of gas about 30 miles from home but fortunately stopped an army truck almost immediately and scrounged a jerry can of the fluid. Arrived home at 3:00 AM very pleased with ourselves because we had drunk a lot of beer but had enough time riding to keep sober and if we had stayed on camp we would have gotten squiffed and gone to the party at the nurses mess and ended up with nothing but a hangover. Today is still a national holiday but our business progresses as per usual.

Got a letter from you today and was certainly pleased to hear that all is per usual. Joan is really her "Mother's" girl and I have been thinking a bit lately – how will she like it when her old man comes home and tries to monopolize a little of her maw's time. It will be interesting to see won't it? All my love, Hamp

August 17, 1945

Dearest Hamp

Well darling how do you feel about all the things that have happened in the last few days? It's really hard to believe that the war is over – if the Japs would only stop fighting. I really can't remember a world not at war it seems so long ago. We'll have fun finding out what it's like to live normally again won't we honey?

I'm a bit behind in my writing but with good reason, celebrating and all you know, but in a very mild manner. Tuesday night Kay B and I went downtown to see how the world was celebrating. We just shoved up and down the street in the milling mob and got quite a bang watching the people. Saw more bottles of beer and 26s being consumed on street corners and no one seemed to mind. There was paper and confetti all over the place and the streets were really jammed with people, cars and bands. It took an hour to come home on the streetcar as kids on the street kept pulling the trolley off. Sure was tired when I got home – just from fighting for my two square feet of ground to stand on. On Wednesday morning went down to Dad's office to see the big parade which was quite good. How did you celebrate? Bet a lot of the boys had bad headaches for a few days after.

Guess you don't know where I am right now. Yes sir your wife sure gets around. I'm sitting in the sun in the front yard of Alix's cottage at Sylvan Lake – hence the awful writing. Came down yesterday by bus. What a trip! It was awfully hot and we had to keep the windows closed as the tar splashed in. Alix, Sandra and Connie have been down since the first of the month and I've come down until Tuesday. Mother is looking after Joan which is really wonderful. Hope Ma won't be too tired. We no longer have a dog. Sent Buddy to the pound yesterday as he was so old and dying a little bit each day. Mother felt it more than any of us as he was more her companion in the last few years.

It's grand down here at the lake and so awfully hot. Should really get some more tan. The other kids are brown as Indians and altho' I'm brown I'll have to go some to catch up. We have a lot of fun kidding each other and are very amiable. Leila comes down tomorrow so we'll be able to play a spot of bridge. Last night we sat and knit sox until midnight and then we slept like logs. And are we eating – boy what an appetite! Just wish you were here and Joan and everything would be grand. Oh well. That's all for now darling. Heaps of love always – Peg

Ordinary Mail: Canadian Red Cross Society Envelope and Stationery with logo "Keep in touch with the folks at home"

August 18, 1945

Dearest Peggy,

Some snap shots taken in front of the mess at 22 CGH at Bramshott. You'll probably recognize Cam Harrison and Leonard Loveseth with MacDonald on the right side of all the pictures.

Please notice in the picture which includes your husband that he is the only one not holding a glass. The air force pilot is a chap from Peach River who was visiting Mac the day Len and Cam arrived.

You don't get much of an idea what the countryside around here is like because the hospital is built on a plateau then there are valleys on all sides with hills on the other side and not visible in the background of the snaps. I'll have to take some more pictures of the countryside one of these days.

No mail from you today but can't grumble because your correspondence is really faithful these days.

Well honey, will sign off and finish on a blue form. All my love, Hamp

August 21, 1945

Dearest Peggy,

Received a letter from you today – Aug. 20 – so we average about 8 to 10 days for our reply. That Eric Duggan used to be the senior admin officer at Topcliffe in Yorkshire where I spent most of my England time. He is a pretty good fellow and was very popular on the station.

Yesterday I went up to London. Went up at 9:00 and came back at 5:10 PM. Went over to Knightsbridge and had lunch with Doug Ritchie and a couple other MOs from the medical board. We went to our favorite pub there and had a few beers and it was quite a pleasant noon hour all told. Went up to accounts and got a 10 pound advance on my pay from Gordon Armstrong – the accts. Joe who I got to know very well in Yorkshire – was a bit broke with our V.J. excursions in the bar. Then came home with the dough (intact).

Saw the W/O from headquarters – he is the bloke who knows all and I got him to tell all he knew. He said that I should be on a boat within three months time – says my repat number will be in about the third draft and there will be approx. one a month. Sounds pretty good eh darling? – even if he is a month out it will be close to Christmas so we have a little something to build on and by the end of September we can maybe start setting a date for that big re-union.

I am getting a little hard to live with at times these days – seem to miss you a little more each day and have got to the day counting stage – which isn't very good for morale – is it honey? However anyone with a wife as wonderful as my own can't be blamed too much.

Move to a new ward tomorrow. I have been treating non specifics and now move to the "incurable ward". All those that don't respond end up there and you monkey around with fever etc. It will be interesting for awhile at least.

Also I move my quarters tomorrow. Get a room over in "B" quarters which is about half a mile further away. A better room and more exercise so it isn't too bad except for the bother of moving my goods and chattels.

Well honey will sign off. All my love, Hamp

August 22, 1945

Dearest Hamp

Don't know just how this letter will progress as Sandy is sitting on a stool at my feet asking questions and moving around, however, we'll see what happens.

It is 10.30 AM and am packed up for the trek back to the city – packed as far as I can that is – for the bus doesn't go until 6.20 PM. Connie is coming back with me so I stayed on another day. We have had a funny week so far. Monday night I got the heebie-jeebies in my stomach and spent the night throwing up – just like Sandy on Saturday.

Felt swell really but couldn't make my stomach behave and yesterday was just like a good hangover – felt like a wet rag. Last night Alix started so it must have been something we ate or some bug or other. Connie is wondering if it will hit her tonight. She threatens to make me get off the bus if she is which I would do anyhow.

Sandra is just getting bawled out for getting in the jam pail and is going around saying "I'm aren't dirty" when Alix wanted to wash her face. She's sure a cute kid but doesn't quite compare with Joan. Oh natch-natch. Gee I sure miss our daughter. Was glad to get away for a while but now can hardly wait to get home. Had a letter from Mother yesterday and they are getting on OK. Also got a letter from you written August 10. Guess you're all over V-J Day by now. We hear more rumors about fellows getting discharged right and left over here. Who cares eh? We are quite settled down to expecting all you fellows next spring but I think we all secretly haven't given up hope for your returns soon. I know I'm still quite optimistic on one hand and quite resigned and philosophical on the other. Guess I won't be disappointed I hope.

The kids are going to town so must away. Heaps of love my darling. As always – Peg

PS – Fred's address is #5 CGH

August 23, 1945

Dearest Peggy,

Two more days gone adrift with not much of special interest. Yesterday Johnnie Young and Dave Moffat blew in. We had quite a lot of talking to do to get caught up on all our gossip and spent a very enjoyable few hours finding out what we didn't know about the boys. In the evening the sister from my ward invited us over to a Wednesday "at home" in the sisters' mess. To sort of get a run at it we had a couple of scotches in the mess and then Dave produced a bottle of cognac and then we went down the local in Liphook and drank dogs' noses (gin and beer). By the time we got over to the Sisters' Mess we were no particular discomfort. Don't think the Air Force was looked on with much favor and the Sister is quite cool towards us today. However we enjoyed ourselves so what the hell. Johnnie went back to his station today – he is up near Cambridge and I hope to get a day off and go up and visit him next week. Dave is possibly going to be posted to the hospital here and went up to London today to find out about it.

I moved my room again today – I am having quite a lot of difficulty in getting settled but guess we will all find a bed eventually. The new quarters are certainly healthy since you walk about three miles a day going to work and meals – won't do me a bit of harm I guess.

Have been sitting around the office here all night. Came over to write this letter right after supper but Mac and Vic Rosenfield (a Jewish lad but really a fine chap) drifted in and we gassed for three hours and then went over to the mess and had tea and a sandwich and it is now 11:00 PM and am just getting around to the writing.

Well honey, will sign off and start the trek for the quarters – miss you an awful lot but maybe it won't be too long now. Give the daughter my love and kisses.

All my love. Hamp

Penciled on envelope: O.K.

August 26, 1945

Dearest Hamp,

I'm home again and letter behind. Just a bum – that's me – just la bum eh darling? Connie Day came back from the lake with me and was I ever glad as had to wait 3 hours in Red Deer as the bus broke down in Olds and so had to be fixed. The Sylvan bus arrives in Red Deer an hour before the north bound bus so we waited that hour by drinking lemonade and smoking in the Club Cafe. Then back to the bus depot to wait 30 minutes before they found out the bus was late and wouldn't be along until 10 PM. It was then 8:30 and were we mad as we didn't have time to go to a show for it was going on 9 by the time we got our bags packed away in the depot – which was a hotel. So we just sat in the lobby and the pay off came when we had to argue with the desk clerk to keep from locking up. I didn't quite get it but that seems to be what they do down there. However we finally got on the bus shortly after ten. The old thing sounded like a train on a bridge but we made town by 1 AM despite everything. Connie got off at Whyte and 109 St. and I got off at the High Level so it wasn't a bad haul with a loaded suitcase.

Joan was certainly glad to see me and kind of sounded like the broken record saying "Mum – me" and finally ending up with "dear Mum-me". It sure sounded cute. Thursday was a bad day as I was tired and not used to so much work after the lake – although I really didn't do a thing but unpack.

Friday morning went downtown to buy a shower gift for Harold Oldring's fiancée. Got a pair of towels. Then Friday night went to the shower at Netta's. Had a good time and it was almost a family affair. Sure were a lot of kith and kin around.

Saturday night went out with a gang of girls from the Club. We were supposed to go hiking but as it rained we went to a member's house in Glenora and had our wieners, buns, do' nuts and beer – yes beer! That is quite a rare treat let me tell you darling. You sure won't know your teetotaler wife now. Two bottles give me quite a glow now. Pretty cheap eh honey? It was a good party and got home around 1:30 AM and of course Joan awakened at 7 AM and me with a mild hangover and Mother not well so she stayed in bed all day. One of those tired spells again. She's always doing so much. We had a prime rib roast and Peggy's apple pie for dinner so really made out OK.

Had a letter from Alix and Fred has been posted to England and has been told he can be discharged over there to take a P.G. course and that Alix and Sandra will be able to go over there in two or three months so Alix is quite excited although nothing may come of it. You may have even seen Fred by now as he knows where you are stationed.

Helen Day got a letter from her husband last week saying he would be home in time to open the school season at Beaverlodge so she thinks he is on his way. He was a Fl Sgt in the Air Force (education) so it's all beginning to look hopeful. Although I'm not too optimistic as yet. Sure hope we see you by Christmas though.

Guess I'll have to be getting Joan a tricycle soon as she thinks there's nothing quite like them, can't get her by one on the street. It's hard to believe that we have a child old enough for a tricycle. Actually she's a bit young for one and as winter is coming I think it'll wait until next spring. Then you can buy it. Ha! Ha! When you get back I'll sure get my nose shoved out as Joan'll sure take to you like a duck to water. And be prepared for no moments of privacy as Joan doesn't care where you are or what you are doing as long as she is there. Dr. Carpenter died in Calgary on Friday so Dad is away to his funeral. He gave me to you. Remember? All my love my darling. Hope you'll be home soon. As always, Peg

August 27, 1945

Dearest Peggy,

Away behind in my correspondence and no good excuse. Haven't been doing anything but the usual so will enumerate. Freddy Day phoned me on Saturday and I wasn't available so he left a message that he was phoning back at noon. I hung around all noon hour and then gave up and he phoned in the afternoon when I was over at the detention barracks seeing some of my clients. I phoned him back and missed him so that's how things stand at the moment. Hope to see him one of these days though. Art Beauchamp was in on Saturday but could only stay a few minutes. Dave Moffat is now here to stay so we were in the bar having a beer or two when Art came in. He is going home and I told him to be sure to phone you to tell you I still love you and wish that I were home 24 hrs a day (wishing 24 hrs. to be home 24 hrs a day).

Yesterday was Sunday and my day off. I had quite a bit to do and came over here until about 2:00 PM and then the sister invited me to cycle over to Borden where her boy friend was stationed. So we set out and rode about 12 miles to get there. Picked him up and rode about 10 miles to Raslemere for something to eat and then back via a long up-hill route to Bramshott. I said thanks very much and went home and collapsed completely in my bed. This outdoor stuff is wonderful but in moderation for me in the future (when I get to the stage where I can walk comfortably). This is lovely country but all hills.

Watched a cricket game when we were cycling and I had to stop and rest. About 20 middle-aged Englishmen were really pounding up the turf. I was quite impressed because we certainly would never see a group of men of comparable age at home exercising that rigorously.

Am in the midst or pouring a little blood into one my G.C. arthritic's before I start him on fever tomorrow. Hope he does OK because he isn't in the best of health at the moment. Too bad that penicillin doesn't reach these people. Well honey, have more to write but will do it tomorrow (for sure, for sure). All my love, Hamp

August 29, 1945

Dearest Peggy,

Nothing of any interest to report. Haven't done anything in the past two days except flap around trying to get our patients out of the ward before they grow too old and gray. My ward doesn't present much interest because they are all more or less chronics and when everyone else gets tired of them, they get shipped to me. Am giving them all fever with intravenous TAPS so you can imagine they are not a happy lot with their chills, headache, and what not.

Had good news today. Canada is apparently getting more shipping and in the next couple of weeks they are sending home enough to get nearly a month ahead in their quotas. Doesn't mean a great deal but it is all encouraging for getting home for Christmas or sooner. Will maybe know more about it on Friday. Am going up to a meeting of RCAF MO's in London and we should hear the latest rumor as least.

Got three letters from you over the weekend. Glad to hear that you got out to Sylvan with Alix – guess the daughter will be able to get along without you for a few days (you are probably back in Edmonton about a week now I suppose).

Am getting pretty impatient to climb in that boat but guess it won't be so long that we can't be patient.

Haven't heard from Camrose Jr. in some time. Guess they aren't speaking. By the way, a little premature but have been thinking – don't worry about sending anything for my birthday or for Christmas. Won't suffer very much even if I don't get home and probably will be home before Christmas and anything I get will have to make that ocean voyage twice. Well honey, miss you more than ever. This letter is a little vague but about 20 people have wandered in and out of the office as I wrote it. All my love, Hamp

This letter ends up in not a very good mood – just ignore! Kind of patched it up a bit so it's not too bad now.

Hello my darling

Yes this is your wife back in the writing beam. I'm a bum and I know it but have really been the social butterfly this week and quite enjoyed it altho' it has made a very busy week and I didn't get a lot of things done I had planned.

Monday afternoon Joan, mother and I were invited to afternoon tea on Henderson's back lawn – quite a do – ice cream and all. There were 3 other kids there Joan being the youngest by 6 months in one case and a year or more in the others. However she held her own and got what she wanted most times.

Tuesday afternoon Doris Fleming phoned. Sandy was in Calgary to get his final discharge papers as he is going to the University of California in San Francisco to take a PG in orthodontics in October (pause for breath) so Doris was lonely (Ha! Ha!). The outcome was that we had dinner in town and went to a show. Then Doris came back with me to spend the evening.

Wednesday afternoon Joan and I boarded the street car and went out to Doris's for dinner. It is quite a trek as the Flemings live 1 ½ blocks from the end of the blue line in the west end. Joan enjoyed the ride and got quite excited at all the men on the car. She called the river "a big bath" and all in all we enjoyed the excursion. We came back about 8.30 so Joan was quite thrilled at all the colored lights.

Thursday afternoon sent down town to bank my cheque and spend some money. Bought myself a brown felt sport hat and a pale green blouse. Sent your birthday parcel and must apologize that it isn't more personal. Ordered it through Eaton's as they can get the rare cans like salmon. They pack and send it so all I did was pay for it. However darling don't feel abused as your real birthday present is waiting for you at home for that big reunion. At night the JWC club held a dinner party at Mrs Cooper's – half way to the country club – for Kay B and Phil Weber who leave on Tuesday for Royal Jubilee Hospital – poor kids! We had a real good meal and a lot of fun and then went bowling – I watched along with some other not very ambitious types. Now I'm writing you and then going to make a coat for Joan.

That news about you coming home in 3 or 4 months (maybe) is too good to be true and I'll only believe it when I see you. But I'm quite excited anyway although I pretend not to be. Bet it was good to see John and Dave again and by now you should have met Fred. If you come home in 3 months time you'd better start tapering off on the drinking as the sudden stop may be too much for your constitution *(said in fun)* and then too I'm a bit leery of home and drinking life mixing to any great extent *(said seriously)* as we know some people *(meaning Mac)* who seem to have quite a time. However that won't stop me from drinking a wee bit and I suppose what you do is *(mostly)* your own affair so we should get along. Dad was just saying tonight that seeing he couldn't get his holidays this summer he'd take them just after you got back and then we could have this house to ourselves for a week or two or so as long as we wanted. Sound pretty well to me darling, what about you? We could make up for lost time then, the three of us, all by ourselves. I sure can't stand much more of fitting in with other people. Am sure going to be stubborn and selfish for a while about some things I'm afraid, dearest, such as a holiday for us. However – see you soon. All my love, as always – Peg

SEPTEMBER 1945

September 2, 1945

Dearest Hamp

Here it is September and another month by the board. It seems only yesterday that August came rolling in. Sure hope the next few months role by as quickly eh honey?

Heard today that Art Beauchamp is at a repat centre now. Perhaps that is old news to you by this time. Did you ever run into Art? You just mentioned that he was to call around one night. Fred is stationed at Taplow Park #11 CGH now. But you've probably seen him by now too. What a reunion that will be. Wish I could be there to see it however we'll all have a big one some day and make Fred crack open some of the champagne he sent back from France. And speaking of that sparkling liquid – he had two bottles of it confiscated by the postal authorities. So he's not as clever after all even though he has managed to get quite a bit of it past the 'Gestapo'.

Alix was over yesterday with Sandy and we sat in the back yard while the kids played in Joan's sand pile and turned somersaults on the grass. Fred expects to be home for Christmas perhaps a bit earlier. Sure hope you're home too coz we could all have a bang up time together New Year's Eve. Of course Alix may be going to England if she gets her exit permit.

Saturday night (last night) I went over to Kay's with some of the kids from the club. It was Kay's last Saturday in Edmonton for sometime as she leaves on Tuesday for Victoria – to go in training as I've mentioned before. She and Phil Weber (who is going too) were quite excited about it all but their glee will pass shortly me thinks. It will be hard on them as they are 25.

Tonight Joan and I went for a ride with Alix, Sandy and her grandparents. We saw all the new houses being built under the Veteran's Land Act. They look like quite nice places and they make quite a settlement – 300 or so.

Joan is quite a demon these days and has a fiendish gleam in her eye on occasion and altho' hard to handle at times is really a cute kid – if I do say so. Sure am glad she's ours as the days would have been very long without her. Almost finished Joan's coat on Friday night and hope to get it done tomorrow. That's all for now. Heaps of love my darling, Peg

September 2, 1945

Dearest Peggy,

Two days into winter. It doesn't seem possible that we are again into fall with more rain and what not approaching. Certainly will keep my fingers crossed against spending another winter here. When I said, don't bother about my birthday or Christmas, I didn't mean to give the idea that I was on a boat but there is such a good chance of being home by Christmas that it would be kind of silly to worry about sending anything over here – can make it all up when we get home.

Have done very little in past few days. Went up to London on Friday after ward rounds. Went to my lending library and drew out 3 more books, bought a new tie for 9 shills, (a ridiculous price for a plain black tie) had a chop-suey dinner, wandered around down Piccadilly, Trafalgar Square etc. and did some window shopping, went to the bank and drew out my money and then went over to Lincoln's Inn Fields and saw the film on cardiac surgery. It was quite good but just a little out of our line. The American surgeon who did the surgery was there and gave quite an interesting talk as the film proceeded. He had removed a good many foreign bodies from heart chamber with no deaths. Since the films were in Technicolor you can imagine how much red there was in them when the stage came up where the heart was actually incised. Came home on the 8:45. Dave Moffat and I went up together and George Elliott (VD Controller) came back with us to wander around the hospital for the weekend. We are still fairly full although not overworked. I have about 2 or 3 on fever every day and since I get all the complications in my ward – it is fairly interesting. Wish more every day that I were with you. But will not get too pressed on the whole situation. Love you and the daughter very much. All my love, Hamp

September 5, 1945

Dearest Hamp

If I used to sit and wait for the postman before you can imagine what I'm doing these days with all the wonderful news and rumors about your posting home. Your letters sure get better all the time and I hope the meeting of MOs last week was good news and not the typical brush-off which has been usual with the services.

Saw Easton the other day with wife and child. He doesn't know me of course but I recognized him from pictures. He has been appointed to Dr McQueen's old job of administer of the Colonel Mewburn Hospital.

Monday – Labor Day Holiday – I stayed close to home. Auntie Lena and Harold and his fiancée were over for supper mainly to see Dad as he is taking the service.

Tuesday was Ma and Pa's 32nd anniversary so gave them a dozen gladioli from the 3 of us. While down town bought myself some panties (and with elastic all the way around too) and a slip and leggings and shoes for Joan. Lingerie has been almost nil the last year and my stock was getting very low. However, am buying whenever I see any now so should have my second trousseau well established when you come home.

Alix, Helen and I went to Thompson and Dynes fall fashion show today and got the lowdown on the fall clothes – also the price. You needn't worry old boy, didn't even have to talk myself out of buying anything. $130 for a suit and $300 for a cloth coat with some fur trim are a bit out of my element.

As you know I sent a parcel of food away for your birthday. Will see how postings are going before I send a Xmas one. There will be nothing personal for either in case you've gone then we won't have to worry about the parcels making that second sea voyage eh darling?

Had a letter from your mother today – first one for over a month – mostly as I haven't written either. Mac and Irene got to Banff for a week as Dad took over. Dad has written Ottawa again to see about getting you out. (Sounds like a prison term; perhaps it is in a way eh honey?) Mother is fine. Have a new maid – reminds her of Margaret. Margaret and Bill went to Jasper over the long weekend. So that's Camrose.

Fred Day is on leave in Ireland as he didn't make it last time. Perhaps you saw him before he got away. Alix had word from Ottawa and she most definitely cannot leave the country – even with the Vealonds pull – so guess Fred will be a-sailing home one of these days too.

Have just about finished Joan's coat – the hand finishing sure takes a long time but am going to sew the lining in tonight and then its all done. The first coat I've made and all on my own hook as Ma leaves me alone now when I'm sewing as we've had some tiffs over it in the past. The coat is part of Joan's trousseau for your homecoming. Heaps of love my darling, always, Peg

PS Forgot to mention it is swell Dave is with you. Say hello to him for me. More love

Dearest Peggy,

Away behind in my letter writing and no excuse because I certainly have been doing nothing which might otherwise occupy. Have been home every evening since last writing and busy in the hospital for a couple of them. Am now rooming with Dave Moffat and we are quite comfortably settled. Am rather glad to get away from Howard Ellis since he is drunk 28 out of every 30 nights and is quite fed up with England. We all are but it doesn't help to have to live with someone like that. Last night Dave and I had a couple of quick ones before the evening meal while we shot a game of pool. Then we looked in at the meal and decided that we would be better off to have another couple of quick ones. After that things looked a little better and we came over to the room and had some cheese and crackers and canned tongue which the previous occupant of the room had willed us when he went home – funny how you can make the time go now that it gets dark so early and the evenings seem longer. It's now quite dark at 8 o'clock. The weather is cooler with little sunshine so winter isn't too far away. On Tuesday I took the sister on my fever ward at nights out to lunch and had a lobster and then walked home. It was quite respectable darling and she is leaving the place which was the reason for the splurge so hope that it's OK.

Had quite a surprise today and yesterday. Got a letter from Mac yesterday and one from Irene today. Mac drew out the plans he has for converting the downstairs of the building in Camrose into offices and it looks pretty good. Irene is sending a parcel. Don't know what came over them all of a sudden but guess that I better answer right back and maybe they'll repeat the proceedings.

Miss you and Joan just a little more each day and wish that you were here with me. Was talking to Jimmy Ralston who was with Freddy Day. Freddy still hasn't any definite plans and it seems more likely that he will go home and then possibly return to England. Well darling, all my love to you and share it with the daughter, Hamp

Dearest Hamp,

I think that's the date. At any rate it's Saturday night and Mother and Dad are at Harold Oldring's wedding and Dad is officiating so Joan and I are at home.

Finished Joan's coat at last. Sure didn't realize that such things as sewing in linings and doing buttonholes etc. take such a long time. The deck is all clear now to start making something else. Have also just finished a pair of mitts for Joan but must do two more pair. Thank goodness she doesn't need any sweaters. Remember that white and blue creation I knit in Claresholm while Joan was on the way? Well she can still wear that, or should I say is at last able to fit in it. Speaking of knitting old boy, you didn't mention whether you liked knitted sox or not. Have two pairs done now and hate to knit any more if you don't like them. So please let me know eh honey?

I've just been bursting since I got your letter prior to going to London on Aug. 31. Can hardly wait for the mail tomorrow to find out what went on if anything but suppose they don't know very much. Three boats docked in Canada this weekend. That's sure bringing them home fast. Here's hoping eh honey?

Don't know how you feel about such things but I'd kind of like (1) to meet you in Saskatoon or Winnipeg.(if you are allowed to break your trip) and have a day or two alone for just the two of us and then pick up Joan and go down to Camrose for as long as you like. (2) Or go down to Camrose for awhile and them come back to this place if Ma and Pa go away. Those are just my two ideas. What are yours darling? I honestly think the two of us and preferably the 3 of us should have a few days alone somewhere without having to fit into anyone's program but our own. Your family will probably want (you, us) for your whole 30 days leave but I'm afraid I'm too selfish to see it all that way. Your mine and I want you, so there! Don't you think we should have some sort of a plan to count on? It would be much easier seeing that we have no real place of our own. What are your views on the subject, darling? That should be good for a couple of letters in case you're out of writing material. But honestly honey I'm serious! What are your plans? Our daughter can carry on quite a conversation now and has got to the "no" stage when asked to say something. Isn't that kind of early? She has to kiss Daddy's picture every night so you're not neglected. Heaps of loves and kisses.

As ever, Peg.

Dearest Peggy,

Got two letters from you – today and yesterday. In today, you apologized for not writing more promptly – boy did that ever make me feel like a heel. Promise you I will write every second day whether there is anything to write about or not. The days go by here and there is nothing to record so you just kind of let them slip.

The pictures of you at the lake came yesterday. I didn't stop looking at them for hours and have made all the MOs of the dept. have a look and after that the comments came quite naturally. Am certainly the luckiest guy in the world and wish I could say that I was worthy of you. I'll have to improve considerably to live up to that beautiful wife of mine. It made me kind of nervous to think about going home and thrusting my attentions on someone who grows more beautiful with each passing month, while I don't improve a bit. Maybe I'll have to propose all over again and just hope for the best.

Interruption – Mac MacDonald and Clarke White (another MO) just wandered in. Everyone seems to drift over to their offices in the hospital these evenings because the rooms are so damn cold now that it's raining every day and fall is coming. It's too chilly to sit in the room and read and can't hang around the mess now that I've taken the pledge (after getting a blast from my little woman by mail today). I quite agree with you honey on the principle of the consumption of alcoholics in the home in excess and will never let you down on that score.

We have just been having a little discussion. Have been reading the nominal roll of everyone in the Can. Army who has ever had VD – about 65,000 names which is one hell of a lot. Most of them aren't to be excused at all and for that reason I get a little fed up with my work around here at times. I can truthfully say darling that I have not been

627

unfaithful to you since I left you (or before) and cannot condone what our patients seem to think nothing of.

Saturday was a big day (here's that drinking again) – Mac got his majority so we had a few drinks and since there was a party in the mess we made it a departmental celebration and everyone had a good time. Unfortunately I had a sore foot and loosened my shoelace and then offered to dance with a sister and shed my shoe and had four toes sticking out of a sock so my face was very red. Last night Bill Carsen – a brother of an MO I know got engaged to the sister on my last ward and had me to dinner and a drink – positively the last one however – even it was quite subdued. All my love, Hamp

September 12, 1945

Dearest Hamp,

You old buggerlugs you! You sure had me over a barrel last weekend waiting for mail expecting great news from your London trip. So what was the letter all about? Cardiac surgery and a tie worth 9/. I'm still laughing at me for getting so excited, but next time I'll be more cautious and won't believe anything until you arrive home. It wasn't anything you really said in your letter other than you might have more rumors but I sure lapped it all up. However it was real fun to be so full of expectation for a change. One of these days it will al come true though eh honey?

The headlines in Monday's Journal was to the effect that all troops except occupation would be home by or shortly after Christmas which sounds too good to be true. Heard a rumor yesterday that all Air Force would be home by the end of November – which is also too good to be true. All these rumors and the arrival of three boats last weekend keeps one on their toes and I'm sure getting my work all caught up. Joan's coat done, mittens made, some sox done and now I'm making your Christmas present. Ha! Ha! You'll never guess what it is!

Sure am spending money lately. Took my fur coat in to be shortened a bit, had my shoes repaired, bought Joan two pair of leggings, white and blue (for winter) and myself a blue dressmaker's shirt. Quite plain but it fits like a glove. (Sound effects here please – a whistle) size 11 – to be exact! Now all I need is a better dress for going places of an evening and I'm all set and awaiting for you. It's fun to buy things to put away knowing that when I wear them you'll be around. Ah! What it is to love one's husband!

Last night went to the Capitol with Alix and Helen to see "Enchanted Cottage" – good and sentimental. Tonight is JW Club so should get some more knitting done. My mind's not on Club this year. Of the 4 other married girls in the club – one's a war widow, one's husband is writing from overseas for a divorce, another has his discharge from the Navy and the fourth had never enlisted so I'm kind of on my own in getting excited.

In case you are interested Art Beauchamp arrives in Calgary tomorrow and Sheila has gone to meet him-pretty fast work once you get on the way eh darling?

Took Joan downtown this AM and she was bug-eyed at the stores and people etc. Heard all about it the rest of the day and probably far into the night. She is really talking a blue streak now and is on to the "No!" and "My!" stage. Everything is "My car, my shoes, my spoon etc." with great emphasis on the my! If you ask her if she'd like to do something or tell her to do something the reply is always "No!!!!!"-but definitely, and with a shake of the head, although with a bit of pressure she usually comes around without a fuss. This bringing up kids is really quite a game as you will find out – the hard way.

Fall is really here. The leaves are turning and the nights are quite cold with some frost so guess winter is not far away. Ron Horner has got his discharge and is back with Vant although Ross is too sick to do anything. He is at home now but really quite a wreck from what I can gather. That seems to all the news right now. Flash! I just killed a mosquito – maybe summer is coming again. Goodness don't tell me time goes that fast! All my love, my darling, and here's hoping for good news soon. As ever, Peg

September 12, 1945

Dearest Peggy,

Another letter from you today which makes 3 days running so figured I'd better follow your good example and set me down with pen in hand and tell you the happenings of the day.

Nothing much out of the ordinary I can assure you what with rising at 7:30 as per routine, breakfast at 10 to 8, the ward at 8:15. Ward rounds 8:30 to 9:30. Squirting fever for half an hour. Fifteen minutes for coffee and then a half mile trek to West Wing to the detention hospital with its double fence of 12 feet barb wire and having to sign in and out through the guard house. Then back by 11:15 and writing up discharge charts until 12:00 noon. Then 1:30 starting instrumentation parade and doing urethroscopes and soundings for about 1/2 an hour and then a few specials, then coffee and then routine physicals on tomorrow's fever patients from 3 to 4:30 and then quitting and back from 7 to 9:15 PM for a little reading and special charting and then to the mess for coffee and sandwiches and a game of pool and then to the room. That is the daily routine and that's what it is seven days a week (if I feel ambitious enough to go back in the evening). So you see – there just isn't much to write about.

Don't know if I told you the one about our penicillin parade – patients parade for it every 3 hours – one man sweeping the floor kind of swept his way into the line up and then was ordered to take down his trousers (for penicillin is given in the hip here) – he did so, got a shot and then had the curiosity to ask "what was that for".

Turned in my helmet and respirator today and a few bits of kit and now I can get all my belongings into that suitcase-trunk of mine with a very few odds and ends of overflow to put in my dunnage bag. That's pretty good going but doesn't say much for the state of the wardrobe. Am going to send my great coat home by parcel post as soon as I get it from Yorkshire – maybe you will get it cleaned just in case I have to wear it for awhile when I get back.

There are 27,000 troops going home by the end of the month and 41,000 total this month. Figure out honey, 3 x 40,000 – Christmas and the majority of the troops. Sure sounds good to me. Love you a lot. Miss you a lot. All my love to you and Joan, Hamp

September 15, 1945

Dearest Hamp

Here it is with half September by the board. It just doesn't seem possible, does it, that the days are going by so quickly.

Have spent the last two days close to home except for yesterday afternoon. Have really been working on our Christmas present and you'd better remember to like it darling coz right now I've a feeling I'll never make another one.

Yesterday afternoon went over to see Clara Garrison and Billy. Clara tells me Gus was around to see you but you were in London. However you may have met now as Gus can't be stationed very far away from you. Joan and Billy got along swell together as there is just a week between them, Joan being older. They played beautifully together in the kitchen while Clare and I chatted in the front room. Suddenly all seemed quiet so we went out to see what was going on and there sat Billy and Joan playing with the shoe polish and plastered from head to toe with the stuff – Joan brown and Billy black. What a mess. However we scrubbed them well, took off polish and skin but couldn't get their clothes clean and Joan of course had on her best dress.

Phoned Margaret today as I hadn't heard from her for quite a while. They all have colds. Your mother is planning on a trip to Wyoming next week by train and bus for a family reunion. It seems like an awful long trip by oneself. It will be good when she gets down tho'. Your Dad is in hospital with an ear infection and Mac and Irene arrived home from Banff. Sure am glad they got a holiday at last. I think they could have taken one before but Mac didn't think so and after all I guess he should know.

Joan chatters away all day and generally runs the show. When I put her to bed at night she kisses your picture and then says, "Mommy knit sox for Daddy. Bye Mommy." – so out I go. She is so darn cute and gets cuter all the time. Of course she's looking more like me all the time. Ahem! At least that's the comment I hear often now. Haven't had any mail since Monday so hope some comes next week. Hope you come home soon. Heaps of love my darling, as always, Peg

September 15, 1945

Dearest Peggy

This one of those unusual mornings so figured I'd better drop you a line while the day still looked pretty good to me. Woke up early and found the sun shining – both unusual occurrences. My watch had

631

stopped so didn't know the time and after meditating a few minutes got up and shaved and then found out that it was just seven AM – it's going to amaze you if this morning insomnia of mine lasts since it's getting to be almost a habit to waken between 6:30 and 7:00 and then not be able to go back to sleep.

The past two days have run according to form. The day before yesterday we had about 20 MO's from nearby units in for the day to see how we run our unit. Had quite a busy day and we convinced them that we have problems even if they are little ones. That evening had a big snooker game in the mess and myself and my partner distinguished ourselves since he is a pretty good player. Last night just sat around and worked on my statistics on our turnover until 10 PM and then went home to bed.

Interruption – time out for a couple of hours work. – have decided to kind of call a halt for the day and just sit and meditate and give the boys a break by not giving any fever today – it makes quite a hectic ward for them when you have 10 or 15 people on fever or just over it.

Good news in the Maple Leaf today (the daily paper of the Canadians overseas) all with 110 points will be in repat depots by the end of September. That will put the 100 pointers in by the middle of Nov. or end of October and since I have 100 points (army calculations) it doesn't look so grim. Time really does slip away and another couple of months won't kill us now that there is an end somewhere in sight.

By the way the sun only lasted an hour today and is now gone. Things are certainly damp these days with a heavy fog every morning. The linoleum floors of the quarters have got a continual film of moisture on them and look like they had just been mopped.

Well honey, will sign off. Love you and certainly am looking forward to spending some time with you and the daughter. (I still insist on that holiday (of some kind). Swell of your Dad and his offer re taking his holidays. All my love, Hamp

September 18, 1945

Dearest Hamp

Time is still flitting by. Guess I'd better not apologize for being a day late in writing eh old boy? As you might feel like a heel – so we'll just skip it – both ways. I know just what you are going through re letters as it is often that way with me – nothing to write about so one night falls away to 3 & 4 before one wakes up to the fact that you owe about 2 letters. So what say we try and write every other night but if we should miss OK – just forget and don't apologize – as long it's not more than 4 days coz I get awfully ratty to live with if a week goes by and no mail and I'll bet you're the same way. Got two letters from you yesterday and I really enjoyed them. For one thing it was a week since I'd had mail and for another you seemed to be in a good mood – I don't mean from alcohol either you goat!

Boy you sure poured on the oil about your wonderful wife. I'm not *that* wonderful but I'll sure take all the compliments I can get. Don't hear many more and do I miss the loving – you have no idea, or have you? No wonder I'm pining away to a shadow while my dear husband – hum. Sure makes one think doesn't it darling? Am just kidding as I really don't think – not that kind of stuff anyway. Thank goodness we don't have to worry about somethings eh honey?

Suppose you know about Fred being accepted to the Orthopedic Hospital for October 1946 for a year plus a few months? Alix is quite excited about the prospect of going to England and is naturally very pleased that their plans are more definite at last and Fred thinks he'll be home the last of October.

It has certainly been wintry these last couple of days. Rained steadily for two days with a cold north wind. There was snow in Calgary and Fort St John so that doesn't promise a warm fall. Speaking of Calgary, Mother is going down for a few days to meet Dad. Wish it was me going to meet you eh honey?

Bet the plan of the new office is really something but guess it will be a dream for a few more years as the government has frozen all building materials except for veteran's homes and hospitals etc. Aunt Lena is duplexing her house and has the bath and toilet upstairs but can't buy any piping to finish the job.

Haven't bought anything new this week mainly because I haven't been down town.

Joan is certainly cute these days. You should see how she rolls her eyes. When Art Henderson left for Winnipeg on Sunday she gave him a great big hug and a kiss and Art, who Joan calls "Da-a-bo" – for some unknown reason – said "Boy can she ever kiss". And I said, "The point is who taught her". At which Art replied, "Your husband is sure missing a lot isn't he?" At which I agreed and decided I was missing a lot too. Yesterday when I brought her in from a walk she ran to mother and said "Nana! It's raining. Wind blow Doney" – so she's really talking. Brother! Are you ever going to get an earful when you get back. That seems to cover all the news for now.

Heaps of love darling – always, Peg

September 18, 1945

Dearest Peggy,

Two more days and not a great deal to report. Saturday night played pool with Claire Schneiderman and Day for an hour or so and since we played for drinks, we got quite cheerful and ended up by stopping in the mess the rest of the evening and continuing the game. Sunday was another day and so was yesterday. Last night went cycling and dropped in at a couple of the locals on the way by for a quick pint and managed to get our exercise in. The time seems to go by somehow but one gets a little fed up with the place at times. Dave went up to London last night for the day today – hope he brings back some more gossip about repat. Harold Kester who came over with me is now on his way home. He has fewer points than I have however since he enlisted in August 41 but the time is drawing shorter.

Our cigarette ration has been reduced to 600/month so it looks like we will be smoking some limey ones but it shouldn't be for long. If they are sent from home the ration apparently will still hold so there isn't very much to do about it.

Our admissions still keep pouring in – 70 yesterday – so the Canadian erk is apparently a damn fool regardless how you look at him.

Yesterday we had a hot day for a change and everyone went around moaning that they wished it would rain. This country just isn't built for warm weather – it was just like a Turkish bath and absolutely steamy. It sure will be nice to get back to that unhealthy dry climate of Alberta.

Have to start shopping around for a birthday present for the daughter. It's quite a problem because there isn't a damn thing in the shops that's worth carrying away.

Everyone seems to take home a suit-length of cloth to their wives and I often think that it is received with some misgivings. If you would like some tweed, please let me know and I'll bring you enough for suit or skirt or what not. If you want some please give me some ideas as to what approximate color or design you like. Well honey, will sign off. All my love, Hamp

September 20, 1945

Dearest Peggy,

More news from down here at Bramshott and therefore very little to write about. We are quite busy as usual with our practice still on the increase. Had to open another ward yesterday so things aren't improving very much. Haven't heard from you for 8 days so I guess the lag in my writing has caught up to you. Had word from George Elliott yesterday and he expects to get posted home in October (that means to go in November). Since he has more points than I have or just about the same, it looks pretty good.

Haven't done anything very startling in the past two days. The night before last about 6 of us walked a couple of miles to a pub and had some beer. Last night Dave and I sat in the room and tore up paper and old letters and tried to lighten our luggage as much as possible – probably won't have to worry about it for months but it's kind of nice to make the preparations. I sure haven't got many souvenirs of my stay in England and I'll have to start doing some shopping. Am going to wait until I go on leave next month – will try to get something for everyone and am going to take lots of pictures of all your relatives at Blackburn, Fleetwood etc. Don't know what to get your parents but that will be a start and will look around for something. Will have two weeks and a 48 in which to meander the countryside so am kind of looking foreword to it. I will be a little pressed for dough and wonder if you would send me 10 pounds to tide me over I may not need it but I have a feeling that I will and will probably not save it. If you could send that as early in October as possible then would be prepared for even the unexpected.

Can't seem to save money here regardless. Dave went up to London, two days ago and saw Fred Day at London House. He will be there today again and am going to phone there this evening to see if I can locate him and persuade him to come down here for the weekend.

Well had better sign off now that I've put the bite on you and wait for comments. Still wish the hell I were home. Give the daughter my love and kisses. All my love, Hamp

September 21, 1945

Dearest Peggy,

Thursday with sunshine and kind of a fall atmosphere and no rain. It looks almost like fall at home except the leaves are still quite green. Am on a day off but have decided to stick around and just not be as busy – that keeps you from getting behind in your work, gives you an excuse for being lazy and is quite economical.

Got your letter yesterday discussing the leave question. Have been going to talk about it but didn't know quite what to say. One thing sure we are going to have some leave. Another is that I'm not going to go to Camrose and just sit – we will be doing enough of that and I think we both deserve a chance to look around and see the sights – particularly yourself since you have been tied down for a year and a half and have been (or always let me feel you were) more or less able to be cheerful and have never complained.

What I had thought to do was this – go home by C.P.R. and meet you in Calgary and then just do as we pleased for a week or so. We could stay there, go to Banff (weather permitting) or do what we wanted. That would save an unpleasant train journey for you if traveling is still difficult and would be a good place to start from. Had planned on letting you alone know just exactly when I got in the country and if you kept it quiet then we could be our own bosses. It sounds kind of selfish but after all I don't think we have been too selfish in the past 4 years and can indulge ourselves and any fancies we may have – regardless how silly anyone else might think them to be. So honey let me know what you think and don't say anything to anyone till we kind of have it talked over. I say Calgary because we know it and it's kind of nice to go back.

We are probably counting our chickens a little prematurely but what the heck, he darling. Miss you very much and love you very much. All my love, Hamp

September 22, 1945

Dearest Hamp

Really must apologize about the letter written last Tuesday. The letter was OK but I didn't mail it until Thursday. Isn't that awful darling? *Actually*. Went down town Wednesday morning with the letter in my purse and even went as far as to buy stamps and blue forms standing right by a mail box and came home with the letter. Guess I'm getting a bit absent minded eh honey? What took it off my mind then I think was that while I was buying stamps at Eaton's I spied some jockey shorts on a counter and I haven't seen any of those since the good old Claresholm days so tore over and bought you 4 pairs – size 38 – hope you aren't insulted at the size darling. Figure your old ones must have had it by now. These unfortunately have no elastic in them – they button – so I have visions of you loosing your shorts like you did once remember? However they'll be something to come home to! Wednesday night went to a show with Alix and Helen – 'The Adventures of Susan' – which had some very good lines in it – and forgot to mail the letter again. However Mother went to Calgary on Thursday for the weekend to meet Dad so Mother mailed it somewhere.

Am not exactly alone as we have two students in the basement – males. But don't worry darling they're just kids – second year dent and engineer – and left high school the year before to come to Varsity. They are really nice kids – Mormons from Cardston (maybe that doesn't help) and know Frank Christie as one of the older boys from town. So you see where that puts me or us as friends of Frank. Am definitely *Mrs* Smith and I guess they think I'm nearing 40. Well, I am too – some days it feels like 60. Gad I'll be 26 next birthday, my oh my, and you old thing will be 28.

Yesterday afternoon went over to see Marg and family. Marg is putting on quite a bit of weight and looks slightly pregnant but don't be alarmed it's only a false impression I think as she would have said something for she is always wondering if she is or isn't while sit back and laugh quite green with envy that she has the chance to be or not to be.

The days are cloudy and very raw with snow all around except in Edmonton so Joan doesn't stay outside more than ½ an hour when she wants in. She won't keep the mitts on so her hands get very cold. She calls me "Mammy" now and it sounds so funny – don't think I've changed color at least I haven't noticed it.

Your Ma didn't go to Sheridan as your Dad was quite sick with his ear – same one he had mastoid in but he's home now as a nurse wakened him up one night to tell him he had his glasses on. He was very mad so went straight home. That's all for now. Heaps of love my darling, always, Peg

September 23, 1945

Dearest Peggy,

Two letters today so am doing very well. Sunday afternoon and not doing very much except have coffee and look out at the rain and hail. It is now beginning to get cold and it won't be very long before the leaves go down and we will be wishing that our room had a stove or some other means of providing heat. One good thing is that it gets you to bed early since it is too cold to sit around.

Last night Dave and Roy Clarke and myself walked down the hill a couple of miles and saw a show. A double feature that wasn't much good but killed the evening. Came home to bed and then Rip Fowler dropped in – he was passing by on his way back to #4 C.M.H. at Horsham. Is quite pleased to be there and has recovered following a broken ankle he got in a car accident on the continent a couple of months ago.

It's funny about hearing about Gus from you. Dave and I had inquired around but haven't been able to find out just where he is stationed and haven't heard from him – small world eh darling. Sure hope Joan begins to look more and more like you – it's every man's ambition to have a good looking daughter. That Christmas present kind of intrigues me – can't guess what it can be but maybe I'll be home to sneak a look at the final stages of it's construction.

Sorry about getting you all excited about my London venture – will keep my big mouth shut for awhile. It's funny how enthusiastic one gets here though – we are in the center of a group of army repat camps and hear all the shipping news. Since the ships go in bunches there is a flurry of optimism as everybody pulls out and then there is two or three weeks with positively nothing happening and everyone kind of settles down and surveys the situation a little more soberly. However it won't be too long anyway honey and guess will just have to be patient.

We hit an all time high of patients this week and so it all goes to show you that when one says, "it seems to be decreasing" they should touch wood.

Well, will sign off. Miss you very much and it'll certainly be wonderful to see you and touch you and talk to you again. Also will be wonderful to see the daughter up close. All my love, Hamp

September 25, 1945

Dearest Peggy,

Wonder if you are beginning to have to worry about winter woollies yet. We are just beginning to start our cool and cold weather and it really does go right through you. From now on we will apparently have to spend our evenings in the hospital or in bed because you can see your breath in the room after 7:00 PM and that's too damn cold.

This afternoon Claire Schneiderman and myself decided to go golfing. Cycled down to Lysbook and it was so chilly that we went into the Anchor to have a beer. Had a couple of gins and a couple of beers and then went out and decided it was too darn cold and cycled around and got 4 cobs of corn each and came home (9 pence a cob which figures out something over 2 dollars a dozen) After we got back we went down the road for tea and into Grayshott while I tried to find a birthday present for Joan.

After arriving back I got under the top blankets to keep warm and woke at 8:00 PM and am now over here in the process of writing one darling wife – which is yourself.

Next week am going up to London for a day and visit the boys and drop into headquarters to get the latest rumor. There won't be any honey so don't get excited. There are big troop movements in the next few days and then things will settle down again for the next push. Oct. will soon be upon us and then is your birthday month coming up – don't know what to do about it but will probably procrastinate and try to deliver the birthday gift in person.

Well honey, will sign off with all my love. Give Joan a little fatherly affection from me. All my love, Hamp

September 12, 1945

Dearest Hamp,

Nothing very much to report except that I got two letters from you today. They sure were wonderful and change of mood of the day entirely. Always around 2 PM I move onto the chesterfield and with some work in hand keep a sharp eye for the postman and then when there's mail from you he always knocks on the door so I'll know to come and get it.

Sure got a big bang out of your insomnia. Better keep it up darling coz our daughter is an early bird and the whole house wakens up when she does. However she doesn't waken up as early as you do but 7:45 is a good average. So it's a good idea to keep up your insomnia so you won't be annoyed at being awakened. I'm always sound asleep at that hour and some mornings you feel like you'd been cheated but then it's really not very early at 8 AM is it darling? Sometimes wonder just how long I would sleep if given the chance.

The news in the Maple Leaf sure was good. It will be grand to have you home. Am glad we agree on the holiday matter any kind, any where, as long as it's just we three. Boy am I selfish but in this case my scruples are all gone and we'll have that holiday or bust.

We sure are having our troubles what with meat rationing and now butchers' strikes. With the ration we could at least get meat but not now that some of the butchers have struck.

Pardon me while I lay the daughter low. She's trying all the tricks of the trade to stay awake – go-go, a drink, dropped her doll and this time I can't imagine what, so had best go and see but it had better be good – or else. Well! Second pair of wet pants in 1/2 hour. Leaky Jo they

640

call her! It's just an excuse to get out of bed. Then she wants to sit on go-go and look around. Sure made her mad though as she got put right back to bed – with dry pants of course. But my, she's really mad and will go to sleep this time. We play this game almost every night. Sure hope we tire of it soon. I'm tired of it now!

The sun shone today for the first time in a week so we went for a real long walk. It was still chilly though 45 was the high for today. The Banff-Calgary road is blocked by snow drifts. Quite a change from last year when Kay and I had such good weather.

We were to go to Robertson's for dinner today but Sandy has a cold however Ma and Pa are coming home tonight so we aren't feeling blue. Alix and Helen were over Saturday night and we sat and knit – just like three old maids. That's us – almost anyhow. Always said you'd be home this fall. May have to stretch fall into winter but at least it's not too far away eh darling. All my love dearest. Always, Peg

September 25, 1945

Dear Hamp,

Long time no see. Long time not write. Glad to get your last letter. Hope we are still friends. Before I forget it may say that I will be glad to see you home, for many things are becoming more or less complicated. Put a note in Canadian today stating that you might and probably would be in Camrose before the end of the year. There are a lot of people looking forward to your return, and it doesn't do any harm, I hope, to create anticipation. I am going to keep this going occasionally, with the help of Ma. Sent a letter to your friend Tice sometime ago. He was out on holiday, but the answer was very satisfactory. Could have done something nasty through King or McKinnon, perhaps, but took the matter up through regular channels Looks fair if I had tried to wrangle you out, you would have been sorry for it in later years, and held it against me. Maybe. Has been making me feel my years. Carried on while Mac took a week out and then, of course, went to the cleaners. Had an otitis media which has taken some of the serum out of me. It is still ornery. Took 100,000,000 units of penicillin in my ass and it came out of my ear a week later. Then took innumerable tablets of sulphadiazine, which always drive me wild. Am now trying to lead a normal life. Haven't heard from Peggy since God finished making little apples. Margaret is just a name that I used to

641

hear at my mother's breast. Eating around for a living. Nobody loves me. Come up and see me sometime. Just sort of fed up. Much love, Dad

September 28, 1945

Dear Hamp,

Little news. Had a week off – got down absolutely flat so had to walk out on work: never came a good time so just left. Right back to 2 cholecystectomies, 2 hysterectomies, a Caesarian, a pelvic abscess, a hand ?ligament egst?, ?abocardys?, and hernia in first week and 13 cuts so am right up. Things are shaking up a lot here. Neville is bringing in a young Norwegian chap – would like to form a clinic so told him would naturally not be able to make any arrangements till you returned – which is a nice pleasant stall and smoother than no, flatly. Rogers wants to sell. Hemmings and son Muig from Calgary were up to see him. They saw me: they annoyed me by suggesting they should just cut in with me and help me so I told them I would welcome them to Camrose and cut their throats from 8AM to 8PM and we should all be good friends every evening, which is as it should be but didn't please them so very much. Roger's price is too high. $12,000 for home and practice. (House assessed at $4,000, $1,000 probably worth of office equipment) Alvith told me he'd pay him $8000. So Rogers approached me and suggested I bring in somebody congenial to myself. Know you wouldn't want his house. So wrote to Bill Strome – he's capable and a good enough egg and considering returning from clinic practice and suggested he buy Roger's., associate with him long enough to transfer the practice and possibly some sort of clinic might be formed here – though naturally not till you were here and I'd consulted with you (fair stall, huh!). Am going to get Dad to fix over downstairs and charge us a real good rent and retire now – he's spending $15000 a year with the greatest of ease and small return – though of course taxes eat up most of it. Well enough business. Haven't seen anybody or done anything for a spell. Family is well.

Will write a more social letter soon, Mac

FLASH

P.S. N.B. operated on an OR nurse from Col Belcher Hosp. visiting here – down sick 1 week. Her sister, a personnel officer working on discharges in RCAF here, states she knows Tice and local situation, took your name and # and is going to work. So here's hoping it works.

Dearest Peggy,

A beautiful fall morning with sunshine and all that stuff so leapt out of bed at 7:00 AM and now have an hour before I can get started on my day's work. Today we have another bunch of visiting Medical Officers descending upon us so we have to wait and demonstrate what goes on everyday.

Am getting a little discouraged again with my boys. One occasionally sits down and reflects the futility of it all – you work hard to empty your beds only to have them filled immediately with the same type of patient – as a matter of fact the only difference in your patients is their faces and you don't treat them. The part of their anatomy in which you are most interested shows remarkably little variation. However – one doesn't suffer.

Have done nothing since my last writing. Puddle along all day and sit around in the evening playing knock or snooker for an hour after the evening meal and then going to the room and sitting until you decide it's too cold and then coming over to the hospital and reading. Not a very rapid fire existence but the time goes quickly and Christmas gets a little closer every day. Think I am gaining weight again with my sedentary existence so that's not very good is it honey? Hope you will claim me regardless. – Well have now got an interruption so will continue later – well that was quite an interruption – it is now 8 AM Sept 28.

– Made rounds yesterday morning with our visiting MOs (another VD clinic day) and then was busy all morning with the routine. Had ward round in the afternoon to show what a hopeless ward I had. Doug Ritchie phoned after lunch. Gus Garrison was with him and arranged to come down this afternoon to spend the weekend. Doug said he expects to be posted about Oct. 10 and told me that I am next in the list for repat. George Elliot arrived down late in the afternoon and confirmed this. He and I and Dave and 2 others are all next on the list and he said that we should be posted to report somewhere between October 15th and 30th. He said the rumors were that shipping was going to be bad in October but we should get away in the 1st half of November (If shipping were really good we would have left in Oct.).

Sure sounds good doesn't it honey – however will take it all with a grain of salt and just keep hoping for the best – should be able to look forward to something now at last though.

All my love – kisses sent to daughter after the big hello from me. Hamp

September 28, 1945

Dearest Hamp,

How's my great big handsome husband making out these days? I suppose you're getting all ready for your wanderings around Lancashire or maybe you are on your way if you take your 48 first. However you probably won't get this until you are back at Bramshott so I hope you had a good time darling. As usual wish we were with you to see the sights.

Mother and Dad got back from Calgary and brought Joan her first real doll with eyes that open and shut – for her birthday they said but just couldn't wait to see her reaction so gave it to her next day. Needless to say Joan was very pleased and has spent busy days being a little mother to "Baby Doll". It eats and sleeps with her and every time you turn around Joan is saying "Mummy look, baby waken up".

Haven't been doing much of note. Went downtown Tuesday and bought me a dress for afternoon and evenings a real super number so now my wardrobe is complete and ready for you to come home. Tuesday night was J.W.C. club so knit on your sox. The other evenings have been spent in finishing your Christmas present. I know you'll like it – it's (Air Force blue with Air Force crests all over it!) How does that suit you darling? No honestly it really isn't like that so wipe that disgusted look from your face, Bumpey.

Got two letters from you today and I'm walking on air. To think you might be home in November is really almost too much to think about. And your ideas of leave are the same as mine. Calgary sounds good to me as we know it and I hope you can arrange to come CPR. Most RCAF for Edmonton come CNR so you may have to do some pulling to come CPR but I don't know about that. As for just letting me know when you arrive would take care of any opposition but remember darling that the paper prints a list of all Edmonton and district men

644

returning as soon as the boat docks and the time they are expected in Edmonton. However you could be delayed – which you will be by your wife. Gosh it all sounds too wonderful to ever happen doesn't it Hamp? But there's the old saying about things coming to those that wait and broth-er we are sure doing just that. You talk about me not complaining, well honestly, darling; I've nothing to complain about. I'm quite happy except that you are not here which is something beyond my control so there's no use complaining about that. And as for not having a place of my own, well I don't want it unless you are here to share it because without you it wouldn't be ours and I only want to work for things that are ours – if you see what I mean. The first 6 months were the worst when there seemed to be so sight of the end or our being together but as 1944 disappeared the end was in sight and it changed things an awful lot. Now that you are nearer home the waiting hasn't seemed so bad and it's hard to realize that a year and a half have gone by. On the other hand it seems like centuries. Sure wouldn't want to do it again though for anything in this world. What about you honey?

We are having sunny weather again but there's a distinct nip in the air. Now that our flowers are all killed I guess we'll have Indian summer. By the way darling there are no comments re £10 as the money is yours to spend any way, anyhow.

Heaps of love and don't work too hard. Hugs and kisses from Joan. As ever, Peg

OCTOBER 1945

October 3, 1945

Dearest Peggy,

Away behind in my writing but have done a lot of running around since last writings. Gus Garrison and George Elliott were down last weekend. Dave and I were so busy being the perfect hosts that we managed to get quite alcoholic while the guests remained comparatively sober. There was a supper dance in the nurses' mess on Sunday night – no meal was served in the officers' mess so we had to go or else starve. A sister named Cailkinson who works for me invited me to go so I reciprocated by asking her to come over to the officers' mess on Saturday. By the time Dave and I got through with our hosting she wasn't very pleased with the whole situation but we were not impressed anyway. Guess you need never have to worry about anyone else admiring your husband and sure hope you'll associate with me darling.

Monday noon I went up to London to see the boss. Stayed at the Maple Leaf Club and managed to get a single room which is quite a luxury. It's a Red Cross Club for officers and is very nice. Gus went back with me and we sat around all evening talking to Bob OPow and Doug Ritchie came over and we had quite a bull session. The next morning went over and saw the DMS and here comes the news – he said that I would be posted to Torquay (the repat centre) between Oct 15 and Oct. 30. We generally stay there about one to three weeks and so will be home in November and possibly near the middle of the month – pretty good eh honey so clear the old women and children from the streets because Edmonton here comes Mrs. Smith complete with husband. Will be home before the end of November anyway so just keep your fingers crossed and hope that it's nearer the middle than the end of the month.

When we get posted to repat we can't get leave so I'm going to try to get away next week so I'm glad I wrote for the dough. That was actually the reason because I was told a while ago that I could expect to be in a boat by the middle of October but didn't write it because I didn't believe it and it was just as well. Go on leave next week I don't get my October money until return so may run short. Gosh it is a wonderful feeling to think that at last there is something more or less definite in the offing. Can hardly believe it and am certainly a little slaphappy today. Didn't get back until last night and that's the reason for the delay in writing. Johnnie Hunt is coming back from the continent this weekend and we should all be coming home together so things look good.

Sure miss you and will be a good boy and not try to have to many alcoholic going away parties with the chaps. All my love, Hamp

October 4, 1945

Dearest Hamp

How time flies eh old boy? It's almost a week since I wrote. Sure hope you are on leave so that you won't miss the mail too much. Have been quite busy though guess I could have found time to write if I could settle down once in a while.

Saturday night Mother and I went to a show. We got a seat after an hour's waiting which wasn't too bad. Sunday I wrote letters to Doris Bothwell and Jean Palmer and as we haven't corresponded for about 6 months there was a lot to write about. Then finished up by writing to your mother.

Monday went downtown and cabled £10 to you. Hope you got it OK. Then came home and got a letter from you and if you think you're going to get a peek at your Christmas present you're mistaken as I finished it last night and it's all ready to put away. Too bad dear. I may be slow at sewing old bean but brother I'm not that slow! So you'll just have to keep your curiosity in check for a couple of months – longer if you aren't home. But what am I saying eh darling? Monday night was church group meeting so went and knit on a soc for you. Everyone else was making stuff for the bazaar we are having but I'm too busy making things for you and Joan. Didn't get to sleep until 3 AM that night for when I got home Joan was just waking up and with a beautiful cold. Her eyes and nose were running so she was very restless and kept saying "Mommy blow my nose" so finally I took her in bed with me so I wouldn't have to keep getting out in the cold. Consequently I was kicked about and then wakened at 6 AM for the day. It was the worst cold she's ever had and don't know where she got it. However it wasn't enough to keep her in bed although she had a few degrees of temperature. Kept her quiet with crayons and books which was an all day job for a couple of days and by nightfall I was just content to sit and do nothing.

Oh! Ye gods! The daughter has just swanked out of the bedroom wearing my new hat and of all things a girdle. Yes sir, has her pants off and is giving a demonstration of putting on a girdle. Hat's off now and there's a curler in the hair. Our daughter will kill me with her escapades one of these days. And we are in the climbing stage again. Yesterday found her sitting on the brick wall of the veranda in the few minutes I had her out. And today found her sitting outside the back gate. What a che-ild! Have some pictures to send taken the first part of September. They are real good of Joan but not so hot of me – not glamour one. Am going to a show with Alix tonight as we feel it's about time we went out together. That's all for now honey. Heaps of love and stuff. As ever, Peg

October 4, 1945

Dearest Peggy,

And here I thought I was behind in my writing – got a letter today starting "Tomorrow you will have been gone a year". Then looked at the date and saw that it was April 16 and then noted that it was addressed to #423 Squadron. You wrote it when you were in Camrose – might almost think that you gave it to Dad to mail and he just located it recently and popped it in the mailbox. In the letter you talked of that homecoming – guess it arrived at an opportune time after all.

I expect to get away on leave on Oct. 12 and will head straight north to Blackburn and Darwen and Fleetwood. That should take about a week and then I hope to go down and visit Stan McMillan at his transport squadron and then just sit and hope that the post isn't too long. Should be posted between the 21st and 30th of October and sure hope I am.

Doug Ritchie came down to see me yesterday. Drove down at mid morning and back in the late afternoon. He just wanted to see the routine of the place so put on a pretty good show for him. The place here is still expanding and we are having to put in double deckers in all the wards but mine. That means 60 pts to a ward for 30 – doesn't leave too much room. Thank goodness mine can't expand any more although I may have to take over another ward to handle my overflow. What a mill! Am just beginning to feel that I want no more of it – my ward has a lot of worries and since you can't give fever indefinitely without a death I just want to finish without a casualty.

What about our leave darling? We could go anywhere you say. I don't care where we go so long as I'm with you and nobody bothering us. Imagine you have a hankering to do something though so make any plans you want and will do them. I can get a leave warrant to Vancouver and we could go there if you wanted to. However if you meet me in Calgary or elsewhere we can take a day off and talk it over. Just remember though that you're the boss because I'm the guy that's been the tourist for the past 18 mos. and now it's your turn.

Tonight there is a formal mess dinner to wish the old CO of the hospital (Co. Young) on his way and to welcome the new one (Col. Coke). Big dinner with a quarter of a chicken for everyone so it should be quite the affair what with speeches and a wine course and all the fixings and a bridge game afterwards for everyone. Quite a mad social whirl here. Well honey, be seeing you and the daughter. All my love, Hamp

October 7, 1945

Dearest Hamp

Don't get excited he says, don't get excited! Don't get excited! Hum! Darling I'm so excited it's wonderful. And so are the glad tidings you wrote in your letter which I got yesterday. Sure hope it all turns out the way it seems to be planned. It's really too good to be true. Of course I realize anything can happen to change it all but we won't think along those lines.

Have decided for us that if you can't arrange to come to Calgary, I'll go to Winnipeg, even if I have to sit up two nights. Won't be sleeping anyway so it doesn't matter. However all that depends on the wire I get when you arrive in this country. Calgary really would be much nicer as we do know the city a bit and have a few friends there if we should decide to find time to go visiting. Ah me! All this planning isn't it wonderful darling?

Alix was all agog on Thursday as she received a phone call from the operator in Montreal asking her to stand by for a call from London in the afternoon. She waited all afternoon and at 4 PM got another call saying everything was cancelled. So now the big question is "What gives?" She has had no further word.

We (Alix and I) went to a show on Friday night – "Blood on the Sun". It was quite entertaining but the typical lone American holds forth against the Japanese. Stayed home last night as it was cold and wet – didn't have anywhere to go anyway – and knit mitts for Joan.

By the way you and I bought Joan a table and two chairs for her birthday. She has it all ready and is getting a big bang out of it. Baby doll

649

sits on one chair and Joan on the other. I'm lucky if I manage to sit down on a chair for ½ a second before Joan comes along trying to push me off saying "my chair" or "Baby Doll's chair". A bit of coaxing and I get a few seconds more. Joan still has her cold and is quite spoiled now as she is in most of the day. Her feelings are quite near the surface as she's not up to scratch and so cries easily. However today was better and she must be recovering as I caught her singing several times. Boy is she a handful. You'll understand how I keep my skinny figure when you see her in action. So be prepared to lose a few pounds.

Mrs Young phoned me last night to see if you'd mentioned Johnny in your letters. Seems he wrote saying he might be home end of October and now she hears via Mac and a returned officer that Johnny is posted to the Continent again and as she hasn't heard form him for quite a time was wondering if you might know something. If so darling, give with the info. Mac Young expects his discharge in January – when you boys get back in the swing I guess – and Carol has a house in 88th avenue so they are all set. Nice going if you can get it eh darling?

Here are bits of the latest news. Helen has had to go back to the sanatorium this week as she took a hemorrhage last Sunday. Ted Bell had his mug in the paper last night for being mentioned in Dispatches. Also "Have" McLennan and Lt Col Ansley – all MOs. The Archers – John and Jessamy – have another son as of Thursday. He is discharged too. J & J sure keep busy eh honey? Marg Norton is going to Dr Vant – for backache she says, so it must be backache. Guy Morton is coming back to the city – to the Mewburn, I guess as he's in the army still unless he just got out. Dr Ken Thomson got married in Victoria a couple of weeks ago. The Loyal Edmontons arrived last night with much fanfare and Bluebell Trowbridge has returned too. You are next so be prepared for a loving you've never had before. All my love dearest. As ever – Peg

Rubber stamped on back of envelope in red:

SIGN YOUR NAME TO VICTORY
INVEST IN CANADA'S
NINTH VICTORY LOAN

October 8, 1945

Dearest Peggy,

October is certainly drifting along without much effort and the day of leaving Bramshott is getting closer and closer. Hope to go on leave on Friday and have applied for 16 days. I really can't afford to stay away that long (financially I mean) since it costs about 2 quid a day just to live and eat when you're moving but will kind of spread out my finances as thinly as possible and cover a maximum of territory! Am going straight to your relatives and then there can't be any diversions or excuses.

Johnnie Hunt flew back from Hamburg yesterday and phoned me at noon. I persuaded him to come down and spend the evening and he has left again this morning to report to H.Q. He hasn't changed a bit and has gained more weight than ever I think. He should be going to repat at the end of this month too and hope he and Doug and I get home together.

Haven't done much since last writing. Saturday night was a party night again and since it was my last one I went over to the mess and sat around and had a few rums and am now officially on the wagon until meeting my little woman in Calgary and from then on my fate is entirely in her hands. Don't know how long we'll be in Calgary before going up to see the daughter – am getting more and more anxious to see how she looks and acts – your letters have brought her practically into my lap and she must be wonderful. How could she help it eh honey with such a wonderful example to follow every day? Sure will be wonderful to see you both. My posting won't come in before the end of October I expect but it may be a few days sooner and so guess we can't expect to see each other before the interval between the 15th and 30th of November.

Gray McClaren was down over the weekend and he is just the same – don't know if you knew him very well. He's at O/S H.Q. and is doing very well by himself and incidentally the army isn't suffering by him either.

Well darling, better get this in the mail and will write quite often this week because there may be quite a lag in mail when I'm on leave. Give the daughter my love. All my love, Hamp

Dearest Hamp

Hope you are somewhat settled down after the good news of your repat posting. It's sure wonderful to live with your head in the clouds but I had to loose a bit of altitude so I could get things done. My feet are far from being on the ground though & everything is just rosy. That was the best news I've heard for ages and sure am hoping everything continues in the same manner – then you'll be home before I've time to turn around. Guess the next four or five weeks will simply crawl away. However still have a few things to accomplish before you arrive so that should keep me occupied.

Gosh! Am fairly busting every time I think of it – which is all the time. Have done some thinking re a holiday for just "us" and here are some conclusions arrived at by various means. Dad can't take a holiday in November as that's his busy month – think he goes East. Haven't talked to Dad yet as he is away. Mother thinks it's too expensive to go East for herself and says that anyway I should have a holiday with just you minus our whirlwind for a while so she has offered to look after Joan for a week or more. However Joan wears Mother out in time and as I don't want Mother to be a total wreck about 7 to 10 days is about as long as we could stay away from our daughter. Could stretch it out for two weeks though as Mother herself has offered that length of time. About going to Vancouver – well if the weather is cold & foggy it will not be good & perhaps we couldn't get reservations in the time of your arrival in Canada & our leaving for Vancouver. Things are very crowded and will be so the nearer to Christmas we get. So think our best bet is to meet in Calgary and stay there for a while & maybe going to Banff for a weekend. Personally what we do doesn't really matter as far as I'm concerned but Calgary seems to offer so many answers to our problem. We might even decide one morning at breakfast to go to the Coast. Who knows about us eh darling? If by any chance you can't come to Calgary I'll meet you in Winnipeg and we can tour that metropolis but I don't see any reason why you couldn't arrange to go to Calgary. Do you honey? Then we could return here and spend a few days with the daughter and then push on to Camrose with the tornado. Guess that's all I've turned over in my mind so far – pro & con.

Monday was Thanksgiving but we didn't have much of a spread as Dad was away and Mother went to a wedding. Tuesday was club night and they are having a dance on Nov 2 but guess we won't be going to that one eh honey? Yesterday got your letters and so was very excited and went out to Marg's in the evening – just told her you would be home next month but didn't mention anything else.

Hope you had a good time on your leave and that you are in Torquay reading this – but probably you'll still be in the same old place – #22. Somehow or other I still can't rely on Air Force things until they actually happen. That seems to be all for now and we are certainly waiting for WE day. Instead of V-day it will be "we day". All my love honey, Peg

October 14, 1945

Dearest Hamp

Where are you now and what are you doing honey? Pardon me for being rude but I hope you are at the Repat Centre doing nothing & that you won't be there long. But better still hope you are on your way. You wouldn't get this letter then but I'll tell you now there isn't much in it – but you'll get this as it's too early yet to think of you coming home. Gee I just can't believe it – it's still like a dream – not sure if it happened and afraid to count on it too much in case it all goes boom! But gosh it can't be long now can it darling?

Everyday I hear about someone else getting out or returning home. Gord Bell got his discharge & is helping Dr Scott – J Scott I guess. They have a house on 85th Ave. You'd think houses were really plentiful with all the people I've heard of with places lately but things are hard to locate.

Wednesday night Alix and I went to "Gaslight" at the Varscona – plus the corniest show I've seen in years. "Gaslight" was good though. If you try to make me believe I'm insane darling I'll just say "Gee darling you must have seen Gaslight too!" So you villain it won't work. Ha! Ha! Foiled again!

Sent a bunch of stuff to the cleaners on Friday and now I've trouble finding something to wear as I won't put on any of my new things until I'm on my way to see you. Oh happy day!

Have no further ideas about *our* holiday. Still think Calgary is a pretty good bet even if you come some other line. What say you old bay?

Eddy Oldring is now a papa. He got a son towards the last of Sept and was I ever laughing at Aunty Lena now. Eddy won't be married for 9 months until the end of October so *of course* the baby is a "premie" and Aunt Lena is sure giving this end all the reason etc for the early arrival and after all the cracks she made at me before Joan arrived. Oh! Ha! Ha! Ain't life wonderful?

Today was a real hot day 75^0 –really terrific after all the cold and wet we've had. Must be warming up the country for you honey.

That is all honey for now. Haven't done a damn thing & what I have accomplished was done in a daze. Please excuse writing. Am curled up in an arm chair. All my love dearest. Be seeing you soon. As always, Peg Kisses from Joan & big hugs too.

October 15, 1945

Dearest Peggy,

Away behind in my writing and guess I'll be further yet before I get this mailed, so please accept my apologies.

Am writing this in Blackburn – 3:20 PM and me sitting on one side of the fireplace and your Aunt Maggie sitting on the other. She's so tied up in reading a murder mystery that she can scarcely take time out to bite her finger nails with the suspense of it all. She's quite an alert character and I'm really enjoying my stay here with her.

Sorry I didn't write before leaving Bramshott. Was fairly busy but that's no excuse. Worked late a few nights cleaning up my statistics on the treatments of the affliction and then puttered around each day initiating my successor into the ways of the place. The day before I left I took the nurse in charge out to tea and to a show – hope you won't be jealous honey but she was a conscientious sort and had done all the work towards making my stay there a success – which I feel it was from the standpoint of treatment, for we ran a ward for complications and we had a lot of them with good results.

Left Friday noon, Oct. 12 and went up to London, Dave went with me and we dashed over to H.Q. to see what about out postings. We were quite disappointed to find that we hadn't been given a date for reporting yet but we should be going to repat at the end of the month. Now that the Queen Mary will carry Canadians things are really looking good – so darling at last it looks quite definite.

Stayed Friday night in London at the Maple Leaf Club and Johnnie and Doug were over for the evening meal and we sat around and talked.

Saturday morning I caught the train for Manchester and then arrived in Blackburn about 4:30 PM Aunt Maggie seemed to more or less take me for granted.

(continued in #2) All love, Hamp

Letter #2, October 15, 1945

Dearest Peggy,

The room at the back was all ready and it was just like coming home.

My birthday parcel from Eaton's (thanks very much darling, it was a swell one) came just before I left so I dumped it all in my suitcase and gave it to Aunt Maggie when I arrived. Made me feel a little less guilty about staying and eating even though I do have my own ration cards. Speaking of rationing – it's been kind of tough on your Aunt but it has been a godsend in a way. Rationing and talking about rationing has provided more excitement and complication in her every day existence that you can guess. Routine living will lose a lot of its appeal when rationing goes off and things don't have to be planned and discussed so carefully.

Your cousin Rex is still in the army and stationed in the south. He is in Group 24 though and should be out around Christmas or shortly after. On the table beside me is a picture of Eddie Oldring and his bride standing on some steps after the wedding. Eddie looked just about as pleased with himself as anyone you can imagine. His wife has been quite ill apparently but is now convalescing fairly well I'd gather.

Saturday evening we sat around and talked until midnight.

Slept in Sunday morning until nearly noon and then read in the afternoon when Aunt Maggie went off to teach Sunday school class.

In the evening we both went to the chapel. (Can you read that all right?) Quite a good service and after it, I spent about 20 minutes (shaking hands all the time) with your Mother and Dad's cousins and friends. Must have met twenty-five people in 10 minutes and got hopelessly confused as to who they were but will get some coaching now and tell you. More love, Hamp

Letter #3, October 15, 1945

Dearest Peggy,

These letters are kind of for family publication – as you may have guessed.

Guess who I met on Sunday evening
– Annie Walmsley (Mrs. Phillip Smalley)
– Mary Alice Walmsley (Mrs. Tom Gittens)
– Harry Best (accused me of being one of Dad Smalley's sons or blood relatives)
– Thom Harris (sang in the choir and went around with the collection plate)
– Dick Grimshaw
– Phillip Smalley (said to be sure to remember him to Will Smalley – so shall do so – more explicitly when I get home)
– Celina Jackson (Mrs. Riding)
– Mr. and Mrs. Arthur Sager (Mrs. Sager was Emma Arnes and said to be sure to remember them both to both my parents-in-law)
– Albert Croft (Aunt Maggie said that your parents and Albert and his wife did a lot of courting together and last time you were in England they toured the rounds they had made in their youth).
– Grace Walmsley (Harry Walmsley's widow).

Monday I was going to go over to Darwen but it became chilly and dense fog came down which didn't lift all day. Stayed home and did four jig saw puzzles, read 3 detective stories and managed to squeeze in breakfast, lunch, tea and supper, listen to the radio and do a lot of talking with Aunt Maggie. Not a bad day's program all told. Morning got up and waited a couple of hours until the sun beat through the fog and then went to the bottom of Redridge Road and caught the tram to the station

and went up to William Pickup's house. More to follow. More love,
Hamp

Letter #4, October 15, 1945

Dearest Peggy,

To continue – was quite disappointed on arrival that they were all
out for the day. Serves me right for not letting them know. However
left a message with maid and got a cup of coffee and decided to come
back to Blackburn since its only half an hour away.

Came back and found myself locked out so took a walk down
through the park. It was (& is) a beautiful afternoon and took a roll of
film of it on the way through. Also got very warm in the process of
navigating the hills. On the way back I passed the house where your
Dad's father and mother were married. (Getting to be quite the tourist
eh honey?) Your Aunt showed it to me the other day as we walked down
Duke's Brow on the way to Chapel.

Am now quite comfortably settled again. Will phone the Pickups
tonight and see if I can arrange to see them tomorrow. On Thursday
will go up to Fleetwood and then go across to Harrogate and then try
to be in London by next Monday or Tuesday and needle them a bit
about my posting and make sure I'm put on.

Your Aunt is giving "the cake basket from the Isle that Aunt Alice
used to have in her display cabinet" to take to you and is giving me a
rose bowl that came when Mrs. Bell died to take back to your Dad &
Mother. The chair for your Dad is just a little too much for me to tackle
unfortunately. It's quite a substantial piece of furniture and what with
current shipping shortages bulks a little large for casual shipment.

Well honey, will sign off and continue as the news comes.

All my love to you and share it with Joan. Hamp

October 16, 1945

Dearest Hamp

Got a letter from you today written on Oct 8. Good service eh

657

honey? Guess by now you are visiting the relatives and putting on the best front. You'll probably have a nice but quiet visit and it should help your budget. By the way darling did you ever get your money? It was cabled on the first & so far no news about you receiving it. Also your birthday box should arrive one of these days as it was ordered Aug 30. However it probably arrived after you went on leave.

Which reminds me. Happy Birthday darling, for Oct 28th. Your real present is waiting for you here, the food was just a substitute. Speaking of birthdays – tomorrow Joan is two. It's hard to believe that the time has gone so. You'll certainly get a jolt when you see her as she's changed so much from 6 months. Of course you've seen snaps of her but you certainly haven't seen her in action. So you better come prepared to meet your Waterloo.

It's funny you mentioning about not staying long in Calgary as you would be anxious to see Joan. 5 days is about all I can take away from her and not get a hankering to return home so guess we are going to get along OK eh honey? Was thinking about that if you return until the end of November it would be OK as then your leave would run into Christmas & New Year. On the other hand if you were posted to Calgary it wouldn't really matter. When do you expect a discharge, not that I'm caring, but was just wondering if you knew anything.

Was over at Alix's last night knitting. Fred is coming back with the 3rd division too so you should be coming back within a week of each other. Then what a reunion we can all have! Isn't it too wonderful to believe honey? If it's all a dream please don't wake me up.

On Thursday we're having a party for Joan – 6 kids and 5 mothers. You work on that one honey until you get the letter about the party but please don't expect it to be written on Thursday night. I don't think I could do it. That's all for now you old dear and don't do too much unofficial seeing that you are officially on the wagon. Big hugs from Joan and all my love darling – as ever – Peg

Letter # 5, Oct 17, 1945

Dearest Peggy

Missed one relative – Edith Walmsley (Mrs Beardwood) – sings in

658

the choir and almost forgot meeting her. Today is the big day in our lives and am ashamed not to have gotten a cable away wishing Joan many happy returns of the day. Will also have to make up a present when I come so tell her her old man won't be a bum all his life. Wish I were there to celebrate the occasion with you both but will have to do a job of no. 3 since that will be the first with all of us together.

Made a mistake in my letters yesterday – letters one to four should have been dated the sixteenth instead of the fifteenth.

After writing you last evening Mrs Riding came in for the evening. She is a very pleasant person and has a good sense of humor. I got quite a kick out of her because she has a broad Lancashire accent and speaks some of the dialect – she prides herself on it I think and it's quite interesting to hear her talk.

Phoned the Pickups yesterday evening – arranged to go over there to see them on Thursday.

Today went up to Fleetwood and saw your aunt and uncle, Mr. and Mrs Taylor. They asked to be remembered to you all.

Left here about 9.00 and got a bus from Preston to Fleetwood and arrived there about 11.30. Was just coming in when I saw their shop and hopped off and went in and introduced myself. They were very busy but took me out and I felt quite at home. For lunch they introduced the biggest and best piece of meat that I have seen in England – it was really good and done really rare with a piece of genuine butter on the top – doesn't it make your mouth water? They are quite rushed there and beginning to feel their years a bit. They have over 700 people rationed with them and just the two of them to do the work so they are very busy. Their son is in the marines and has returned from Italy & is stationed near Liverpool. They are trying to get him out so he can help with the business but haven't had much luck to date. They can't take a day off or time out because the shop must carry on. More to follow. All my love, Hamp

Letter #6, October 17, 1945

Dearest Peggy,

Only stayed a couple of hours in Fleetwood because they were so darned busy but wouldn't carry on until I left so I went early.

Got some pictures of them in the shop and I hope they turn out

OK. Aunt Annie gave me some handkerchiefs to take to you and Maw so will deliver same shortly (I hope).

Got back from Fleetwood about 4 PM and we had tea. Mrs. Sweeting (Aunt Maggie's sister-in-law) had queued this morning and obtained some tripe for the two of them. I wasn't enthusiastic however so they were welcome to it – not that tripe has any flavor one could either like or dislike – it's quite a neutral dish. But I seem to see the peristalsis of that old cow's stomach with each bite.

Well darling will sign off for the night and write you tomorrow and give you a blow-by-blow account of Willie Pickup and his family. (If I hang around here much longer I'm going to end up by calling your Dad and Mother, Will and Margaret – everyone asks me about them by their first names and I almost have to talk about them in the same way or the questioner gets my "Smalleys" confused with some of the local ones.)

October 18/45

To continue – have just completed a most delightful day and have enjoyed as much (or more) as any day I have spent in England.

Went over to Darwen and arrived at Pickup's at about 11:30. Mrs. Pickup was waiting for me and we had coffee and kind of got introduced. She is a very charming individual and made me feel completely at home. They have a lovely home which they are now in the midst of adding improvements which were delayed during the war.

About 12:00 we went down to the mill and had lunch in the mill canteen with Joan (the daughter – aged 19 who works in the office) and Will Pickup. Had a good lunch and then made a tour. All love, Hamp

Letter #7, October 18, 1945

Dearest Peggy,

To continue – he showed me over the mill from start to finish and I now have a vague idea how one makes cloth. The thing that impressed me most was the noise of it all when those 500 looms were going full blast – quite deafening.

After that we drove over to Stanley Pickup's and sat and talked with him for an hour or more and had tea. He has been ill for some time and is just beginning to recuperate. He seems a pretty good egg – although William Pickup is unbelievable – made me feel just as if I'd known him always and was the perfect host.

After that we drove back to the house and he proceeded with his work and Mrs. Pickup and Joan and myself went for a walk up through the park and finally climbed to the moor overlooking Darwen and about the same height as Darwen Tower. It was quite misty but we got a good look at Darwen (As well as a bit of exercise).

Took a little over an hour and I sat around and read on coming home and then Gwenda got home. She is about 16 and a nice kid. She is going to a tech school in Blackburn and taking art. Both she and Joan just finished school last month and are home for the first time in several years (to stay that is).

Then we had tea – (I'd call it supper and a full meal but they insisted that it was tea so I guess it was.

After supper Mr. Pickup had to go out so the rest of us sat around and gassed and then played quite a bit of ping pong and after a bottle of beer for me they drove me home to Blackburn at 10:00 PM and here I am. Quite a nice day. Now to fill in. I said that we came home and then Wm. Pickup went to work. All through the war he has operated a radio listening post. That is he listened to short wave German broadcasts for 3 to 5 hours for 5 days a week and took down the code as it came and passed it along. Quite a war effort I'd say since he also ran a cotton mill. Continued All love, Hamp

Letter #8, October 18, 1945

Dearest Peggy,

Yes, this radio job of Mr. Pickup's quite impressed me. He was a wireless operator in the last war and that explains how he got into it. He is still working because they get a certain amount of stuff from the German underground still.

Another funny thing – I'm off tomorrow to Harrogate to go to the little village of Lintman Wharfe. I told them about this and found that the son Arthur is going to school there – small world, eh? Quite a coincidence that I should happen to land in the same place. I am going to go over the school on Saturday and look him up and on Sunday the Pickups are going to drive up to see him. They will pick me up and I am going to drive back to Darwen with them on Monday. Quite a break for me to drive around by private automobile and to be able to make all my visits in the process.

I would like to stay a couple of days with the Pickups and may do so. Want to phone London on Saturday and see if there is anything new on when I might expect to be posted – don't expect that there will be, but don't want to miss anything. If there isn't then I will stay up here until the middle of the week and just bum around.

Well darling will sign off for the time being and add to this as I go along.

October 22, 1945

Well honey, have covered quite a bit more territory since I left off writing the above. Friday morning (Oct. 19) went to Manchester to Leeds and then by bus to Weatherby, York. Phoned Frank and Margot Toas the night before found that they had room for me so I didn't arrive totally unexpected for a change. Got a big reception from the two kids at home – which made me feel quite important of course. The oldest girl is off at a boarding school.

The night I arrived they were going to a masquerade party insisted that I go along with them. Everyone met for drinks at one of the locals first and I renewed a lot of acquaintances I had made last January when there on leave. The party was a lot of fun and although I did little but watch, I got quite a kick out of watching them. Many of the men were the typical Englishmen in ordinary dress but had on ridiculous costume and thoroughly amused themselves and everyone else making fools of themselves.

All my love, Hamp

Dearest Peggy,

To continue – Finished up with the masquerade party at about 2:00 Am and then slept in until 10 on Saturday morning and then Frank got me up and we drove into York. He had to go in on business and took me along as a tourist. I have been in York several times but that was the first time I had a guide. He had lived there for some time and knew the history of the place well. He drove me all over it around the walls and then took me to the places in the old city that are of most interest. I quite enjoyed the day. Came back about 2:00 PM and picked up Broeya (the oldest girl) aged (10 or so) at her school on the way back. Had lunch and then went to sleep until 7:00 PM on the sofa by the fire. Phoned Darwen in the evening to let the Pickup's know we had accommodation for them for Sunday evening at a local inn.

In the evening later Frank and I went down to the Windmill and had a couple of beers and then brought one back for Margot.

Slept in Sunday morning. After lunch the Pickups arrived from Darwen and picked up Arthur and came down to the house with him and sat for an hour or so. Then I went down with them to the Inn for tea (supper) and drove out to the school to take Arthur back. In the evening we went to the Windmill and met the local lights and a party of them came back to the Toas' for sandwiches. It was quite nice and I think Alice and "Willy" Pickup quite enjoyed it.

Monday morning the Pickups collected me at 10:00 AM and we drove to Bradford. Billy had some business and dropped us off. Alice and I had lunch, did some shopping (bought some buttons for my trench coat) and then went to a show. Met Billy at 2:00 PM and then drove on Skyston and had tea and then proceeded home.

On the way home we stopped at Mrs. Eva Barnes. She asked to be remembered to you all, as also did the children at home. Young Eva Barnes (who was a bridesmaid of Mother's wedding) was in the fire service and is now demobilized and at home. Dick Barnes was also home. He is a sergeant major in the army and at present stationed in the South of England. He expects to be demobilized next spring. More to follow. Love Hamp

Dearest Hamp,

Hello, old thing, this is your wife again. I don't feel too badly as me thinks you missed several nights before you went on leave. You'd best come home so I can give you the wifely blast properly. However that can wait. The question now is "Where are you?" I'm only up to Oct. 8 in my news from you so a lot has probably happened – at any rate the days go by very quickly which is a good thing eh honey?

Wednesday night Maw and I baked for Joan's party and were quite busy what with the cake and ice cream etc. Thursday morning I slapped up the sandwiches and then in the afternoon, Marion and Arthur Carlyle and Clare Henderson Carlyle; Lorry Campbell and Helen Hedley Campbell; Alix and Sandy; Maribeth and Nora Horner, Carol Lynn and Carol Young arrived for the party. The kids got along sweet – no fights and everyone blew out the candles at least once. So all in all a good time was had.

Bought Joan a blue sheer dress and with blue sox and blue bow and new white shoes she looked kind of cute. Margaret and David were to come but Marg. couldn't seem to muster up the energy for the long trek.

Next day Joan relived the party and had to blow out the candles again. She got some plastic dishes from David to go with her table and chairs and I caught her talking, then nodding "Joany wants a cup of tea?" and put the empty cup to her mouth.

She is really a treat now and continually surprises me with the things she says and does. Today she pretended she had some candy and went around saying "one for Mummy" "one for Nana" "One for Doany Mith". She is trying to sing too and one song has a line "And play the whole day through" which comes out as "N pay the o' day do". It's really a panic.

Friday night went to a show with Clare Henderson and Saturday went over to Connie Day's to play bridge. Took Joan to the Nursery Class at Church on Sunday and she had a great time. Kept asking to go next day. Looks like I've lost my good excuse eh darling? Last night went to the Col Mewburn Hosp. to visit the boys for War Services Council. I still think they hate it as much as I do. So tonight I'm writing you. Ain't you a lucky boy! Mrs. Young had a cable from Johnnie to say he'll be in Canada on Nov. 4 but I guess you know all that too. Hope you'll be home soon now darling but it really can't be long now. Heaps of love dearest, as ever Peg

October 26, 1945

Dearest Hamp,

Well you old goat where's all that mail you were going to write before you went on leave? Me thinks you are a bum! And it's a mighty good thing you are so far away so that you miss all the remarks being sent in your direction. Mean aren't I honey? Don't really mean it all – for I'll forget all about it when I hear you are coming home but right now my feathers are ruffled somewhat.

Haven't been out at night since Monday so life is quiet. Last night the snow hit us and today everything is blanketed in five inches of snow so winter is upon us. Joan had a wonderful time playing outside today and kept shouting at the top of her voice "I ply 'n no". Her pronunciation for snow. She is really talking these days but has a very funny accent. She calls me "mammy". Says "mo" for more, "comb" for come, which sounds very silly as "I wanna comb up". Last night she wakened me up by raising an awful fuss – sobbing and wailing and saying "I want my hair combed" so at 2 AM I combed her hair for a few minutes and she settled right down. Am wondering what she can dream up tonight.

Johnny Young and Charlie Duke arrived on the Queen Elizabeth today, guess they had a pretty rough trip across. Hope it isn't stormy when you come over next month.

Am certainly waiting for the word that you are coming then I can hop to those last minute details so please give me a bit of warning before you leave England.

Am going to serve at an afternoon tea at Alix's tomorrow so am becoming social for ½ a day. Fred has given up trying to contact you as all attempts have failed. I know you couldn't get him either but perhaps you had better luck on your leave.

Guess I'd better stop this dribble because as you can see I have positively nothing new to write about.

Still love you, more each day – even if I do get a bit irked with you at times – and can hardly wait for our day. It can't be long now and oh boy am "I going to love my guy like he's never been loved before!" As always, Peg

Dearest Peggy,

Back to camp late last night and feel a little deflated but its swell to come back and get a pile of mail from you. Got five letters – one with snaps – you both get better looking every day and don't know how I'm going to be able to live up to my beautiful family. Joan is getting to be quite a young lady and she will take a little time to get to know I imagine.

Now about my repat – went into London yesterday and found that my name hadn't gone in for posting yet and since it takes ten days after it goes go in, then I probably won't leave here much before the middle of November and won't be home much before the end of November. Quite a disappointment honey. But I guess a couple of weeks or three more won't make that much difference now that we have waited so long. Shouldn't have raised your hopes so high and am sorry. However, honey, it won't be too long as you say – it will be nice to be on leave at Christmas time and have all those days to kind of take a run-up on Christmas. November 30 and Dec. 1 sound kind of far away but there are only 30 days in the month after all and the month is just about beginning.

Wrote quite a bunch of letters while on leave (ten to be exact). Hope they all get there OK. For I'm sure I can't remember half the names of the people if the mail goes astray. Think it will take me about half a day to tell your mother all the news and gossip. Really had a marvelous time there. Yesterday morning the Pickups got up at seven and had breakfast with me and then Billy drove me down to the station. The day before I went only to Blackburn at noon and took Gwenda Pickup out to lunch and was going to spend the day with Mrs. Horsfall. She was out so killed time by going to a show and then back to Mrs. Horsfall's at teatime and spent the evening. Brought back the rose bowl for your parents and the cake dish she sent to you. All in all it was a good leave and kept quite busy with my traveling around.

Say honey – that grey suit of mine – if it's still in one piece I wonder if you could get it cleaned and also the overcoat – don't know where that is. Would like to be able to climb out of blue occasionally when on leave.

Well darling – will see you before too long and will not fall of the wagon "unofficially" to quote my charming wife. Miss you and warn Joan to look out for an awful lot of attention from your husband before too long. All my love, Hamp

October 25, 1945

Dearest Peggy

A couple more days have eased by with a little to report. I imagine that you are thoroughly disgusted with me by now with the big mail famine that started when I was on leave. Hope all the leave letters get to you intact and in order.

Saturday afternoon Mac and Dave Moffat and I went down to Bournemouth to see Mac's brother who is just back from India. We went to Portsmouth and then across to Southampton and then caught another train from there. From Southampton to Bournemouth we had a compartment to ourselves in a train with no corridor. So we sat and drank rum and coca cola and got feeling quite cheerful and even passed many favorable comments on how pleasant the English trains were to travel on. Arrived at Bournemouth and went to the RCAF staff mess which is housed in a residential hotel. We knew several of the MOs there and so we went into a very pleasant evening with a good meal and sitting around chewing the fat. Slept at the hotel and got up in the morning and wandered around Bournemouth and caught the train at 3.30 PM & arrived back here in the early evening. All in all it was very pleasant.

Went back to work today & it was quite a struggle. About 3.00 PM got on the bus and rode down to Grayshott a couple of miles away and took films in to be developed. Had acquired 8 rolls on leave and around here so should get about 2 dozen pictures that turn out (that's about my average). Then shopped for something for the daughter and you. Got her a little sweater that's kind of cute and will look further afield for you. Don't know what to get you. I'm sure and it's kind of hopeless to get something half decent for your Mother & Dad but will keep looking. Anything from the jewelers has a 100 percent luxury tax & is just pure junk since they only get plastics or second hand stuff to deal in for the past 3 or 4 years. Well honey, no more news. Sure miss you I do. All my love. Say hello to the one & only. Hamp

November 2, 1945

Dearest Peggy,

Time seems to move faster than I do. Haven't heard any word about posting to report and it looks like it may be a couple of weeks yet – certainly hope it isn't any longer. Am back in the routine and it's worse than not having left it at all but guess it's to be expected. We have had four nice days this week and one afternoon went cycling and another went shopping. However Dave and I didn't think that it was Wednesday afternoon so the shopping wasn't very successful.

Got a letter from you yesterday giving me the blast for nor writing just before going on leave. Sorry honey but guess the mail will have caught to you by now unless these Atlantic storms delayed the airmail for a day or so.

Wednesday night was a masquerade party. Dave and I went over with an Air Force MO who is visiting the unit. We didn't have costumes but quite enjoyed watching everyone else and got feeling quite cheerful on the punch and having several dances. My dancing seems to get worse so I guess you'll have to take me in hand and give me a few lessons in a little while.

Got a very hurt letter from Dad today giving me the blast also for not writing. I haven't heard from him after my last letter until I received it but guess I also deserved it. Sure am being kicked around these days honey but kind of like it from you – want nothing more than to be a little hen-pecked for awhile.

Gosh it will be good to leave the place – am fed up to the gills with it but it won't be too long I hope. Am going up to London on my next day off – Nov. 6 – to do a little more inquiring. Well darling will sign off. Love you an awful lot. All my love, Hamp

November 5, 1945

Dearest Peggy,

Well today our news came through. W/C MacLochlen phoned from

London that he had posted Dave and I to repat effective Nov. 15. That is pretty good but I'm getting to the stage that I'll believe it when I see it. However we should be there by then and then it will take awhile to get a boat. It may be one week and it may be four but will be home sometime near the first of Dec. and so we will have Christmas and New Years on leave at least and can't grumble too much. Was just beginning to feel a little desperate and a lot fed up with the place and its contents but guess I can hold out for another ten days.

Got a letter from you yesterday with another blast for not writing. Gee whiz honey I'm almost getting afraid to open my mail. Sure hope it's all blown over by the time I get home. (Actually am not too worried but realize that I was quite a bum not to write. Sure hope that leave mail has caught up by now.)

Have not been doing very much since last writing. Last Saturday afternoon Dave and I went down to a show and walked around the countryside. Sat in at night until we got desperate and went over and had a couple of beers and shot snooker.

Sunday was a repetition except we went for a walk in the afternoon.

Tonight spent the evening in the sisters' mess with Carmen and Dick Whittington. He is a Captain in the provost corps and went to school in Camrose with me. We sat around for a couple of hours and talked, had tea and sandwiches and then I came back to the mess and had an onion sandwich, shot a game of snooker with Dave and now I'm back in the damn room again. Sure will be glad to leave it and go elsewhere. Funny how the place kind of closes in on you occasionally isn't it. Well honey, will sign off and write sooner. Be seeing you. All my love, Hamp

Nov 7/ 45

Dearest Peggy

Another couple of days gone by and it seems hard to believe that theoretically I have only one more week to spend in the place. Went up to London yesterday & went to Headquarters & talked over the general situation with the boss. I am definitely in for posting to the repat on the 15th and it should come about that time. Then may sail a couple of weeks

669

or three after that – not more than three weeks I hope but you never know your luck.

When we get to Canada we apparently have to spend a couple of days at Lachine & that will give us time to get in touch with each other & then oh boy! –It surely will be wonderful won't it honey.

While in London I bought myself a pair of Oxfords. Had been putting it off, hoping to get home first but was just beginning to find the pavement a little bit cold. They seem to rob you for shoes but guess it's about the same as at home. That reminds me – I promised to try and get some shoes for the Pickups and they gave me £10 to do the buying – so that's one of the first bits of Christmas shopping that we do I guess. They gave me the sizes but I'm damned if I know how they expect to get them to fit. Also want a subscription to the Saturday Evening Post and to one of the Ladies Home Journal sort of things. Something more to do.

Got a ride home by road yesterday. They were sending a patient down to the hospital so rode along. The traffic in London has just about returned to its peacetime hell and it's quite amazing how the cars manage to move at all. The highways are also crowded so I guess that basic ration is probably being added to by the black market.

Well darling hope you have got over your mad at me & will wait hopefully for mail. Miss you (for not much longer I hope) and give Joan a little warning of the horrors of having her old mad at home. All my love, Hamp

November 11, 1945

Dearest Peggy,

Time goes on doesn't it. Just counting days and hours now and keeping my fingers crossed. No posting in yet but it is fairly definite that we will go to repat on the 10th and then wait there. Once you get there you at least can start looking forward to something a little more concrete. Have done absolutely nothing of note – since last writing. Every afternoon Dave and I go out for a walk or visit one of the local towns. Thursday walked into Haslemere and toured the town window shopping. Absolutely nothing to buy – we ended up by going to the local museum and looking at a lot of stuffed birds and then having tea and bought a pound of mushrooms – sneaked into the mess at night and cooked them.

Yesterday was cold so worked a bit and in the evening went over the mess for the usual Saturday night routine.

Today Bob Bergman came over to see me – he is working at one of the near by camps and seems quite happy with his lot. He came over last March and hasn't started to panic too much about going home.

Don't know if I told you or not – got all the pictures developed that I took on leave. Had about 6 rolls. They all turned out fairly well except the ones I took in Fleetwood – you aunt's picture was the only one that turned out and the others of the shop etc. were no good – don't know what went wrong but it can't be helped.

Haven't heard from you this week and guess I must be in the doghouse for sure. Hope that Fido moves me out before I get home.

Got a letter from Mother yesterday and was quite amazed to hear that Irene was expecting. Mother quoted the date as May – that seems to be a call in considerable advance of the event. Must have been pretty well calculated.

I hear they aren't very busy now at the RCAF release centers – sure hope that they don't need much help by the time I get home. Well honey, will sign off hoping to hear from you soon. Hope you aren't too disgusted with me for not being on a boat by now but just couldn't do much about it. Prepare yourself for being loved like *you* have never been loved before. All my love, Hamp

November 13, 1945

Dearest Peggy,

Today I got the best news of a long, long time. We are posted to report on the 15th. Dave and I got cleared today at the hospital and tomorrow we go up to London and get cleared from headquarters. Don't know if we go to Torquay or Bournemouth but I imagine that it will be Torquay – certainly hope so because it's warmer there and also I want to see a bit of Cornwall before we move off. We will be billeted in hotels and since they will probably have only fireplaces and no coal to

671

go in them, it would be better not to stay there too long. The sailings I know are the Empress of Scotland on the 22nd and the Queen Elizabeth on the 2nd and 19th of December. We will probably make the Queen Elizabeth's first sailing since the Empress of Scotland's no doubt all booked up by now. Will go on anything that sails however (except a grain boat going back via the Panama – have already had the opportunity to reject one of these that sails in a month or so – you would scarcely make it home for Christmas on that!).

Now we can start counting days at last – will let you know as soon as we get down to Torquay just how things are going. Will be traveling around tomorrow and stay the night in London and then leave the following morning. Gee it's wonderful to finally begin to see a glimmer of light on this boat trip.

Dave and I were kind of hoping to have a couple of days to tour London and take pictures of its historic sights but guess we'll have to skip that and you and I can come back some day and be tourists.

I heard that Johnnie and Doug have already sailed but I don't know for sure. Hope they have because the less MOs there are around the sooner we'll sail – so honey don't get too impatient and don't start counting on seeing me at once. Haven't heard from you for 10 days and guess it'll be another week now for the mail to catch up. All my love, Hamp

Box 494, Camrose, Alberta
November 13, 1945

Dearest Peggy,

Cheerio! Received your letter, also one from Hampton last night. He was to be posted in a day or so from Nov 2 to a depot where he will get a boat when his turn comes. It is the first step on the way home he says – so hope it is the one leaving Nov 15. Not long anyway. Isn't it great?

Well, we got Hampton's clothes together. Aired them yesterday. Sent his over-coat and tweed coat to the cleaners. I had the pants cleaned and pressed when he left here. They are still wrapped in his club bag. Just as soon as the cleaner has them ready, I will be sending them with his club bag. No worry about the charges. Shall I have the old blue suit and his dress suit cleaned and pressed? The light greenish sport suit is clean and pressed – needs a little pressing – we will do it –

Home Talent. Francour's[28] *is not busy now as they may be in December so let me know. The dress suit needs cleaning all right.*

Hampton gave a glowing account of his visits with your relatives. Said he was amazed how hospitable all these people were to a complete stranger. Lovely of them – was it not?

We were disappointed not to see Dr. Smalley last Friday night for the burning of the mortgage. All went well. The substitute sent, Rev. Smith, was splendid. Gave a wonderful message. He said your father was not so well. Am sorry. It would have been a hard trip for such a little. I was allowed to hold one side of the mortgage while it burned, since I am the last Charter Member of the eleven left – thirty years ago. The Church presented me with a sheaf of chrysanthemums – I felt rather over come – wonder why I am the last leaf on the tree.

Am just not so sure about Irene. She is on a diet now. Does not look at all well. Margaret says she is well enough but gets tired. She always works so much.

Mac operated all forenoon and another at one o'clock.

Dad no better – same thing. Will be so glad when Hampton can take over. I surely need a holiday. Would like to get a good distance from him.

We are trying to be ready for a happy homecoming for all.

Have my cranberries, mince meat and fruit for a light cake and the plum puddings.

Had a letter from Mrs. Forbes yesterday. Her mother, Mrs. Patrick, has broken one hip. She was too old for an operation so a bone specialist pinned the bone. Later pneumonia developed. Penicillin saved her. She is home. Up and down. Hoping the bone will knit. Terrible for a woman 86 years old.

We had a hectic week last – all sick with flu. Fern home the whole week. She was down two days. My arm was bandaged three weeks – all healed now – quite a red scar left.

Will write Hampy once more though am hoping he is on his way home. Won't you be a happy little girl. Do as you feel you should. Mac will be overjoyed to have Hampton when he comes.

Remember me to all and please write. Letters sustain me.

Lots of love, Mother

Nov 15/45

Dearest Peggy

Will not repeat my sins of leave & neglect the correspondence. Dave and I came up to London yesterday expecting to go to repat today. However we found that records had changed our reporting date to Nov 19 and that we report to Bournemouth not Torquay. Therefore we are still attached to the hospital but since we are cleared from there we decided not to go back and just go AWOL for 4 days. Both of us have spent a lot of time in London but have neglected to see all the historical spots that one is supposed to visit and so are now catching up on them with a vengeance.

We had a busy morning yesterday going to the bank, checking in at headquarters, going to our lending library for the final check out and then coming over here to the Maple Leaf Club and getting a room. This is really a nice place to stay – an officer's club run by the Red Cross & quite cheap & quite good meals cooked in Canadian style.

Yesterday afternoon we got on the tube and went to London Bridge and walked around a bit and then went through the Tower of London. It was just a heap of old rock but the guide made it seem fairly interesting. Didn't see the crown jewels however since it is not yet back to full peace time swing. In the evening we went & saw a show – The Seventh Veil – stood in a queue form 7:15 to 8:45 and finally got in. It was quite a good show and it was damn nice to get inside and warmed up.

This morning we got up at 08:00 and after breakfast went down town – walked through the end of Hype Park along the Serpentine and then over to Westminster Abbey. Spent a couple of hours wandering through the Abbey and then back to the club for lunch. The Abbey was quite impressive and we looked at it quite carefully. On the way back I bought tickets to a revue called "Fine Feathers".

This afternoon we went over to the Victoria & Albert museum and spent a couple of hours getting brushed up on old English art and what have you. Then went down town and looked up Gardiner Craig. He is MO examining wives of Canadians before they are sent to Canada. Spent half an hour with him and then dashed out and had a meal of chop suey and then went over to the theatre to see our "Fine Feathers". It was good – nice costumes, good-looking gals and the gags were not too corny. Got the tube back and now at home –lying on my stomach writing on a chair beside the bed. Well honey, Bournemouth on the 19th – may not sail for 3 weeks. Will write soon. All my love, Hamp

Dearest Peggy

Another couple of days gone by without a great deal to report. Yesterday we managed to keep quite busy. Went down to St Paul's in the morning and did quite a good job of looking it over. Started at the crypt, saw Nelson & Wellington & so forth, all safely laid away & gradually progressed up to the whispering gallery. Were whispered at by a guide (for six pence) and then went up to the dome and surveyed London. It's amazing that St Paul's didn't suffer more damage when you look at the acres of blank spaces around it. It's in the area of the docks which were pretty heavily hit. I guess most of the surrounding buildings were burnt and that accounts for its preservation. It's a very beautiful spot however.

In the afternoon we saw a show – Rhapsody in Blue – the life of George Gershwin – I quite enjoyed it. The prices of movies in London would amaze you. The seat range from 4/6 to 15 bob – that's down town. Seems funny to have to pay between $1.00 & $3.50 to just see a movie.

In the evening Gardiner [Craig] came over to the club & had the evening meal with us & then we went to a nearby pub & had a few beers & then came back here at 10.00 for coffee and sandwiches.

Today we spent the morning at Base accounts at Knightsbridge and then went over to Dave's bank, had lunch near there & then walked from St Paul's along the embankment to Westminster. The Embankment is a nice spot to walk along to watch the river traffic on the Thames & watch old codgers feed sea gulls etc. When we got to Westminster we went through the Houses of Parliament since Saturday is visitors' day. Saw the Houses of Lords & Commons & bought our usual quota of pictures of them. Then had tea & walked for an hour along Holborn and down Gray's Inn to Kings Cross Station where we caught a tube back here. Quite an athletic afternoon. This evening we saw a show – Valley of Decision – at the local theatre and have now collapsed in bed where I am about to go to sleep so I can dream of you. All my love, Hamp

675

Dearest Peggy

Well, am now in Bournemouth & pretty much over the business of getting settled into the place. We got here yesterday afternoon & started right in on the business of getting through reception. They have 3 divisions – reception, holding & repat & you progress from one to the next. However we cleared reception and go into the repat squadron tomorrow so it looks like they will try to push us right along. The first sailing we have a chance for will probably be the Queen Eliz on the 2nd of Dec and I think we have a fair chance of getting on it. Keep your fingers crossed anyway please honey.

Haven't heard from you in quite a time now – hope all is well and you still love me. May get a letter soon I hope since Dave's mail caught up with him today.

We are billeted in one of the hotels that have been requisitioned. It's pretty bare but we are quite comfortable and there are only 2 in a room where we are. Another good thing is the fact that there is central heating and they turn it up enough to take the chill out of the air. Developed a real head cold yesterday and woke up this morning with a head like s barrel and a temp of 101. However after wandering around all day felt practically cured and am actually going to make sure that nothing keeps me off that boat if ever I get the chance to get on it.

Spent Sunday in London after I last wrote. Dave and I and Bill Prowse got up and wandered through Hyde Park and listened to the orators – it was quite a lot of fun to hear them and the hecklers. Met [Tom Otto?] who says his wife nee Dorothy Stephens knows you quite well.

Well honey will let you know as soon I as hear anything definite. All my love, Hamp

Dearest Peggy

Another couple of days gone by without much to report. We are now on repat squadron which means we parade every day at 9.30 AM

& answer our names on roll call and then break off & have until the next morning at the same time. The days seem quite long but guess we aren't suffering too much. We seem to be working out a routine of getting up and dashing for the roll call & then having a cup of coffee at 10.00 & then going for a walk for an hour and then waiting for lunch. Have tea in mid-afternoon and just bum around before & after. Have seen a show every night but we are getting a little fed up with seeing the same newsreels. We won't know anything of a posting for at least another 7 days. The QE sails on Dec 2 and I'm just praying that I'll be on it. If we miss that we should get the Mauritania though no sailing date has been announced for it as yet.

Got a letter from Mother yesterday – she seems to think I am on board ship going home. Said she had gotten the clothes cleaned and was sending them up to you – anything that was in the stuff in Camrose at least.

I gave my address as the Palliser Hotel in Calgary as a stop over en route home. Sure hope that is OK honey and if not we'll have to contact each other soon. Sure hope I hear from you this week – it's going on for 3 weeks since I heard from you and will wire and find out what goes if I don't hear from you pretty soon.

Seems funny getting so impatient to be home in the last few days when we have waited patiently for so many months. Oh well honey, we have 30 days regardless where it starts and you had better resign yourself to having to give me your undivided attention for that period.

Saw by the Maple Leaf of about 5 days ago that Freddy Day is sailing home as crew of a freighter. Hope I get there about the time that he does. If I sail on Dec 2 (IF!), I'll get home about the 15th. If I don't sail then we may have a rush to get there by Christmas. Well honey – it won't be long. All my love, Hamp

November 25, 1945

Dearest Peggy,

Many Happy Returns of the day! Sorry I can't help you celebrate it but will try to make amends. Hope you got the flowers all right. Sent them from London on the 15th so they should have arrived on time.

Tomorrow is the day that is hanging over our heads like Damocles sword – the draft for the Lizzie is to be announced. There are about 500 berths and I'm sure I have talked to 1000 people who expect to be on it. I think I'll break down and bawl if I miss it. Some of the boys have been waiting 2 mo. in repat sqdn for it though so I guess I should consider myself fortunate to have gotten this far.

Yesterday Dave and I went to Salisbury – it's a two-hour bus ride from here. We had lunch and then went through the Cathedral. I think the Cathedral building itself is one of the most beautiful I have seen in England. We did a thorough job of reading our guidebooks and touring it. Got back for supper and then played knock-rummy all evening with Lorne Oatway (just back from India and also wanting to go home) and another chap. That filled up Saturday pretty well (started the day by standing in a line for two hours at roll call and what have you).

The day before yesterday (Friday) we went out to Christchurch (5 miles from here) and went through the priory there. It was very old and quite nice but kind of put in the background compared to Salisbury.

Have seen a number of people here from Claresholm – don't know if you remember them or not. Robinson a pilot – he was married. Also Woodson and Al Nichols – they weren't married and you may not remember them. Len Jenner (an M.O. who preceded us at Claresholm) is also here waiting repat. He has a higher number than we have though – came over here last March. Seems funny so many like him have been here less than 6 months and have been repatriated on points.

This is Sunday morning and am still in bed since we don't report on Sunday. Can't sleep for the church bells ringing. Sure am looking forward to home and Sunday morning breakfast with a genuine orange and an egg and good coffee – say I'd better stop before I starve to death here. Well honey, please be patient.

All my love, Hamp

Nov 26/45

Dearest Peggy
    Just a note.
    I sail on the Q Eliz on Dec 2 – next Sunday. Will probably take 4

678

days to cross and then a day to Lachine (allow to Dec 8) – spend about 2 days in Lachine & then home. Ain't it wonderful?

Will contact you from Lachine. Do you still want to come to Calgary I hope? Am going to write the Palliser for reservations from Lachine so you had better count on a 48 in Calgary. All my love, Hamp

DECEMBER 1945

2RN AV 21 MARCONI

SANSORIGIN 28

NLT MRS C H SMITH

11024 89TH AVE EDMONTON ALTA

SAILING DEC SECOND ON ELIZABETH WILL CONTACT YOU FROM LACHINE

LOVE

HAMP

1250A

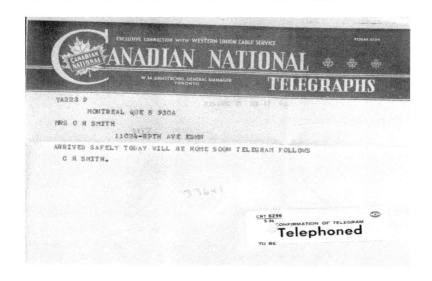

YA223 9

MONTREAL QUE 8 930A

MRS C H SMITH

11024-89TH AVE EDMN

ARRIVED SAFELY TODAY WILL BE HOME SOON TELEGRAM FOLLOWS

C H SMITH.

CNT 6296
5 36 CONFIRMATION OF TELEGRAM
Telephoned
TO BE

CRA56 7/5   1945 DEC 9 AM 11 48

    MONTREAL QUE 9 104P
MRS C H SITH   490
11024-89TH AVE EDMONTON

ARRIVE CALGARY 9.20 AM WEDNESDAY

                  HAMP

APPENDICES

APPENDICES

I. Doug's Eulogy for Hamp's Funeral

Christopher Hampton Smith

We are here today to remember and pay tribute to my father. He was many things to each of us here: a husband, a brother, a father, an uncle, a physician, a surgeon, a business partner, an active participant in this community and, of course, a friend. I have been asked by our family to share with you some of our memories – in many respects they are my memories – of this unique and talented man. Hopefully it will allow each of you to reflect in your own private way.

I suppose like all children my early images of my father were exactly that – images from photos and stories that grew into memories. I did not have a true recollection of him until I was relatively old. I think this was because of the nature of his work and the fact that he spent several months studying medicine in Edinburgh in 1952.

But the images are clear. They begin with a photograph of my parents on their wedding day, 15th January 1943. I recognised very early that my mother by every standard was a very attractive woman. At that time my father was in the Air Force and struck a very smart pose in his uniform. These images that had remained still in a dresser photograph for so many years leapt to full life and colour at Norton's fiftieth wedding anniversary a few months ago. David had made a video of Uncle Mac's colour movie of Norton 's wedding and this was replayed. What seemed to me to be a large portion of the film showed my parents in living, moving colour just a few months before they too were to be married. It showed the vibrancy of my mother despite her nervousness in meeting many new faces. And to me it showed the striking resemblance of my father and grandfather and how their mannerisms and habits were so similar. It showed my father's roots as described for me many times by my grandmother. And for me it confirmed the perceptions of my father as a quietly confident man who enjoyed people but was not necessarily outgoing by nature. He was always alert to imposing himself on others.

Dad did not talk about his childhood in Camrose often but I always pictured it as being very typical. He belonged to the Boy Scouts, went hunting on occasion with his friends and I suspect spent a lot of time reading – given the number of books around my grandmother's house in which his name and handwriting were present. And he must have done some homework and studying because he graduated from high school at the age of sixteen with an amazing report card. The lowest mark was ninety-eight and the rest were all one-hundreds. My kids would say that it must have been easier because there was not that much to know then. But I have looked through his schoolbooks of the day and it was no less challenging for the time than today.

He talked once about his first day at university. The story retold was of how Grandpa Smith loaded him into his car, drove to Edmonton, enrolled him in a route towards Medicine and returned to Camrose. There was little or no discussion on the matter. Dad suggested if he could have had anything to say about it he would have taken Law. His new home became St. Stephens College at the university and it was a time of his life that he greatly enjoyed. Somewhere in the house are pictures of those days at university and at Steves, up in the alcove rooms on the top floor – I saw them many times many years later. This was the domicile of a group of med students including my father. Their loosely formed club was specially named after the epicranium, a particular portion of the brain described in *Gray's Anatomy* text as possessing four fleshy bellies. I recall thinking at the time that it was clear from the photos that the group did justice to the name.

After university, Dad joined the Air Force. Immediately following their honeymoon in Vancouver Mom and Dad were posted to Claresholm. Mom recalls arriving in Claresholm a day late because Dad had misread his posting orders. They had five cents between them and moved into a room above the bar at the Claresholm Hotel.

In March 1944 Dad was posted overseas as a Medical Officer first to Bomber Command at Yorkshire and then to the Sunderland Squadron in Ireland. He obviously had pull to get there in the first place. Not only did he have flat feet but also he had a bad ankle as a result of a break as a child. He often spoke of his good and bad experiences in England and Ireland during the war and while obviously not enjoying the time away from Mom and Joan, he was pleased in hindsight to have made a contribution. His last posting was in London to the School of Tropical Medicine. For reasons that I have never understood, he felt if he could get posted to the Pacific theatre he could get discharged sooner. Fortunately the war ended and Dad returned home after VE day in December 1945. Mom and Dad immediately came to Camrose to help out at the clinic 'for just a few months'. They of course never left.

In June 1952, Dad went to Edinburgh to earn his FRCS and the rest of us remained in Camrose. He never completed the course because while there he had an operation to improve the situation with his ankle. Unfortunately there were complications and he became seriously ill. Mom joined him that December and the rest of us were left under the charge of Grandma Smalley – Nana to us. I refer to this period of our lives as the 'tapioca and riced-potatoes' phase. Dad of course recovered. He and Mom were able to spend the early part of 1953 travelling in Europe together. This was probably one of the few times that they had a chance to get away without the rest of is.

Their early years in Camrose were obviously busy ones. Dad worked continuously and Mom had the joy of the rest of us to contend with. I expect for them it was a blur until the lake cottage came along. This became Dad's retreat. He designed it and had the initial shell constructed by a local contractor. The rest of it he finished himself. How he gained a mastery of carpentry skills was a mystery to me – he referred to it as 'wood butchery'. And for what seemed like years, he would pack in a full weeks' work in Camrose and then on Saturday afternoon race to the lake only to work non-stop until Sunday night. I had lots of time to reflect on this as I fetched and carried lumber, nails, etc.

But the lake cottage was his salvation. It was started in 1953. It was a sanctuary from the pressures of his work that were impossible for him to ignore when he was in Camrose. It was a place for the family to be together and later congregate on special occasions. It was a place to relax and be with friends. It was a source of many new and lasting friends. And it became a retirement home. For Dad it was home and he hated to leave it for too long. I suspect for Mom it was at times a bit confining but she never complained.

I remember those early years as carefree days for the family, mostly centered on the summer at the lake. Saturday nights were often nights with many friends of Mom and Dad's getting together. It strikes me in hindsight that they seemed to have a lot more fun than our generation did at a similar time in our lives. The group from Camrose seemed to know how to work hard and play hard. The lake was a place for them to enjoy themselves. And for all of us in the family it was a place of many memories. The nature of the activities changed over the years but it was always a place that their friends dropped by to visit.

One of the many lake memories that came to mind as I thought about this involved the purchase of our first outboard motor. It was a 5hp Firestone that

Happy Hales had brought out to the lake for Dad to try on the boat he constructed in the basement at home the winter before. I was sceptical. This was the only Firestone motor on the lake and probably in captivity. But it was just a test and surely we would not buy it. Happy confidently placed the motor on the boat and with some quick verbal instructions Dad started the motor, forced it into reverse and turned the throttle. The audience on shore watched as the boat progressively descended into the water in submarine-like fashion. Of course we were obliged to buy the motor and we were the proud owners of a one-of-a-kind Firestone. It was the first of many motors and boats that my father would curse frequently for the rest of his days. It was also not the only major incident he would have with his 'fleet' but those are other stories.

My father's number one priority in his life was his work. He was good at it and obviously earned a great deal of respect from his colleagues and his patients. As I travel throughout Western Canada now I am continually amazed at the number of people who know of my father through personal experience or reputation. When conversations got around to where one was from, as they inevitably do, the next question always was, "Was Hamp or Mac your father?"

He got a great deal of satisfaction from his accomplishments but I think he got even more satisfaction from those of his patients. Many of you here have first-hand knowledge of working with him as a colleague or a patient. I don't believe I could do justice to him to attempt to put his years of practicing medicine in Camrose into proper perspective in these few brief moments.

I had few opportunities to observe him at work first-hand but when I did I was always fascinated. I recall an unfortunate gentleman coming to the cottage door one summer after a fishing accident. While following through with his cast he had hooked his tackle box and brought it with considerable force into contact with the back of his head. He had an amazing collection of hooks but they were now in plain view and deeply imbedded in his scalp. Dad's manner immediately switched upon seeing the nature of the problem. He got down to the business of confidently and quickly removing the hooks while at the same time distracting the man with a humorous line of chat. It was a performance that we saw many times over the years as people came to the door needing assistance.

There were many opportunities to see the compassion which he felt for the people he served. One incident that comes to mind occurred one winter when he went around the house gathering up winter clothes that he felt were not particularly needed. When I asked him what they were for he replied: "For a family that needs them more than us". The next day at school I would see a girl in my class wearing some recognisable things.

Even though my father seemed to always be at the clinic, at the hospital or in his living room chair either asleep or reading, he still seemed to find time for a number of hobbies and interests. Probably his favourite pastime was reading. Every relaxing moment was spent reading. He would race through an enormous number of pocket books in a year. In addition he subscribed to a wide variety of magazines and generally read them all. The first year of his retirement, he pulled out the *Encyclopedia Britannica* and started reading the first volume. All of this made him a great Trivial Pursuit player but his sense of humour could not allow him to resist making up most of the questions himself. It took us a while to catch on to that.

Another favourite pastime was gardening. The back yard at the house in Camrose was always a floral showcase. It represented an enormous amount of work but for those few short weeks in the summer the effort always seemed worth it. In the spring and summer he was always out in the garden by 6 am. I can still remember one early morning in which he had thrown me out the door to weed. I was dutifully defoliating a piece of the flowerbed when a roar came out of the bathroom window. From 200 feet away in the early morning light he could see that I was ripping out a prized perennial. To me at five feet away, the length of the hoe, it seemed nothing more than a common weed.

He also loved to cook and entertain. He was never satisfied unless there was enough food to feed twice the number of people expected. And as the years advanced he became more of a dominant force in the kitchen during these occasions. His portion of the meal preparation was always well done but the kitchen always needed a major hose down when he was finished. The fact that this was left to others never seemed to bother him. He loved to have people in and to entertain but he was always uncomfortable when people tried to reciprocate.

Another favourite pastime of my father's was giving advice. Accepting it of course was not held with the same esteem. I am sure that part of his joy in this pastime was always having THE last word. After many discussions of course we caught onto this and eventually learned how to end a conversation. But he always had the upper hand with telephone calls. These would begin when he called with either no greeting at all – right to the message – or a sharp "Hampton here", or "This is your father speaking" (there was never any doubt). But it was with the closing where he had you. When he finished what he had to say he would simply hang up. You never had the opportunity to say goodbye – I am sure he felt it was redundant.

One of his brief but fascinating hobbies was beekeeping. The backyard had the flowers and one of his elderly patients was giving up his hobby of beekeeping. He provided Dad with all the equipment and the backyard instantly became a honey farm. This went on for several years and once a year the rumpus room turned into the honey processing room. It would become progressively stickier as harvest week wore on. It was always with the piano that this became most noticeable.

Farming first became one of his interests when he was involved in the purchase of the Hills ranch. He loved this place and regretted not retaining some attachment to it. When he gave up his interest in it, he purchased other farming properties near Pigeon Lake. These have provided much enjoyment for him over the years. Fond memories for us were the multi-coloured tractor, created by the neighbours painting it every conceivable colour from the remains of paint cans. Also the community garden plots that became a focal point for several years. The farms also provided him with the opportunity to take on the big government when he repealed his income tax one year. He prepared and presented the case himself and to his own surprise, won. I can recall him tearing apart the income tax act with more enthusiasm than most corporate lawyers.

Probably a favourite family memory was the summer-long trip to nine of the ten provinces with the entire family of six plus the dog and a trailer just for excitement. With an evening's practice driving the trailer – which consisted of driving only forwards and clockwise around the block. The backing up lesson was halted when one fin on the 1959 Chrysler punctured the front of the trailer. The next morning we set off on five weeks of high adventure. It was a dream of Dad's to take us across Canada and he was particularly proud that he was able to accomplish it.

My final image of Dad is from last Saturday when we visited him in the hospital. When we arrived he was asleep in an easy chair in his room. He claimed his pull with the management had provided it. For me this was the natural place to see my father sleep when he was uncomfortable. He had probably slept more hours of his life sitting in a chair than he had in a bed. At first he appeared physically uncomfortable but as he became more awake he became of good spirits and humour. He spoke of how he had stubbornly delayed his trip to the hospital so he could renew his driver's license. He suggested that the only way he would be able to get past St. Peter and the Pearly

Gates was to drive on through. And he spoke of how pleased he had been to have a visit each day that week from a group of ladies who had been patients of his. He spoke of particular admiration of one whom he counted as a dear friend. He had many flowers but it was clear that hers were to be treated with the most respect as Lauren watered them. When we noticed him growing weary, we decided it was time to leave. As we left the room and said our goodbyes, I held back briefly. He looked up with a smile. His face was relaxed, his blue eyes were clear and bright and smiling as well. He was obviously at peace – more so than I had seen him in a long time. I felt he knew exactly what was happening with him and finally said goodbye.

I would like to close with a poem that Gail remembers from her valedictory address when she graduated from nursing. It seems appropriate now, with apologies to the author whom we can't remember:

I walked along the sands of time and, oh, the years went fast.
But, as I walked, I stopped
and picked the mementos from the past. Some were bright and some
were small for so our life is planned.
But when I'm gone, they'll linger on, those pebbles in the sand.

All of us here today represent my father's pebbles in the sand. We are overwhelmed by the number of you here and on behalf of the family, thank you for joining us this afternoon.

Doug Smith
29th October 1992

II. Eulogy for Peggy's funeral[29]

**IN LOVING MEMORY
OF
MARGARET (PEGGY) C. SMITH**

The Smiths at PigeonLake

**Camrose United Church
Camrose, Alberta
1:00 p.m. Wednesday, April 27, 1994**

**Margaret Cowell Smith
25th November 1919 – 22nd April 1994**

Peggy was born Smalley. The family lived in Winnipeg and Ottawa, moving to Edmonton in 1929, where Peggy completed high school and attended university. In 1943 she graduated in nursing from the University of Alberta. In January of the same year, she and Hamp were married. Hamp joined the R.C.A.F. and they were posted to Claresholm shortly after their marriage. They lived there for a year during which time Joan was born. When Hamp was posted overseas Peggy returned to Edmonton to live with her parents. During this time

690

she worked as a nurse at the University Hospital. Hamp returned from overseas in 1945 and the family moved to Camrose where Hamp joined his father and brother in the family medical practice. Doug and Pat were born during the first two years in Camrose and the family moved to their home at 4718-51 Street. Ian was born in 1955.

During those years Peggy made the home at 51st Street and the cottage at Pigeon Lake an important focus of family life. This was no easy task as Hamp was working very long and irregular hours at the clinic, hospital and 'on-call'.

In 1978 Hamp retired and they moved to the lake. Their home was a meeting place always open to their family and many friends. The family gathered there at Christmas, Thanksgiving and Easter and Peggy made each a special occasion.

Peggy was also active outside the home, being a member of the U.C.W., the church choir, the Eastern Star and the I.O.D.E. She was an avid curler and participated enthusiastically in many bonspiels.

Peggy was predeceased by Hamp in 1992. Peggy is survived by her four children and families: Joan (Peter Noble and sons Michael and Peter Hollihn), Doug (Gail and children Christopher, Cameron and Lauren), Pat (Bob Adamson and sons Rob and Jeff), Ian (Cheryl and children Stewart, Andy, Erin and Caroline).

Peggy created a home that was an important centre for all the family and gave her children and grandchildren many happy memories of their times at the lake together. She was much loved and will be dearly missed.

III. Michael's note about Hamp

Grandpa

My grandfather is a man with a heavy-set frame. He walks with a limp, shuffles his dentures around in his mouth and slouches when he sits. He fits a good description of the cartoon character 'Herman'. My grandfather is a very successful and intelligent man. I have a great deal of respect for what he is and what he has done. My grandfather was one of my best friends during my childhood. I had a lot of good times with him and I still do. The best times seemed to be when we were kids though.

My grandparents used to live in Camrose, Alberta Canada where they had a big, beautiful, old white house on the top of a hill. It had big, towering white pillars in the front that seemed to protect everyone inside. There was a dusty old attic with a bunch of old memories I could rummage around in. In the living room it smelt of Grandpa's pipes and cigars where my grandpa, my dad and my uncles used to smoke Cuban cigars whenever they used to sit down and drink.

When my grandpa was through practicing his medicine, he and my grandma retired to Pigeon Lake where they turned their cabin into their home. Every summer they had all their grandchildren out to the lake for a few weeks; this was the part of the summer that I looked forward to the most. We went for boat rides in the big pink boat, skipping across the lake to visit friends of my parents at Ma-Me-O Beach. One summer we built a fire pit in front of the cabin, right next to the beach. We spent all day lugging big round stones out of the lake to build it. Many summer nights were spent roasting marshmallows and making smores around that pit. To this day our names are still etched in the cement. That fall my grandpa built a tree house with us that we called 'The Falcon's Lair'.

He always took us for rides on the multi-coloured tractor to the store to buy candy. Every morning there would be a dollar bill for each of us on the table to blow at the store on junk food. He insisted we blow it on junk food; he always kept a basket full of chocolate bars for us too. When I think about my grandpa I can always hear him saying, "Why aren't you eating a chocolate bar dummer?" I would say "They're all gone dummer." We used to call each other 'dummer' or Grandpa would call everyone 'boob'. When we would be out of chocolate bars Grandpa would say, "What are you waiting for ya boob, get on the tractor and let's go get some more cavity bars!"

The bright red paddleboards he built us must have a couple of thousand kilometres on them from paddling up and down the shore. Grandpa even taught us how to drive the little 9.9 horsepower fishing boat so we could learn how to water-ski behind it.

It was so nice to wake up in the morning to the crash of the waves on the shore, or the slam of the screen door, to find Grandpa sitting in his pyjamas, in his lawn chair, drinking his coffee. The mornings were spent feeding the ducks or talking about my college plans of going to medical school.

My grandfather has and always will be a best friend. We have grown apart now but those memories are everlasting. I can't wait to see him again; now we can talk about the good old days as adults.

Michael Hollihn, 1988

IV. Ode to the lake cottage

the smell of poplar

we set out across the lake searching for the cottage
straight as a boat can skip across the water we made our way
memories of the big pink fibreglass whale heaving its way across the lake
the smell of gasoline, the deep gargling roar of the outboard motor
moving push rods and blue smoke
a beach towel shielding my body from rain and wind
my face welcoming the reminder of childhood
i keep trying to look out past the canopy
past the stinging spray
there it was
we hit it straight as a destined arrow might
the bull's-eye was now blue instead of the dark green i had remembered
it took a few looks to be sure
i glanced at the surrounding cabins
they had changed
but the reed grasses crowding the old slough two cabins to the right seemed
    just as before
but smaller
we tied the boat and i shook hands with a man that came out to greet us
"hellooo! sorry to intrude but i grew up here, i'm hamp smith's grandson,
    are you middletons or pendletons?"
"not any more, we bought from them before hamp passed on... he used to
    come over in his pyjamas and give the kids candy bars...
"we call pyjama pants 'hamp pants' to this day"
we laugh
i ask if it's ok to look around
he says sure there is no one there
"the dentist that bought from hamp has it up for sale, he's asking $560,000"

as i walk down the pier i lock my eyes onto the cabin and i am overwhelmed
    with a strong emotion
my eyes scan the three upstairs windows and the screened porch
i notice the tree missing that used to house the falcon's lair
the fire pit is gone and there's a newer one in its place
i walk up to the front steps and press my face into the screen beside the door
i smell screen and porch and can't quite believe where i am
i yearn to hear the screen door slam shut but it's locked
there's no more finger hole to help me
i step down to the grass and head around the side where the paddle boards
    used to live
i expect to see an old brown cabin deeply shaded by poplars and covered in
    cob webs and fuzz
i remember stepping on soft gnarled branches of poplar in my bare feet, the
    cool earth of a pathway
there is a modern summer retreat of a home that can't be called a cottage
    any longer
i feel a sense of entitlement and belonging so i open the gate to the back
    yard
i am pleased to see that not much has changed but some colour and surface
    details
the garden is still a garden and in the same place grandma and grandpa
    turned the earth,
the outhouse is gone but grandpa's work-bench is still there covered in what
    looks like ten coats of grey paint
the book nook and shelves are still there that had all the *Life* and *National
    Geographics*
amazed how a garage can bring back so much memory
realise how much time was spent there snooping, combing books, reading,
    building
the number '13' with the horse-shoe still protects the garage
i walk out onto the back road and get hit by another flood of wonderful
    memory
the road lamp that buzzed with electricity and the lives of a million moths
i could hear our voices running in the twilight playing hide and seek
the cow field across the road is now home to some other lake lovers
the smell of balsam pitch intoxicates me as i head back towards the cabin

i step the small step onto the back porch
the sound the wood makes under the green carpet still sounds the same
a welcoming creak and sound that always told grandma and grandpa that
    we had finally made it
a deep freeze is still humming in the room to the left
i look in the window and think of grandma getting freezies or fudgsicles for
    all of us
i look in the door window, the window above the kitchen sink and the
    sliding glass door,
they've done a little remodelling
the bathroom where grandpa's teeth were in a cup,
'no hair combings, please use the basket, there's a darn good reason why we
    ask it'
the smell of sulphur
you can't see up into the upstairs hallway anymore
the kitchen sink where all the adults helped grandma with the dishes
reminded me how short she really was; cute but feisty
the fireplace gave me the biggest jolt
i felt tears and a warmth well up in my heart and throat
i had forgotten how beautiful a fireplace it is and was
a lot of milk cartons met their end there
grandma doing her crossword puzzles in her green chair with her glasses
    on the end of her nose
grandpa reading his pulp fiction in his yellow chair threatening to light
    himself on fire
steven fay waved to me from the front porch through the big front window
i walked around between the wood shed and the cabin

Michael Hollihn
June 2011

The family home, 4718-51st Street, Camrose painted by J C Brager

The Camrose house in winter

697

Smith Cottage at Pigeon Lake

Hamp and his colourful tractor

Hamp's early morning coffee at the lake

From back left clockwise: Robbie, Hamp, Jeff, Michael, Peggy, Christopher, Cameron, Peter

The fire pit at the lake built by Hamp and the grandchildren

Peggy and Hamp on their fortieth wedding anniversary 1983

Grandchildren taken at Peggy's funeral in 1994 from the back left clockwise:
Christopher, Robbie, Michael, Jeff, Cameron, Stewart, Lauren, Andy, Caroline and
Erin. Peter Hollihn is missing.

Ian, Pat, Joan and Doug, April 1994

Grampa had a long life and he was happy most of it. And he gave me a teddy Bear thats named Grumpy. And I sleep

with him every night to remember him. I dream of the happy times I had with him. to Grandma love from Erin XoXoXoXoXoXoXoXo

Grampa

Erin

Grandma

NOTES

1   William Arthur (Bill) Waterton wrote 'The Quick and the Dead', a book about the perils of post-war test pilot flying. They remained good friends and corresponded until Hamp's death.

2   He refers to his sister Margaret's wedding. She married Bill Norton. Hamp and Peggy both attended the wedding and appear in a home movie given to me by their son David Norton. JN

3   They must have decided to get married. JN

4   She brings this up in her letter of 11 July 1945. "Aunty Lena phoned and came over for supper… Her latest news – Eddie and his English bride are expecting a baby Ha! Ha! So now watch me count the months like Aunty Lena did with us."

5   Buddy was the Smalley's dog.

6   D-Day, the Normandy Landings.

7   Eddie Oldring was a cousin of Peggy (the son of Auntie Lena who was a sister of Peggy's father William Smalley).

8   Mrs Williams lived in Camrose by the dam off what is now the highway. She used to babysit us occasionally.

9   The Henderons lived next door to the Smalleys.

10   She never did smoke in front of them! I remember, about age 16, being on a road trip to the coast with Mother and Ba (our name for her father) and covering up for her. JN

11   Actually when he did come home I apparently went for the taxi driver. Dad often brought up the story of his arrival home and how I cried and screamed whenever he came near me but took to and adored the taxi driver, even calling him "Daddy". It seemed to me that it had quite upset him. JN

12   Peter Hollihn has this silver cake holder – Peggy gave it to Joan when she moved to England and Joan sent it back to Canada with Peter in 2013.

13   Very scrawling scribble all over the page.

14   Probably enlistment date.

15   Hamp's birth date.

16   An orthopedic surgeon at the University of Alberta Hospital, Edmonton.

17 St. Mary's Hospital in Camrose was founded and managed by the Sisters of Providence of St. Vincent de Paul. They wore traditional ankle-length habits including hooded head covers.

18 The walls of the den were hung with the hunting trophies of Hamp's father. This particular one was the head of a white mountain goat from the Rockies.

19 Assume blackout blinds.

20 The Wellington "Wimpy" Bomber was a British produced aircraft introduced before the war.

21 Some words are missing due to big hole in the letter where stamp has been removed. I recall as a child of taking stamps from a few letters for my stamp collection. JN

22 I went to Dublin for the weekend with two friends in 1999 and stayed at the same hotel! It was right on the sea and very nice. JN

23 Canadian General Hospital.

24 This was the Smith family lake cottage at Ma Me O Beach, Pigeon Lake, Alberta.

25 Grandfather Smalley (we called him 'Ba') loved to row and in later years I remember him taking the rowboat out for long rows along the shore from our cottage at Grandview, Pigeon Lake. JN

26 PF (Grandfather Smith) grew rows of gladioli like corn in a large backyard garden.

27 The local dry cleaners in Camrose.

28 Drawing of the Smith Cottage at Pigeon Lake by Erin Smith, age six.